BAREFOOT GEN

VOLUME THREE:
LIFE AFTER THE BOMB

KEIJI NAKAZAWA

Translated by Project Gen

LAST GASP OF SAN FRANCISCO

Barefoot Gen: A Cartoon Story of Hiroshima
Volume Three: Life After the Bomb

By Keiji Nakazawa

Published by Last Gasp of San Francisco
777 Florida Street, San Francisco, California, 94110
www.lastgasp.com

First serialized under the title Hadashi no Gen in Japan, 1972-3.
Published by Last Gasp with a new translation, 2005.
First hardcover Last Gasp edition, 2016.
ISBN 978-0-86719-833-1

Translation by Project Gen
Volume 3 Translators: Kiyoko Nishita, George Stenson, Alan Gleason,
Jared Cook, Frederik Schodt.

Project Gen Volunteers: Namie Asazuma, Kazuko Futakuchi, Michael
Gordon, Kyoko Honda, Yukari Kimura, Nobutoshi Kohara, Nante Kotta,
Michiko Tanaka, Kazuko Yamada.

Edited by Alan Gleason and Colin Turner
Production: Colin Turner
Cover design: Evan Hayden

Printed in China by Prolong Press Ltd.

For more information visit www.barefootgen.net

The Bomb Did Not Just "Fall"

Jun Ishiko

From *Kuroi Ame ni Utarete* (*Struck by Black Rain*) to *Barefoot Gen*, Keiji Nakazawa has drawn many works over the years about the atomic bomb and the people who were its victims. In the world of comic books, this sort of cartoonist is extremely rare. Nakazawa has consistently pursued a single theme without compromise and without quitting.

Barefoot Gen begins with a child's view of life in Japan during the last days of the Second World War, casts an unwavering eye on the atrocity that occurred on August 6, 1945, then goes on to tell about the lives of Gen and other survivors of the bomb. This is not only a history of Japan in defeat, but a history of the atomic bomb itself. As a graphic chronicle of the city of Hiroshima in the aftermath of the bomb, *Gen* matches the best efforts of prominent photographers like Yuichiro Sasaki, who documented the same period through a camera lens.

Keiji Nakazawa always planned to continue depicting the lives of his characters as they grew up in postwar Hiroshima. So when Ryuta, the orphan who resembles Gen's dead brother Shinji, is taken away by a gangster, or when Gen's Korean neighbor Mr. Pak briefly reappears as a black marketeer, we should realize that these are hints of plot developments to come.

When a cartoonist tries to tell the truth, he often runs into interference. It was true of the French caricaturist and social satirist Honoré Daumier. Nor is the wartime suppression of Japanese "proletarian" comic books ancient history. Even in postwar Japan, with freedom of speech supposedly restored, negative pressure remains. *Gen*, despite its popularity, was cancelled in mid-serialization. The reasons were never given, but it smacked of an attempt to suppress *Gen's* message while avoiding a messy frontal attack. Nor were the serialized installments of *Gen* immediately compiled for publication in book form, as is usually the case. Why was that?

For these reasons I am especially happy to be writing this on the occasion of the first publication of the *Gen* serial in four book-length volumes. As one of the people who worked hard to make this happen, I hope it will mean that more readers can now become acquainted with *Gen*.

I have been friends with Keiji Nakazawa for a long time. It began when I read *Struck by Black Rain* in a comic magazine and was amazed to discover the existence of such a cartoonist. A few years ago, before the serialization of *Gen*, an anthology was published of seven of Nakazawa's earlier works, including *Struck by Black Rain*. Even then there were rumors that Nakazawa would have a hard time finding a publisher for any more comic books on themes like these. But through his own persistence, and his dedication to constantly improving his craft and his powers of expression, he paved the way for eventual publication of works like *Gen*.

As the years go by, Japanese textbooks have less and less to say about the atomic bomb, and as a consequence schoolchildren today have a poor understanding of what really happened. In these circumstances, *Gen* has already had a powerful impact. While it was being serialized in a weekly children's comic magazine, letters from readers constantly poured in, a clear indication of how much these kids learned from Gen's story.

A boy who is at once innocent, active, thoughtful, worried, stubborn, and full of life, Gen often stumbles but never falls, never succumbs to the horrors of the bomb, and thereby earns the reader's sympathy and admiration. Through their friendship with Gen, children can experience a bit of what it was like to survive the bomb.

Nowadays, however, we often hear about how the atomic bombs "fell" on Hiroshima and Nagasaki. "Fell" sounds as if the bombs were natural phenomena, like rain falling from the sky. We must not forget that in fact, these bombs did not simply fall but were dropped -- by human beings. They were not an act of nature. People built them, and people used them. Rarely are we reminded that these bombs killed hundreds of thousands of people and left many more to suffer from radiation sickness for decades after the war ended. When we talk about the bombs "falling," it is easy to end the conversation with cheap platitudes about the poor victims, or to simply feel relieved that we weren't living in Hiroshima at the time ourselves.

Even the expression "was dropped" does not tell the whole story. It is passive, it lacks a subject. Who dropped the bomb? Who is responsible? In *Gen*, Nakazawa is unafraid to answer these questions. He faces the truth, and the truth can lead to accusations, to protests. It can lead to our accepting the victims' pain and anger as our own. It can lead to a vow that the same atrocity must never be repeated.

But when we ask who is responsible for dropping the bomb, we cannot simply accuse the United States of doing wrong. The Japanese government is culpable too. Even today it continues to take an evasive stance toward its own responsibility. Nor has it provided adequate compensation to the survivors of the atomic bombs. When we insist on talking about the "dropping," not the "falling" of the bombs, it is not just wordplay; it symbolizes our determination to force those responsible to own up to it.

It is the fundamental difference between "falling" and "dropping" that distinguishes Keiji Nakazawa's comic books from the euphemistic descriptions of the atomic bomb seen in school textbooks, and occasionally in other comics.

(Jun Ishiko, a literary critic, wrote this essay in 1975 for the first printing of *Hadashi no Gen Volume Three,* published in Japan by Chobunsha.)

The Birth of Barefoot Gen

Keiji Nakazawa

The atomic bomb exploded 600 meters above my hometown of Hiroshima on August 6, 1945 at 8:15 a.m. I was a little over a kilometer away from the epicenter, standing at the back gate of Kanzaki Primary School, when I was hit by a terrible blast of wind and searing heat. I was six years old. I owe my life to the school's concrete wall. If I hadn't been standing in its shadow, I would have been burned to death instantly by the 5,000-degree heat flash. Instead, I found myself in a living hell, the details of which remain etched in my brain as if it happened yesterday.

My mother, Kimiyo, was eight months pregnant. She was on the second floor balcony of our house, had just finished hanging up the wash to dry, and was turning to go back inside when the bomb exploded. The blast blew the entire balcony, with my mother on it, into the alley behind our house. Miraculously, my mother survived without a scratch.

The blast blew our house flat. The second floor collapsed onto the first, trapping my father, my sister Eiko, and my brother Susumu under it. My brother had been sitting in the front doorway, playing with a toy ship. His head was caught under the rafter over the doorway. He frantically kicked his legs and cried out for my mother. My father, trapped inside the house, begged my mother to do something. My sister had been crushed by a rafter and killed instantly.

My mother frantically tried to lift the rafters off them, but she wasn't strong enough to do it by herself. She begged passersby to stop and help, but nobody would. In that atomic hell, people could only think of their own survival; they had no time for anyone else. My mother tried everything she could, but to no avail. Finally, in despair, she sat down in the doorway, clutching my crying brother and helplessly pushing at the rafter that was crushing him.

The fires that followed the blast soon reached our house. It was quickly enveloped in flame. My brother yelled that he was burning; my father kept begging my mother to get some help. My mother, half-mad with grief and desperation, sobbed that she would stay and die with them. But our next-door neighbor found my mother just in time and dragged her away.

For the rest of her days, my mother never forgot the sound of the voices of her husband and son, crying out for her to save them. The shock sent my mother into labor, and she gave birth to a daughter by the side of the road that day. She named the baby Tomoko. But Tomoko died only four months later -- perhaps from malnutrition, perhaps from radiation sickness, we didn't know.

After escaping the flames near the school, I found my mother there by the roadside with her newborn baby. Together we sat and watched the scenes of hell unfolding around us.

My father had been a painter of lacquer work and traditional-style Japanese painting. He was also a member of an anti-war theater group that performed plays like Gorky's "The Lower Depths." Eventually the thought police arrested the entire troupe and put them in the Hiroshima Prefectural Prison. My father was held there for a year and a half. Even when I was a young child, my father constantly told me that Japan had been stupid and reckless to start the war.

Thanks, no doubt, to my father's influence, I enjoyed drawing from an early age. After the war I began reading Osamu Tezuka's comic magazine *Shin-Takarajima* (*New Treasure Island*); that had a huge impact on me. I began slavishly copying Tezuka's drawings and turned into a manga maniac. Hiroshima was an empty, burnt-out wasteland and we went hungry every day, but when I drew comics, I was happy and forgot everything else. I vowed early on to become a professional cartoonist when I grew up.

In 1961 I pursued my dream by moving to Tokyo. A year later I published my first cartoon serial in the manga monthly *Shonen Gaho* (*Boys' Pictorial*). From then on I was a full-time cartoonist.

In 1966, after seven years of illness, my mother died in the A-Bomb Victims Hospital in Hiroshima. When I went to the crematorium to collect her ashes, I was shocked. There were no bones left in my mother's ashes, as there normally are after a cremation. Radioactive cesium from the bomb had eaten away at her bones to the point that they disintegrated. The bomb had even deprived me of my mother's bones. I was overcome with rage. I vowed that I would never forgive the Japanese militarists who started the war, nor the Americans who had so casually dropped the bomb on us.

I began drawing comics about the A-bomb as a way to avenge my mother. I vented my anger through a "Black" series of six manga published in an adult manga magazine, starting with *Kuroi Ame ni Utarete* (*Struck by Black Rain*). Then I moved to *Shukan Shonen Jump* (*Weekly Boys' Jump*), where I began a series of works about the war and the A-bomb starting with *Aru Hi Totsuzen ni* (*One Day, Suddenly*). When the monthly edition of *Jump* launched a series of autobiographical works by its cartoonists, I was asked to lead off with my own story. My 45-page manga autobiography was titled *Ore wa Mita* (*I Saw It*). My editor at *Jump*, Tadasu Nagano, commenting that I must have more to say that wouldn't fit in 45 pages, urged me to draw a longer series based on my personal experiences. I gratefully began the series right away. That was in 1972.

I named my new story *Hadashi no Gen* (*Barefoot Gen*). The young protagonist's name, Gen, has several meanings in Japanese. It can mean the "root" or "origin" of something, but also "elemental" in the sense of an atomic element, as well as a "source" of vitality and happiness. I envisioned Gen as barefoot, standing firmly atop the burnt-out rubble of Hiroshima, raising his voice against war and nuclear weapons. Gen is my alter ego, and his family is just like my own. The episodes in *Barefoot Gen* are all based on what really happened to me or to other people in Hiroshima.

Human beings are foolish. Thanks to bigotry, religious fanaticism, and the greed of those who traffic in war, the Earth is never at peace, and the specter of nuclear war is never far away. I hope that Gen's story conveys to its readers the preciousness of peace and the courage we need to live strongly, yet peacefully. In *Barefoot Gen*, wheat appears as a symbol of that strength and courage. Wheat pushes its shoots up through the winter frost, only to be trampled again and again. But the trampled wheat sends strong roots into the earth and grows straight and tall. And one day, that wheat bears fruit.

BAREFOOT GEN

LIFE AFTER THE BOMB

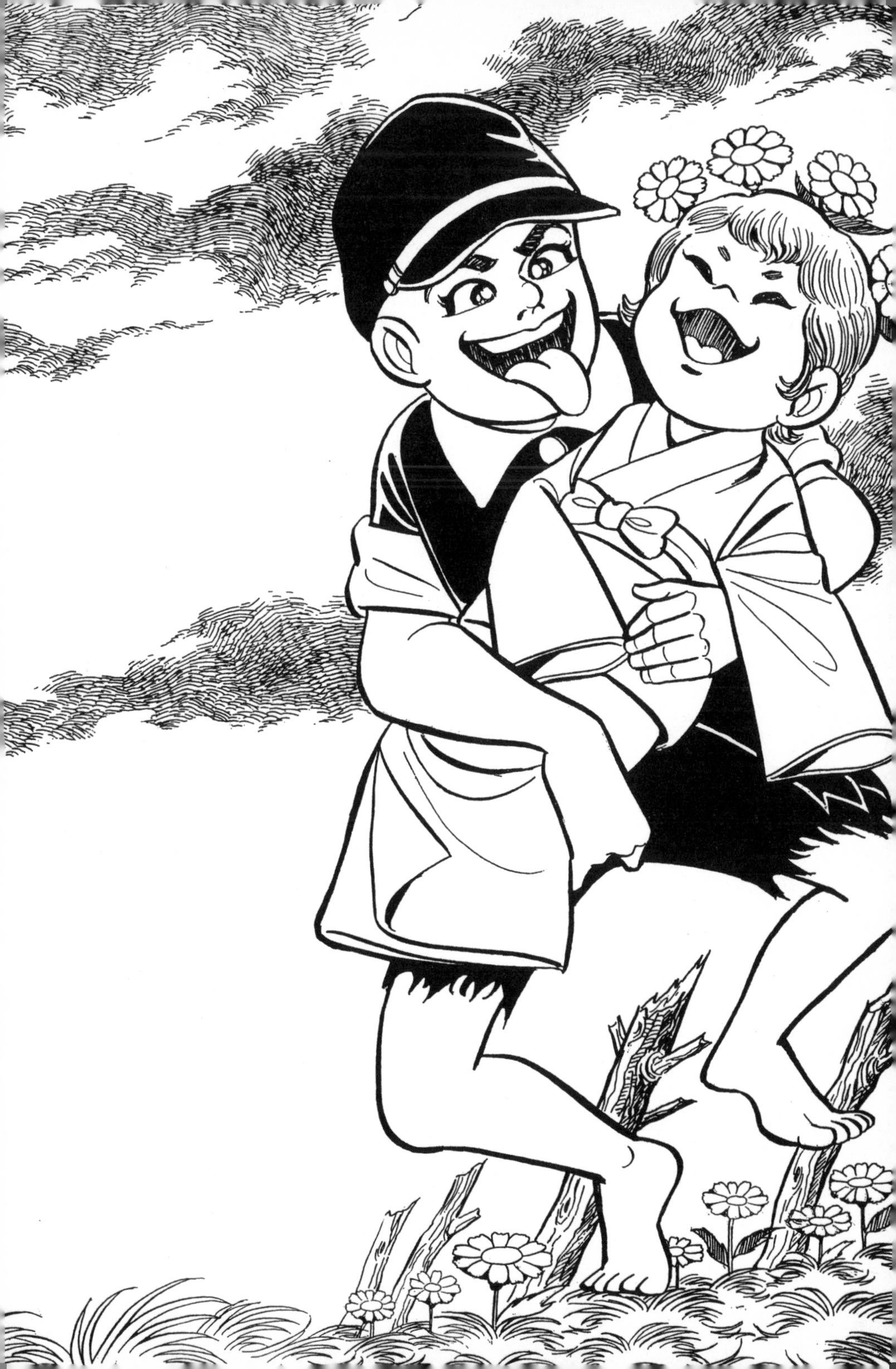

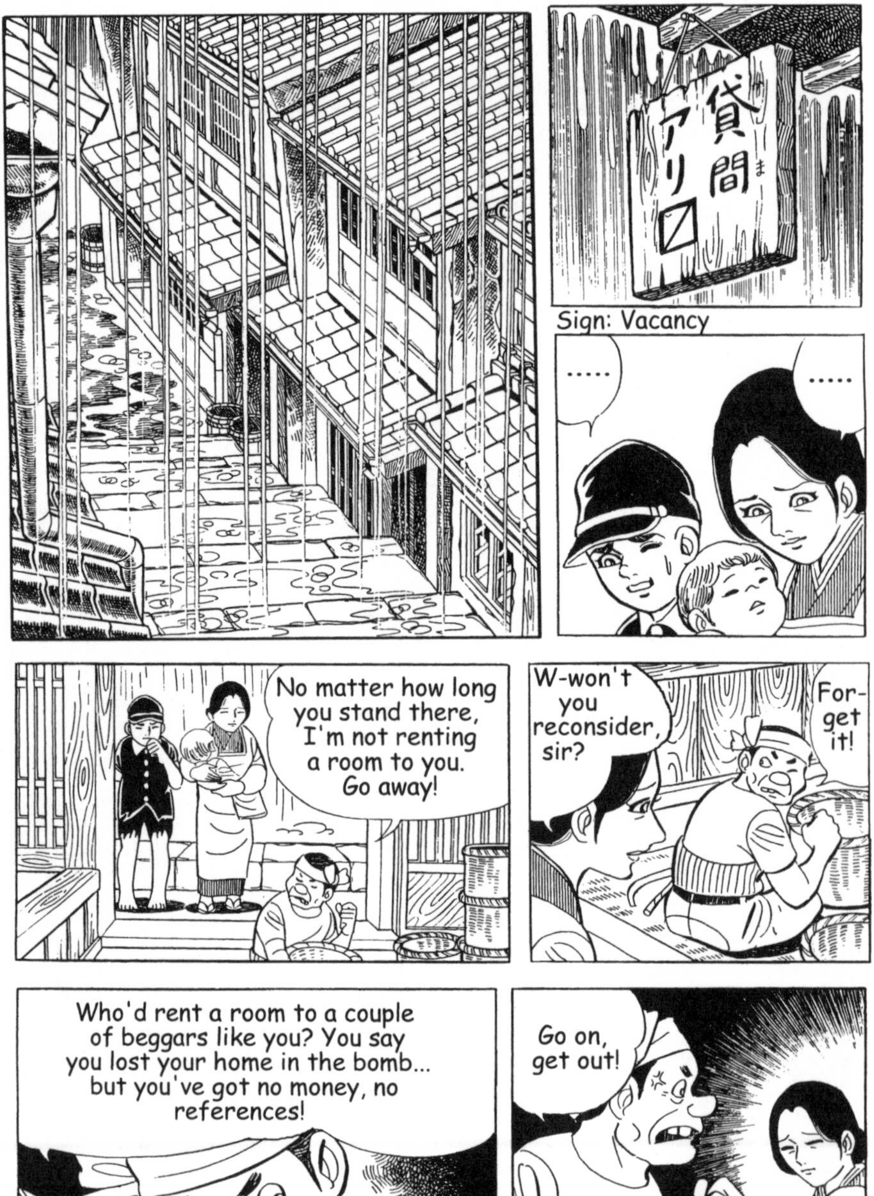
貸間アリ
Sign: Vacancy
.....
.....
No matter how long you stand there, I'm not renting a room to you. Go away!
W-won't you reconsider, sir?
For-get it!
Who'd rent a room to a couple of beggars like you? You say you lost your home in the bomb... but you've got no money, no references!
Go on, get out!

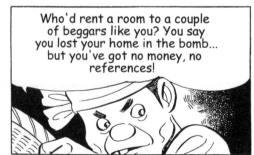

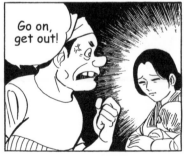

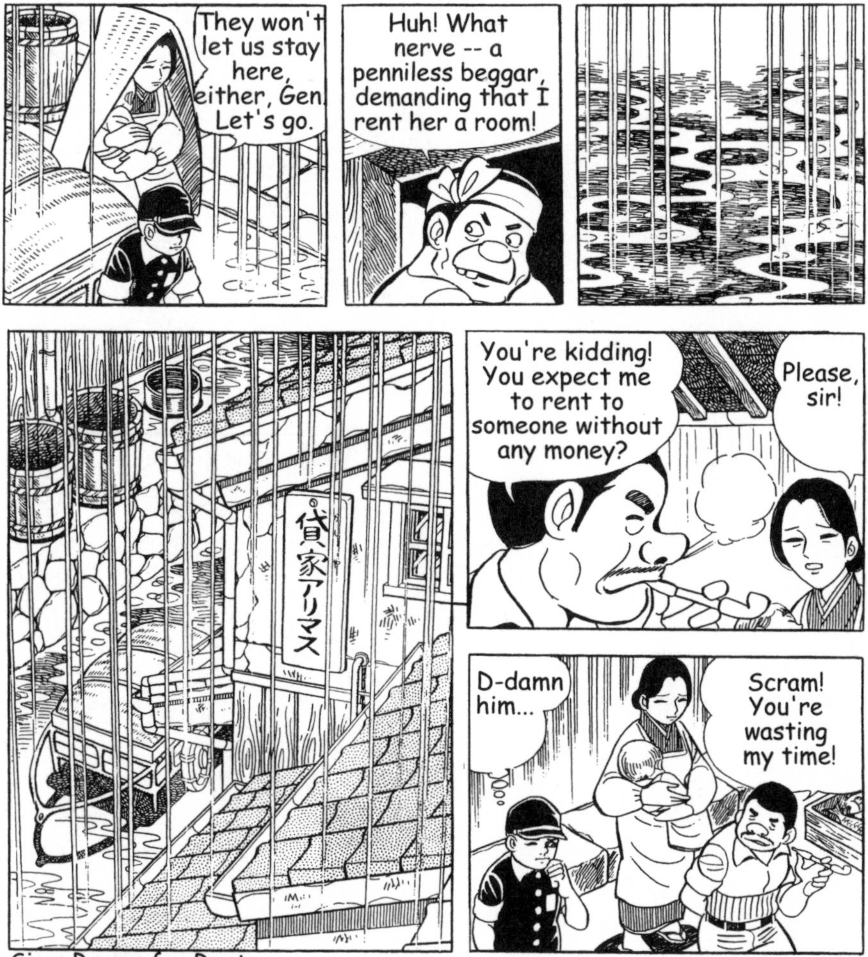
They won't let us stay here, either, Gen. Let's go.
Huh! What nerve -- a penniless beggar, demanding that I rent her a room!
貸家アリマス
You're kidding! You expect me to rent to someone without any money?
Please, sir!
D-damn him...
Scram! You're wasting my time!

Sign: Rooms for Rent

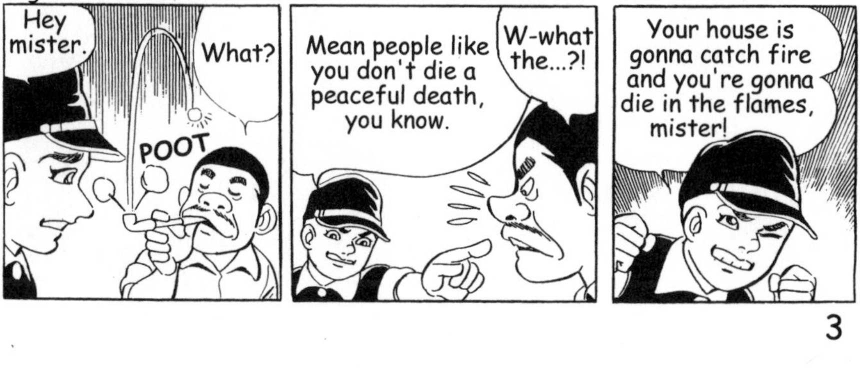
Hey mister.
What?
POOT
Mean people like you don't die a peaceful death, you know.
W-what the...?!
Your house is gonna catch fire and you're gonna die in the flames, mister!

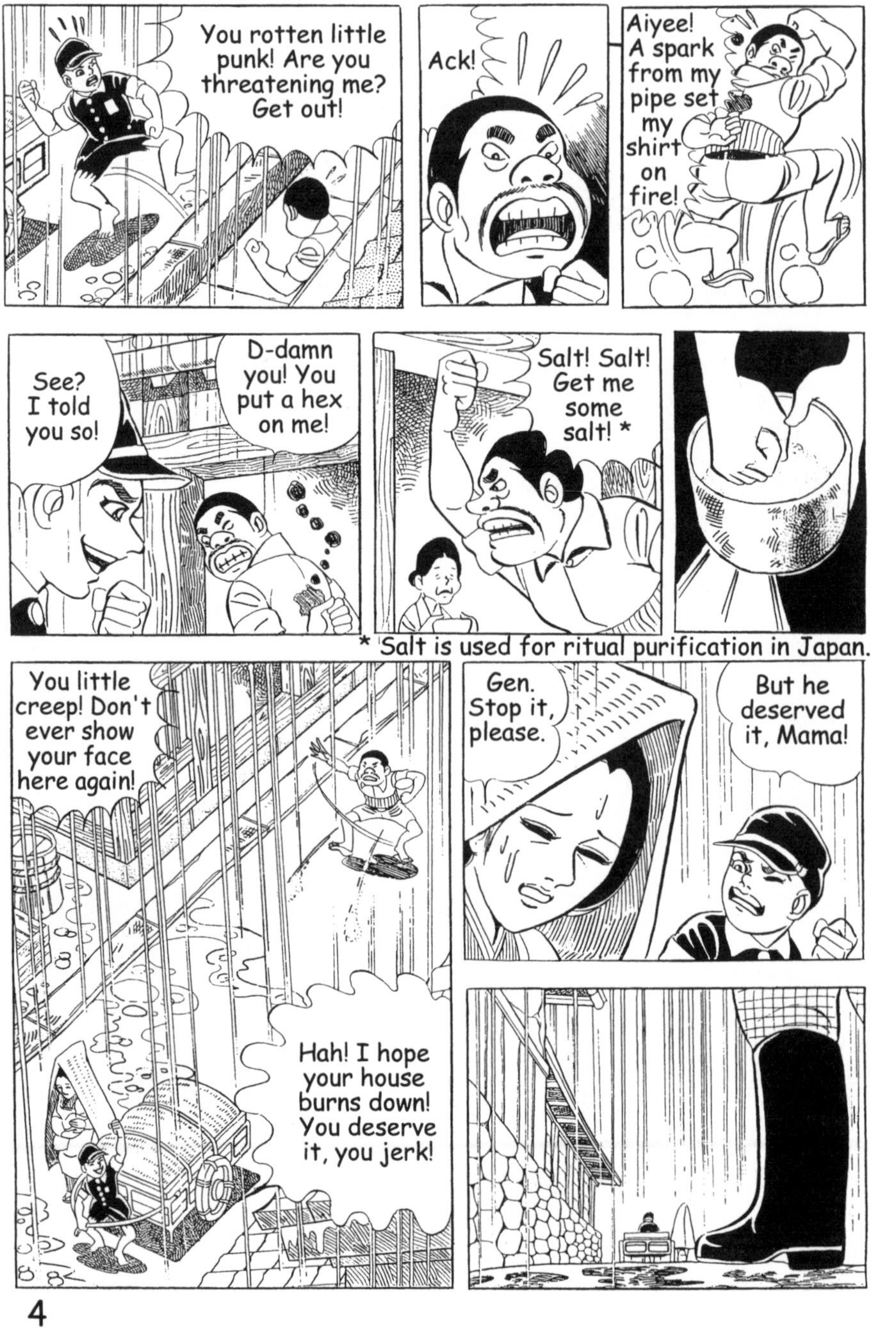
You rotten little punk! Are you threatening me? Get out!
Ack!
Aiyee! A spark from my pipe set my shirt on fire!
See? I told you so!
D-damn you! You put a hex on me!
Salt! Salt! Get me some salt! *
You little creep! Don't ever show your face here again!
Hah! I hope your house burns down! You deserve it, you jerk!
Gen. Stop it, please.
But he deserved it, Mama!
* Salt is used for ritual purification in Japan.

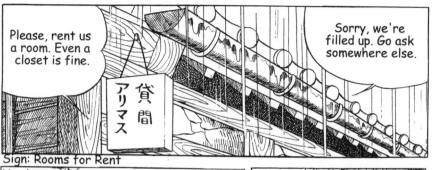

Please, rent us a room. Even a closet is fine.

Sorry, we're filled up. Go ask somewhere else.

貸間
アリマス

Sign: Rooms for Rent

You have nothing?

If you're looking for shelter, go over to the primary school. They're putting up homeless bomb victims there.

T-thank you.

Why didn't you give her a room, dear? We have plenty of vacancies, don't we?

Don't be an idiot! If we rented them a room, all we'd do is lose money.

When Mr. Gan rented a room to a bomb victim, the tenant died and no one claimed the body. He had to pay for the cremation, lost a ton of money!

We're better off having nothing to do with those bomb victims, I tell you!

Oh...

.....

5

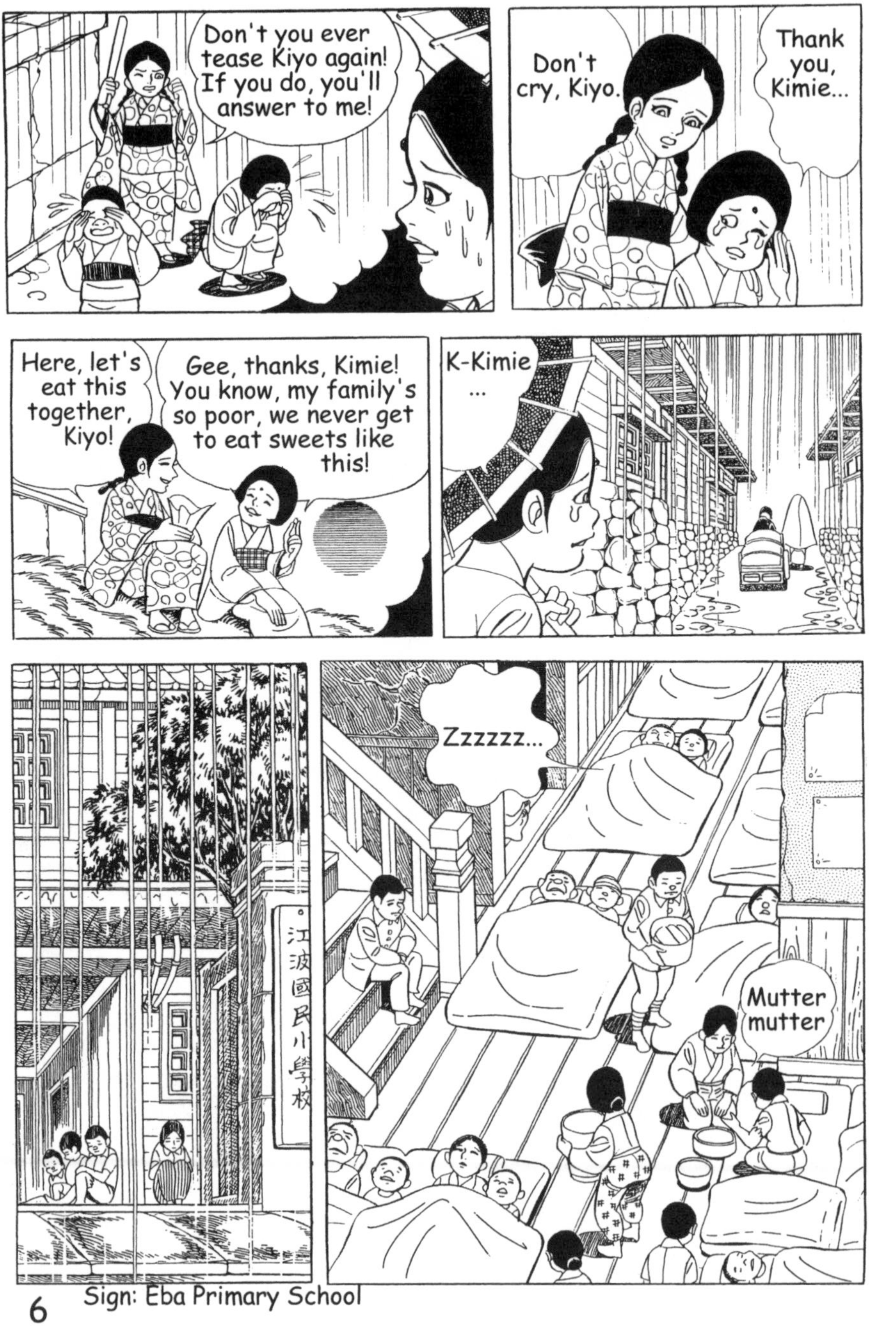
Don't you ever tease Kiyo again! If you do, you'll answer to me!
Don't cry, Kiyo.
Thank you, Kimie...
Here, let's eat this together, Kiyo!
Gee, thanks, Kimie! You know, my family's so poor, we never get to eat sweets like this!
K-Kimie ...
江波國民小學校
Zzzzzz...
Mutter mutter

 Sign: Eba Primary School

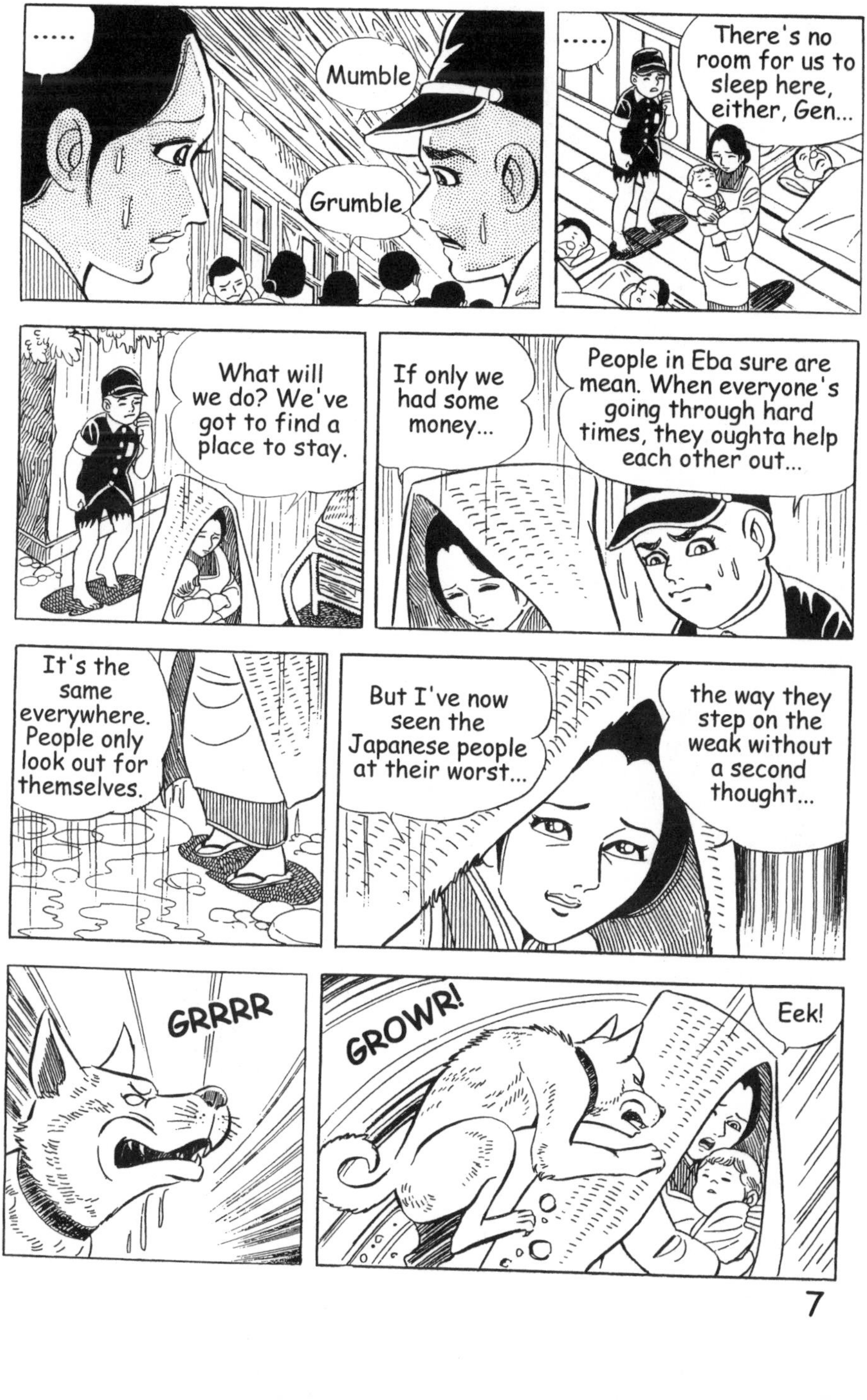
.....
Mumble
Grumble
.....
There's no room for us to sleep here, either, Gen...
What will we do? We've got to find a place to stay.
If only we had some money...
People in Eba sure are mean. When everyone's going through hard times, they oughta help each other out...
It's the same everywhere. People only look out for themselves.
But I've now seen the Japanese people at their worst...
the way they step on the weak without a second thought...
GRRRR
GROWR!
Eek!

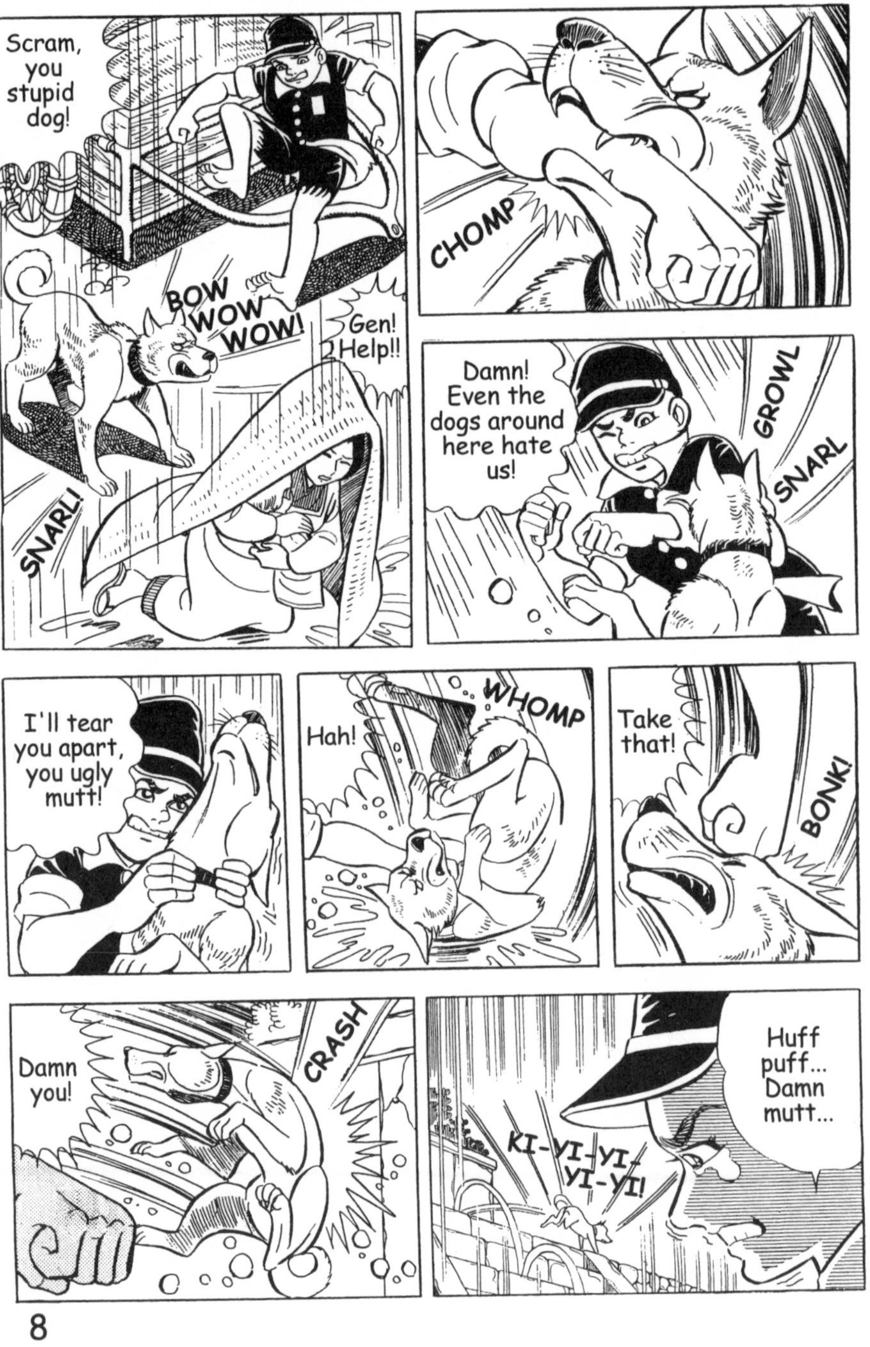

Scram, you stupid dog!
BOW WOW WOW!
Gen! Help!!
SNARL!
CHOMP
Damn! Even the dogs around here hate us!
GROWL
SNARL
I'll tear you apart, you ugly mutt!
Hah!
WHOMP
Take that!
BONK!
Damn you!
CRASH
KI-YI-YI-YI-YI!
Huff puff... Damn mutt...

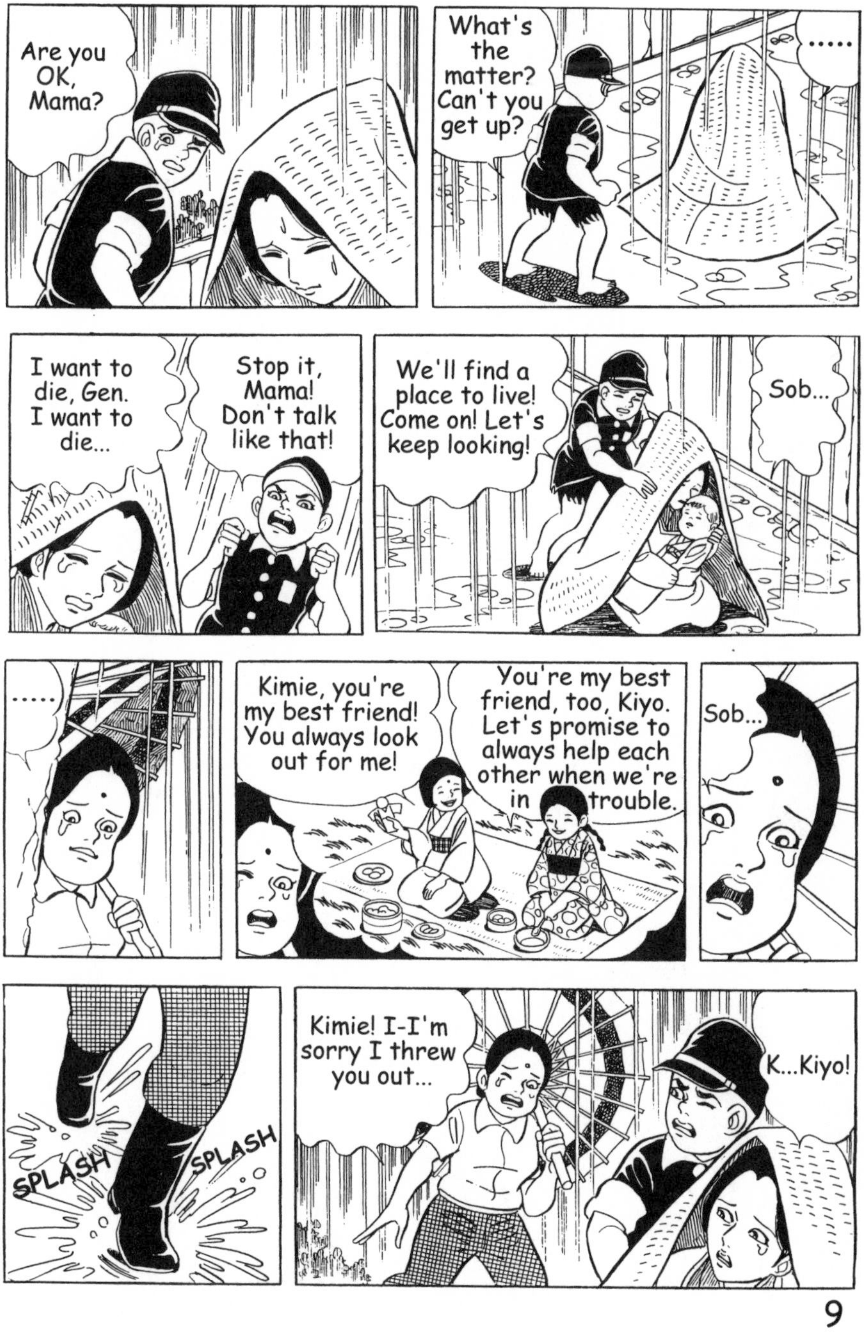

Are you OK, Mama?
What's the matter? Can't you get up?
.....
I want to die, Gen. I want to die...
Stop it, Mama! Don't talk like that!
We'll find a place to live! Come on! Let's keep looking!
Sob...
.....
Kimie, you're my best friend! You always look out for me!
You're my best friend, too, Kiyo. Let's promise to always help each other when we're in trouble.
Sob...
SPLASH
SPLASH
Kimie! I-I'm sorry I threw you out...
K...Kiyo!

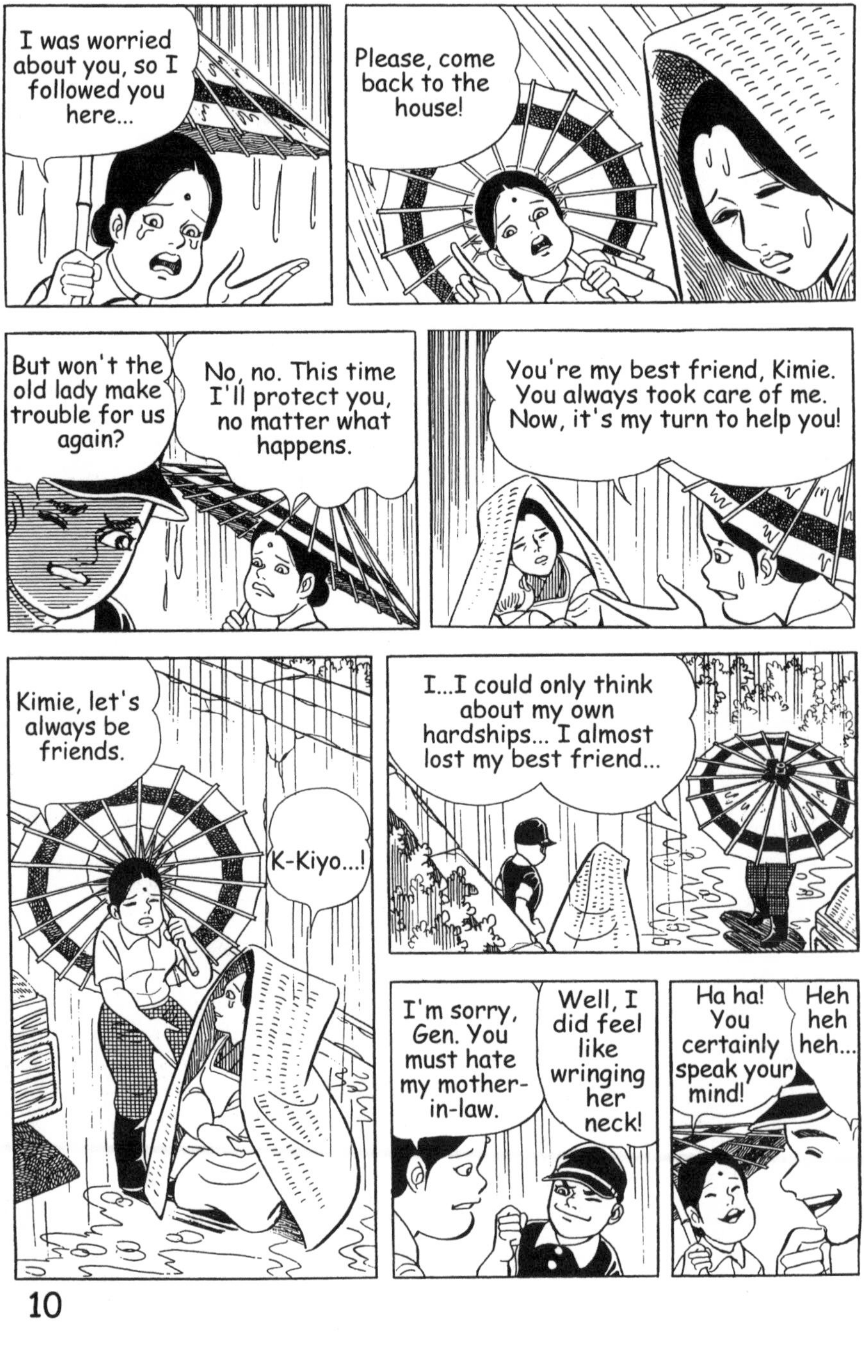
I was worried about you, so I followed you here...
Please, come back to the house!
But won't the old lady make trouble for us again?
No, no. This time I'll protect you, no matter what happens.
You're my best friend, Kimie. You always took care of me. Now, it's my turn to help you!
Kimie, let's always be friends.
K-Kiyo...!
I...I could only think about my own hardships... I almost lost my best friend...
I'm sorry, Gen. You must hate my mother-in-law.
Well, I did feel like wringing her neck!
Ha ha! You certainly speak your mind!
Heh heh heh...

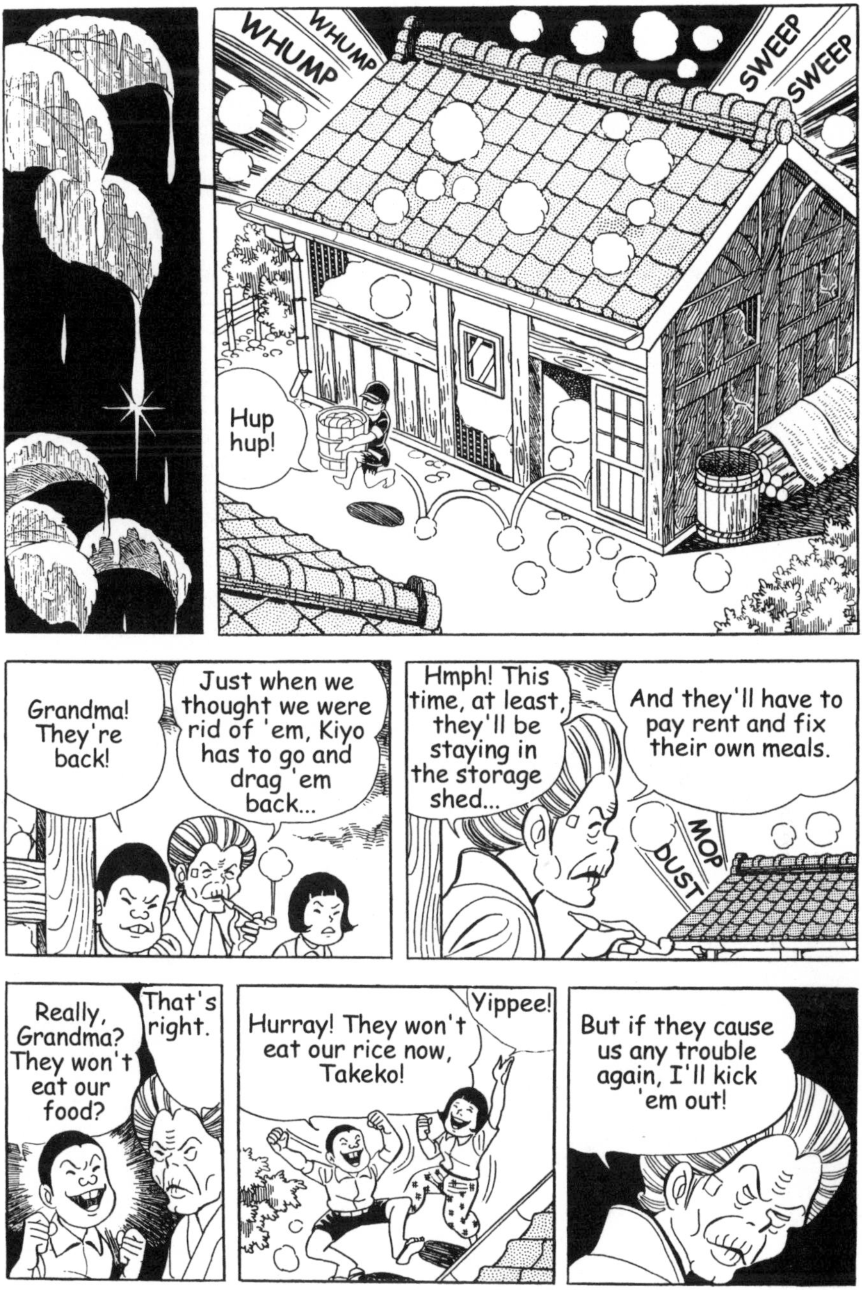
WHUMP
WHUMP
SWEEP
SWEEP
Hup hup!
Grandma! They're back!
Just when we thought we were rid of 'em, Kiyo has to go and drag 'em back...
Hmph! This time, at least, they'll be staying in the storage shed...
And they'll have to pay rent and fix their own meals.
MOP
DUST
Really, Grandma? They won't eat our food?
That's right.
Hurray! They won't eat our rice now, Takeko!
Yippee!
But if they cause us any trouble again, I'll kick 'em out!

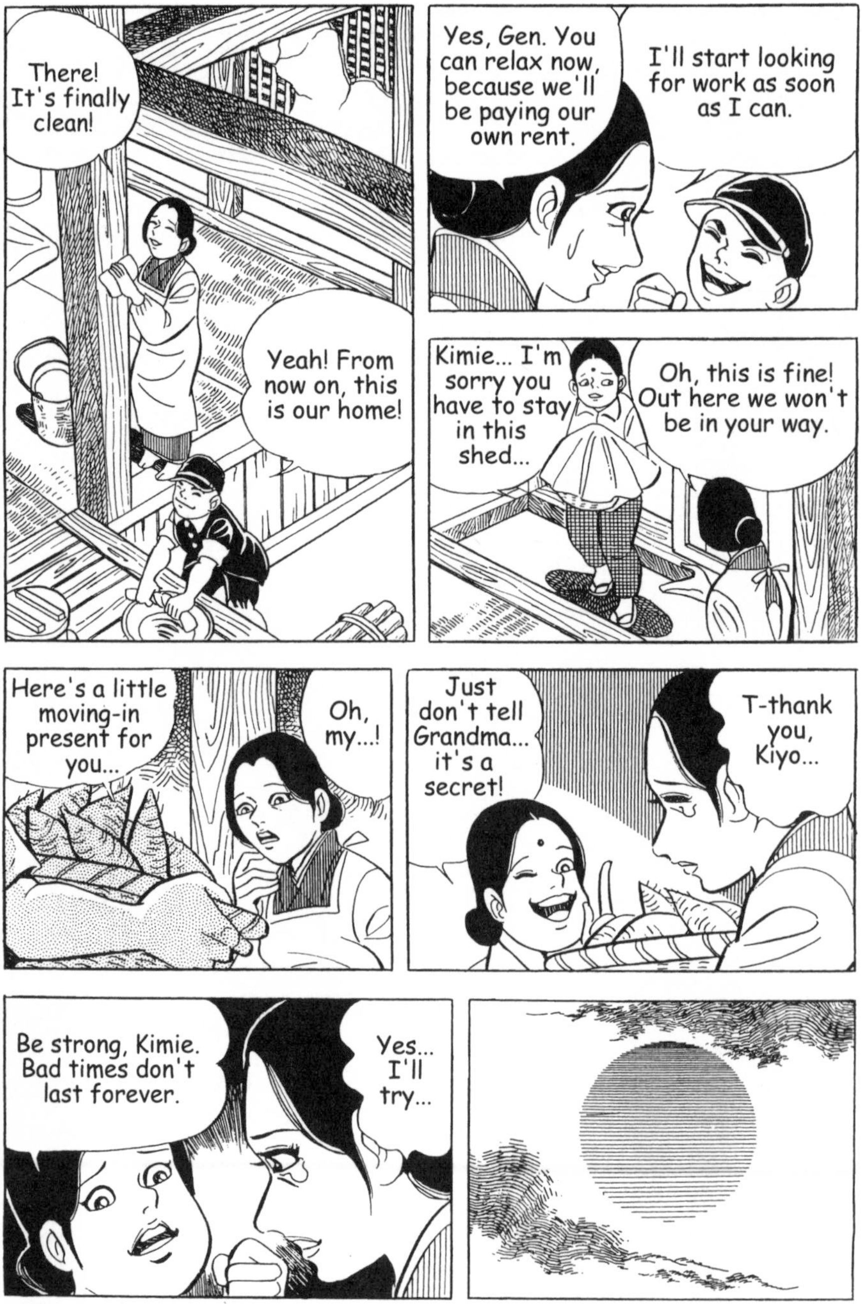
There! It's finally clean!
Yeah! From now on, this is our home!
Yes, Gen. You can relax now, because we'll be paying our own rent.
I'll start looking for work as soon as I can.
Kimie... I'm sorry you have to stay in this shed...
Oh, this is fine! Out here we won't be in your way.
Here's a little moving-in present for you...
Oh, my...!
Just don't tell Grandma... it's a secret!
T-thank you, Kiyo...
Be strong, Kimie. Bad times don't last forever.
Yes... I'll try...

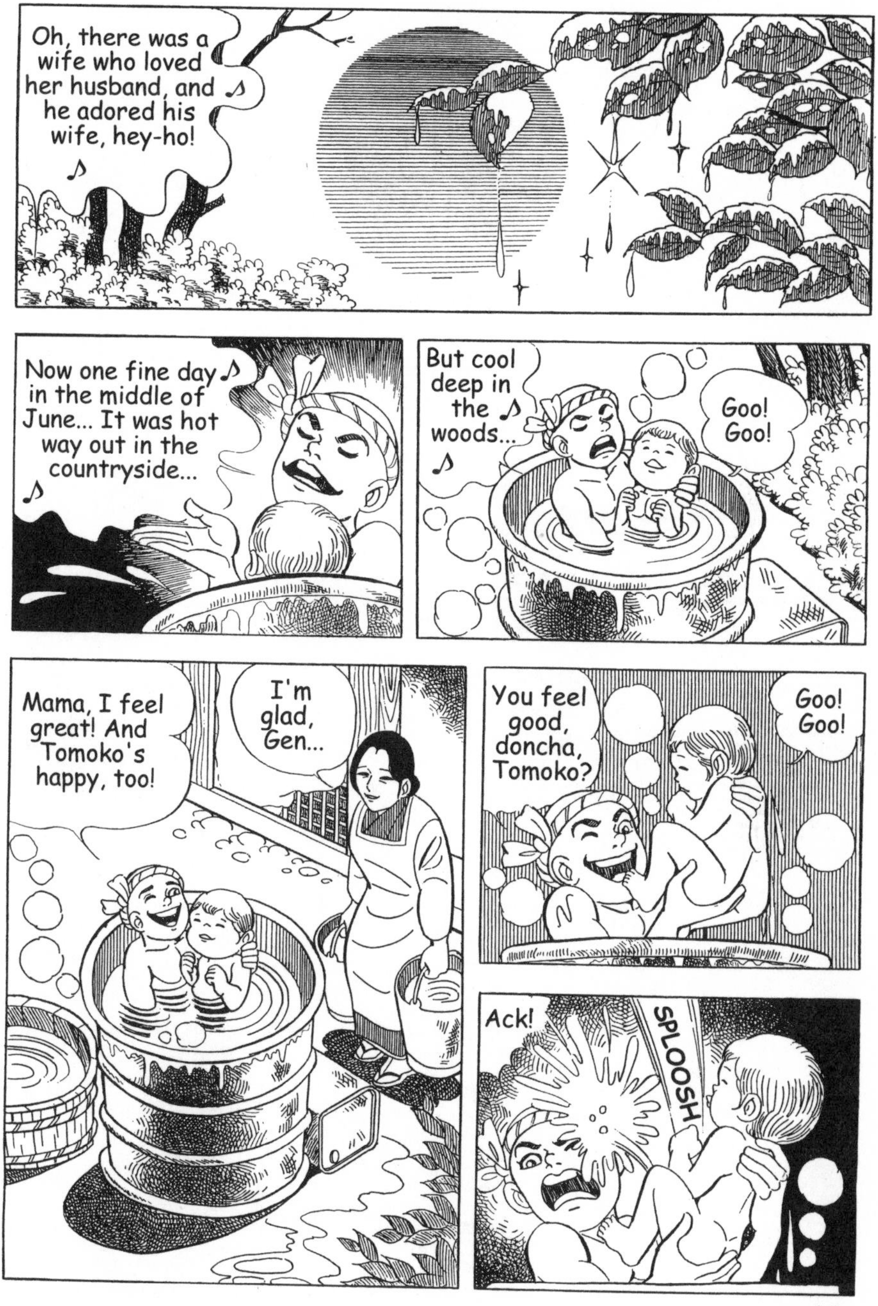
Oh, there was a wife who loved her husband, and ♪ he adored his wife, hey-ho! ♪
Now one fine day ♪ in the middle of June... It was hot way out in the countryside... ♪
But cool deep in the ♪ woods... ♪
Goo! Goo!
Mama, I feel great! And Tomoko's happy, too!
I'm glad, Gen...
You feel good, doncha, Tomoko?
Goo! Goo!
Ack!
SPLOOSH

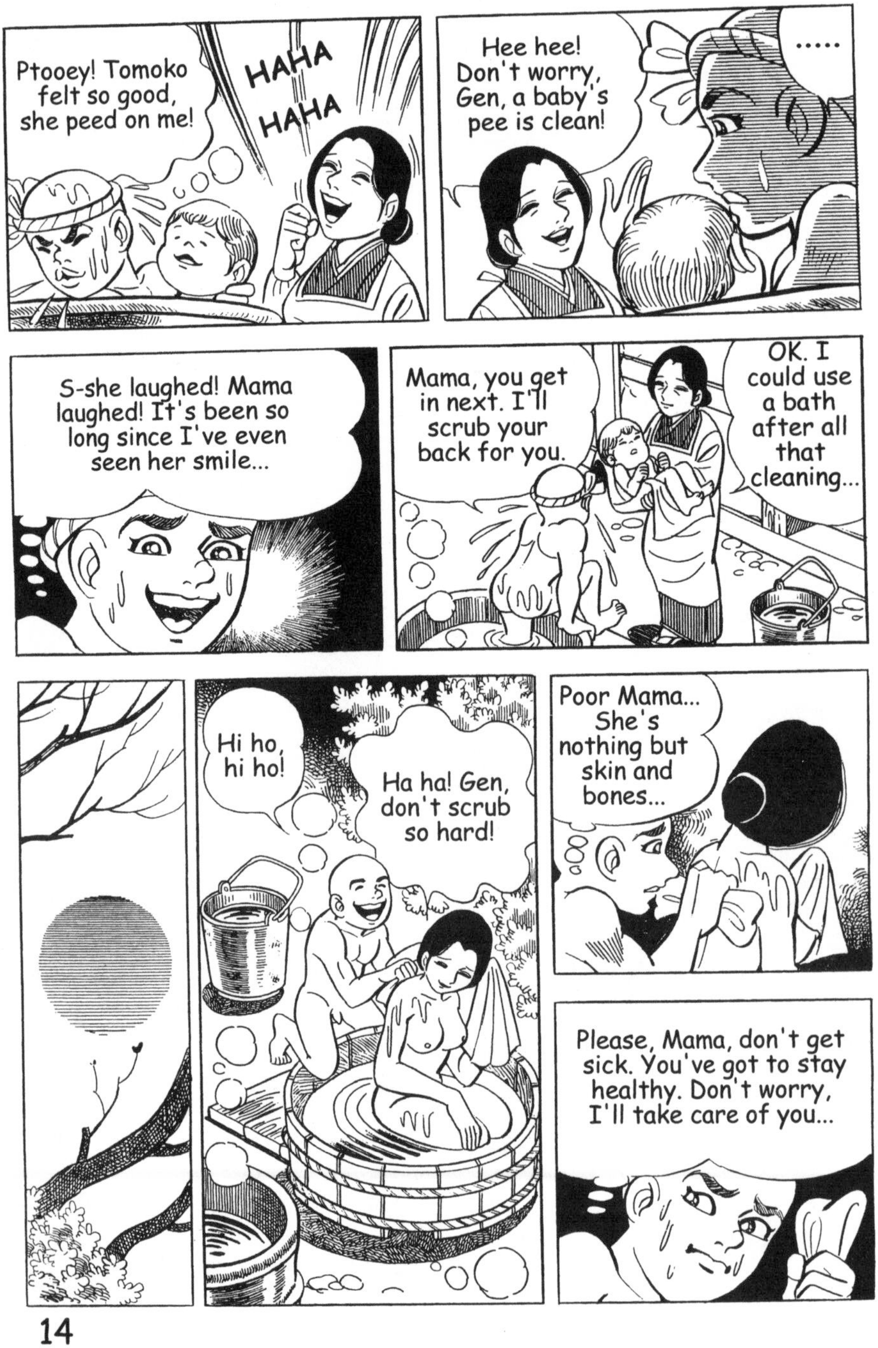
Ptooey! Tomoko felt so good, she peed on me!
HAHA HAHA
Hee hee! Don't worry, Gen, a baby's pee is clean!
.....
S-she laughed! Mama laughed! It's been so long since I've even seen her smile...
Mama, you get in next. I'll scrub your back for you.
OK. I could use a bath after all that cleaning...
Hi ho, hi ho!
Ha ha! Gen, don't scrub so hard!
Poor Mama... She's nothing but skin and bones...
Please, Mama, don't get sick. You've got to stay healthy. Don't worry, I'll take care of you...

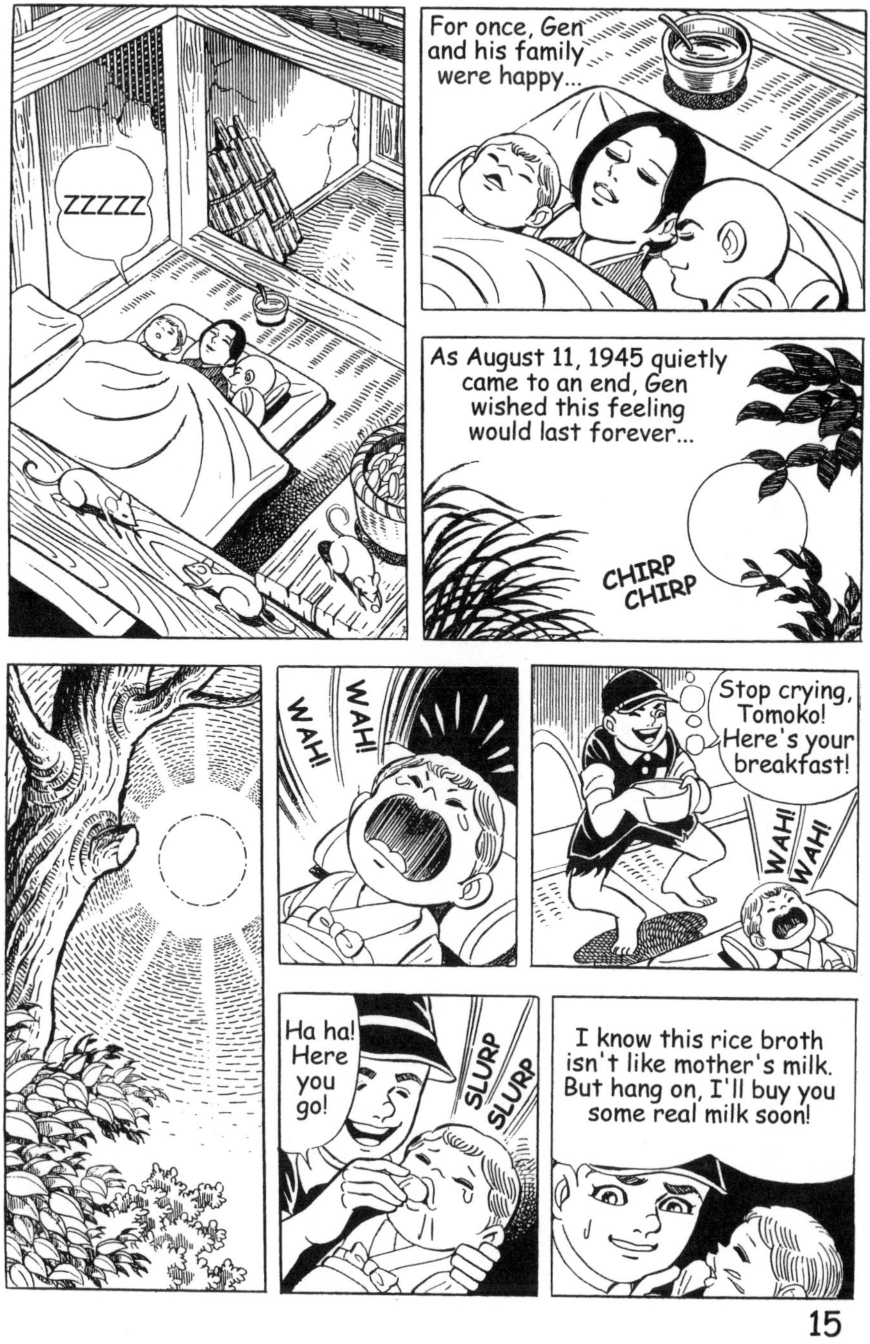
ZZZZZ
For once, Gen and his family were happy...
As August 11, 1945 quietly came to an end, Gen wished this feeling would last forever...
CHIRP CHIRP
WAH! WAH!
Stop crying, Tomoko! Here's your breakfast!
WAH! WAH!
Ha ha! Here you go!
SLURP SLURP
I know this rice broth isn't like mother's milk. But hang on, I'll buy you some real milk soon!

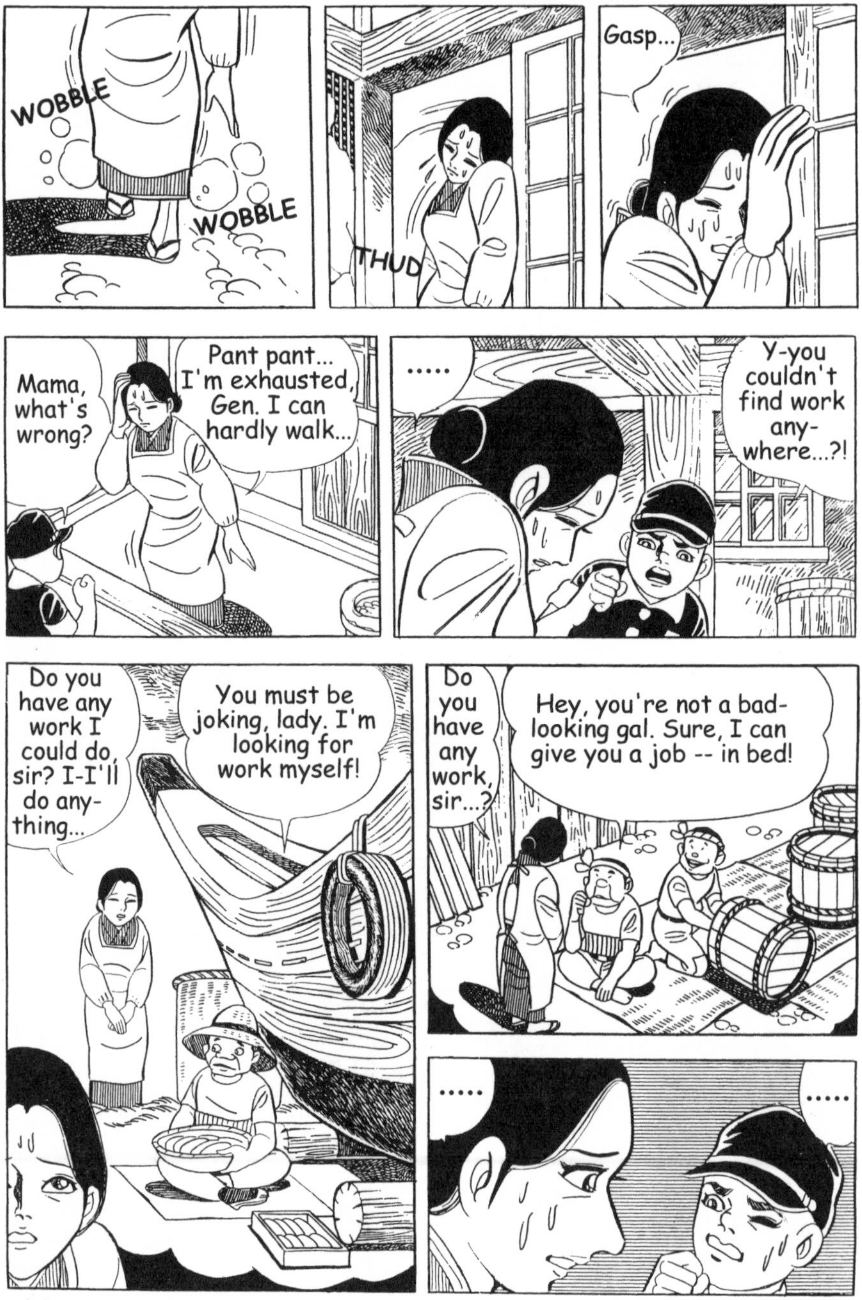
WOBBLE
WOBBLE
THUD
Gasp...
Mama, what's wrong?
Pant pant... I'm exhausted, Gen. I can hardly walk...
.....
Y-you couldn't find work any-where...?!
Do you have any work I could do, sir? I-I'll do any-thing...
You must be joking, lady. I'm looking for work myself!
Do you have any work, sir...?
Hey, you're not a bad-looking gal. Sure, I can give you a job -- in bed!
.....
.....

With Hiroshima in ashes, it's no wonder there's no work anywhere...

What'll I do? We need money to buy food. Without money, we can't live! If I had any clothes to spare, I'd sell them, but...

I can't stand it, Gen, I can't stand it... Sob...

.....

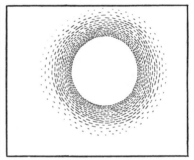

BAM! BAM! BAM!

Look at that!

Ha ha!

Please, give me a job!

Any job!

ぼくに仕事をさせてください

Sign: PLEASE GIVE ME WORK!

17

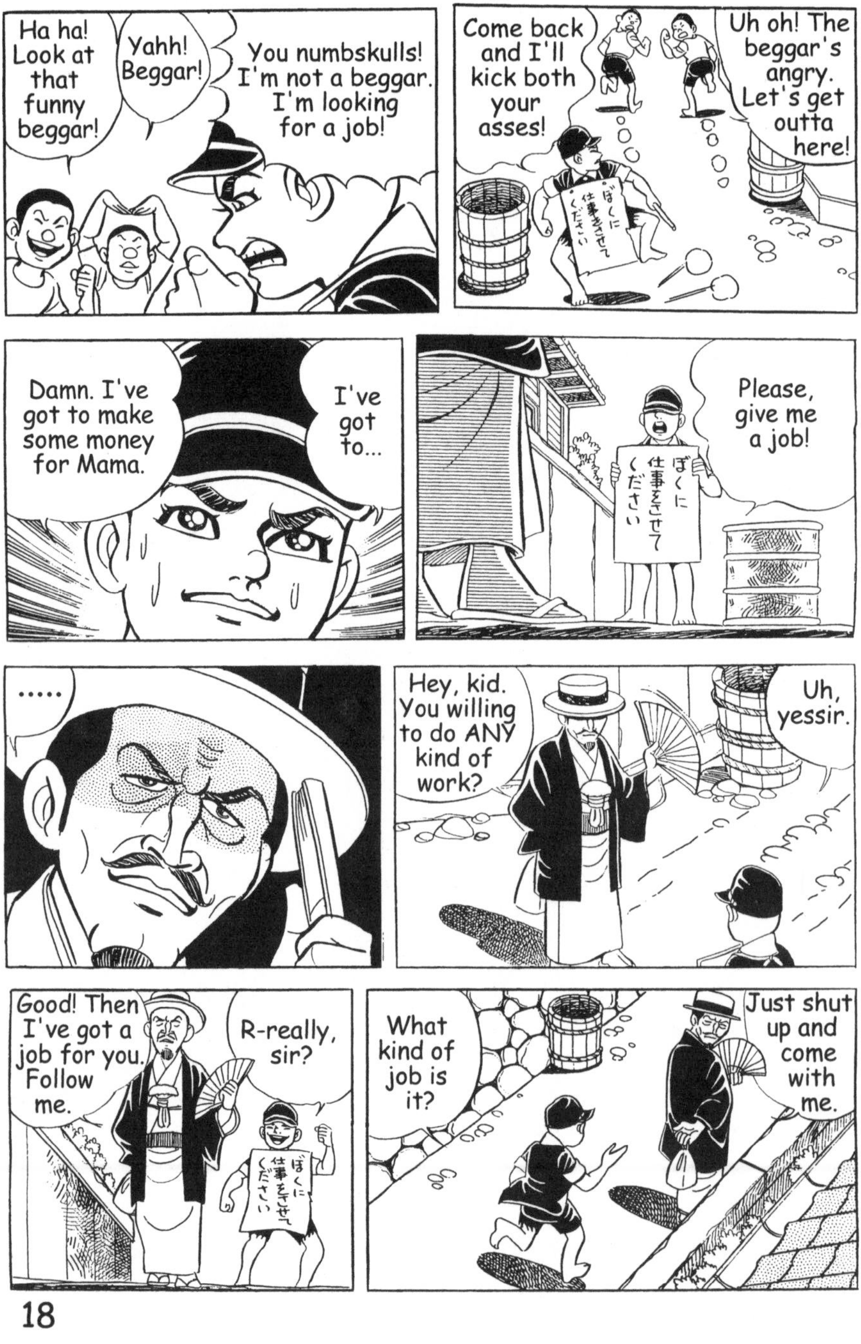
Ha ha! Look at that funny beggar!
Yahh! Beggar!
You numbskulls! I'm not a beggar. I'm looking for a job!
Come back and I'll kick both your asses!
ぼくに仕事をさせてください
Uh oh! The beggar's angry. Let's get outta here!
Damn. I've got to make some money for Mama.
I've got to...
ぼくに仕事をさせてください
Please, give me a job!
.....
Hey, kid. You willing to do ANY kind of work?
Uh, yessir.
Good! Then I've got a job for you. Follow me.
R-really, sir?
ぼくに仕事をさせてください
What kind of job is it?
Just shut up and come with me.

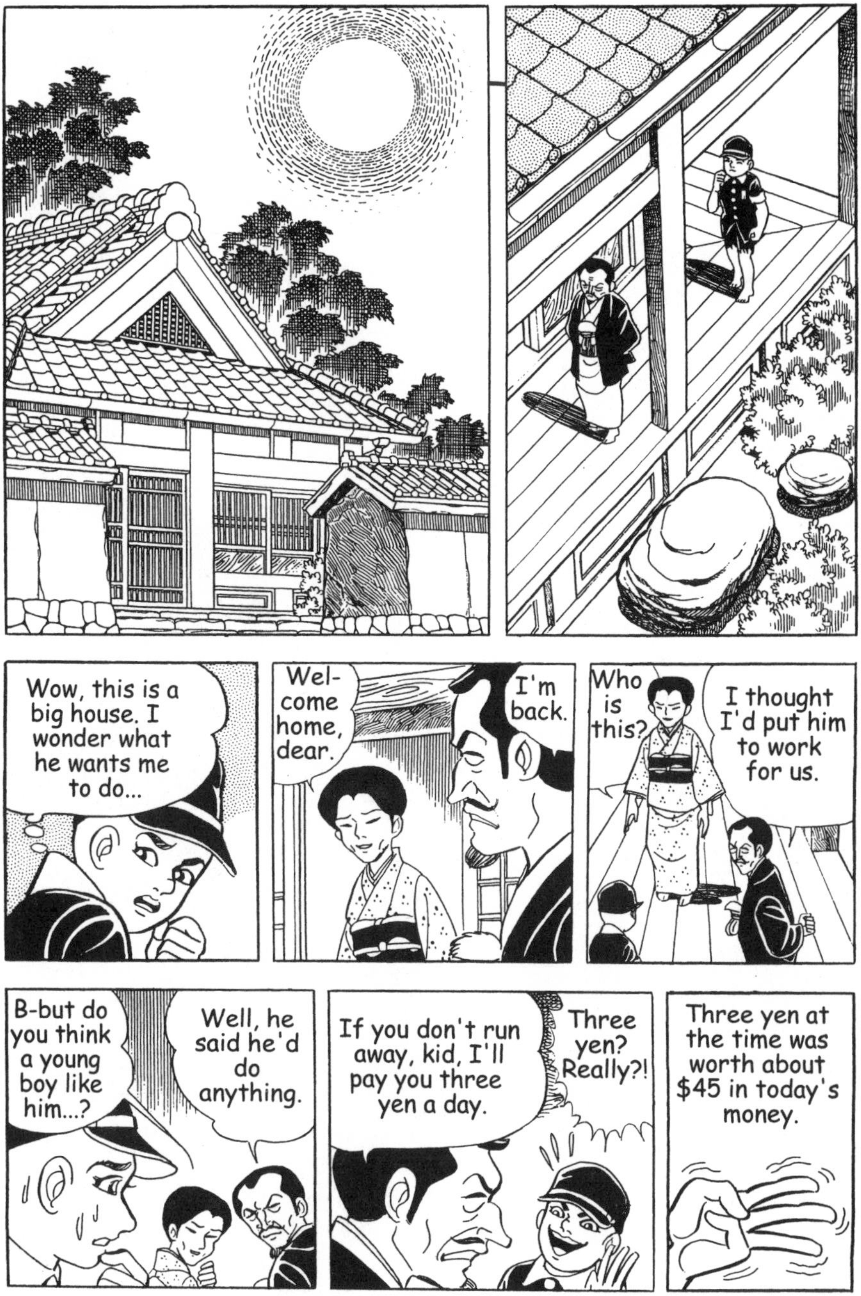

Wow, this is a big house. I wonder what he wants me to do...
Wel- come home, dear.
I'm back.
Who is this?
I thought I'd put him to work for us.
B-but do you think a young boy like him...?
Well, he said he'd do anything.
If you don't run away, kid, I'll pay you three yen a day.
Three yen? Really?!
Three yen at the time was worth about $45 in today's money.

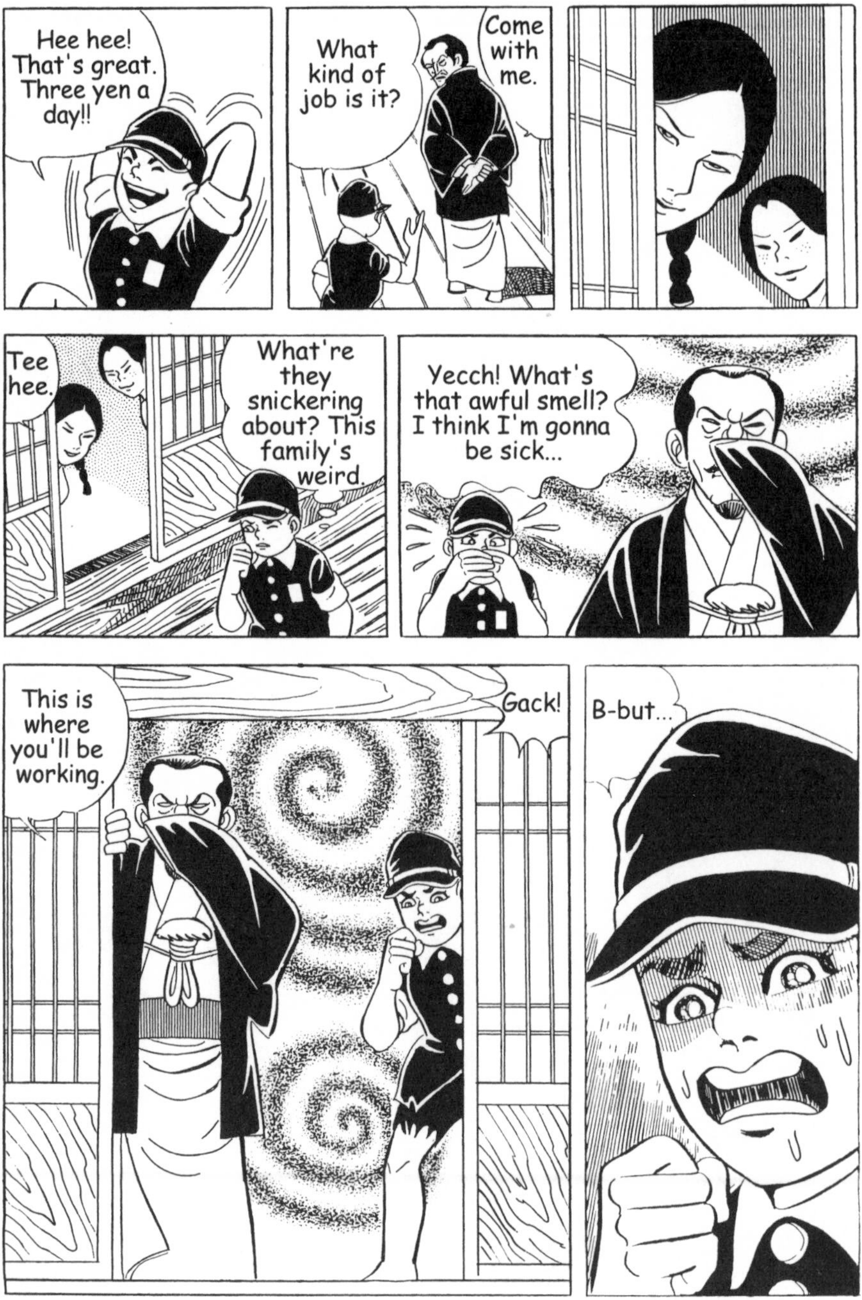
Hee hee! That's great. Three yen a day!!
What kind of job is it?
Come with me.
Tee hee.
What're they snickering about? This family's weird.
Yecch! What's that awful smell? I think I'm gonna be sick...
This is where you'll be working.
Gack!
B-but...

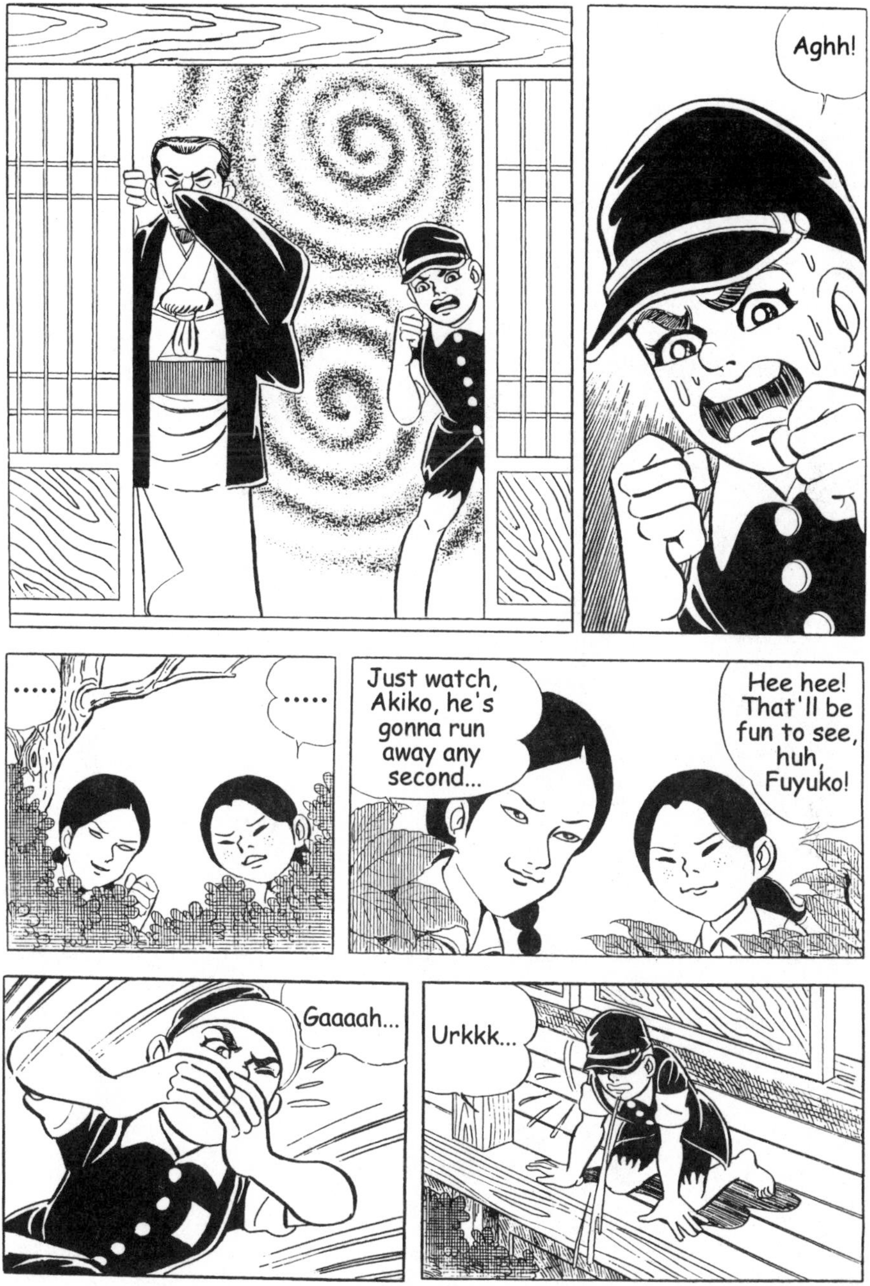

Aghh!
.....
.....
Just watch, Akiko, he's gonna run away any second...
Hee hee! That'll be fun to see, huh, Fuyuko!
Gaaaah...
Urkkk...

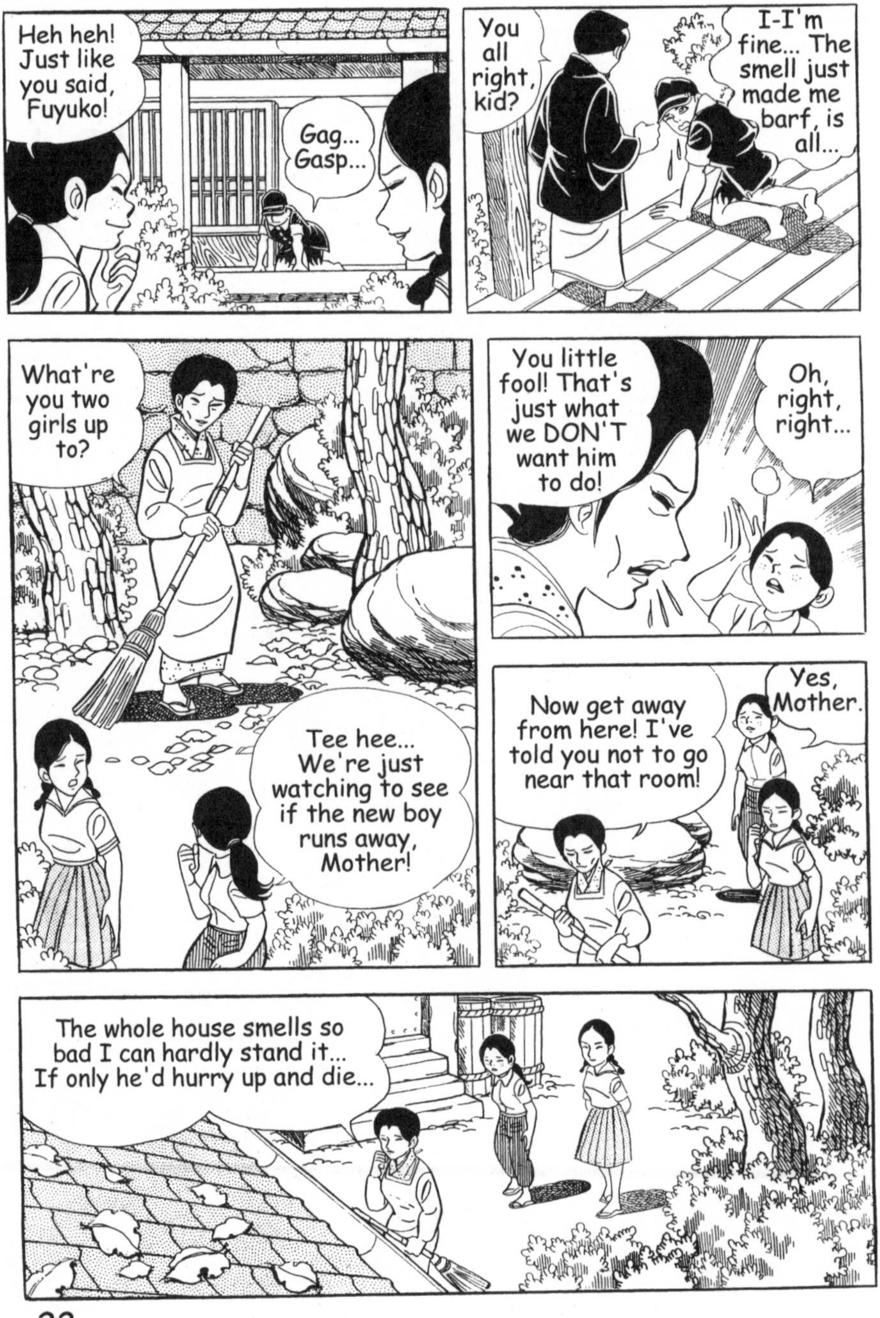

Heh heh! Just like you said, Fuyuko!
Gag... Gasp...
You all right, kid?
I-I'm fine... The smell just made me barf, is all...
What're you two girls up to?
Tee hee... We're just watching to see if the new boy runs away, Mother!
You little fool! That's just what we DON'T want him to do!
Oh, right, right...
Now get away from here! I've told you not to go near that room!
Yes, Mother.
The whole house smells so bad I can hardly stand it... If only he'd hurry up and die...

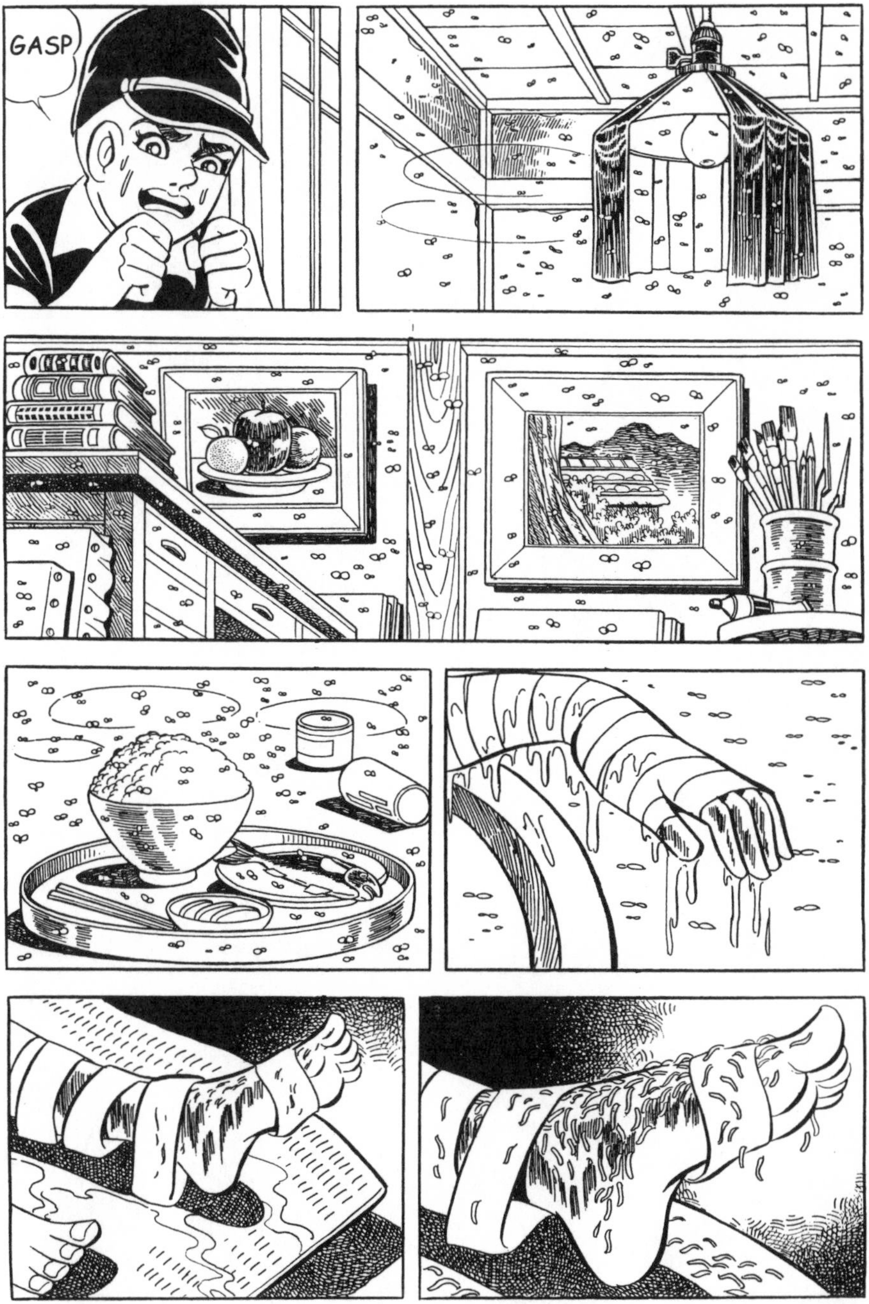
GASP

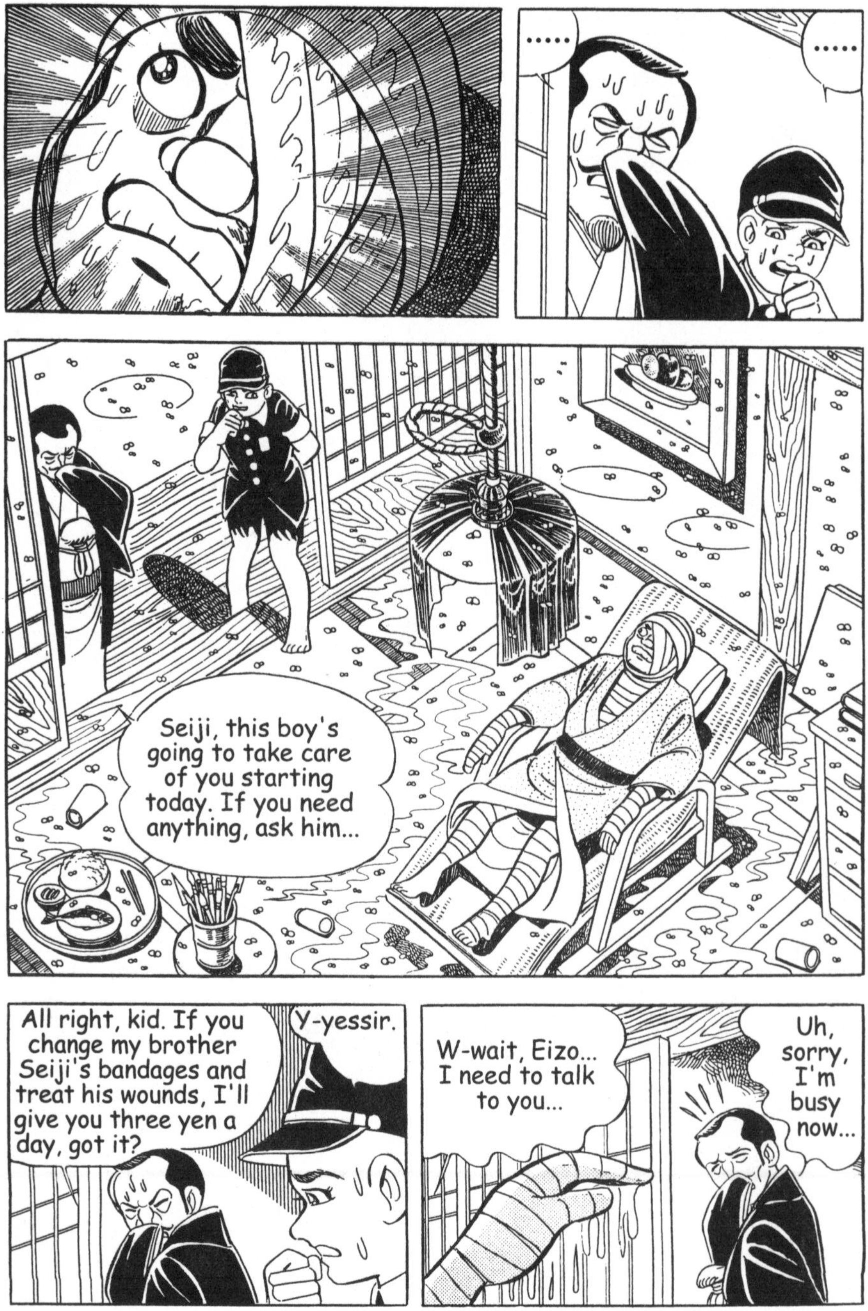
.....
.....
Seiji, this boy's going to take care of you starting today. If you need anything, ask him...
All right, kid. If you change my brother Seiji's bandages and treat his wounds, I'll give you three yen a day, got it?
Y-yessir.
W-wait, Eizo... I need to talk to you...
Uh, sorry, I'm busy now...

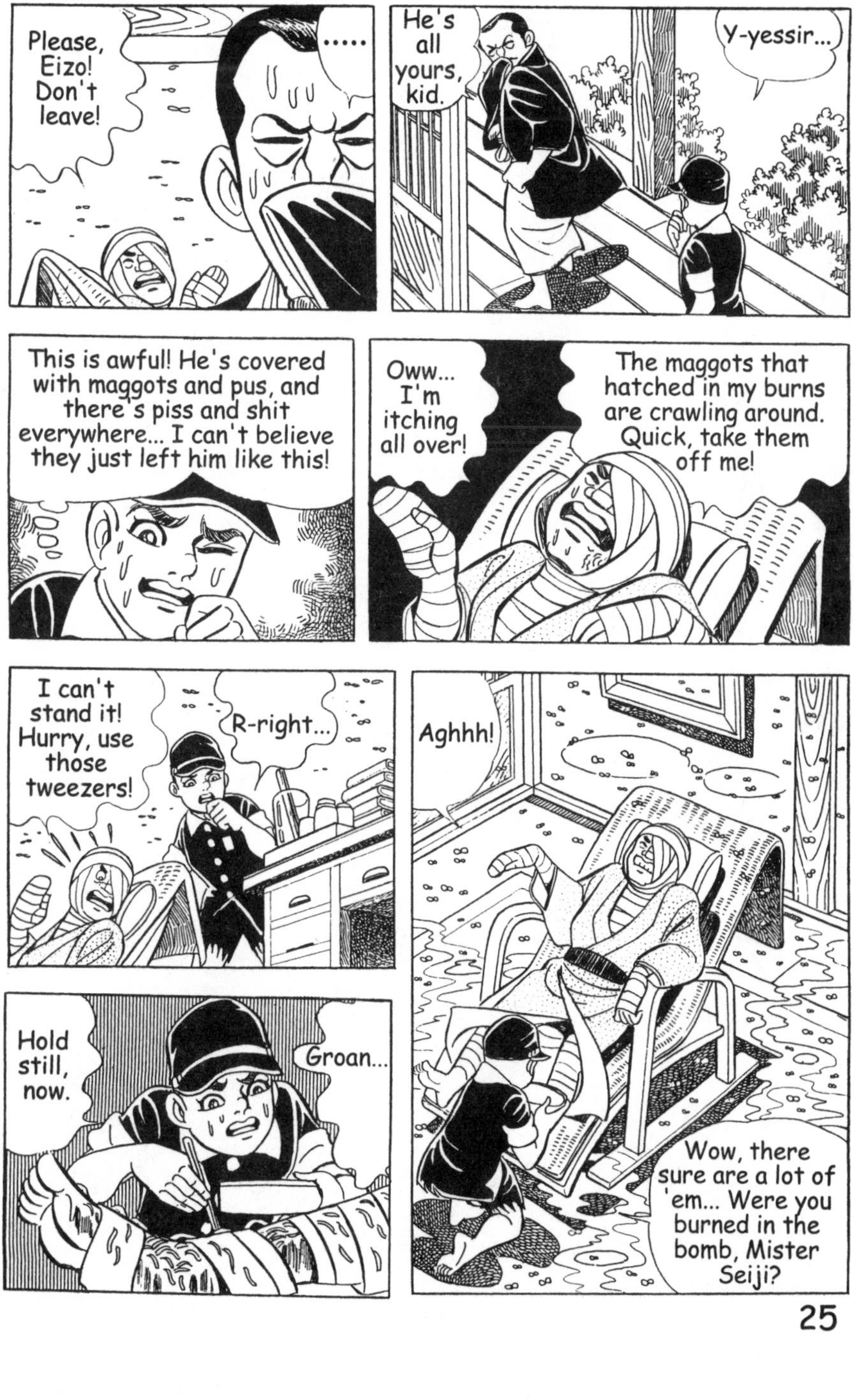

Please, Eizo! Don't leave!
.....
He's all yours, kid.
Y-yessir...
This is awful! He's covered with maggots and pus, and there's piss and shit everywhere... I can't believe they just left him like this!
Oww... I'm itching all over!
The maggots that hatched in my burns are crawling around. Quick, take them off me!
I can't stand it! Hurry, use those tweezers!
R-right...
Hold still, now.
Groan...
Aghhh!
Wow, there sure are a lot of 'em... Were you burned in the bomb, Mister Seiji?

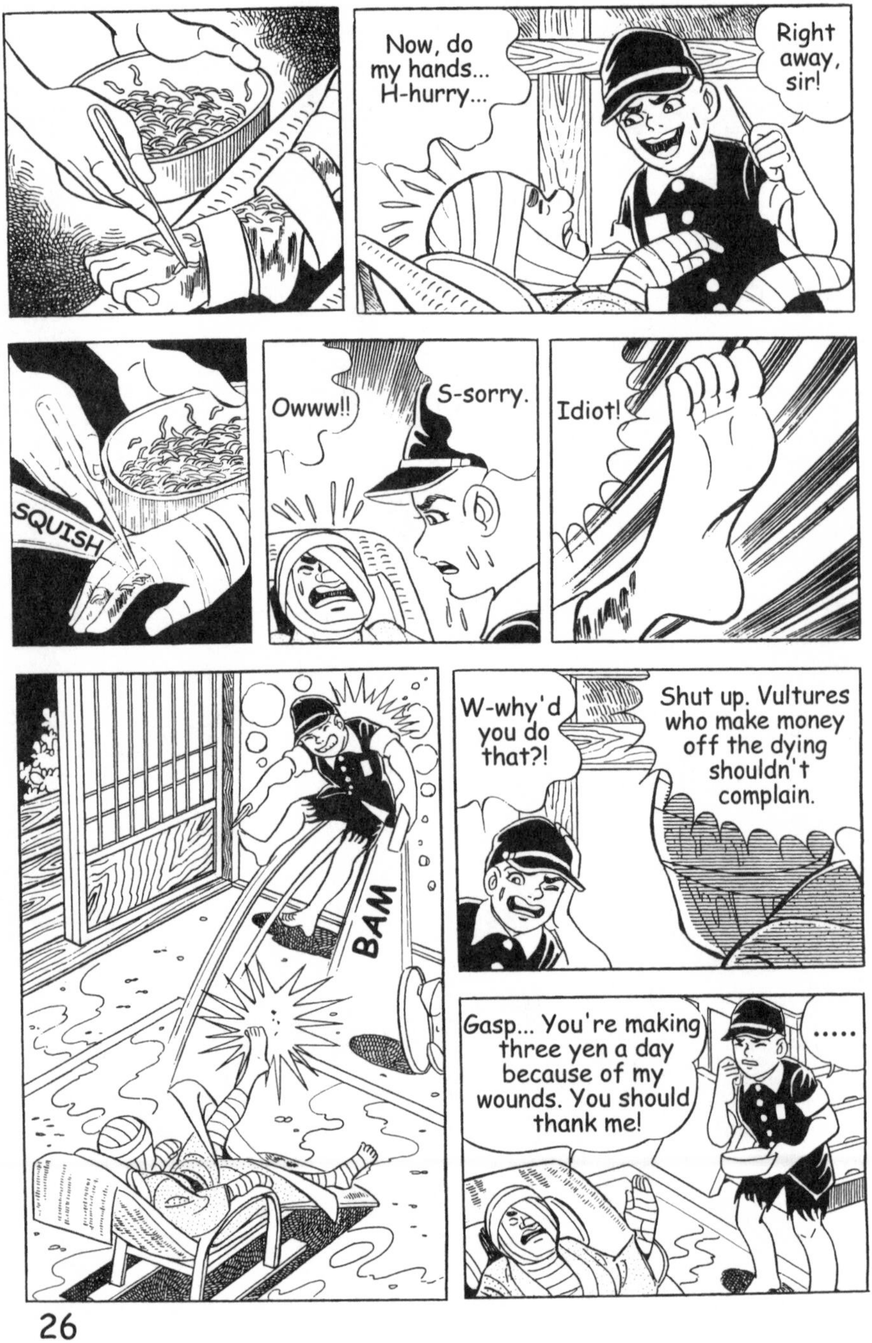
Now, do my hands... H-hurry...
Right away, sir!
SQUISH
Owww!!
S-sorry.
Idiot!
BAM
W-why'd you do that?!
Shut up. Vultures who make money off the dying shouldn't complain.
Gasp... You're making three yen a day because of my wounds. You should thank me!
.....

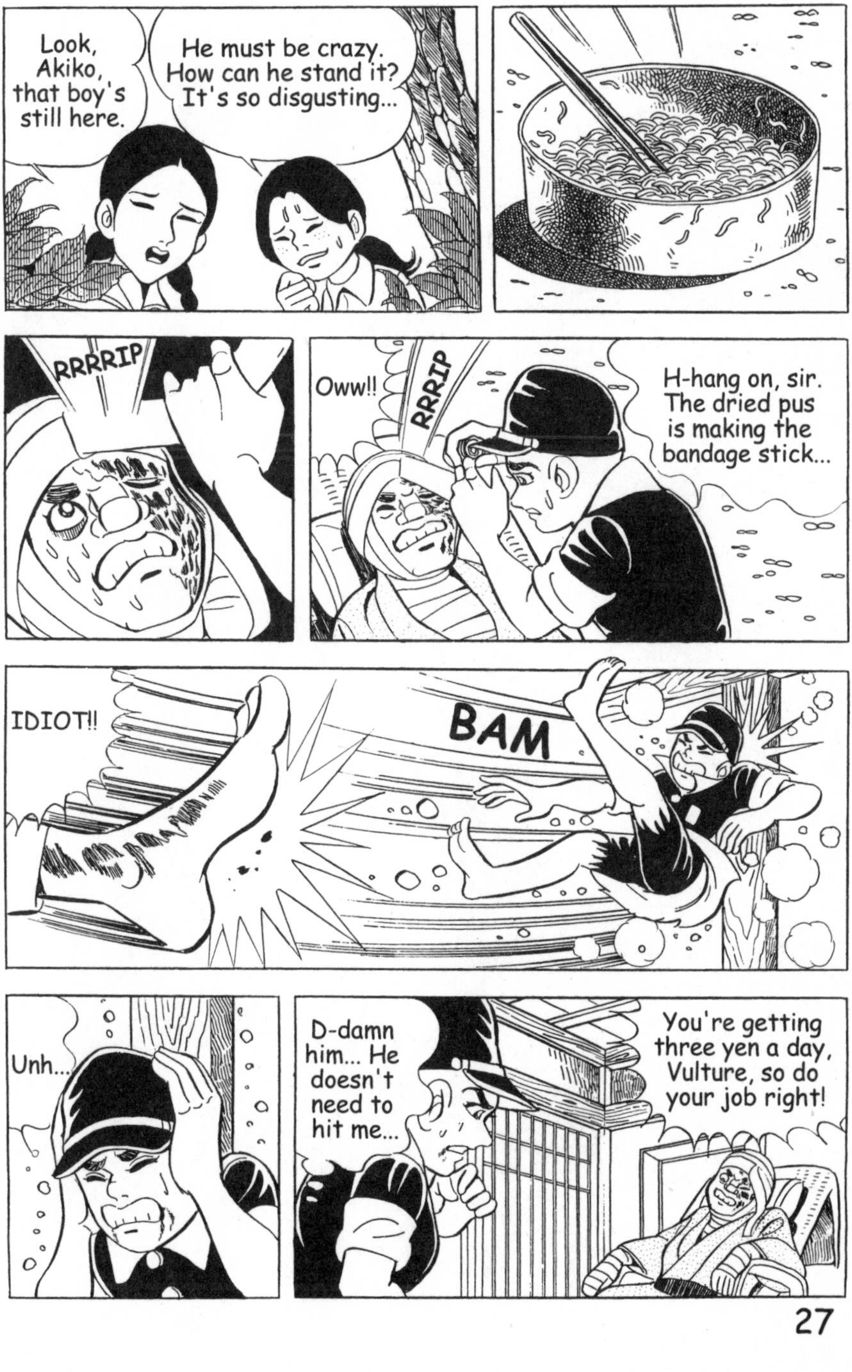
Look, Akiko, that boy's still here.
He must be crazy. How can he stand it? It's so disgusting...
RRRRIP
Oww!!
RRRIP
H-hang on, sir. The dried pus is making the bandage stick...
IDIOT!!
BAM
Unh...
D-damn him... He doesn't need to hit me...
You're getting three yen a day, Vulture, so do your job right!

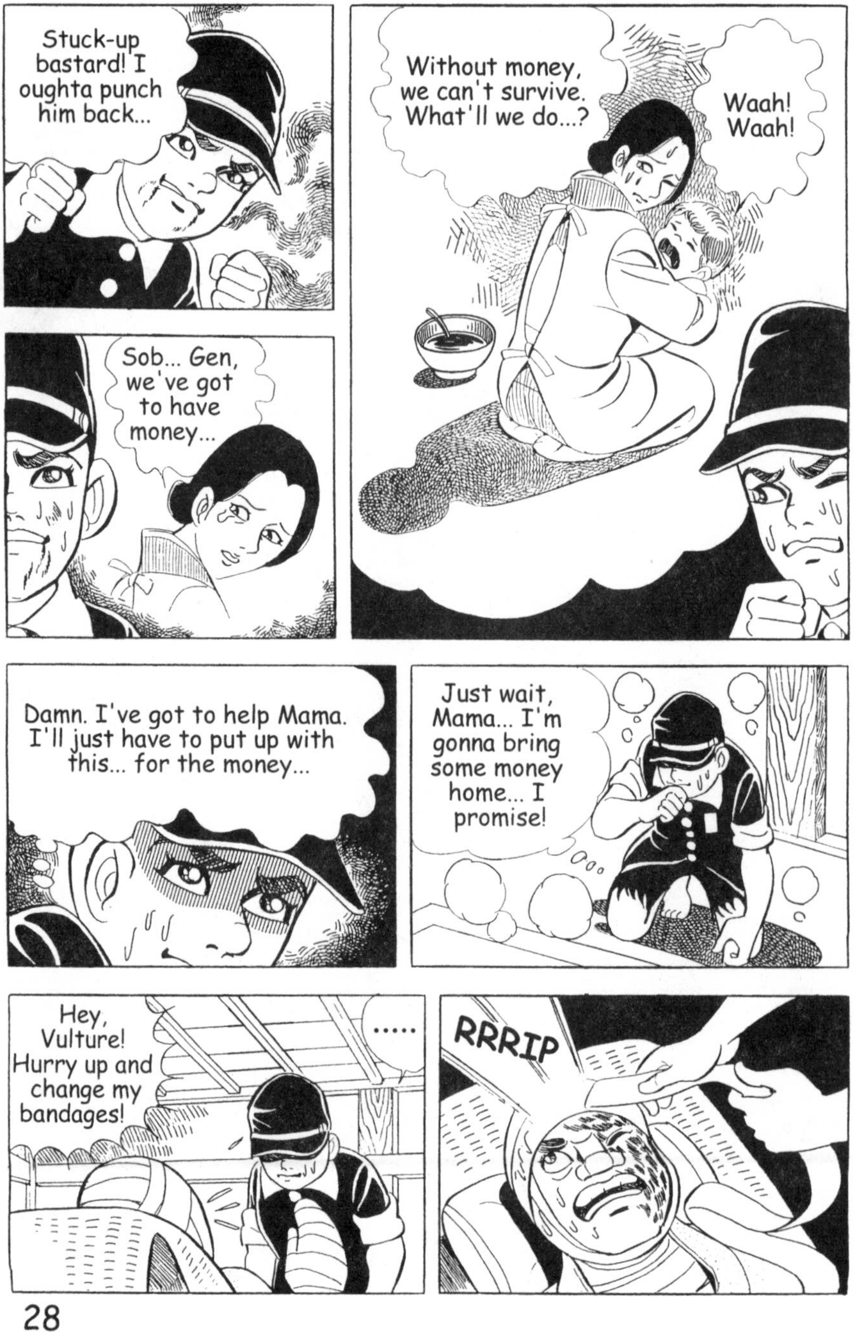
Stuck-up bastard! I oughta punch him back...
Sob... Gen, we've got to have money...
Without money, we can't survive. What'll we do...?
Waah! Waah!
Damn. I've got to help Mama. I'll just have to put up with this... for the money...
Just wait, Mama... I'm gonna bring some money home... I promise!
Hey, Vulture! Hurry up and change my bandages!
.....
RRRIP

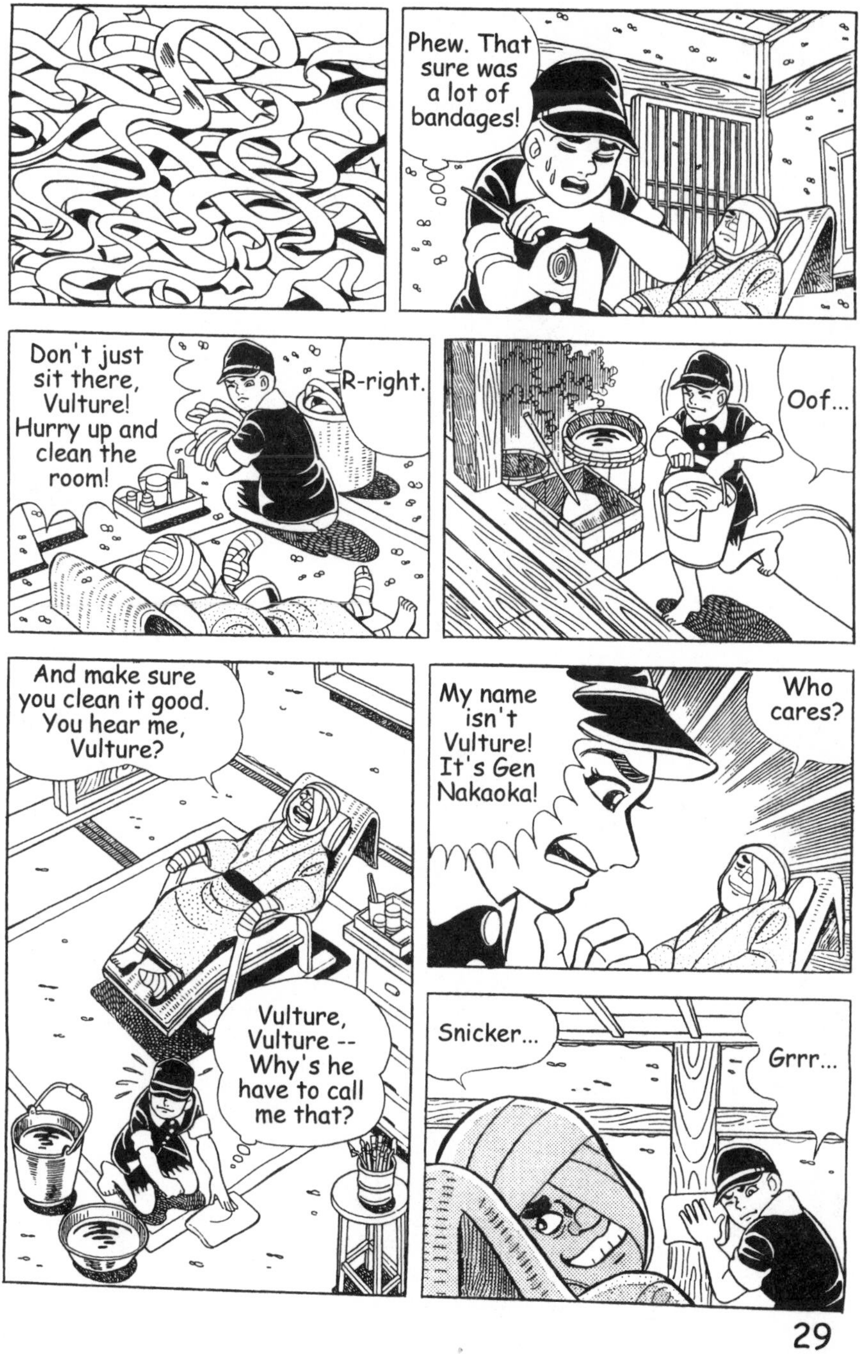
Phew. That sure was a lot of bandages!
Don't just sit there, Vulture! Hurry up and clean the room!
R-right.
Oof...
And make sure you clean it good. You hear me, Vulture?
Vulture, Vulture -- Why's he have to call me that?
My name isn't Vulture! It's Gen Nakaoka!
Who cares?
Snicker...
Grrr...

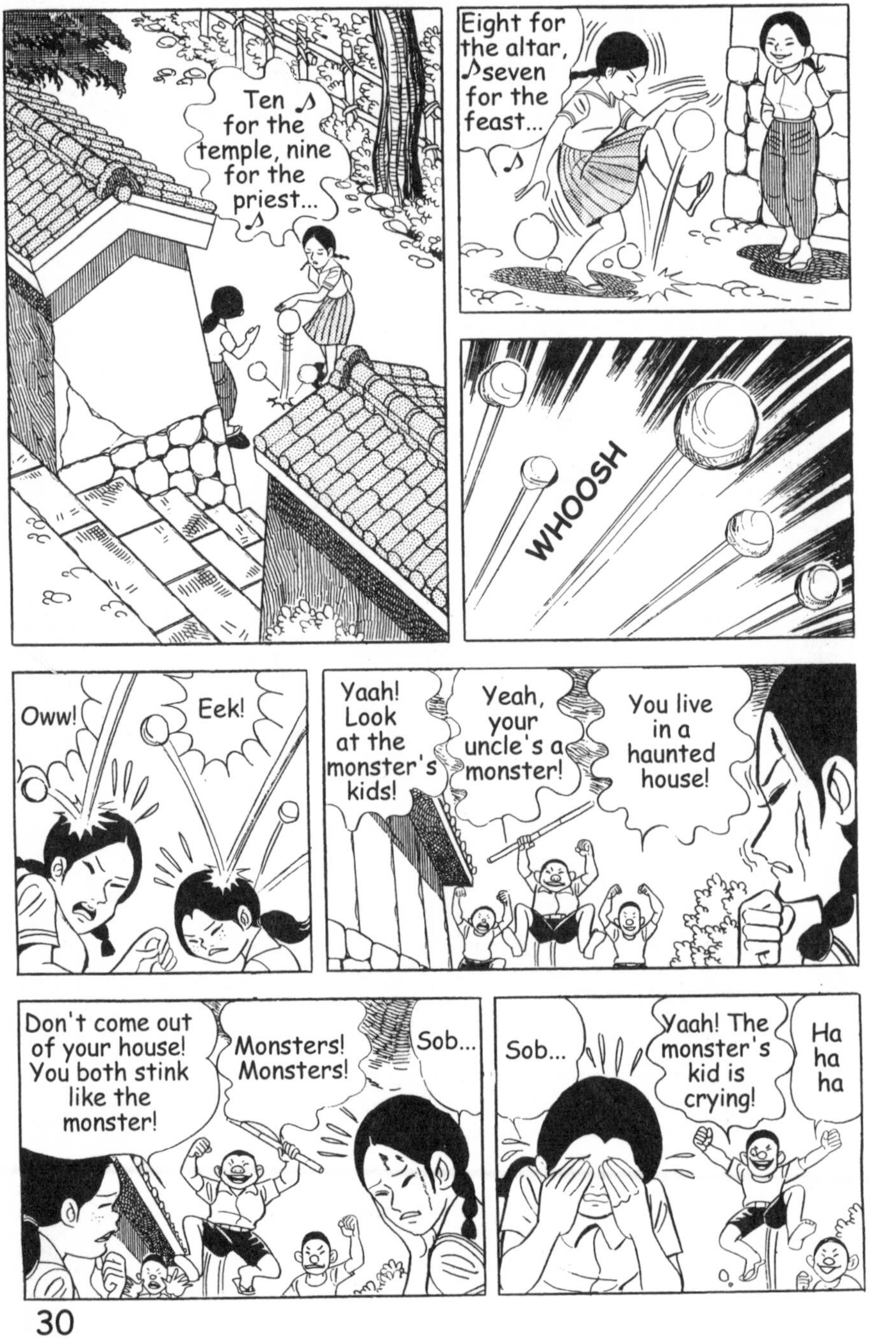
Ten ♪ for the temple, nine for the priest... ♪
Eight for the altar, ♪seven for the feast... ♪
WHOOSH
Oww!
Eek!
Yaah! Look at the monster's kids!
Yeah, your uncle's a monster!
You live in a haunted house!
Don't come out of your house! You both stink like the monster!
Monsters! Monsters!
Sob...
Sob...
Yaah! The monster's kid is crying!
Ha ha ha

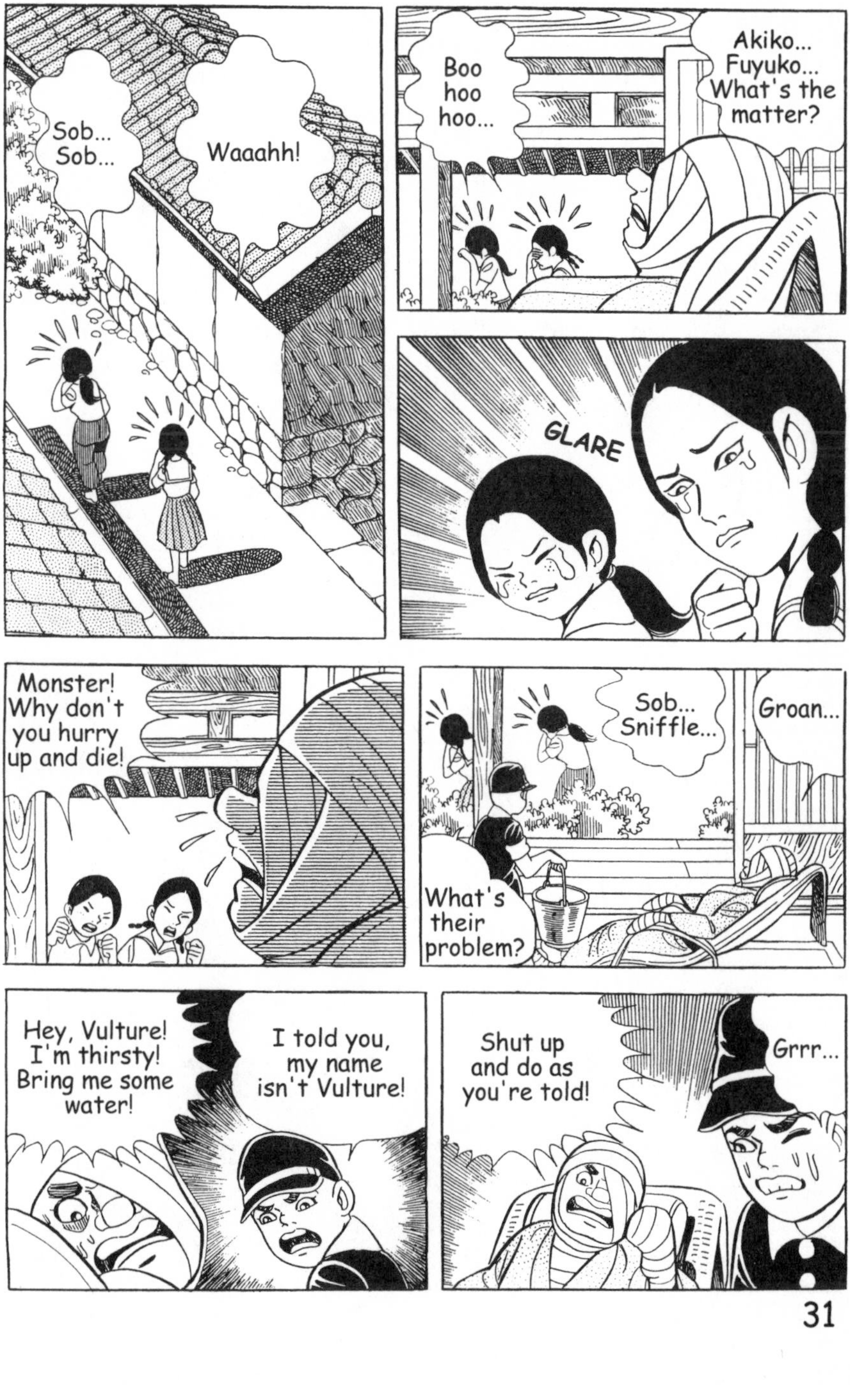
Sob... Sob...
Waaahh!
Boo hoo hoo...
Akiko... Fuyuko... What's the matter?
GLARE
Monster! Why don't you hurry up and die!
Sob... Sniffle...
Groan...
What's their problem?
Hey, Vulture! I'm thirsty! Bring me some water!
I told you, my name isn't Vulture!
Shut up and do as you're told!
Grrr...

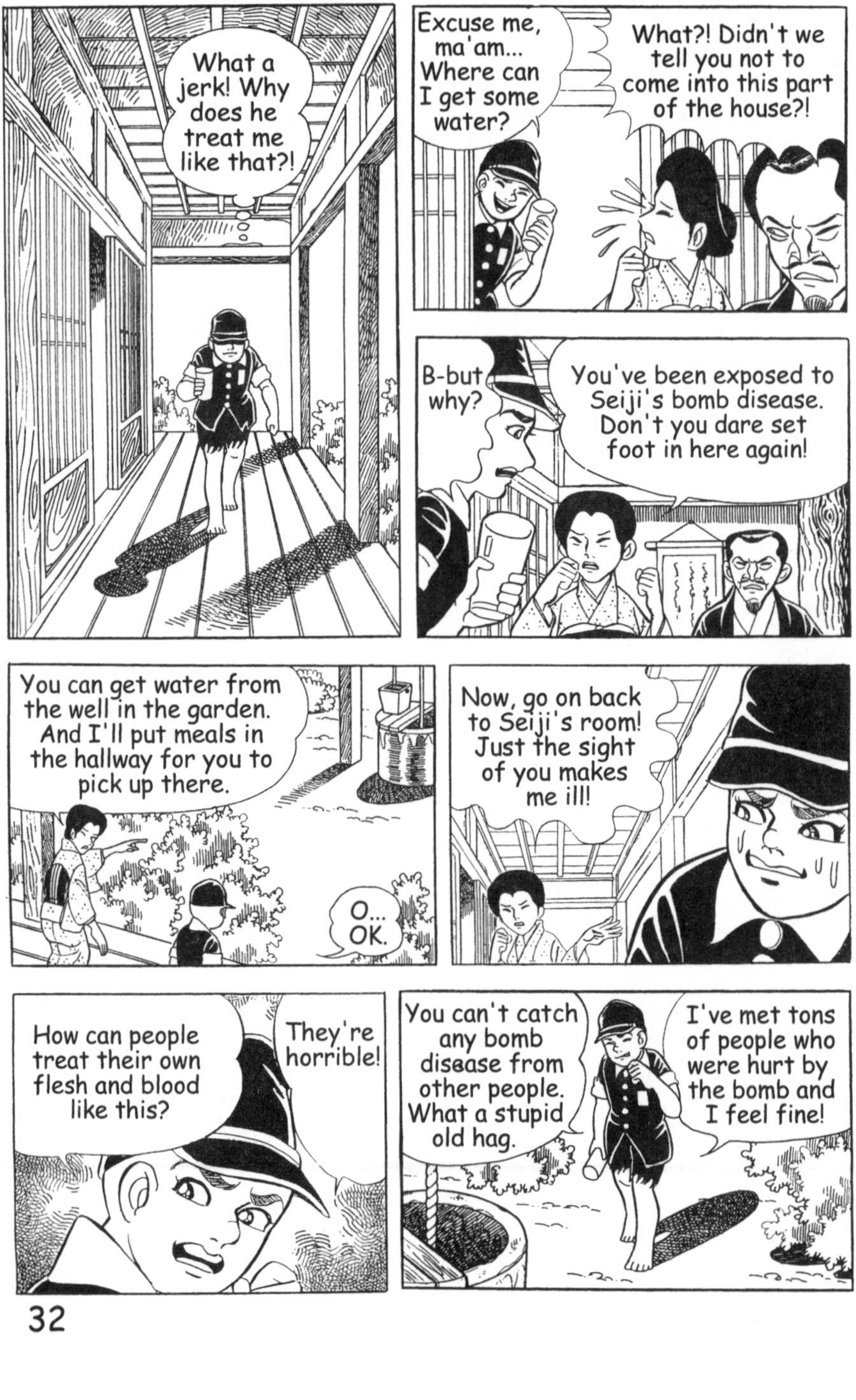
What a jerk! Why does he treat me like that?!
Excuse me, ma'am... Where can I get some water?
What?! Didn't we tell you not to come into this part of the house?!
B-but why?
You've been exposed to Seiji's bomb disease. Don't you dare set foot in here again!
You can get water from the well in the garden. And I'll put meals in the hallway for you to pick up there.
O... OK.
Now, go on back to Seiji's room! Just the sight of you makes me ill!
How can people treat their own flesh and blood like this?
They're horrible!
You can't catch any bomb disease from other people. What a stupid old hag.
I've met tons of people who were hurt by the bomb and I feel fine!

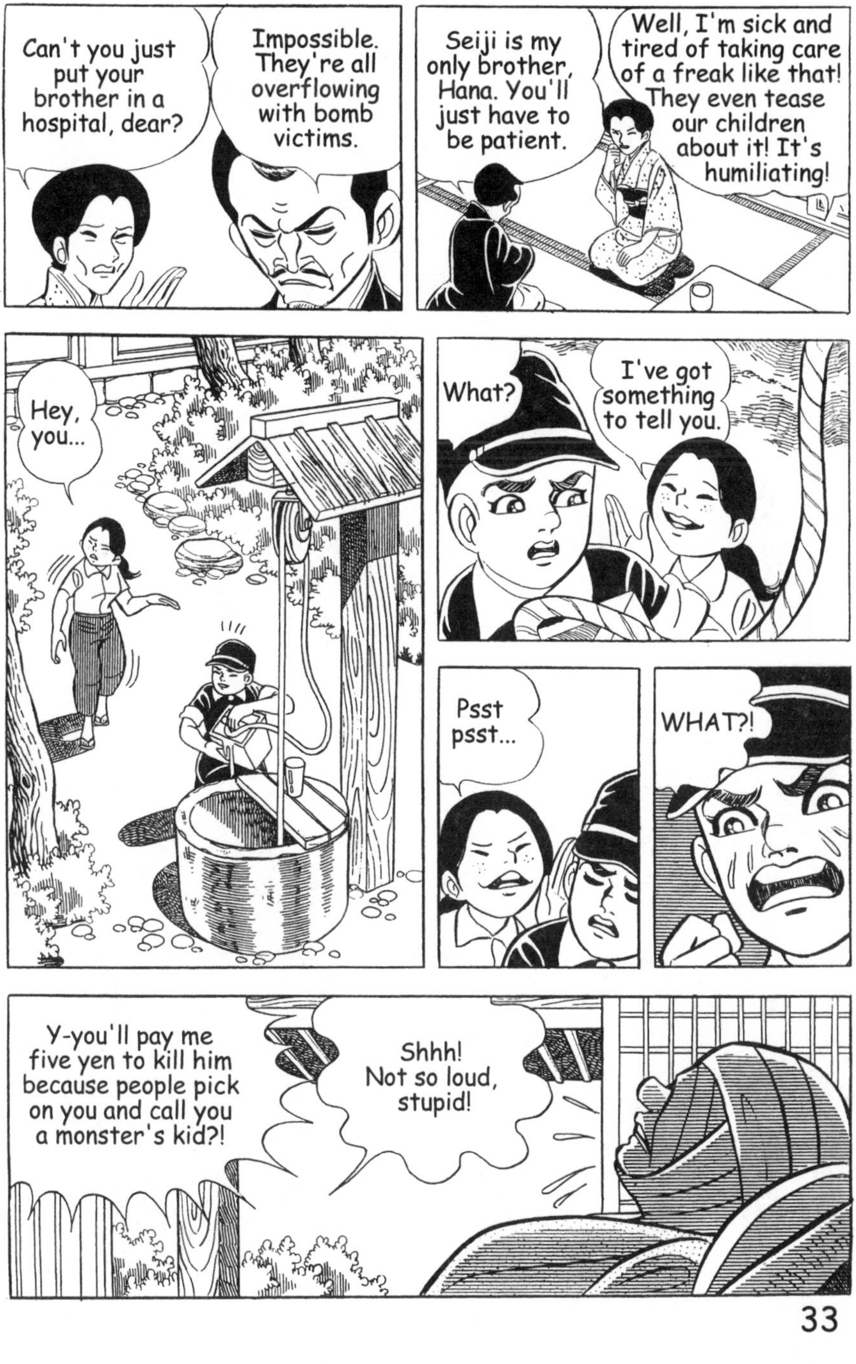
Can't you just put your brother in a hospital, dear?
Impossible. They're all overflowing with bomb victims.
Seiji is my only brother, Hana. You'll just have to be patient.
Well, I'm sick and tired of taking care of a freak like that! They even tease our children about it! It's humiliating!
Hey, you...
What?
I've got something to tell you.
Psst psst...
WHAT?!
Y-you'll pay me five yen to kill him because people pick on you and call you a monster's kid?!
Shhh! Not so loud, stupid!

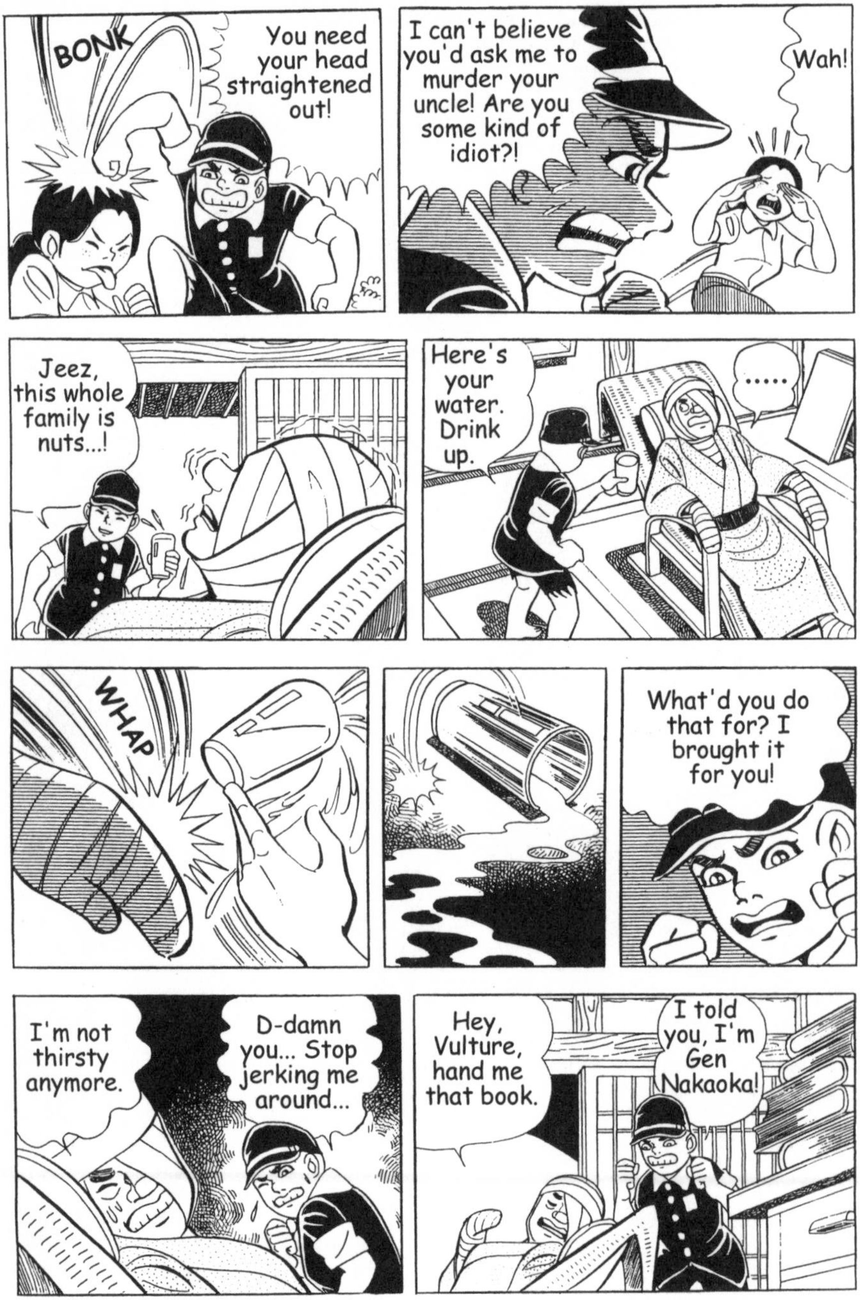
BONK
You need your head straightened out!
I can't believe you'd ask me to murder your uncle! Are you some kind of idiot?!
Wah!
Jeez, this whole family is nuts...!
Here's your water. Drink up.
.....
WHAP
What'd you do that for? I brought it for you!
I'm not thirsty anymore.
D-damn you... Stop jerking me around...
Hey, Vulture, hand me that book.
I told you, I'm Gen Nakaoka!

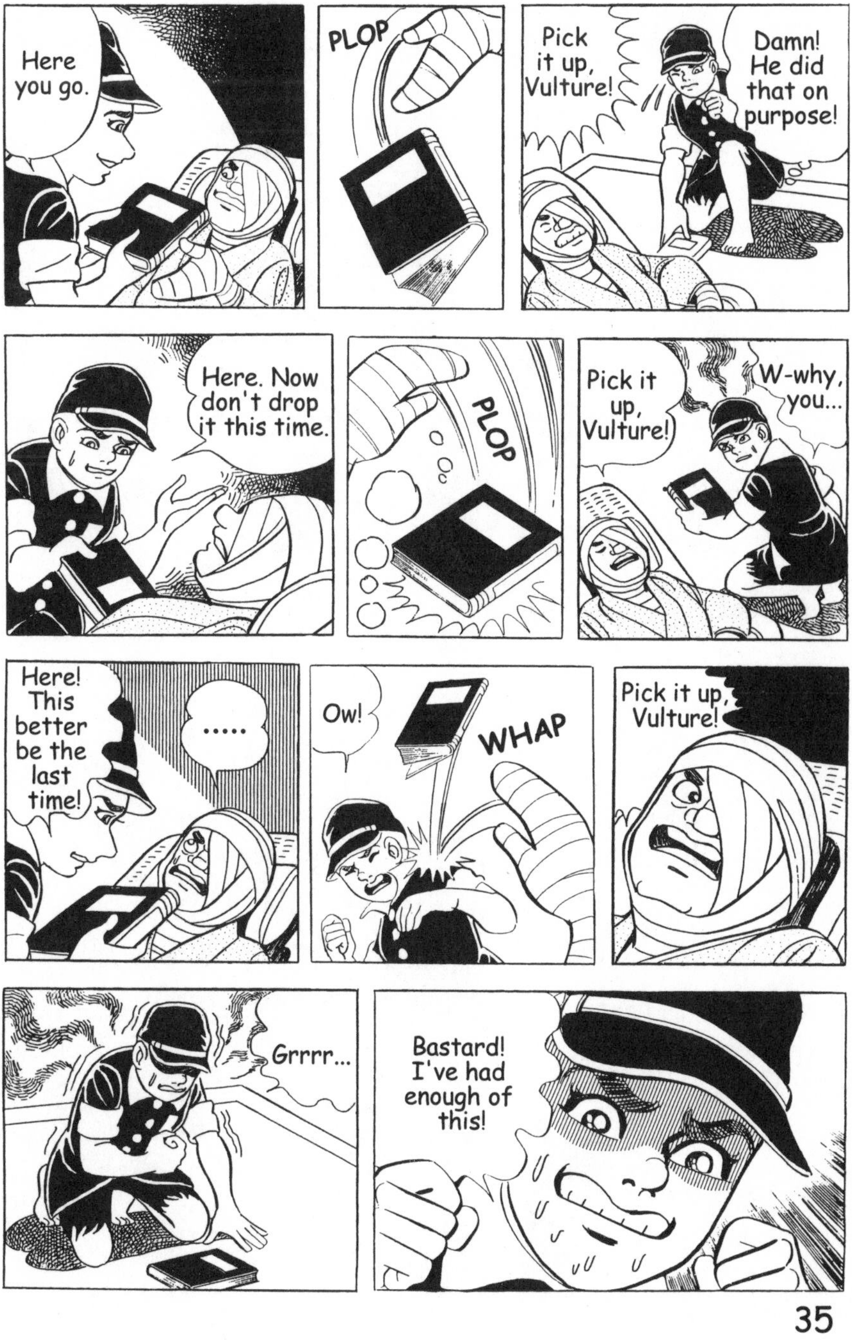
Here you go.
PLOP
Pick it up, Vulture!
Damn! He did that on purpose!
Here. Now don't drop it this time.
PLOP
Pick it up, Vulture!
W-why, you...
Here! This better be the last time!
.....
Ow!
WHAP
Pick it up, Vulture!
Grrrr...
Bastard! I've had enough of this!

Act your age, mister! Not like some spoiled brat!!

SLAP

You jerk!!

I can't take care of you if you act like that!

I'm going home!

You can lie in your own shit, see if I care!!

Sob...

G-Gen... Wait... Gen Nakaoka... Wait...

Y-you called me by my real name...!

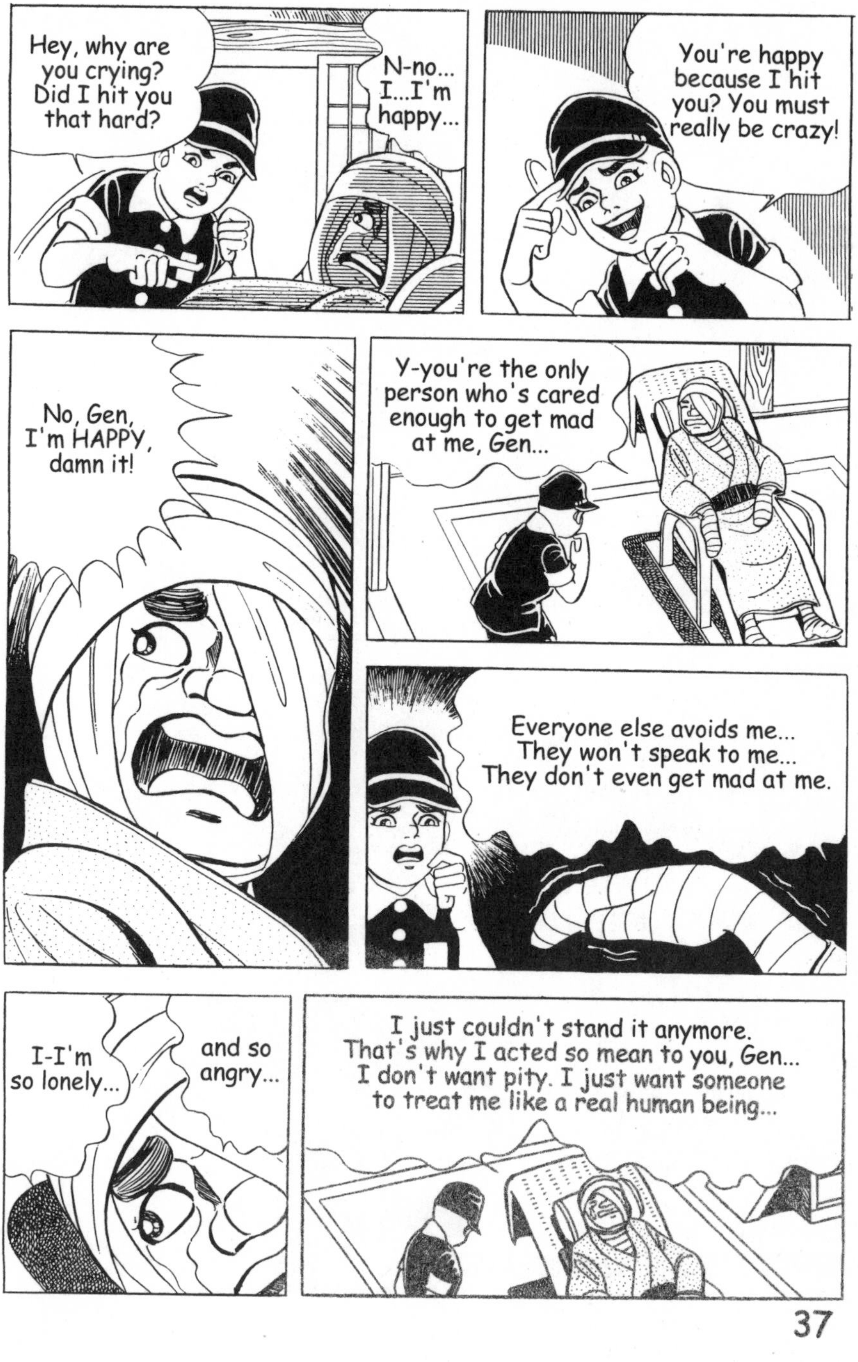
Hey, why are you crying? Did I hit you that hard?
N-no... I...I'm happy...
You're happy because I hit you? You must really be crazy!
No, Gen, I'm HAPPY, damn it!
Y-you're the only person who's cared enough to get mad at me, Gen...
Everyone else avoids me... They won't speak to me... They don't even get mad at me.
I-I'm so lonely...
and so angry...
I just couldn't stand it anymore. That's why I acted so mean to you, Gen... I don't want pity. I just want someone to treat me like a real human being...

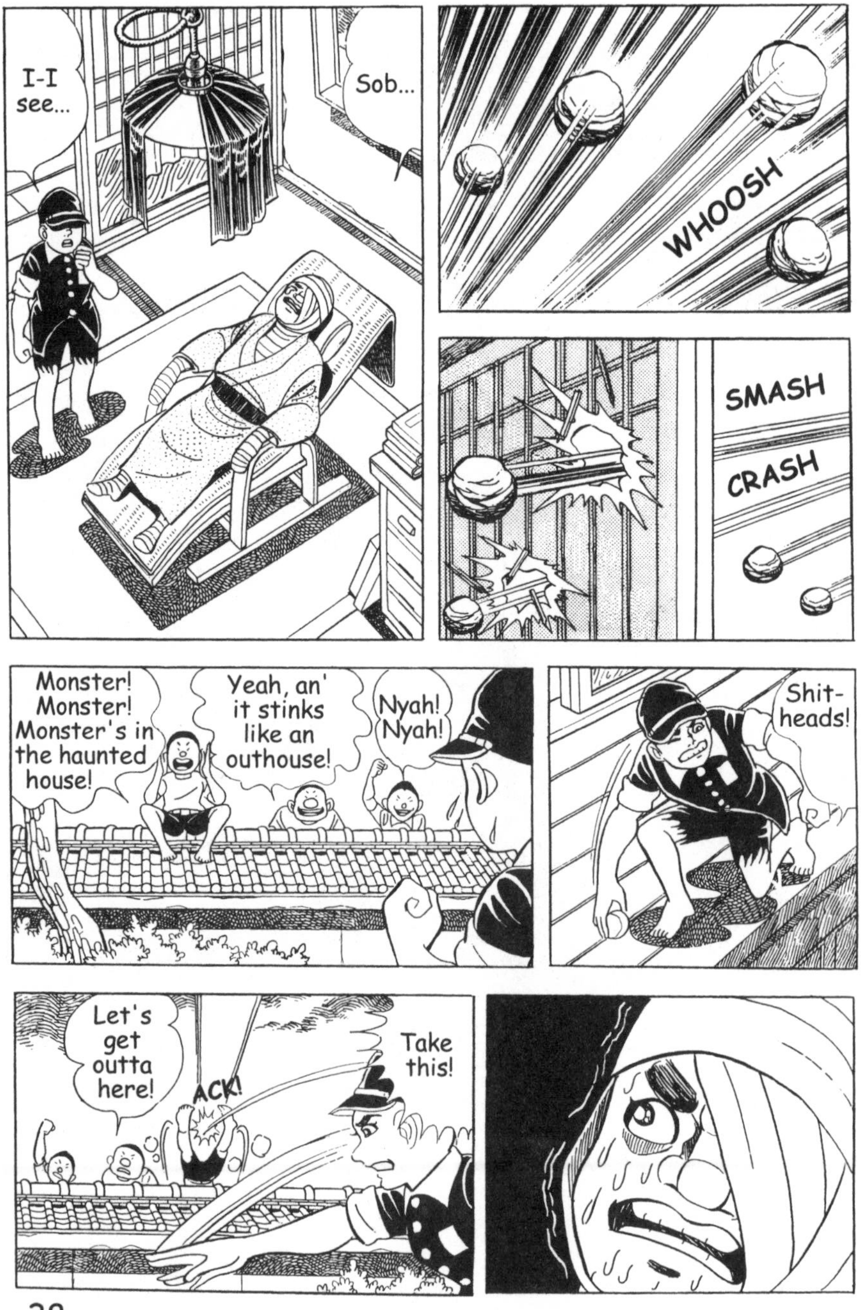
I-I see...
Sob...
WHOOSH
SMASH
CRASH
Monster! Monster! Monster's in the haunted house!
Yeah, an' it stinks like an outhouse!
Nyah! Nyah!
Shit-heads!
Let's get outta here!
ACK!
Take this!

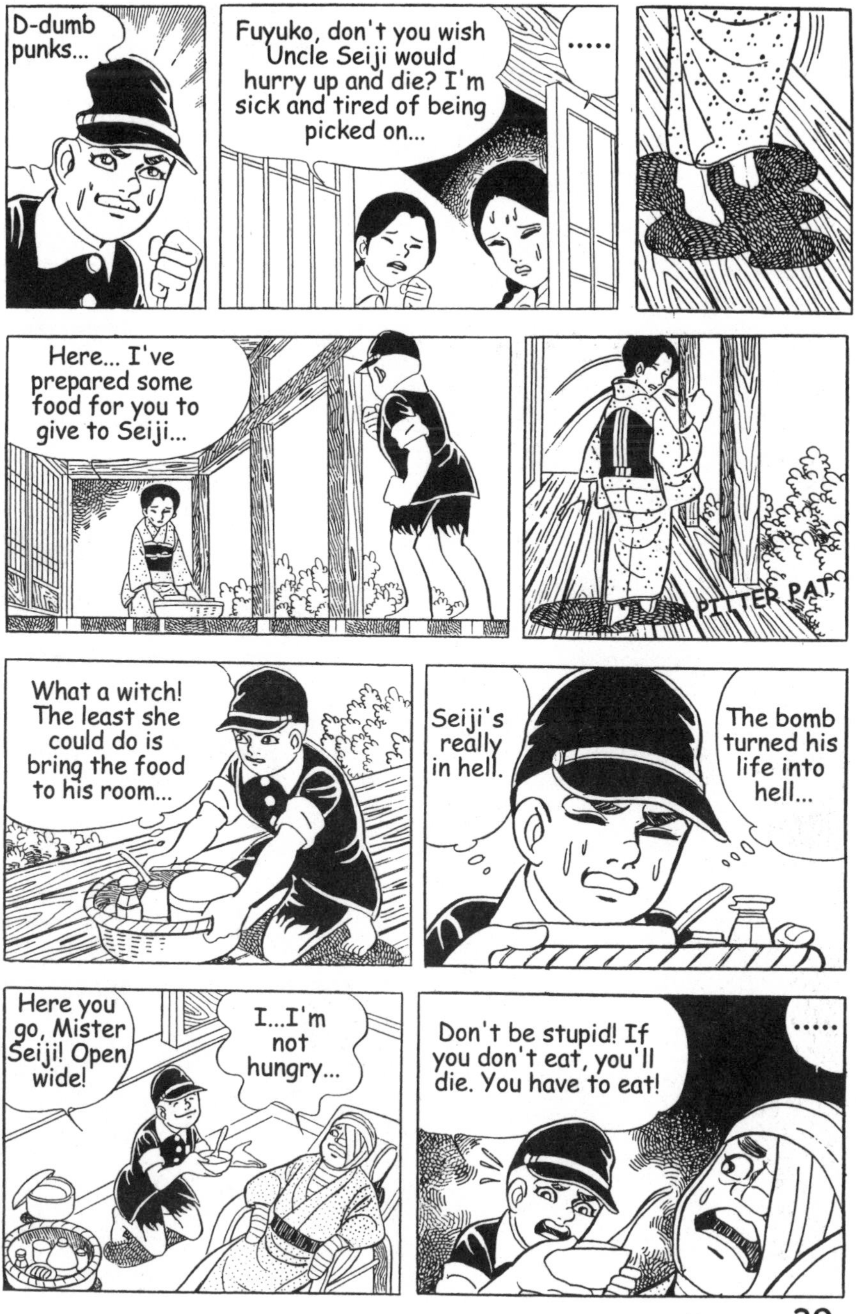

D-dumb punks...
Fuyuko, don't you wish Uncle Seiji would hurry up and die? I'm sick and tired of being picked on...
.....
Here... I've prepared some food for you to give to Seiji...
PITTER PAT
What a witch! The least she could do is bring the food to his room...
Seiji's really in hell.
The bomb turned his life into hell...
Here you go, Mister Seiji! Open wide!
I...I'm not hungry...
Don't be stupid! If you don't eat, you'll die. You have to eat!
.....

C'mon, eat up! Eat and you'll feel better!

G-Gen...

You...you're a good fellow, Gen...

Stop bawling like a baby! Act your age!

I'm sorry, kid... Take good care of Seiji...

Please forgive me, Seiji...

This is the best I can do for you...

40

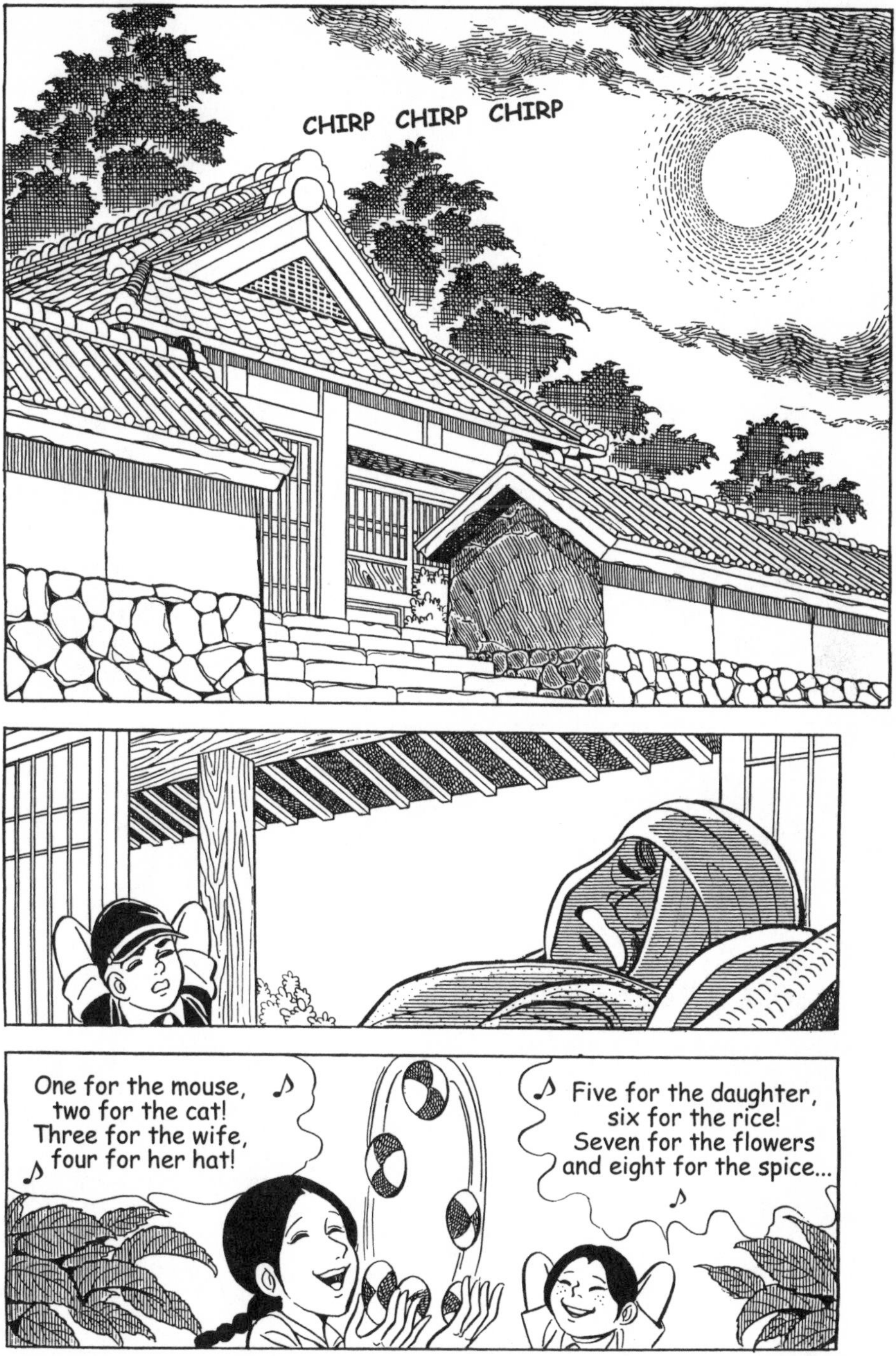
CHIRP CHIRP CHIRP
One for the mouse, two for the cat! Three for the wife, four for her hat!
Five for the daughter, six for the rice! Seven for the flowers and eight for the spice...

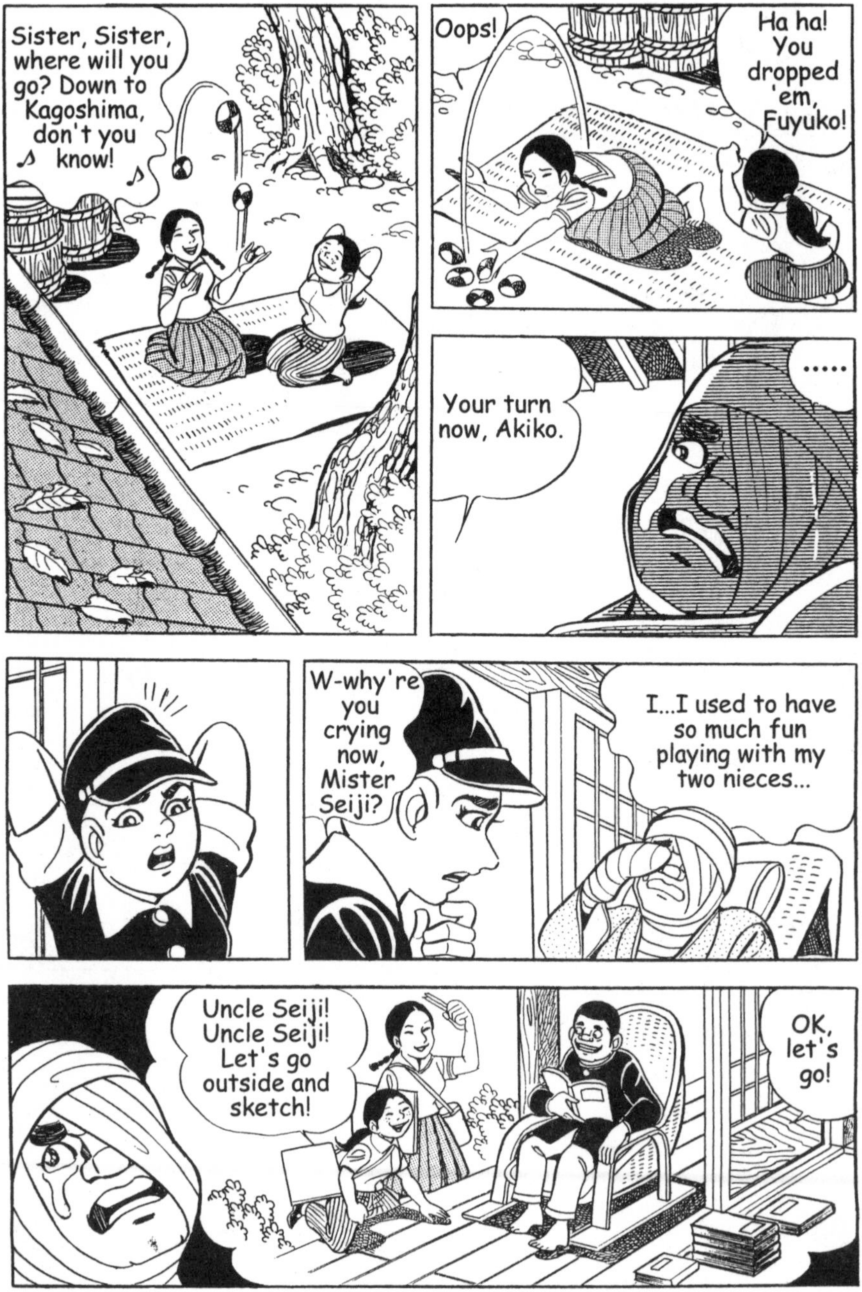
Sister, Sister, where will you go? Down to Kagoshima, don't you know!
Oops!
Ha ha! You dropped 'em, Fuyuko!
Your turn now, Akiko.
.....
W-why're you crying now, Mister Seiji?
I...I used to have so much fun playing with my two nieces...
Uncle Seiji! Uncle Seiji! Let's go outside and sketch!
OK, let's go!

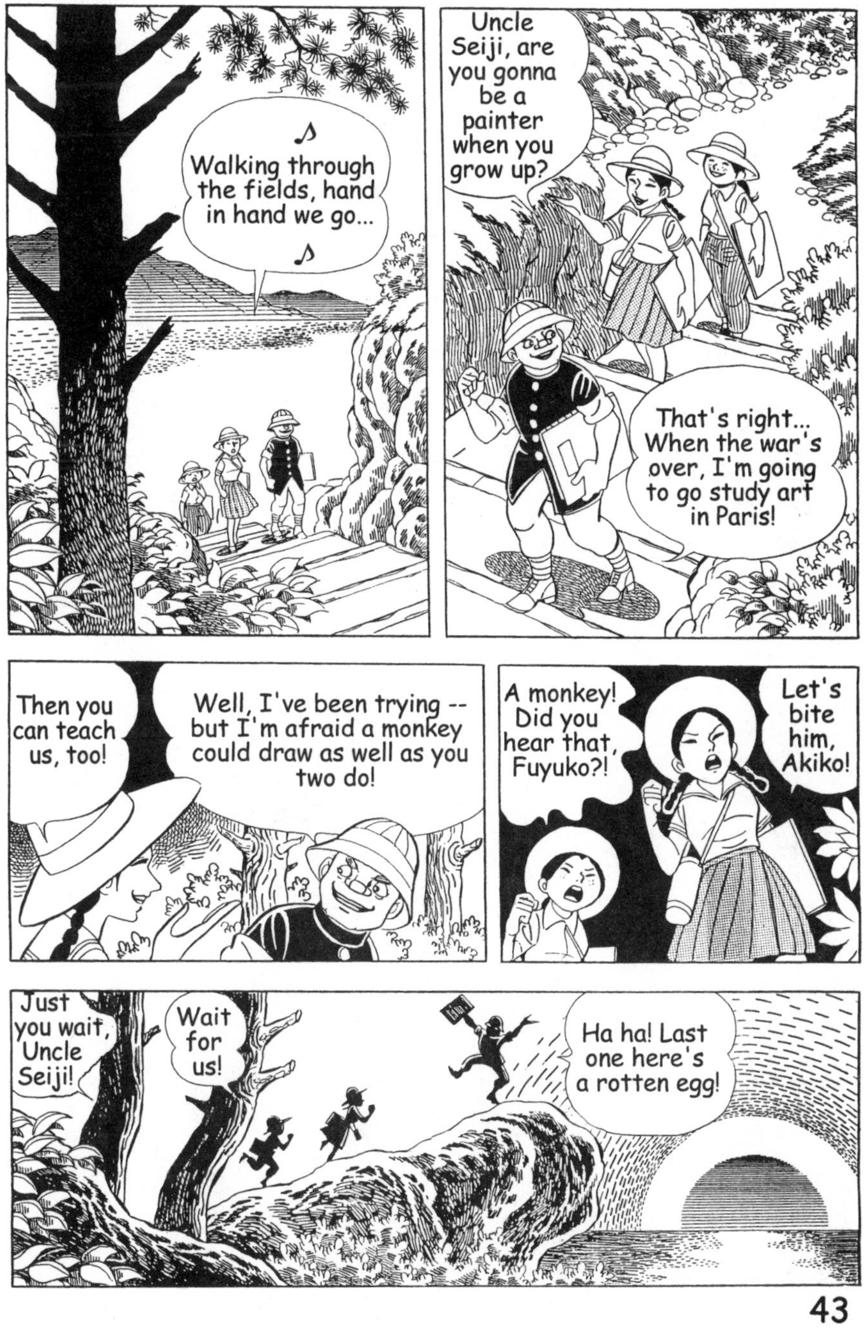
♪ Walking through the fields, hand in hand we go... ♪
Uncle Seiji, are you gonna be a painter when you grow up?
That's right... When the war's over, I'm going to go study art in Paris!
Then you can teach us, too!
Well, I've been trying -- but I'm afraid a monkey could draw as well as you two do!
A monkey! Did you hear that, Fuyuko?!
Let's bite him, Akiko!
Just you wait, Uncle Seiji!
Wait for us!
Ha ha! Last one here's a rotten egg!

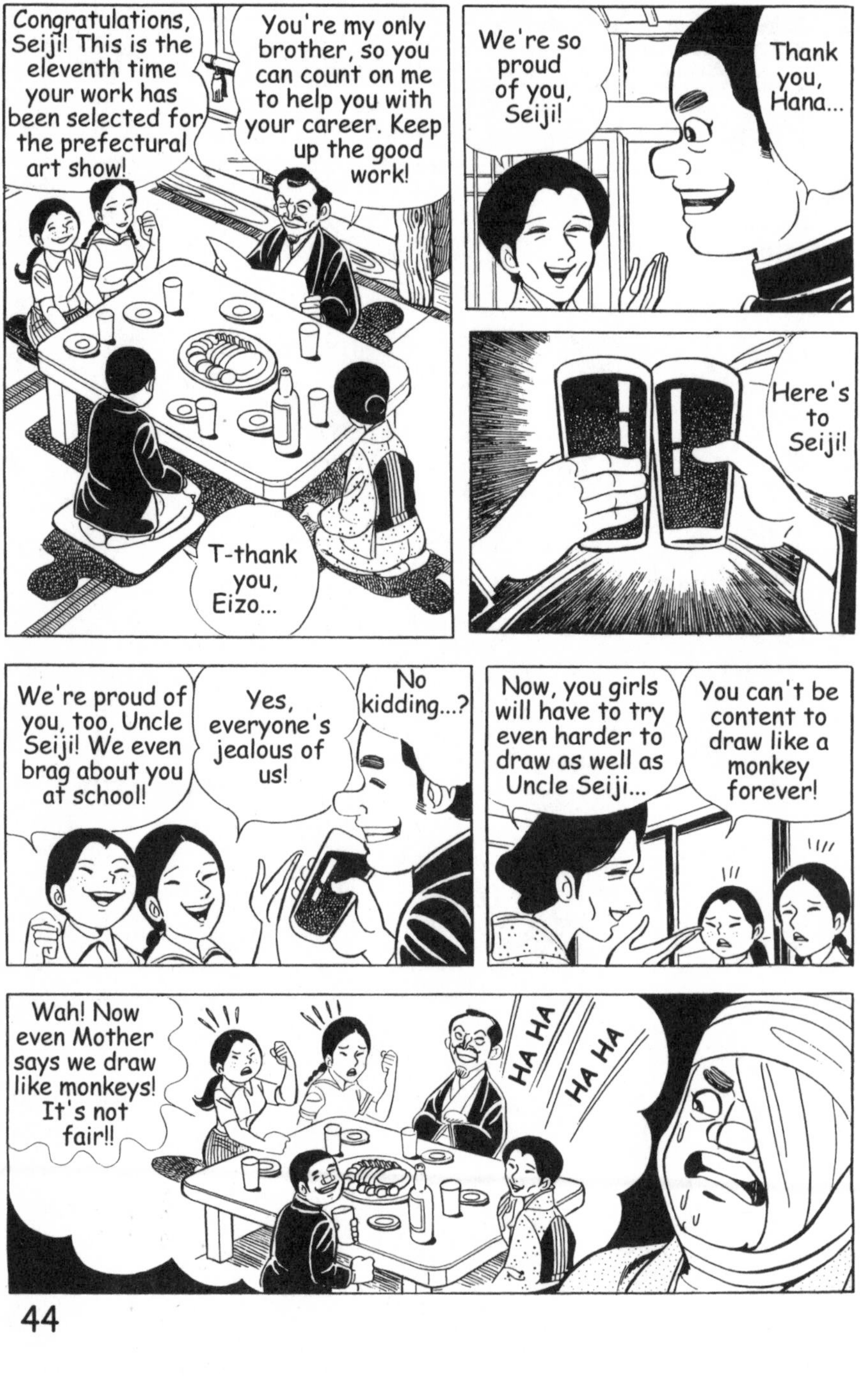
Congratulations, Seiji! This is the eleventh time your work has been selected for the prefectural art show!
You're my only brother, so you can count on me to help you with your career. Keep up the good work!
T-thank you, Eizo...
We're so proud of you, Seiji!
Thank you, Hana...
Here's to Seiji!
We're proud of you, too, Uncle Seiji! We even brag about you at school!
Yes, everyone's jealous of us!
No kidding...?
Now, you girls will have to try even harder to draw as well as Uncle Seiji...
You can't be content to draw like a monkey forever!
Wah! Now even Mother says we draw like monkeys! It's not fair!!
HA HA
HA HA

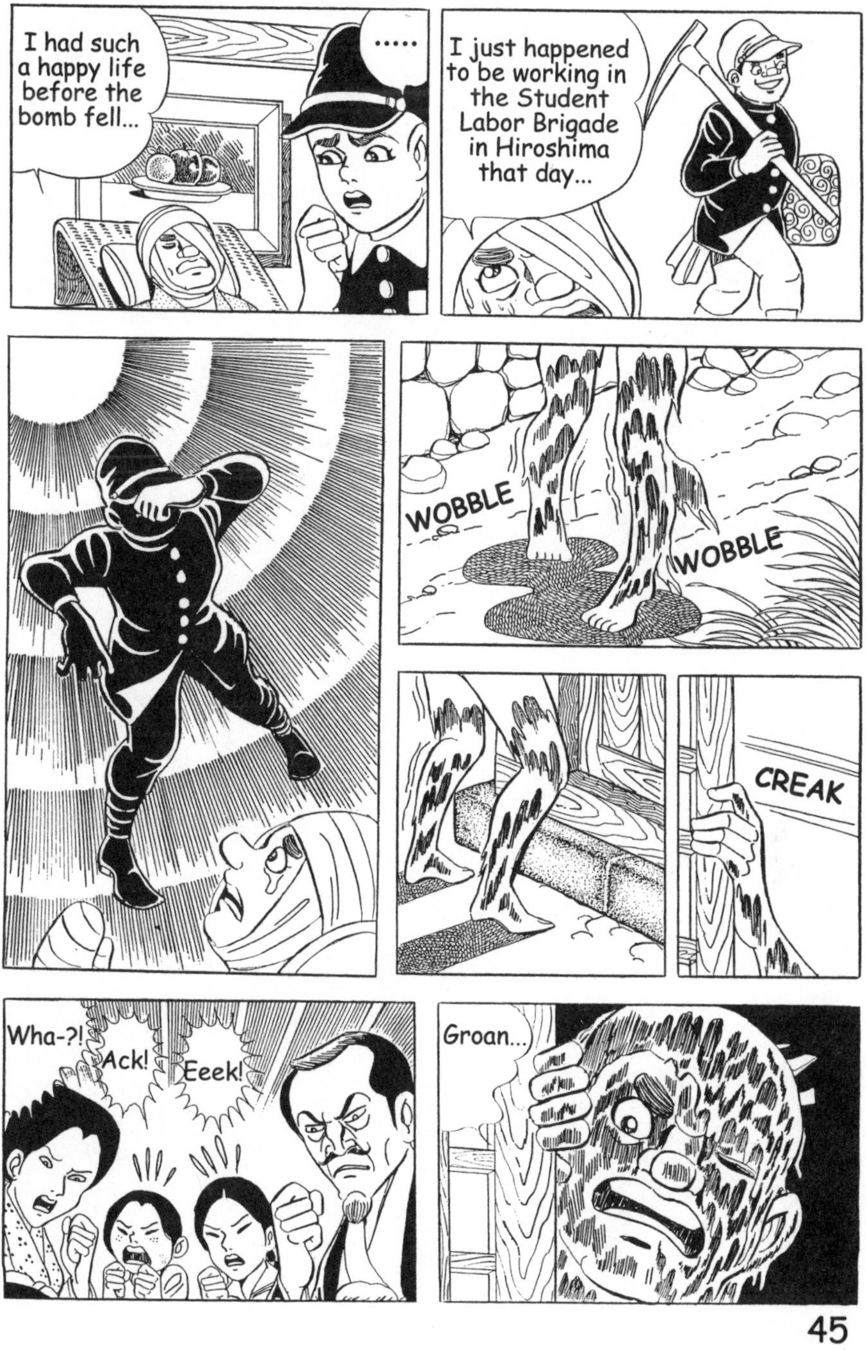

I had such a happy life before the bomb fell...
.....
I just happened to be working in the Student Labor Brigade in Hiroshima that day...
WOBBLE
WOBBLE
CREAK
Wha-?!
Ack!
Eeek!
Groan...

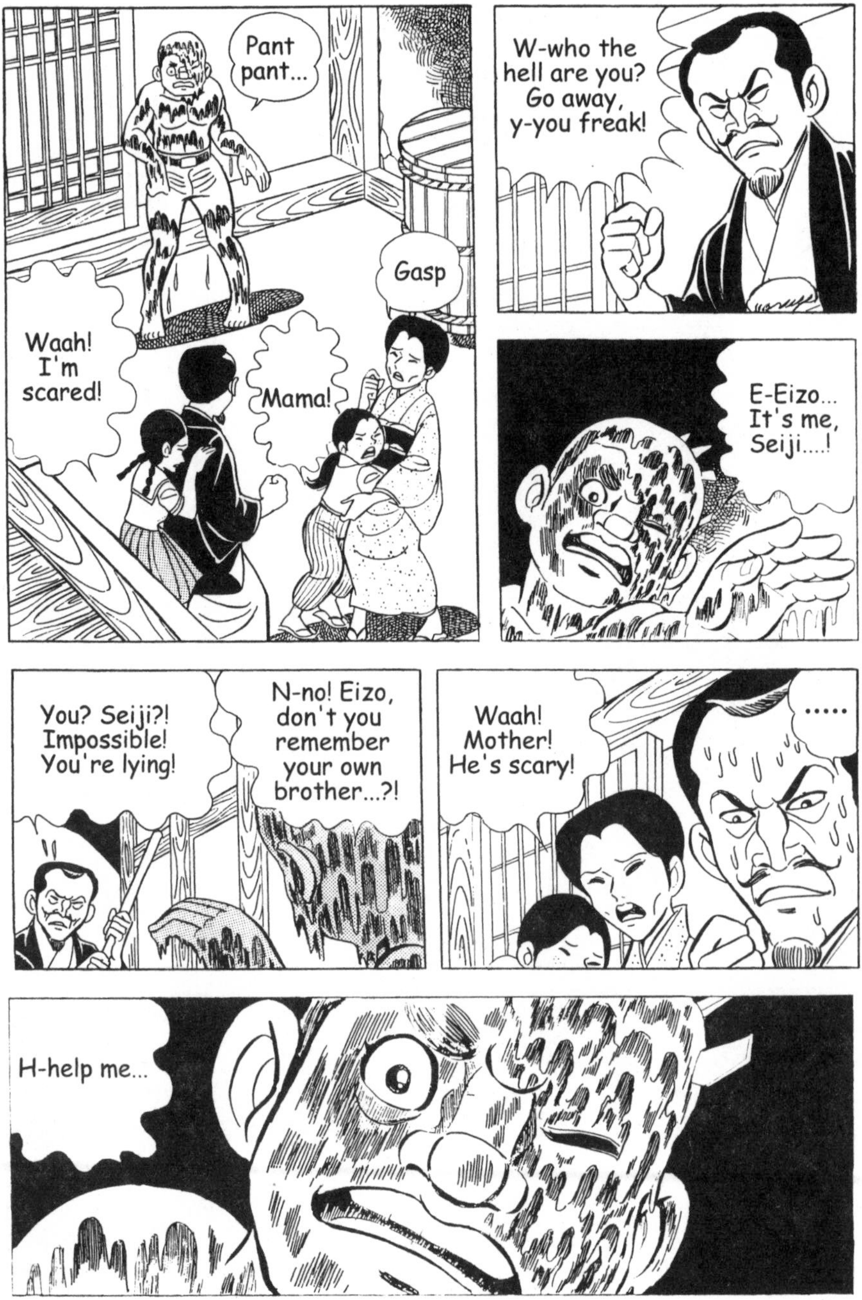
Pant pant...
Waah! I'm scared!
Mama!
Gasp
W-who the hell are you? Go away, y-you freak!
E-Eizo... It's me, Seiji....!
You? Seiji?! Impossible! You're lying!
N-no! Eizo, don't you remember your own brother...?!
Waah! Mother! He's scary!
.....
H-help me...

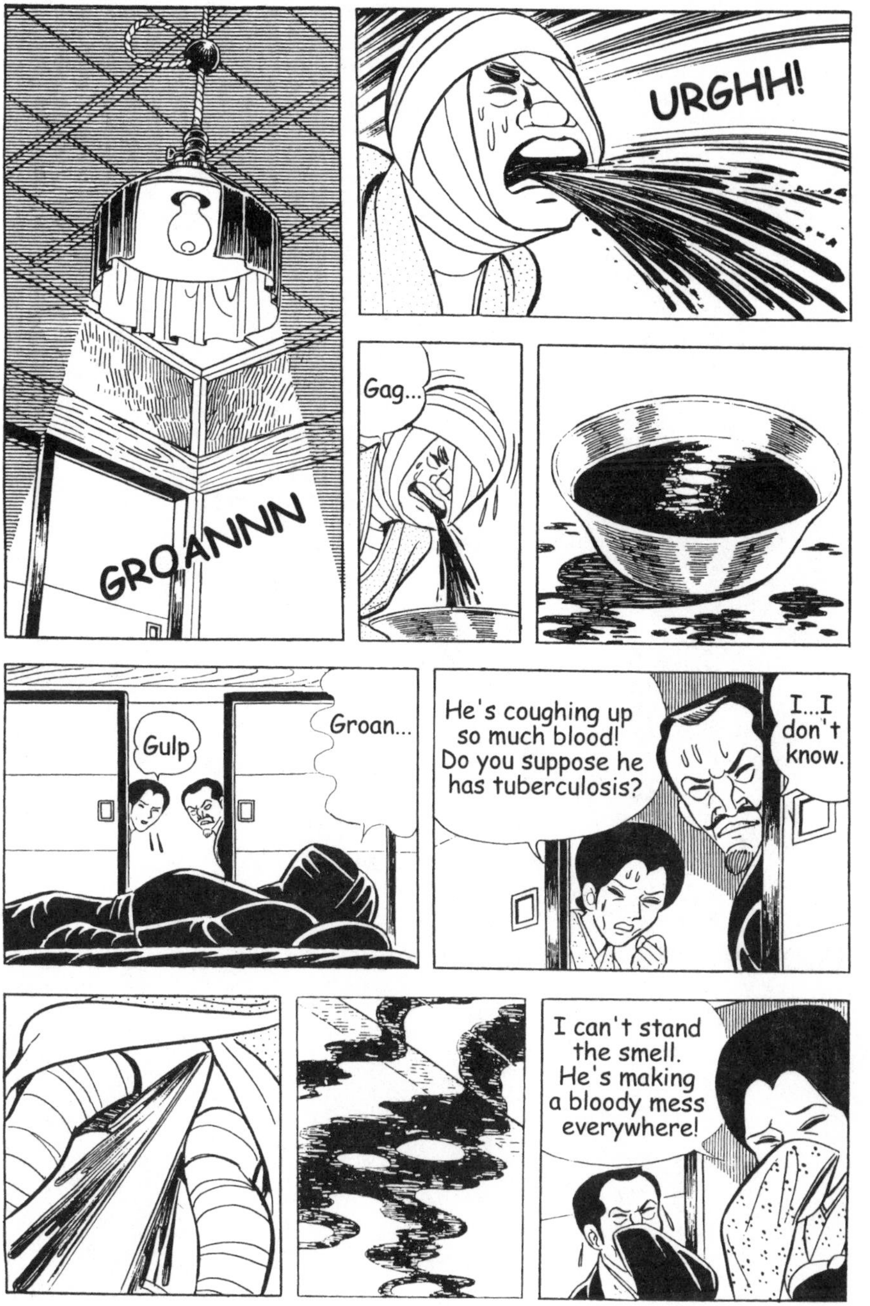
GROANNN
URGHH!
Gag...
Gulp
Groan...
He's coughing up so much blood! Do you suppose he has tuberculosis?
I...I don't know.
I can't stand the smell. He's making a bloody mess everywhere!

Akiko and Fuyuko shouldn't go near him. We can't risk their catching his disease!

I-I suppose you're right...

You two girls must never go into Seiji's room. Understand?

Y-yes, Mother...

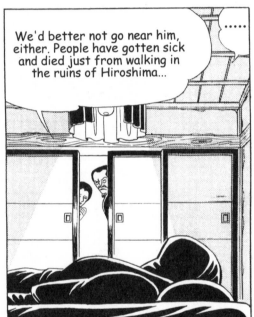

We'd better not go near him, either. People have gotten sick and died just from walking in the ruins of Hiroshima...

.....

What a terrifying thought! We could all catch his disease and die!

Let's nail the doors shut so he can't leave his room...

.....

Eizo! Hana! Akiko! Fuyuko!

Please, somebody, bring me water! I'm dying of thirst!

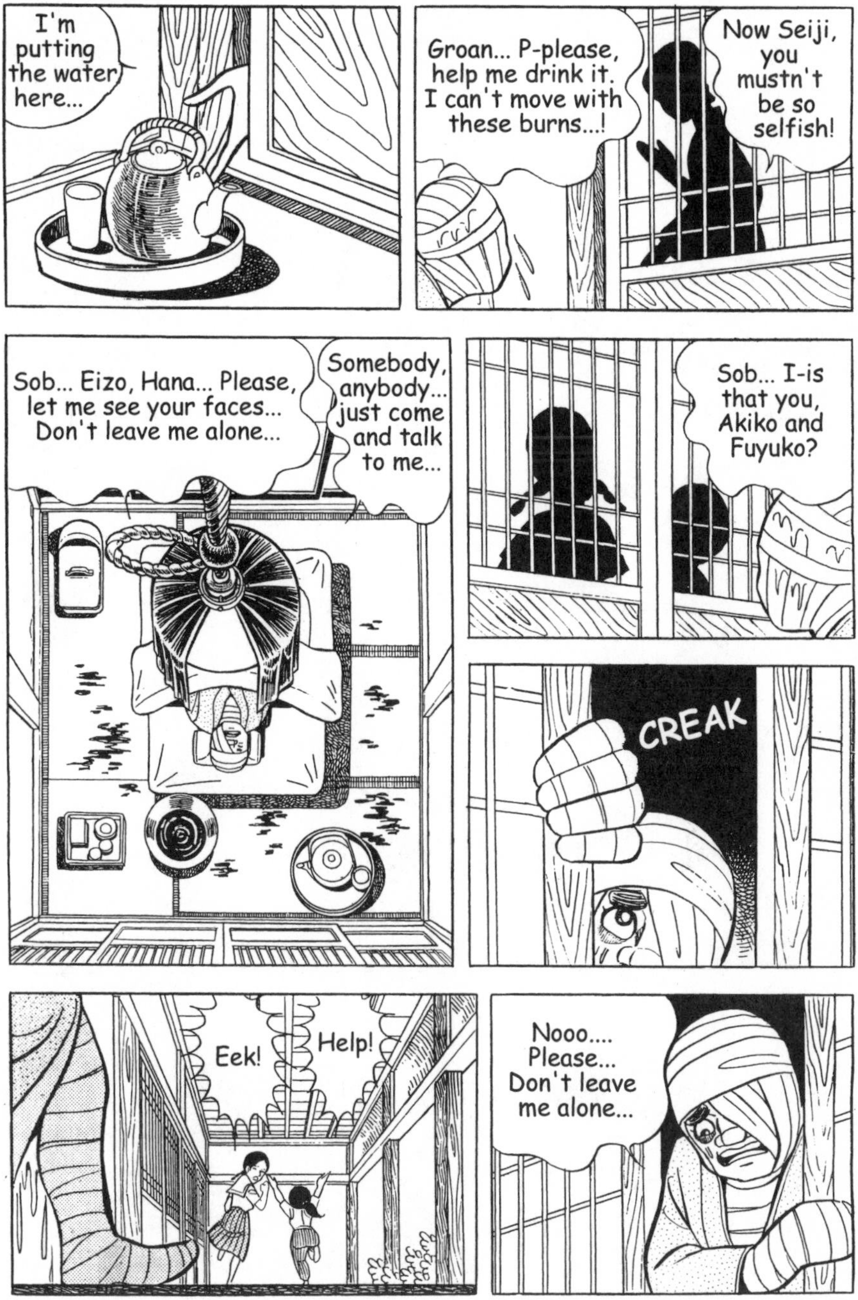

I'm putting the water here...
Groan... P-please, help me drink it. I can't move with these burns...!
Now Seiji, you mustn't be so selfish!
Sob... Eizo, Hana... Please, let me see your faces... Don't leave me alone...
Somebody, anybody... just come and talk to me...
Sob... I-is that you, Akiko and Fuyuko?
CREAK
Eek!
Help!
Nooo.... Please... Don't leave me alone...

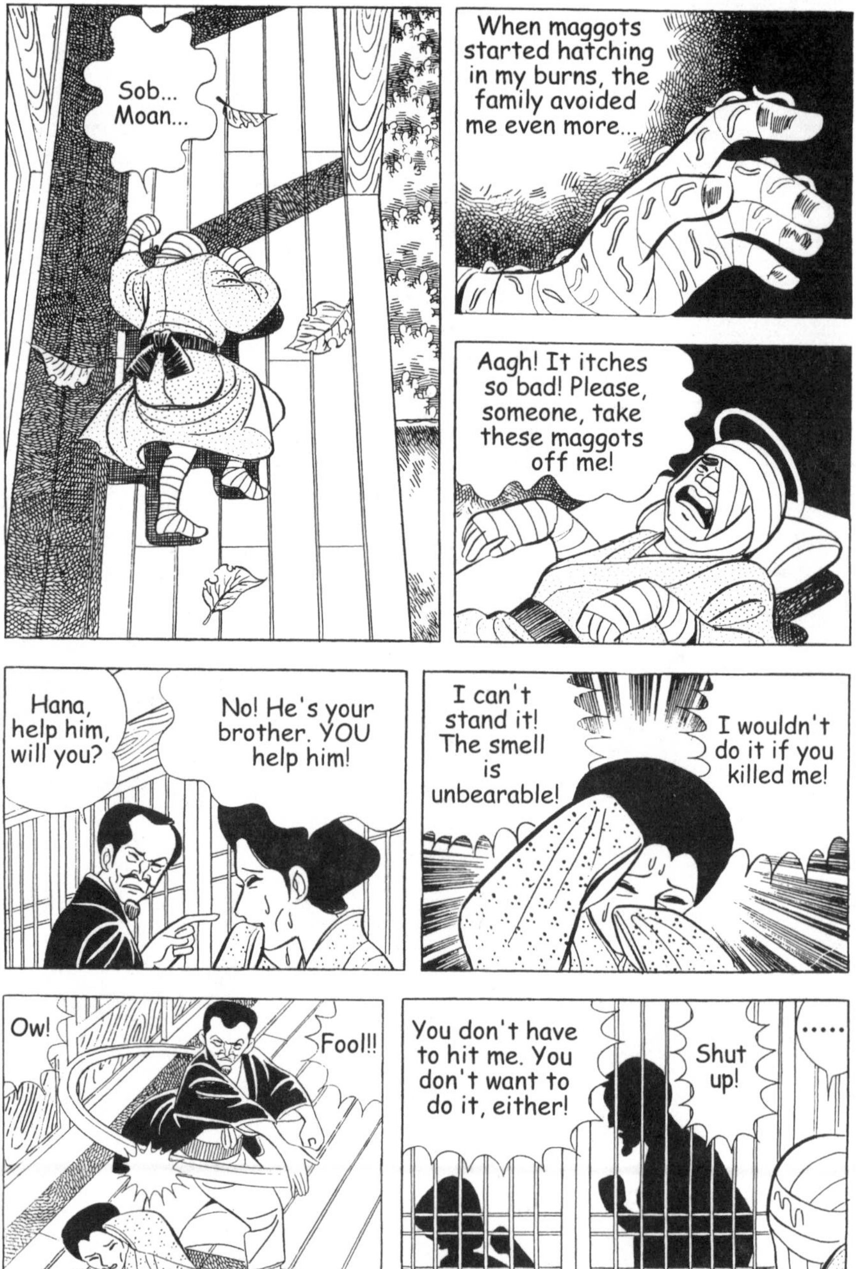
Sob... Moan...
When maggots started hatching in my burns, the family avoided me even more...
Aagh! It itches so bad! Please, someone, take these maggots off me!
Hana, help him, will you?
No! He's your brother. YOU help him!
I can't stand it! The smell is unbearable!
I wouldn't do it if you killed me!
Ow!
Fool!!
You don't have to hit me. You don't want to do it, either!
Shut up!
.....

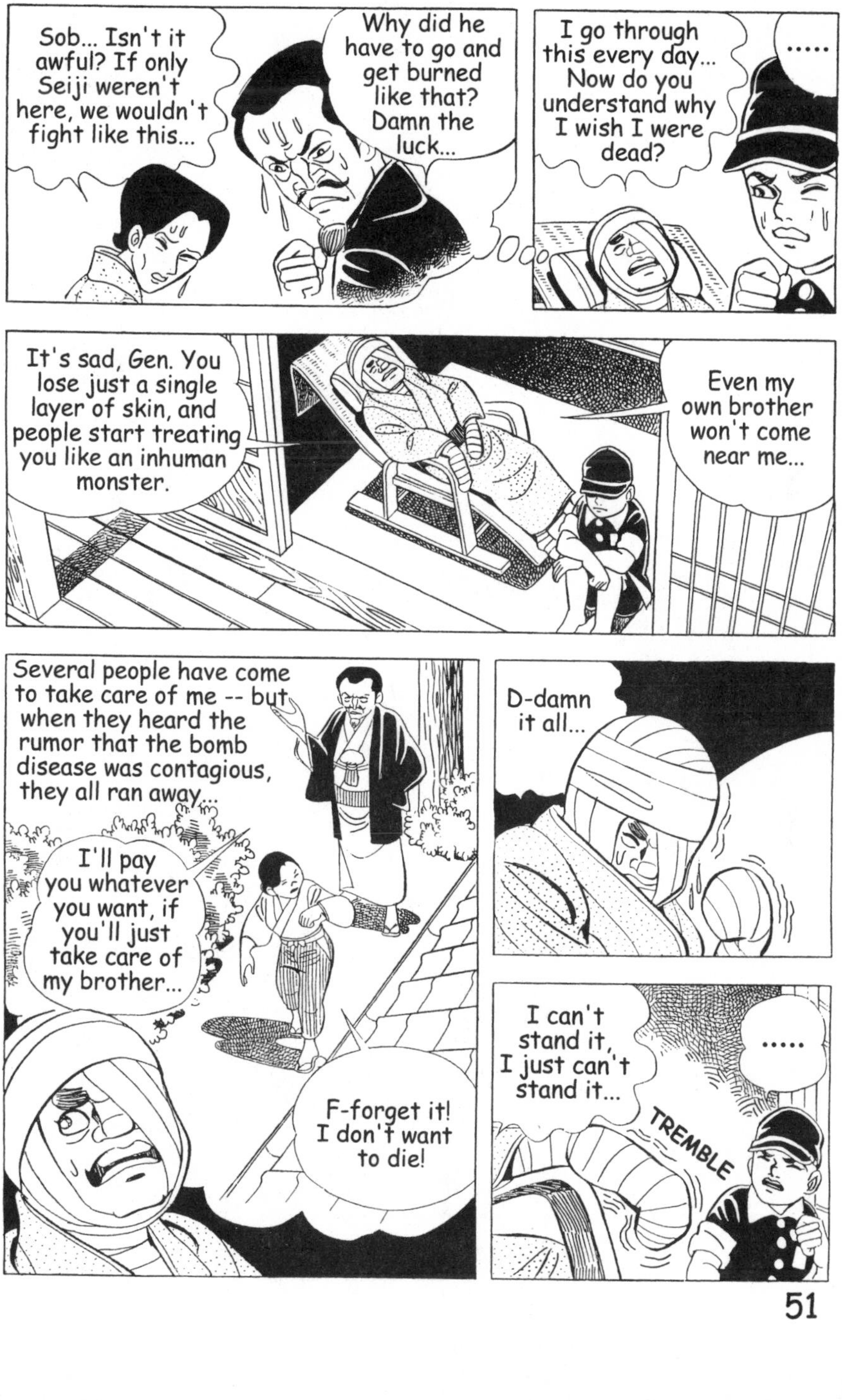
Sob... Isn't it awful? If only Seiji weren't here, we wouldn't fight like this...
Why did he have to go and get burned like that? Damn the luck...
I go through this every day... Now do you understand why I wish I were dead?
.....
It's sad, Gen. You lose just a single layer of skin, and people start treating you like an inhuman monster.
Even my own brother won't come near me...
Several people have come to take care of me -- but when they heard the rumor that the bomb disease was contagious, they all ran away...
I'll pay you whatever you want, if you'll just take care of my brother...
F-forget it! I don't want to die!
D-damn it all...
I can't stand it, I just can't stand it...
.....
TREMBLE

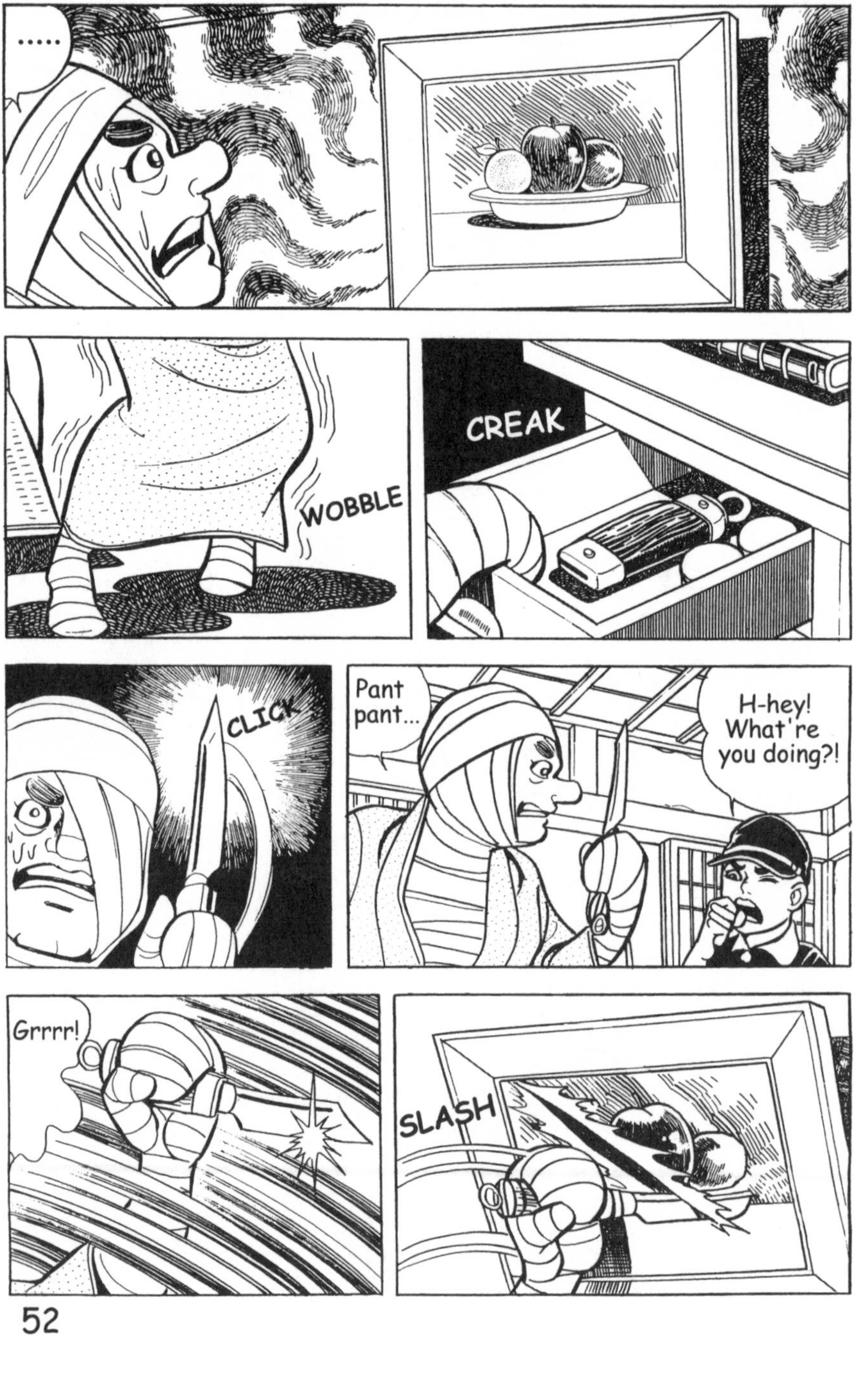
......
WOBBLE
CREAK
CLICK
Pant pant...
H-hey! What're you doing?!
Grrrr!
SLASH

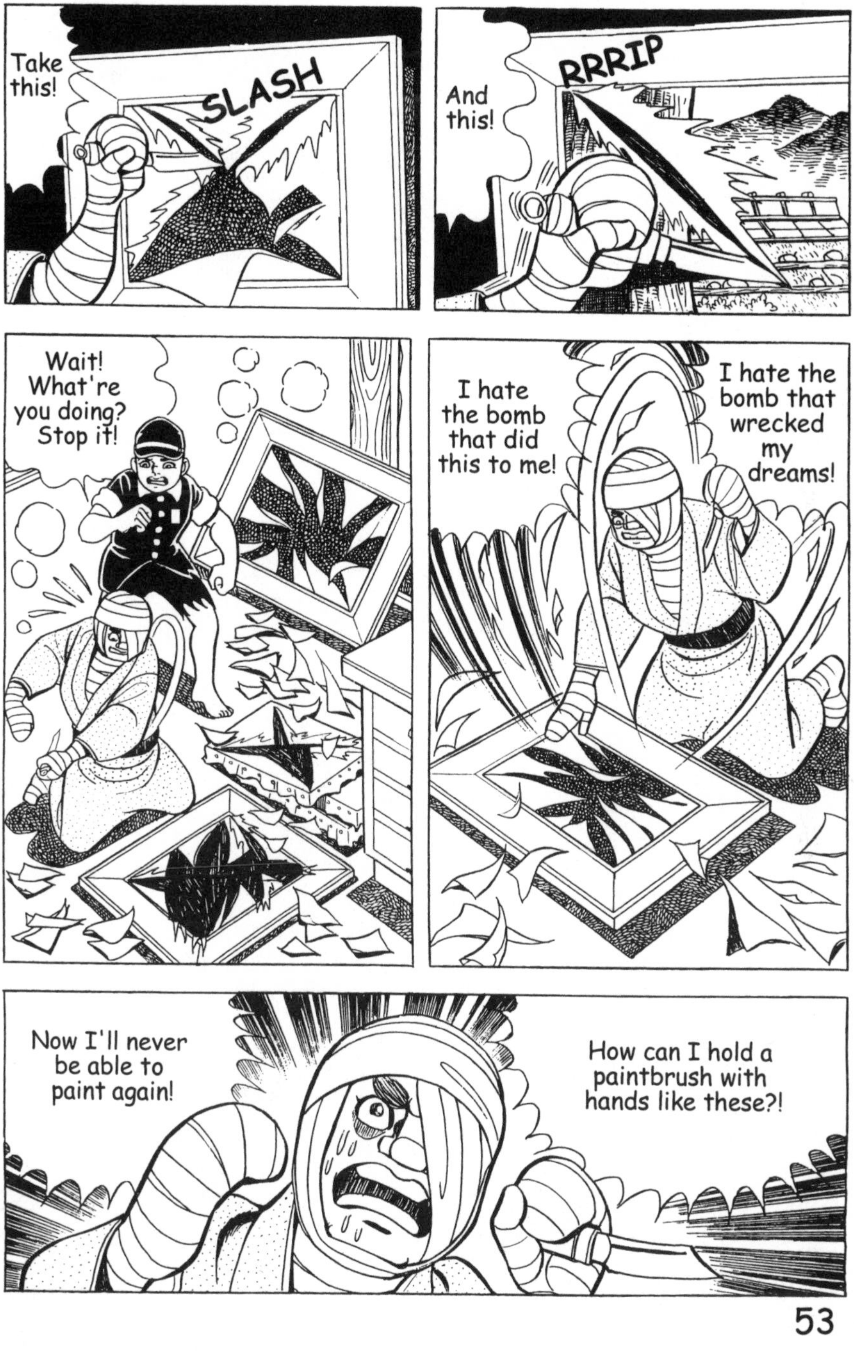
Take this!
SLASH
And this!
RRRIP
Wait! What're you doing? Stop it!
I hate the bomb that did this to me!
I hate the bomb that wrecked my dreams!
Now I'll never be able to paint again!
How can I hold a paintbrush with hands like these?!

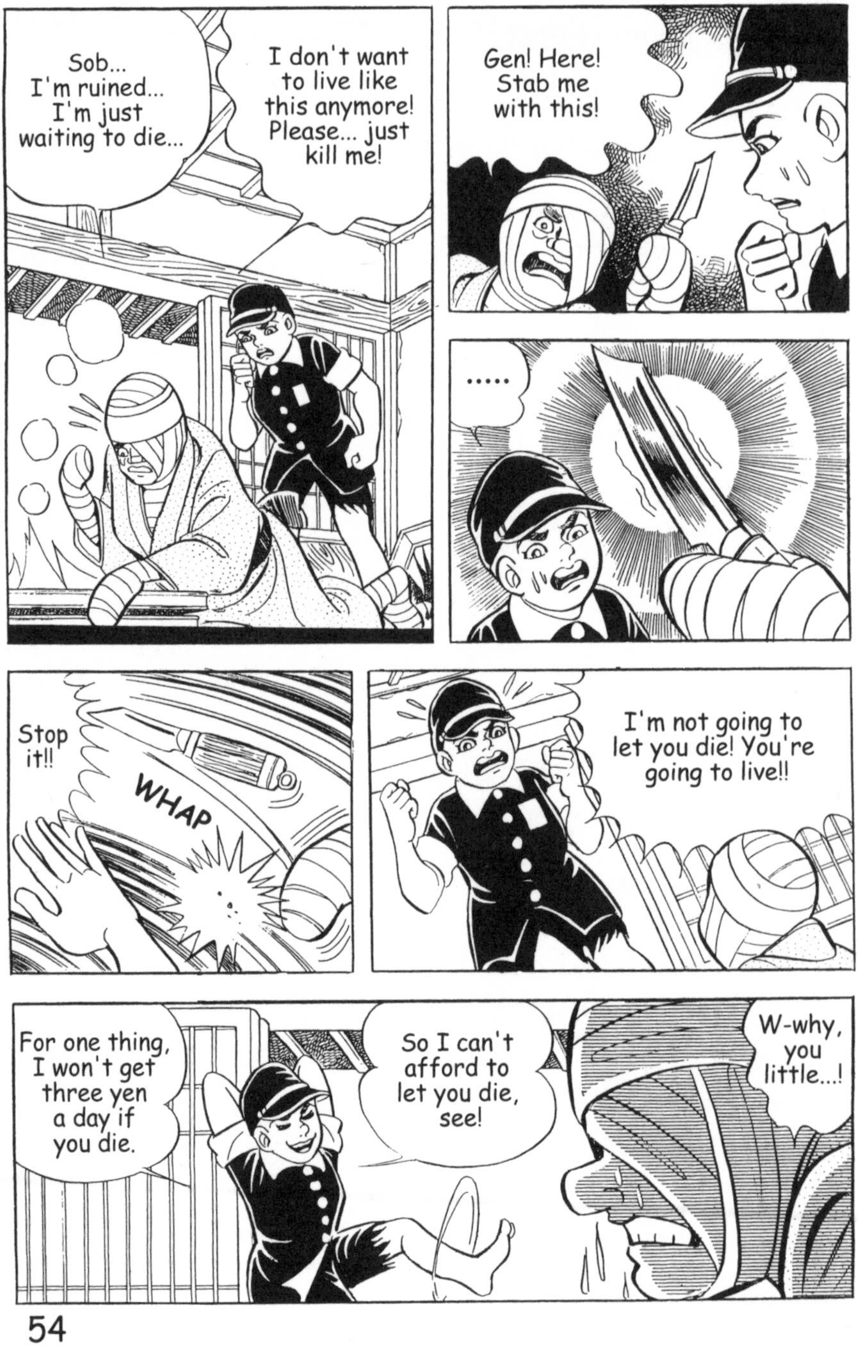

Sob... I'm ruined... I'm just waiting to die...
I don't want to live like this anymore! Please... just kill me!
Gen! Here! Stab me with this!
.....
Stop it!!
WHAP
I'm not going to let you die! You're going to live!!
For one thing, I won't get three yen a day if you die.
So I can't afford to let you die, see!
W-why, you little...!

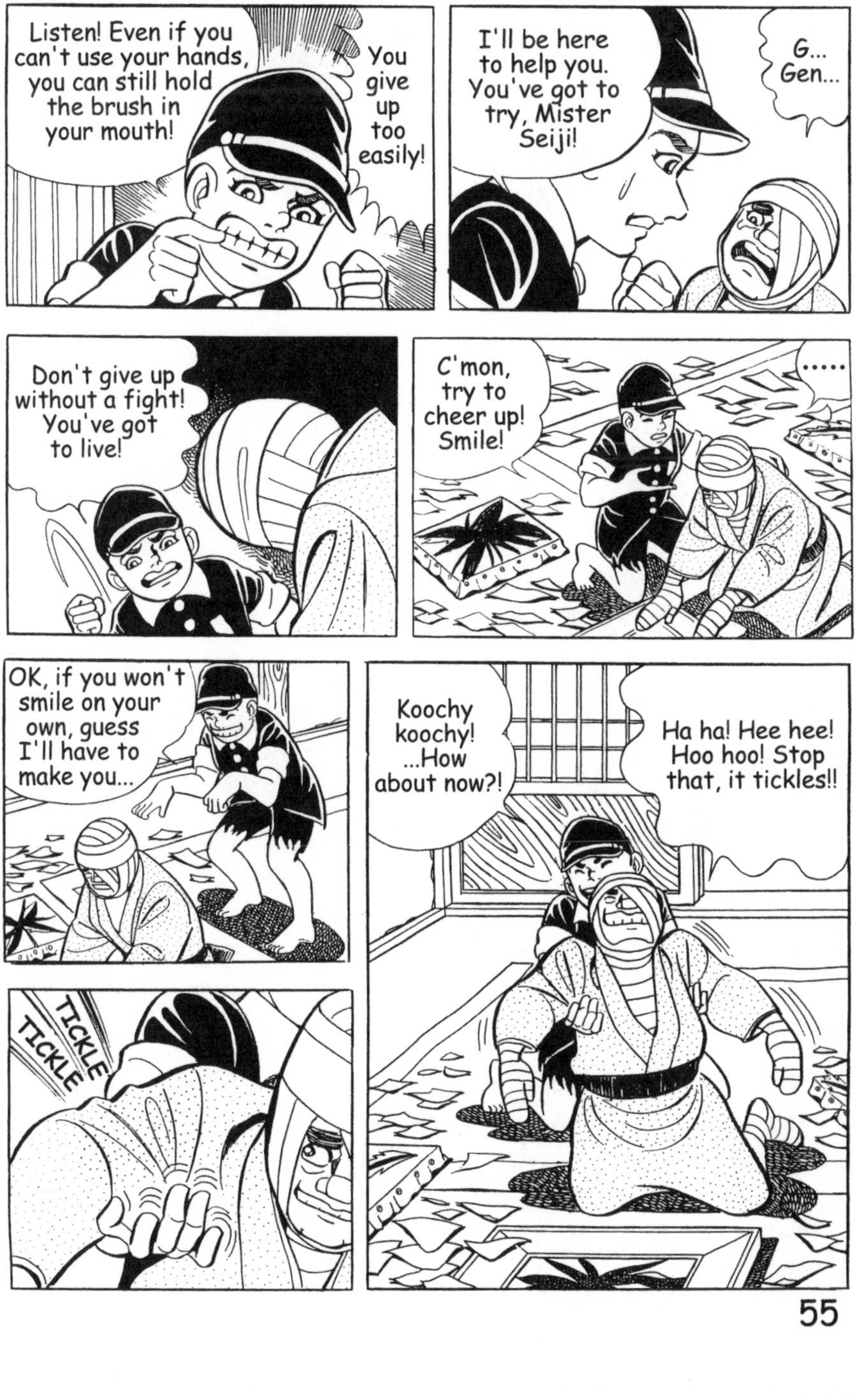
Listen! Even if you can't use your hands, you can still hold the brush in your mouth!
You give up too easily!
I'll be here to help you. You've got to try, Mister Seiji!
G... Gen...
Don't give up without a fight! You've got to live!
C'mon, try to cheer up! Smile!
.....
OK, if you won't smile on your own, guess I'll have to make you...
TICKLE
TICKLE
Koochy koochy! ...How about now?!
Ha ha! Hee hee! Hoo hoo! Stop that, it tickles!!

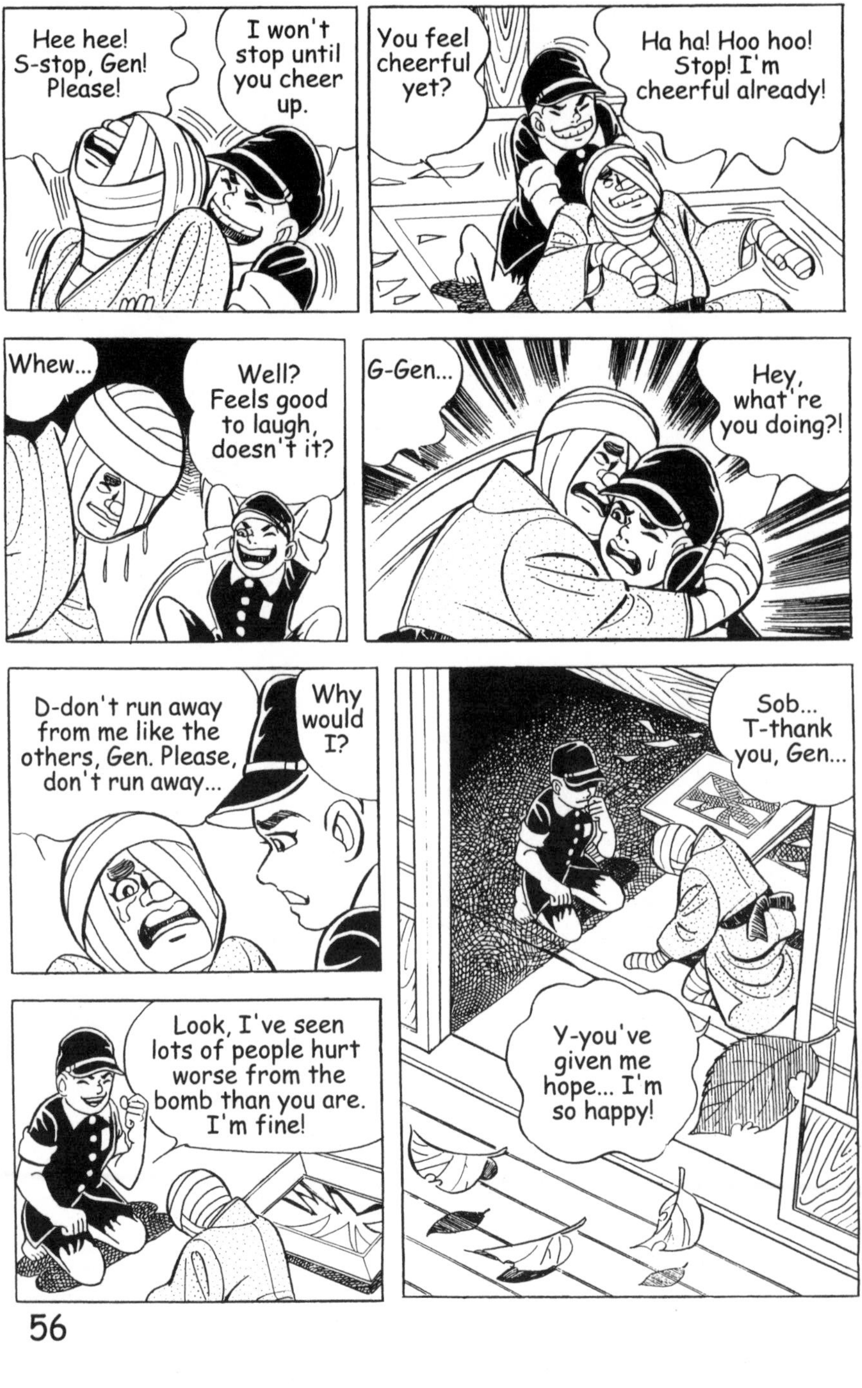
Hee hee! S-stop, Gen! Please!
I won't stop until you cheer up.
You feel cheerful yet?
Ha ha! Hoo hoo! Stop! I'm cheerful already!
Whew...
Well? Feels good to laugh, doesn't it?
G-Gen...
Hey, what're you doing?!
D-don't run away from me like the others, Gen. Please, don't run away...
Why would I?
Look, I've seen lots of people hurt worse from the bomb than you are. I'm fine!
Sob... T-thank you, Gen...
Y-you've given me hope... I'm so happy!

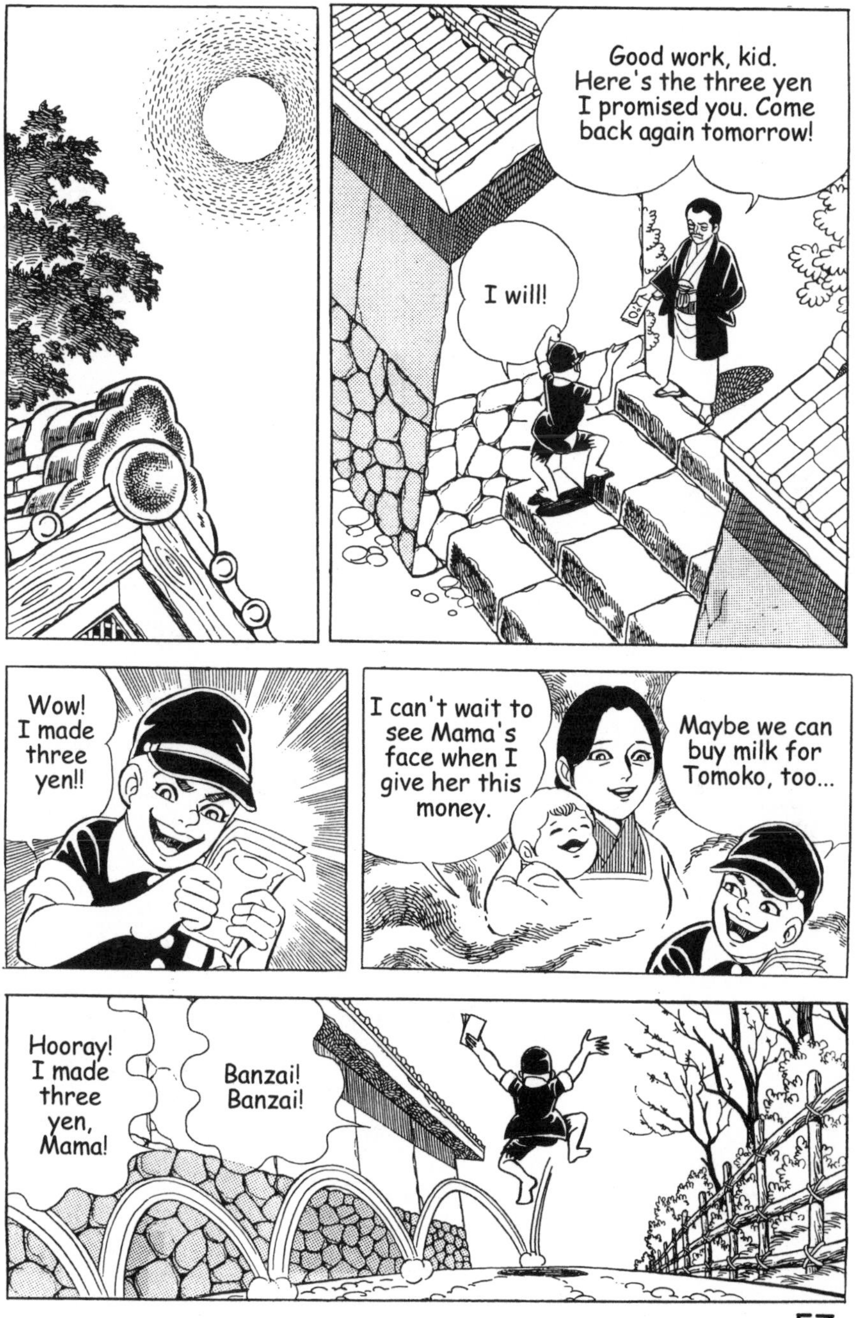
Good work, kid. Here's the three yen I promised you. Come back again tomorrow!
I will!
Wow! I made three yen!!
I can't wait to see Mama's face when I give her this money.
Maybe we can buy milk for Tomoko, too...
Hooray! I made three yen, Mama!
Banzai! Banzai!

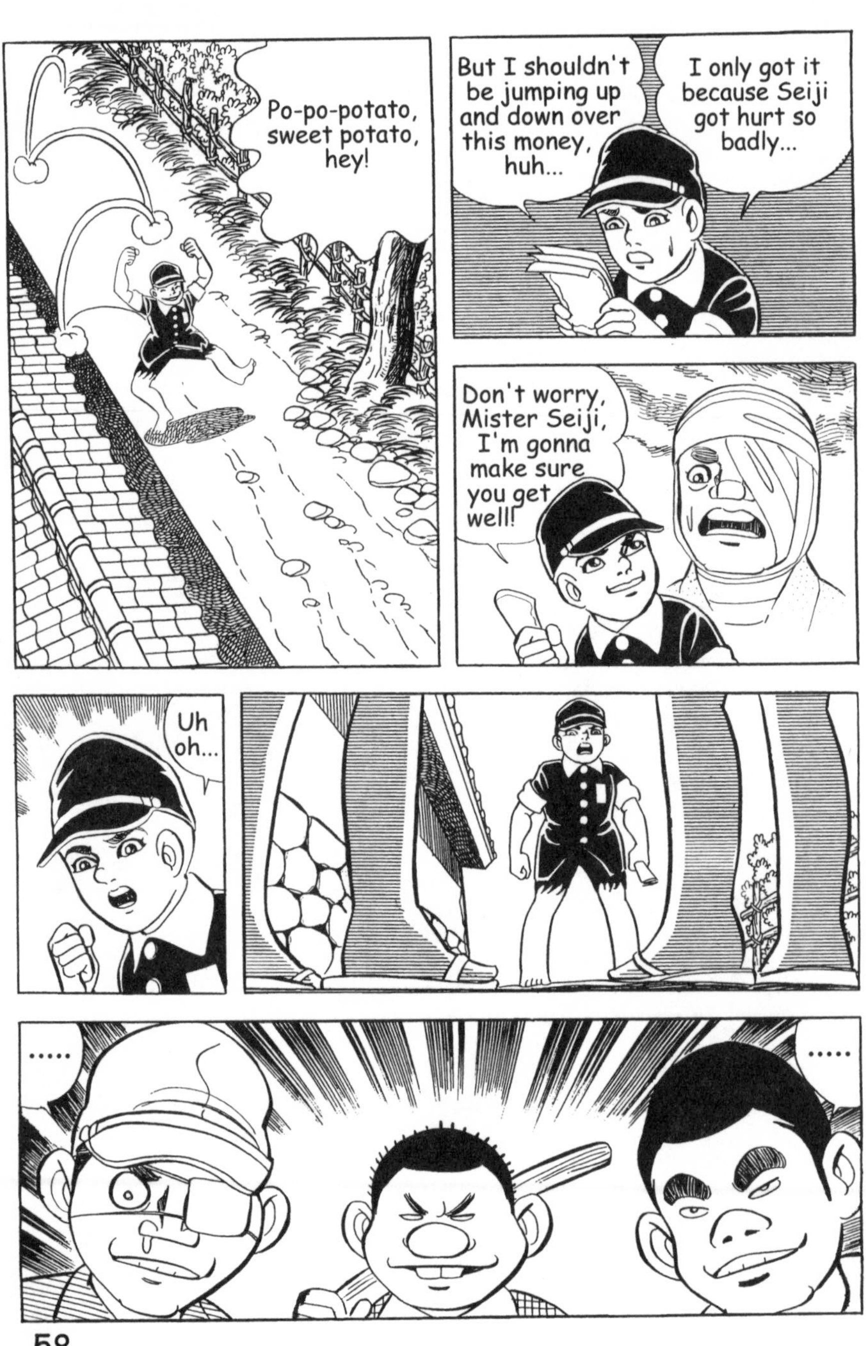
Po-po-potato, sweet potato, hey!
But I shouldn't be jumping up and down over this money, huh...
I only got it because Seiji got hurt so badly...
Don't worry, Mister Seiji, I'm gonna make sure you get well!
Uh oh...
.....
.....

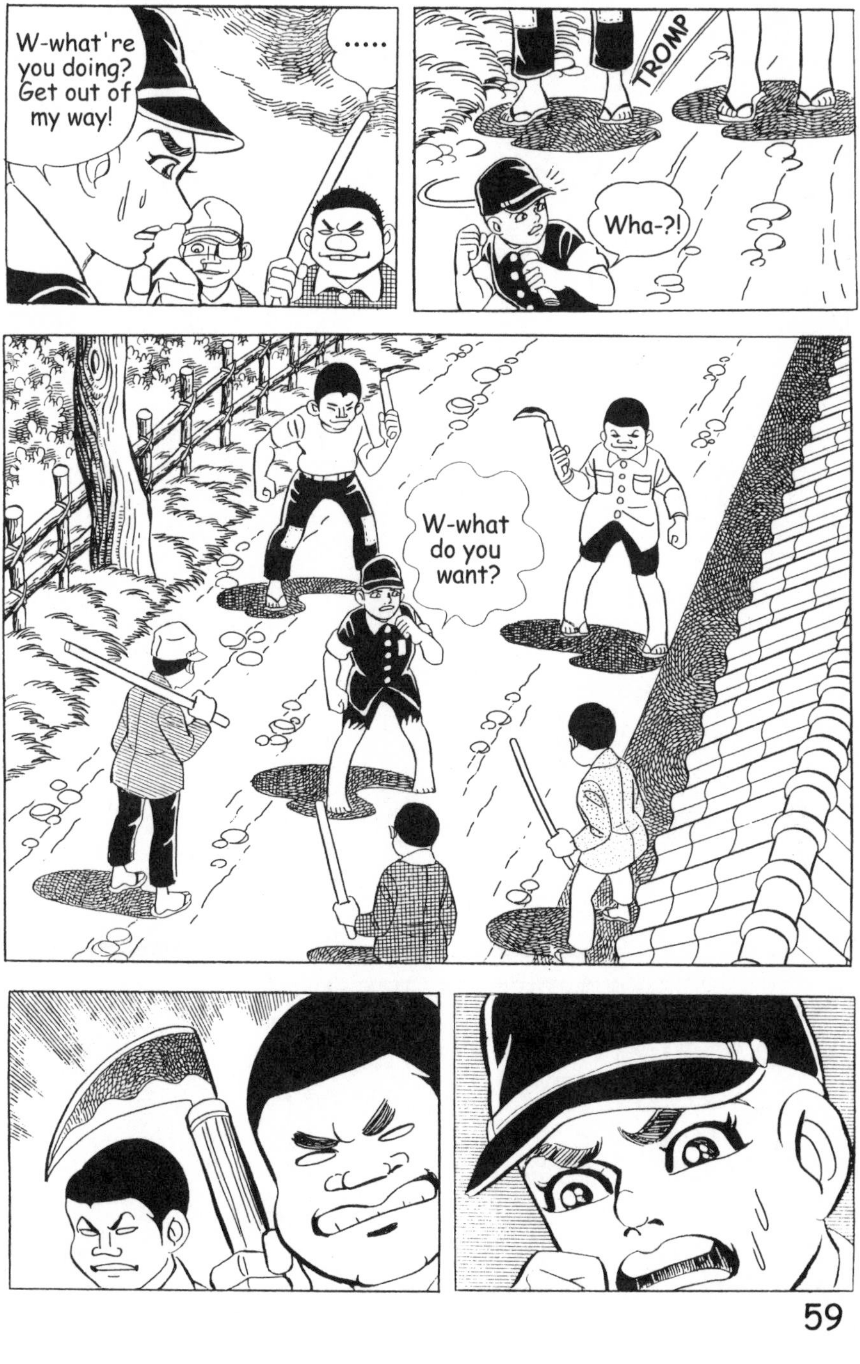
W-what're you doing? Get out of my way!
.....
TROMP
Wha-?!
W-what do you want?

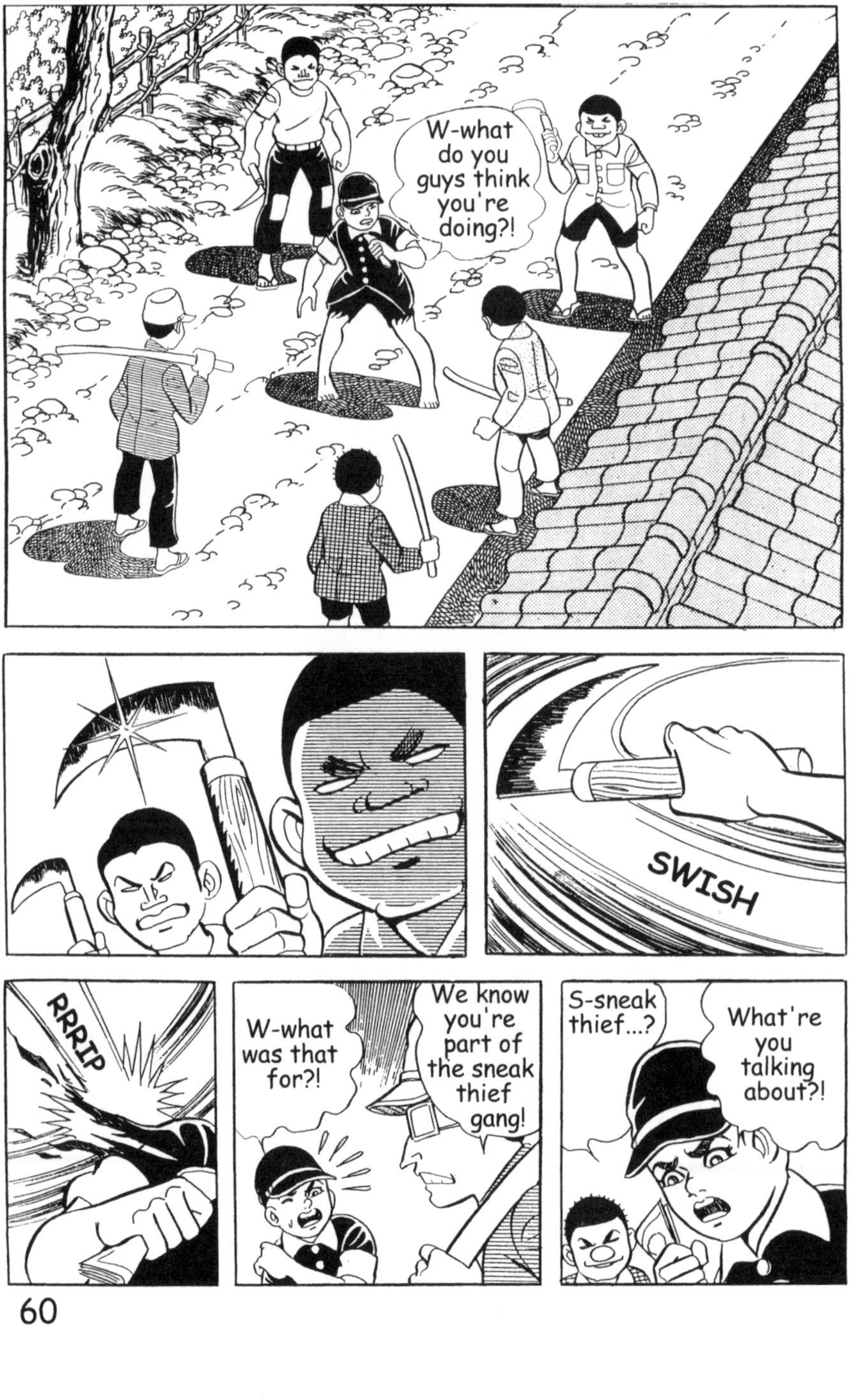
W-what do you guys think you're doing?!
SWISH
RRRIP
W-what was that for?!
We know you're part of the sneak thief gang!
S-sneak thief...?
What're you talking about?!

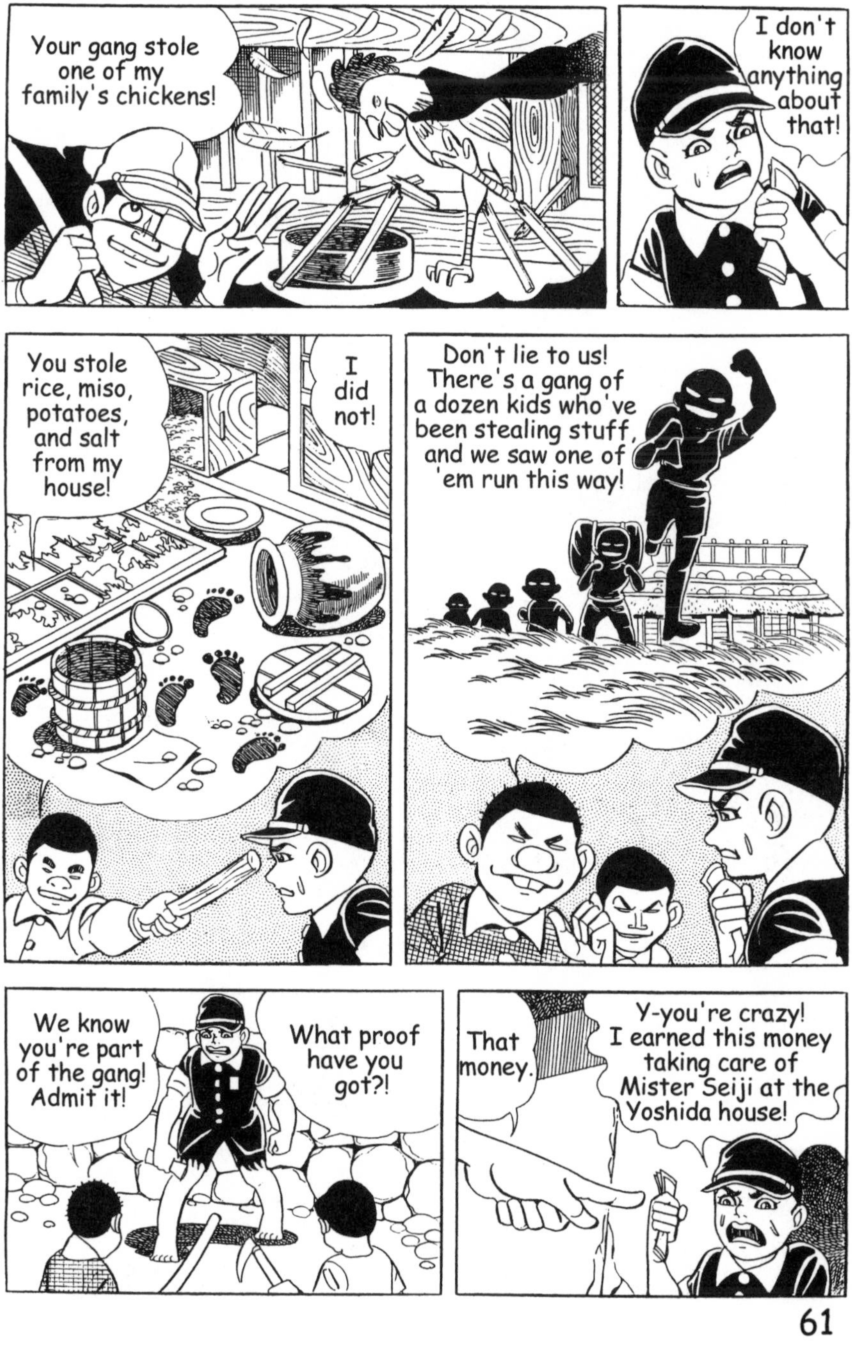
Your gang stole one of my family's chickens!
I don't know anything about that!
You stole rice, miso, potatoes, and salt from my house!
I did not!
Don't lie to us! There's a gang of a dozen kids who've been stealing stuff, and we saw one of 'em run this way!
We know you're part of the gang! Admit it!
What proof have you got?!
That money.
Y-you're crazy! I earned this money taking care of Mister Seiji at the Yoshida house!

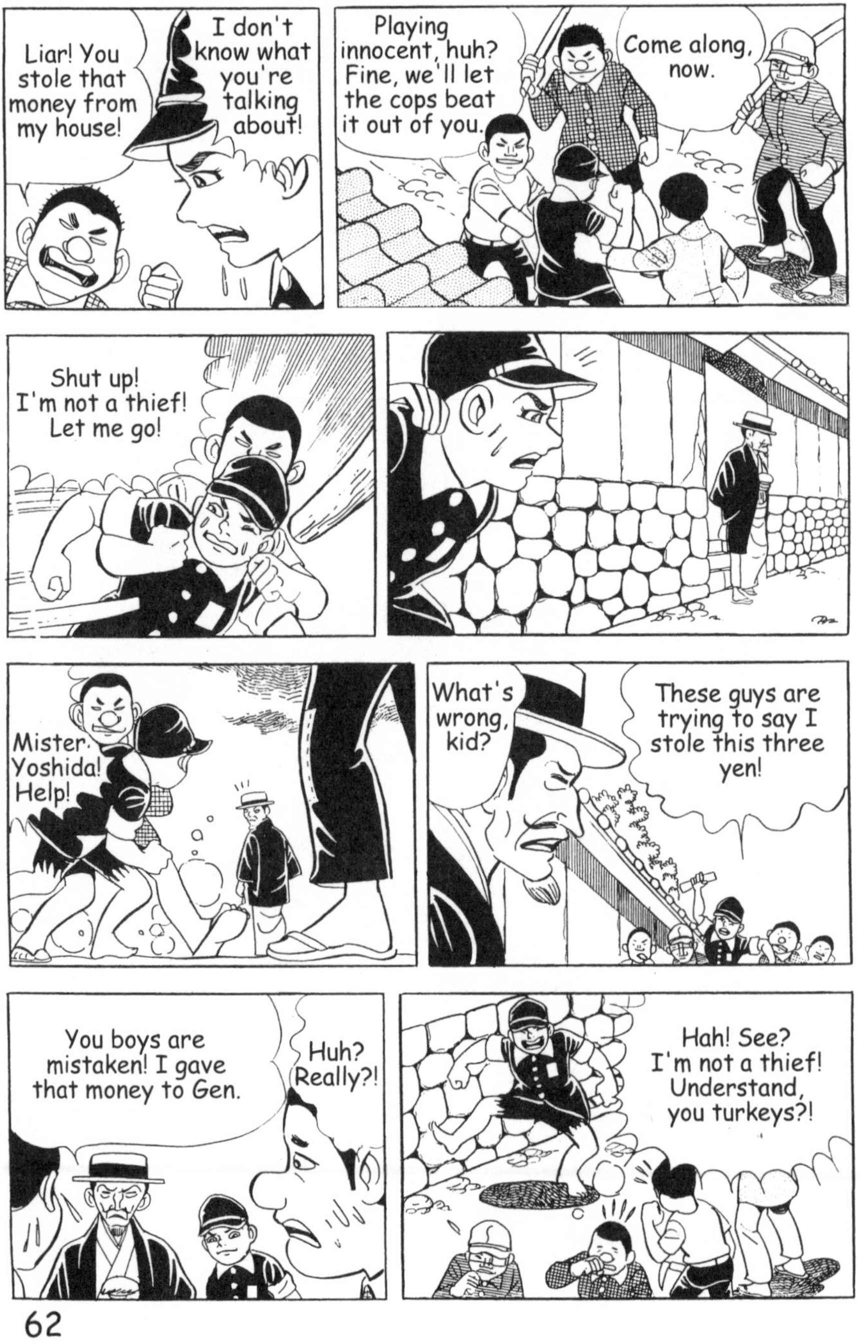
Liar! You stole that money from my house!
I don't know what you're talking about!
Playing innocent, huh? Fine, we'll let the cops beat it out of you.
Come along, now.
Shut up! I'm not a thief! Let me go!
Mister Yoshida! Help!
What's wrong, kid?
These guys are trying to say I stole this three yen!
You boys are mistaken! I gave that money to Gen.
Huh? Really?!
Hah! See? I'm not a thief! Understand, you turkeys?!

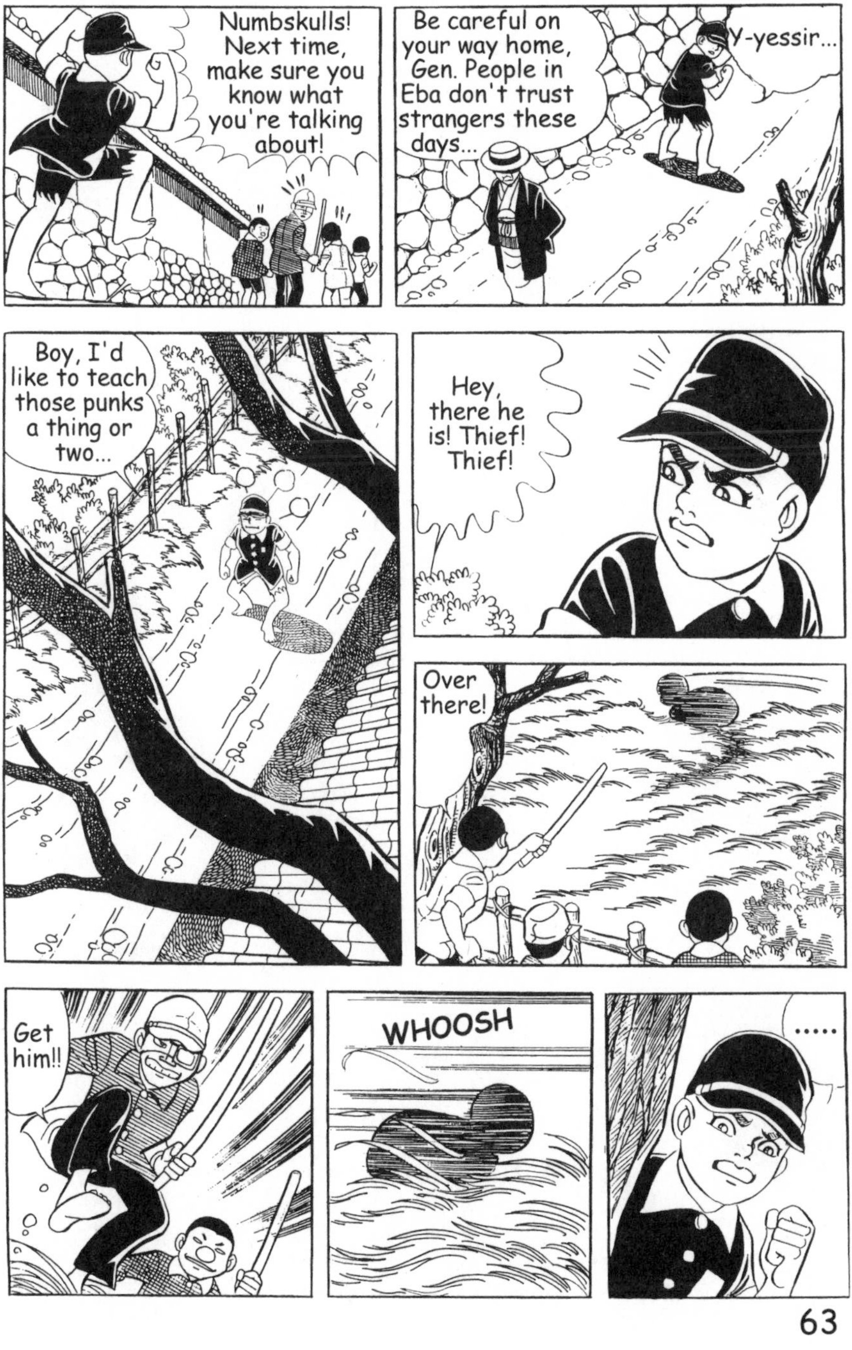
Numbskulls! Next time, make sure you know what you're talking about!
Be careful on your way home, Gen. People in Eba don't trust strangers these days...
Y-yessir...
Boy, I'd like to teach those punks a thing or two...
Hey, there he is! Thief! Thief!
Over there!
Get him!!
WHOOSH
.....

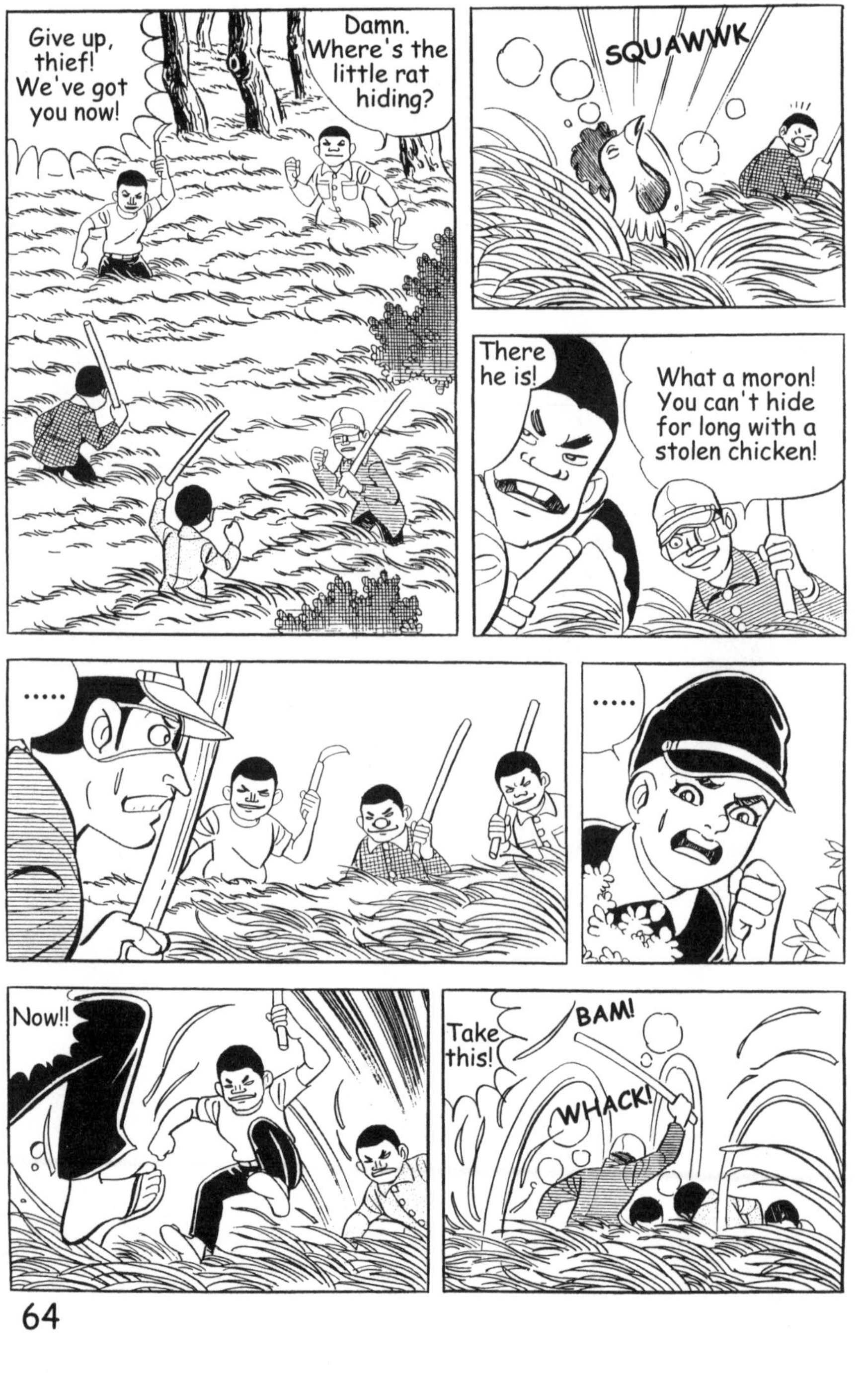
Give up, thief! We've got you now!
Damn. Where's the little rat hiding?
SQUAWWK
There he is!
What a moron! You can't hide for long with a stolen chicken!
.....
.....
Now!!
Take this!
BAM!
WHACK!

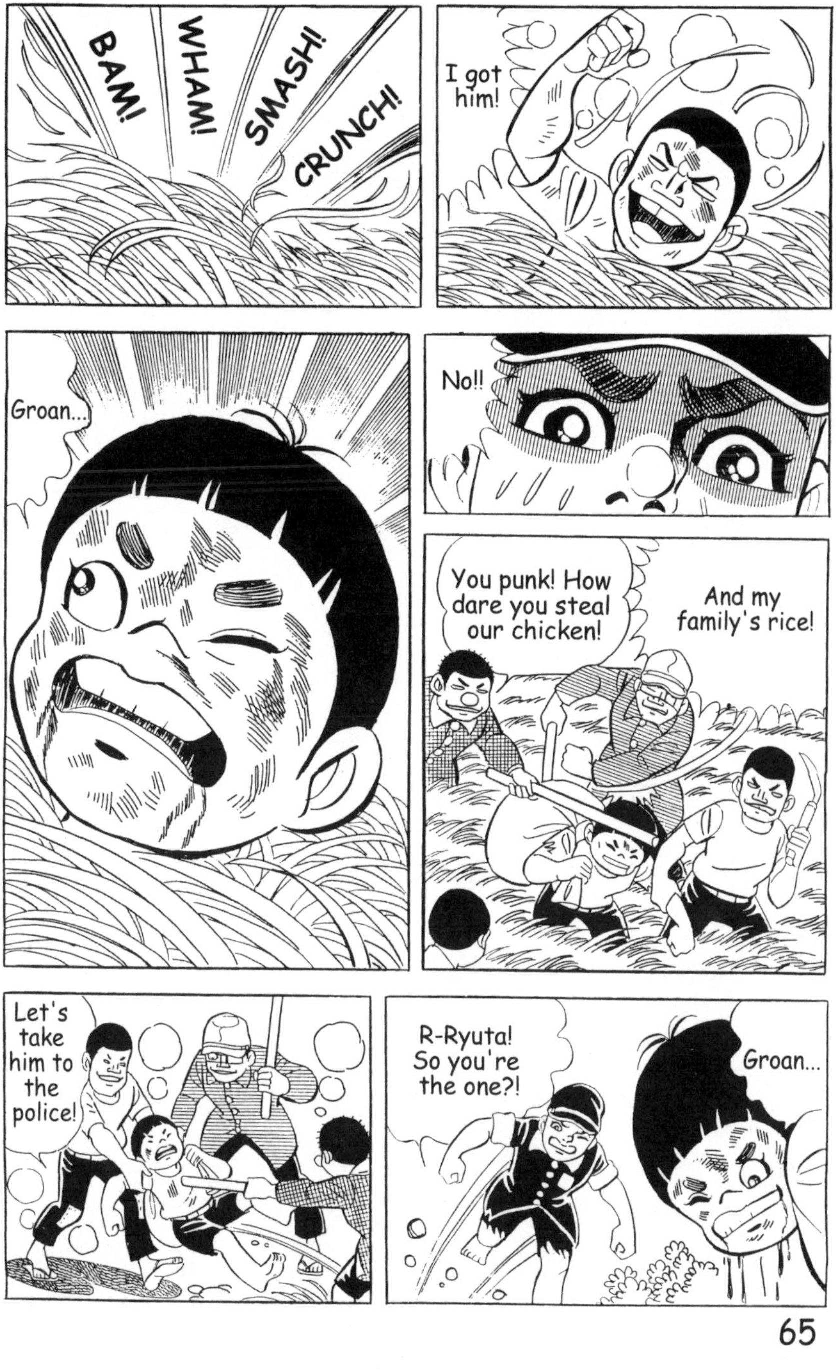
BAM!
WHAM!
SMASH!
CRUNCH!
I got him!
Groan...
No!!
You punk! How dare you steal our chicken!
And my family's rice!
Let's take him to the police!
R-Ryuta! So you're the one?!
Groan...

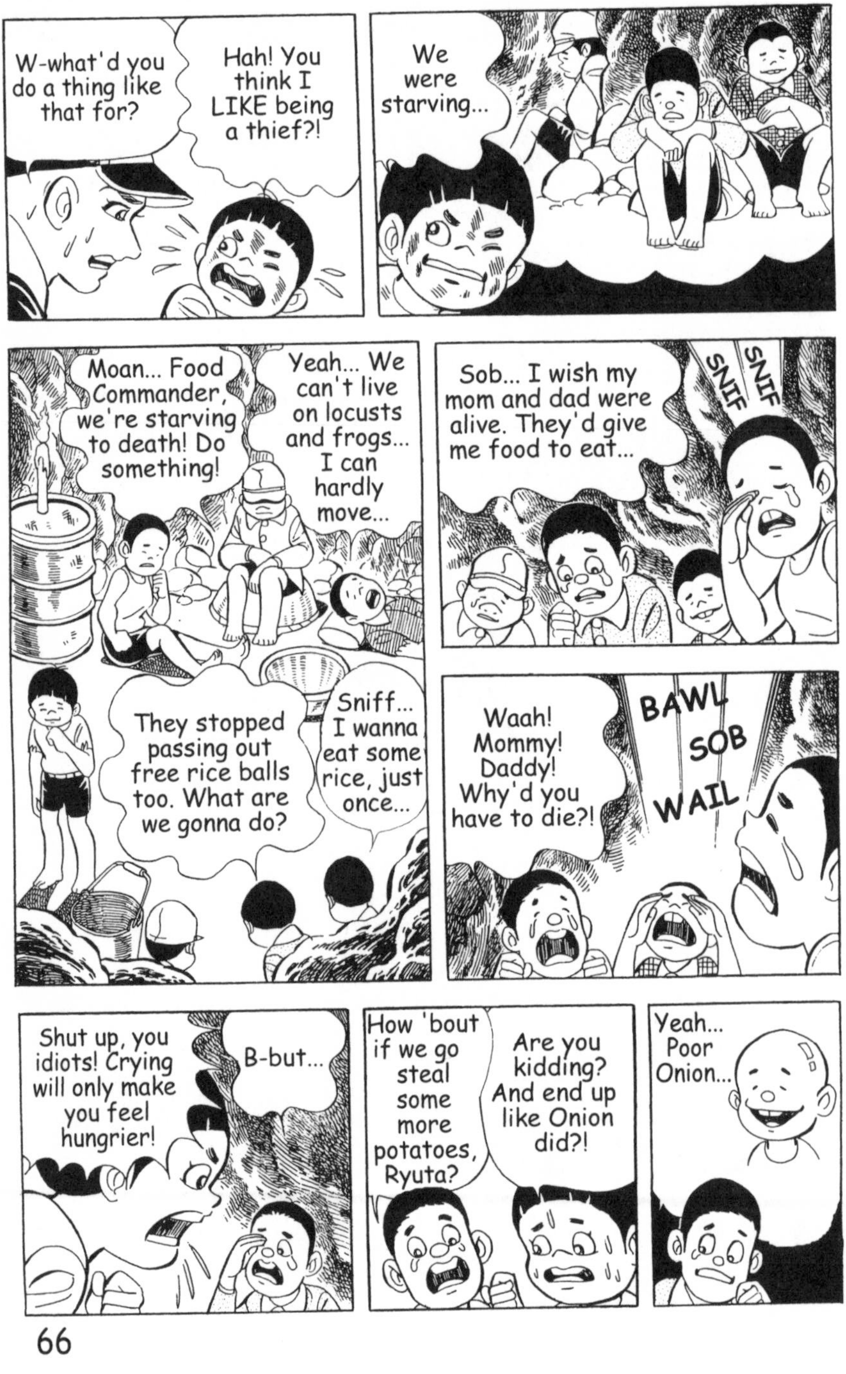
W-what'd you do a thing like that for?
Hah! You think I LIKE being a thief?!
We were starving...
Moan... Food Commander, we're starving to death! Do something!
Yeah... We can't live on locusts and frogs... I can hardly move...
They stopped passing out free rice balls too. What are we gonna do?
Sniff... I wanna eat some rice, just once...
Sob... I wish my mom and dad were alive. They'd give me food to eat...
SNIFF
SNIFF
Waah! Mommy! Daddy! Why'd you have to die?!
BAWL
SOB
WAIL
Shut up, you idiots! Crying will only make you feel hungrier!
B-but...
How 'bout if we go steal some more potatoes, Ryuta?
Are you kidding? And end up like Onion did?!
Yeah... Poor Onion...

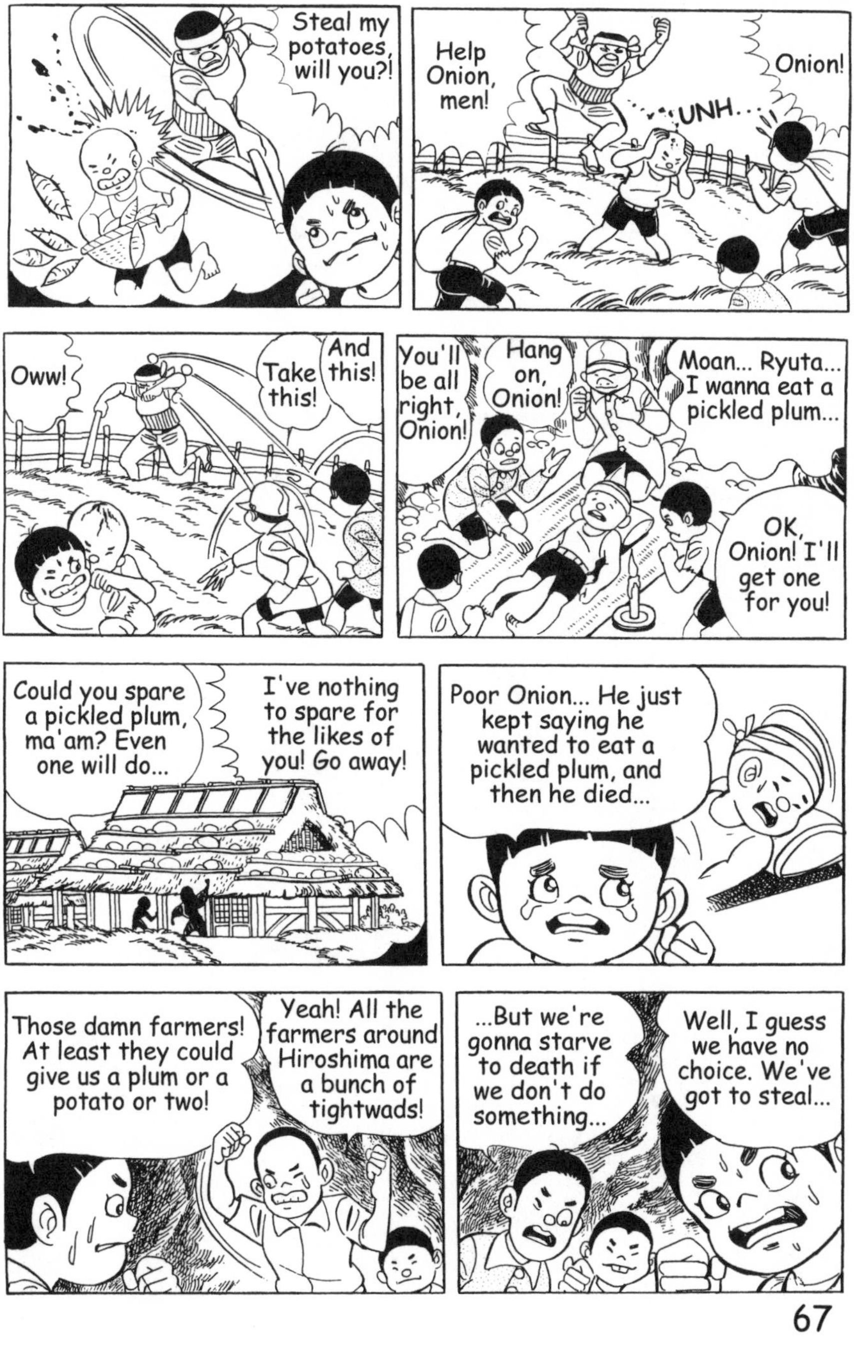

Steal my potatoes, will you?!
Help Onion, men!
UNH...
Onion!
Oww!
Take this!
And this!
You'll be all right, Onion!
Hang on, Onion!
Moan... Ryuta... I wanna eat a pickled plum...
OK, Onion! I'll get one for you!
Could you spare a pickled plum, ma'am? Even one will do...
I've nothing to spare for the likes of you! Go away!
Poor Onion... He just kept saying he wanted to eat a pickled plum, and then he died...
Those damn farmers! At least they could give us a plum or a potato or two!
Yeah! All the farmers around Hiroshima are a bunch of tightwads!
...But we're gonna starve to death if we don't do something...
Well, I guess we have no choice. We've got to steal...

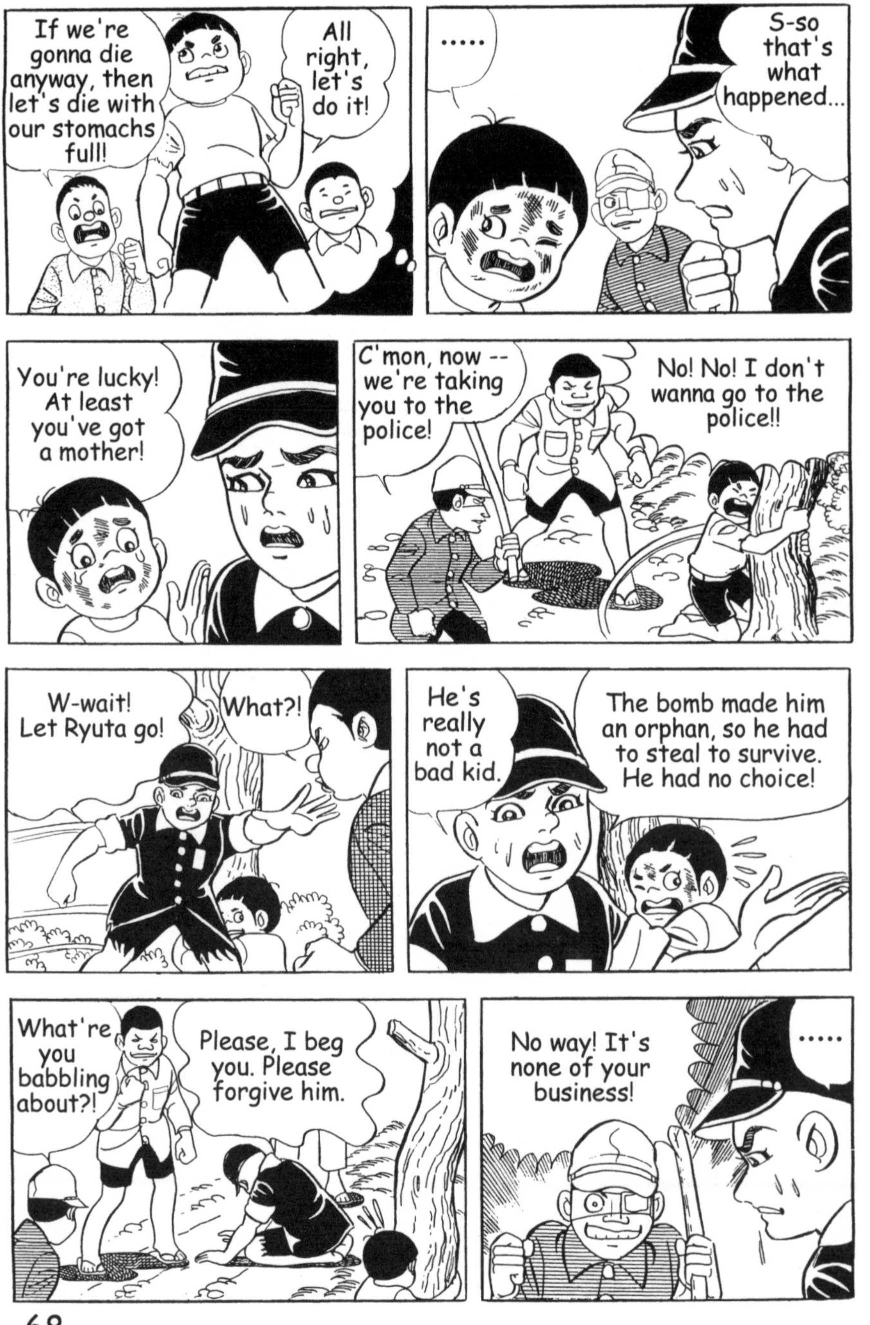
If we're gonna die anyway, then let's die with our stomachs full!
All right, let's do it!
.....
S-so that's what happened...
You're lucky! At least you've got a mother!
C'mon, now -- we're taking you to the police!
No! No! I don't wanna go to the police!!
W-wait! Let Ryuta go!
What?!
He's really not a bad kid.
The bomb made him an orphan, so he had to steal to survive. He had no choice!
What're you babbling about?!
Please, I beg you. Please forgive him.
No way! It's none of your business!
.....

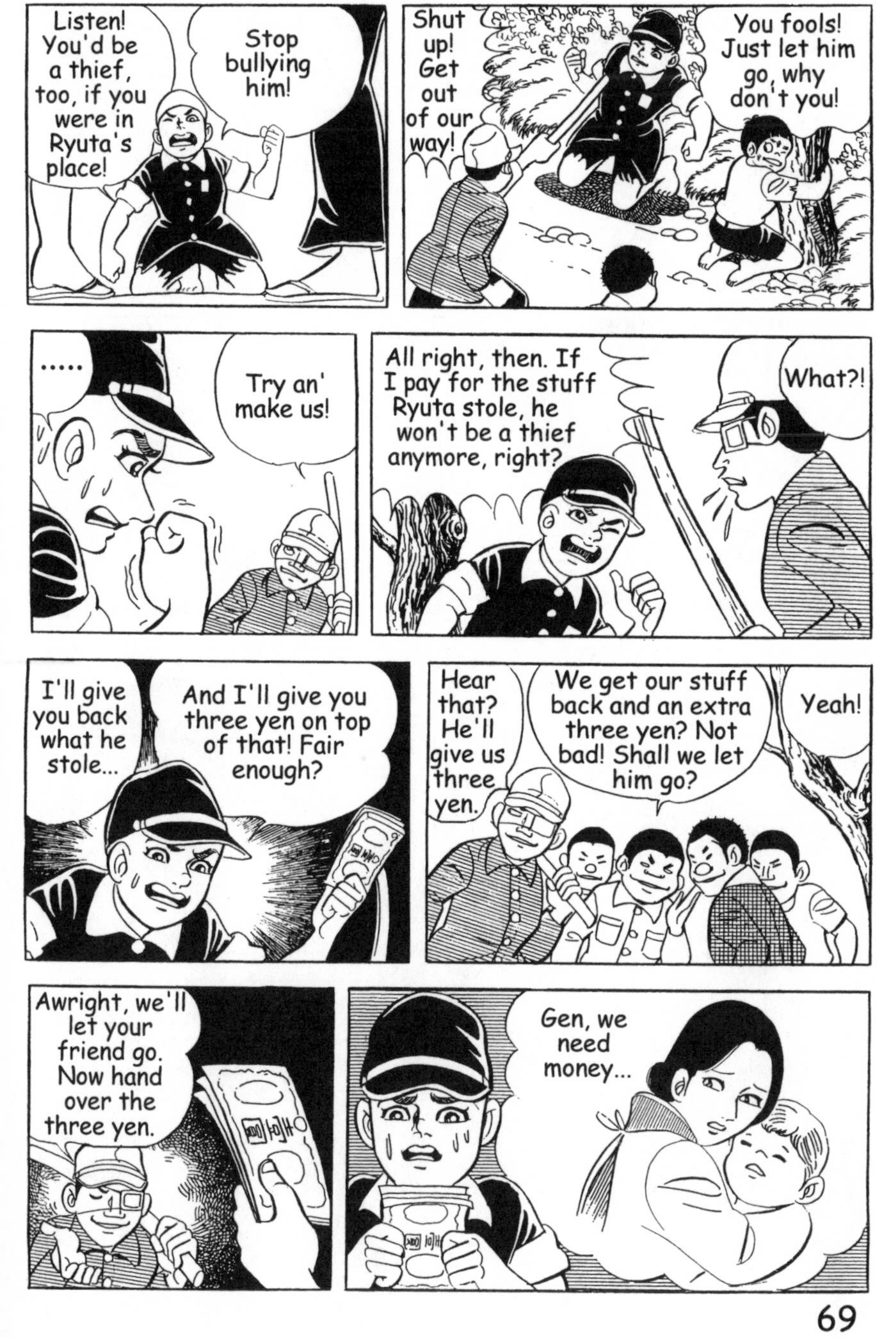
Listen! You'd be a thief, too, if you were in Ryuta's place!
Stop bullying him!
Shut up! Get out of our way!
You fools! Just let him go, why don't you!
.....
Try an' make us!
All right, then. If I pay for the stuff Ryuta stole, he won't be a thief anymore, right?
What?!
I'll give you back what he stole...
And I'll give you three yen on top of that! Fair enough?
Hear that? He'll give us three yen.
We get our stuff back and an extra three yen? Not bad! Shall we let him go?
Yeah!
Awright, we'll let your friend go. Now hand over the three yen.
Gen, we need money...

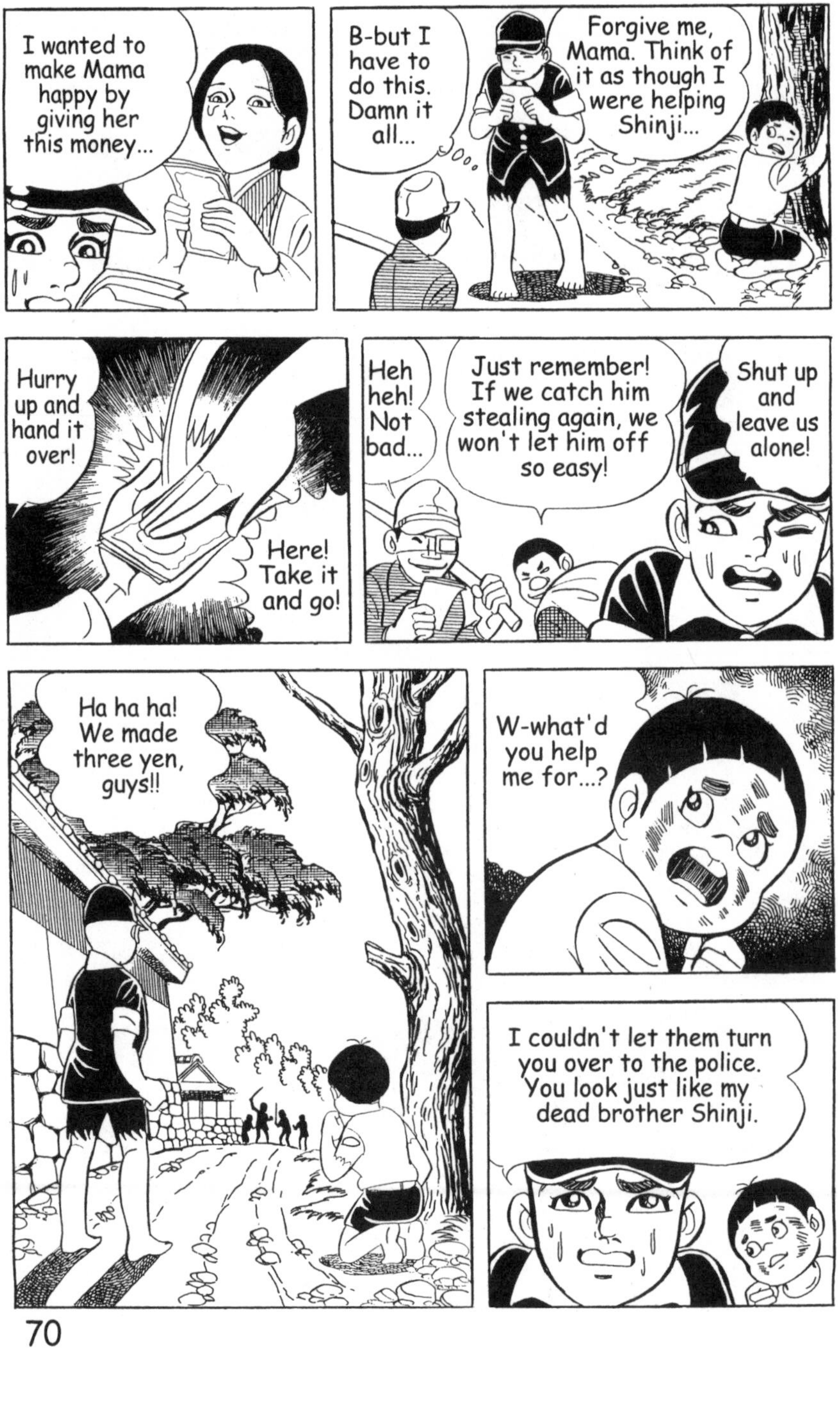
I wanted to make Mama happy by giving her this money...
B-but I have to do this. Damn it all...
Forgive me, Mama. Think of it as though I were helping Shinji...
Hurry up and hand it over!
Here! Take it and go!
Heh heh! Not bad...
Just remember! If we catch him stealing again, we won't let him off so easy!
Shut up and leave us alone!
Ha ha ha! We made three yen, guys!!
W-what'd you help me for...?
I couldn't let them turn you over to the police. You look just like my dead brother Shinji.

I can't help it, I think of you as my little brother. No matter what happens, I'll help you out!
.....
I know life's hard for you, Ryuta, but you can't give up!
.....
WAAAH
WAH
SOB
SNIF
WAIL
Don't cry, you fool. You'll just feel hungrier.
Waah! I'm happy, Gen!!
W-what did you just call me?
Sob... I-I called you Gen.
Big brother Gen!
Hee hee! You sound just like my little brother calling me!

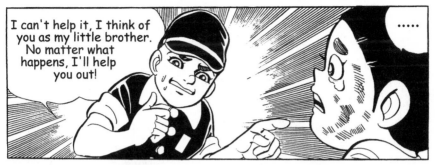

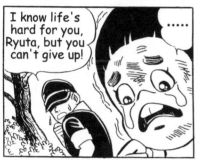

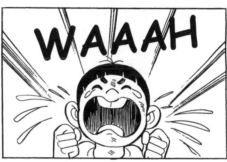

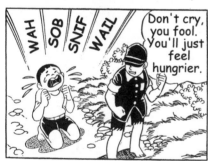

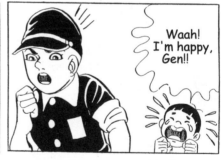

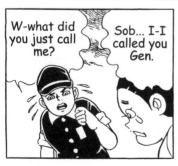

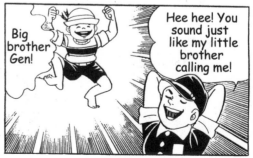

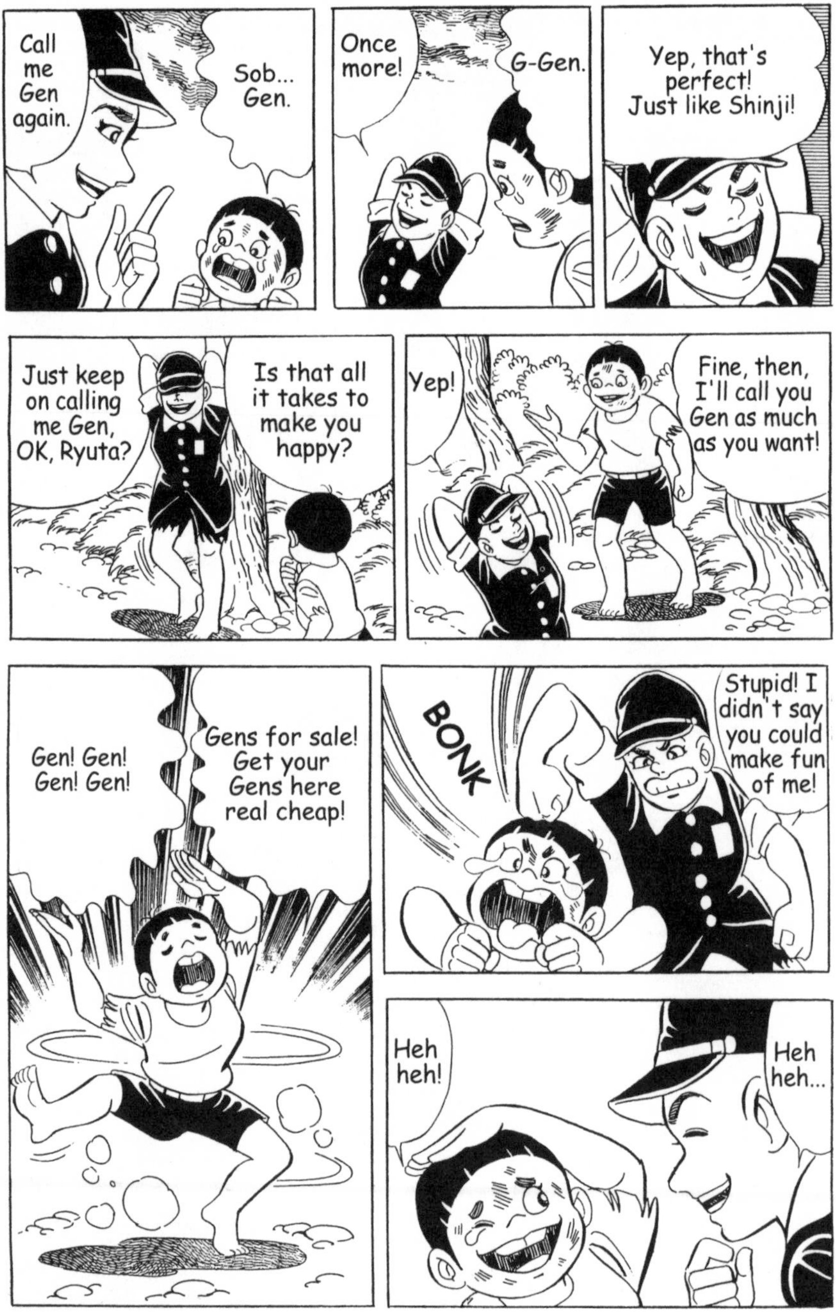
Call me Gen again.
Sob... Gen.
Once more!
G-Gen.
Yep, that's perfect! Just like Shinji!
Just keep on calling me Gen, OK, Ryuta?
Is that all it takes to make you happy?
Yep!
Fine, then, I'll call you Gen as much as you want!
Gen! Gen! Gen! Gen!
Gens for sale! Get your Gens here real cheap!
BONK
Stupid! I didn't say you could make fun of me!
Heh heh!
Heh heh...

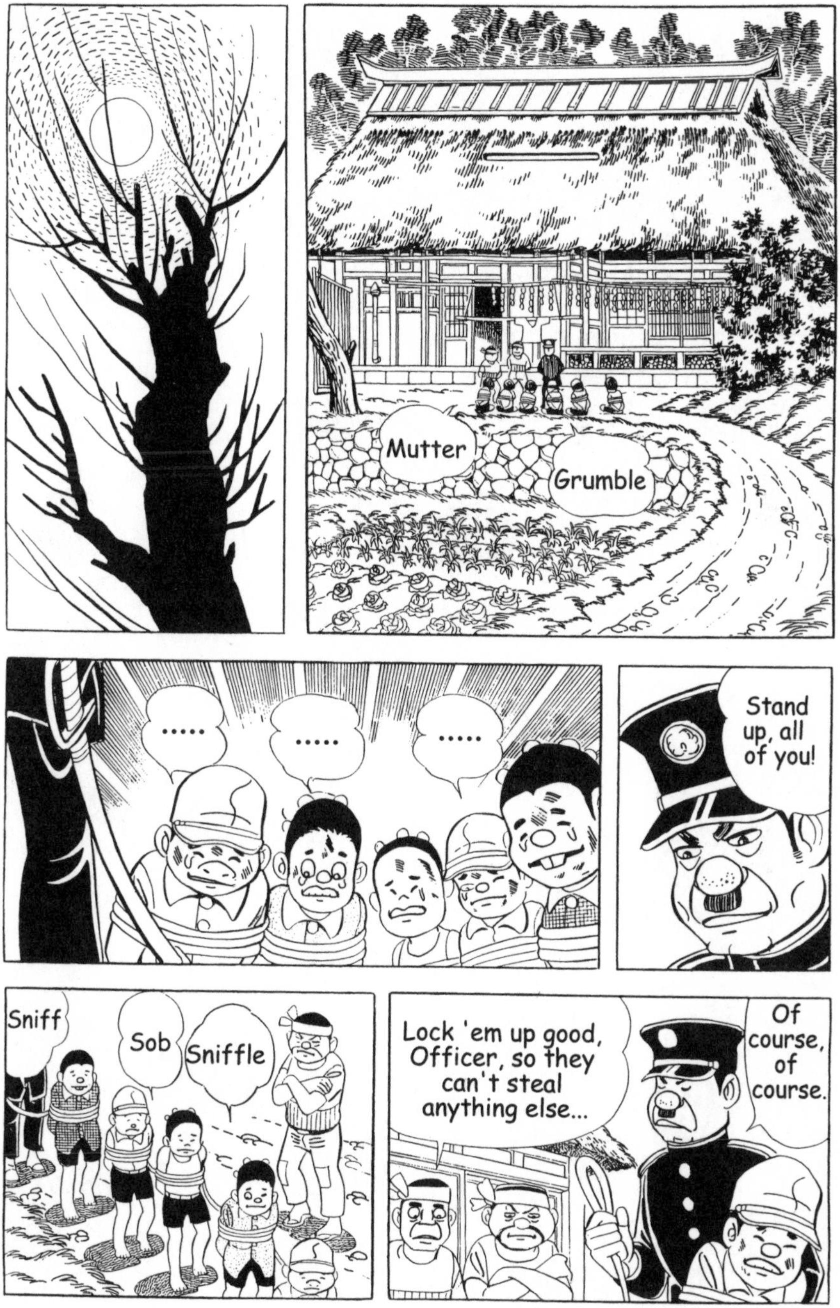
Mutter
Grumble
.....
.....
.....
Stand up, all of you!
Sniff
Sob
Sniffle
Lock 'em up good, Officer, so they can't steal anything else...
Of course, of course.

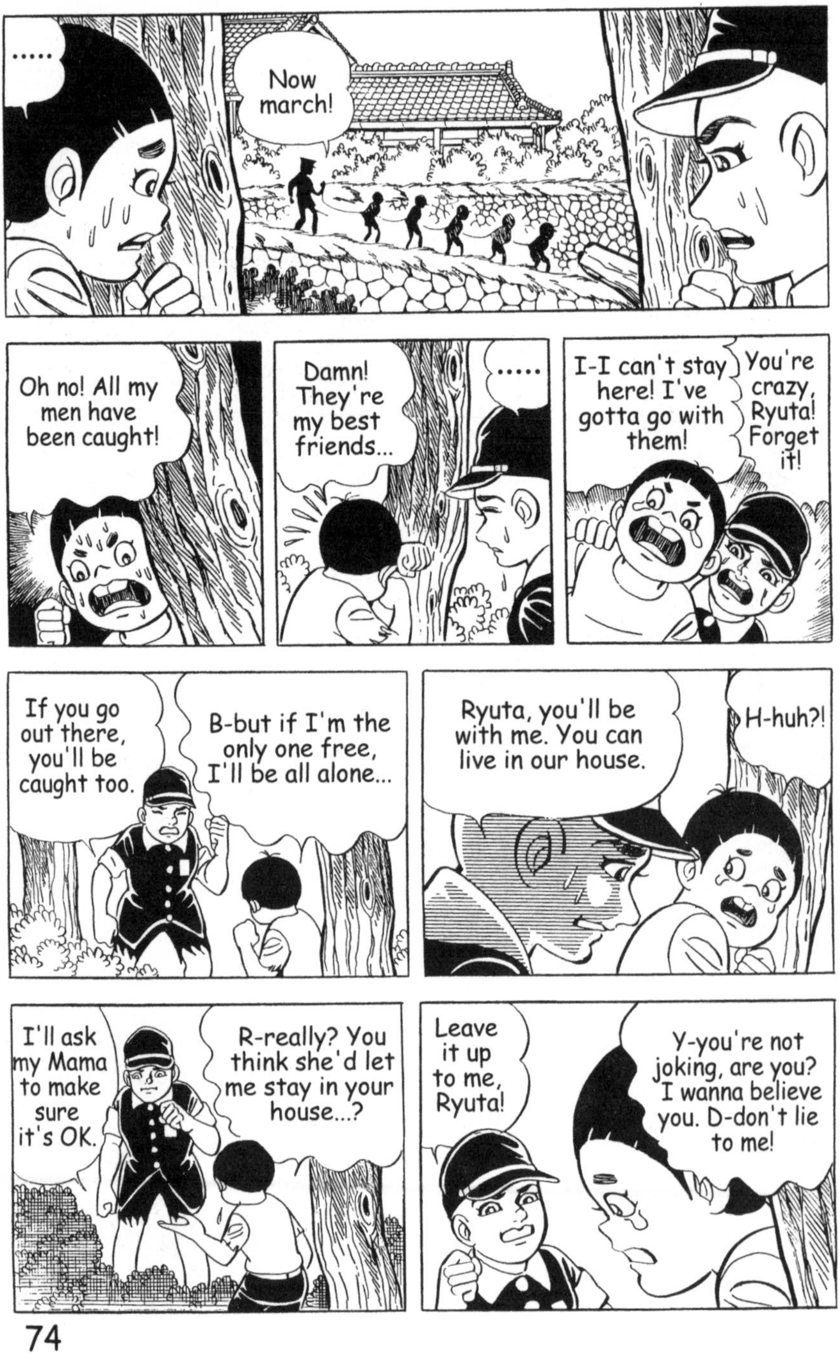
.....
Now march!
Oh no! All my men have been caught!
Damn! They're my best friends...
.....
I-I can't stay here! I've gotta go with them!
You're crazy, Ryuta! Forget it!
If you go out there, you'll be caught too.
B-but if I'm the only one free, I'll be all alone...
Ryuta, you'll be with me. You can live in our house.
H-huh?!
I'll ask my Mama to make sure it's OK.
R-really? You think she'd let me stay in your house...?
Leave it up to me, Ryuta!
Y-you're not joking, are you? I wanna believe you. D-don't lie to me!

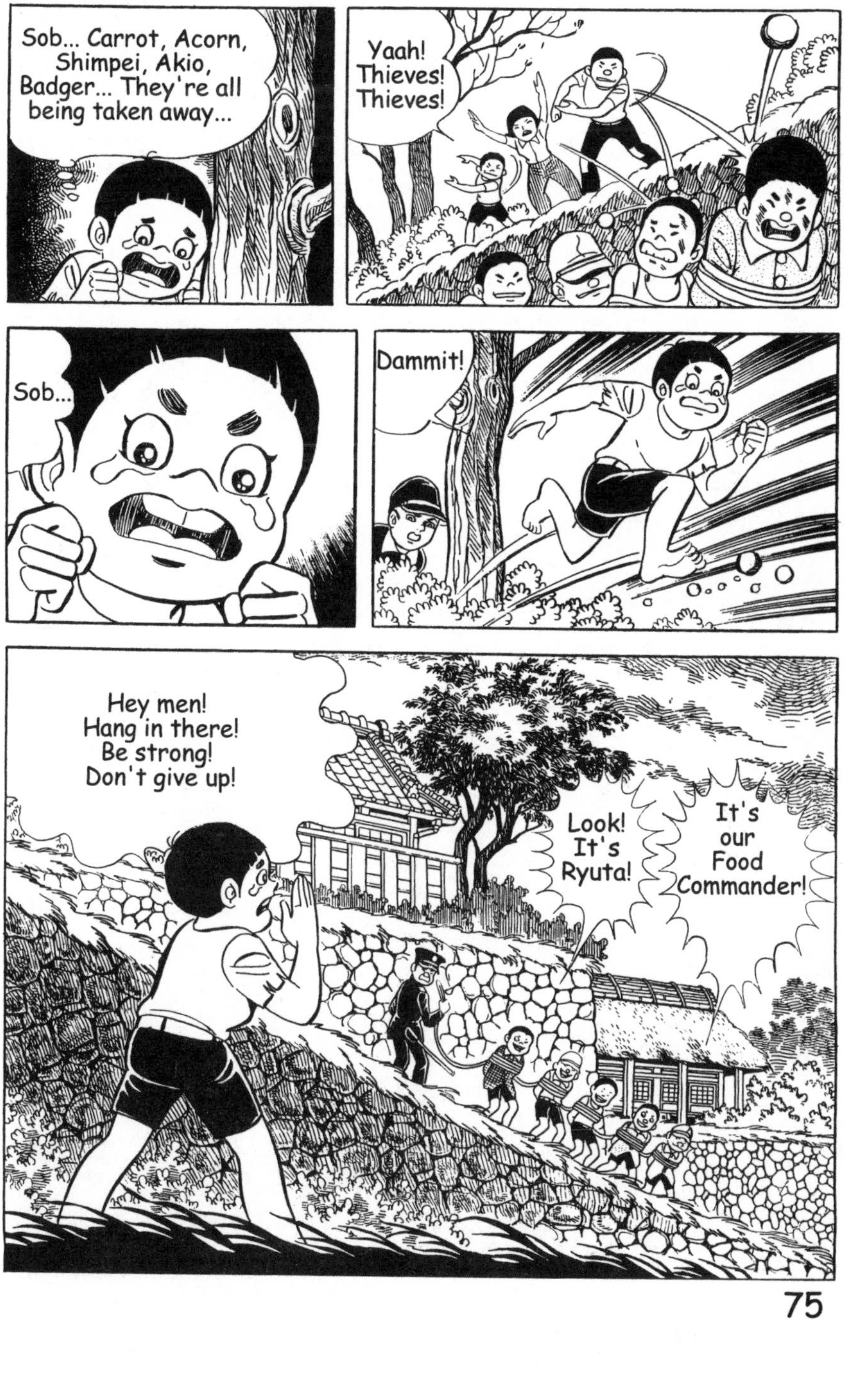

Sob... Carrot, Acorn, Shimpei, Akio, Badger... They're all being taken away...
Yaah! Thieves! Thieves!
Sob...
Dammit!
Hey men! Hang in there! Be strong! Don't give up!
Look! It's Ryuta!
It's our Food Commander!

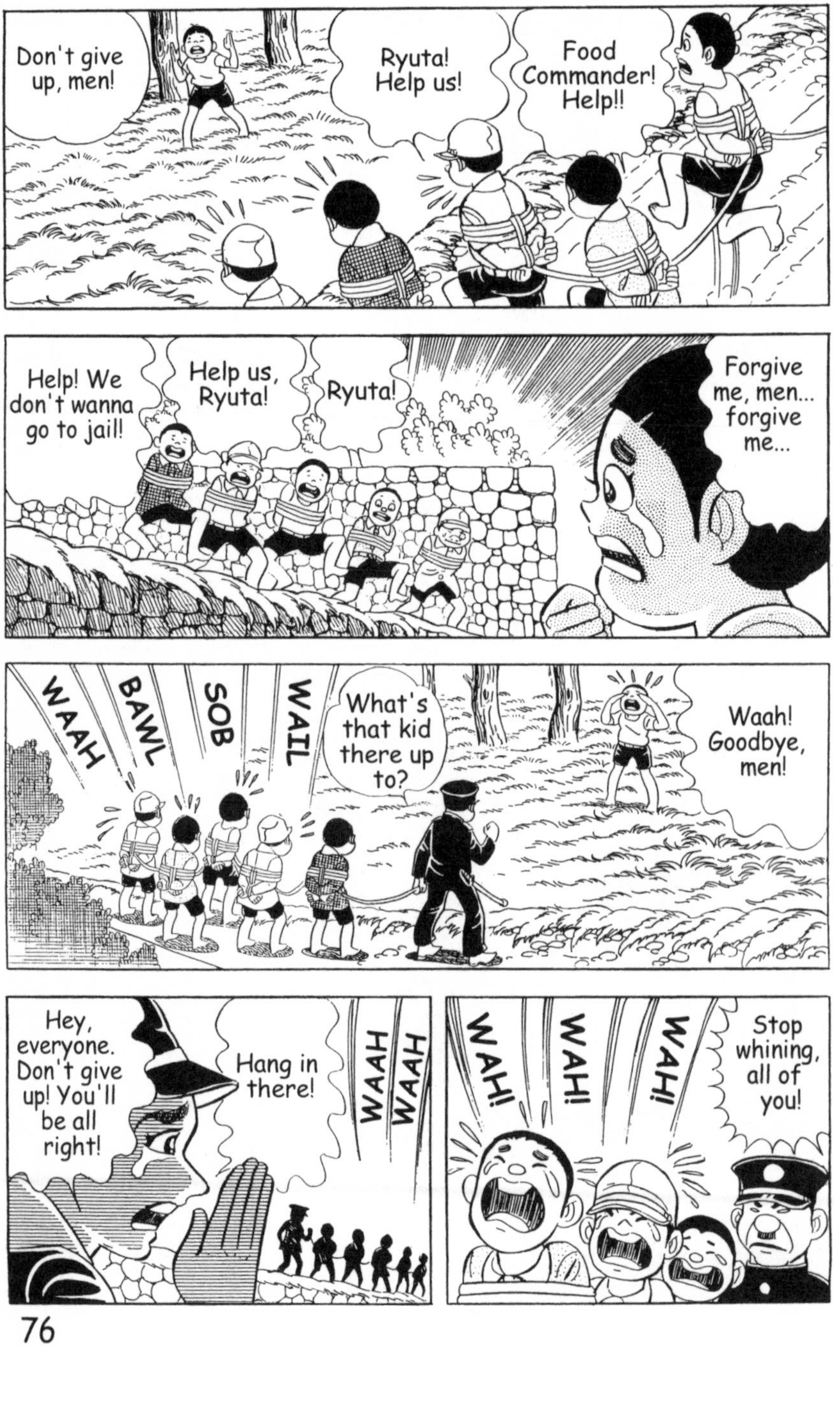
Don't give up, men!
Ryuta! Help us!
Food Commander! Help!!
Help! We don't wanna go to jail!
Help us, Ryuta!
Ryuta!
Forgive me, men... forgive me...
WAAH
BAWL
SOB
WAIL
What's that kid there up to?
Waah! Goodbye, men!
Hey, everyone. Don't give up! You'll be all right!
Hang in there!
WAAH
WAAH
WAH!
WAH!
WAH!
Stop whining, all of you!

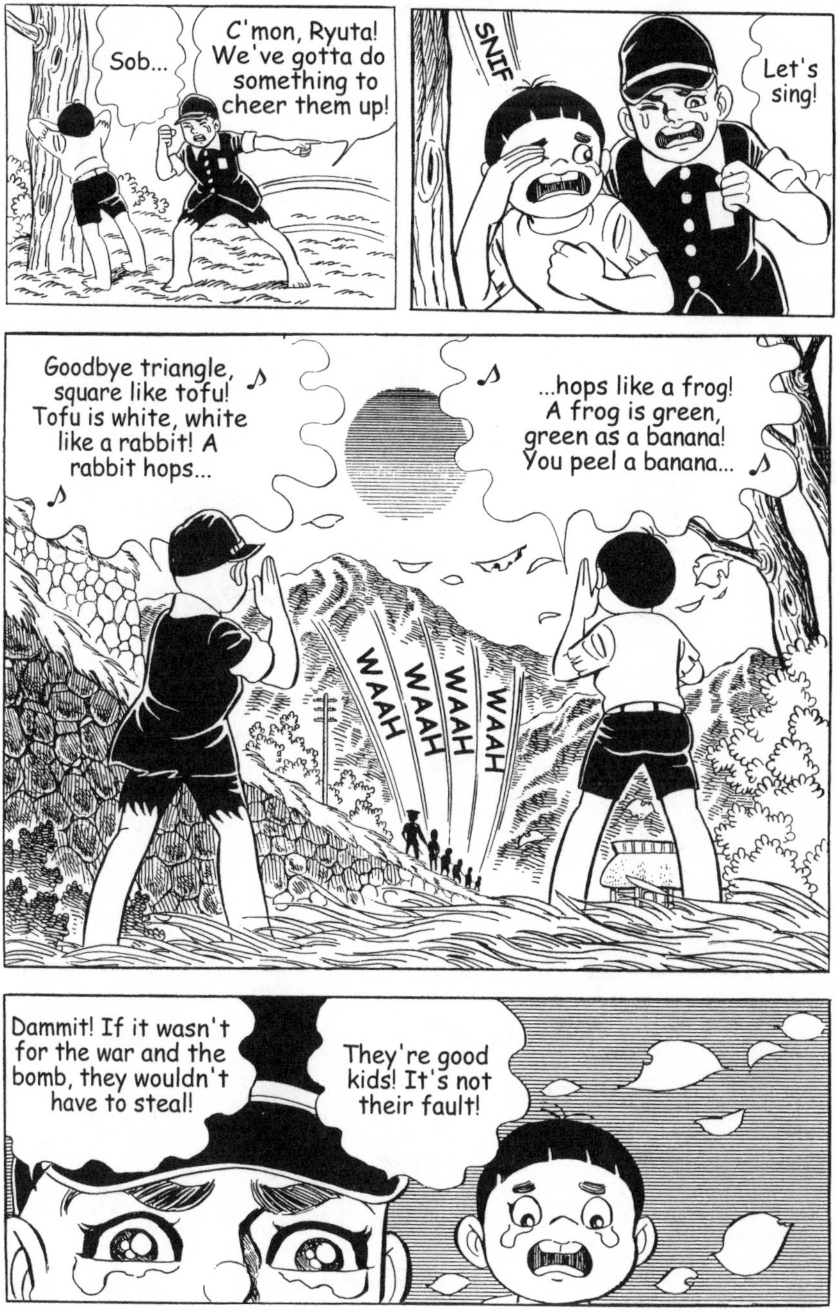
Sob...
C'mon, Ryuta! We've gotta do something to cheer them up!
SNIF
Let's sing!
Goodbye triangle, square like tofu! Tofu is white, white like a rabbit! A rabbit hops...
...hops like a frog! A frog is green, green as a banana! You peel a banana...
WAAH
WAAH
WAAH
WAAH
Dammit! If it wasn't for the war and the bomb, they wouldn't have to steal!
They're good kids! It's not their fault!

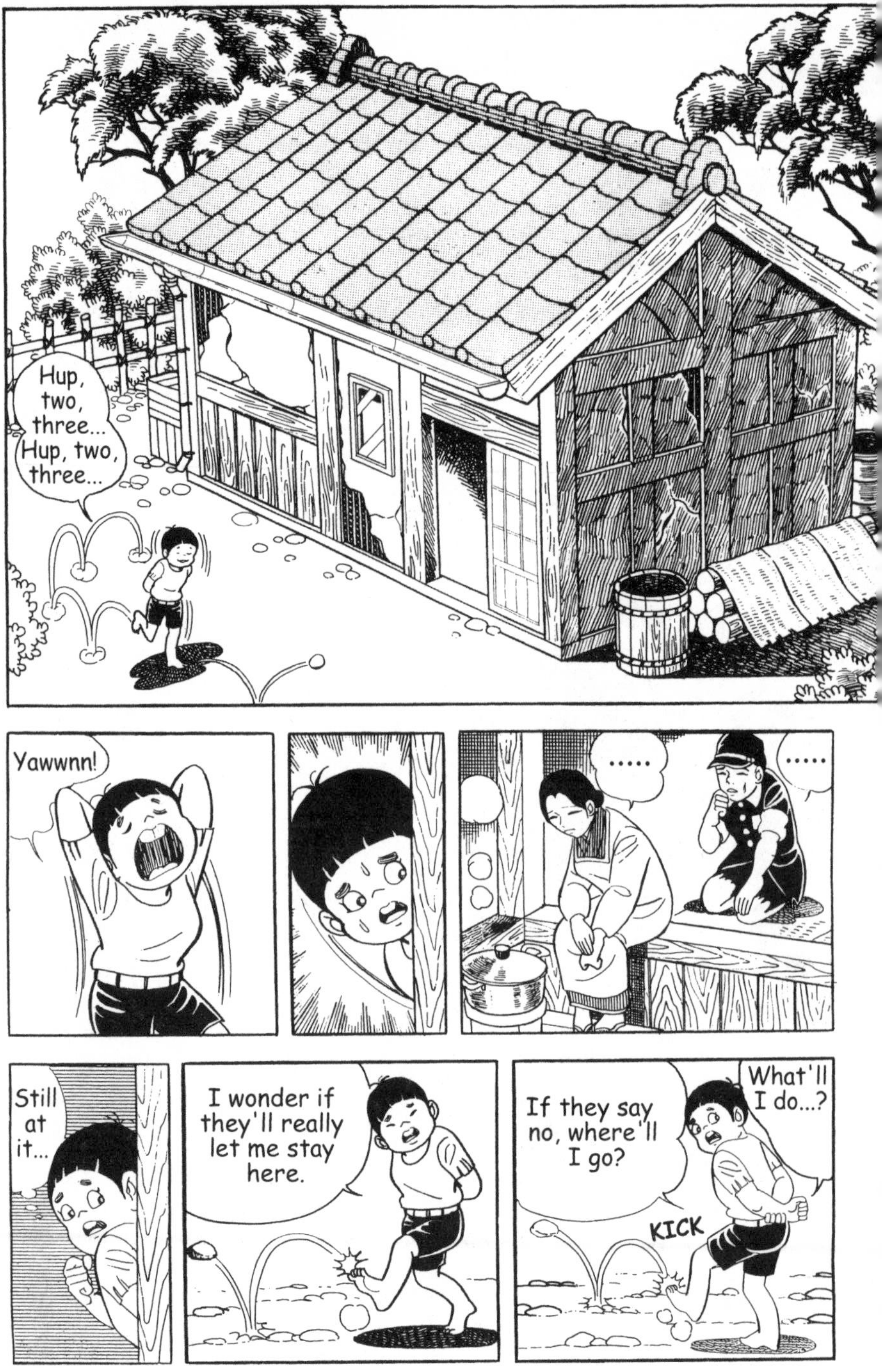
Hup, two, three... Hup, two, three...
Yawwnn!
.....
.....
Still at it...
I wonder if they'll really let me stay here.
If they say no, where'll I go?
KICK
What'll I do...?

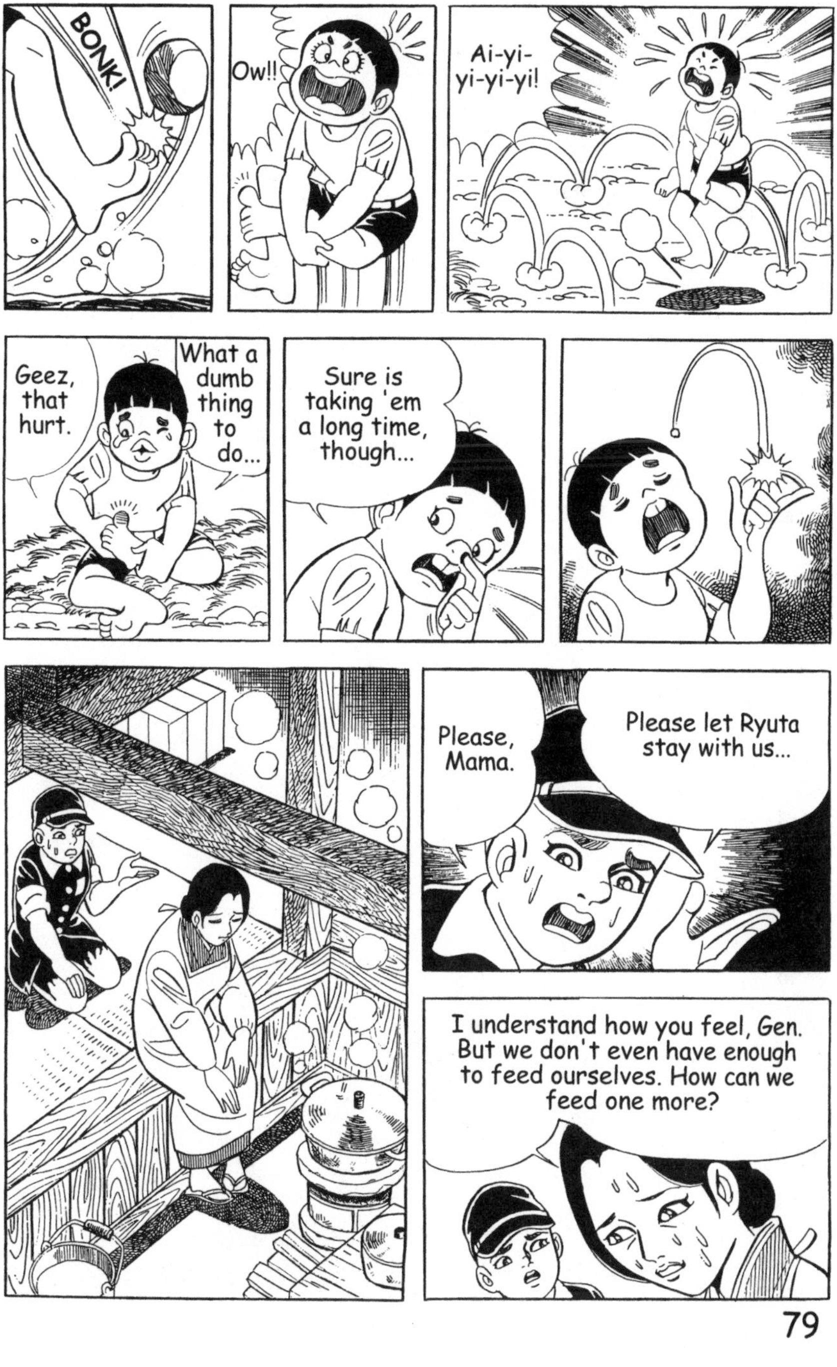
BONK!
Ow!!
Ai-yi-yi-yi-yi!
Geez, that hurt.
What a dumb thing to do...
Sure is taking 'em a long time, though...
Please, Mama.
Please let Ryuta stay with us...
I understand how you feel, Gen. But we don't even have enough to feed ourselves. How can we feed one more?

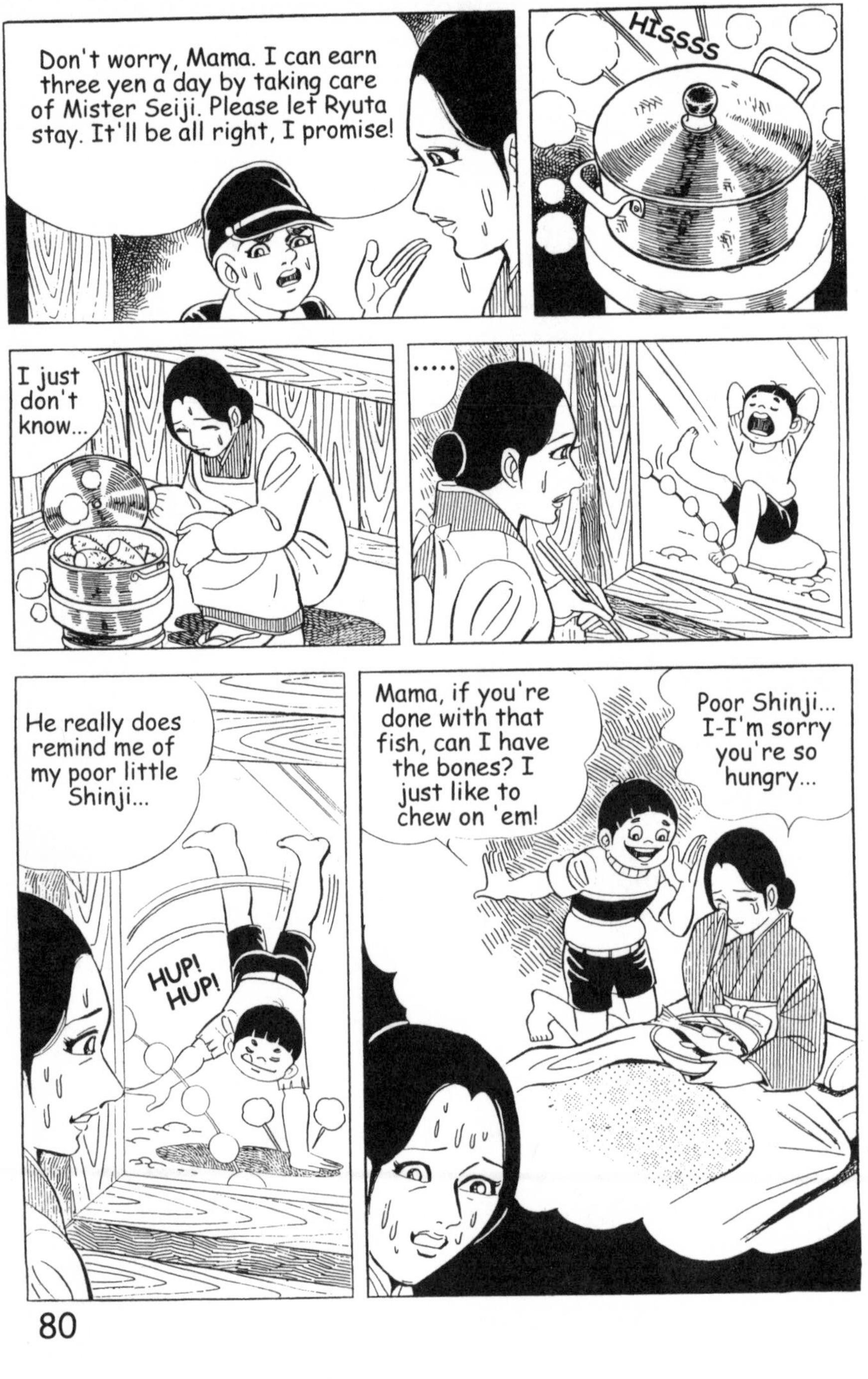

Don't worry, Mama. I can earn three yen a day by taking care of Mister Seiji. Please let Ryuta stay. It'll be all right, I promise!
HISSSS
I just don't know...
.....
He really does remind me of my poor little Shinji...
HUP! HUP!
Mama, if you're done with that fish, can I have the bones? I just like to chew on 'em!
Poor Shinji... I-I'm sorry you're so hungry...

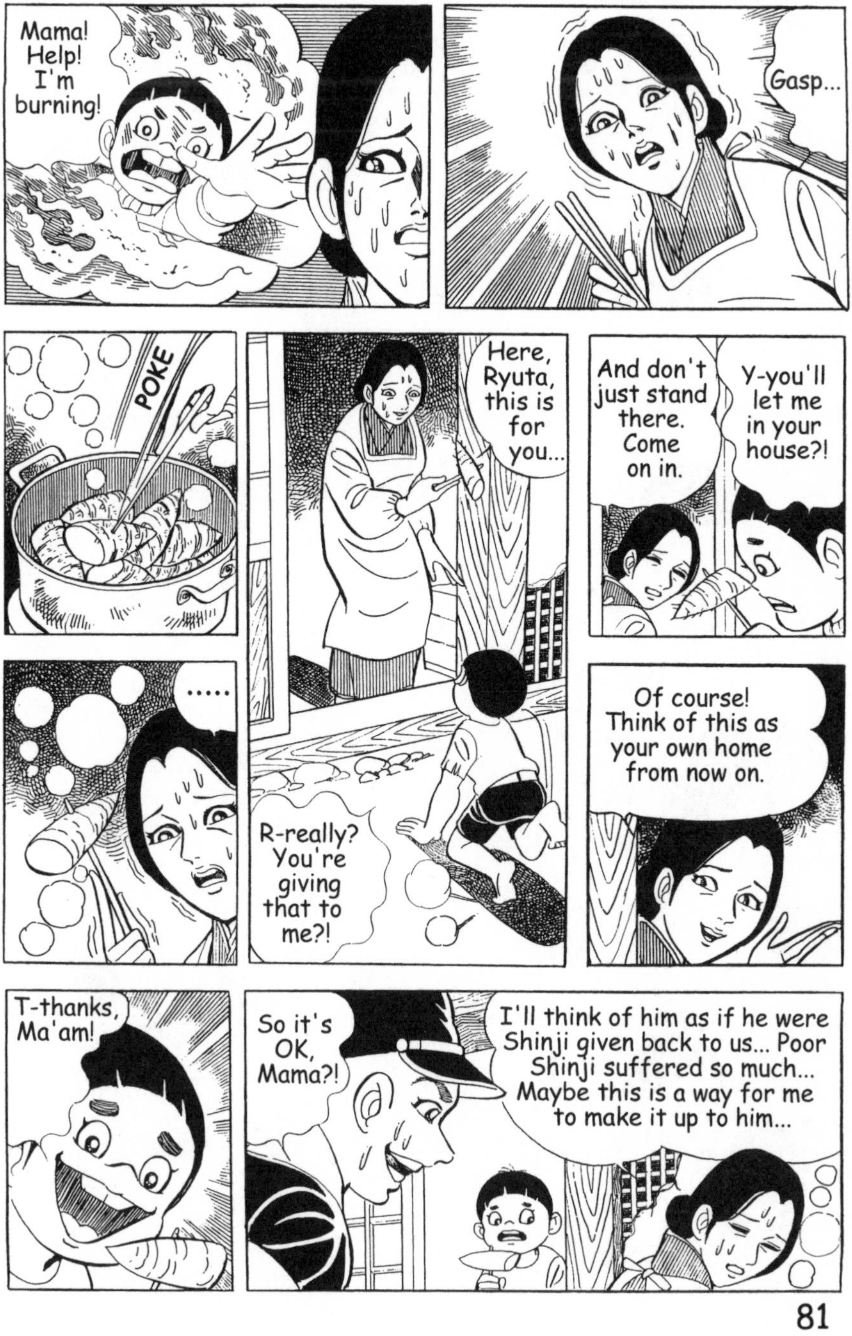
Mama! Help! I'm burning!
Gasp...
POKE
.....
Here, Ryuta, this is for you...
R-really? You're giving that to me?!
And don't just stand there. Come on in.
Y-you'll let me in your house?!
Of course! Think of this as your own home from now on.
T-thanks, Ma'am!
So it's OK, Mama?!
I'll think of him as if he were Shinji given back to us... Poor Shinji suffered so much... Maybe this is a way for me to make it up to him...

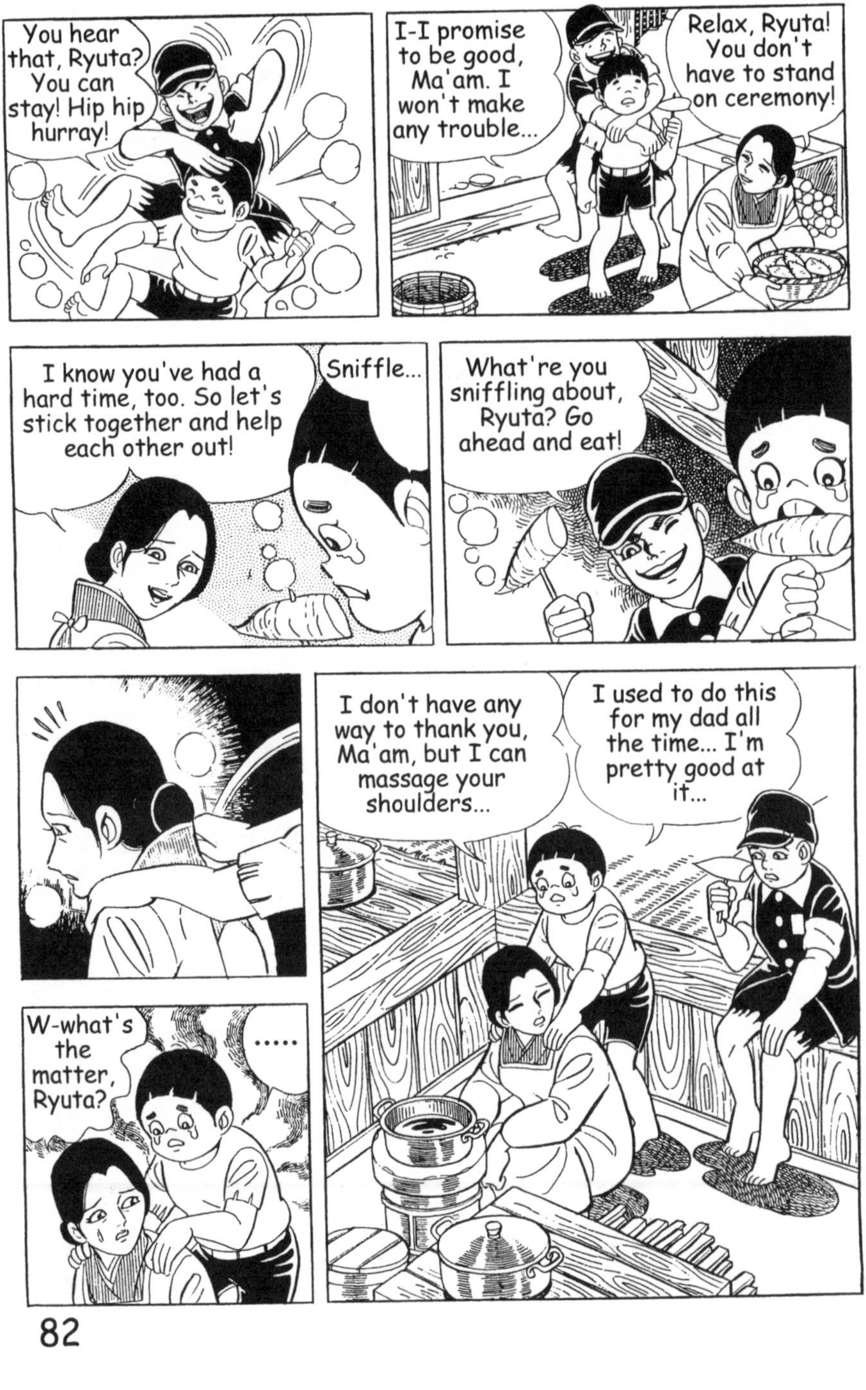
You hear that, Ryuta? You can stay! Hip hip hurray!
I-I promise to be good, Ma'am. I won't make any trouble...
Relax, Ryuta! You don't have to stand on ceremony!
I know you've had a hard time, too. So let's stick together and help each other out!
Sniffle...
What're you sniffling about, Ryuta? Go ahead and eat!
I don't have any way to thank you, Ma'am, but I can massage your shoulders...
I used to do this for my dad all the time... I'm pretty good at it...
W-what's the matter, Ryuta?
.....

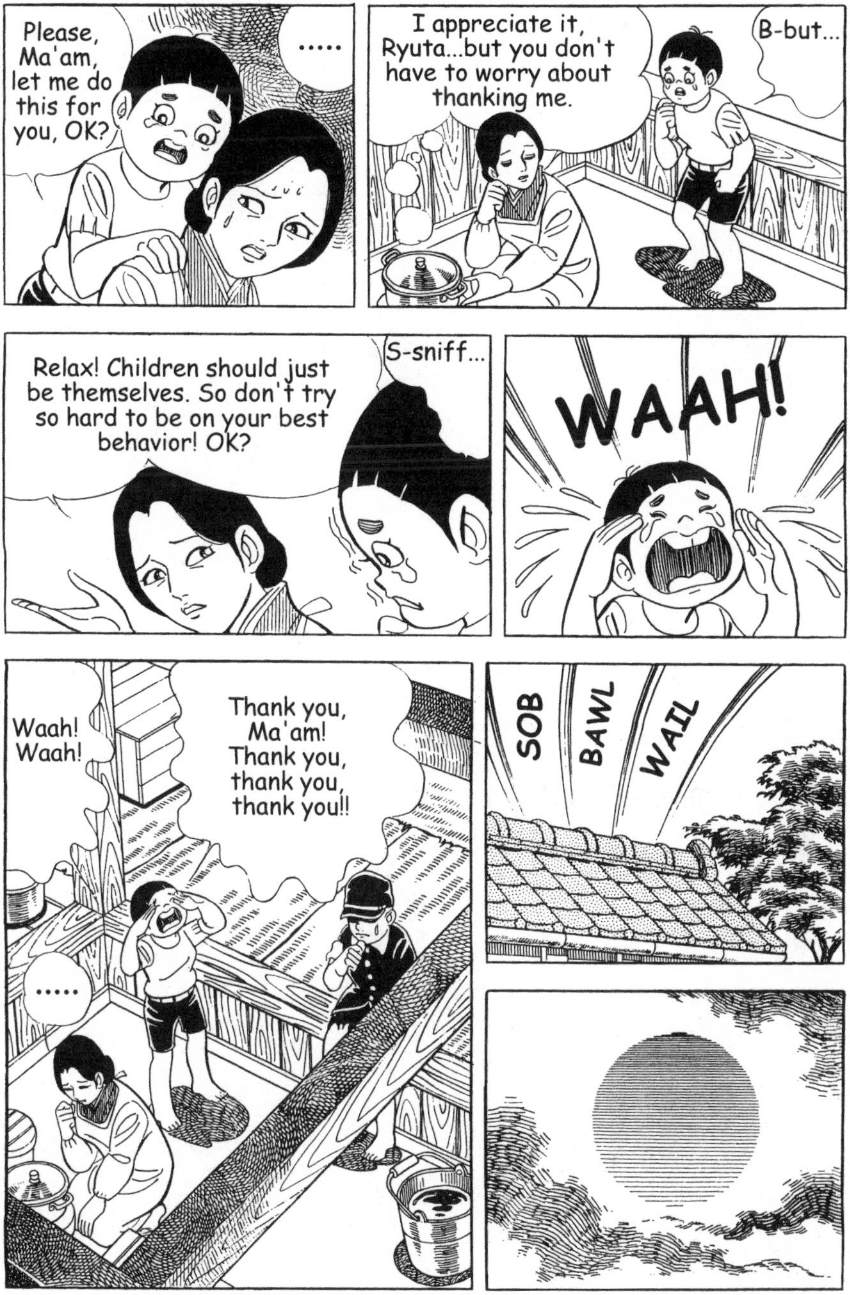
Please, Ma'am, let me do this for you, OK?
.....
I appreciate it, Ryuta...but you don't have to worry about thanking me.
B-but...
Relax! Children should just be themselves. So don't try so hard to be on your best behavior! OK?
S-sniff...
WAAH!
Waah! Waah!
Thank you, Ma'am! Thank you, thank you, thank you!!
.....
SOB
BAWL
WAIL

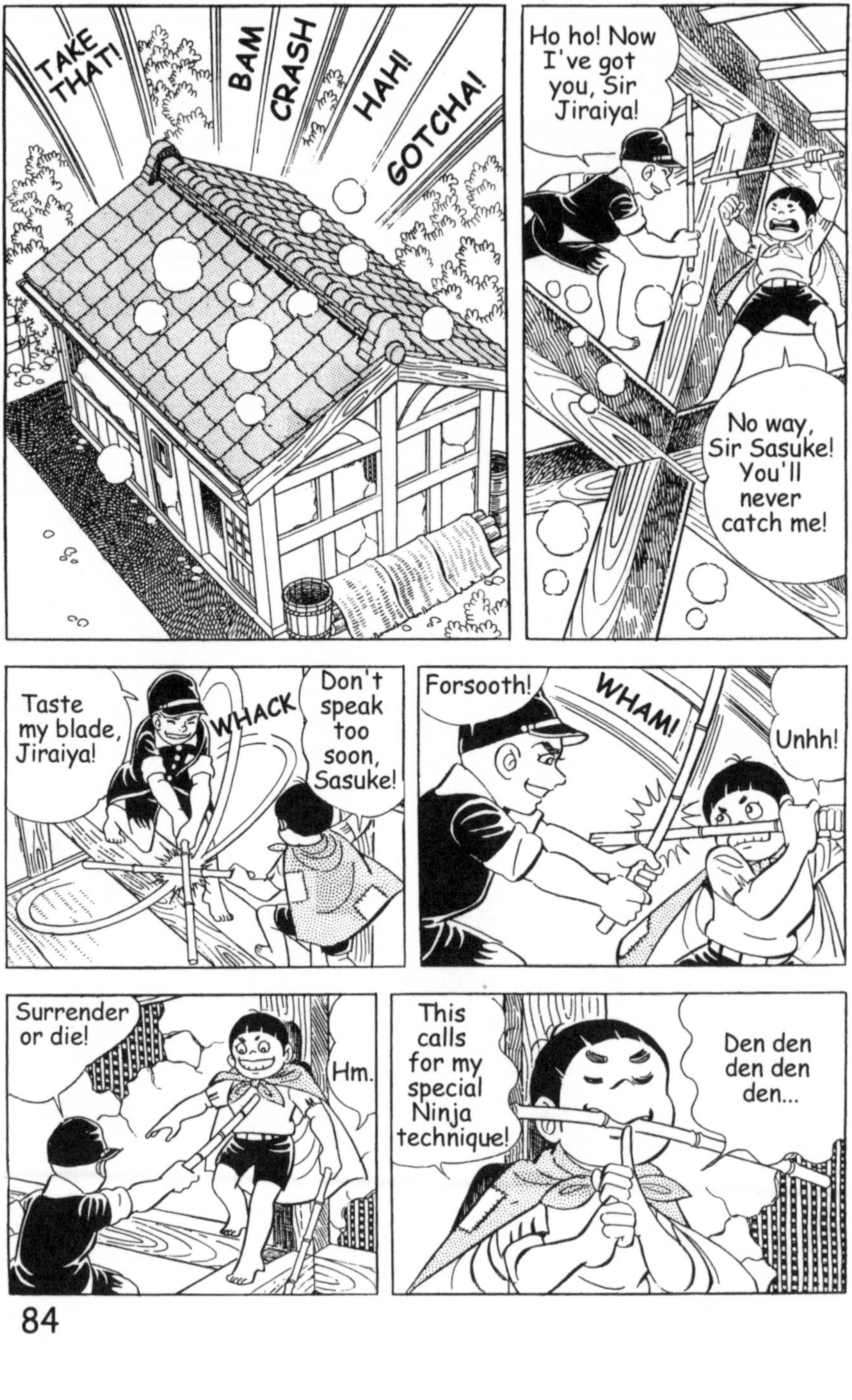
TAKE THAT!
BAM
CRASH
HAH!
GOTCHA!
Ho ho! Now I've got you, Sir Jiraiya!
No way, Sir Sasuke! You'll never catch me!
Taste my blade, Jiraiya!
WHACK
Don't speak too soon, Sasuke!
Forsooth!
WHAM!
Unhh!
Surrender or die!
Hm.
This calls for my special Ninja technique!
Den den den den den...

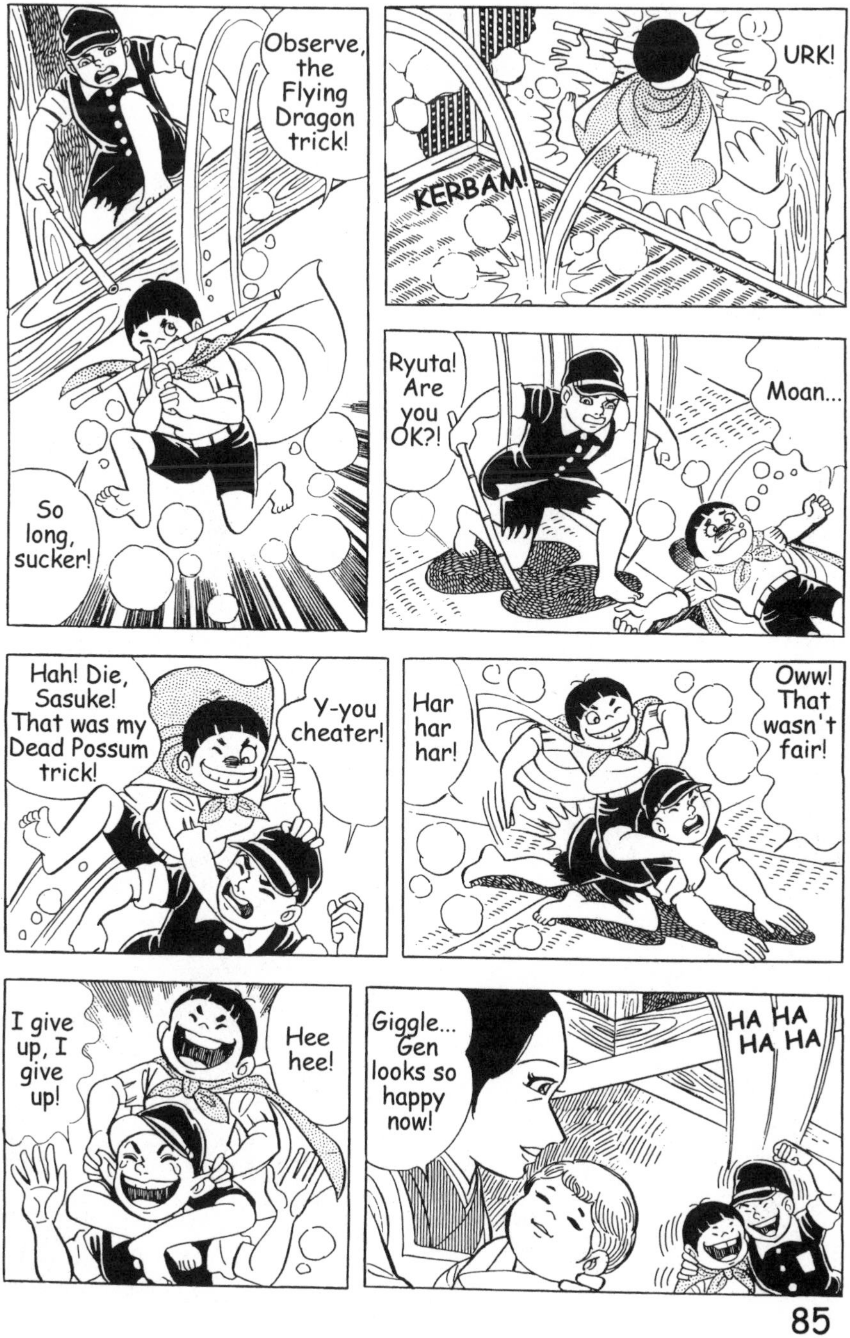
Observe, the Flying Dragon trick!
So long, sucker!
URK!
KERBAM!
Ryuta! Are you OK?!
Moan...
Hah! Die, Sasuke! That was my Dead Possum trick!
Y-you cheater!
Har har har!
Oww! That wasn't fair!
I give up, I give up!
Hee hee!
Giggle... Gen looks so happy now!
HA HA HA HA

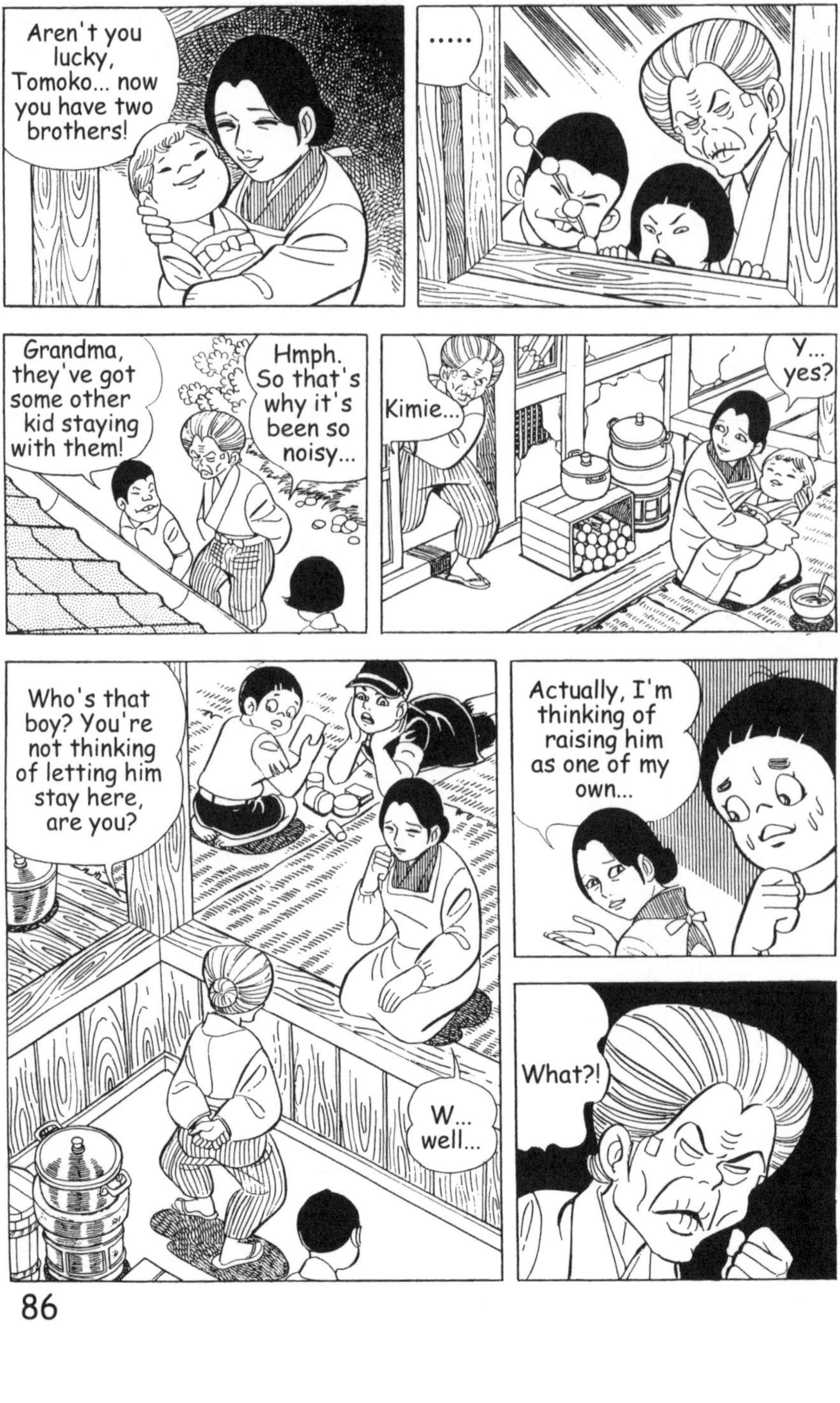
Aren't you lucky, Tomoko... now you have two brothers!
.....
Grandma, they've got some other kid staying with them!
Hmph. So that's why it's been so noisy...
Kimie...
Y... yes?
Who's that boy? You're not thinking of letting him stay here, are you?
W... well...
Actually, I'm thinking of raising him as one of my own...
What?!

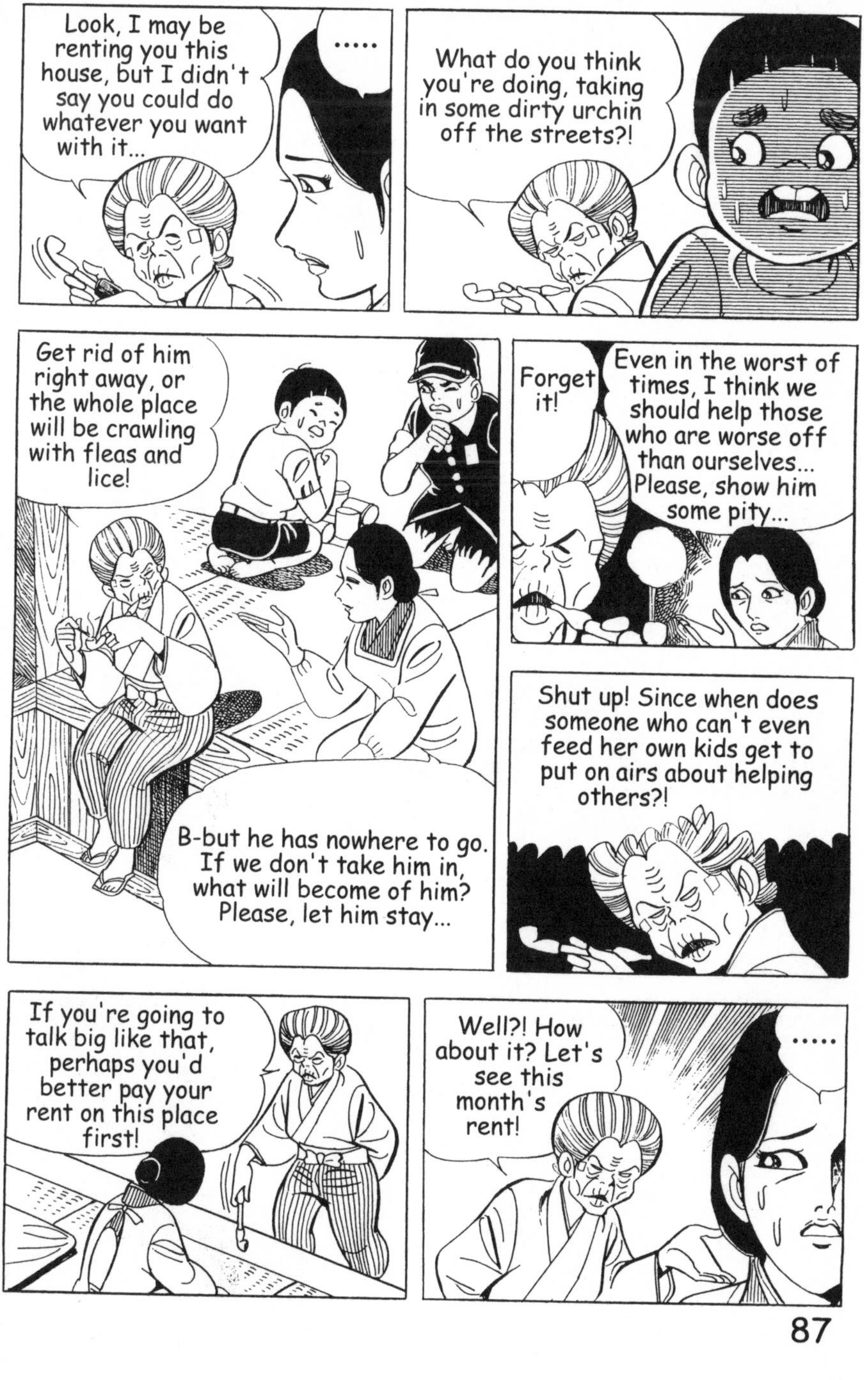
Look, I may be renting you this house, but I didn't say you could do whatever you want with it...
.....
What do you think you're doing, taking in some dirty urchin off the streets?!
Get rid of him right away, or the whole place will be crawling with fleas and lice!
B-but he has nowhere to go. If we don't take him in, what will become of him? Please, let him stay...
Forget it!
Even in the worst of times, I think we should help those who are worse off than ourselves... Please, show him some pity...
Shut up! Since when does someone who can't even feed her own kids get to put on airs about helping others?!
If you're going to talk big like that, perhaps you'd better pay your rent on this place first!
Well?! How about it? Let's see this month's rent!
.....

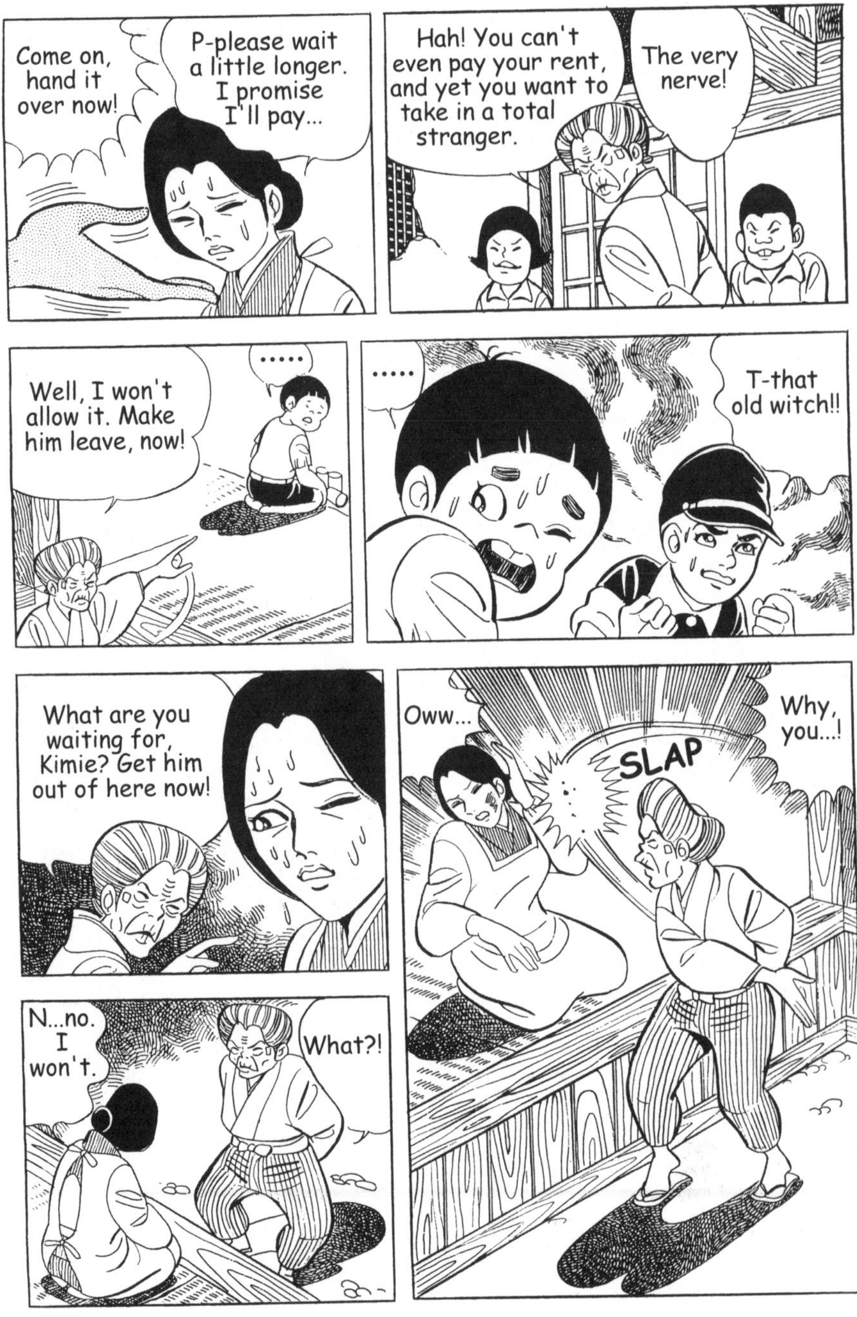
Come on, hand it over now!
P-please wait a little longer. I promise I'll pay...
Hah! You can't even pay your rent, and yet you want to take in a total stranger.
The very nerve!
Well, I won't allow it. Make him leave, now!
.....
.....
T-that old witch!!
What are you waiting for, Kimie? Get him out of here now!
N...no. I won't.
What?!
Oww...
SLAP
Why, you...!

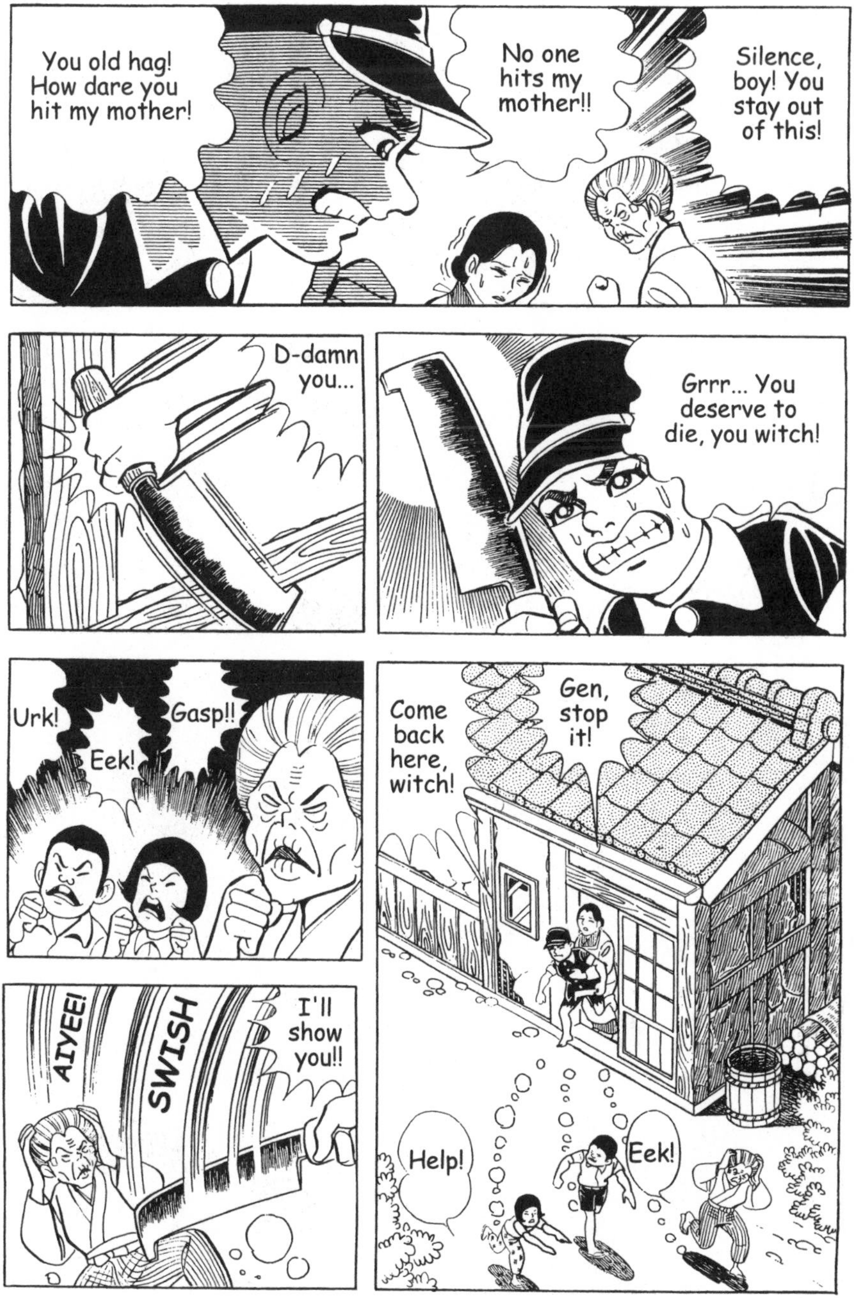
You old hag! How dare you hit my mother!
No one hits my mother!!
Silence, boy! You stay out of this!
D-damn you...
Grrr... You deserve to die, you witch!
Urk!
Gasp!!
Eek!
Come back here, witch!
Gen, stop it!
Help!
Eek!
AIYEE!
SWISH
I'll show you!!

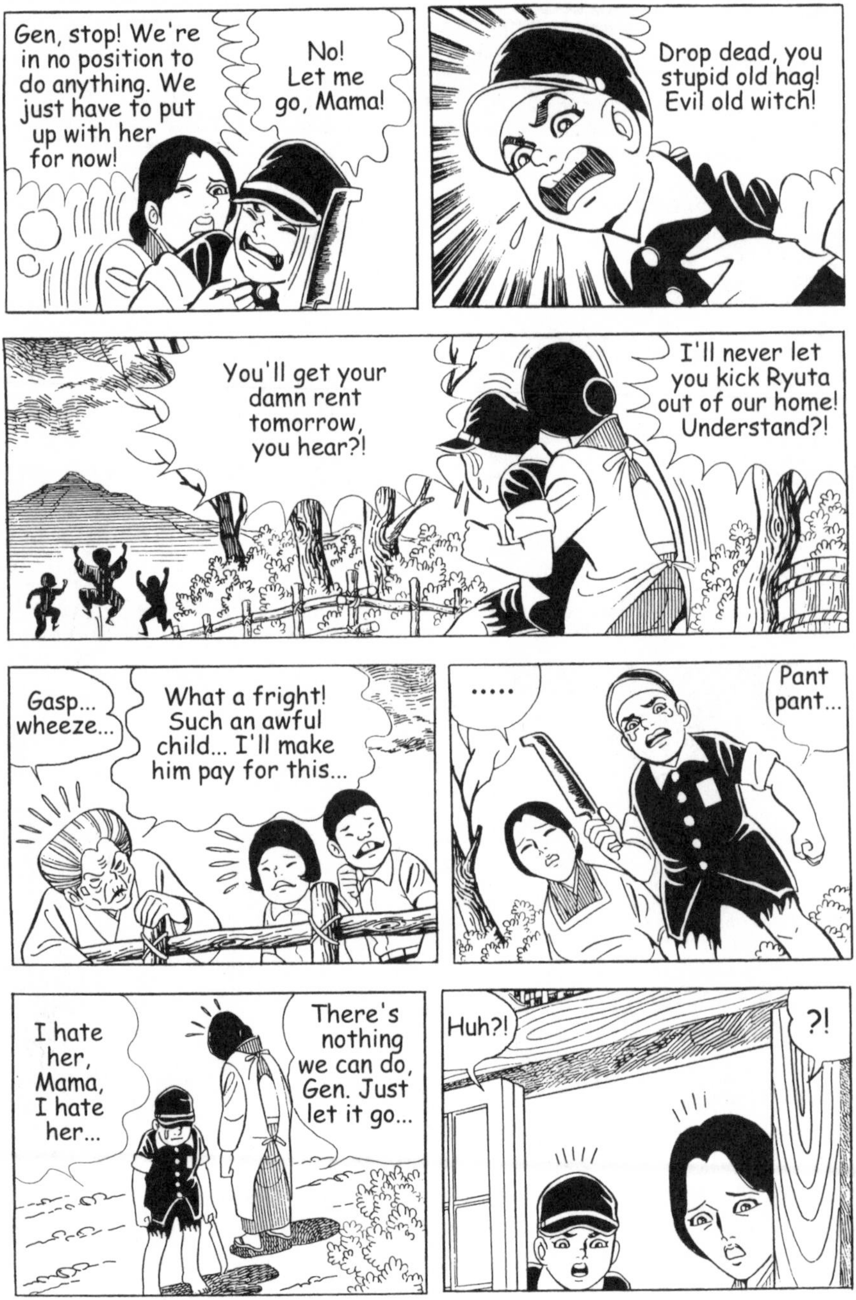
Gen, stop! We're in no position to do anything. We just have to put up with her for now!
No! Let me go, Mama!
Drop dead, you stupid old hag! Evil old witch!
You'll get your damn rent tomorrow, you hear?!
I'll never let you kick Ryuta out of our home! Understand?!
Gasp... wheeze...
What a fright! Such an awful child... I'll make him pay for this...
.....
Pant pant...
I hate her, Mama, I hate her...
There's nothing we can do, Gen. Just let it go...
Huh?!
?!

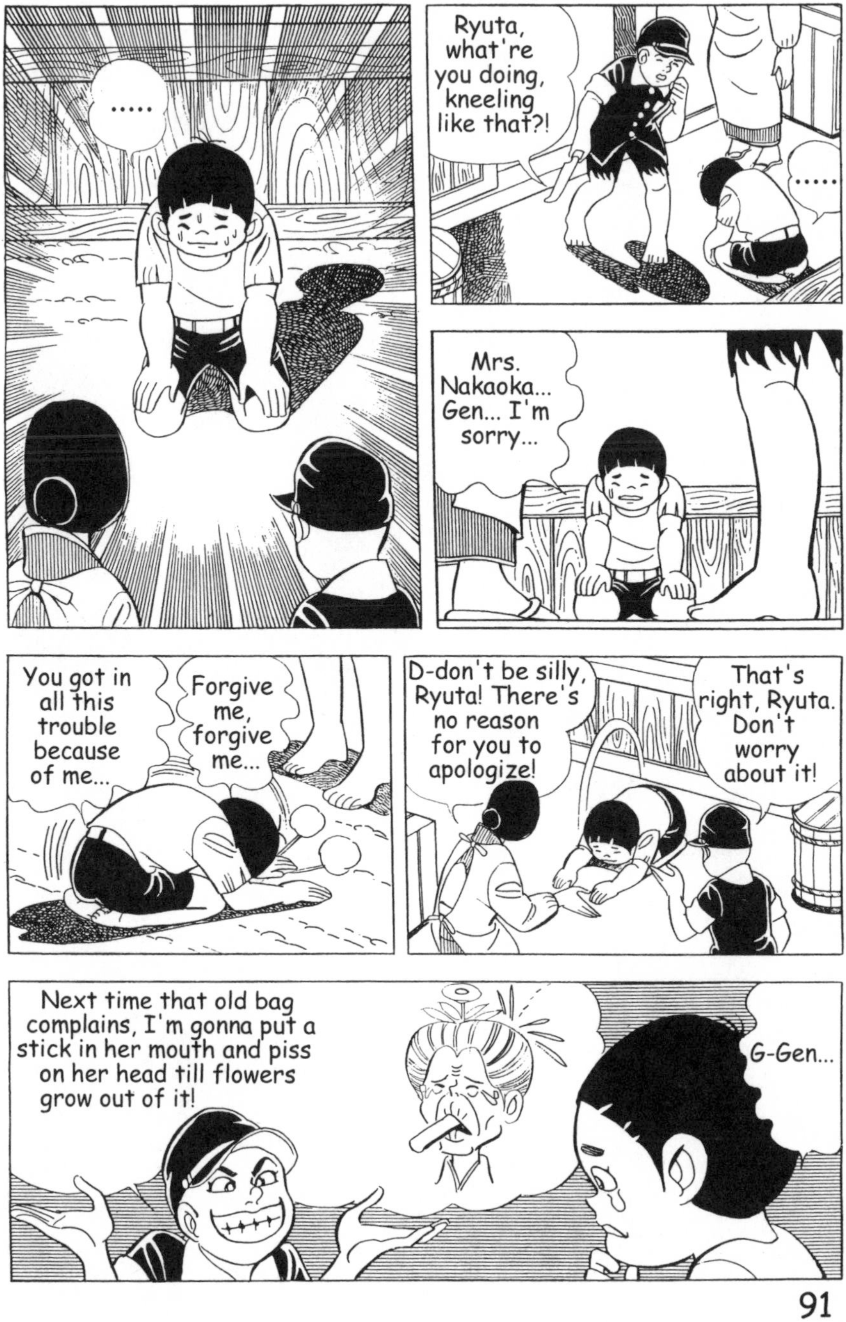
.....
Ryuta, what're you doing, kneeling like that?!
.....
Mrs. Nakaoka... Gen... I'm sorry...
You got in all this trouble because of me...
Forgive me, forgive me...
D-don't be silly, Ryuta! There's no reason for you to apologize!
That's right, Ryuta. Don't worry about it!
Next time that old bag complains, I'm gonna put a stick in her mouth and piss on her head till flowers grow out of it!
G-Gen...

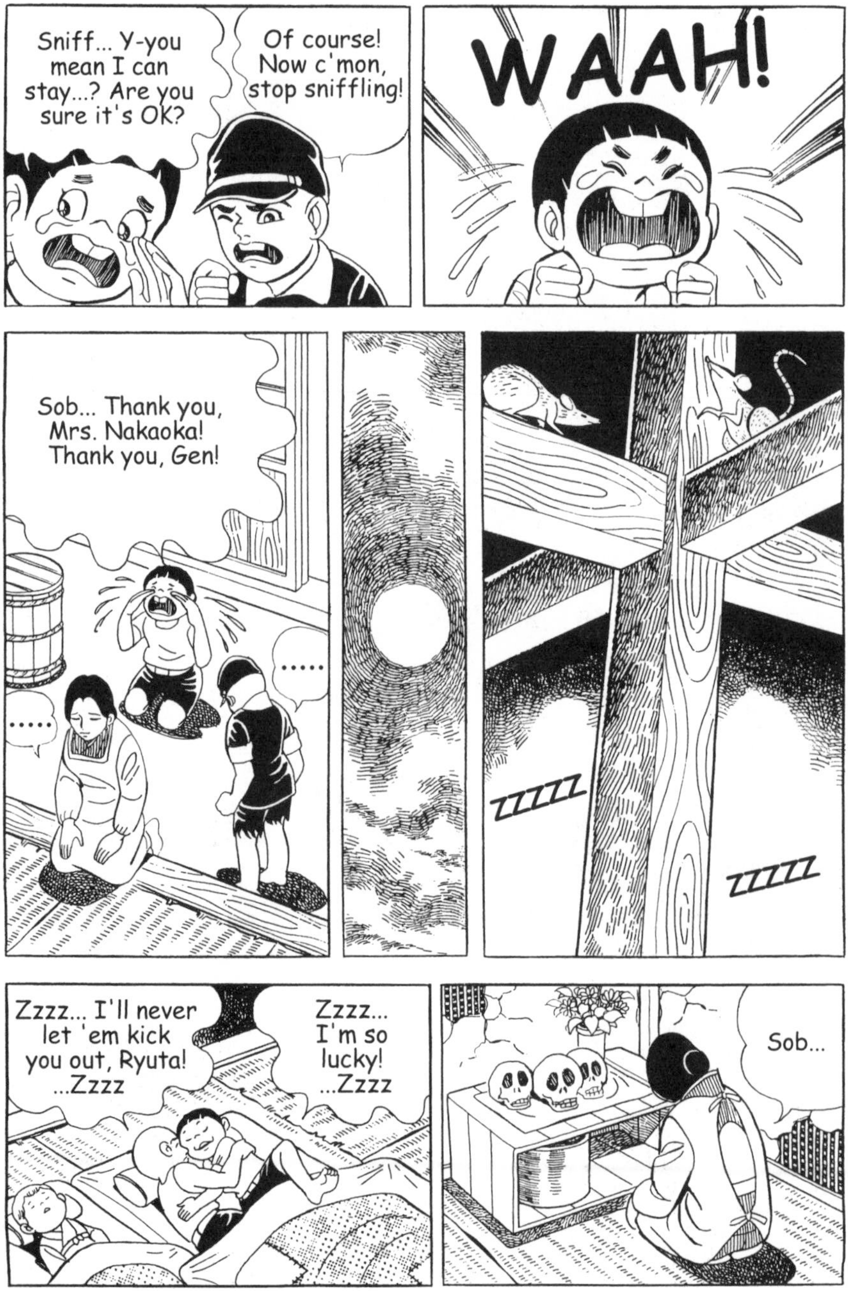

Sniff... Y-you mean I can stay...? Are you sure it's OK?
Of course! Now c'mon, stop sniffling!
WAAH!
Sob... Thank you, Mrs. Nakaoka! Thank you, Gen!
.....
.....
ZZZZZ
ZZZZZ
Zzzz... I'll never let 'em kick you out, Ryuta! ...Zzzz
Zzzz... I'm so lucky! ...Zzzz
Sob...

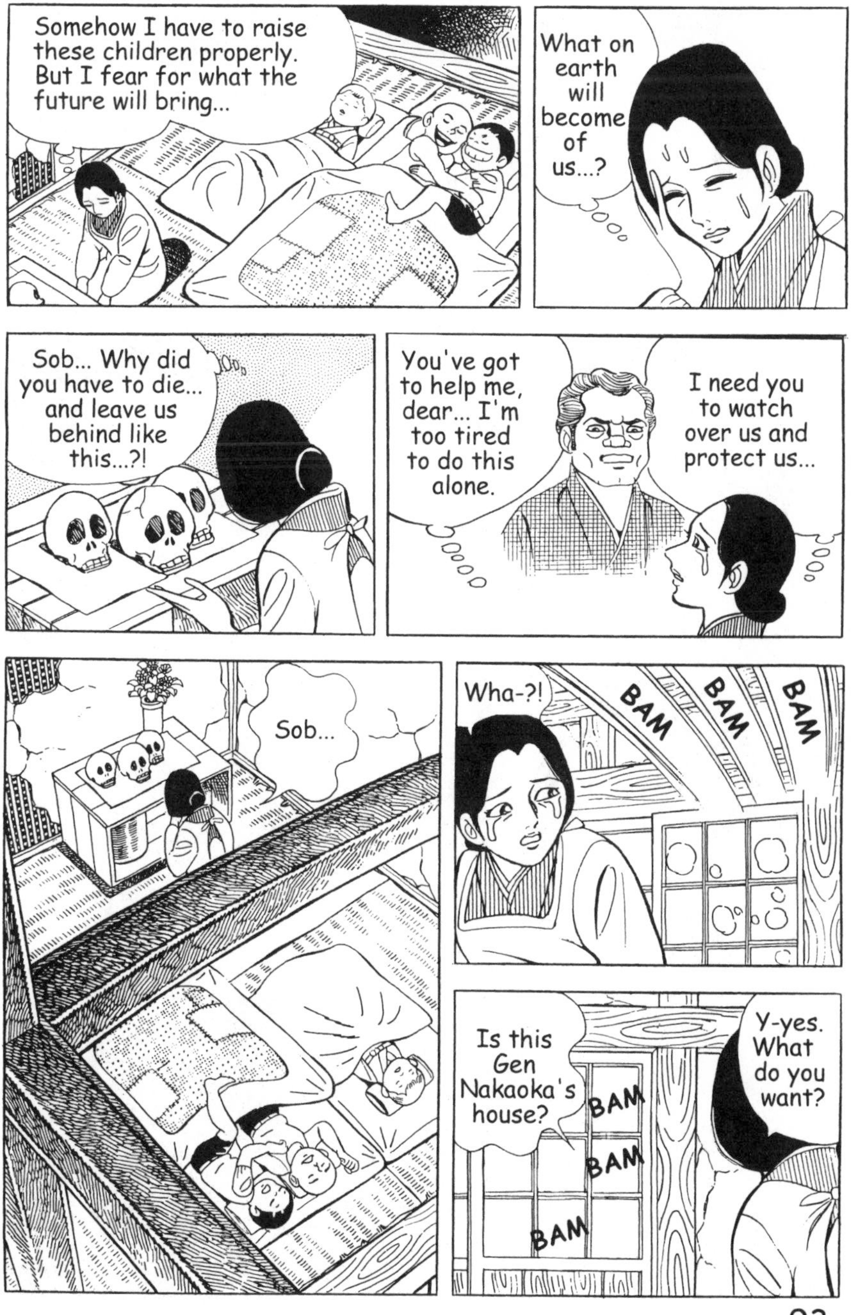
Somehow I have to raise these children properly. But I fear for what the future will bring...
What on earth will become of us...?
Sob... Why did you have to die... and leave us behind like this...?!
You've got to help me, dear... I'm too tired to do this alone.
I need you to watch over us and protect us...
Sob...
Wha-?!
BAM
BAM
BAM
Is this Gen Nakaoka's house?
BAM
BAM
BAM
Y-yes. What do you want?

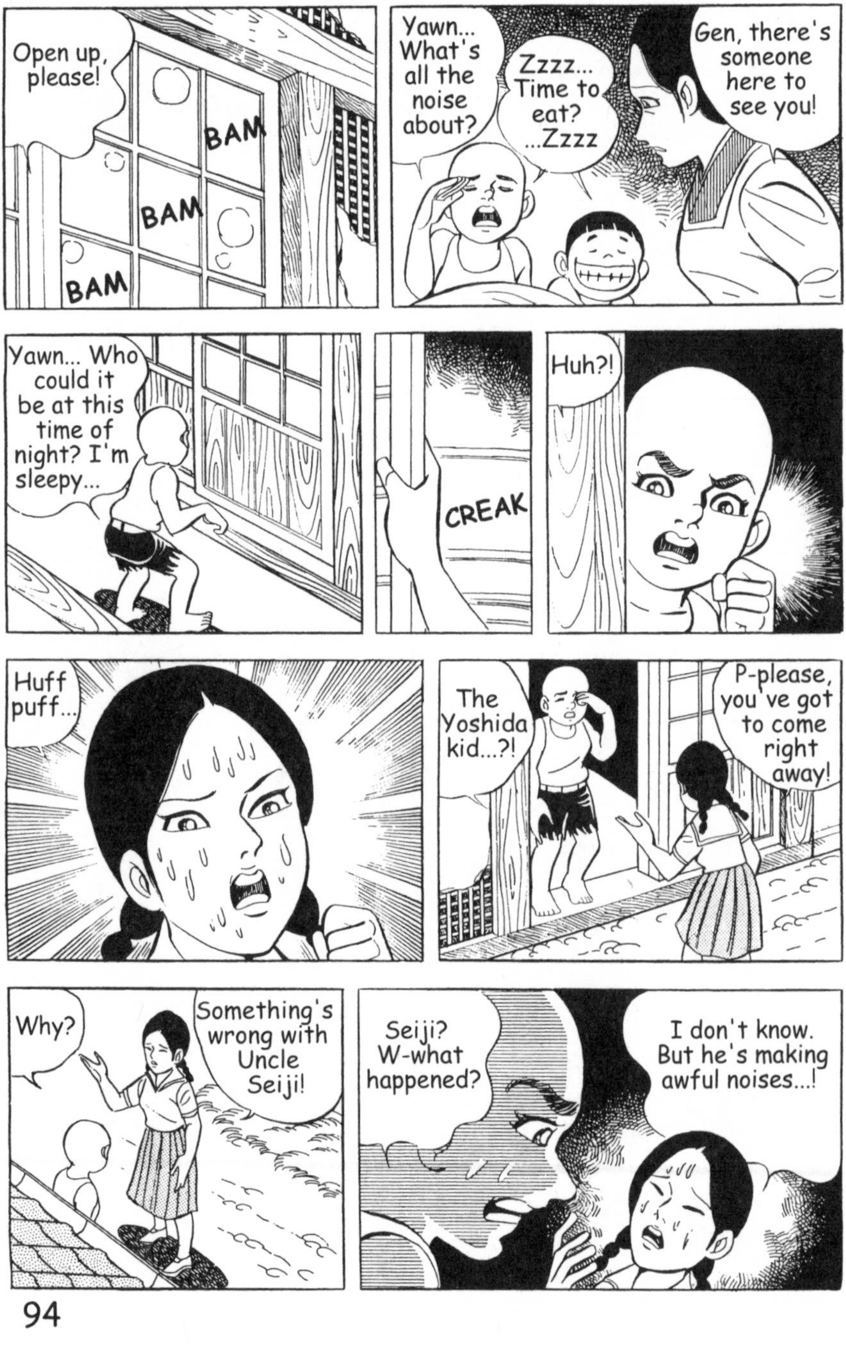
Open up, please!
BAM
BAM
BAM
Yawn... What's all the noise about?
Zzzz... Time to eat? ...Zzzz
Gen, there's someone here to see you!
Yawn... Who could it be at this time of night? I'm sleepy...
CREAK
Huh?!
Huff puff...
The Yoshida kid...?!
P-please, you've got to come right away!
Why?
Something's wrong with Uncle Seiji!
Seiji? W-what happened?
I don't know. But he's making awful noises...!

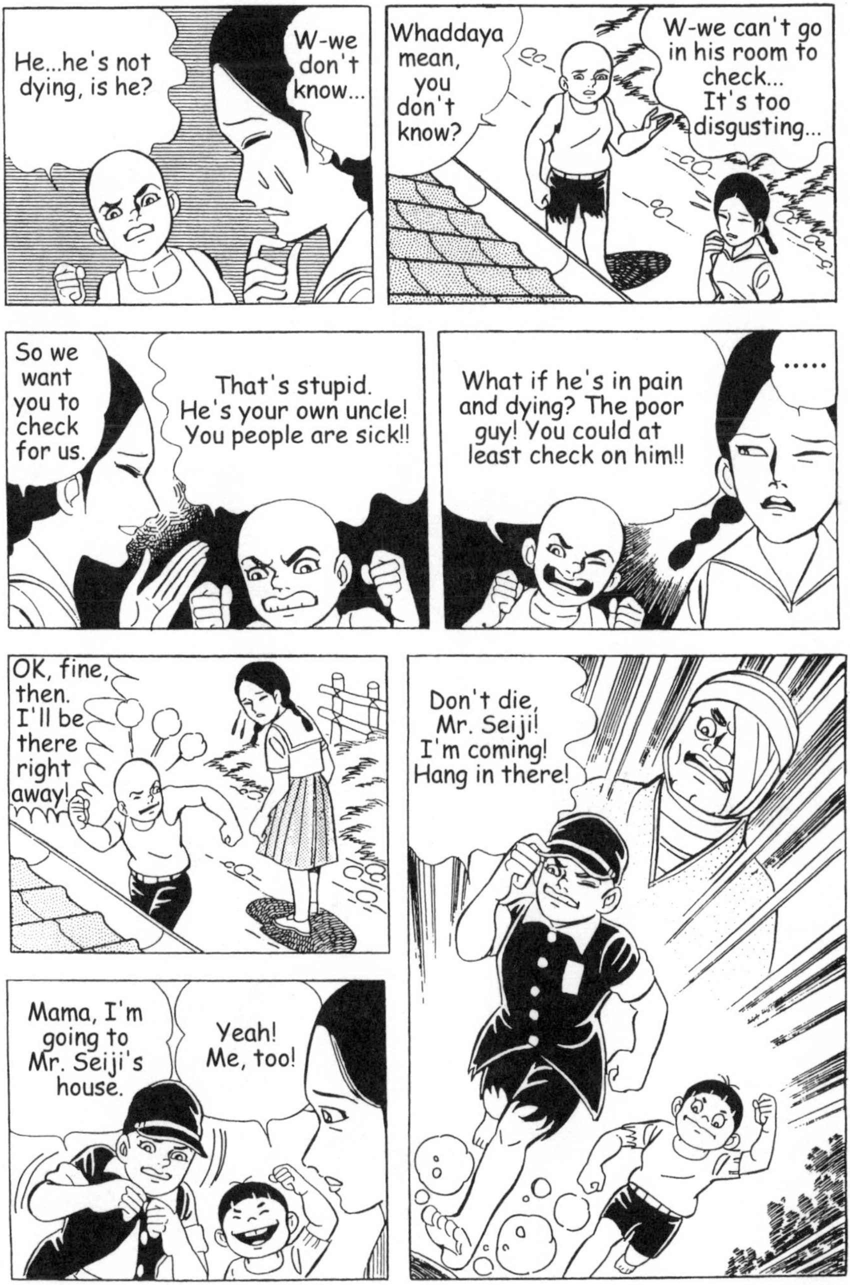
He...he's not dying, is he?
W-we don't know...
Whaddaya mean, you don't know?
W-we can't go in his room to check... It's too disgusting...
So we want you to check for us.
That's stupid. He's your own uncle! You people are sick!!
What if he's in pain and dying? The poor guy! You could at least check on him!!
.....
OK, fine, then. I'll be there right away!
Mama, I'm going to Mr. Seiji's house.
Yeah! Me, too!
Don't die, Mr. Seiji! I'm coming! Hang in there!

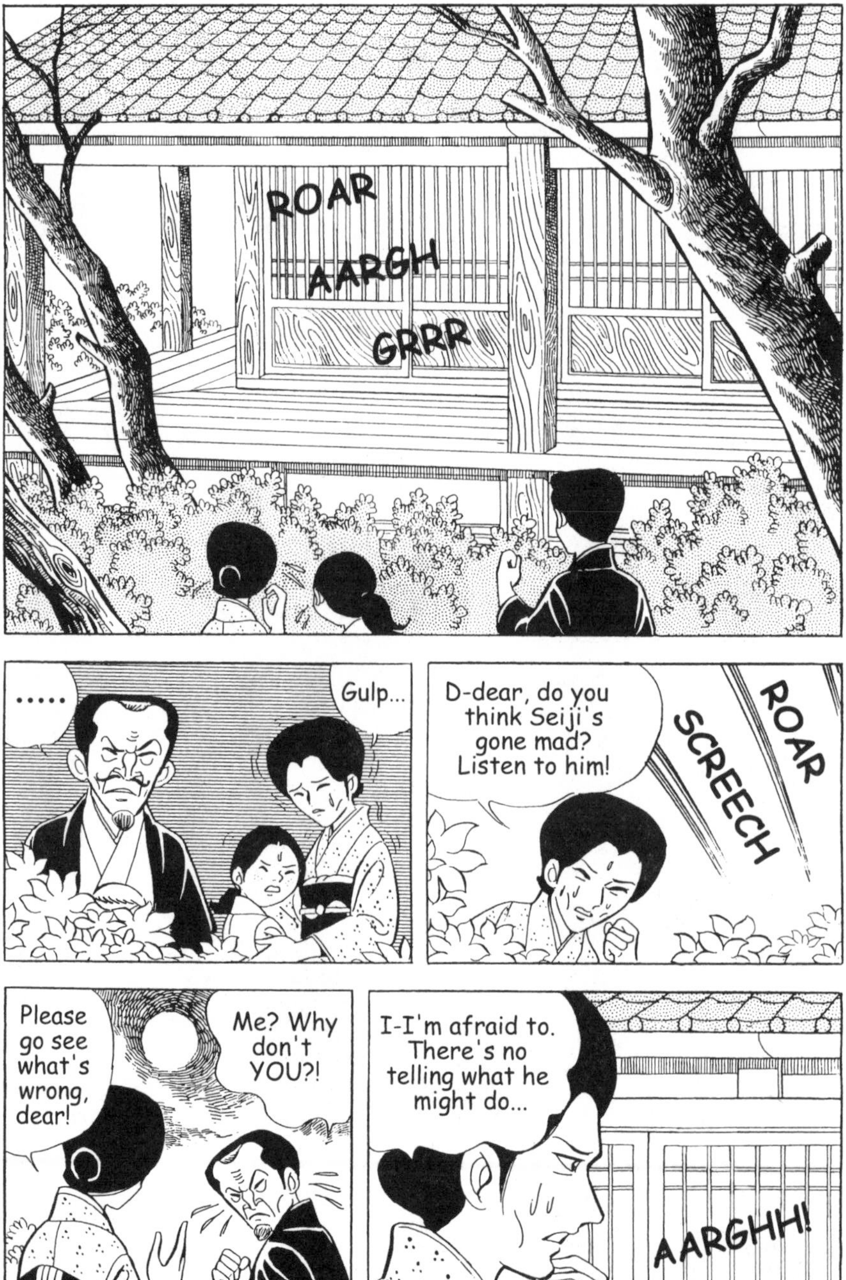
ROAR
AARGH
GRRR
.....
Gulp...
D-dear, do you think Seiji's gone mad? Listen to him!
ROAR
SCREECH
Please go see what's wrong, dear!
Me? Why don't YOU?!
I-I'm afraid to. There's no telling what he might do...
AARGHH!

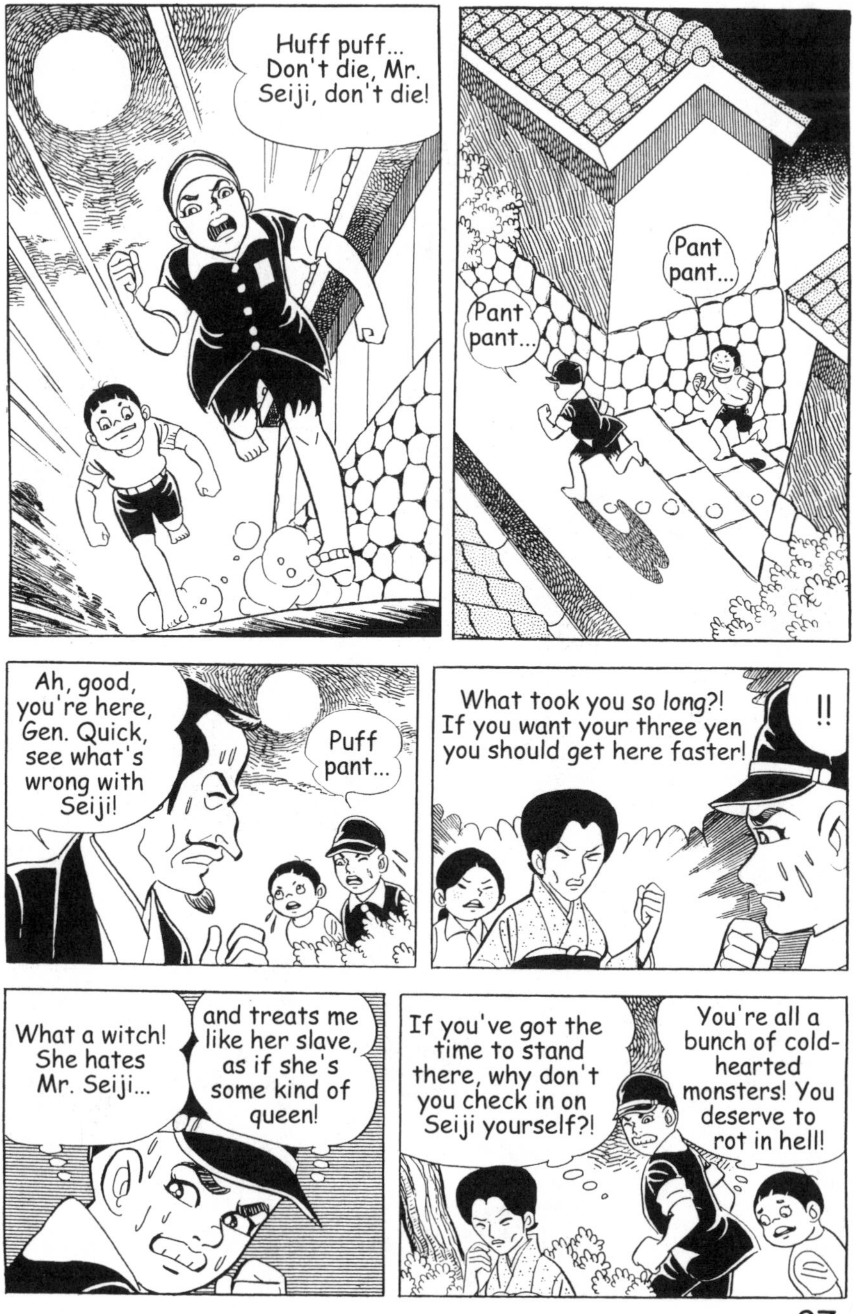
Huff puff... Don't die, Mr. Seiji, don't die!
Pant pant...
Pant pant...
Ah, good, you're here, Gen. Quick, see what's wrong with Seiji!
Puff pant...
What took you so long?! If you want your three yen you should get here faster!
!!
What a witch! She hates Mr. Seiji...
and treats me like her slave, as if she's some kind of queen!
If you've got the time to stand there, why don't you check in on Seiji yourself?!
You're all a bunch of cold-hearted monsters! You deserve to rot in hell!

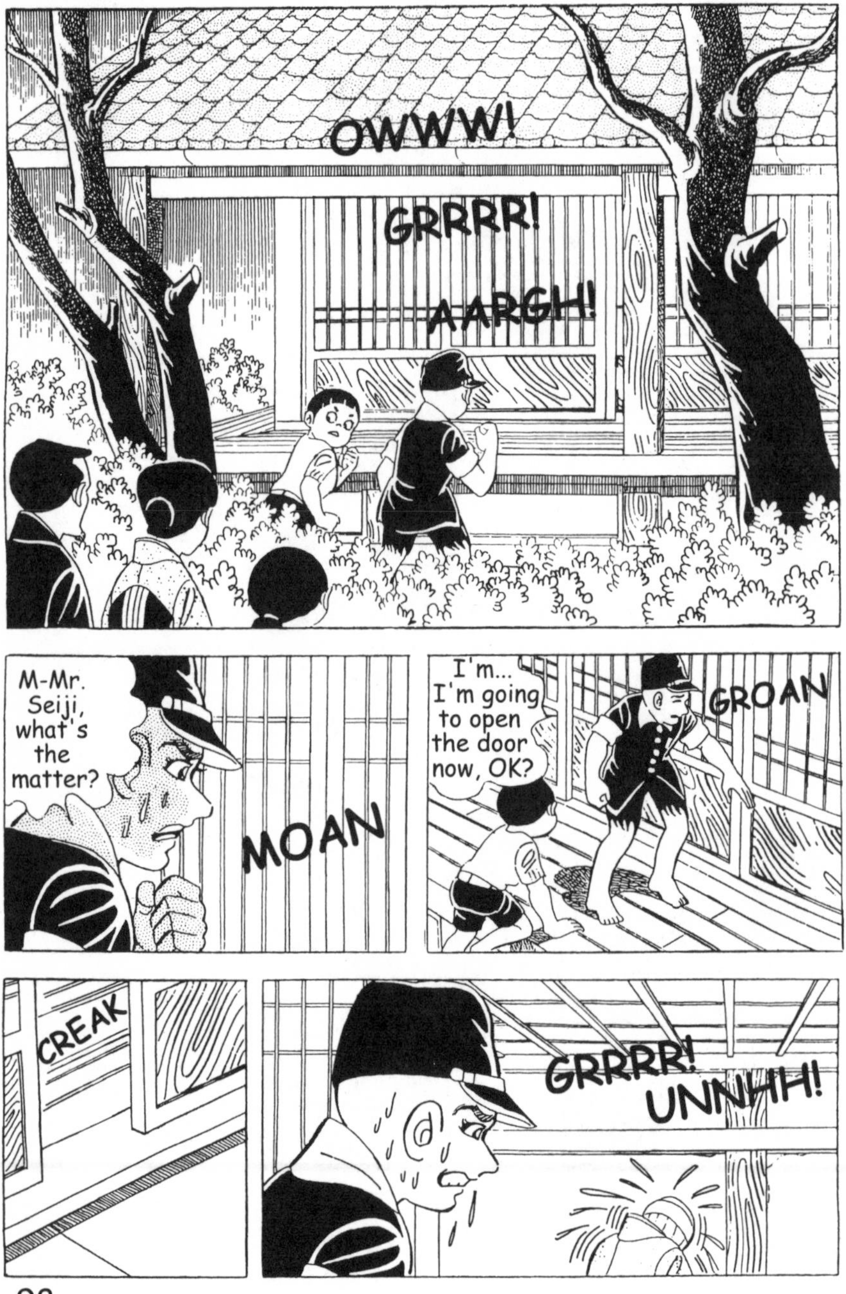
OWWW!
GRRRR!
AARGH!
M-Mr. Seiji, what's the matter?
MOAN
I'm... I'm going to open the door now, OK?
GROAN
CREAK
GRRRR!
UNNHH!

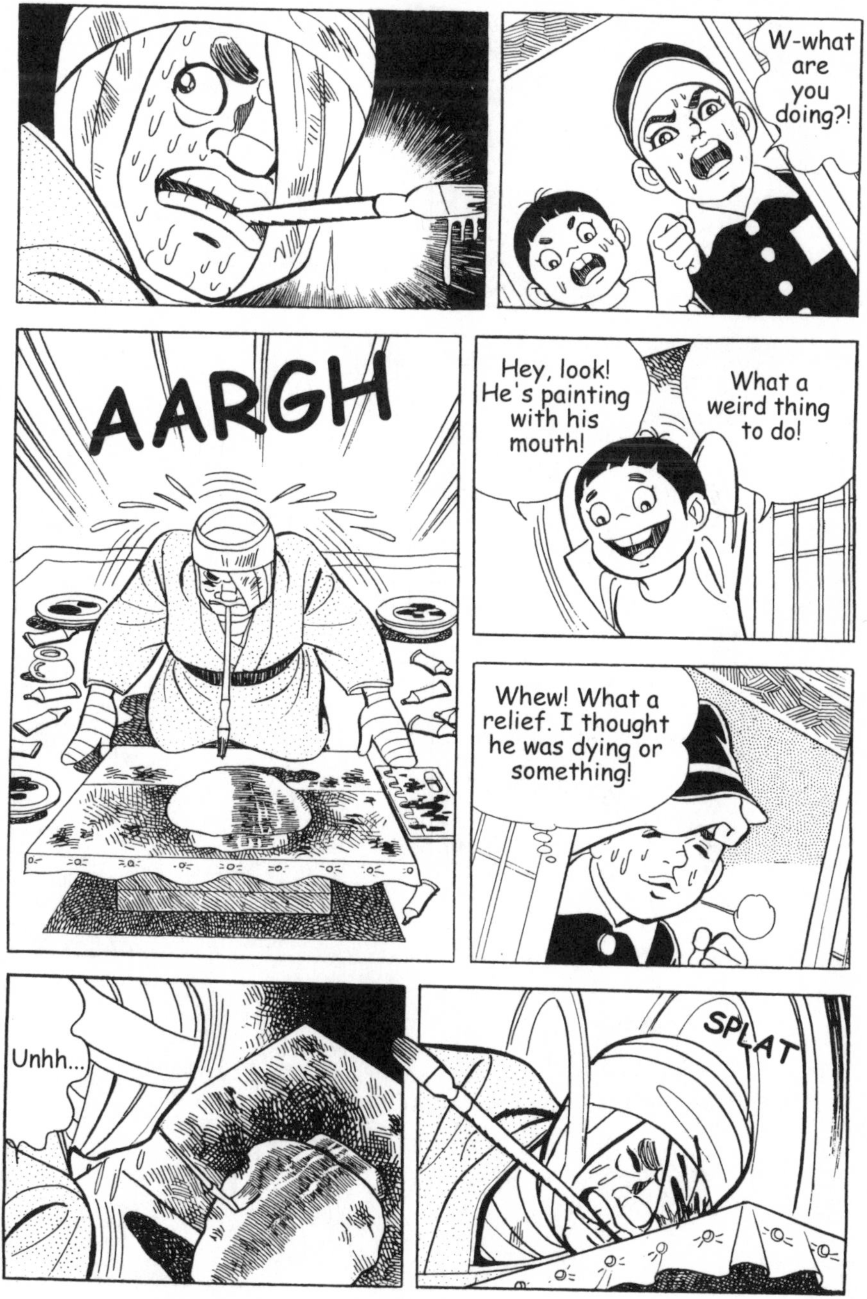
W-what are you doing?!
AARGH
Hey, look! He's painting with his mouth!
What a weird thing to do!
Whew! What a relief. I thought he was dying or something!
Unhh...
SPLAT

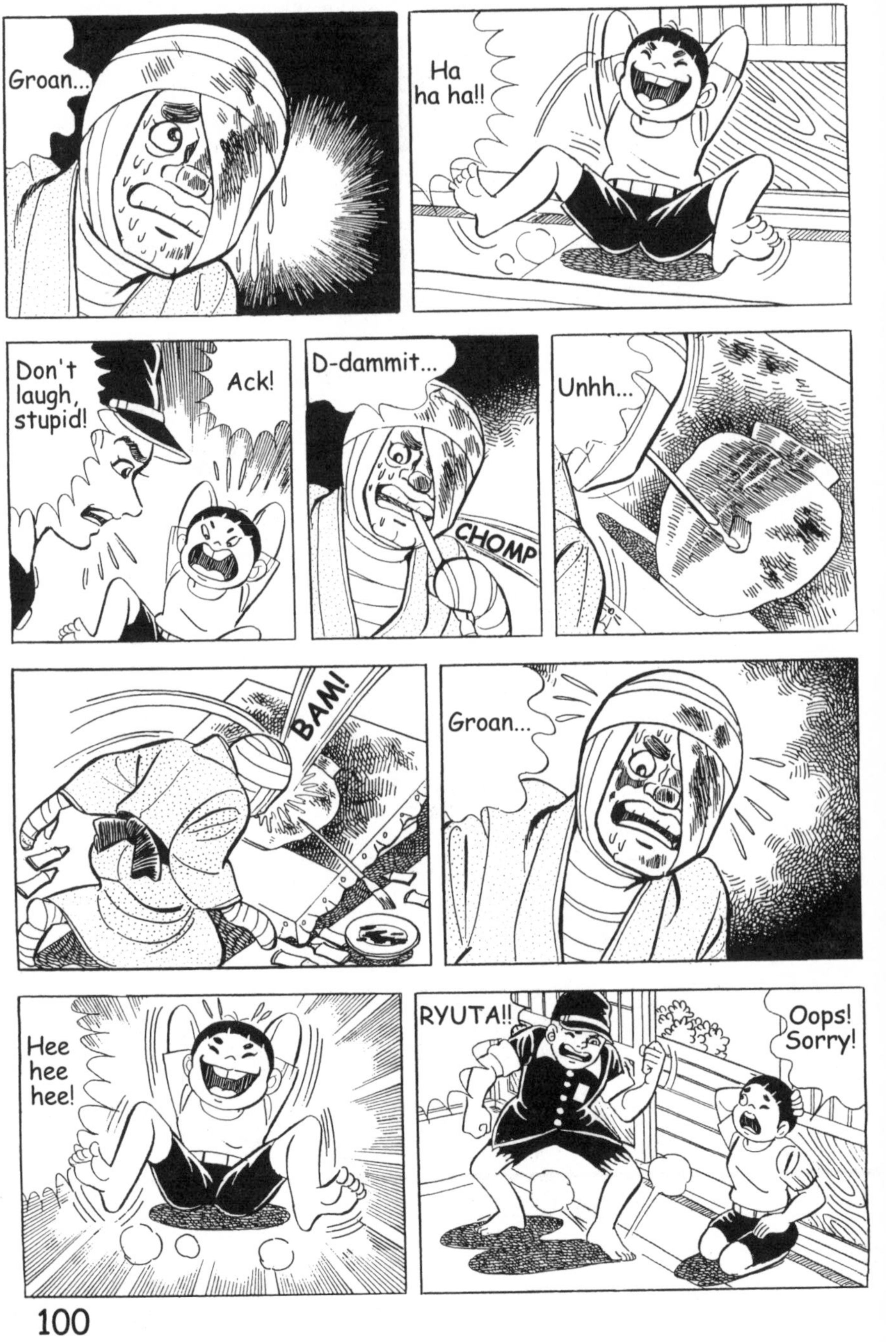
Groan...
Ha ha ha!!
Don't laugh, stupid!
Ack!
D-dammit...
CHOMP
Unhh...
BAM!
Groan...
Hee hee hee!
RYUTA!!
Oops! Sorry!

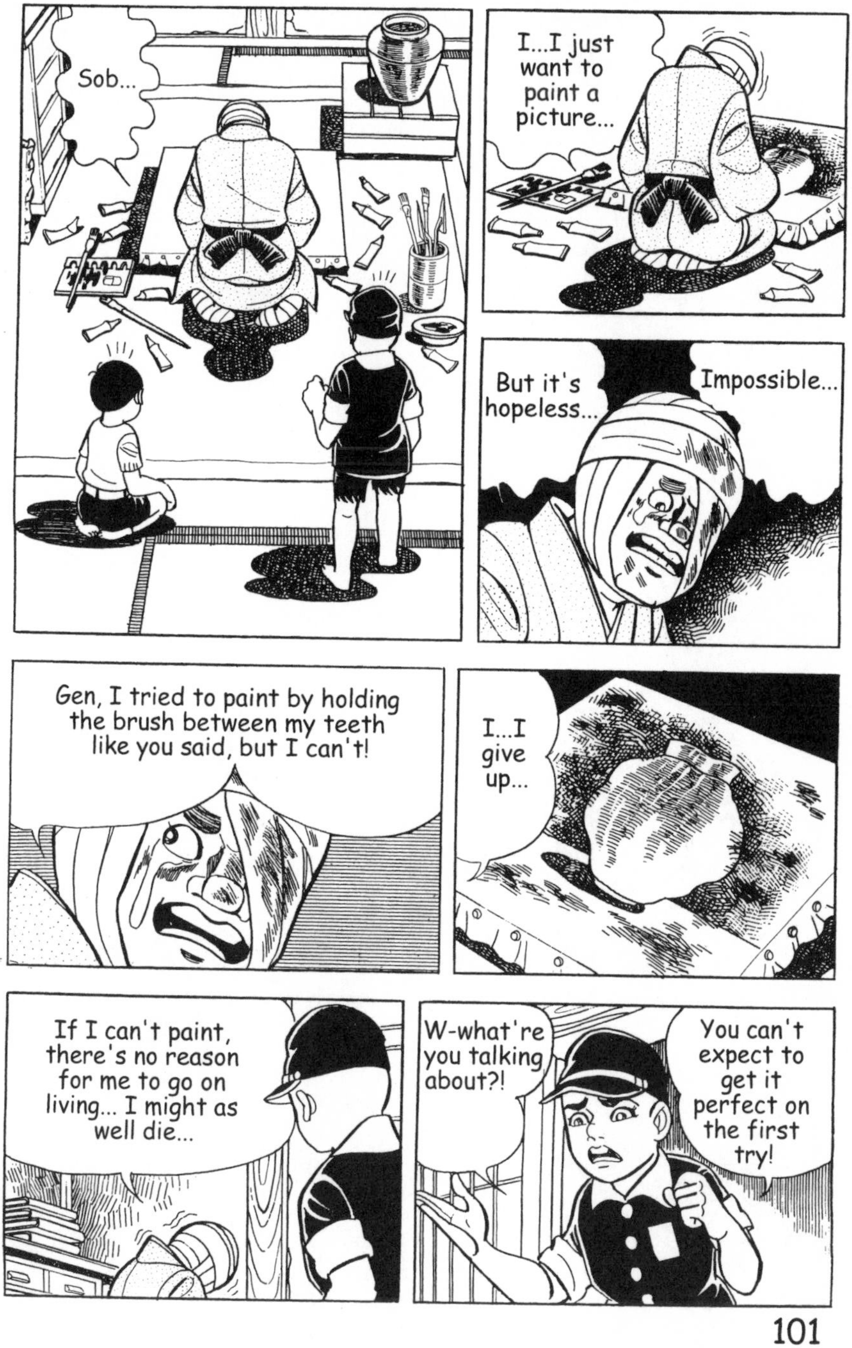
Sob...
I...I just want to paint a picture...
But it's hopeless...
Impossible...
Gen, I tried to paint by holding the brush between my teeth like you said, but I can't!
I...I give up...
If I can't paint, there's no reason for me to go on living... I might as well die...
W-what're you talking about?!
You can't expect to get it perfect on the first try!

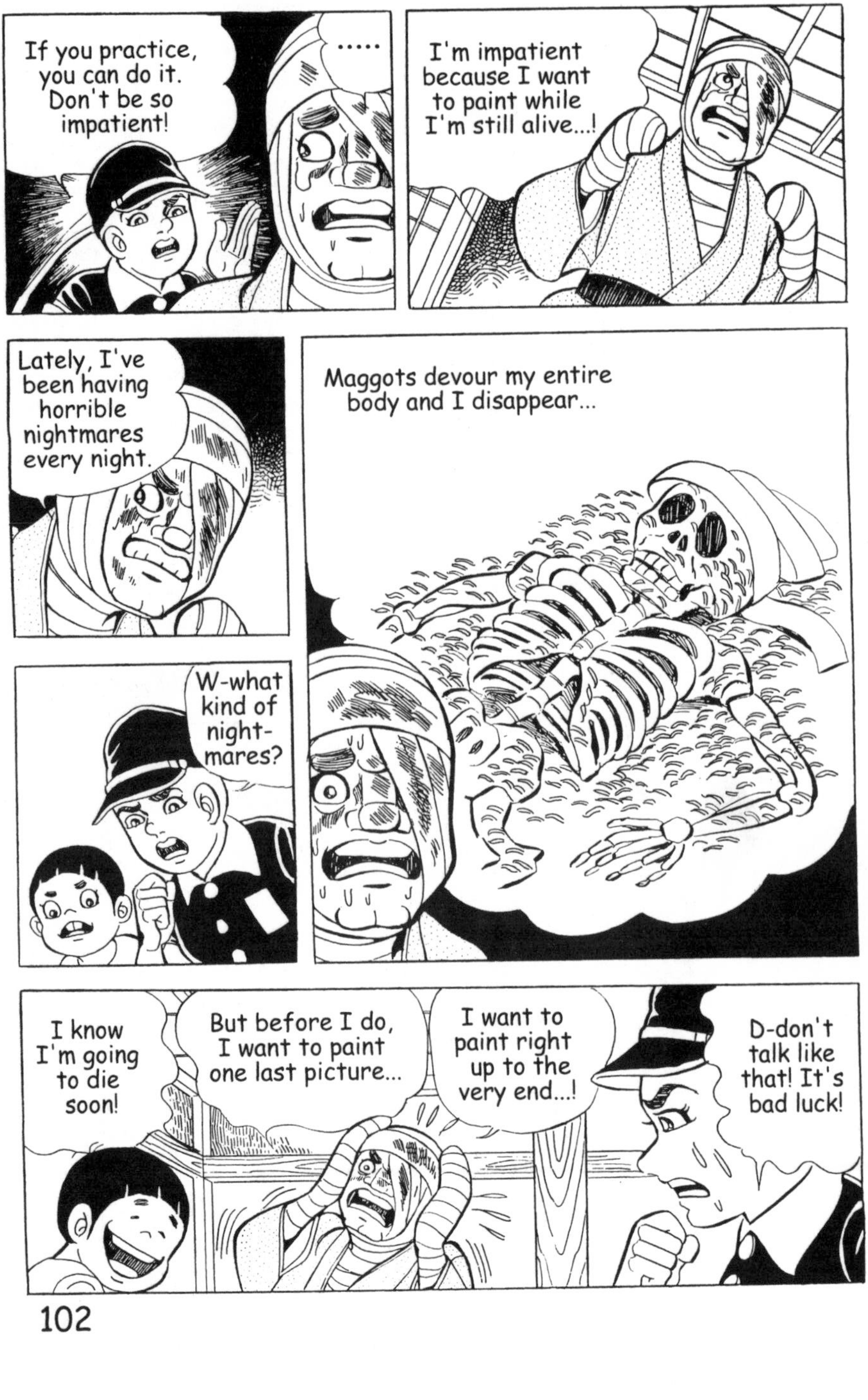
If you practice, you can do it. Don't be so impatient!
.....
I'm impatient because I want to paint while I'm still alive...!
Lately, I've been having horrible nightmares every night.
W-what kind of night-mares?
Maggots devour my entire body and I disappear...
I know I'm going to die soon!
But before I do, I want to paint one last picture...
I want to paint right up to the very end...!
D-don't talk like that! It's bad luck!

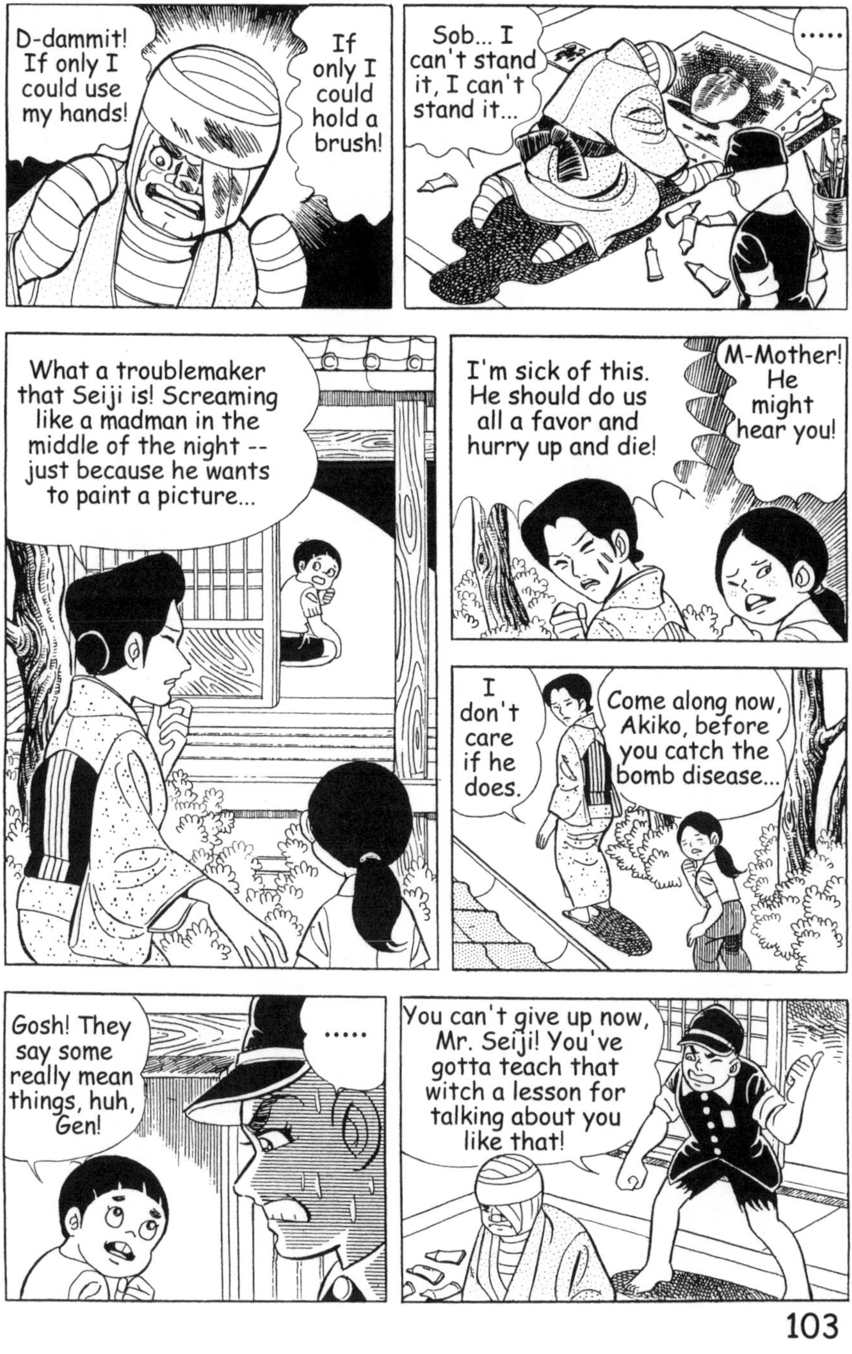
D-dammit! If only I could use my hands!
If only I could hold a brush!
Sob... I can't stand it, I can't stand it...
.....
What a troublemaker that Seiji is! Screaming like a madman in the middle of the night -- just because he wants to paint a picture...
I'm sick of this. He should do us all a favor and hurry up and die!
M-Mother! He might hear you!
I don't care if he does.
Come along now, Akiko, before you catch the bomb disease...
Gosh! They say some really mean things, huh, Gen!
.....
You can't give up now, Mr. Seiji! You've gotta teach that witch a lesson for talking about you like that!

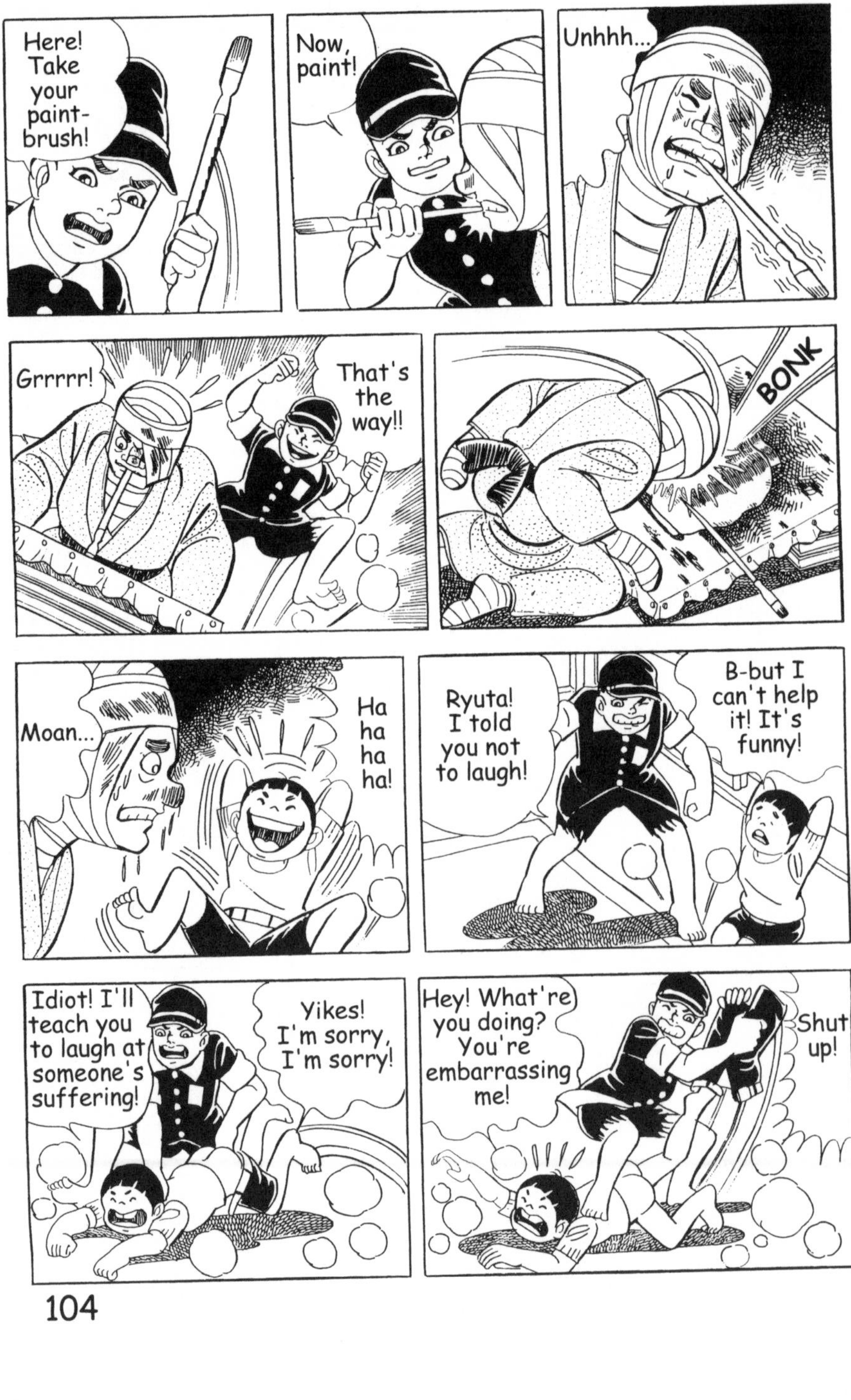
Here! Take your paint-brush!
Now, paint!
Unhhh...
Grrrrr!
That's the way!!
BONK
Moan...
Ha ha ha ha!
Ryuta! I told you not to laugh!
B-but I can't help it! It's funny!
Idiot! I'll teach you to laugh at someone's suffering!
Yikes! I'm sorry, I'm sorry!
Hey! What're you doing? You're embarrassing me!
Shut up!

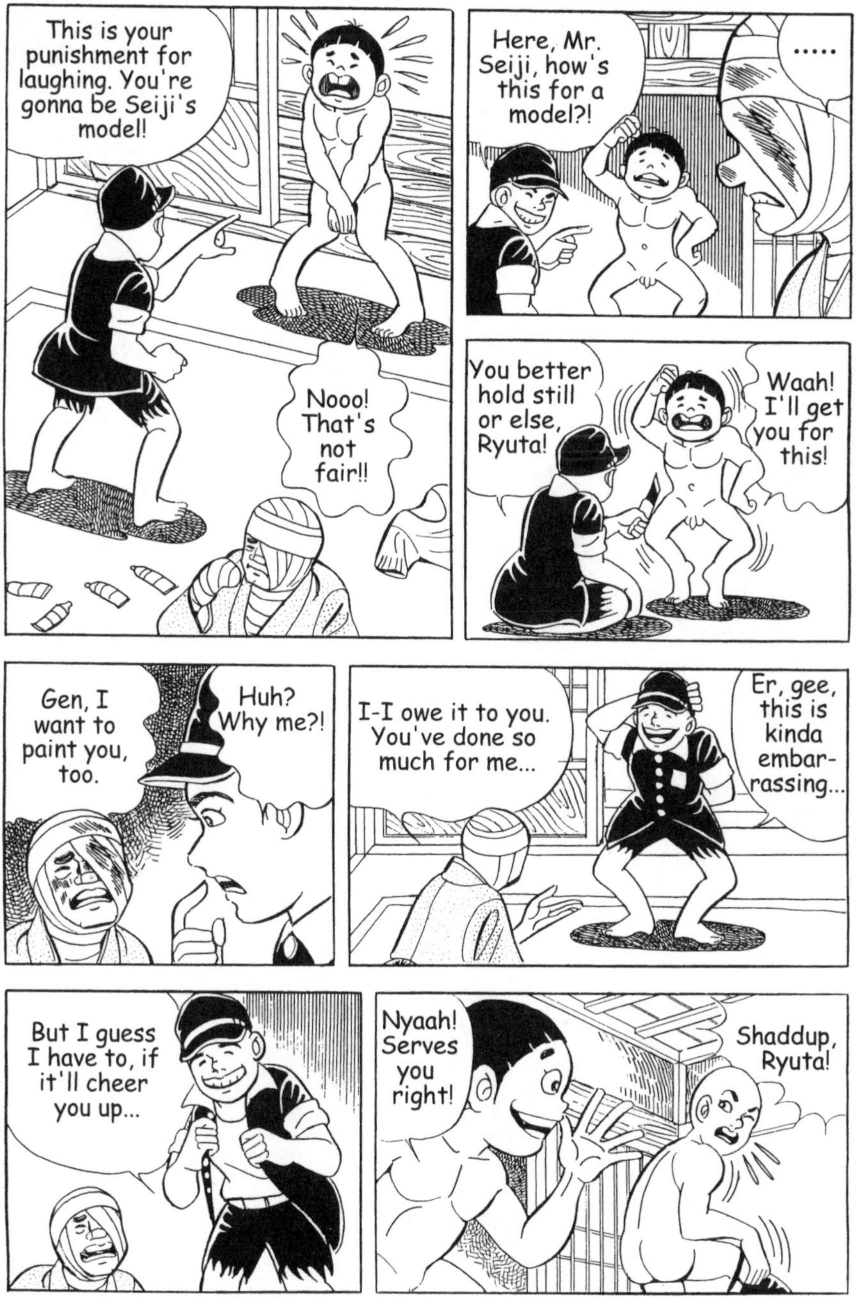
This is your punishment for laughing. You're gonna be Seiji's model!
Nooo! That's not fair!!
Here, Mr. Seiji, how's this for a model?!
.....
You better hold still or else, Ryuta!
Waah! I'll get you for this!
Gen, I want to paint you, too.
Huh? Why me?!
I-I owe it to you. You've done so much for me...
Er, gee, this is kinda embar-rassing...
But I guess I have to, if it'll cheer you up...
Nyaah! Serves you right!
Shaddup, Ryuta!

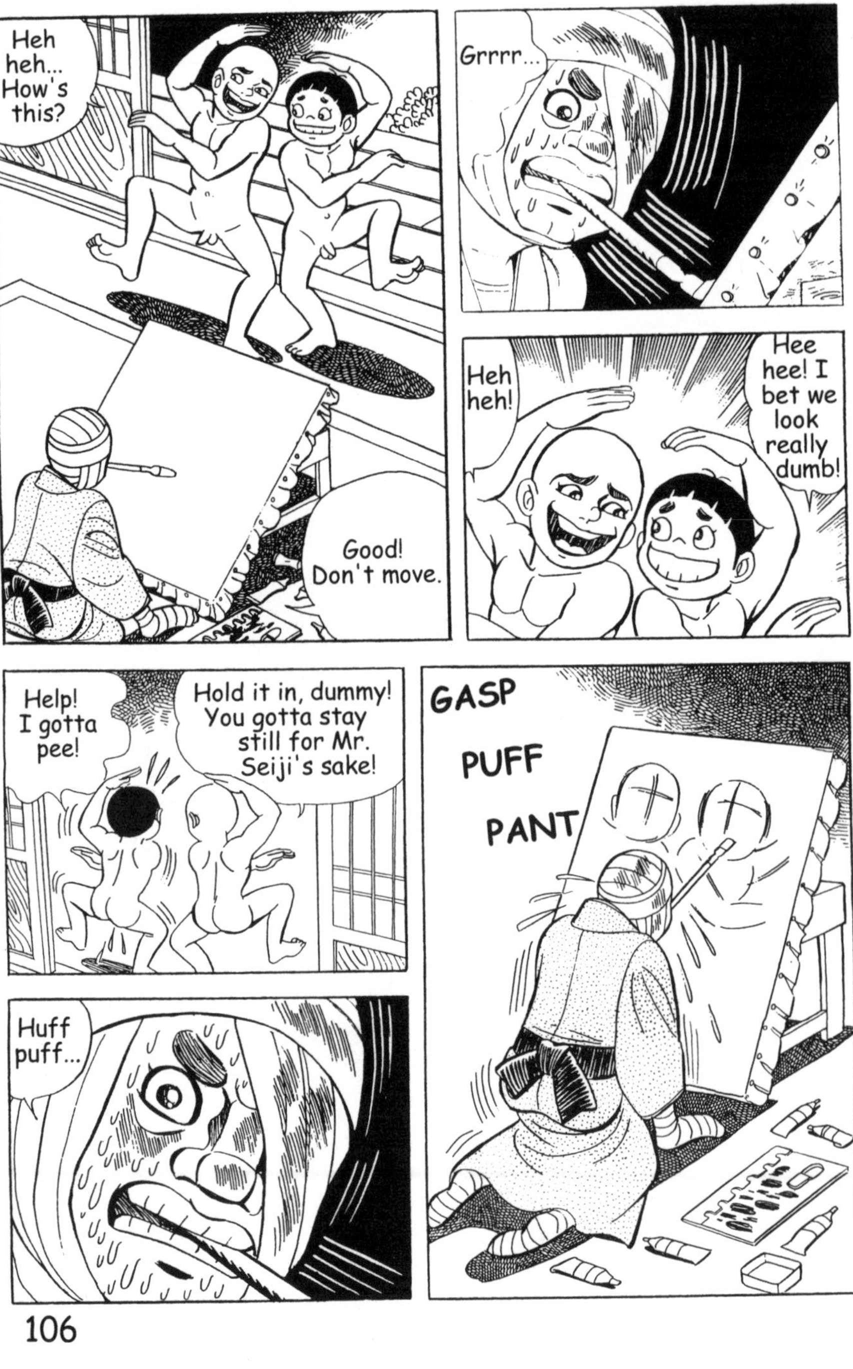

Heh heh... How's this?
Good! Don't move.
Grrrr...
Heh heh!
Hee hee! I bet we look really dumb!
Help! I gotta pee!
Hold it in, dummy! You gotta stay still for Mr. Seiji's sake!
Huff puff...
GASP
PUFF
PANT

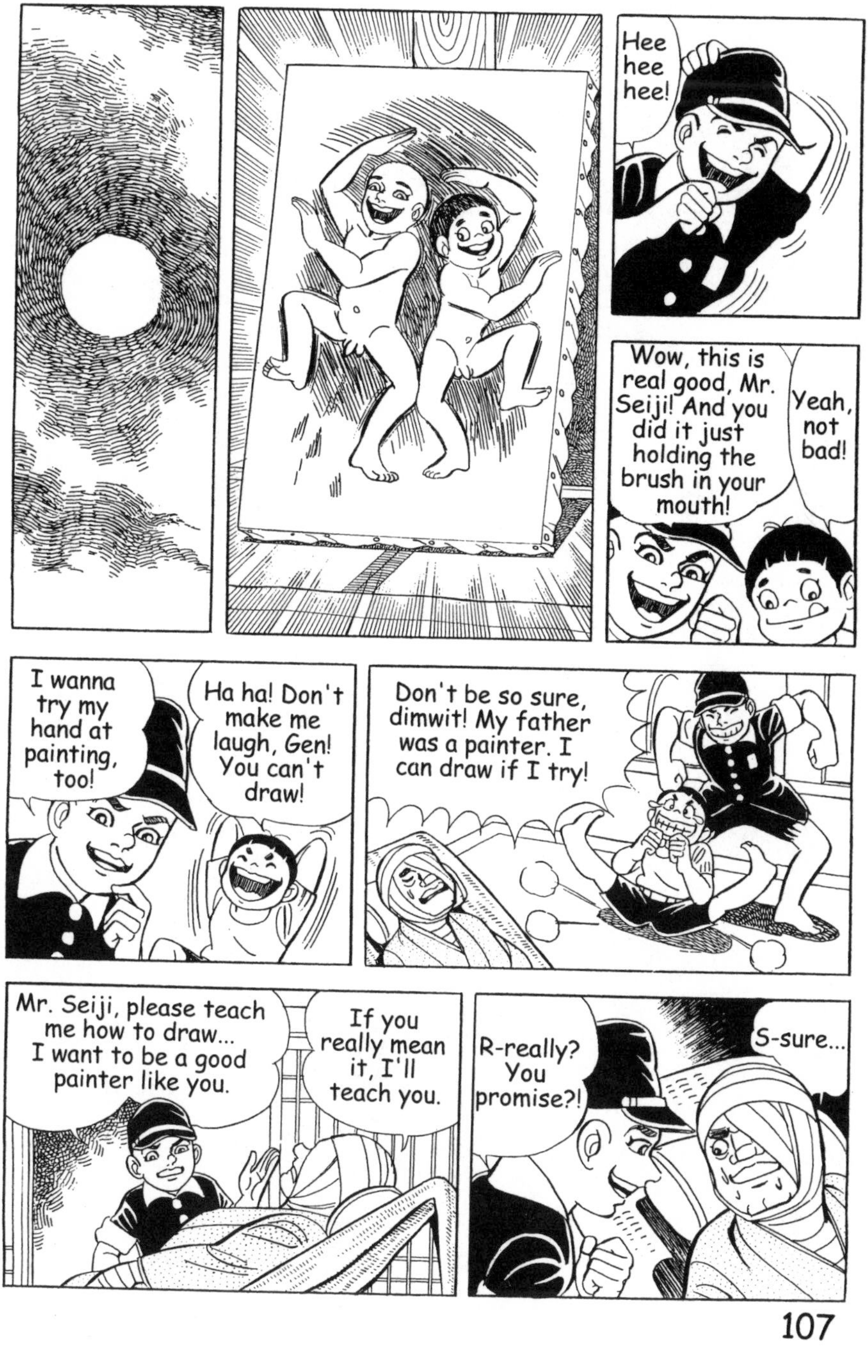
Hee hee hee!
Wow, this is real good, Mr. Seiji! And you did it just holding the brush in your mouth!
Yeah, not bad!
I wanna try my hand at painting, too!
Ha ha! Don't make me laugh, Gen! You can't draw!
Don't be so sure, dimwit! My father was a painter. I can draw if I try!
Mr. Seiji, please teach me how to draw... I want to be a good painter like you.
If you really mean it, I'll teach you.
R-really? You promise?!
S-sure...

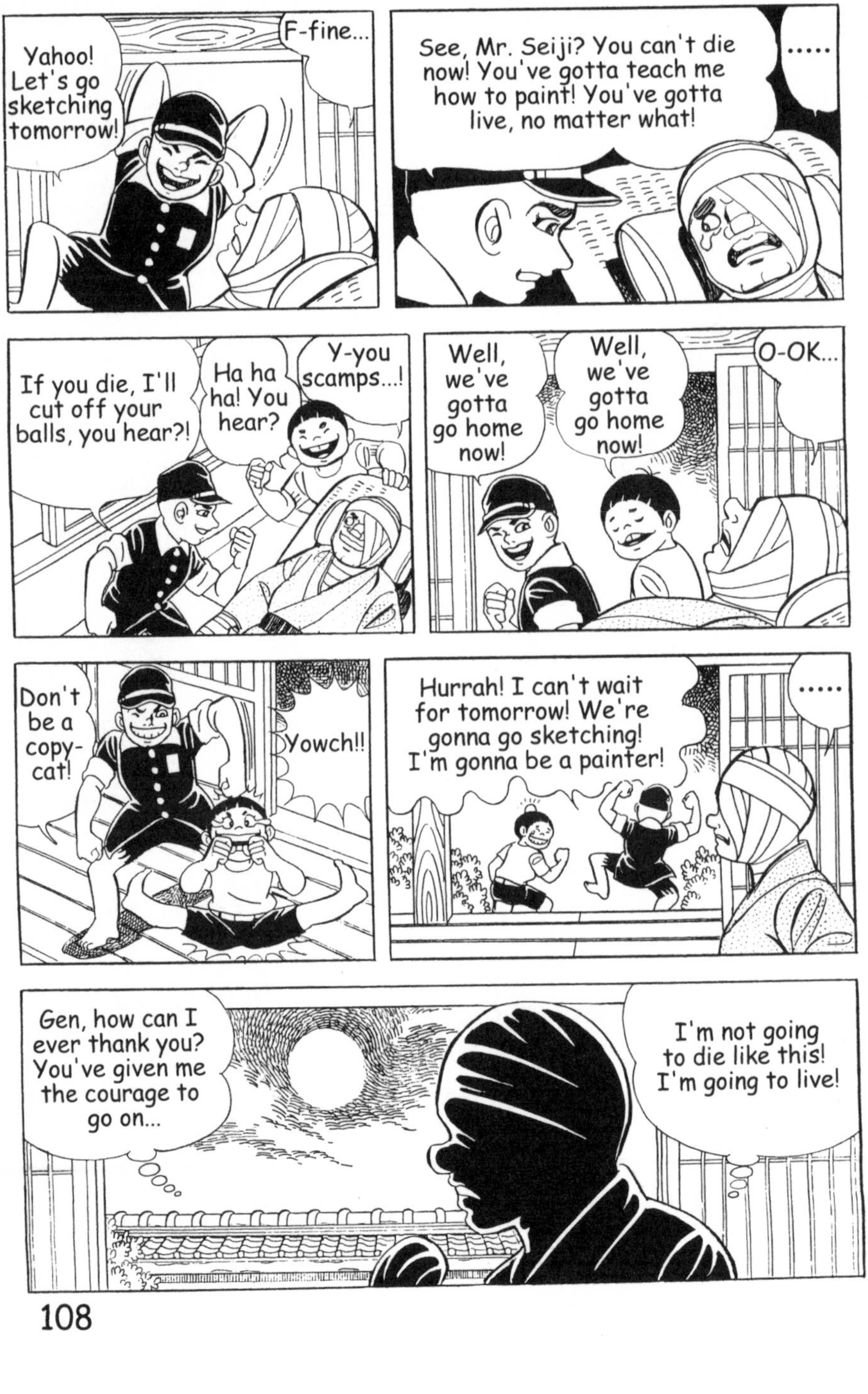
Yahoo! Let's go sketching tomorrow!
F-fine...
See, Mr. Seiji? You can't die now! You've gotta teach me how to paint! You've gotta live, no matter what!
.....
If you die, I'll cut off your balls, you hear?!
Ha ha ha! You hear?
Y-you scamps...!
Well, we've gotta go home now!
Well, we've gotta go home now!
O-OK...
Don't be a copy-cat!
Yowch!!
Hurrah! I can't wait for tomorrow! We're gonna go sketching! I'm gonna be a painter!
.....
Gen, how can I ever thank you? You've given me the courage to go on...
I'm not going to die like this! I'm going to live!

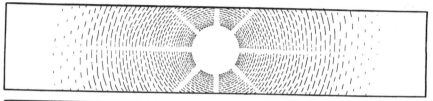

Oh, once upon a time there was a mountain, a little mountain near a grove of oaks...

Aaah, the fresh air feels good!

And everybody laughed at the little mountain, 'cuz it was bald on top...

.....

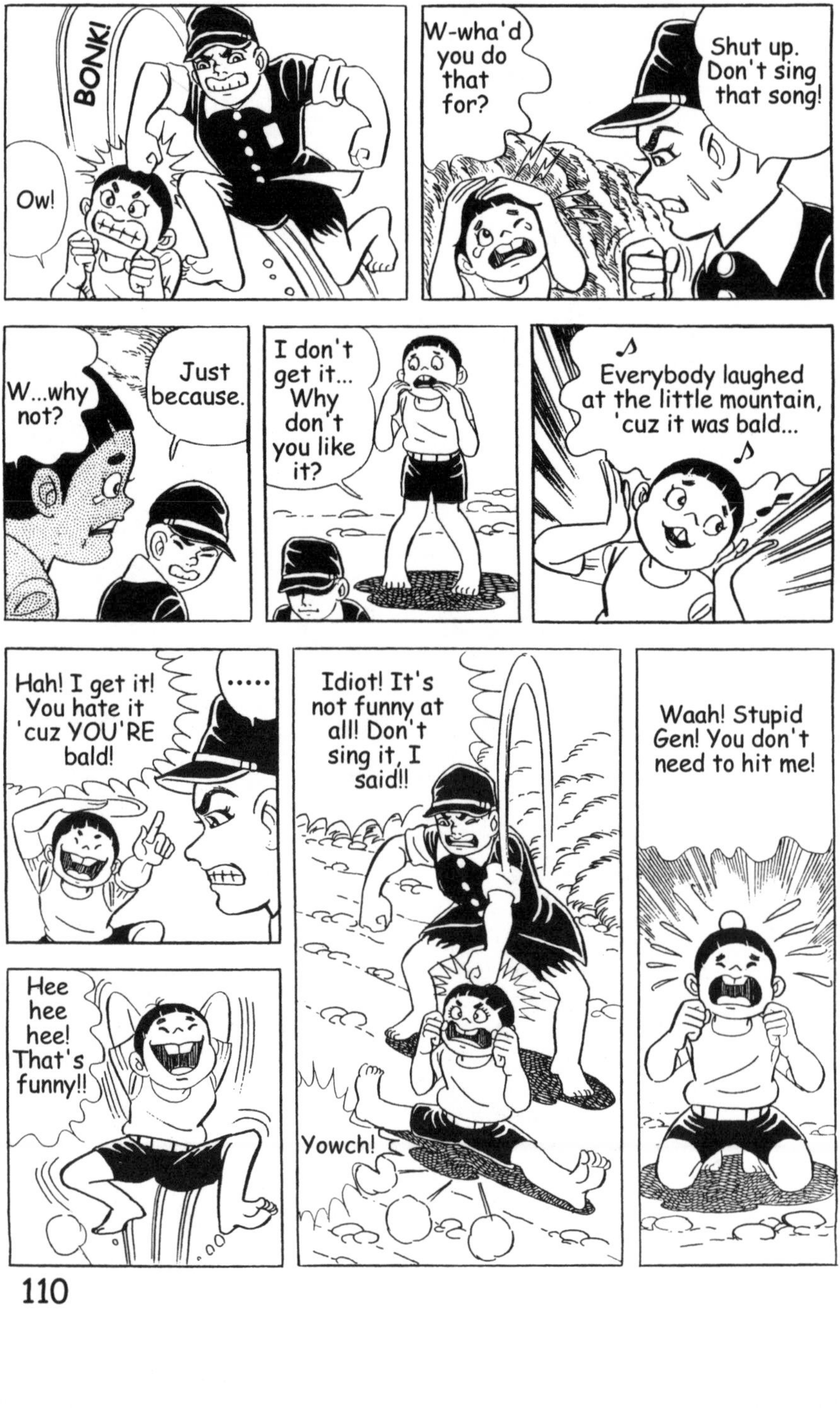
BONK!
Ow!
W-wha'd you do that for?
Shut up. Don't sing that song!
W...why not?
Just because.
I don't get it... Why don't you like it?
Everybody laughed at the little mountain, 'cuz it was bald...
Hah! I get it! You hate it 'cuz YOU'RE bald!
.....
Hee hee hee! That's funny!!
Idiot! It's not funny at all! Don't sing it, I said!!
Yowch!
Waah! Stupid Gen! You don't need to hit me!

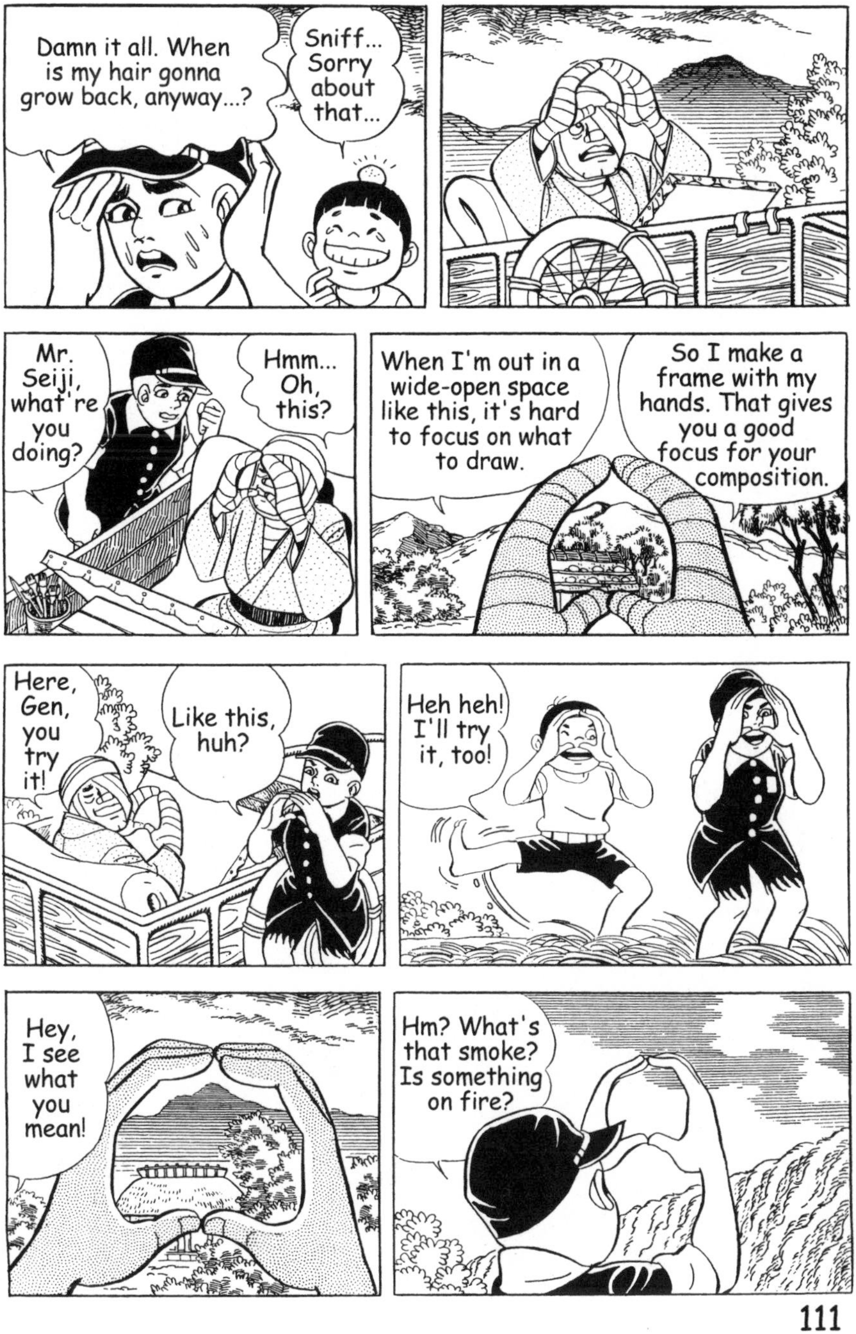
Damn it all. When is my hair gonna grow back, anyway...?
Sniff... Sorry about that...
Mr. Seiji, what're you doing?
Hmm... Oh, this?
When I'm out in a wide-open space like this, it's hard to focus on what to draw.
So I make a frame with my hands. That gives you a good focus for your composition.
Here, Gen, you try it!
Like this, huh?
Heh heh! I'll try it, too!
Hey, I see what you mean!
Hm? What's that smoke? Is something on fire?

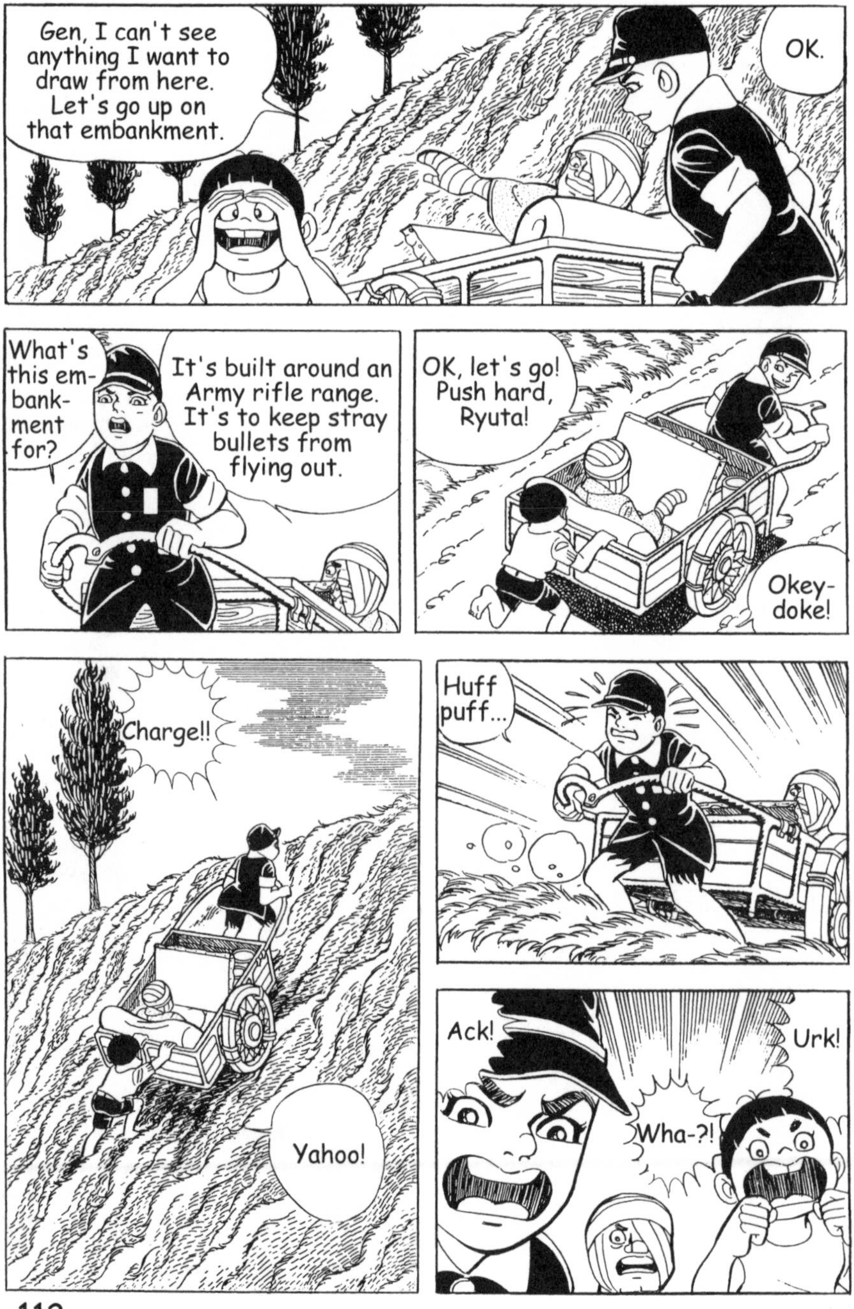
Gen, I can't see anything I want to draw from here. Let's go up on that embankment.
OK.
What's this em-bank-ment for?
It's built around an Army rifle range. It's to keep stray bullets from flying out.
OK, let's go! Push hard, Ryuta!
Okey-doke!
Charge!!
Yahoo!
Huff puff...
Ack!
Urk!
Wha-?!

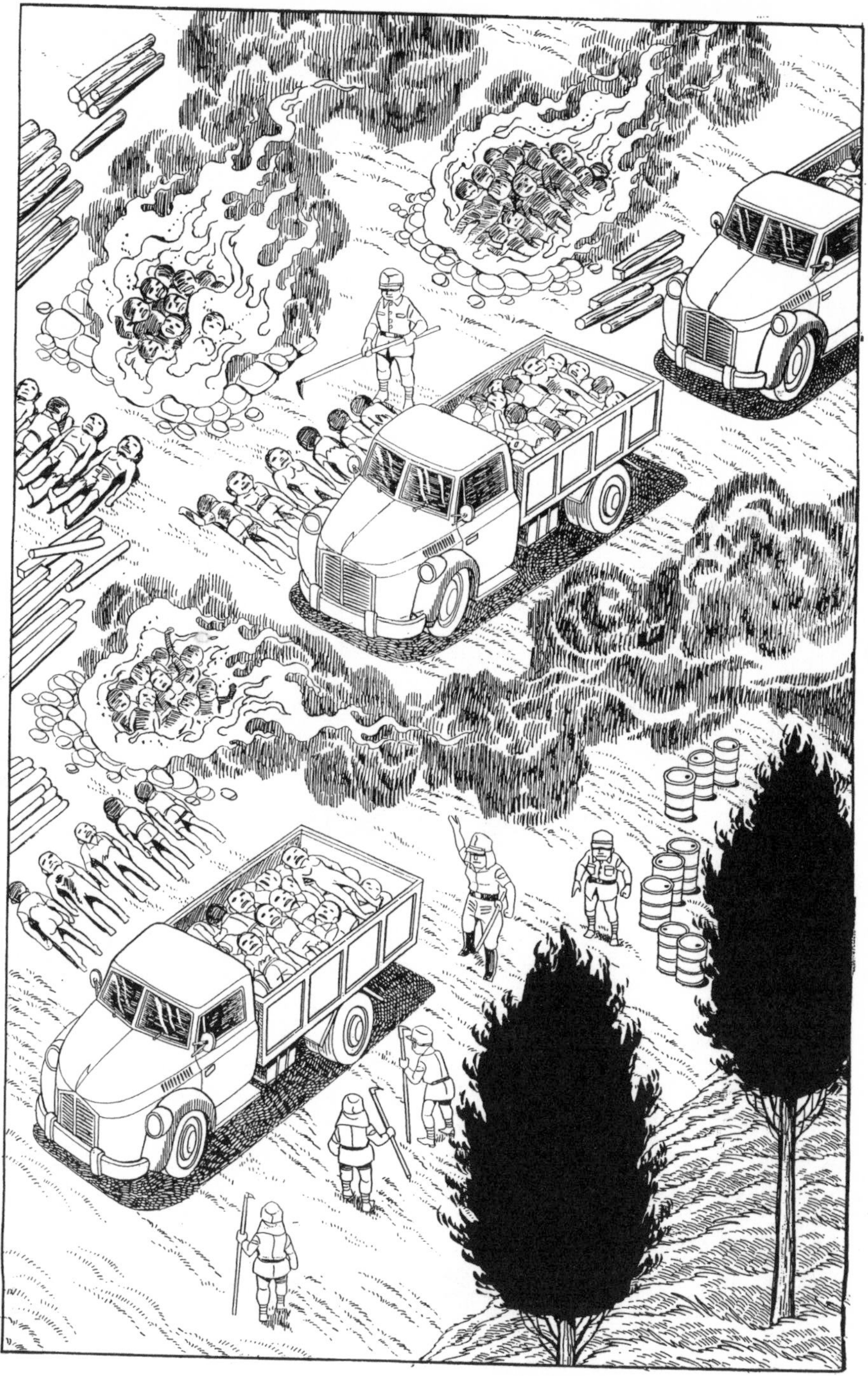

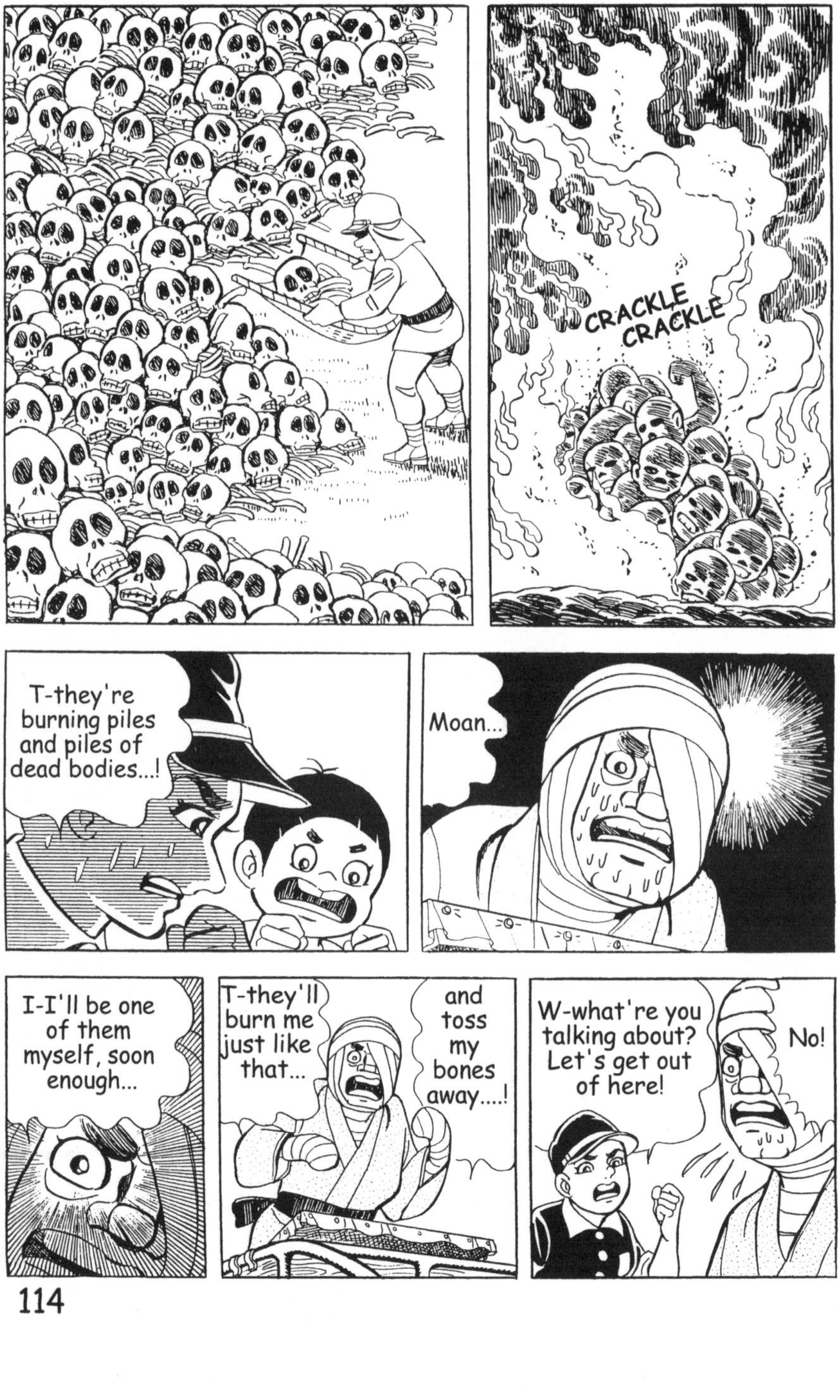
CRACKLE CRACKLE
T-they're burning piles and piles of dead bodies...!
Moan...
I-I'll be one of them myself, soon enough...
T-they'll burn me just like that...
and toss my bones away....!
W-what're you talking about? Let's get out of here!
No!

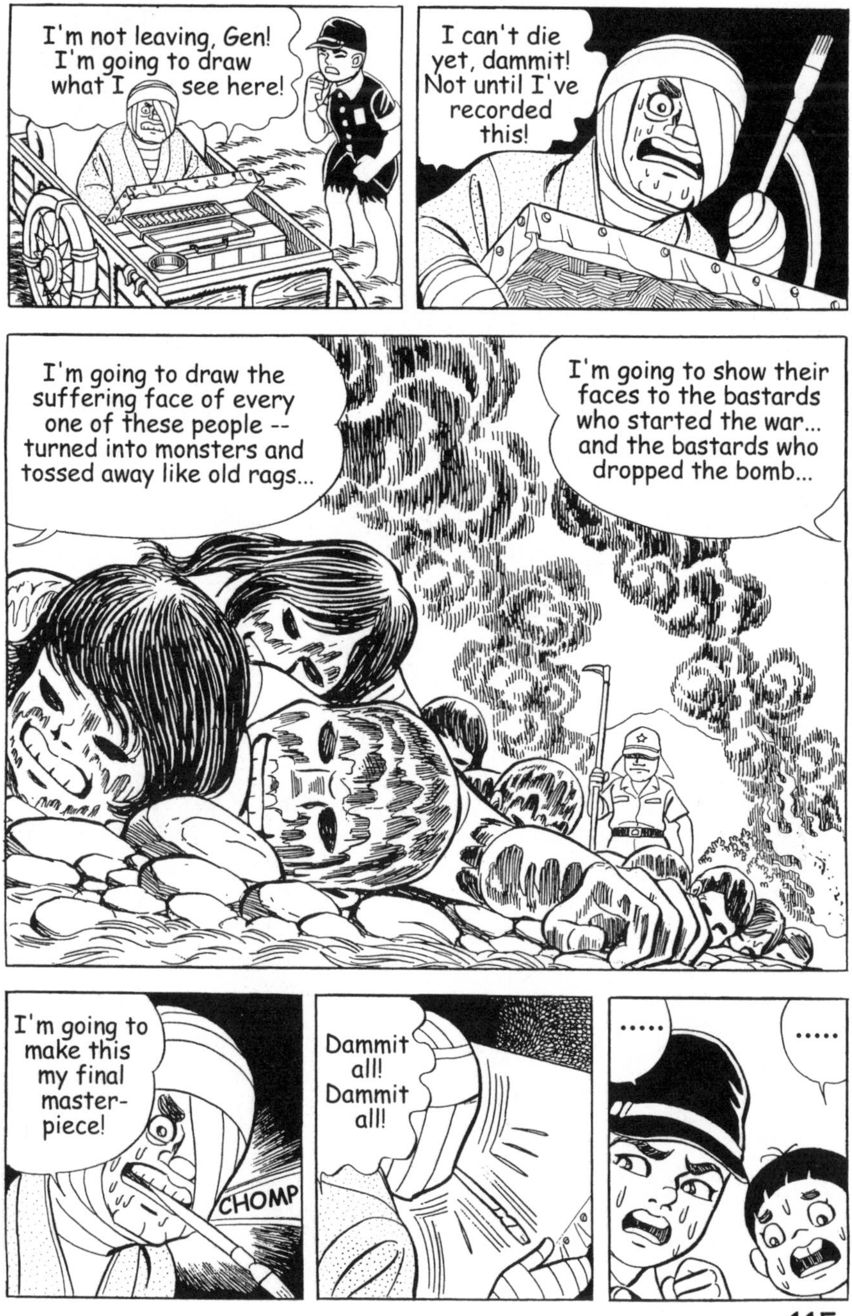
I'm not leaving, Gen! I'm going to draw what I see here!
I can't die yet, dammit! Not until I've recorded this!
I'm going to draw the suffering face of every one of these people -- turned into monsters and tossed away like old rags...
I'm going to show their faces to the bastards who started the war... and the bastards who dropped the bomb...
I'm going to make this my final master-piece!
CHOMP
Dammit all! Dammit all!
.....
.....

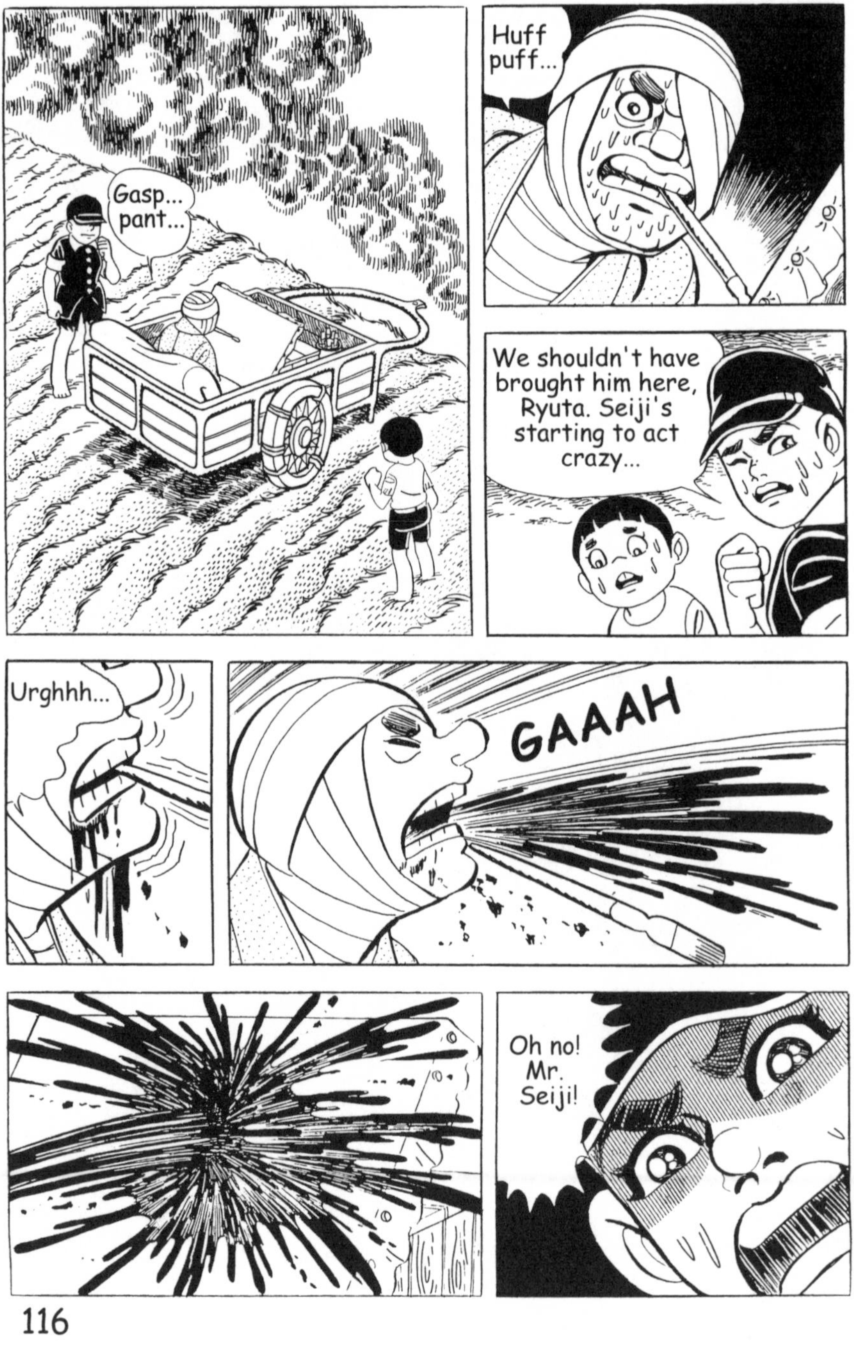
Gasp... pant...
Huff puff...
We shouldn't have brought him here, Ryuta. Seiji's starting to act crazy...
Urghhh...
GAAAH
Oh no! Mr. Seiji!

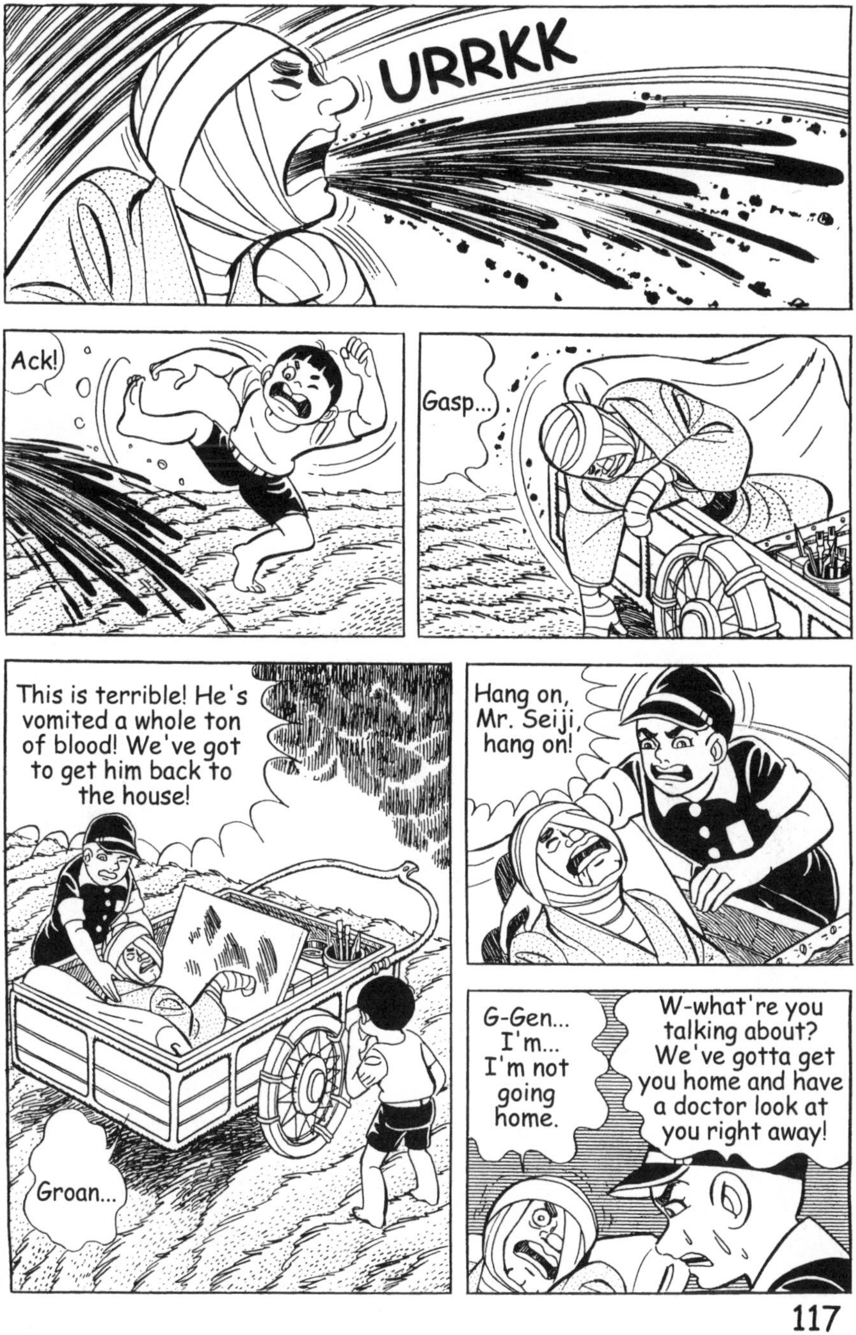
URRKK
Ack!
Gasp...
This is terrible! He's vomited a whole ton of blood! We've got to get him back to the house!
Groan...
Hang on, Mr. Seiji, hang on!
G-Gen... I'm... I'm not going home.
W-what're you talking about? We've gotta get you home and have a doctor look at you right away!

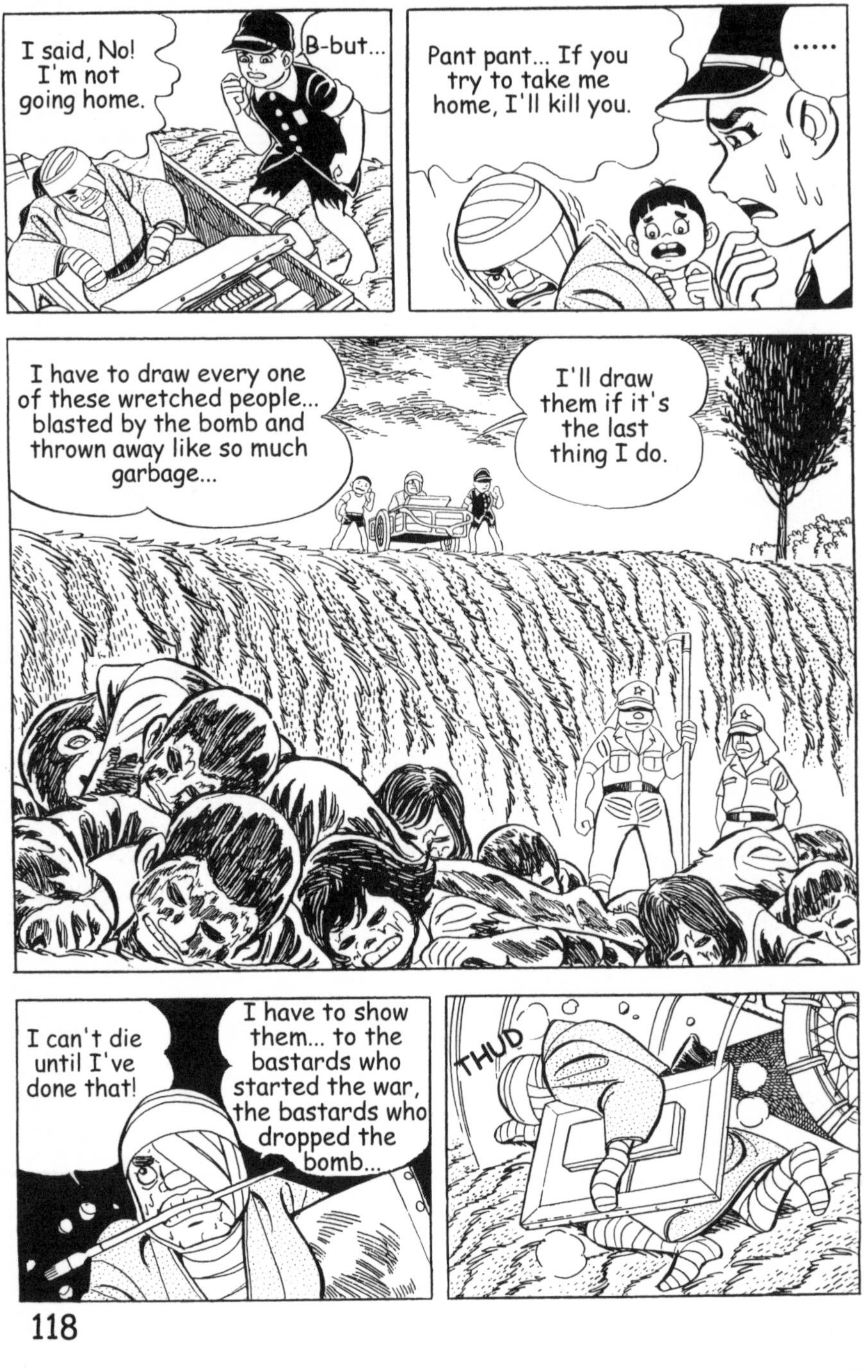
I said, No! I'm not going home.
B-but...
Pant pant... If you try to take me home, I'll kill you.
.....
I have to draw every one of these wretched people... blasted by the bomb and thrown away like so much garbage...
I'll draw them if it's the last thing I do.
I can't die until I've done that!
I have to show them... to the bastards who started the war, the bastards who dropped the bomb...
THUD

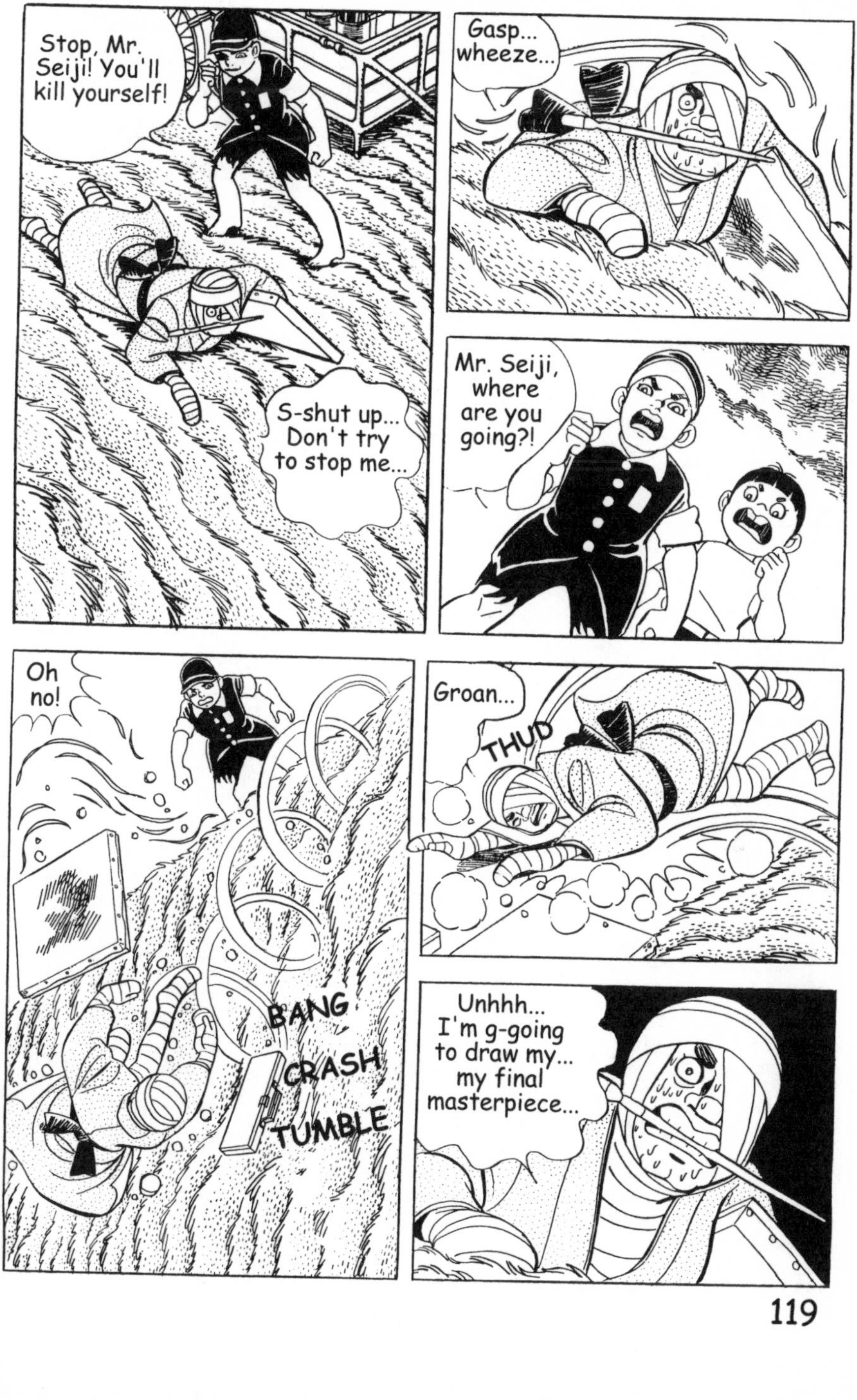
Stop, Mr. Seiji! You'll kill yourself!
S-shut up... Don't try to stop me...
Gasp... wheeze...
Mr. Seiji, where are you going?!
Oh no!
BANG
CRASH
TUMBLE
Groan...
THUD
Unhhh... I'm g-going to draw my... my final masterpiece...

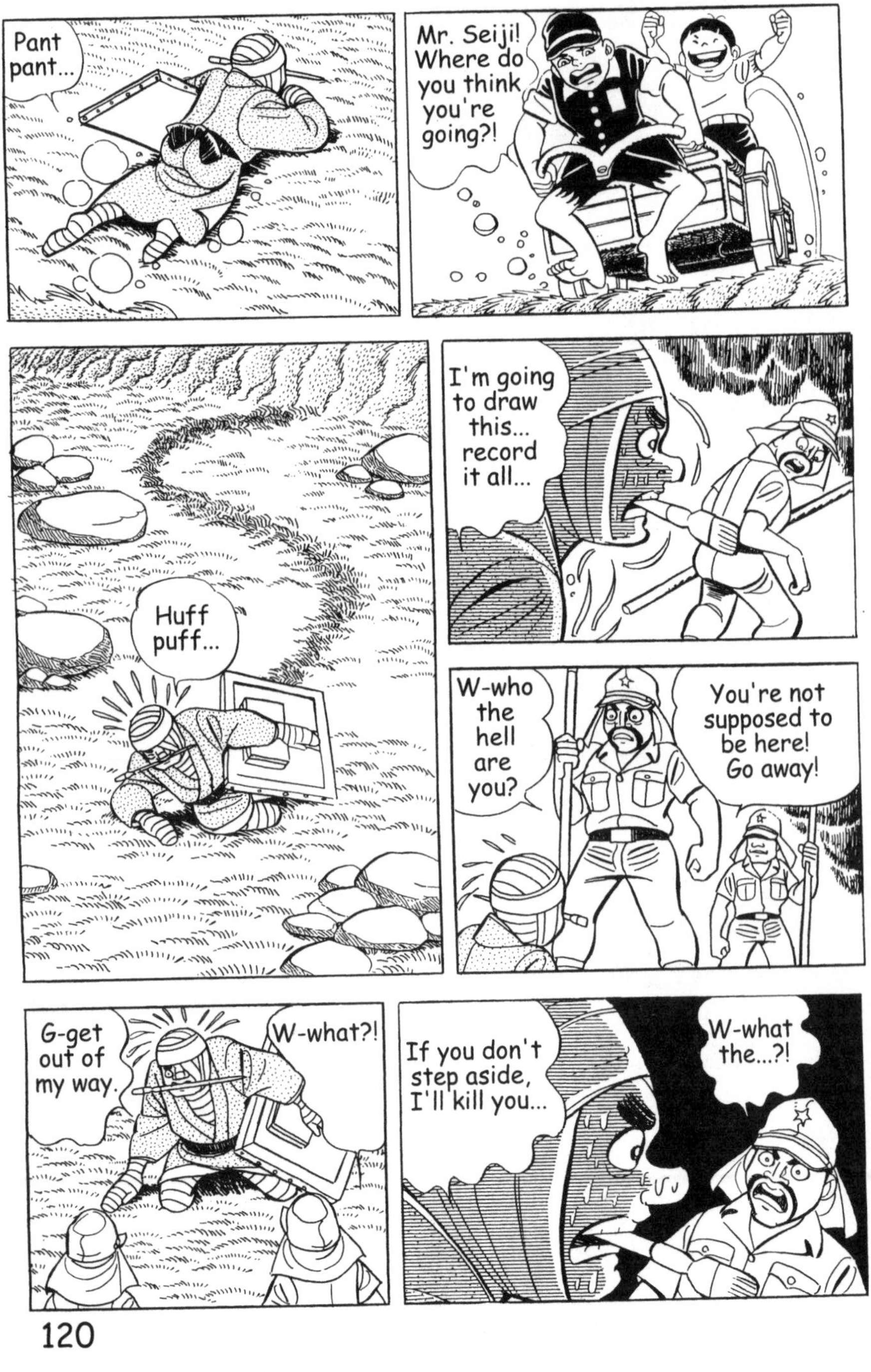
Pant pant...
Mr. Seiji! Where do you think you're going?!
Huff puff...
I'm going to draw this... record it all...
W-who the hell are you?
You're not supposed to be here! Go away!
G-get out of my way.
W-what?!
If you don't step aside, I'll kill you...
W-what the...?!

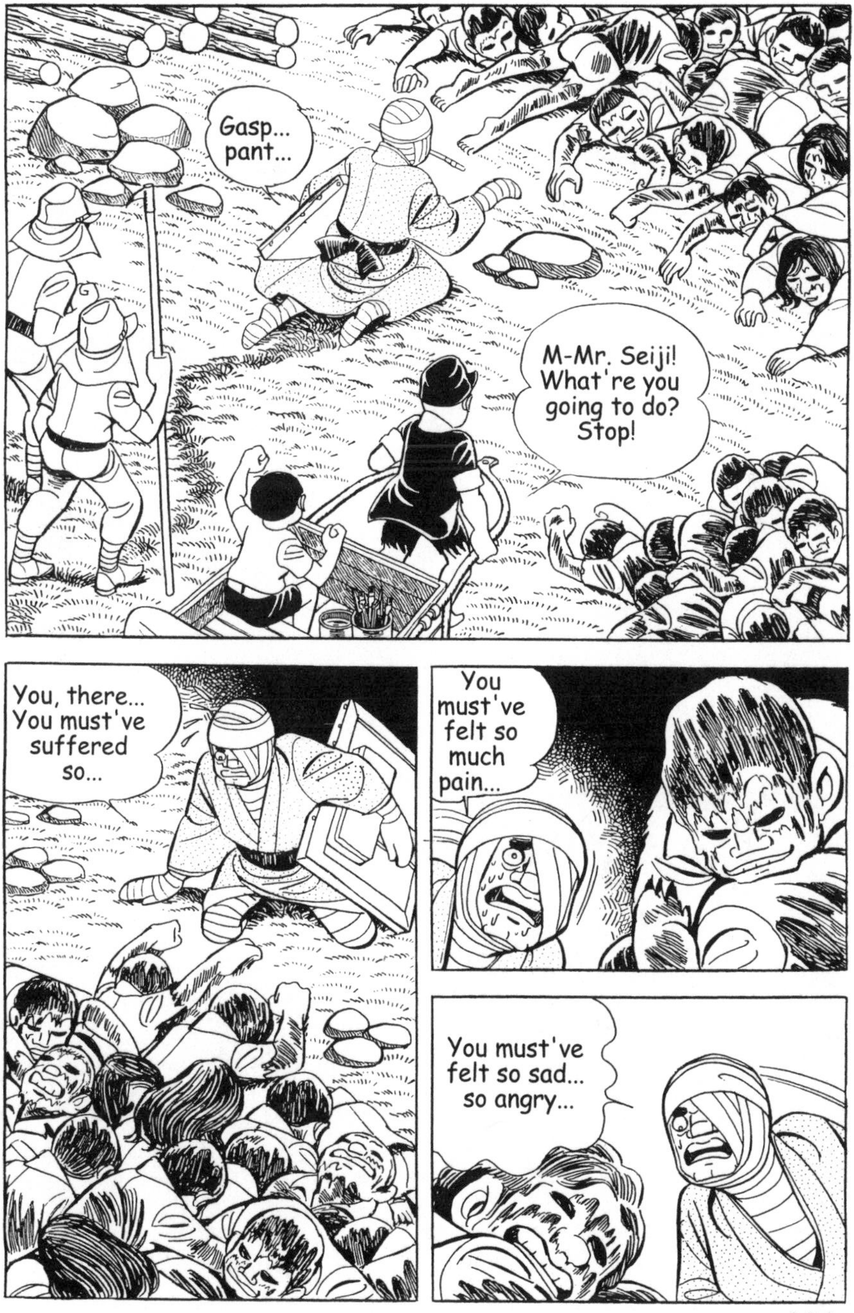
Gasp... pant...
M-Mr. Seiji! What're you going to do? Stop!
You, there... You must've suffered so...
You must've felt so much pain...
You must've felt so sad... so angry...

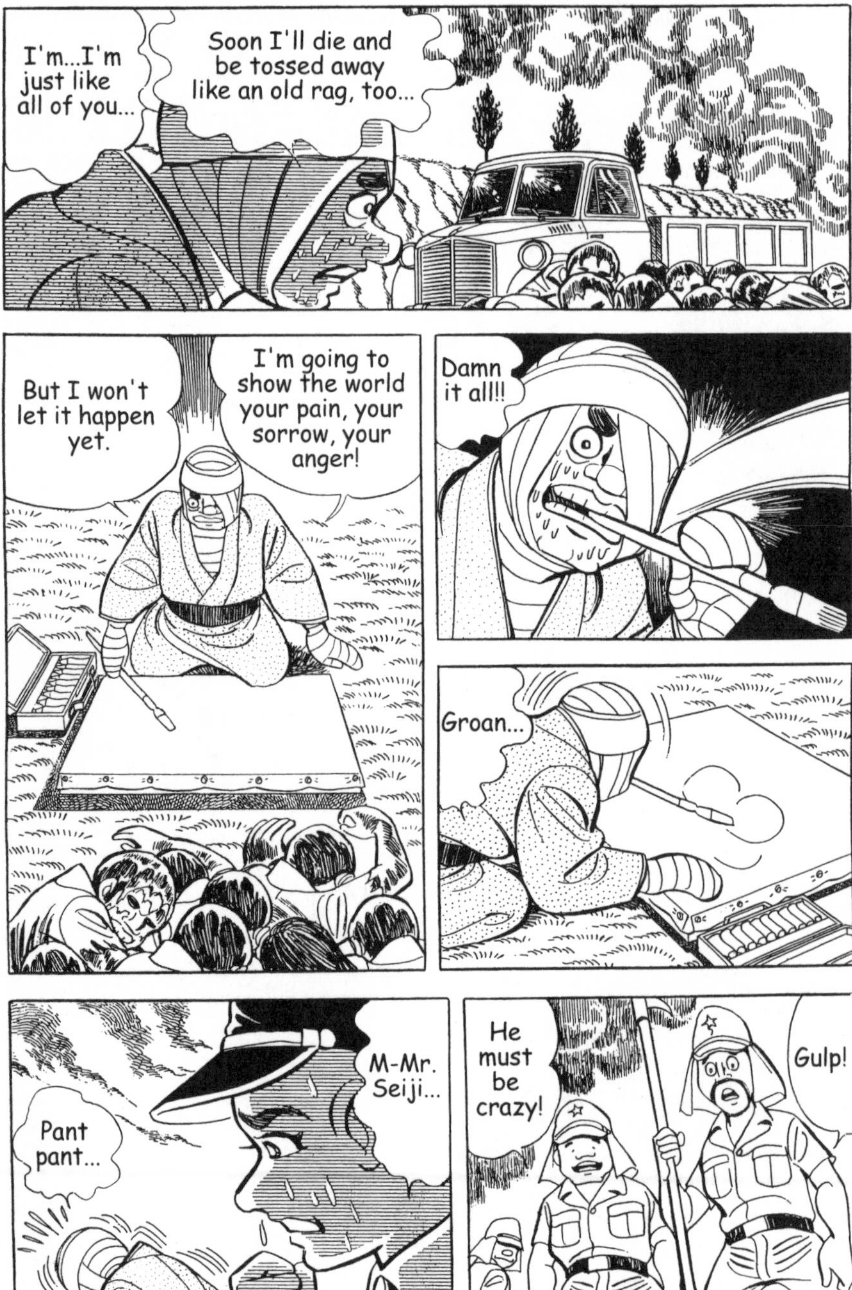

I'm...I'm just like all of you...
Soon I'll die and be tossed away like an old rag, too...
But I won't let it happen yet.
I'm going to show the world your pain, your sorrow, your anger!
Damn it all!!
Groan...
Pant pant...
M-Mr. Seiji...
He must be crazy!
Gulp!

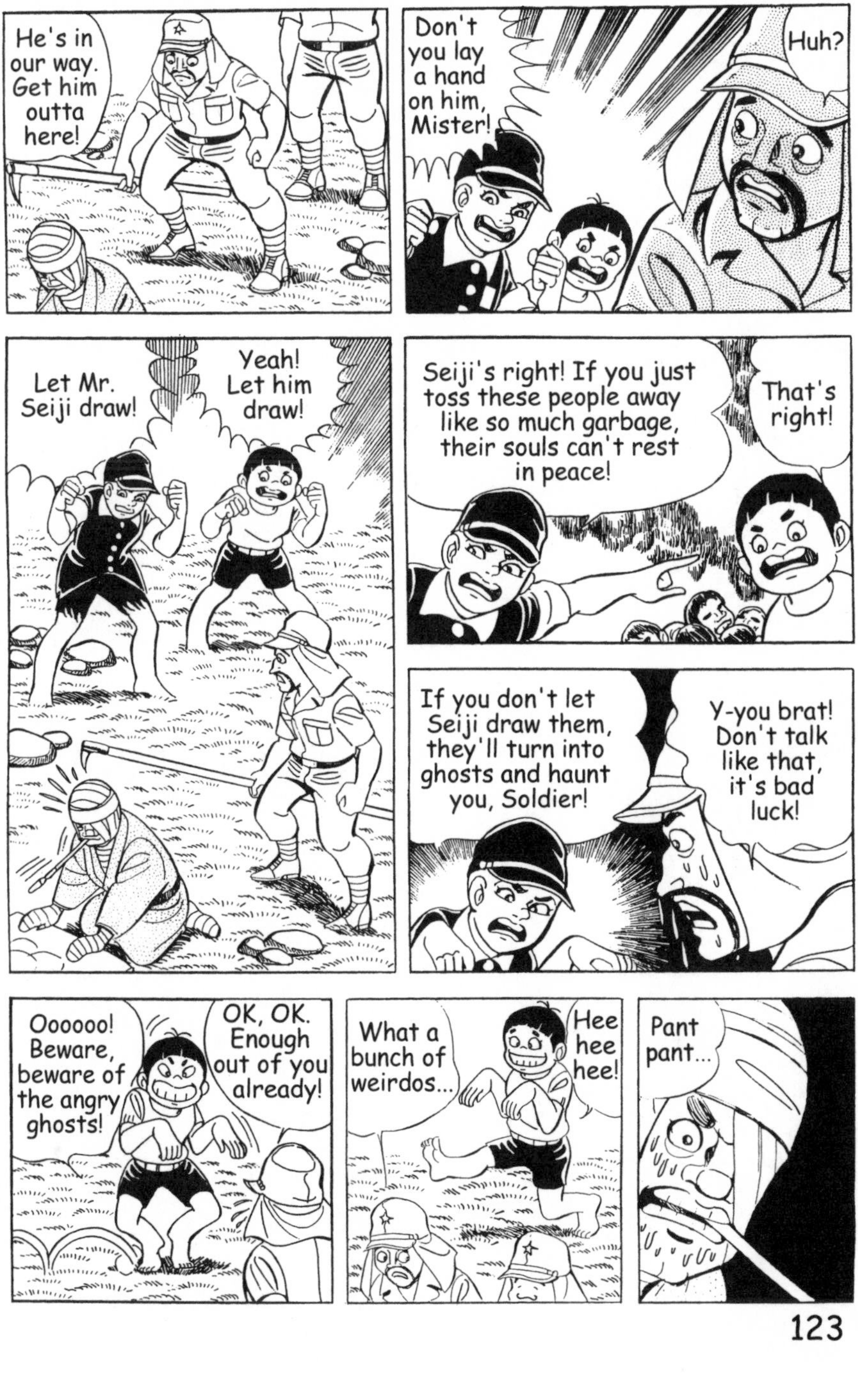

He's in our way. Get him outta here!
Don't you lay a hand on him, Mister!
Huh?
Let Mr. Seiji draw!
Yeah! Let him draw!
Seiji's right! If you just toss these people away like so much garbage, their souls can't rest in peace!
That's right!
If you don't let Seiji draw them, they'll turn into ghosts and haunt you, Soldier!
Y-you brat! Don't talk like that, it's bad luck!
Oooooo! Beware, beware of the angry ghosts!
OK, OK. Enough out of you already!
What a bunch of weirdos...
Hee hee hee!
Pant pant...

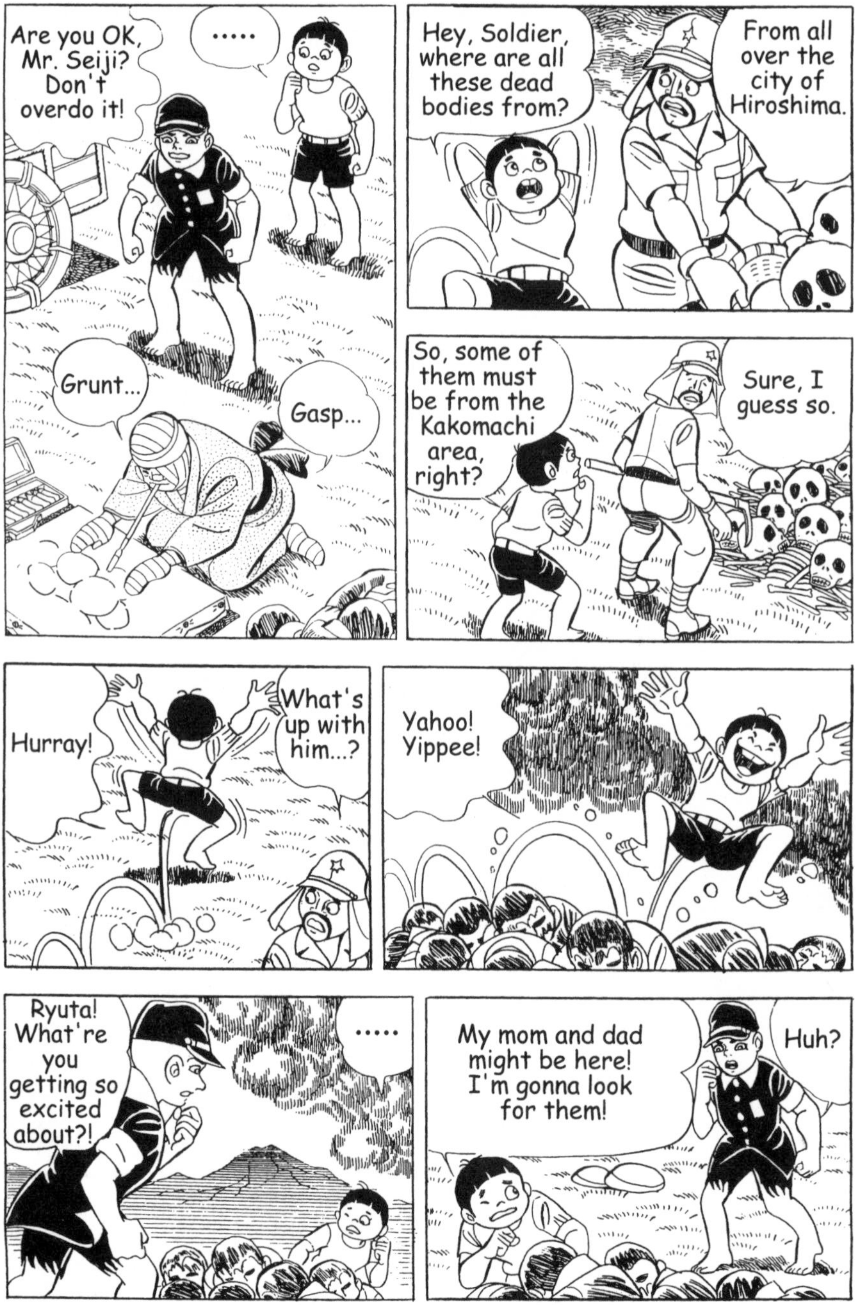
Are you OK, Mr. Seiji? Don't overdo it!
.....
Grunt...
Gasp...
Hey, Soldier, where are all these dead bodies from?
From all over the city of Hiroshima.
So, some of them must be from the Kakomachi area, right?
Sure, I guess so.
Hurray!
What's up with him...?
Yahoo! Yippee!
Ryuta! What're you getting so excited about?!
.....
My mom and dad might be here! I'm gonna look for them!
Huh?

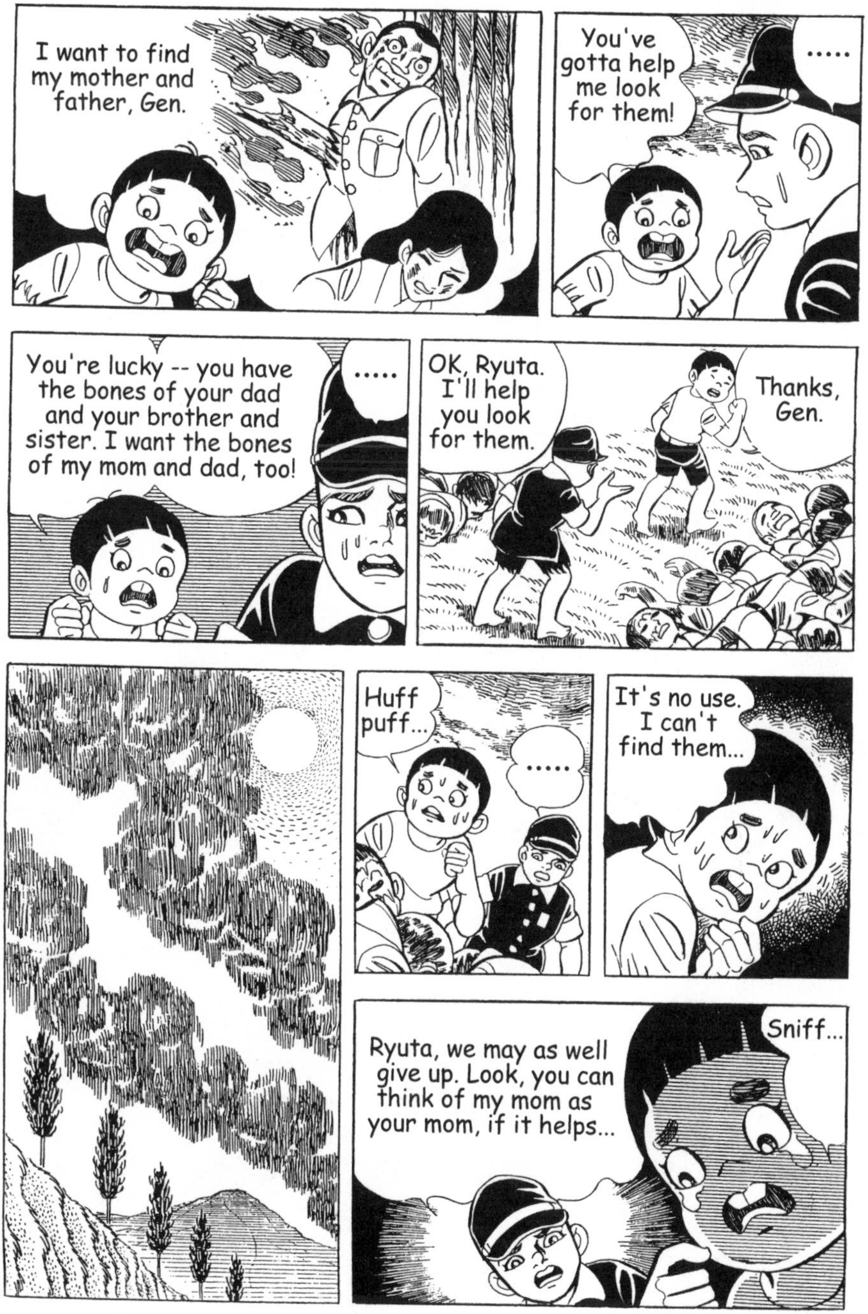
I want to find my mother and father, Gen.
You've gotta help me look for them!
.....
You're lucky -- you have the bones of your dad and your brother and sister. I want the bones of my mom and dad, too!
.....
OK, Ryuta. I'll help you look for them.
Thanks, Gen.
Huff puff...
.....
It's no use. I can't find them...
Ryuta, we may as well give up. Look, you can think of my mom as your mom, if it helps...
Sniff...

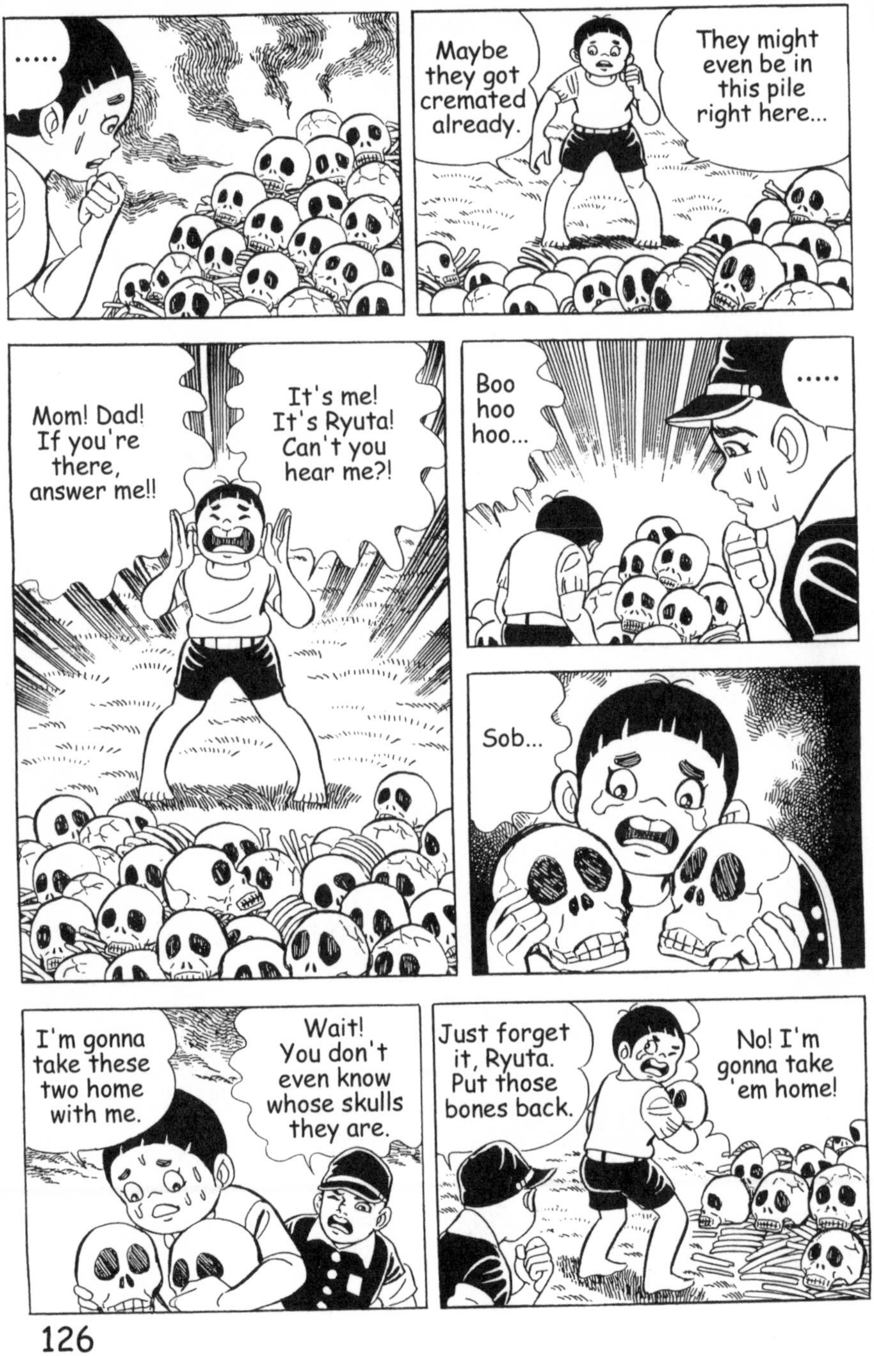
.....
Maybe they got cremated already.
They might even be in this pile right here...
Mom! Dad! If you're there, answer me!!
It's me! It's Ryuta! Can't you hear me?!
Boo hoo hoo...
.....
Sob...
I'm gonna take these two home with me.
Wait! You don't even know whose skulls they are.
Just forget it, Ryuta. Put those bones back.
No! I'm gonna take 'em home!

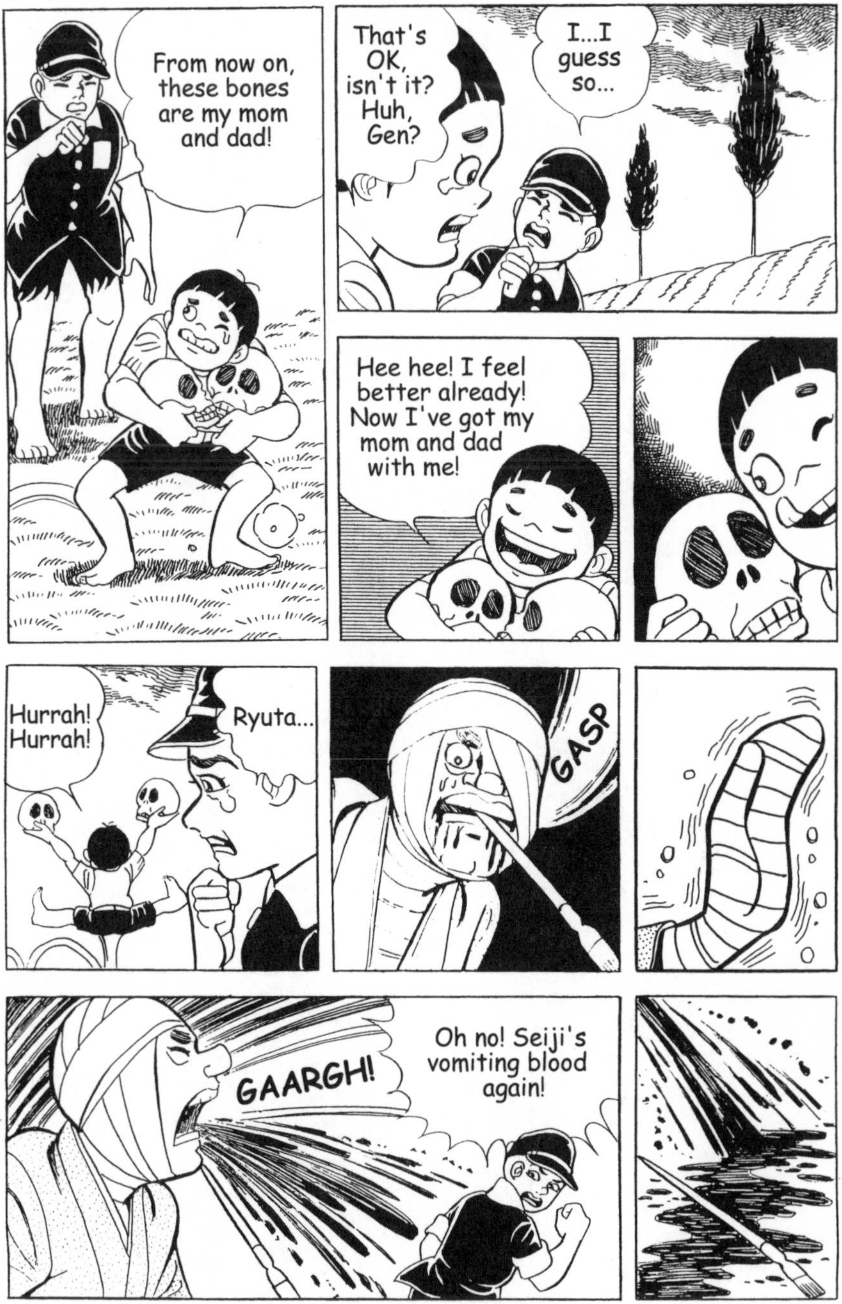
From now on, these bones are my mom and dad!
That's OK, isn't it? Huh, Gen?
I...I guess so...
Hee hee! I feel better already! Now I've got my mom and dad with me!
Hurrah! Hurrah!
Ryuta...
GASP
GAARGH!
Oh no! Seiji's vomiting blood again!

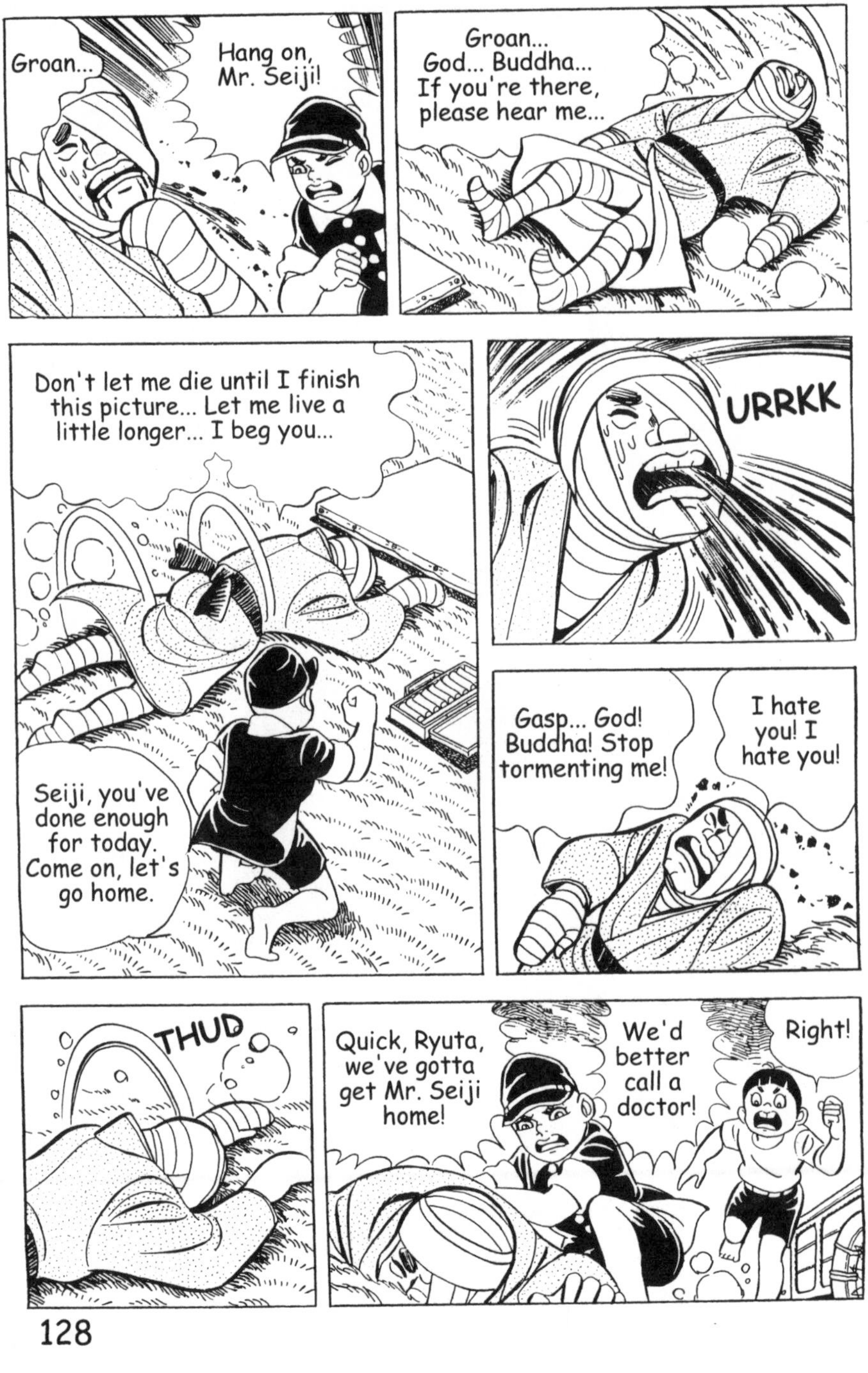
Groan...
Hang on, Mr. Seiji!
Groan... God... Buddha... If you're there, please hear me...
Don't let me die until I finish this picture... Let me live a little longer... I beg you...
Seiji, you've done enough for today. Come on, let's go home.
URRKK
Gasp... God! Buddha! Stop tormenting me!
I hate you! I hate you!
THUD
Quick, Ryuta, we've gotta get Mr. Seiji home!
We'd better call a doctor!
Right!

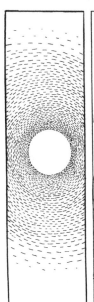

Pant pant...

Huff puff...

Gasp... Wheeze...

Don't die, Mr. Seiji, don't die!

Gen... G-get me some w-water...

Water...?

I'll ask for some water at this house.

Hey mister, can you spare us some water?

Sure.

Groan...

129

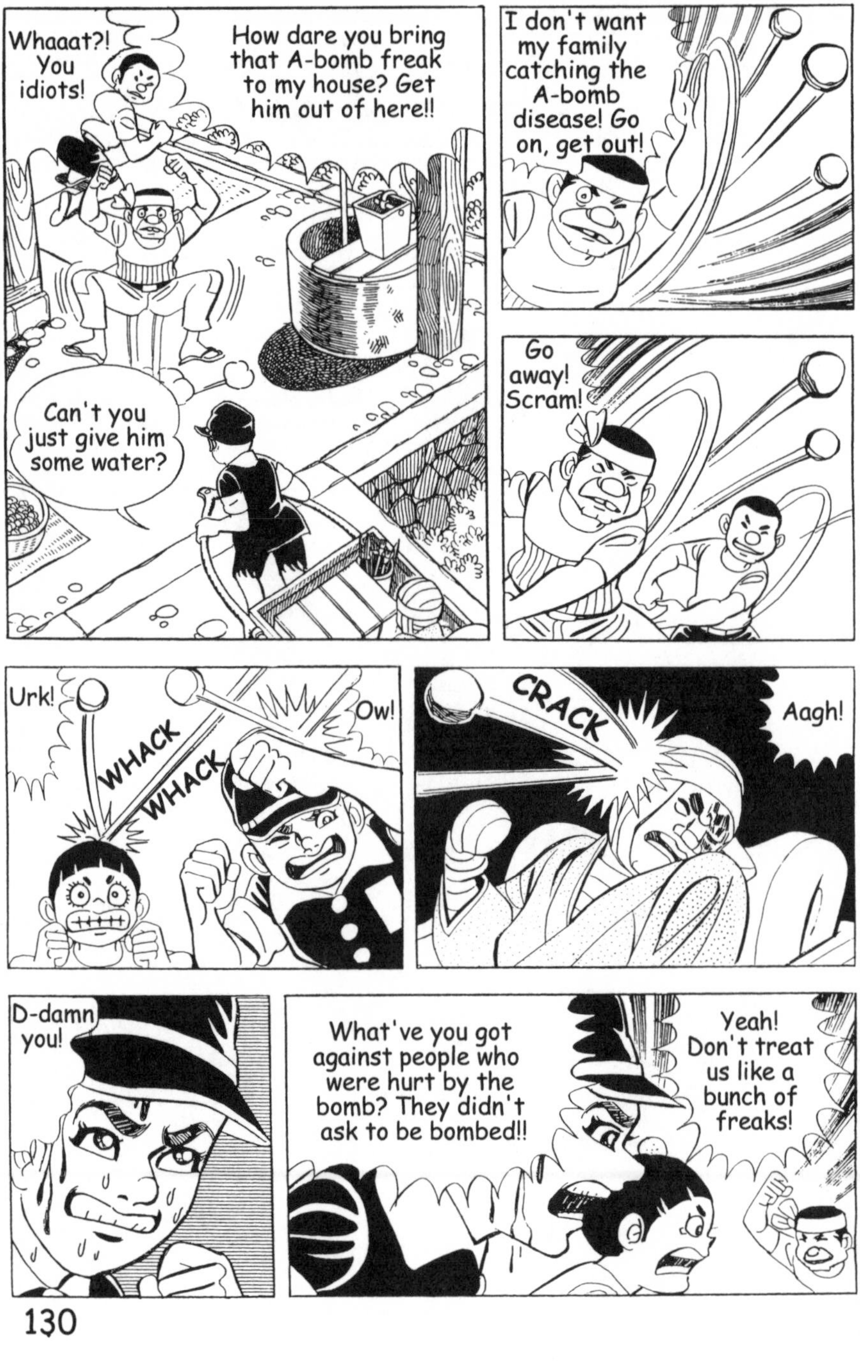
Whaaat?! You idiots!
How dare you bring that A-bomb freak to my house? Get him out of here!!
Can't you just give him some water?
I don't want my family catching the A-bomb disease! Go on, get out!
Go away! Scram!
Urk!
WHACK
WHACK
Ow!
CRACK
Aagh!
D-damn you!
What've you got against people who were hurt by the bomb? They didn't ask to be bombed!!
Yeah! Don't treat us like a bunch of freaks!

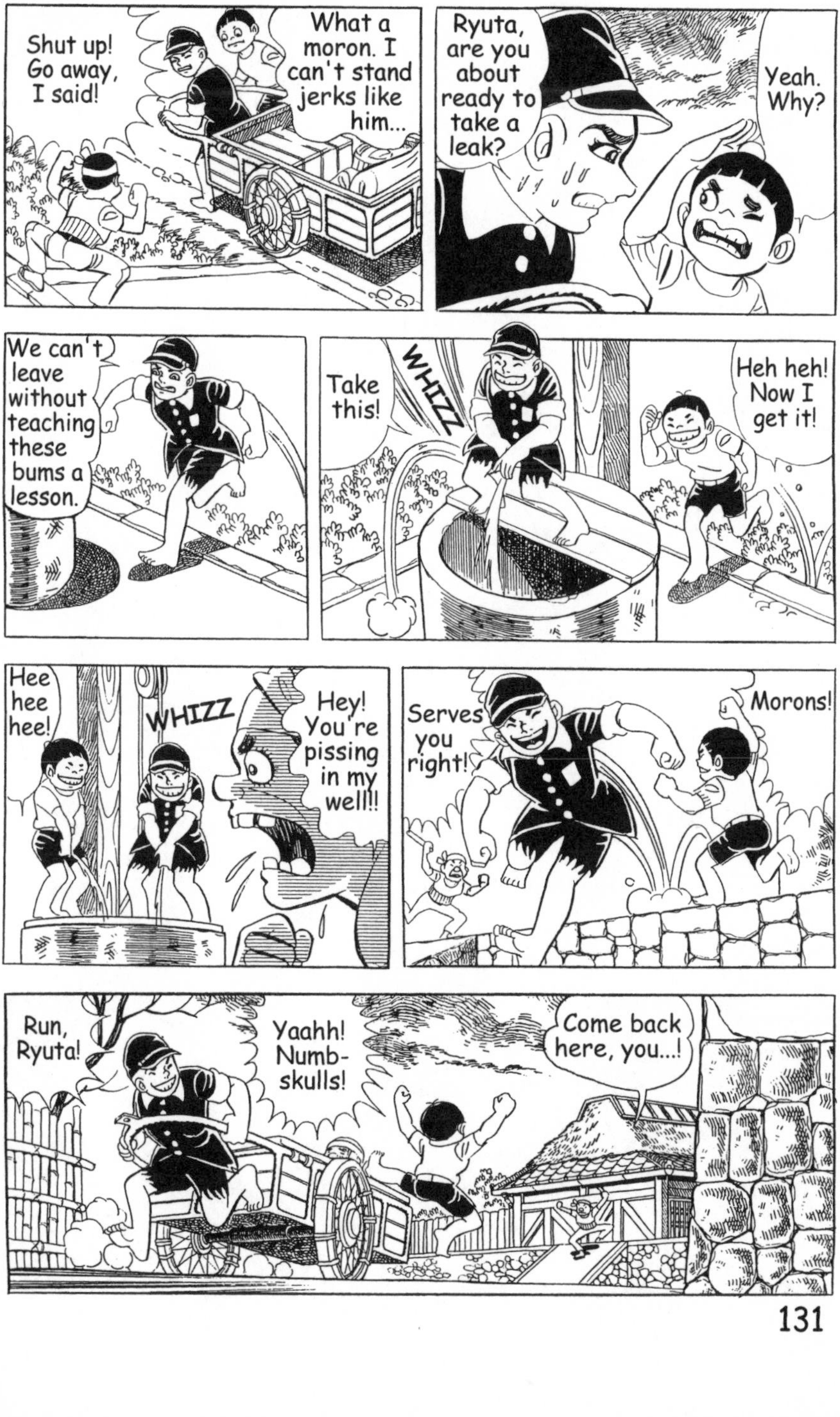
Shut up! Go away, I said!
What a moron. I can't stand jerks like him...
Ryuta, are you about ready to take a leak?
Yeah. Why?
We can't leave without teaching these bums a lesson.
Take this!
WHIZZ
Heh heh! Now I get it!
Hee hee hee!
WHIZZ
Hey! You're pissing in my well!!
Serves you right!
Morons!
Run, Ryuta!
Yaahh! Numb-skulls!
Come back here, you...!

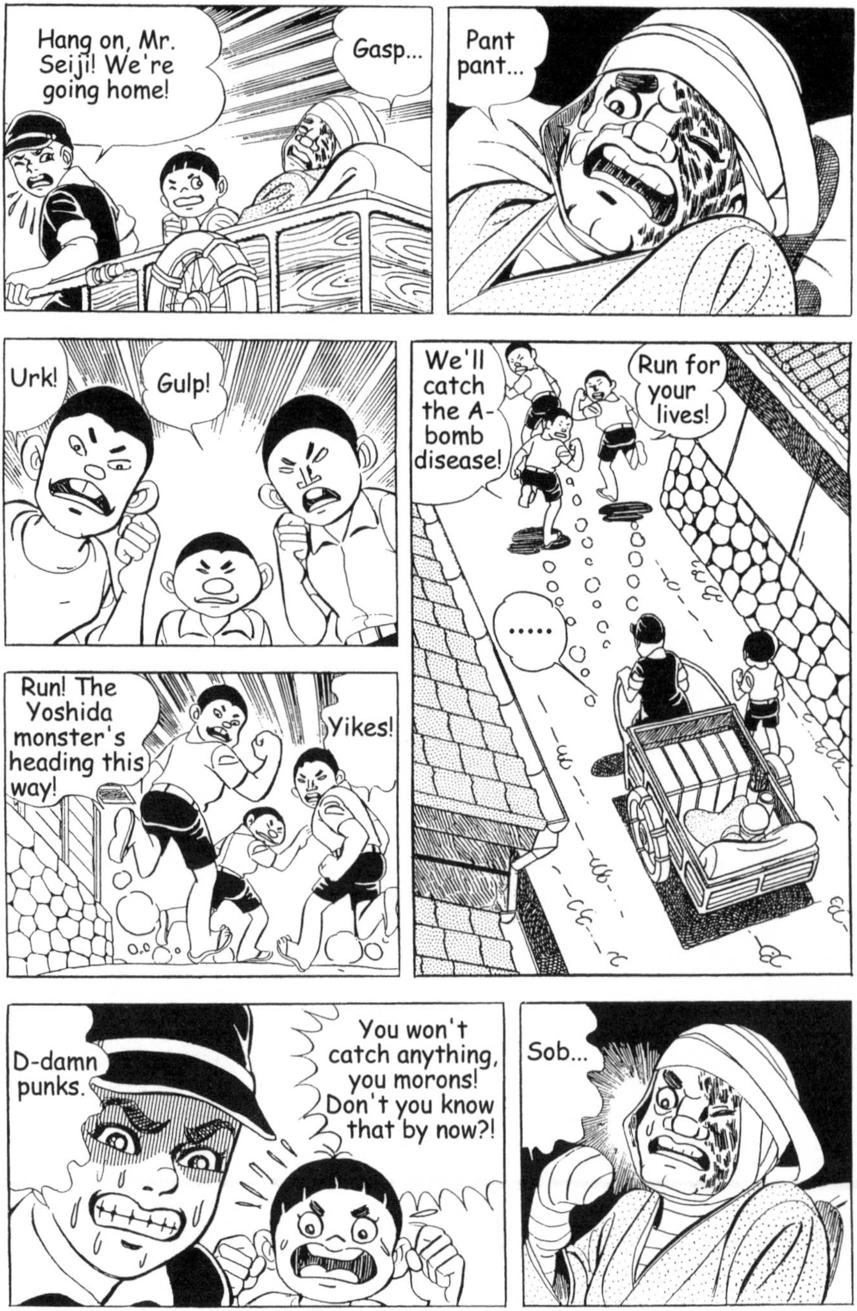
Hang on, Mr. Seiji! We're going home!
Gasp...
Pant pant...
Urk!
Gulp!
We'll catch the A-bomb disease!
Run for your lives!
......
Run! The Yoshida monster's heading this way!
Yikes!
D-damn punks.
You won't catch anything, you morons! Don't you know that by now?!
Sob...

M-Mr. Seiji! What're you doing?

I'm going to show everybody what I really look like.

Take me through the middle of town, Gen. Show everyone how ugly I really am.

W-what're you talking about?!

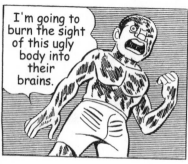

I'm going to burn the sight of this ugly body into their brains.

This is the only way I have to pay them back...

for the way they've treated an innocent bomb victim...

133

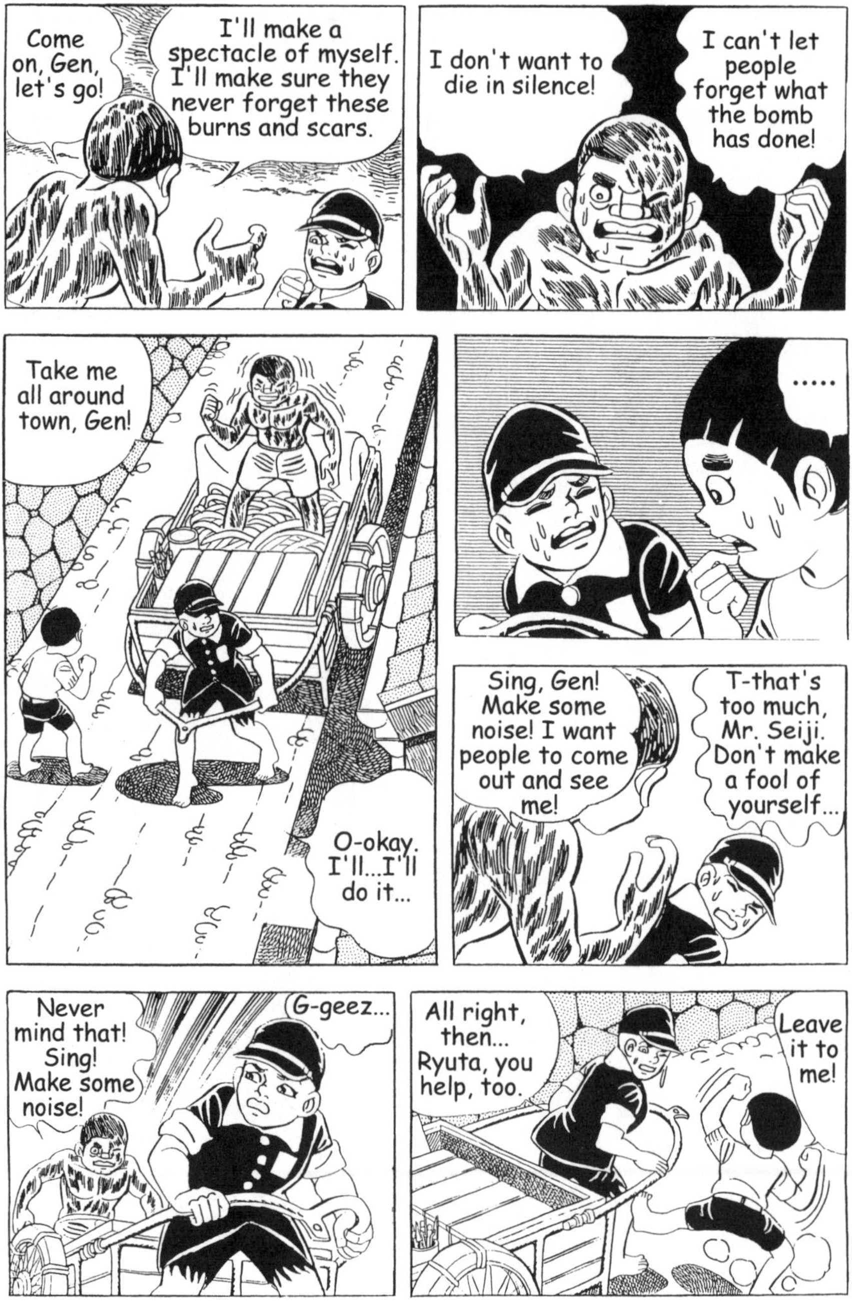
Come on, Gen, let's go!
I'll make a spectacle of myself. I'll make sure they never forget these burns and scars.
I don't want to die in silence!
I can't let people forget what the bomb has done!
Take me all around town, Gen!
O-okay. I'll...I'll do it...
.....
Sing, Gen! Make some noise! I want people to come out and see me!
T-that's too much, Mr. Seiji. Don't make a fool of yourself...
Never mind that! Sing! Make some noise!
G-geez...
All right, then... Ryuta, you help, too.
Leave it to me!

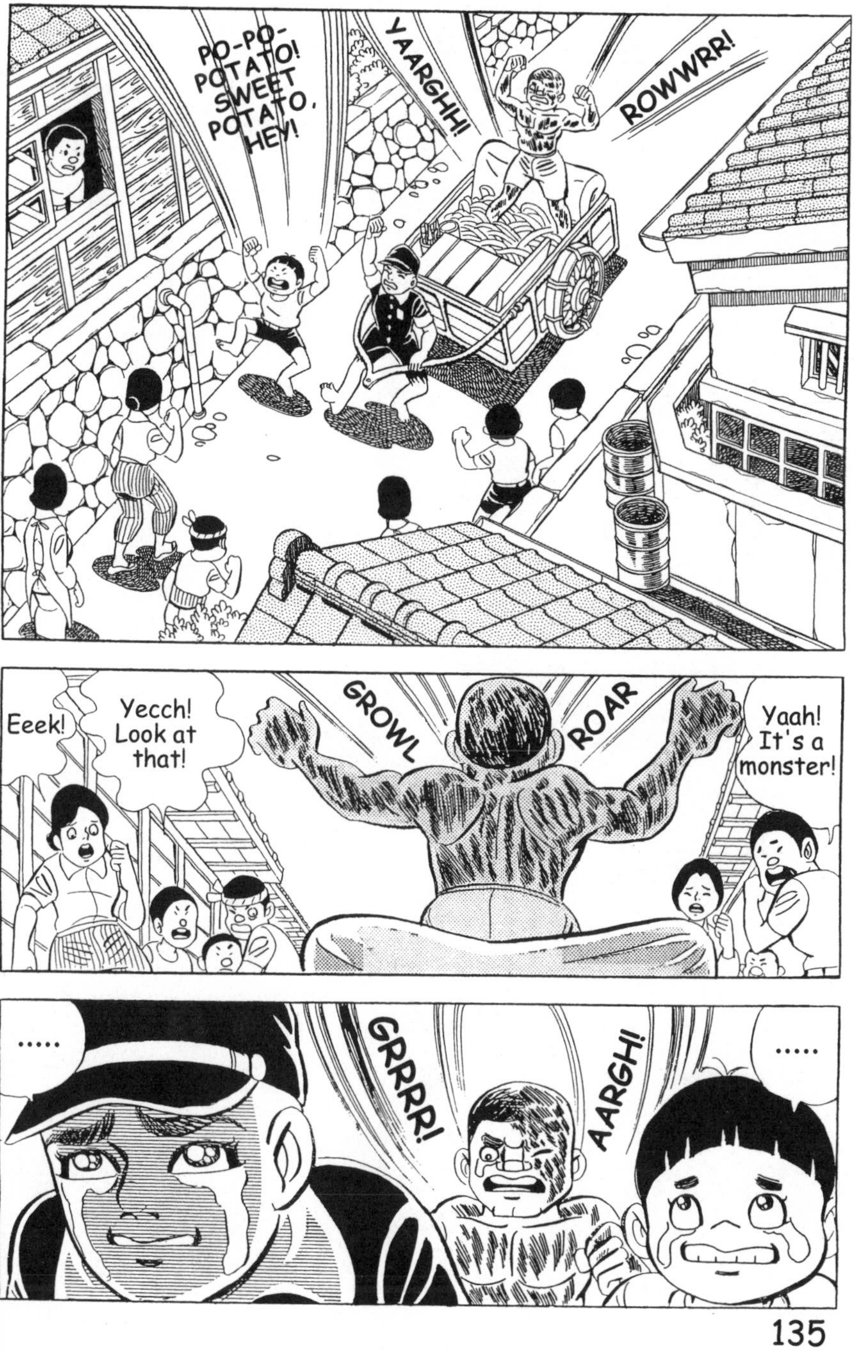
PO-PO-POTATO! SWEET POTATO, HEY!
YAARGHH!
ROWWRR!
Eeek!
Yecch! Look at that!
GROWL
ROAR
Yaah! It's a monster!
.....
GRRRR!
AARGH!
.....

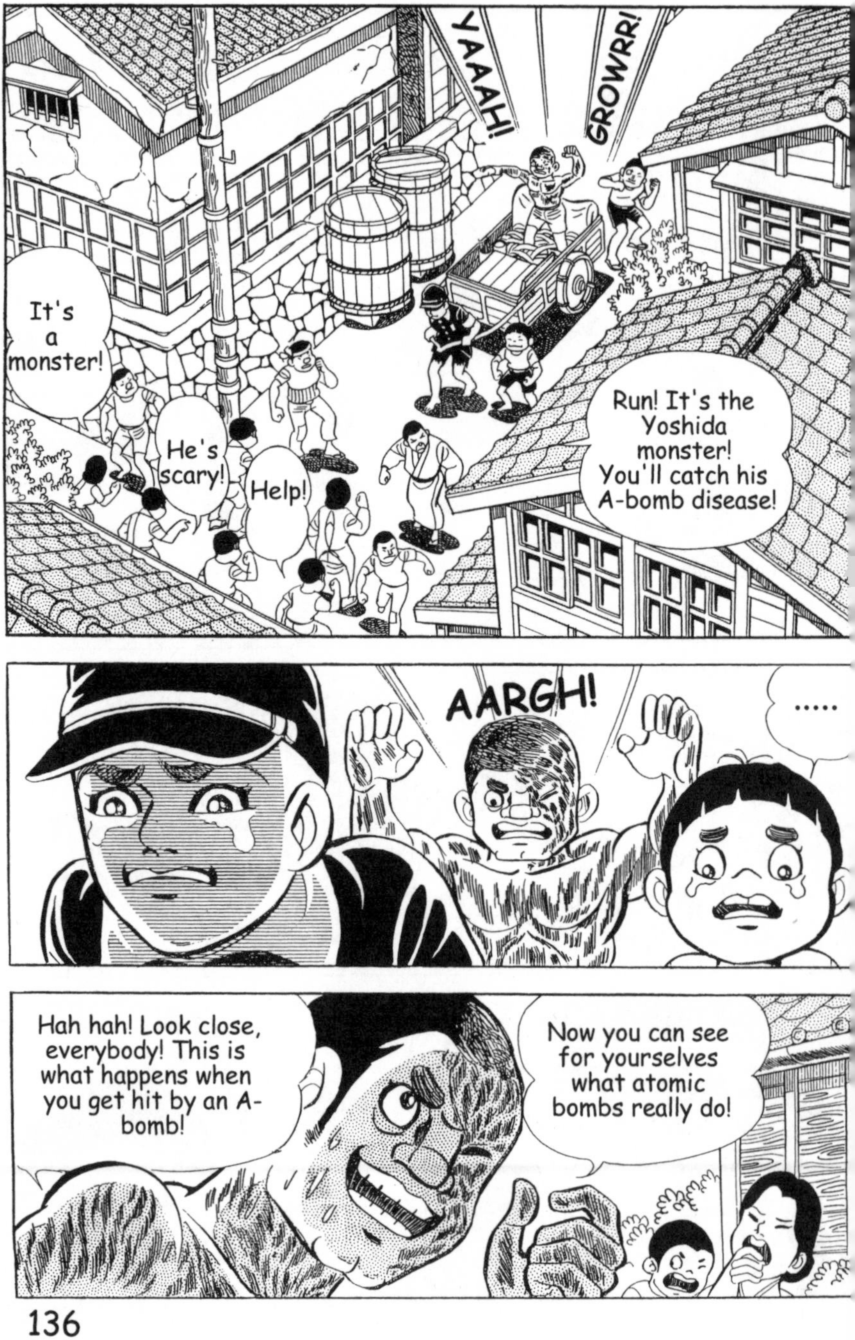
YAAAH!
GROWRR!
It's a monster!
He's scary!
Help!
Run! It's the Yoshida monster! You'll catch his A-bomb disease!
AARGH!
.....
Hah hah! Look close, everybody! This is what happens when you get hit by an A-bomb!
Now you can see for yourselves what atomic bombs really do!

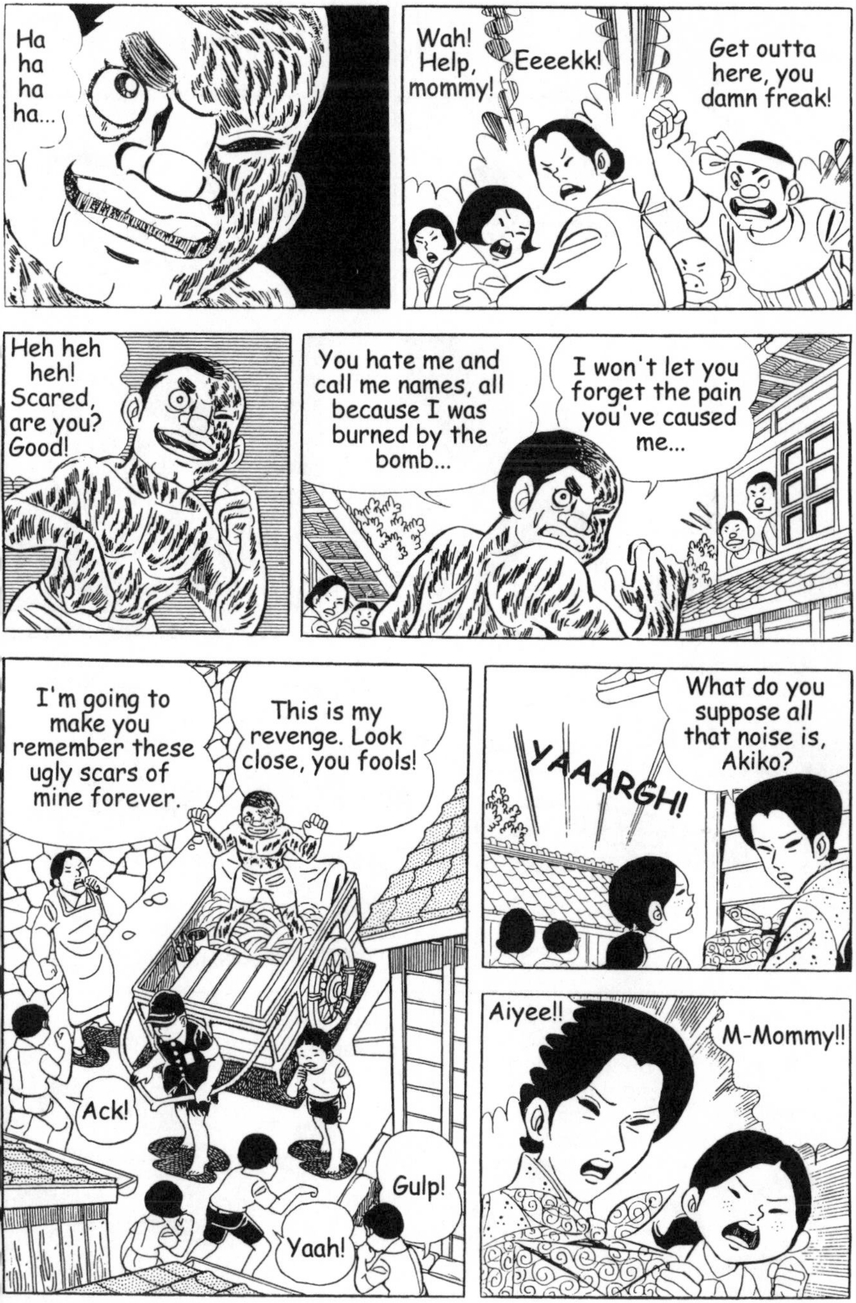
Ha ha ha ha...
Wah! Help, mommy!
Eeeekk!
Get outta here, you damn freak!
Heh heh heh! Scared, are you? Good!
You hate me and call me names, all because I was burned by the bomb...
I won't let you forget the pain you've caused me...
I'm going to make you remember these ugly scars of mine forever.
This is my revenge. Look close, you fools!
Ack!
Gulp!
Yaah!
YAAARGH!
What do you suppose all that noise is, Akiko?
Aiyee!!
M-Mommy!!

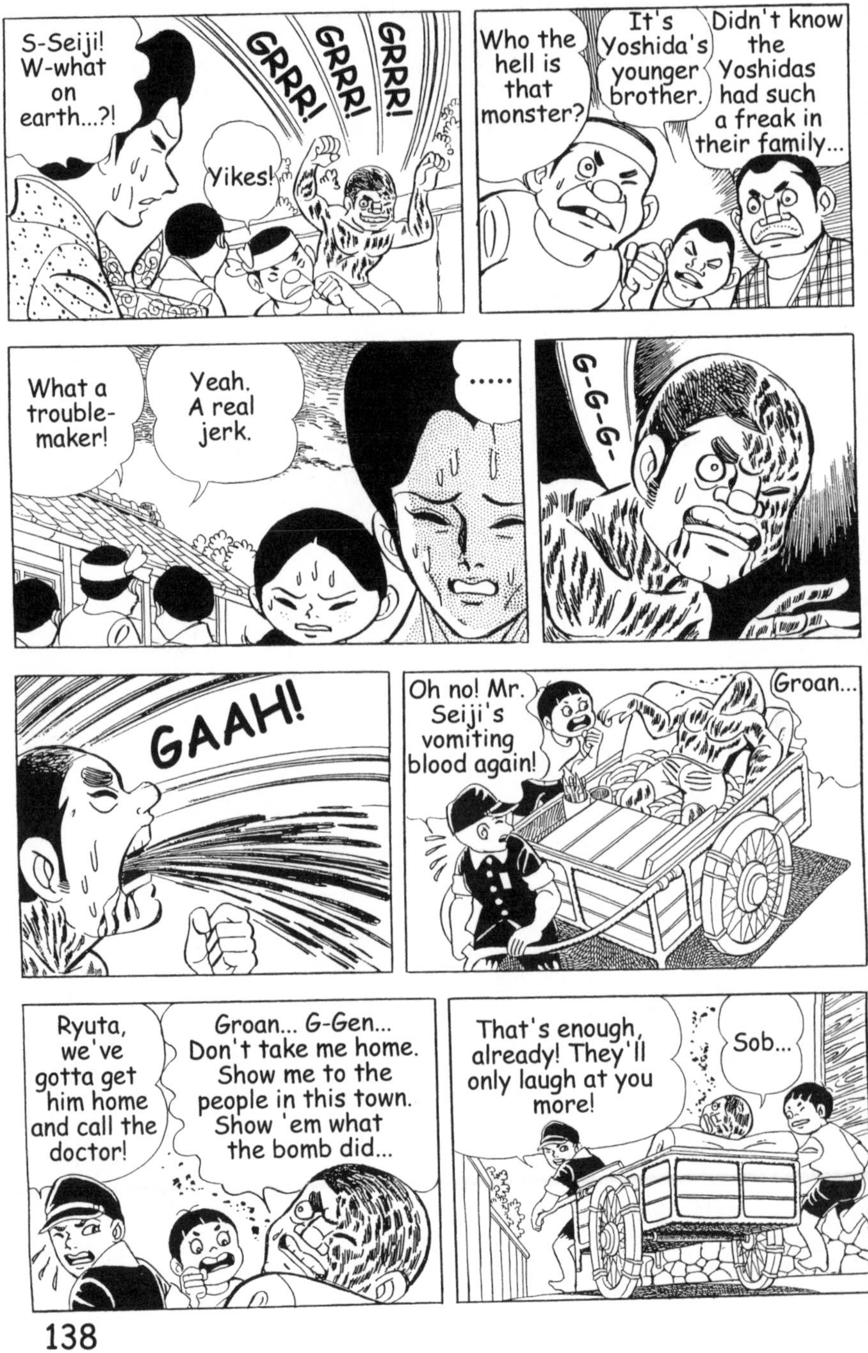
S-Seiji! W-what on earth...?!
GRRR! GRRR! GRRR!
Yikes!
Who the hell is that monster?
It's Yoshida's younger brother.
Didn't know the Yoshidas had such a freak in their family...
What a trouble-maker!
Yeah. A real jerk.
.....
G-G-G-
GAAH!
Oh no! Mr. Seiji's vomiting blood again!
Groan...
Ryuta, we've gotta get him home and call the doctor!
Groan... G-Gen... Don't take me home. Show me to the people in this town. Show 'em what the bomb did...
That's enough, already! They'll only laugh at you more!
Sob...

Pant
pant...

.....

.....

Pant
pant...

.....

Please, Doctor!
Please help
Mr. Seiji!

It's too late.
His internal
organs are a
mess...

D-don't be
stupid! You've
gotta save
him!

I've seen a lot of
victims of the bomb.
The ones that die, their
innards are always
completely ravaged...

W...why?

I don't know. Maybe
the bomb really was
poisonous... It's unlike
anything we've ever seen,
that bomb they dropped
on Hiroshima...

139

I'm sorry, but there's nothing more I can do. Standard medical treatment can't save him.

Y-you damn quack!

You can't die, Mr. Seiji! You've got lots to do yet!

You want to finish this painting, don't you? Open your eyes! Get well!

You haven't taught me how to draw yet, either. Please don't die, Mr. Seiji...

Pant pant...

Pant pant...

Dammit. Isn't there some way to save him...?

.....

I've got it! Ryuta, let Mr. Seiji have some of those bones, okay?

Huh? W-why?!

I've heard you can cure the sick by feeding 'em ground-up bones.

Y-you're joking!

Even if it doesn't work, we have to try.

N-no! This is my papa...

Ryuta, you stingy bastard! We only need a little. Your father would be happy he could help save someone!

I-I guess. But only a little bit.

Only a little, promise?

Right, right. Hurry, let's grind it up quick.

We've gotta help Seiji. We can't let him die like this...

Huh?

141

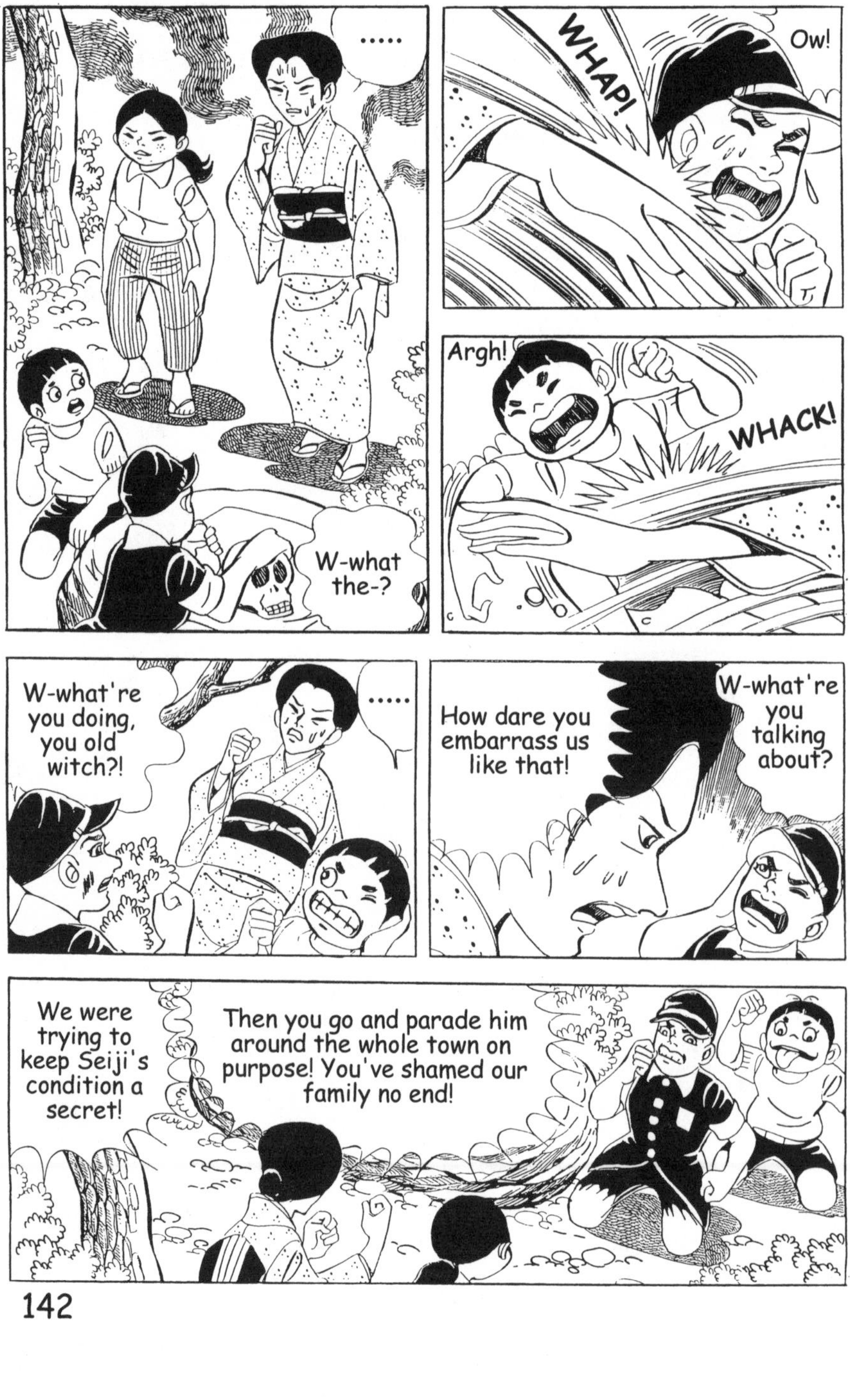
.....
W-what the-?
WHAP!
Ow!
Argh!
WHACK!
W-what're you doing, you old witch?!
.....
How dare you embarrass us like that!
W-what're you talking about?
We were trying to keep Seiji's condition a secret!
Then you go and parade him around the whole town on purpose! You've shamed our family no end!

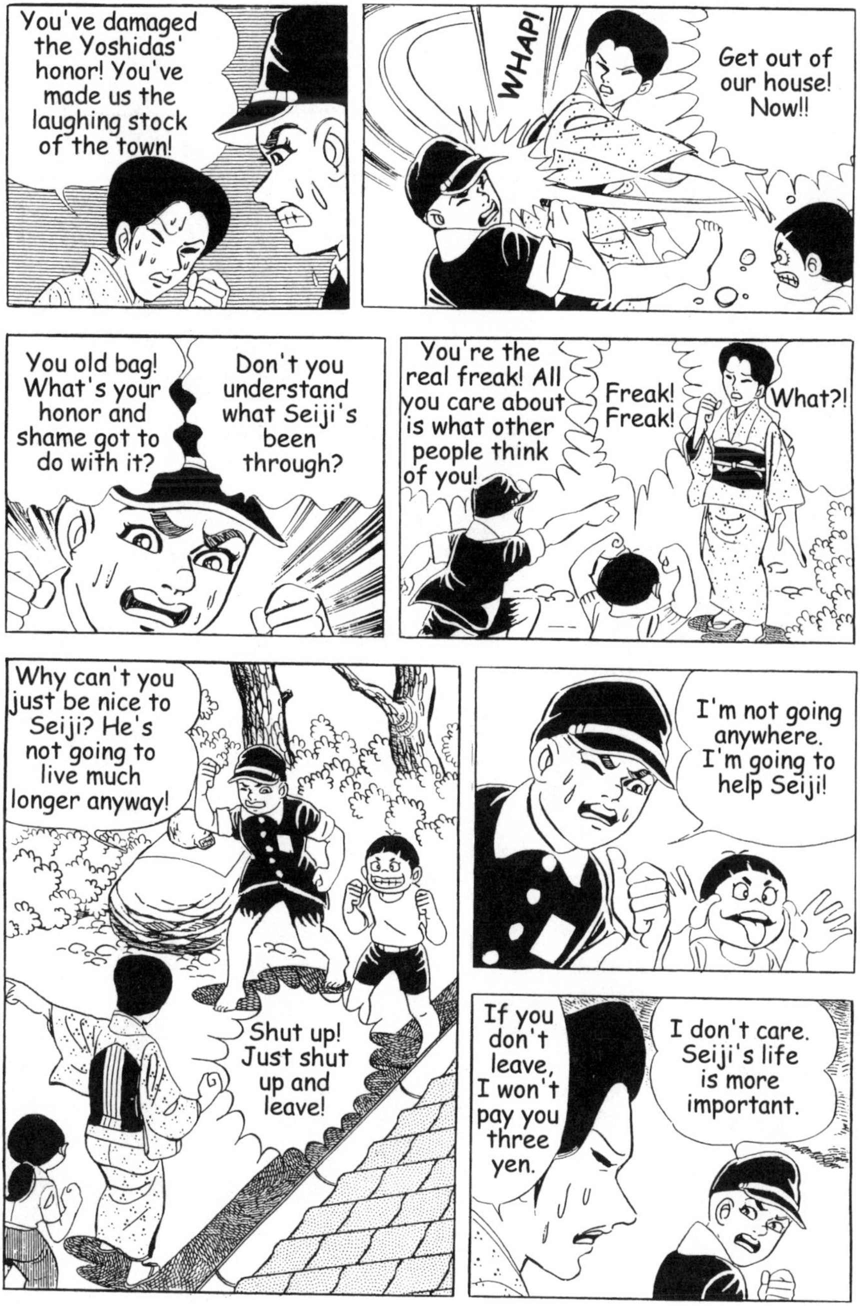
You've damaged the Yoshidas' honor! You've made us the laughing stock of the town!
WHAP!
Get out of our house! Now!!
You old bag! What's your honor and shame got to do with it?
Don't you understand what Seiji's been through?
You're the real freak! All you care about is what other people think of you!
Freak! Freak!
What?!
Why can't you just be nice to Seiji? He's not going to live much longer anyway!
Shut up! Just shut up and leave!
I'm not going anywhere. I'm going to help Seiji!
If you don't leave, I won't pay you three yen.
I don't care. Seiji's life is more important.

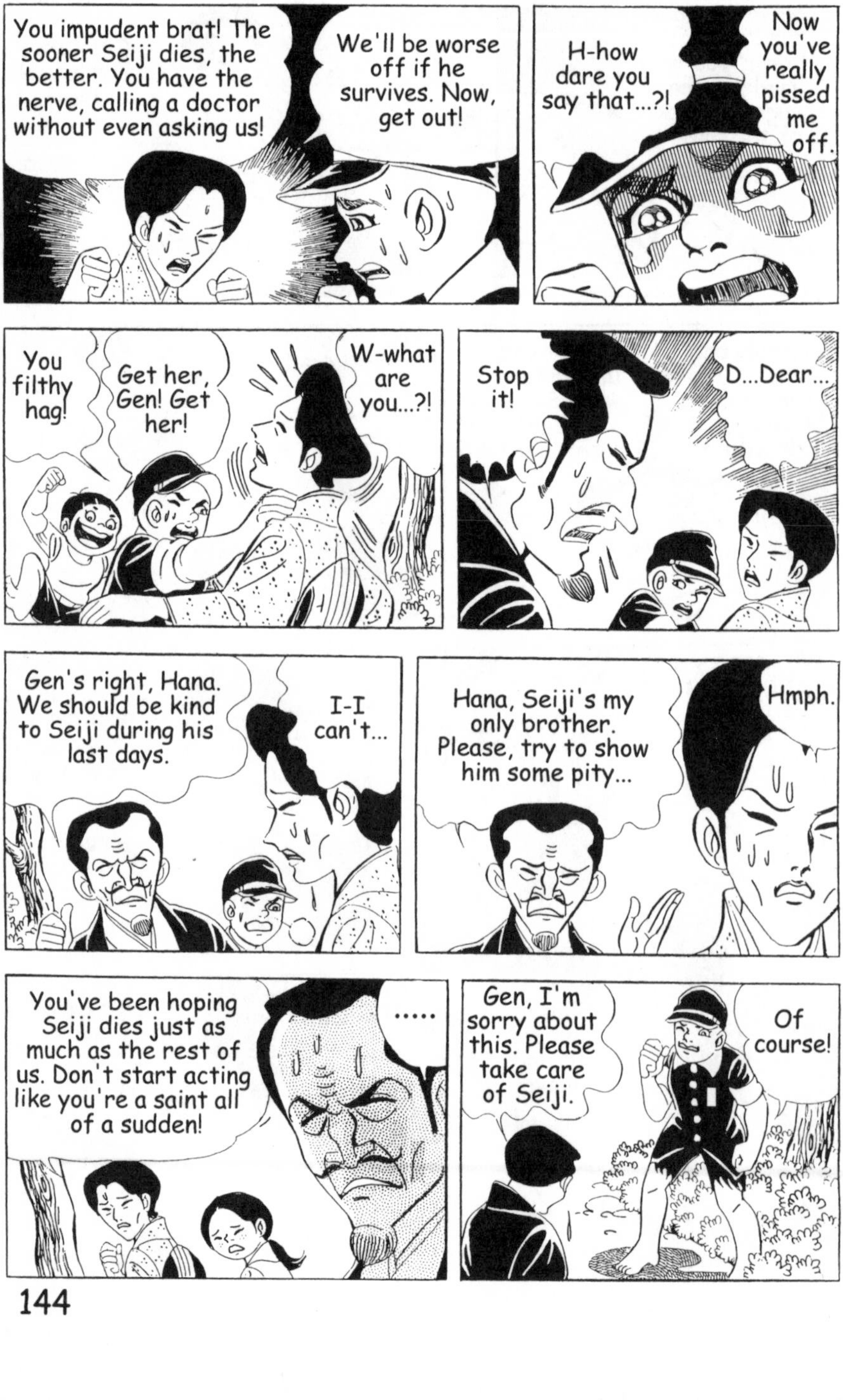
You impudent brat! The sooner Seiji dies, the better. You have the nerve, calling a doctor without even asking us!
We'll be worse off if he survives. Now, get out!
H-how dare you say that...?!
Now you've really pissed me off.
You filthy hag!
Get her, Gen! Get her!
W-what are you...?!
Stop it!
D...Dear...
Gen's right, Hana. We should be kind to Seiji during his last days.
I-I can't...
Hana, Seiji's my only brother. Please, try to show him some pity...
Hmph.
You've been hoping Seiji dies just as much as the rest of us. Don't start acting like you're a saint all of a sudden!
.....
Gen, I'm sorry about this. Please take care of Seiji.
Of course!

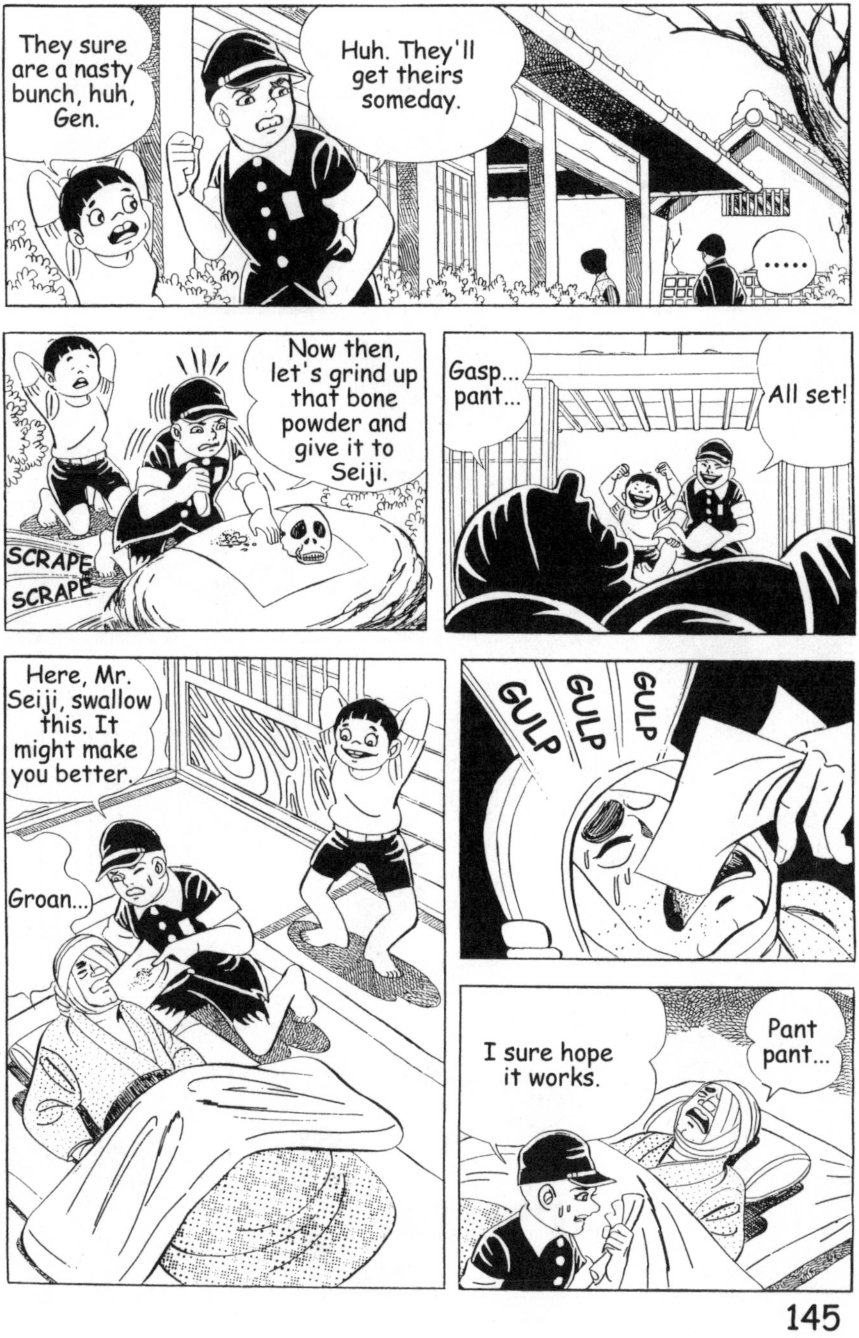
They sure are a nasty bunch, huh, Gen.
Huh. They'll get theirs someday.
.....
Now then, let's grind up that bone powder and give it to Seiji.
SCRAPE
SCRAPE
Gasp... pant...
All set!
Here, Mr. Seiji, swallow this. It might make you better.
Groan...
GULP
GULP
GULP
I sure hope it works.
Pant pant...

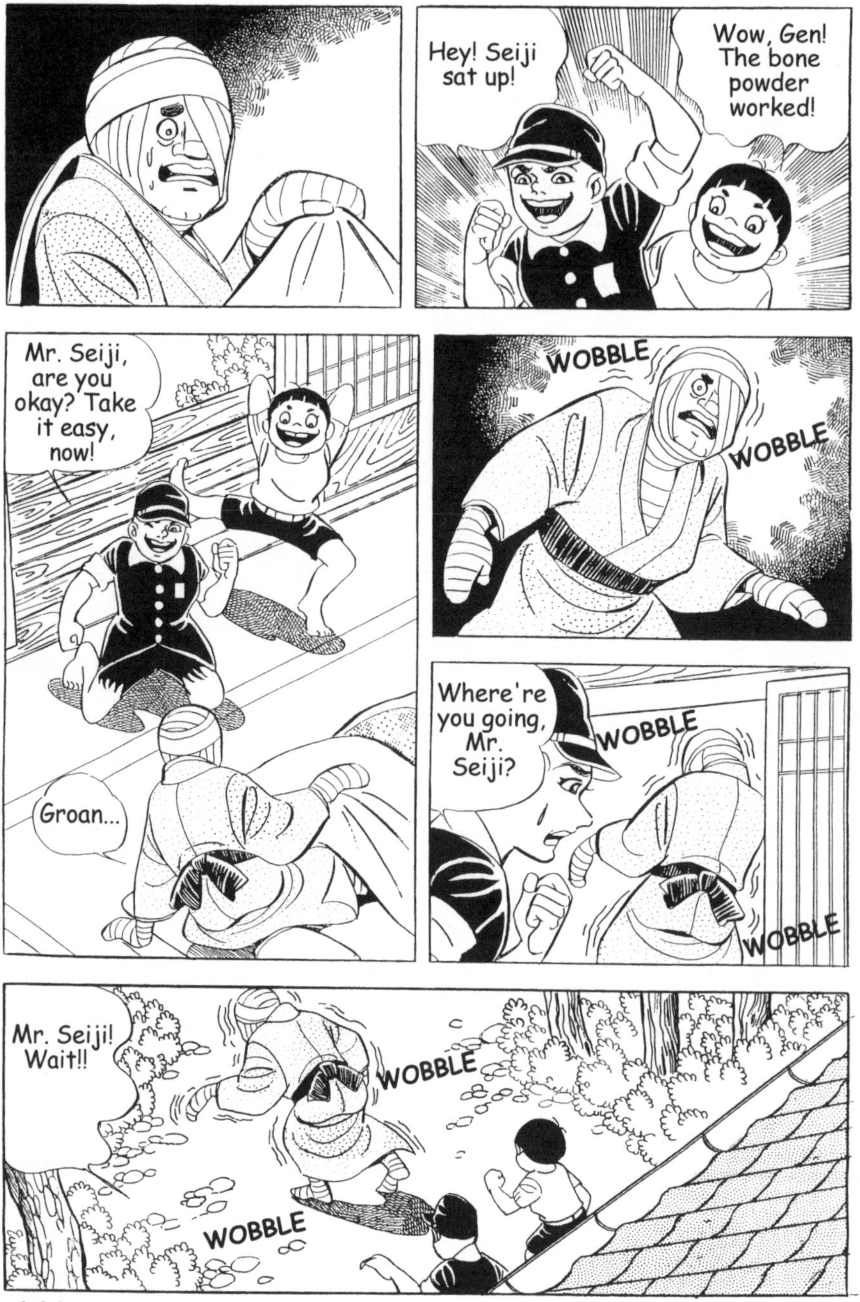
Hey! Seiji sat up!
Wow, Gen! The bone powder worked!
Mr. Seiji, are you okay? Take it easy, now!
Groan...
WOBBLE
WOBBLE
Where're you going, Mr. Seiji?
WOBBLE
WOBBLE
Mr. Seiji! Wait!!
WOBBLE
WOBBLE

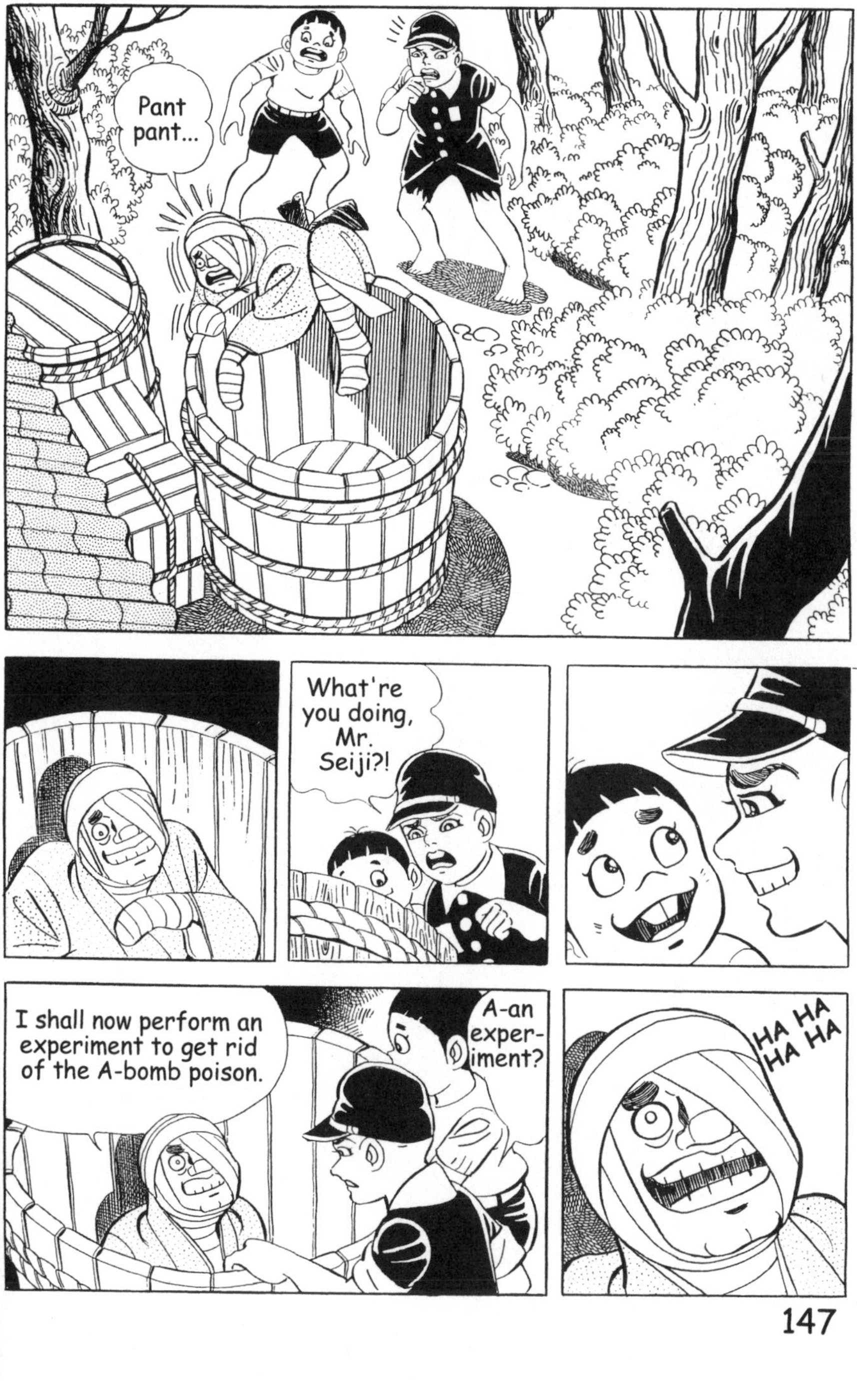
Pant
pant...
What're you doing, Mr. Seiji?!
I shall now perform an experiment to get rid of the A-bomb poison.
A-an experiment?
HA HA HA HA

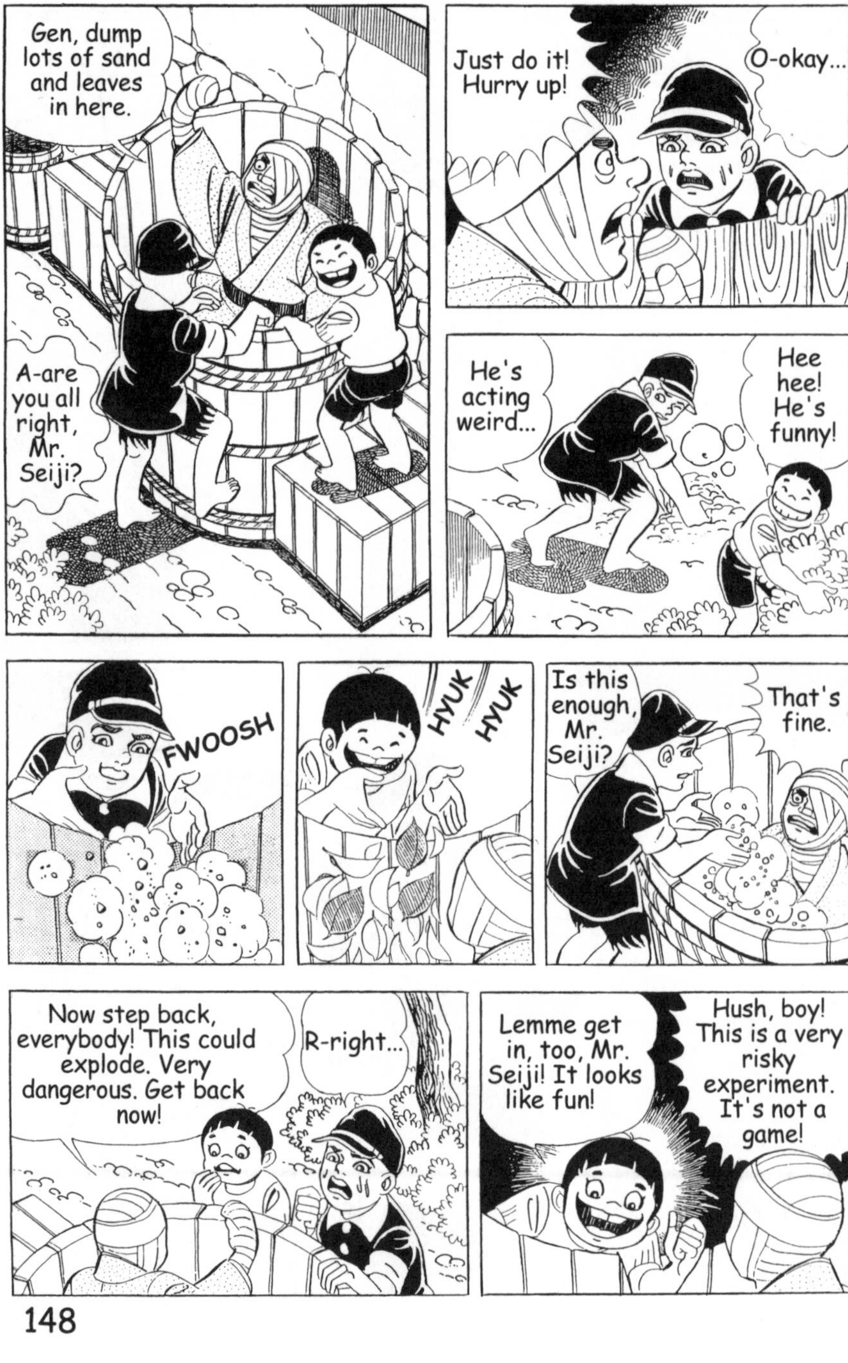
Gen, dump lots of sand and leaves in here.
A-are you all right, Mr. Seiji?
Just do it! Hurry up!
O-okay...
He's acting weird...
Hee hee! He's funny!
FWOOSH
HYUK HYUK
Is this enough, Mr. Seiji?
That's fine.
Now step back, everybody! This could explode. Very dangerous. Get back now!
R-right...
Lemme get in, too, Mr. Seiji! It looks like fun!
Hush, boy! This is a very risky experiment. It's not a game!

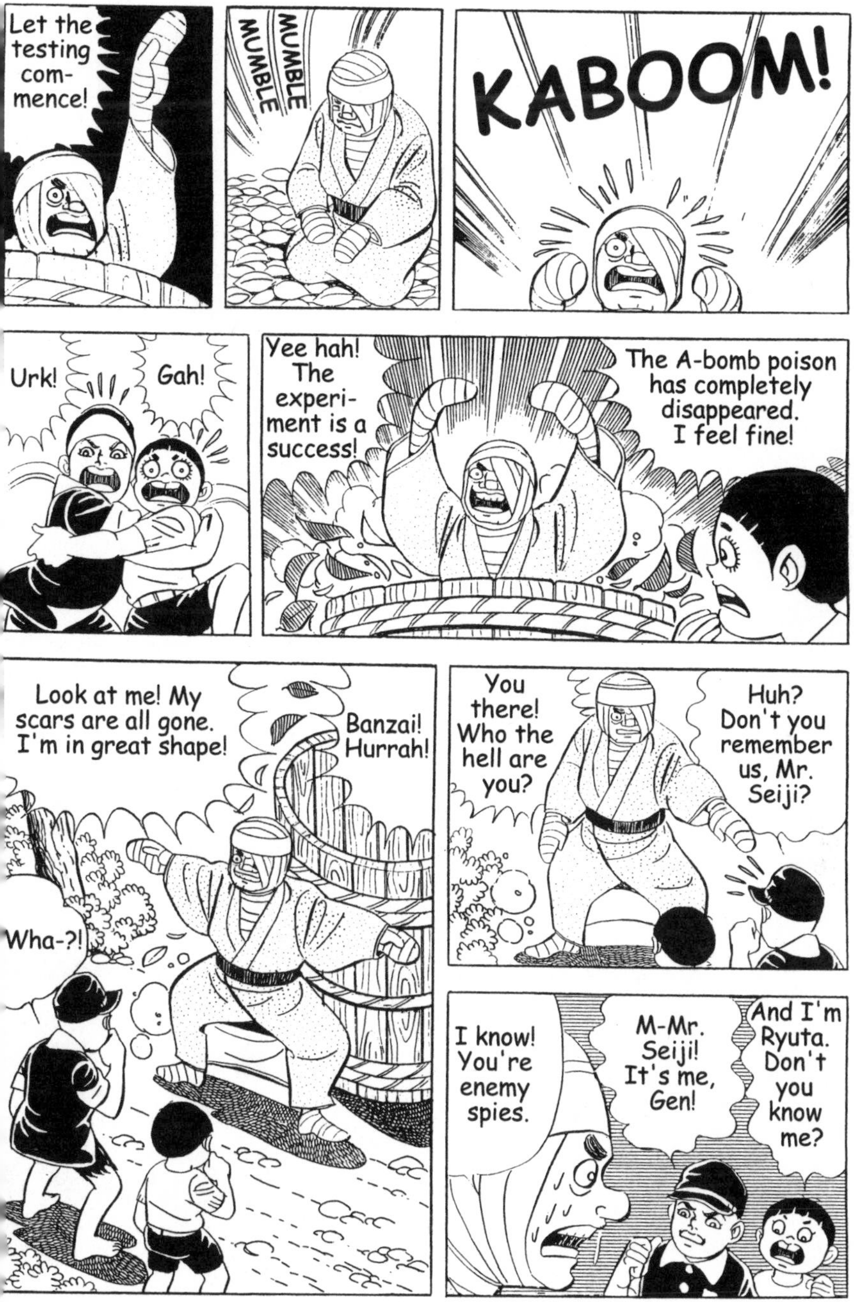

Let the testing com- mence!
MUMBLE MUMBLE
KABOOM!
Urk!
Gah!
Yee hah! The experi- ment is a success!
The A-bomb poison has completely disappeared. I feel fine!
Look at me! My scars are all gone. I'm in great shape!
Banzai! Hurrah!
Wha-?!
You there! Who the hell are you?
Huh? Don't you remember us, Mr. Seiji?
I know! You're enemy spies.
M-Mr. Seiji! It's me, Gen!
And I'm Ryuta. Don't you know me?

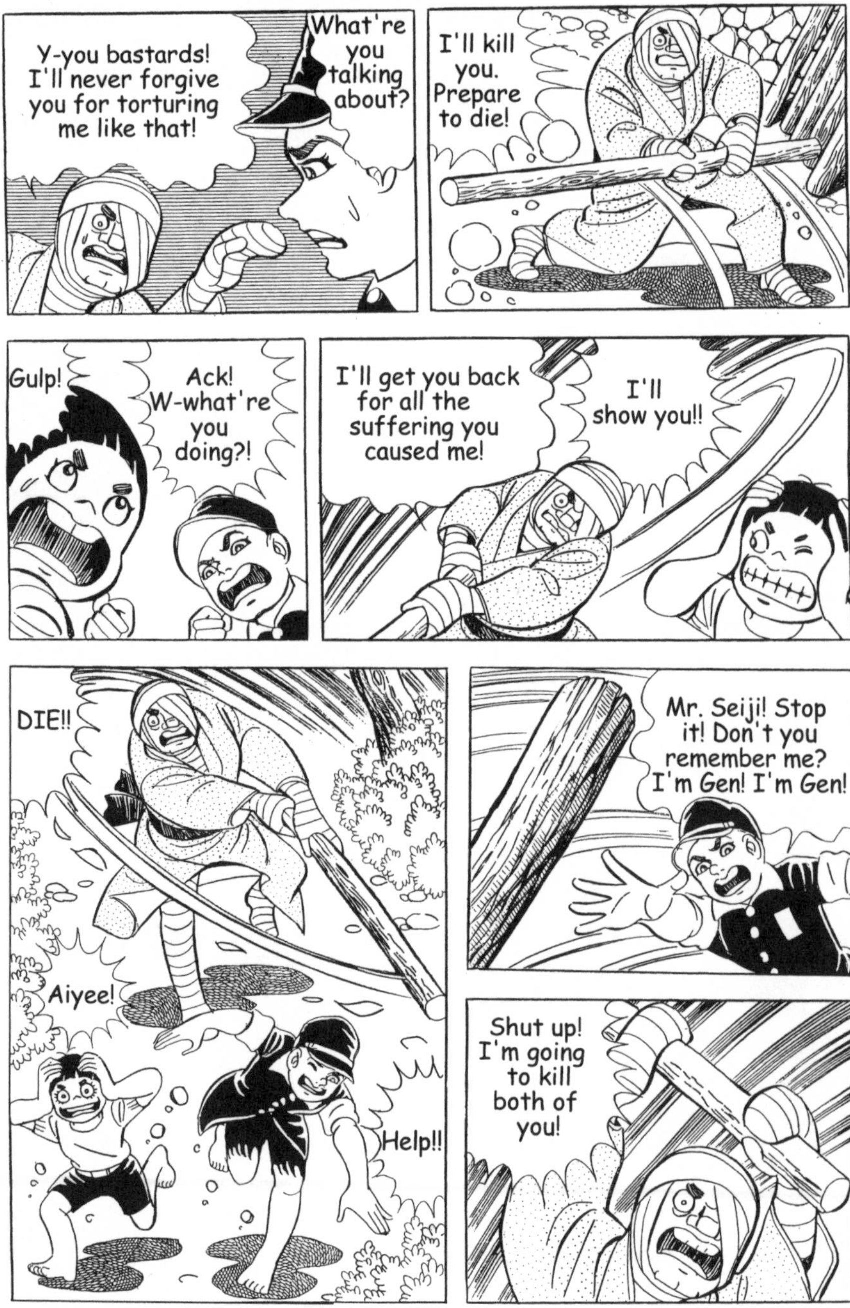
Y-you bastards! I'll never forgive you for torturing me like that!
What're you talking about?
I'll kill you. Prepare to die!
Gulp!
Ack! W-what're you doing?!
I'll get you back for all the suffering you caused me!
I'll show you!!
DIE!!
Aiyee!
Help!!
Mr. Seiji! Stop it! Don't you remember me? I'm Gen! I'm Gen!
Shut up! I'm going to kill both of you!

Come back here, you spies!

Gaaah!

Run, Ryuta!

He's crazy!

Seiji's gone insane!

TROT

TROT

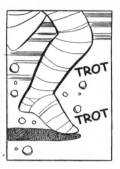

Wait!

Urk!

Die!!

YOW!

WHUMP

Gen! Help!!

Ryuta! Climb up here!

YARRGH!

151

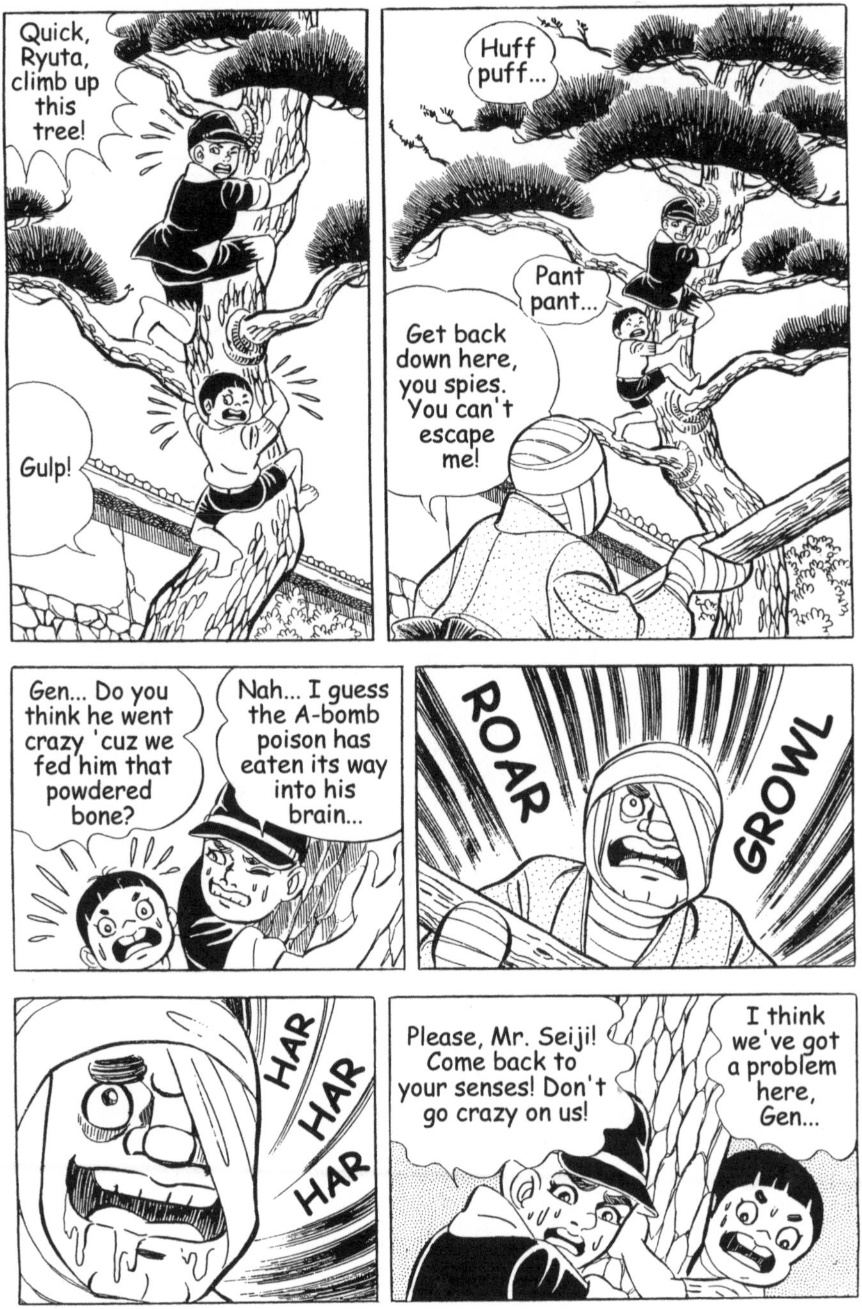
Quick, Ryuta, climb up this tree!
Gulp!
Huff puff...
Pant pant...
Get back down here, you spies. You can't escape me!
Gen... Do you think he went crazy 'cuz we fed him that powdered bone?
Nah... I guess the A-bomb poison has eaten its way into his brain...
ROAR
GROWL
HAR
HAR
HAR
Please, Mr. Seiji! Come back to your senses! Don't go crazy on us!
I think we've got a problem here, Gen...

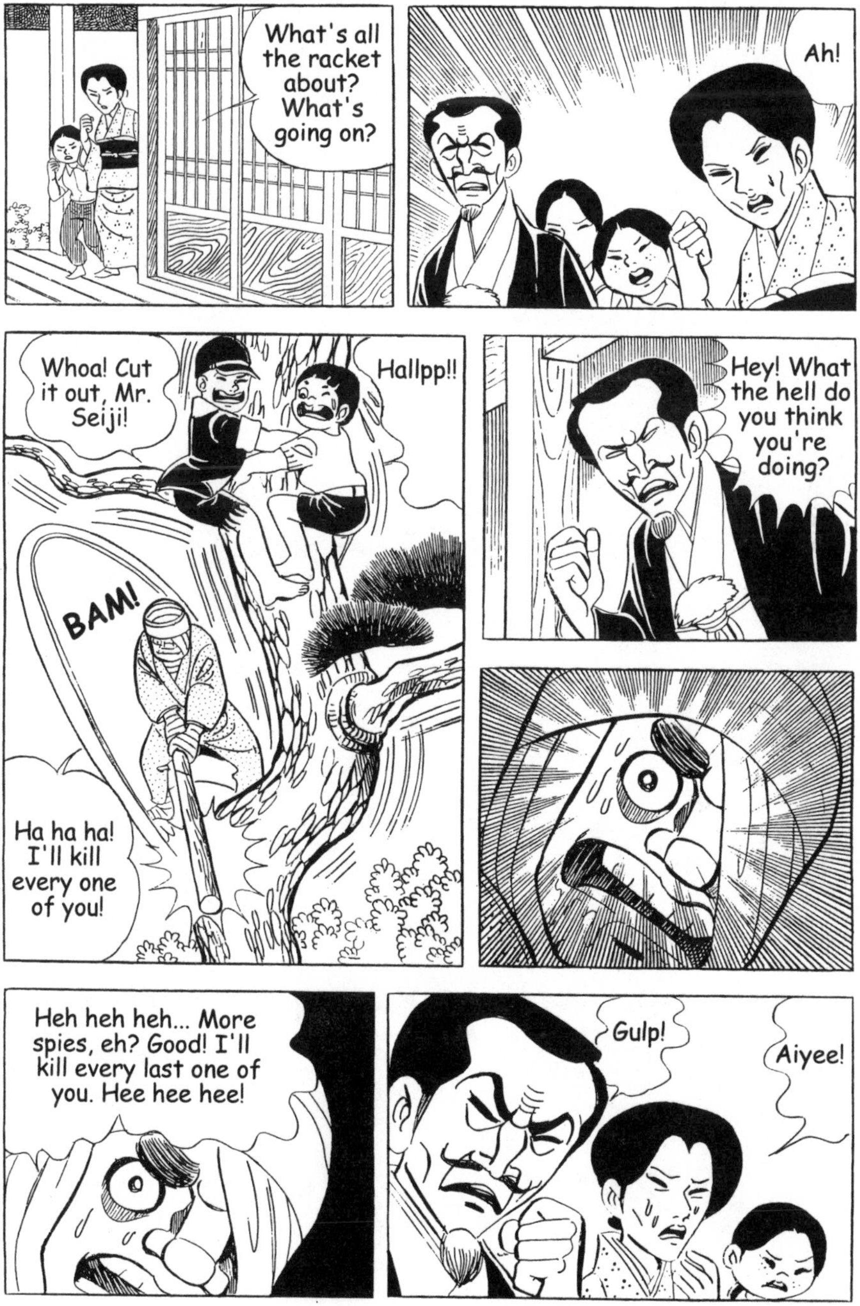

What's all the racket about? What's going on?
Ah!
Whoa! Cut it out, Mr. Seiji!
Hallpp!!
BAM!
Ha ha ha! I'll kill every one of you!
Hey! What the hell do you think you're doing?
Heh heh heh... More spies, eh? Good! I'll kill every last one of you. Hee hee hee!
Gulp!
Aiyee!

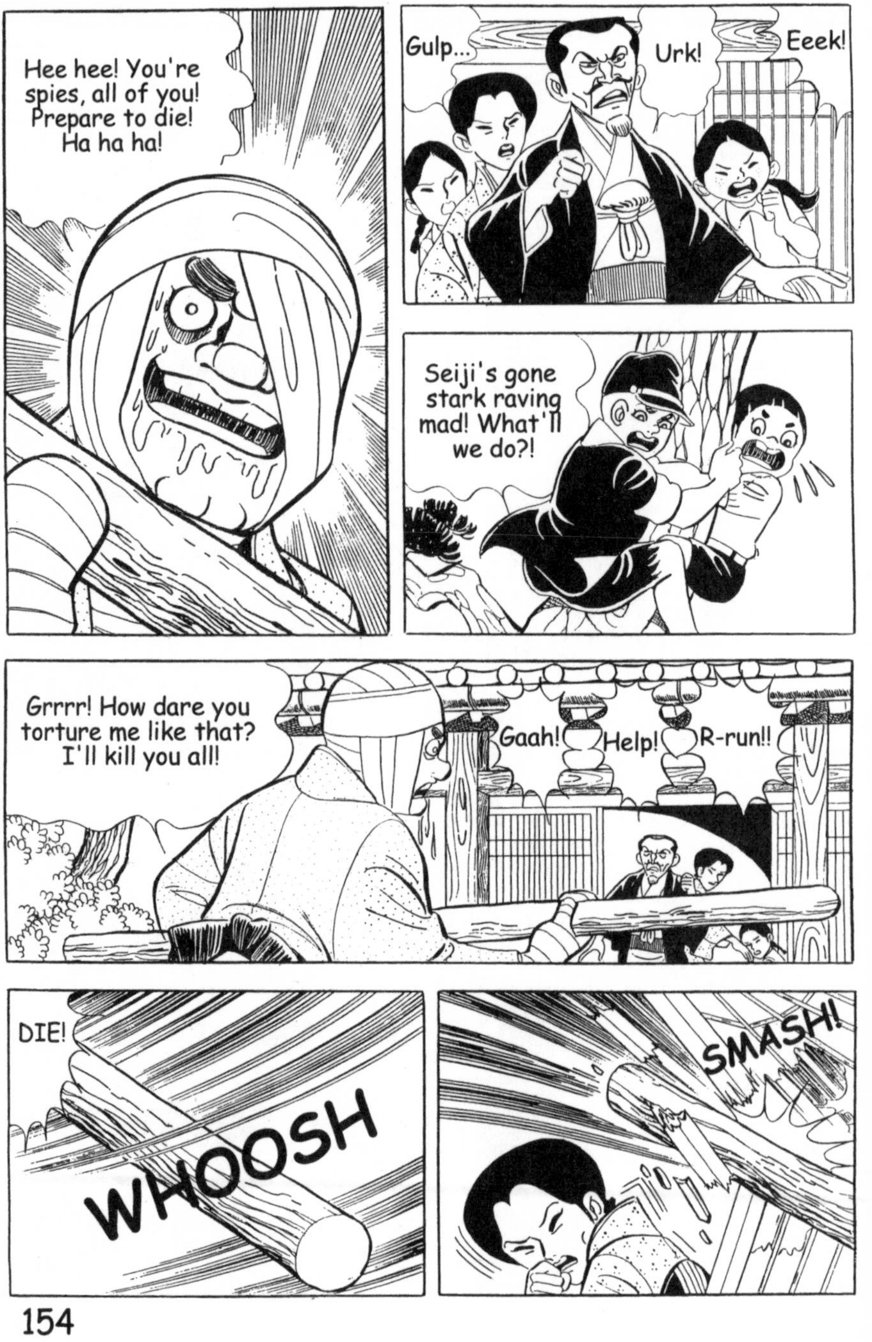
Hee hee! You're spies, all of you! Prepare to die! Ha ha ha!
Gulp...
Urk!
Eeek!
Seiji's gone stark raving mad! What'll we do?!
Grrrr! How dare you torture me like that? I'll kill you all!
Gaah!
Help!
R-run!!
DIE!
WHOOSH
SMASH!

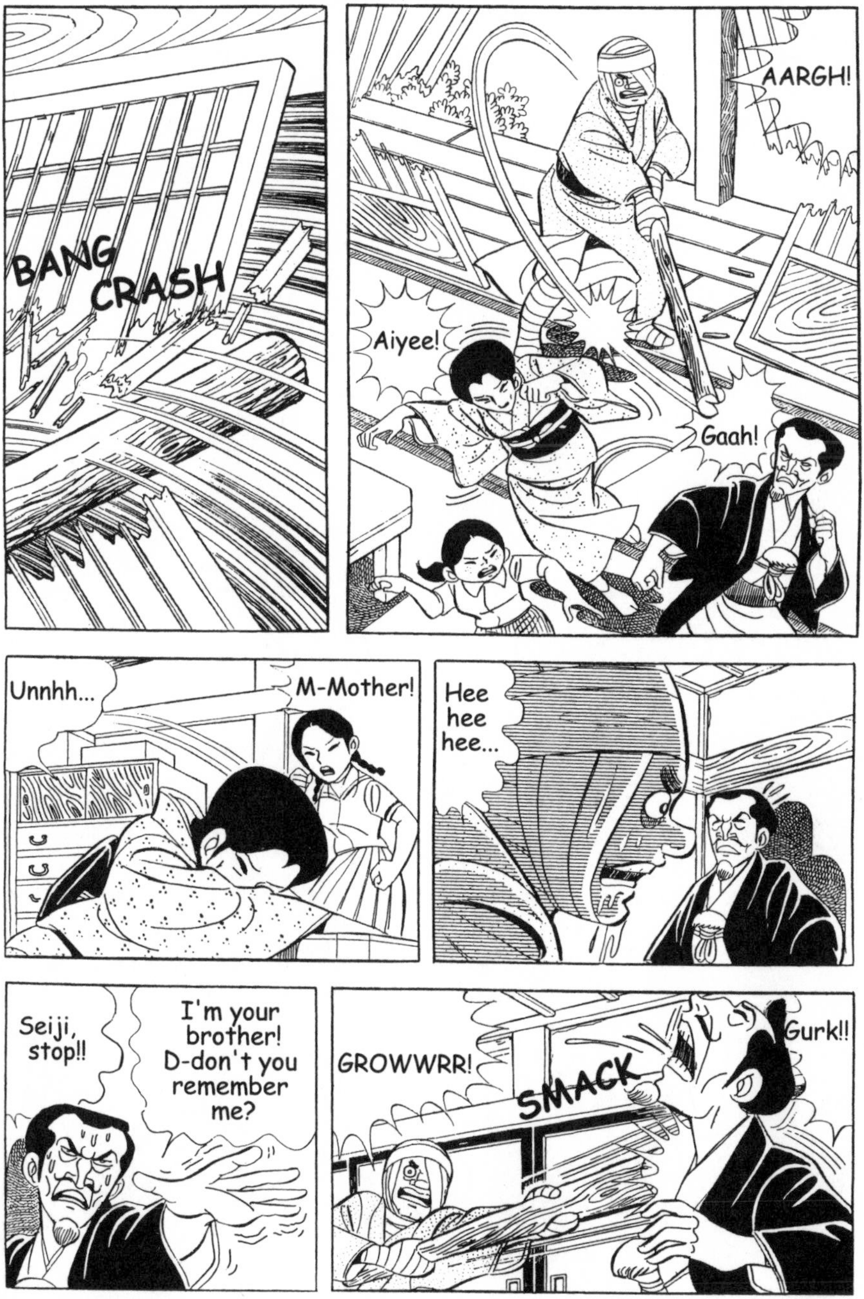
BANG
CRASH
AARGH!
Aiyee!
Gaah!
Unnhh...
M-Mother!
Hee hee hee...
Seiji, stop!!
I'm your brother! D-don't you remember me?
GROWWRR!
SMACK
Gurk!!

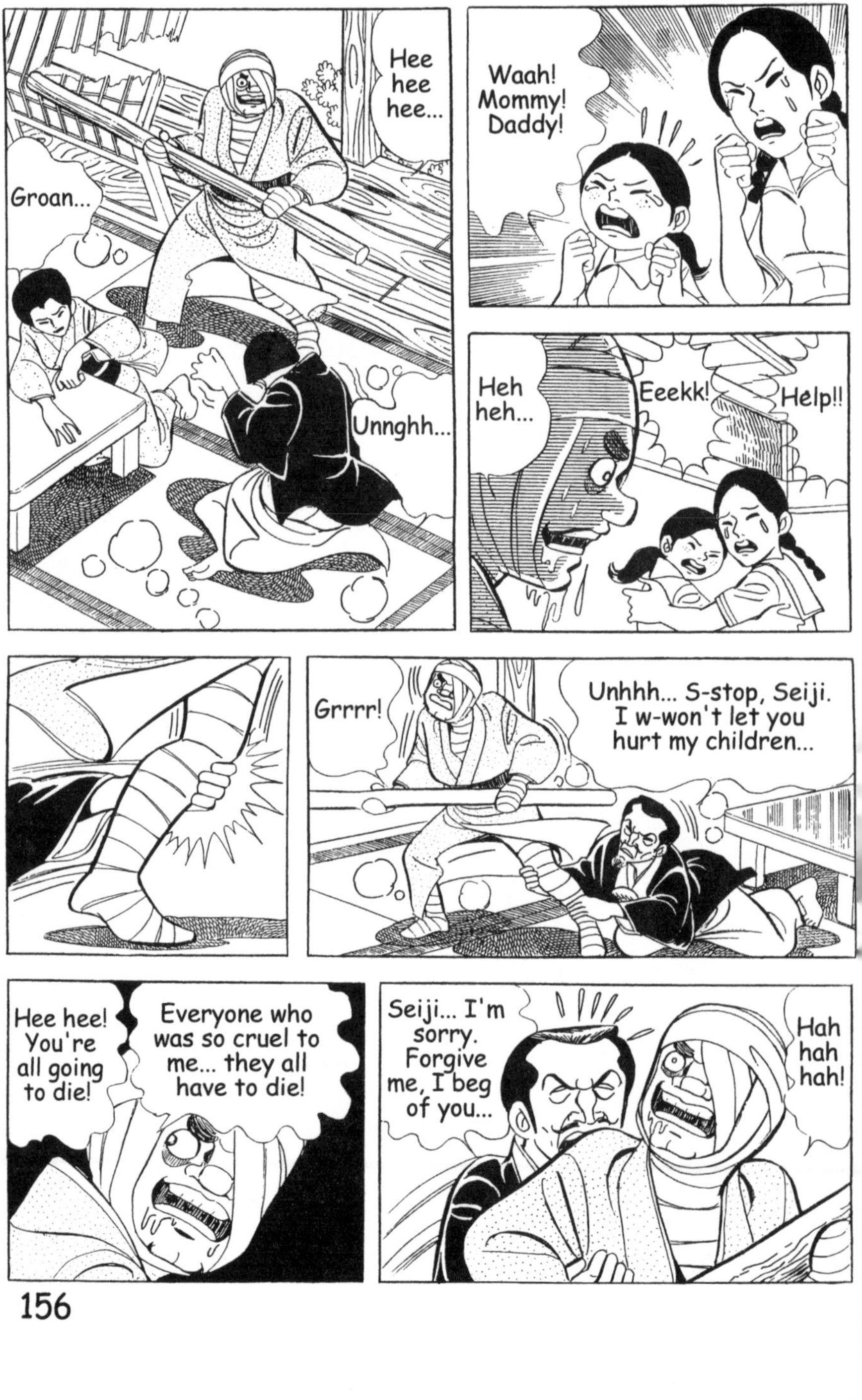
Hee hee hee...
Groan...
Unnghh...
Waah! Mommy! Daddy!
Heh heh...
Eeekk!
Help!!
Grrrr!
Unhhh... S-stop, Seiji. I w-won't let you hurt my children...
Hee hee! You're all going to die!
Everyone who was so cruel to me... they all have to die!
Seiji... I'm sorry. Forgive me, I beg of you...
Hah hah hah!

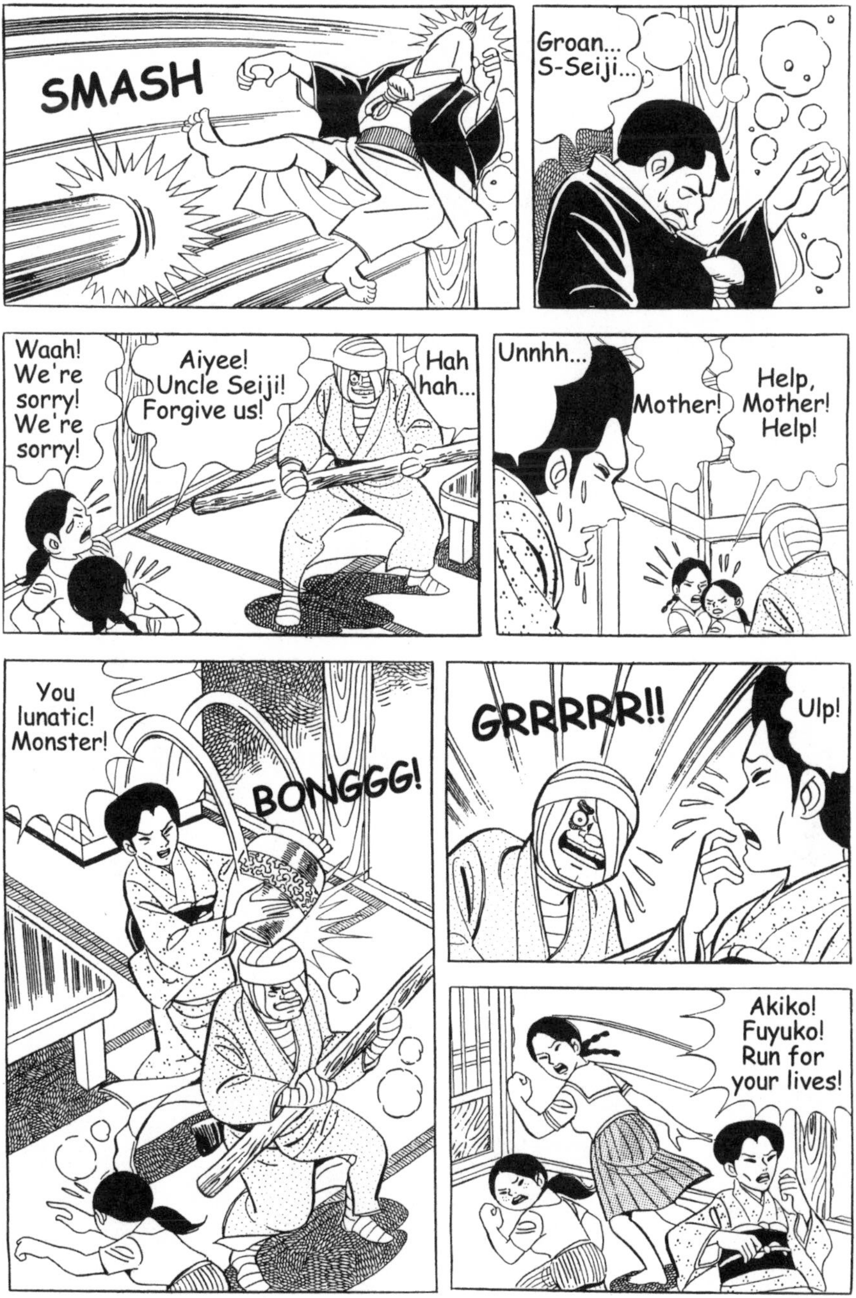
SMASH
Groan... S-Seiji...
Waah! We're sorry! We're sorry!
Aiyee! Uncle Seiji! Forgive us!
Hah hah...
Unnhh...
Mother!
Help, Mother! Help!
You lunatic! Monster!
BONGGG!
GRRRRR!!
Ulp!
Akiko! Fuyuko! Run for your lives!

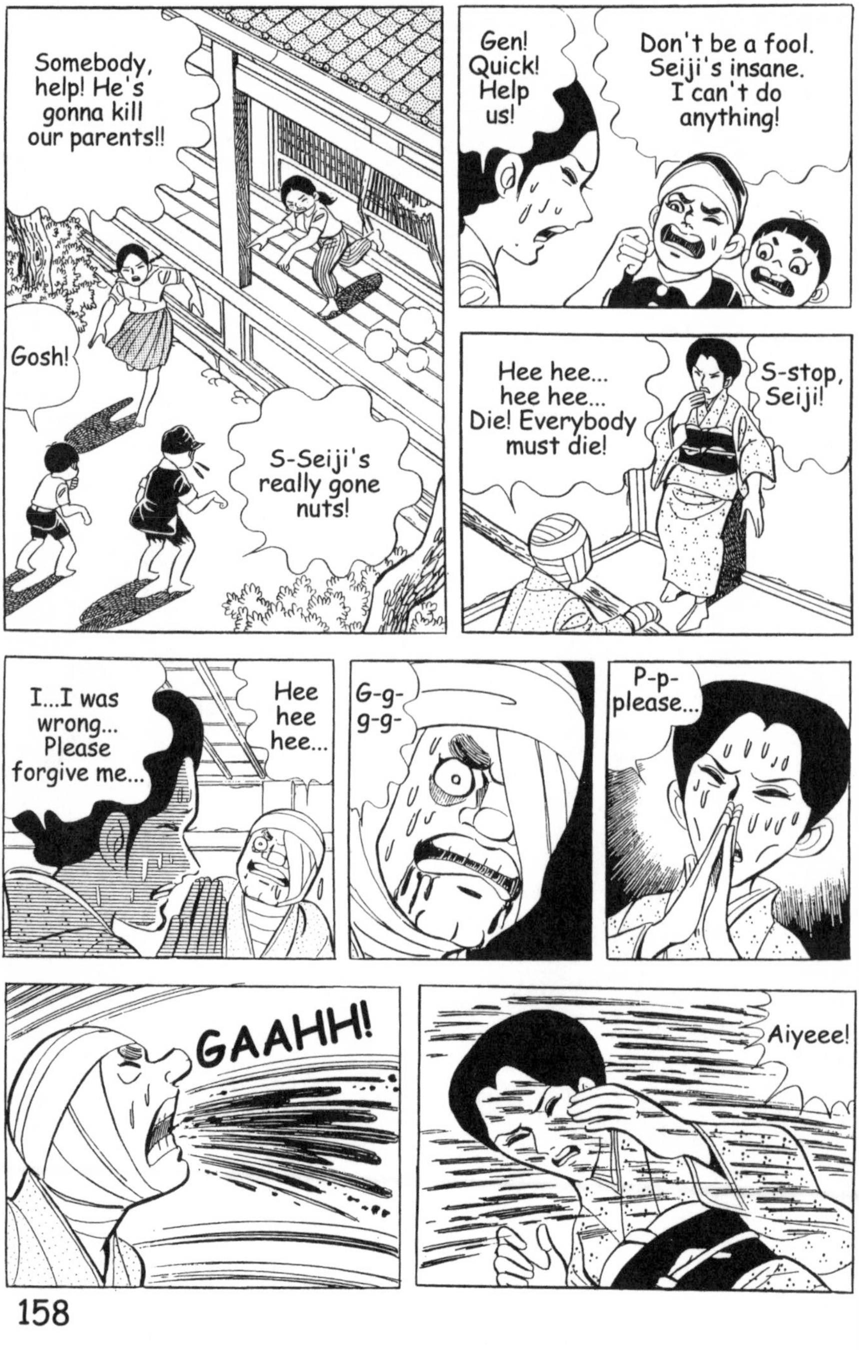
Somebody, help! He's gonna kill our parents!!
Gosh!
S-Seiji's really gone nuts!
Gen! Quick! Help us!
Don't be a fool. Seiji's insane. I can't do anything!
Hee hee... hee hee... Die! Everybody must die!
S-stop, Seiji!
I...I was wrong... Please forgive me...
Hee hee hee...
G-g-g-g-
P-p-please...
GAAHH!
Aiyeee!

GURGLE
Aagh! H-help me... I'll catch his disease...!
WOBBLE
WOBBLE
CRASH
Oh no! Mr. Seiji!
Gulp...
Mr. Seiji! Mr. Seiji!
A-are you okay, Mr. Seiji?
Weird! He's not moving at all!

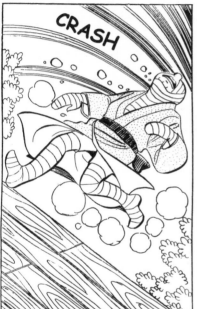

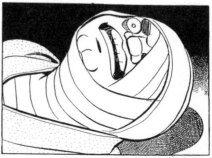

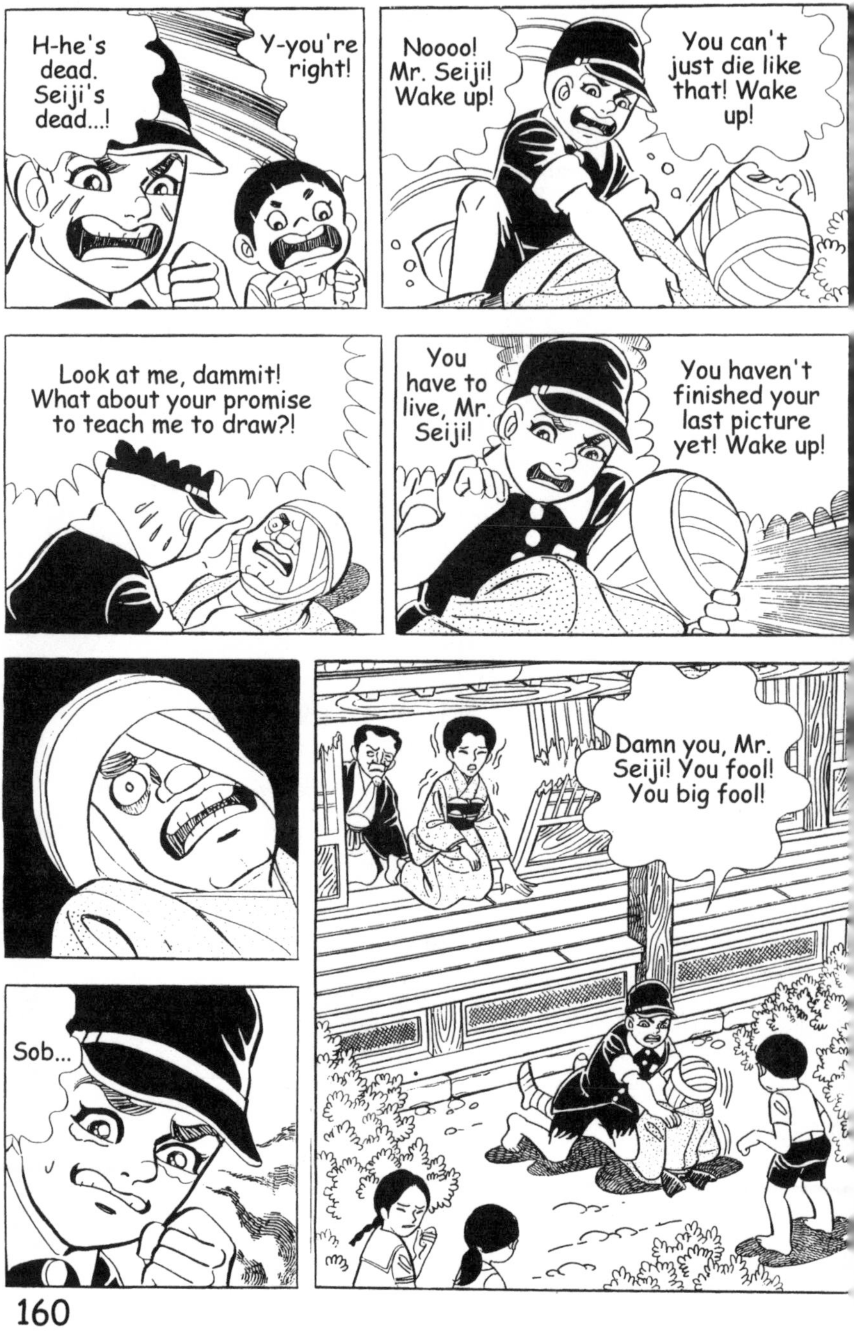
H-he's dead. Seiji's dead...!
Y-you're right!
Noooo! Mr. Seiji! Wake up!
You can't just die like that! Wake up!
Look at me, dammit! What about your promise to teach me to draw?!
You have to live, Mr. Seiji!
You haven't finished your last picture yet! Wake up!
Sob...
Damn you, Mr. Seiji! You fool! You big fool!

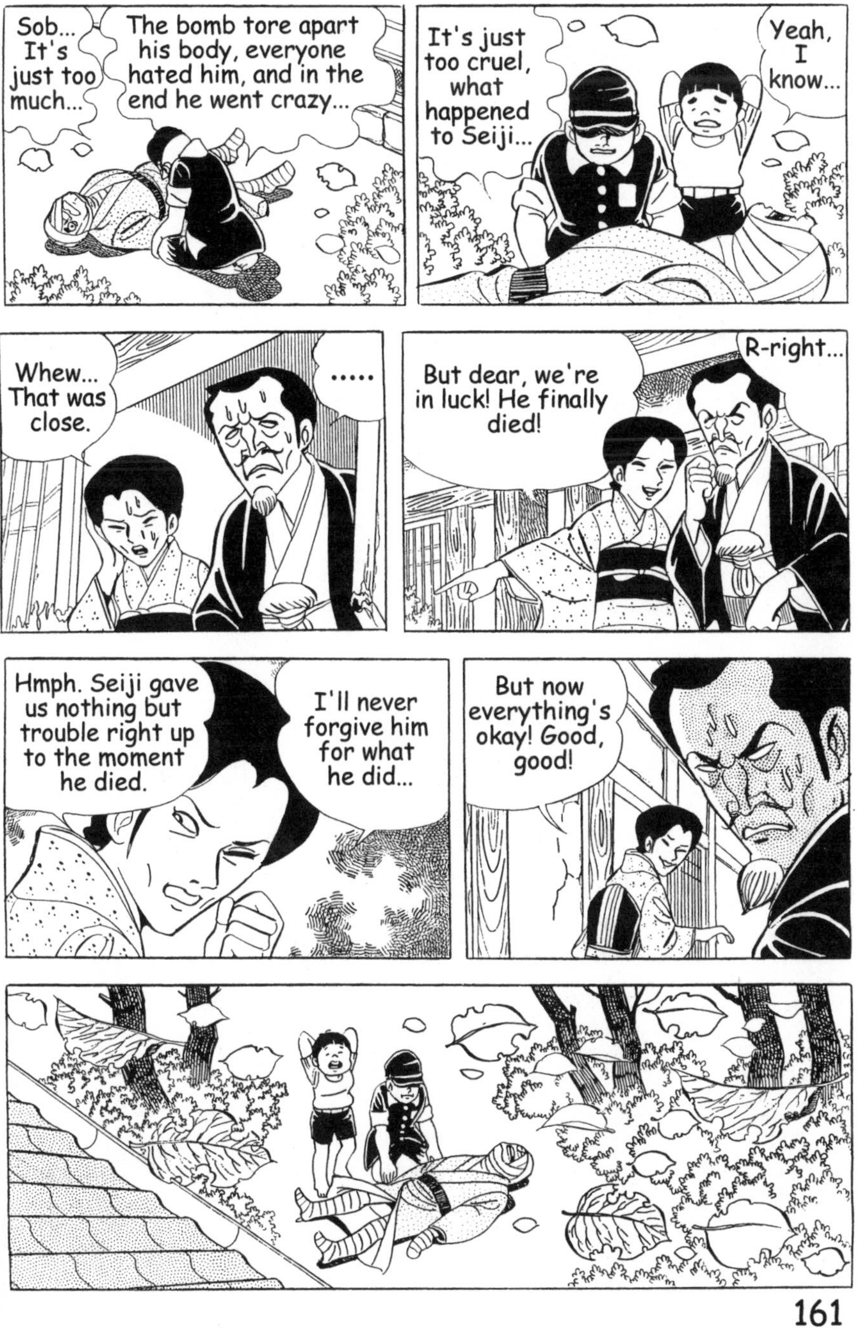
Sob... It's just too much...
The bomb tore apart his body, everyone hated him, and in the end he went crazy...
It's just too cruel, what happened to Seiji...
Yeah, I know...
Whew... That was close.
.....
But dear, we're in luck! He finally died!
R-right...
Hmph. Seiji gave us nothing but trouble right up to the moment he died.
I'll never forgive him for what he did...
But now everything's okay! Good, good!

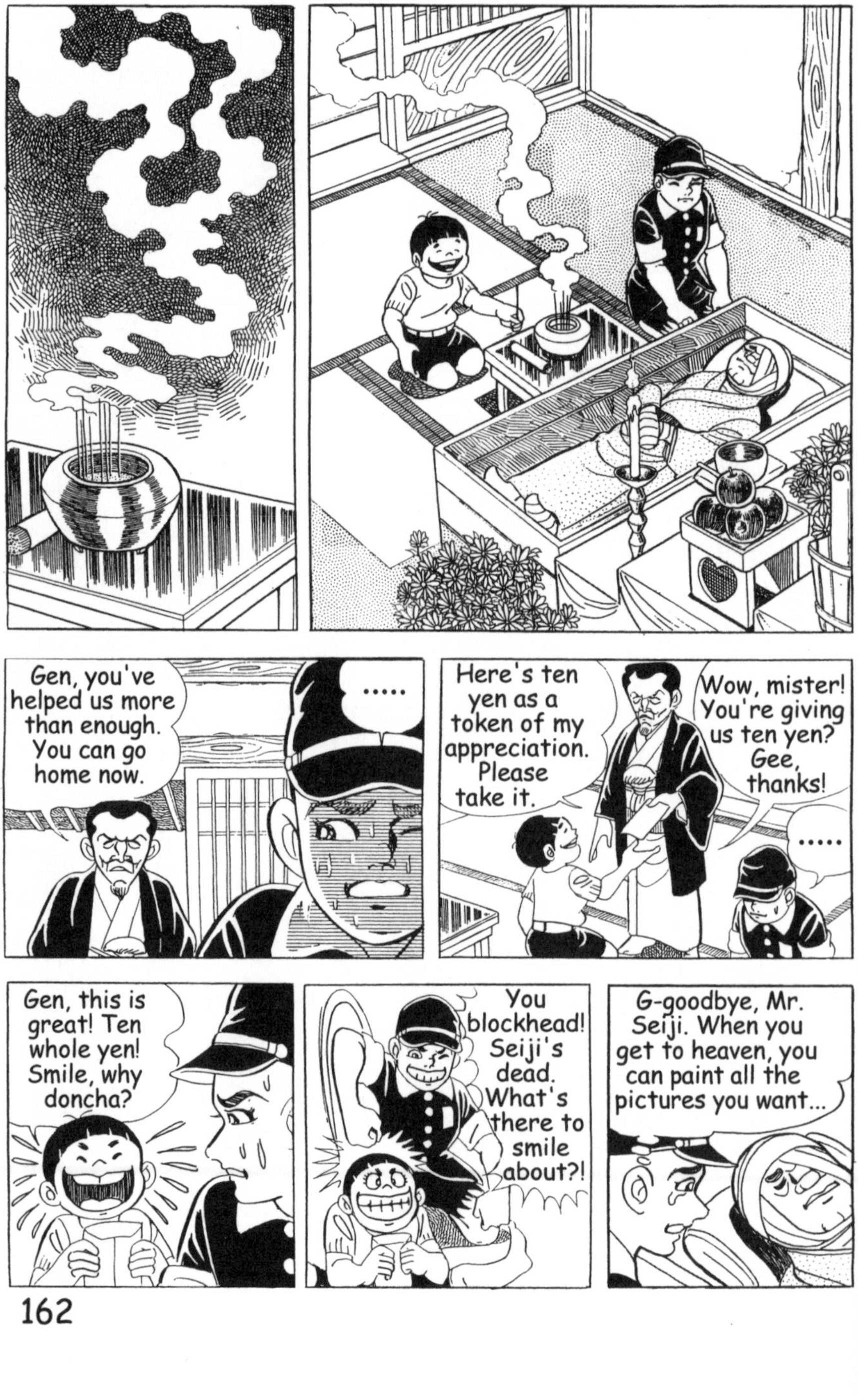

Gen, you've helped us more than enough. You can go home now.
.....
Here's ten yen as a token of my appreciation. Please take it.
Wow, mister! You're giving us ten yen? Gee, thanks!
.....
Gen, this is great! Ten whole yen! Smile, why doncha?
You blockhead! Seiji's dead. What's there to smile about?!
G-goodbye, Mr. Seiji. When you get to heaven, you can paint all the pictures you want...

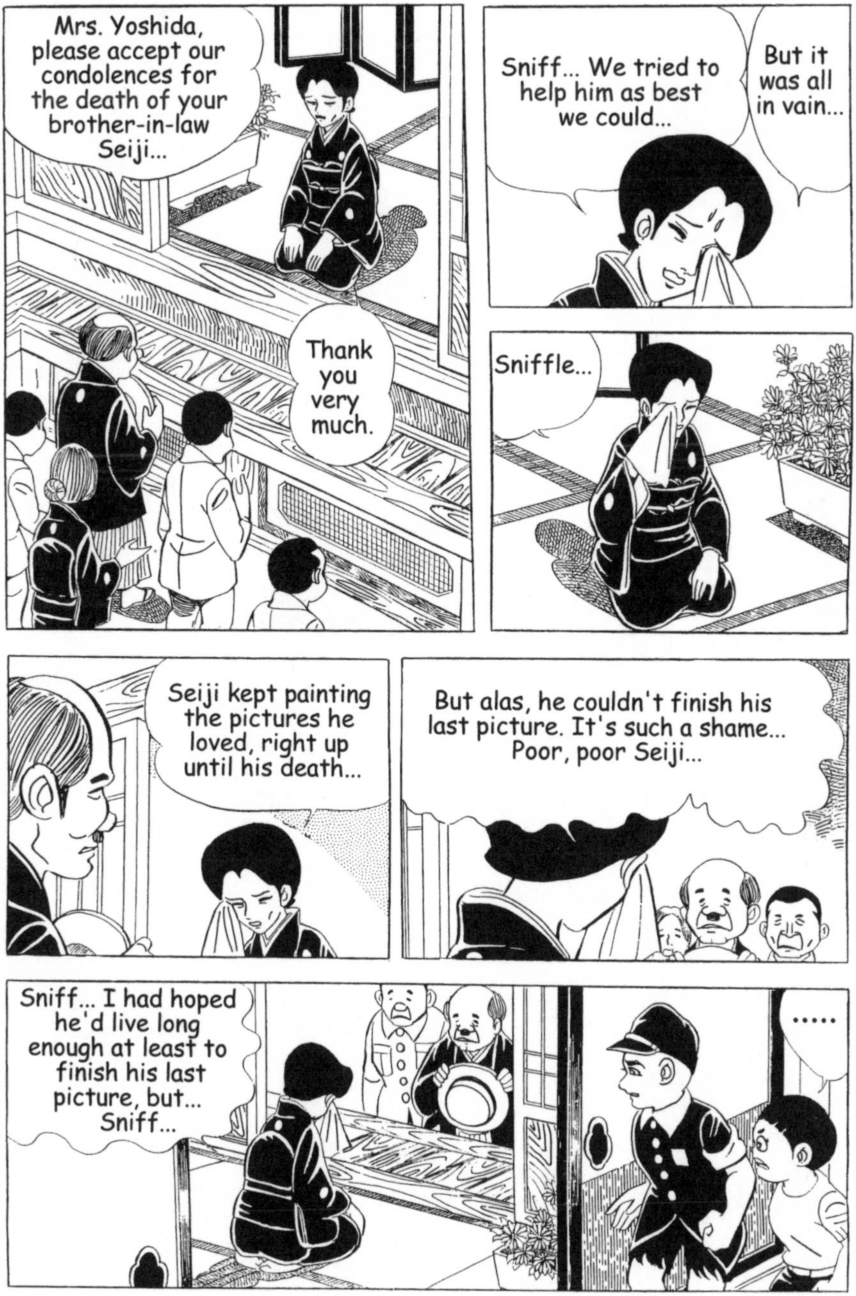
Mrs. Yoshida, please accept our condolences for the death of your brother-in-law Seiji...
Thank you very much.
Sniff... We tried to help him as best we could...
But it was all in vain...
Sniffle...
Seiji kept painting the pictures he loved, right up until his death...
But alas, he couldn't finish his last picture. It's such a shame... Poor, poor Seiji...
Sniff... I had hoped he'd live long enough at least to finish his last picture, but... Sniff...
.....

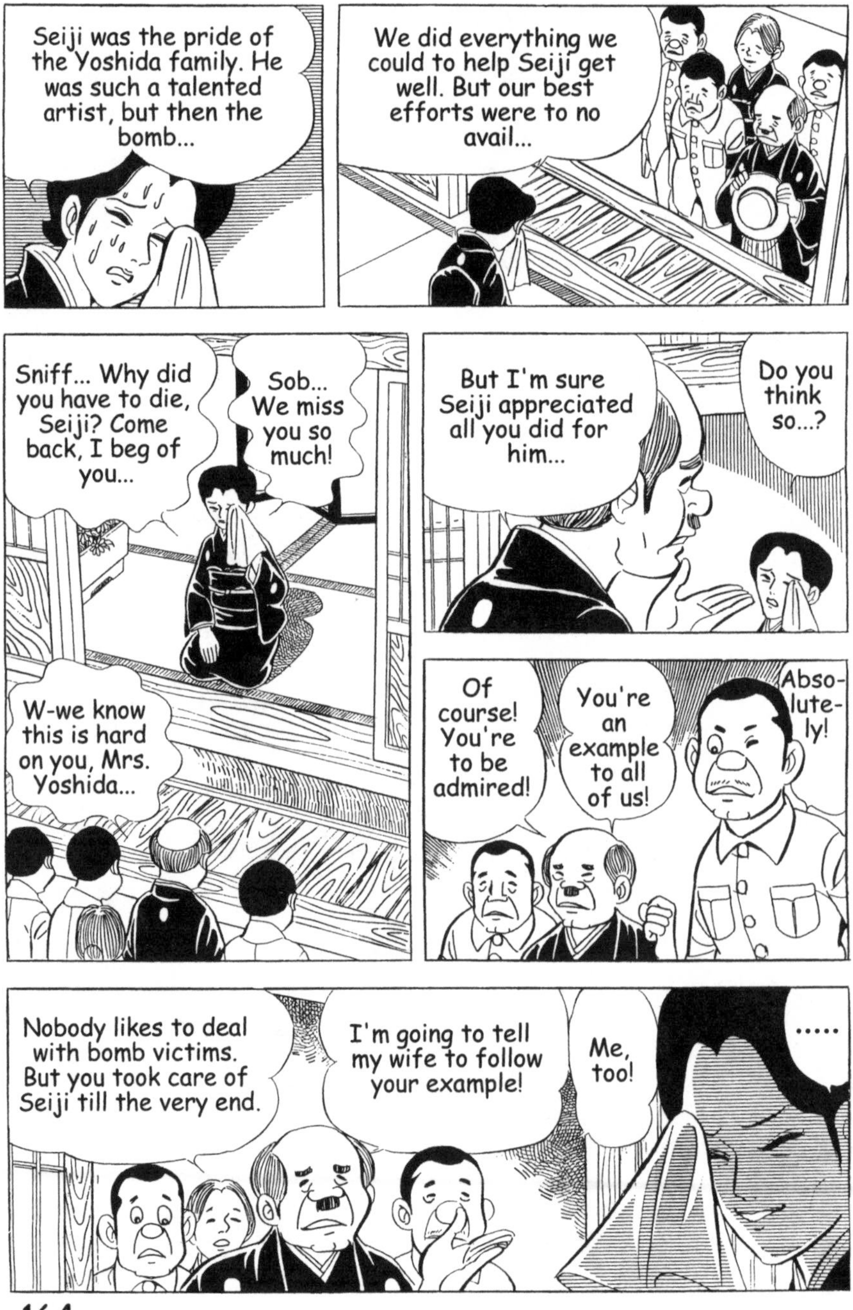
Seiji was the pride of the Yoshida family. He was such a talented artist, but then the bomb...
We did everything we could to help Seiji get well. But our best efforts were to no avail...
Sniff... Why did you have to die, Seiji? Come back, I beg of you...
Sob... We miss you so much!
W-we know this is hard on you, Mrs. Yoshida...
But I'm sure Seiji appreciated all you did for him...
Do you think so...?
Of course! You're to be admired!
You're an example to all of us!
Absolutely!
Nobody likes to deal with bomb victims. But you took care of Seiji till the very end.
I'm going to tell my wife to follow your example!
Me, too!
.....

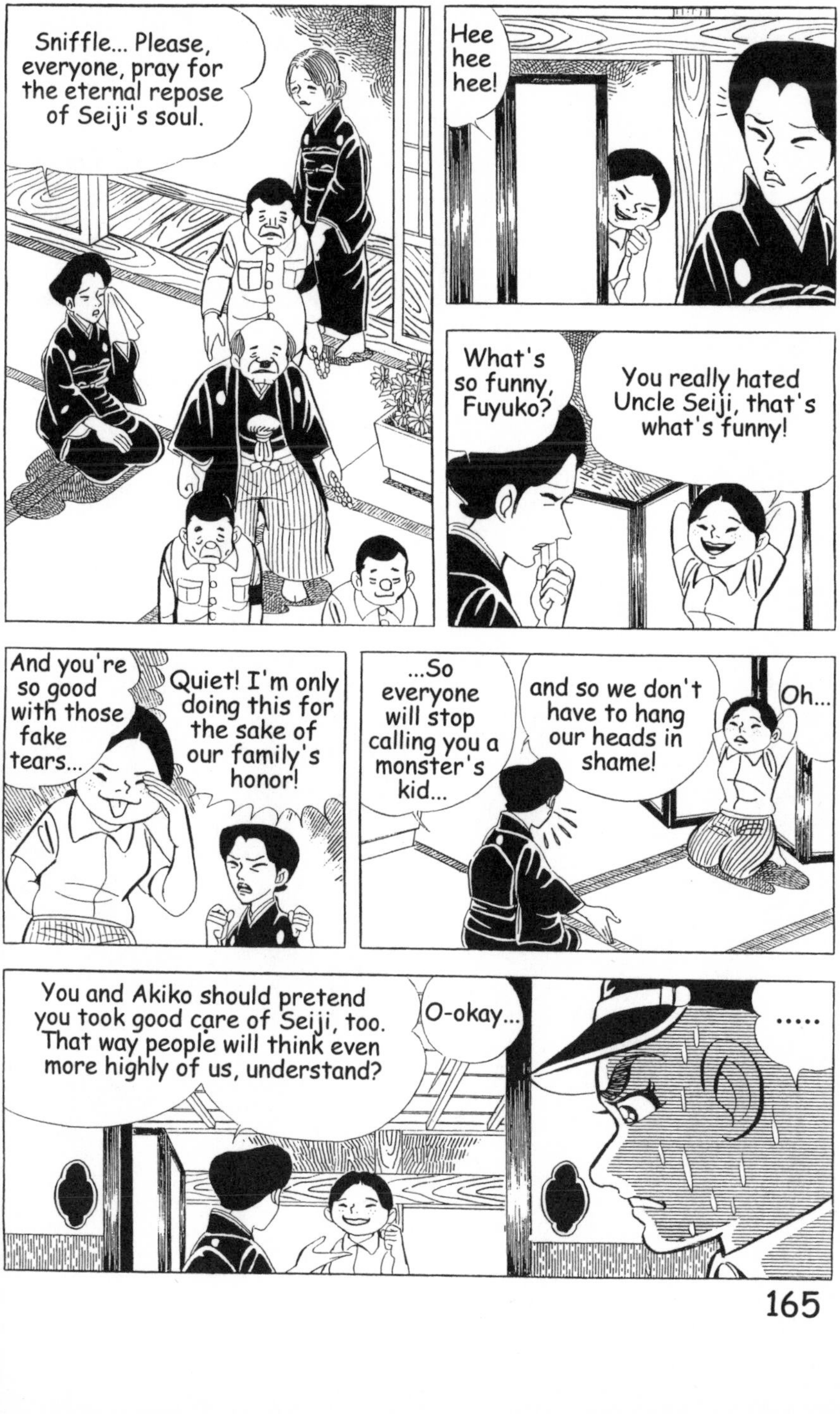
Sniffle... Please, everyone, pray for the eternal repose of Seiji's soul.
Hee hee hee!
What's so funny, Fuyuko?
You really hated Uncle Seiji, that's what's funny!
And you're so good with those fake tears...
Quiet! I'm only doing this for the sake of our family's honor!
...So everyone will stop calling you a monster's kid...
and so we don't have to hang our heads in shame!
Oh...
You and Akiko should pretend you took good care of Seiji, too. That way people will think even more highly of us, understand?
O-okay...
.....

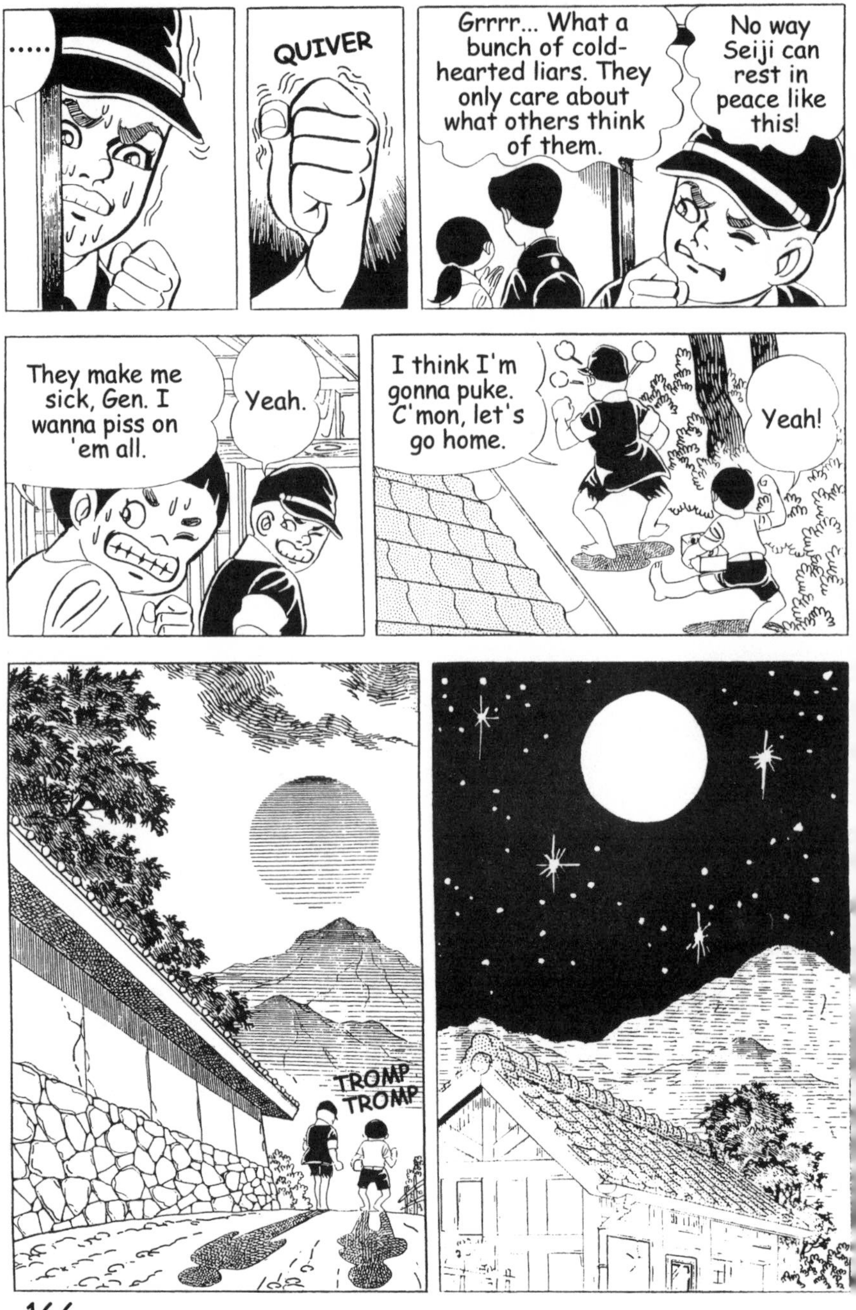
.....
QUIVER
Grrrr... What a bunch of cold-hearted liars. They only care about what others think of them.
No way Seiji can rest in peace like this!
They make me sick, Gen. I wanna piss on 'em all.
Yeah.
I think I'm gonna puke. C'mon, let's go home.
Yeah!
TROMP TROMP

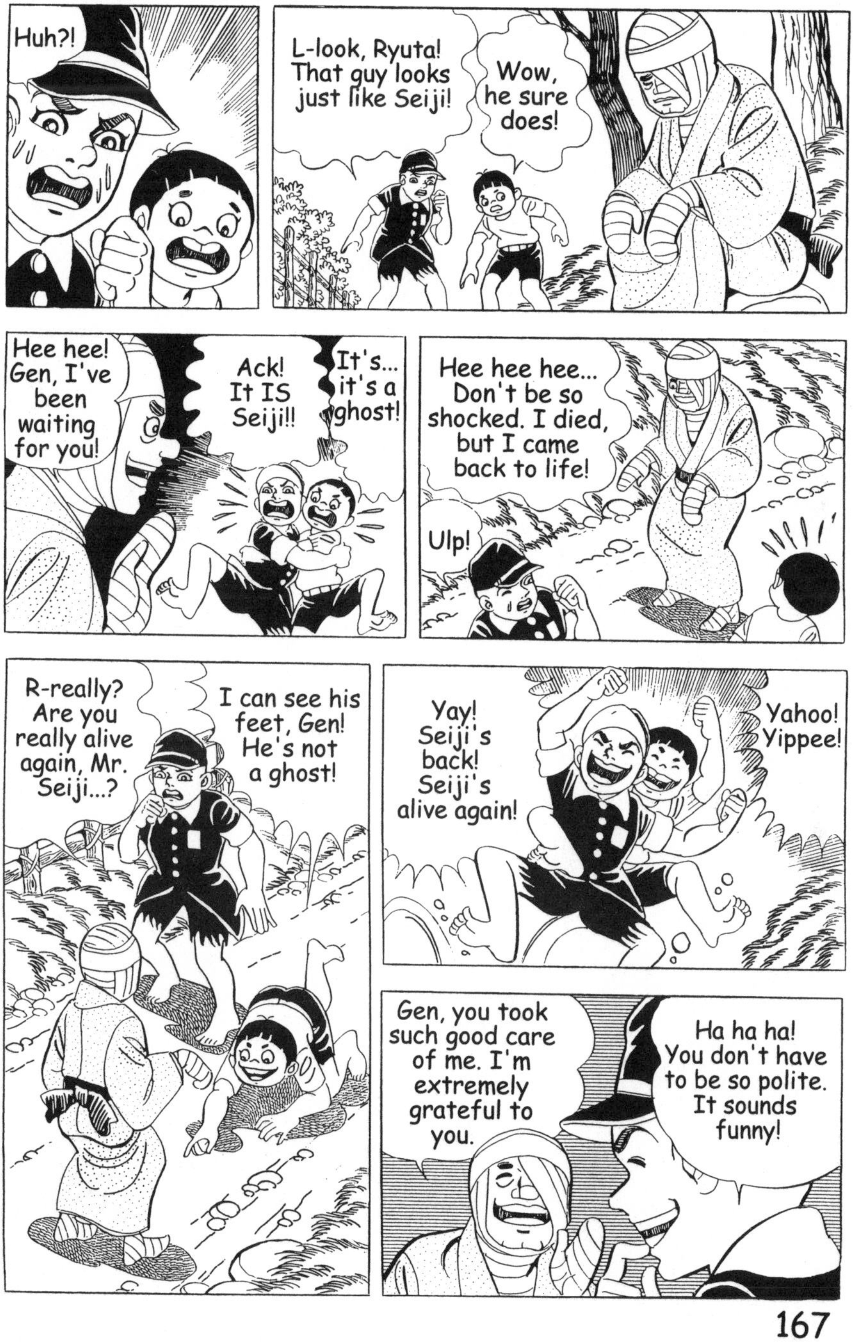
Huh?!
L-look, Ryuta! That guy looks just like Seiji!
Wow, he sure does!
Hee hee! Gen, I've been waiting for you!
Ack! It IS Seiji!!
It's... it's a ghost!
Hee hee hee... Don't be so shocked. I died, but I came back to life!
Ulp!
R-really? Are you really alive again, Mr. Seiji...?
I can see his feet, Gen! He's not a ghost!
Yay! Seiji's back! Seiji's alive again!
Yahoo! Yippee!
Gen, you took such good care of me. I'm extremely grateful to you.
Ha ha ha! You don't have to be so polite. It sounds funny!

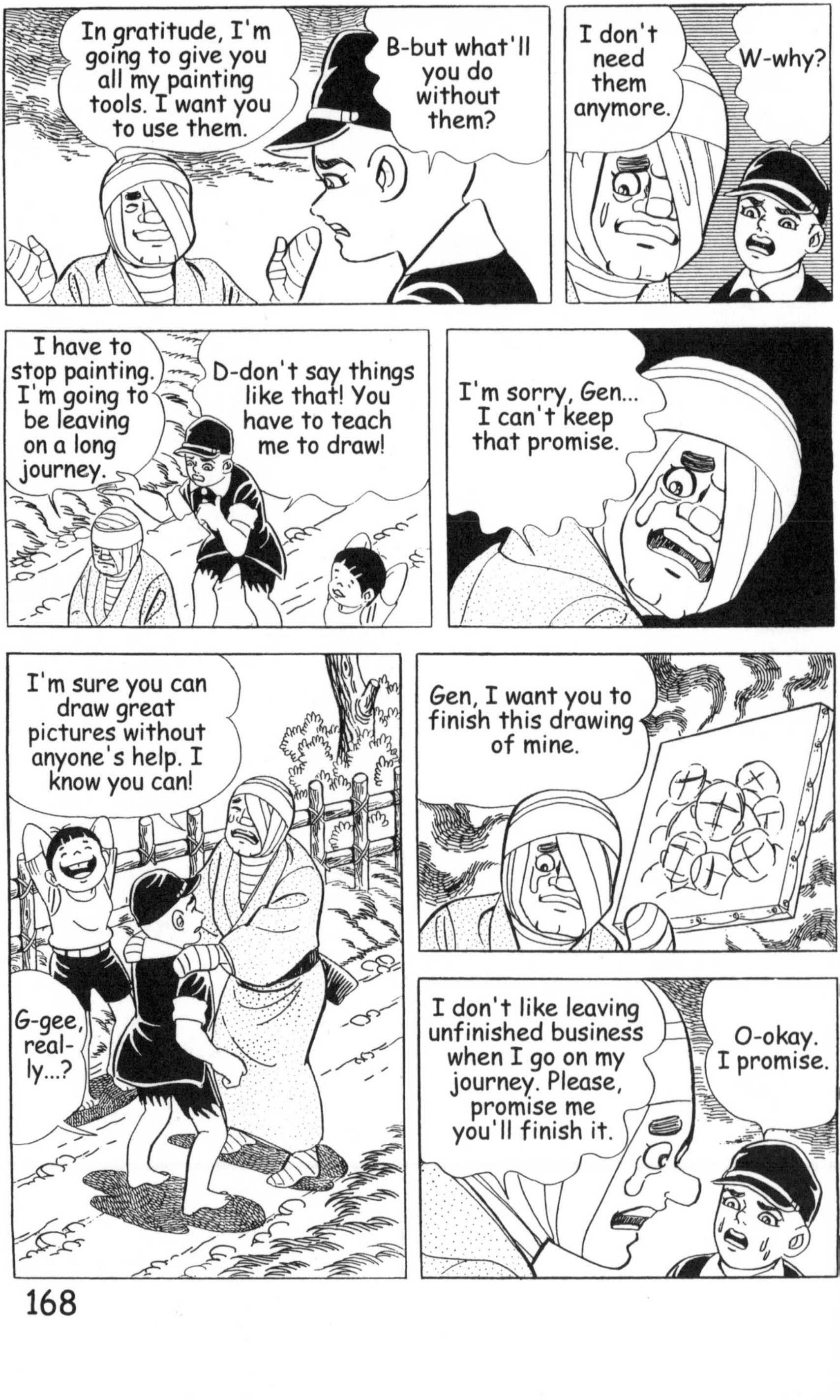
In gratitude, I'm going to give you all my painting tools. I want you to use them.
B-but what'll you do without them?
I don't need them anymore.
W-why?
I have to stop painting. I'm going to be leaving on a long journey.
D-don't say things like that! You have to teach me to draw!
I'm sorry, Gen... I can't keep that promise.
I'm sure you can draw great pictures without anyone's help. I know you can!
G-gee, real-ly...?
Gen, I want you to finish this drawing of mine.
I don't like leaving unfinished business when I go on my journey. Please, promise me you'll finish it.
O-okay. I promise.

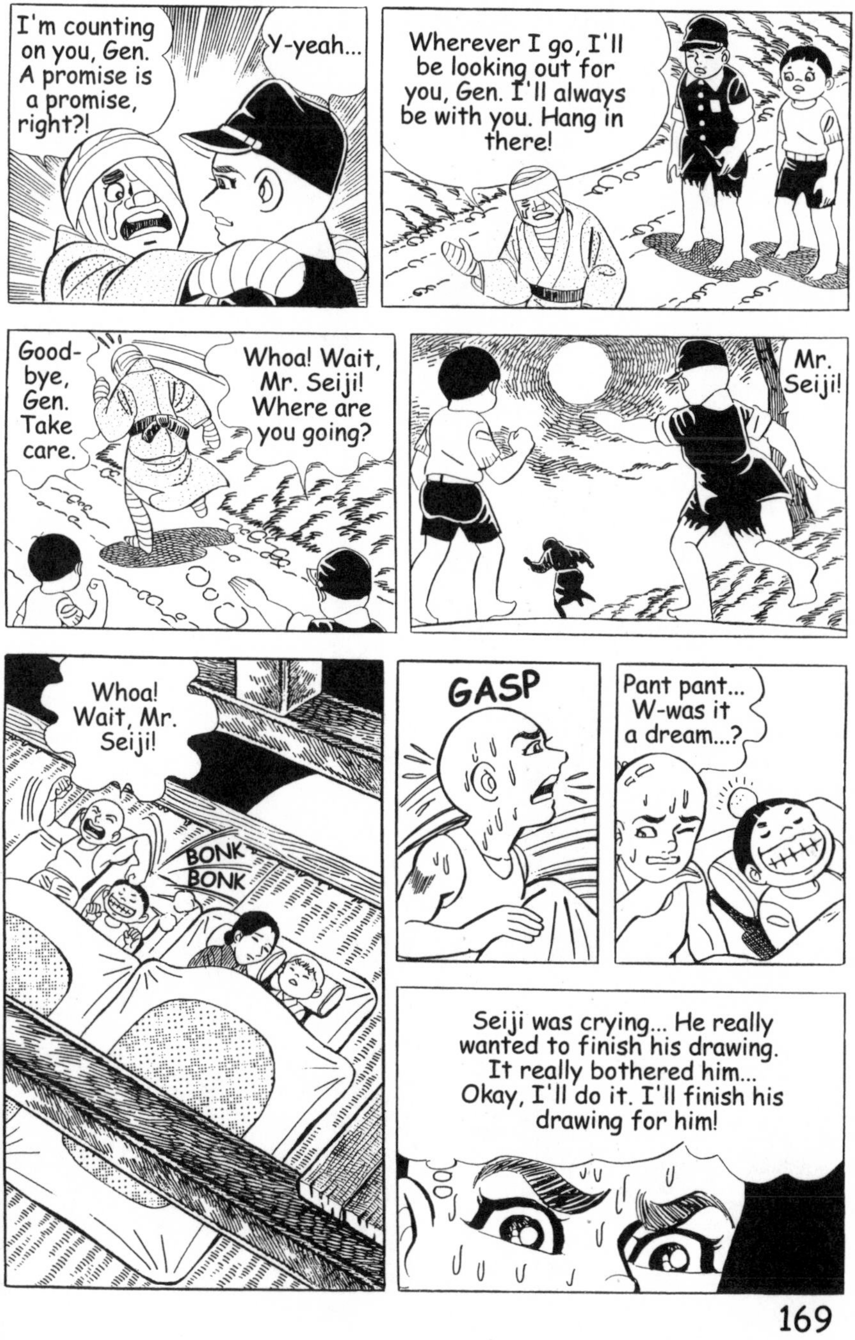
I'm counting on you, Gen. A promise is a promise, right?!
Y-yeah...
Wherever I go, I'll be looking out for you, Gen. I'll always be with you. Hang in there!
Good-bye, Gen. Take care.
Whoa! Wait, Mr. Seiji! Where are you going?
Mr. Seiji!
Whoa! Wait, Mr. Seiji!
BONK
BONK
GASP
Pant pant... W-was it a dream...?
Seiji was crying... He really wanted to finish his drawing. It really bothered him... Okay, I'll do it. I'll finish his drawing for him!

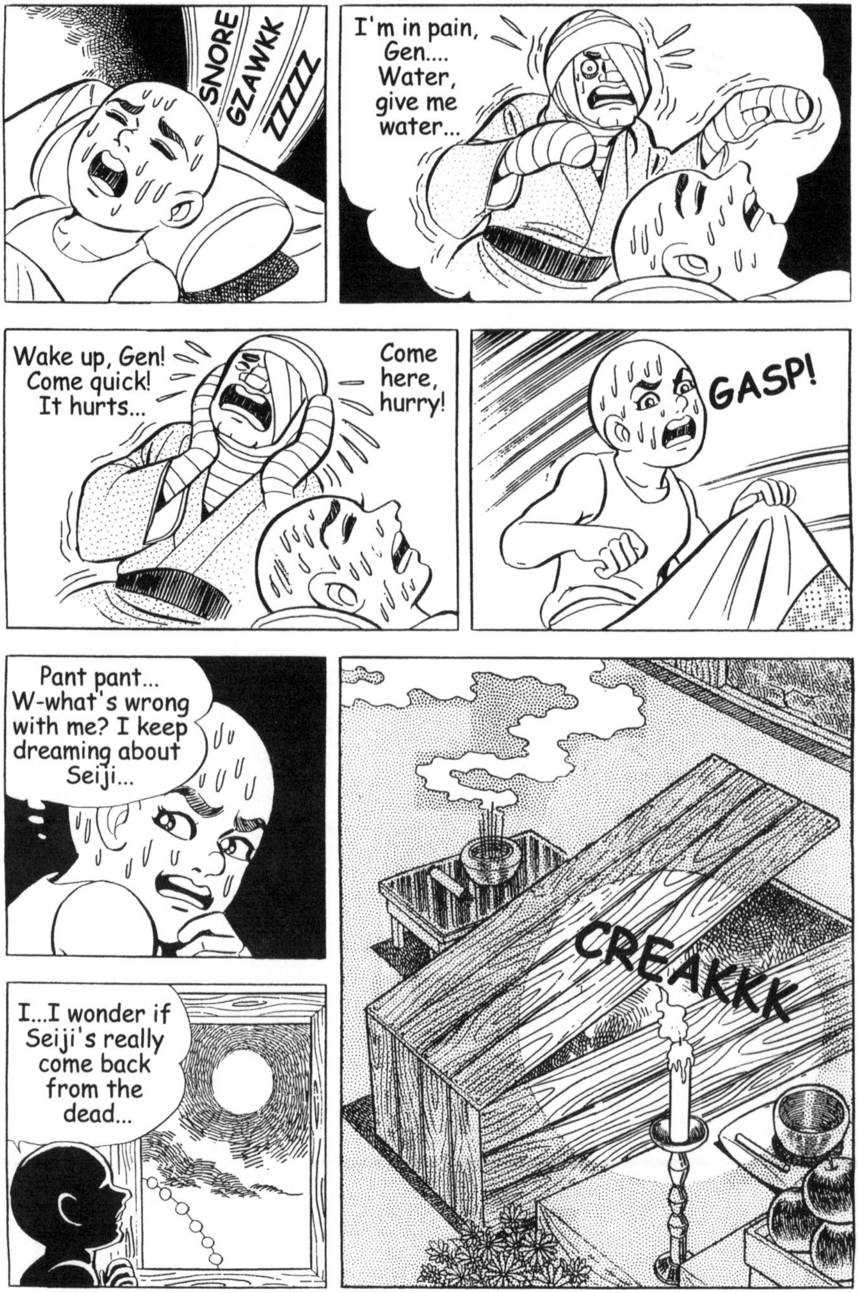
SNORE
GZAWKK
ZZZZZ
I'm in pain, Gen.... Water, give me water...
Wake up, Gen! Come quick! It hurts...
Come here, hurry!
GASP!
Pant pant... W-what's wrong with me? I keep dreaming about Seiji...
I...I wonder if Seiji's really come back from the dead...
CREAKKK

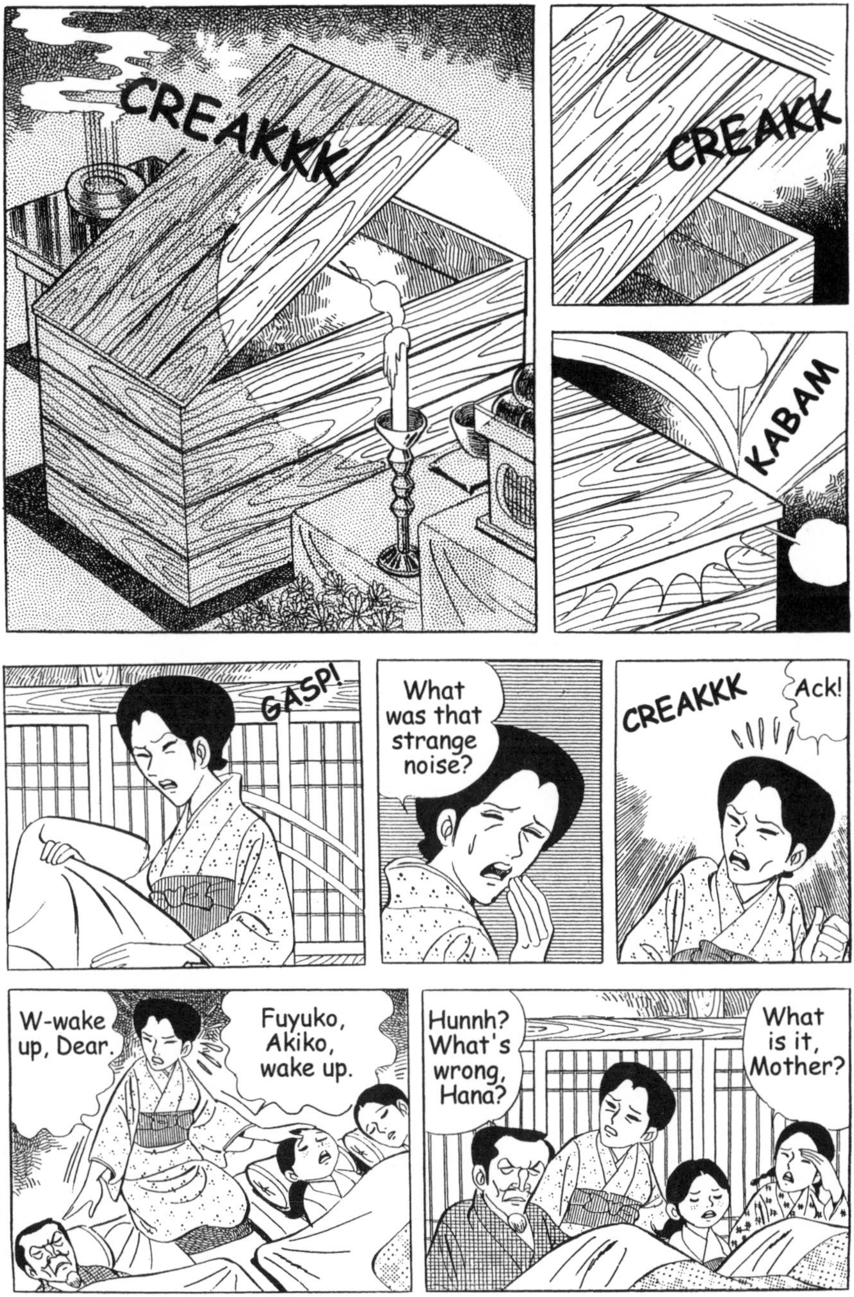
CREAKKK
CREAKK
KABAM
GASP!
What was that strange noise?
CREAKKK
Ack!
W-wake up, Dear.
Fuyuko, Akiko, wake up.
Hunnh? What's wrong, Hana?
What is it, Mother?

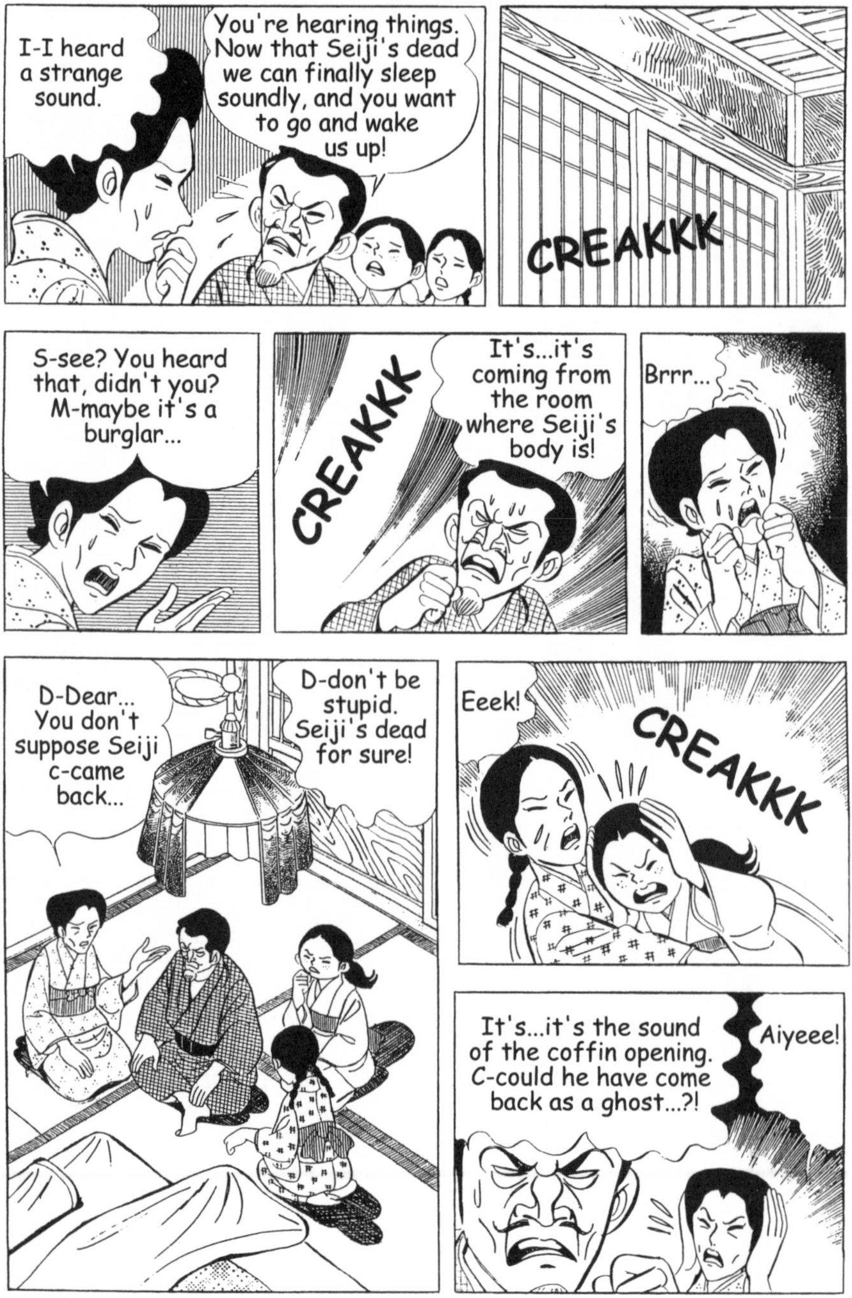
I-I heard a strange sound.
You're hearing things. Now that Seiji's dead we can finally sleep soundly, and you want to go and wake us up!
CREAKKK
S-see? You heard that, didn't you? M-maybe it's a burglar...
CREAKKK
It's...it's coming from the room where Seiji's body is!
Brrr...
D-Dear... You don't suppose Seiji c-came back...
D-don't be stupid. Seiji's dead for sure!
Eeek!
CREAKKK
It's...it's the sound of the coffin opening. C-could he have come back as a ghost...?!
Aiyeee!

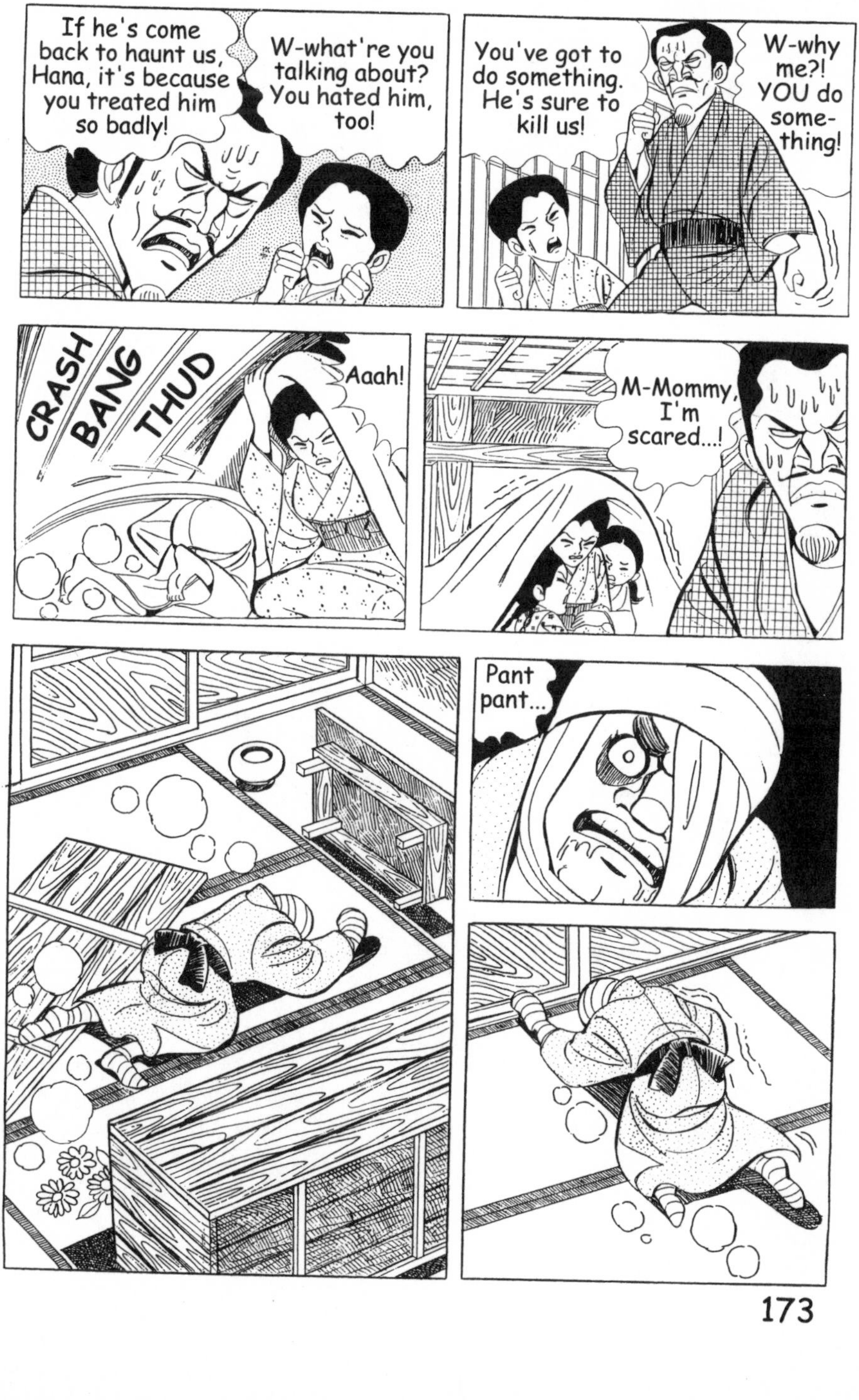

If he's come back to haunt us, Hana, it's because you treated him so badly!
W-what're you talking about? You hated him, too!
You've got to do something. He's sure to kill us!
W-why me?! YOU do some-thing!
CRASH
BANG
THUD
Aaah!
M-Mommy, I'm scared...!
Pant pant...

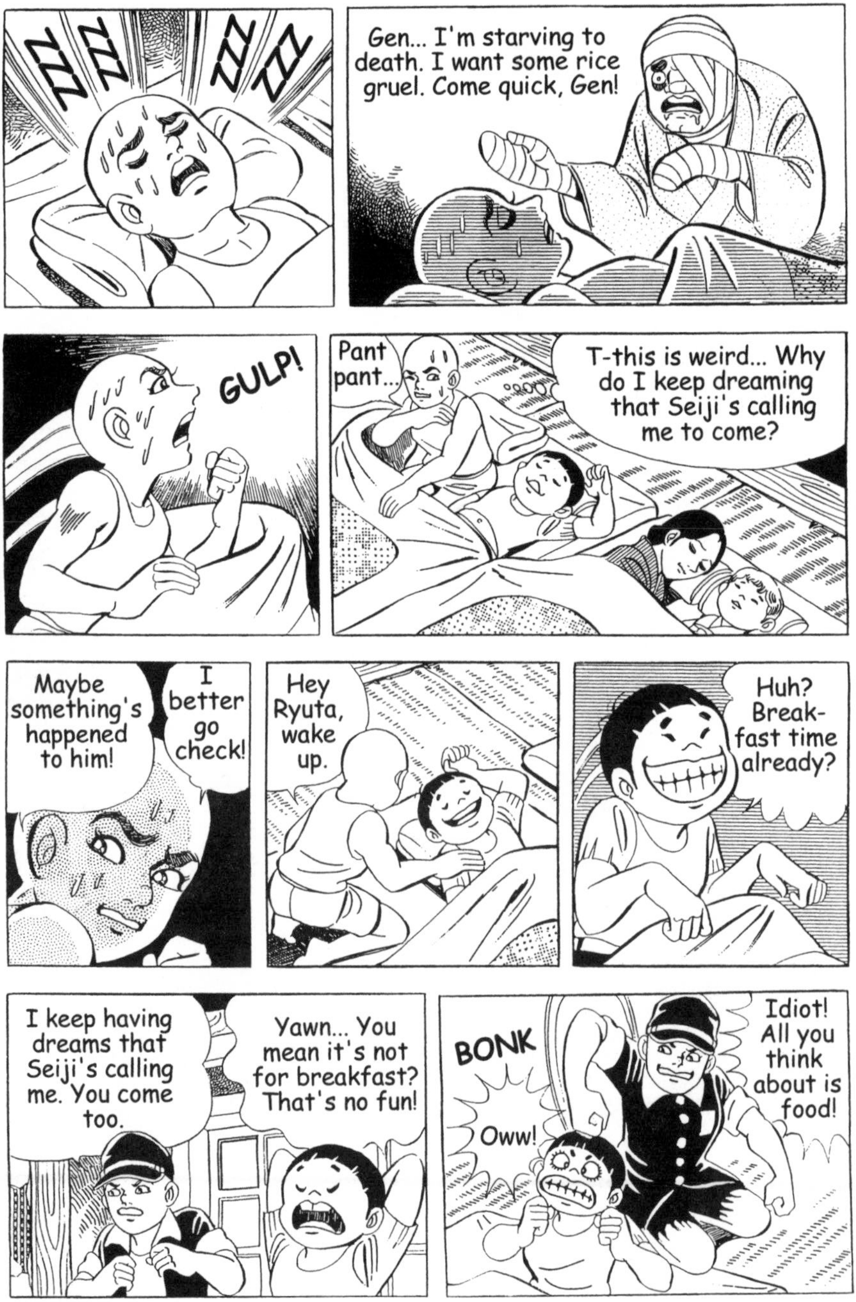
ZZZZ ZZZZ ZZZZ ZZZZ
Gen... I'm starving to death. I want some rice gruel. Come quick, Gen!
GULP!
Pant pant...
T-this is weird... Why do I keep dreaming that Seiji's calling me to come?
Maybe something's happened to him!
I better go check!
Hey Ryuta, wake up.
Huh? Break-fast time already?
I keep having dreams that Seiji's calling me. You come too.
Yawn... You mean it's not for breakfast? That's no fun!
BONK
Idiot! All you think about is food!
Oww!

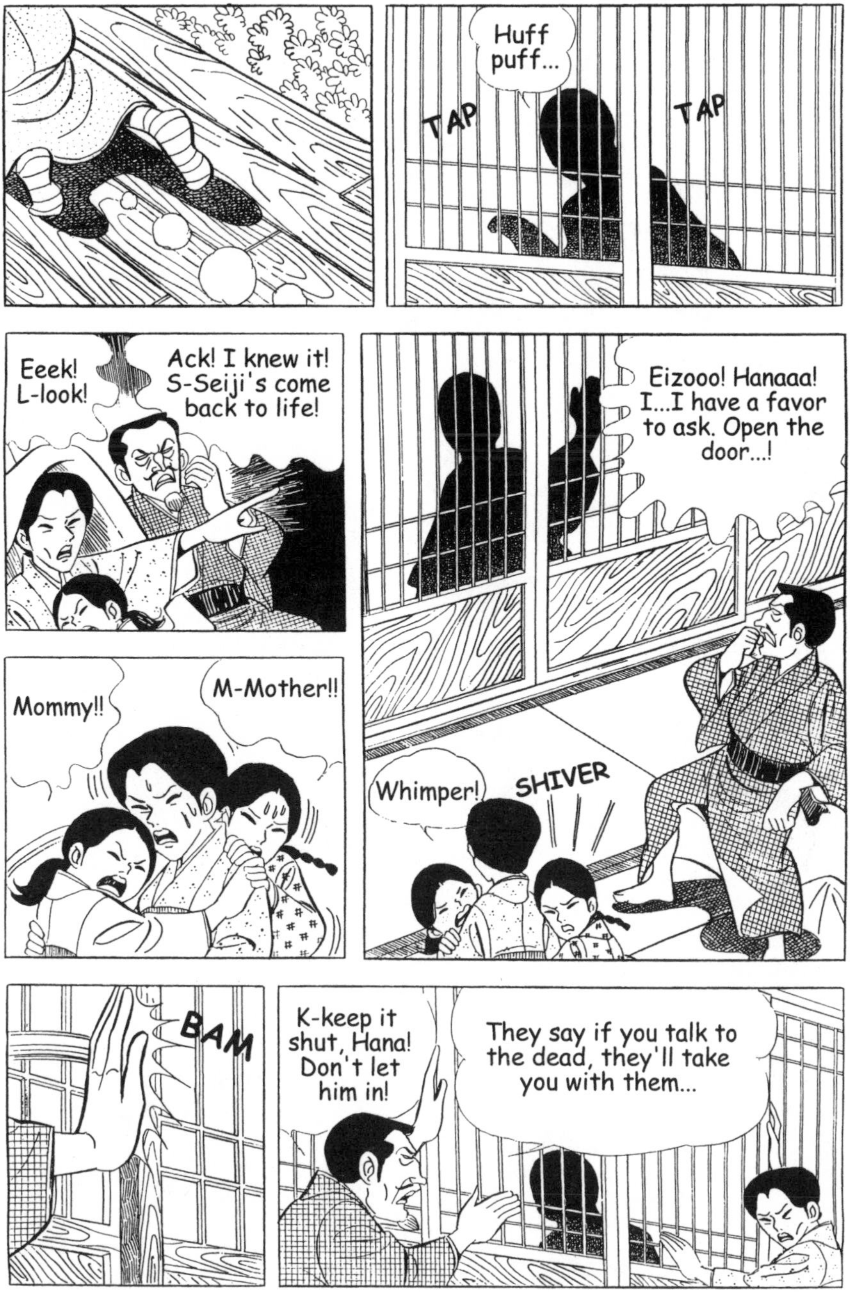
Huff puff...
TAP
TAP
Eeek! L-look!
Ack! I knew it! S-Seiji's come back to life!
Mommy!!
M-Mother!!
Eizooo! Hanaaa! I...I have a favor to ask. Open the door...!
Whimper!
SHIVER
BAM
K-keep it shut, Hana! Don't let him in!
They say if you talk to the dead, they'll take you with them...

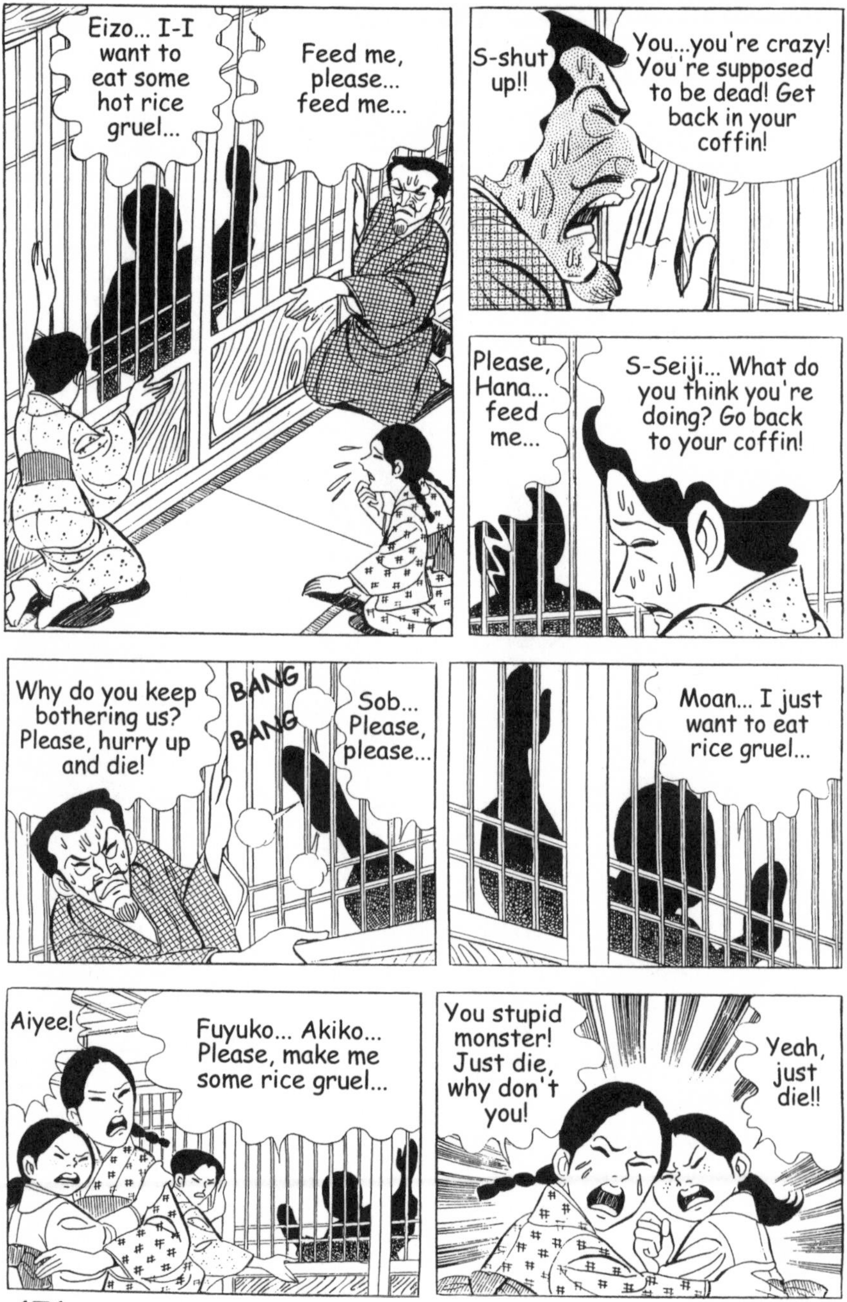

Eizo... I-I want to eat some hot rice gruel...
Feed me, please... feed me...
S-shut up!!
You...you're crazy! You're supposed to be dead! Get back in your coffin!
Please, Hana... feed me...
S-Seiji... What do you think you're doing? Go back to your coffin!
Why do you keep bothering us? Please, hurry up and die!
BANG
BANG
Sob... Please, please...
Moan... I just want to eat rice gruel...
Aiyee!
Fuyuko... Akiko... Please, make me some rice gruel...
You stupid monster! Just die, why don't you!
Yeah, just die!!

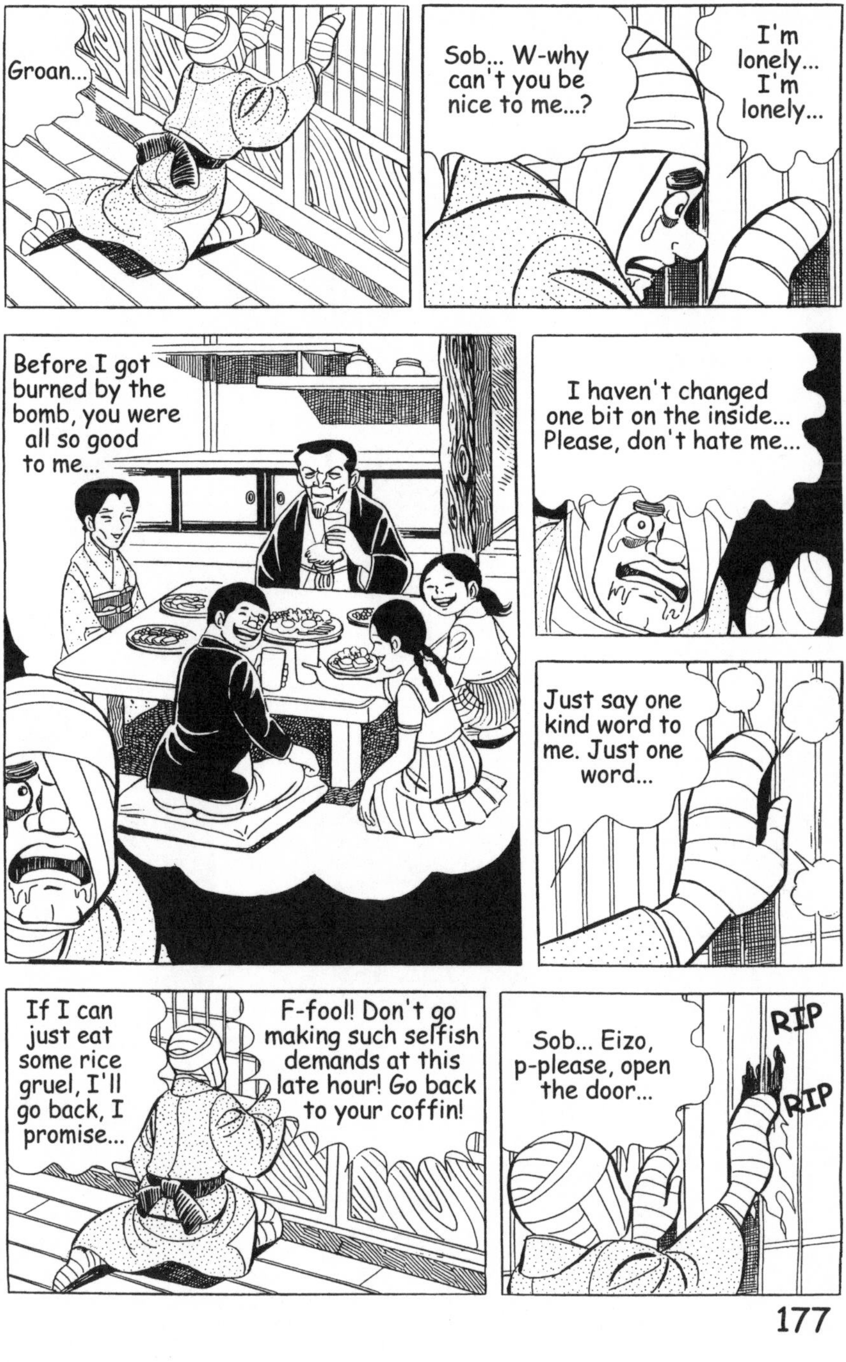
Groan...
Sob... W-why can't you be nice to me...?
I'm lonely... I'm lonely...
Before I got burned by the bomb, you were all so good to me...
I haven't changed one bit on the inside... Please, don't hate me...
Just say one kind word to me. Just one word...
If I can just eat some rice gruel, I'll go back, I promise...
F-fool! Don't go making such selfish demands at this late hour! Go back to your coffin!
Sob... Eizo, p-please, open the door...
RIP
RIP

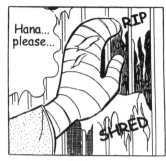
Hana... please...

Fuyuko, Akiko, please...

EEEK!

Please...
Please...

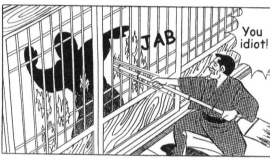
You idiot!

CRASH

Urghh...

Eizo! Hana! Fuyuko! Akiko...!

G...Gen... I...I want to eat rice gruel...

THUD

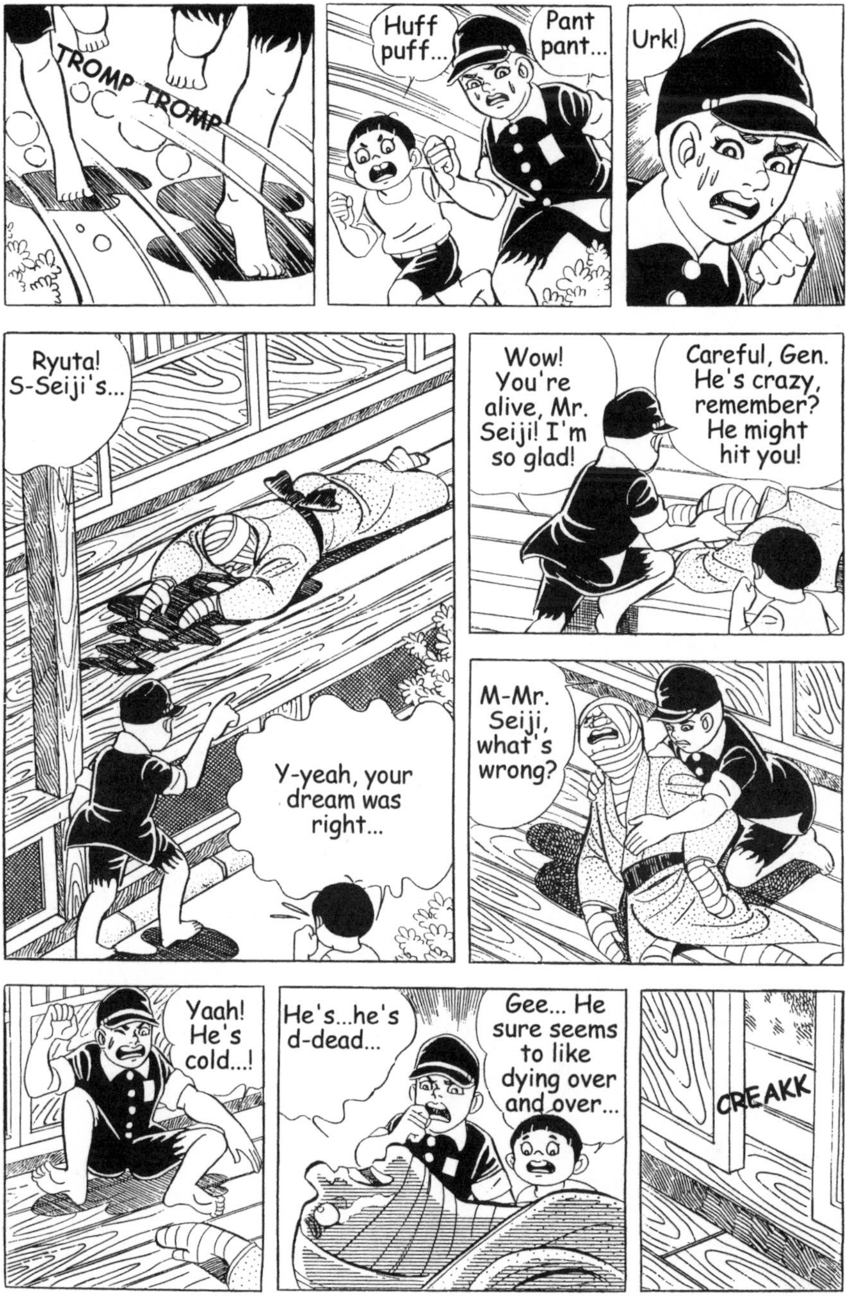
TROMP TROMP
Huff puff...
Pant pant...
Urk!
Ryuta! S-Seiji's...
Y-yeah, your dream was right...
Wow! You're alive, Mr. Seiji! I'm so glad!
Careful, Gen. He's crazy, remember? He might hit you!
M-Mr. Seiji, what's wrong?
Yaah! He's cold...!
He's...he's d-dead...
Gee... He sure seems to like dying over and over...
CREAKK

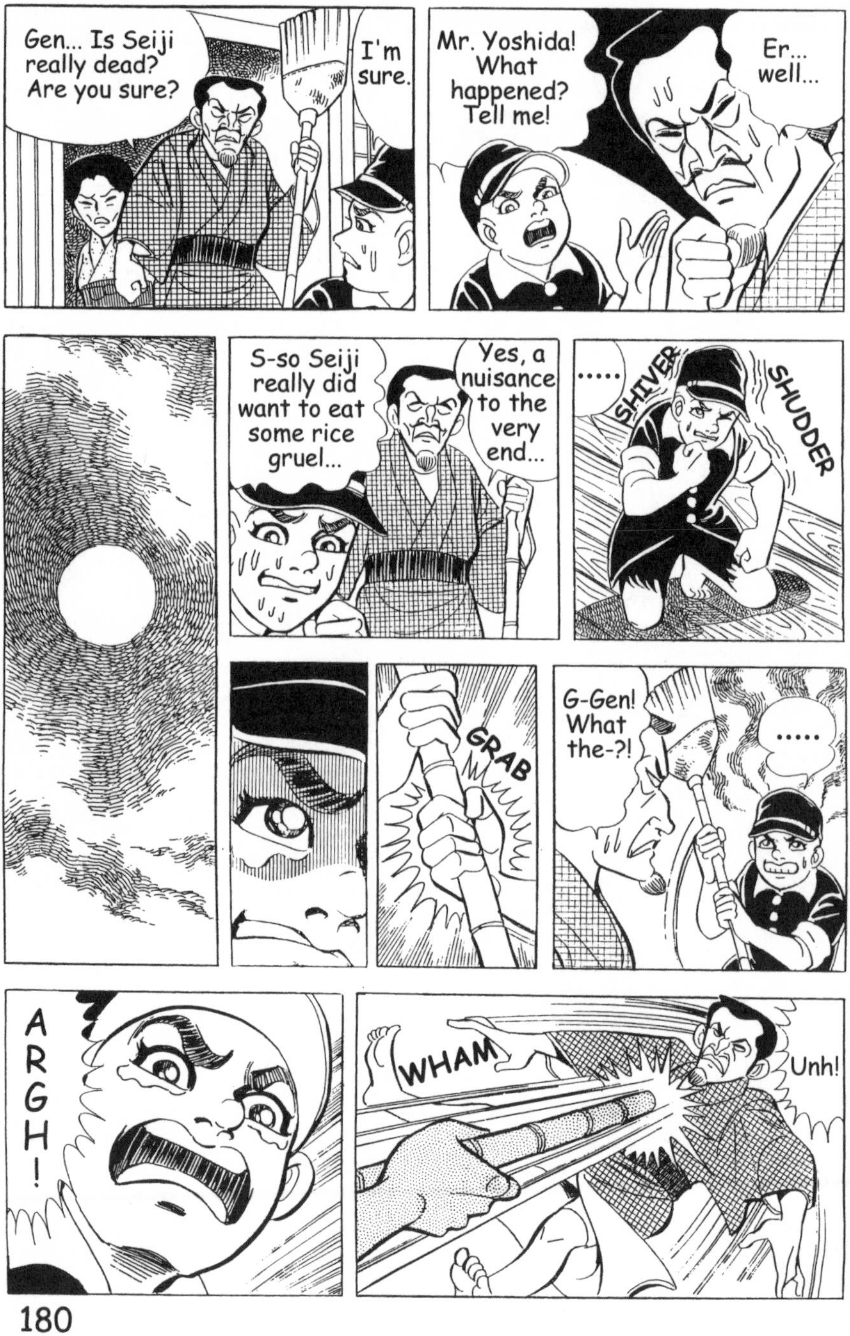
Gen... Is Seiji really dead? Are you sure?
I'm sure.
Mr. Yoshida! What happened? Tell me!
Er... well...
S-so Seiji really did want to eat some rice gruel...
Yes, a nuisance to the very end...
.....
SHIVER
SHUDDER
GRAB
G-Gen! What the-?!
.....
ARGH!
WHAM
Unh!

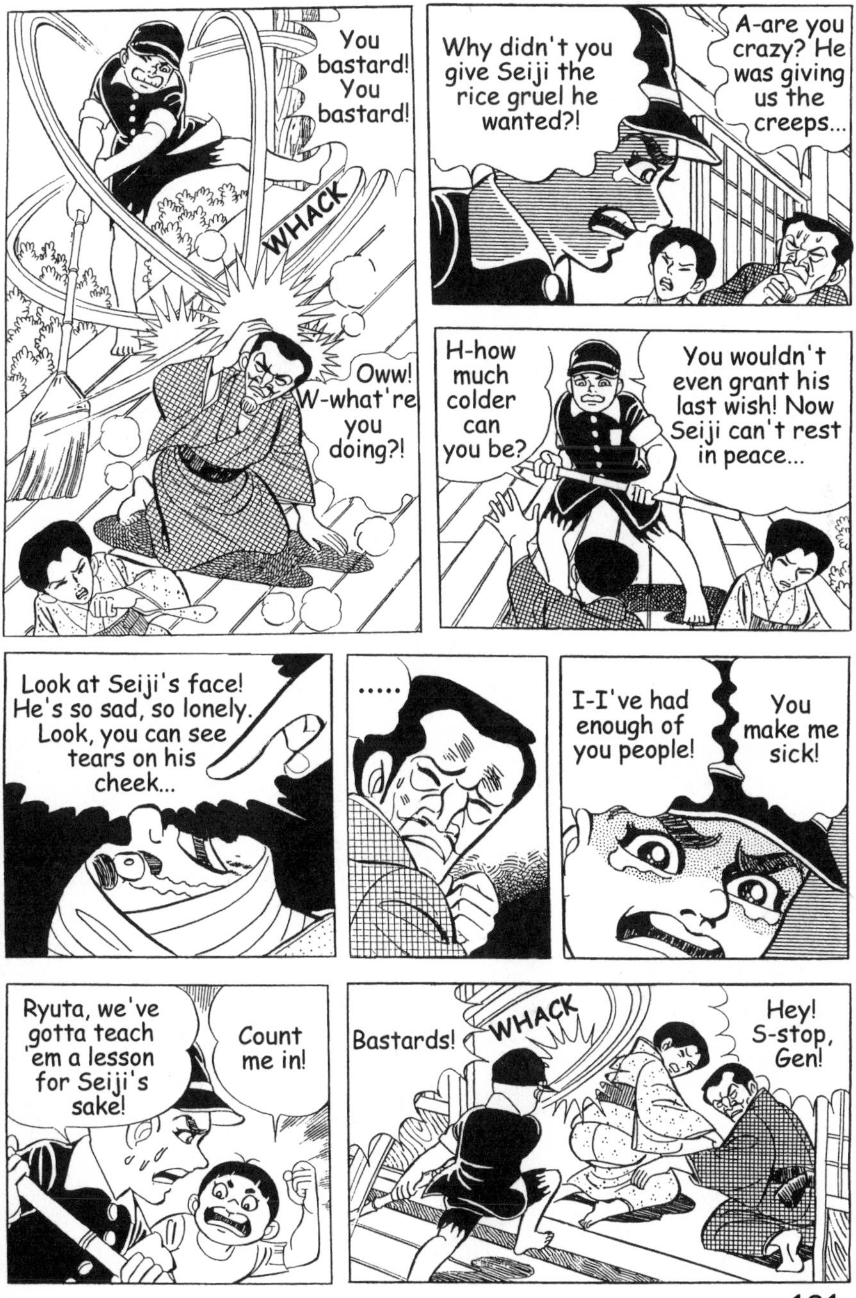
You bastard! You bastard!
WHACK
Oww! W-what're you doing?!
Why didn't you give Seiji the rice gruel he wanted?!
A-are you crazy? He was giving us the creeps...
H-how much colder can you be?
You wouldn't even grant his last wish! Now Seiji can't rest in peace...
Look at Seiji's face! He's so sad, so lonely. Look, you can see tears on his cheek...
.....
I-I've had enough of you people!
You make me sick!
Ryuta, we've gotta teach 'em a lesson for Seiji's sake!
Count me in!
Bastards!
WHACK
Hey! S-stop, Gen!

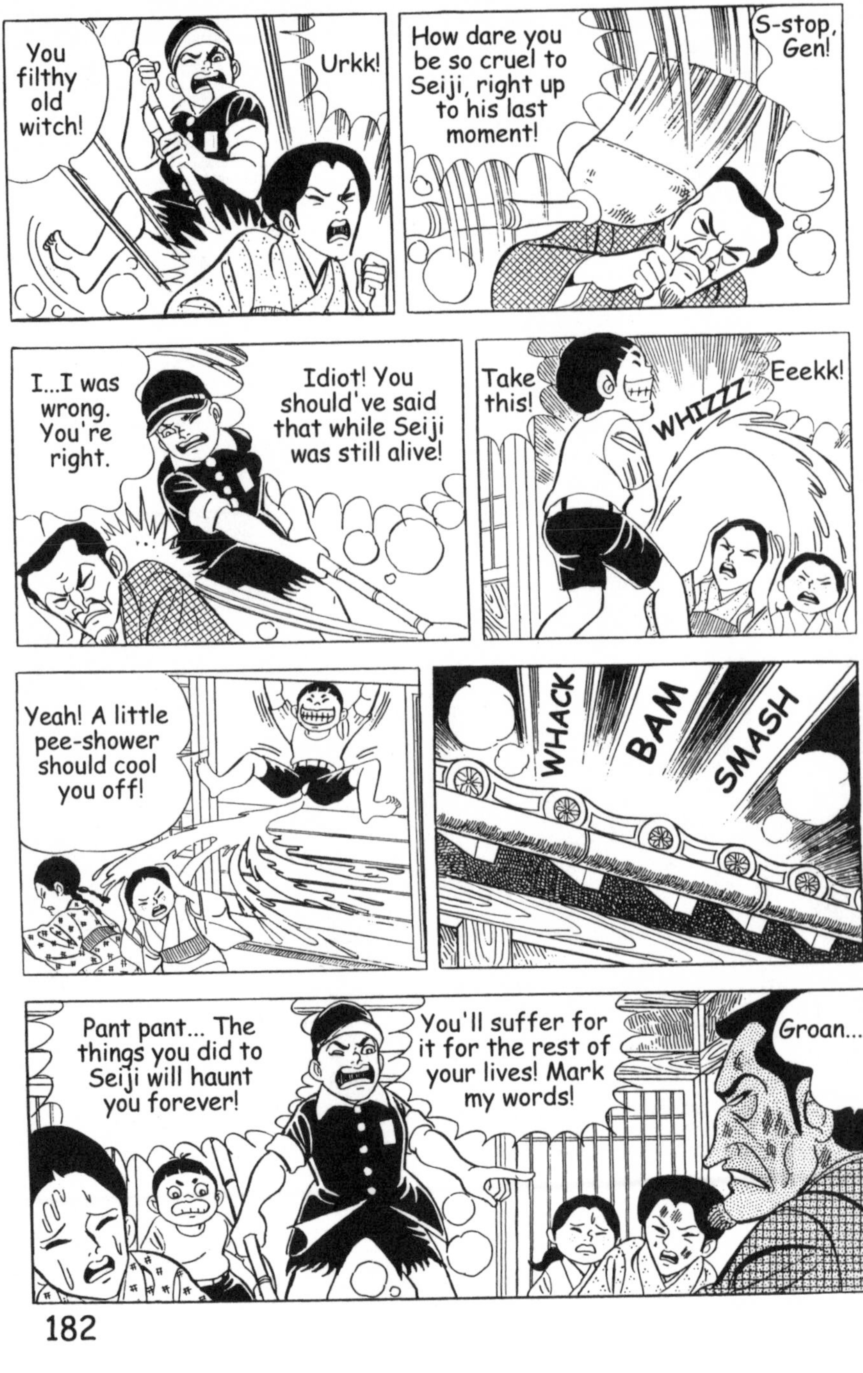
You filthy old witch!
Urkk!
How dare you be so cruel to Seiji, right up to his last moment!
S-stop, Gen!
I...I was wrong. You're right.
Idiot! You should've said that while Seiji was still alive!
Take this!
WHIZZZ
Eeekk!
Yeah! A little pee-shower should cool you off!
WHACK
BAM
SMASH
Pant pant... The things you did to Seiji will haunt you forever!
You'll suffer for it for the rest of your lives! Mark my words!
Groan...

You don't even deserve to cremate Seiji's body! If I let you do that, Seiji will never get to heaven!

C'mon, Ryuta. We'll cremate Seiji ourselves. Y-yeah. .....

Damn them... Damn them...

.....

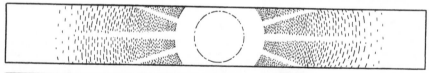

....

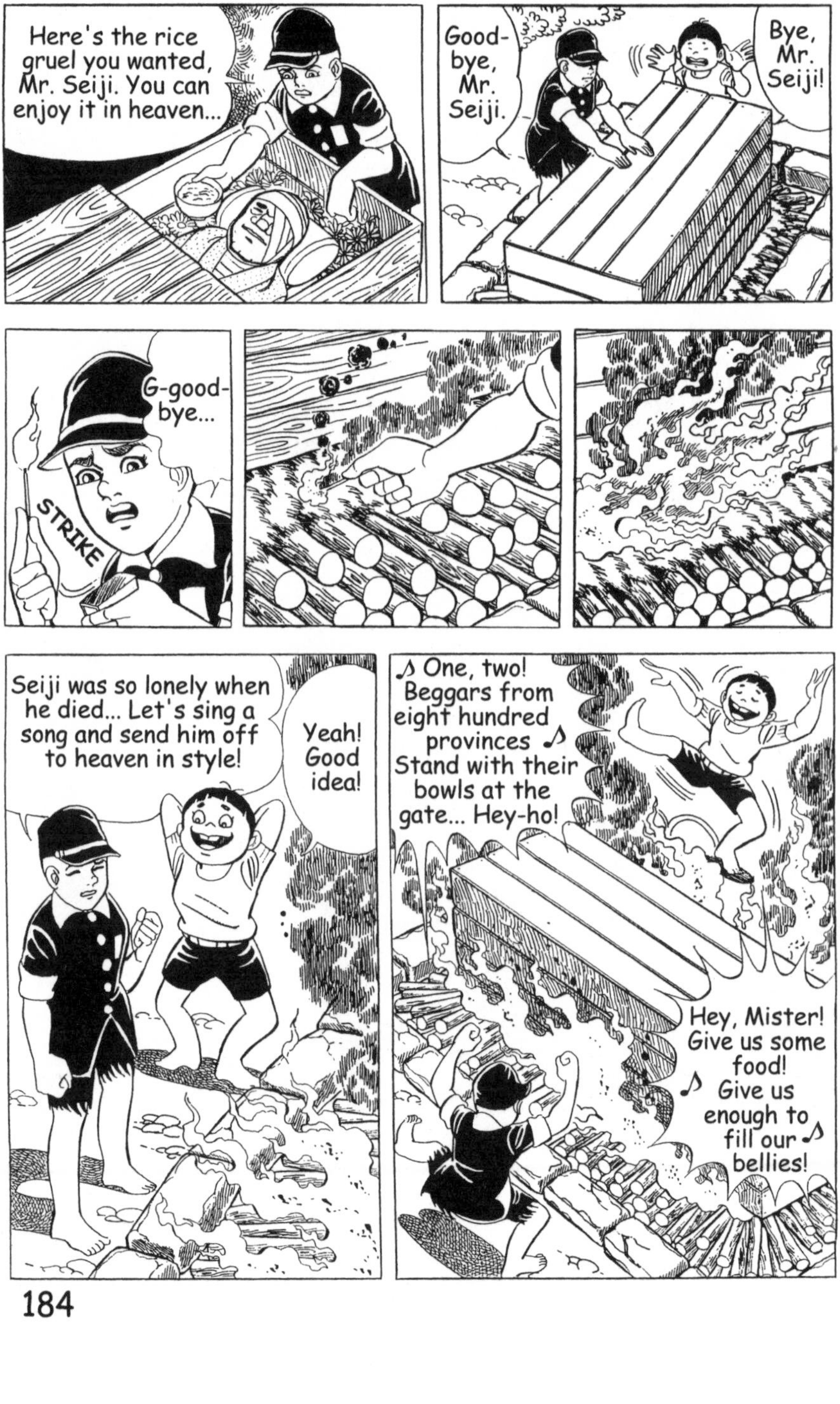
Here's the rice gruel you wanted, Mr. Seiji. You can enjoy it in heaven...
Good-bye, Mr. Seiji.
Bye, Mr. Seiji!
G-good-bye...
STRIKE
Seiji was so lonely when he died... Let's sing a song and send him off to heaven in style!
Yeah! Good idea!
♪ One, two! Beggars from eight hundred provinces ♪ Stand with their bowls at the gate... Hey-ho!
Hey, Mister! Give us some food! ♪ Give us enough to fill our ♪ bellies!

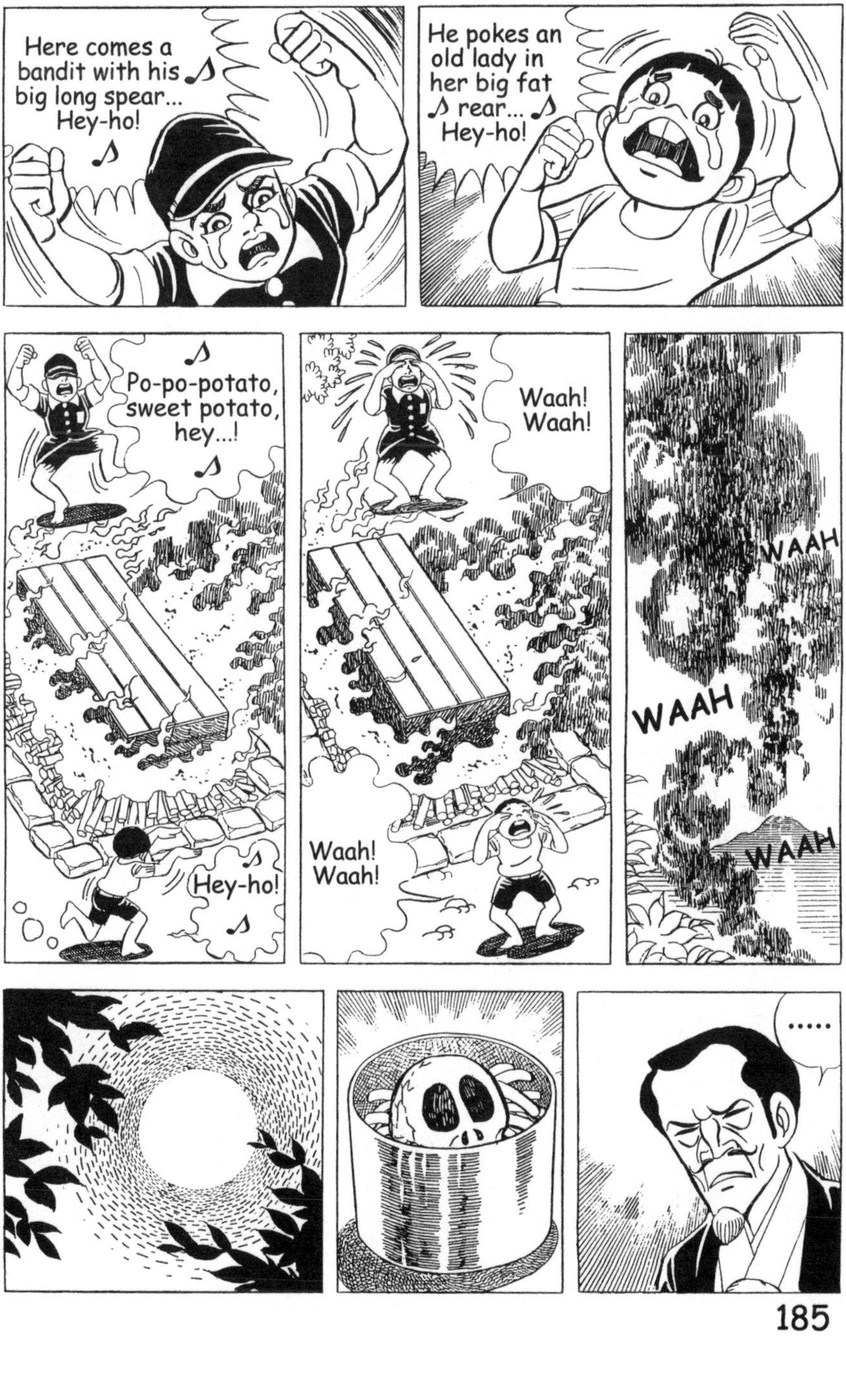
Here comes a bandit with his ♪ big long spear... Hey-ho! ♪
He pokes an old lady in her big fat ♪ rear... ♪ Hey-ho!
♪ Po-po-potato, sweet potato, hey...! ♪
♪ Hey-ho! ♪
Waah! Waah!
Waah! Waah!
WAAH
WAAH
WAAH
......

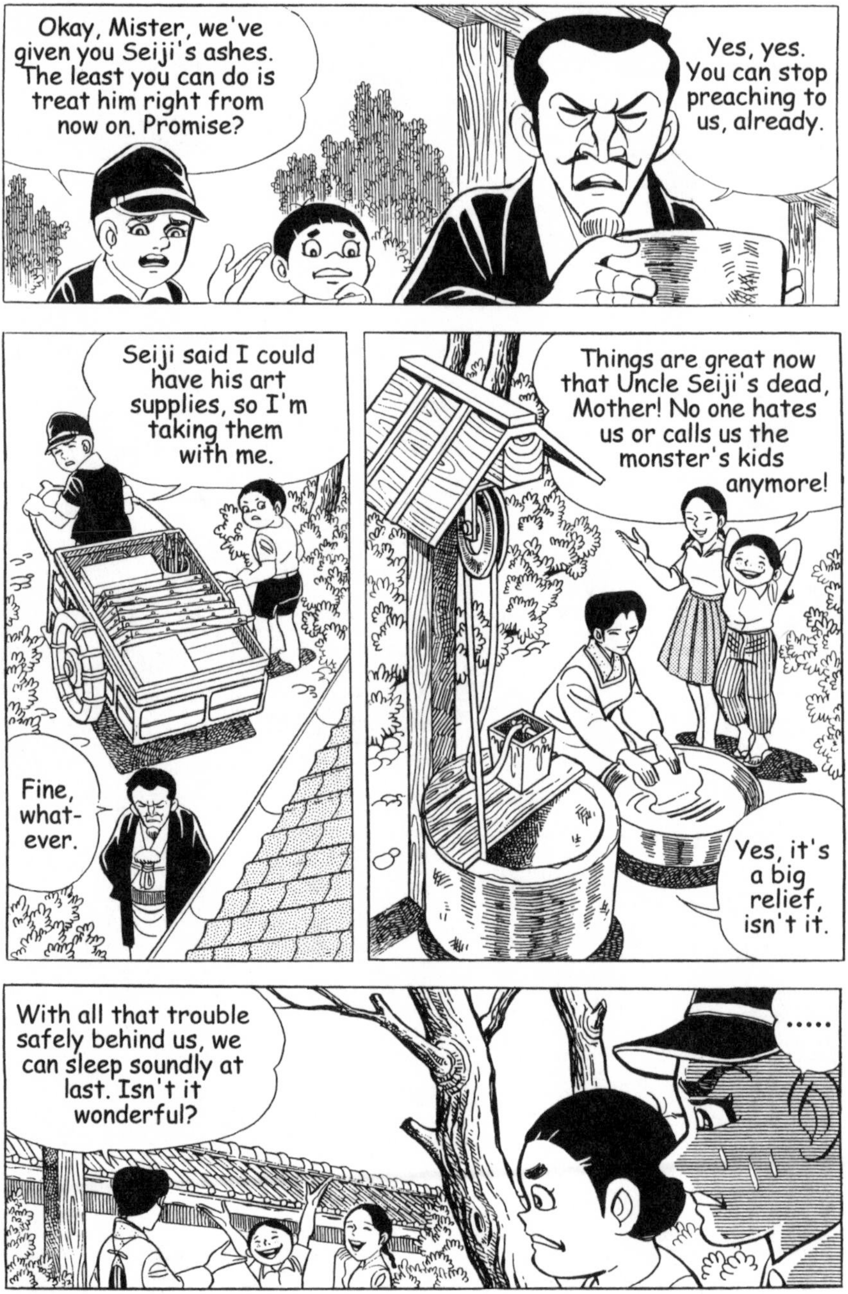
Okay, Mister, we've given you Seiji's ashes. The least you can do is treat him right from now on. Promise?
Yes, yes. You can stop preaching to us, already.
Seiji said I could have his art supplies, so I'm taking them with me.
Fine, whatever.
Things are great now that Uncle Seiji's dead, Mother! No one hates us or calls us the monster's kids anymore!
Yes, it's a big relief, isn't it.
With all that trouble safely behind us, we can sleep soundly at last. Isn't it wonderful?
.....

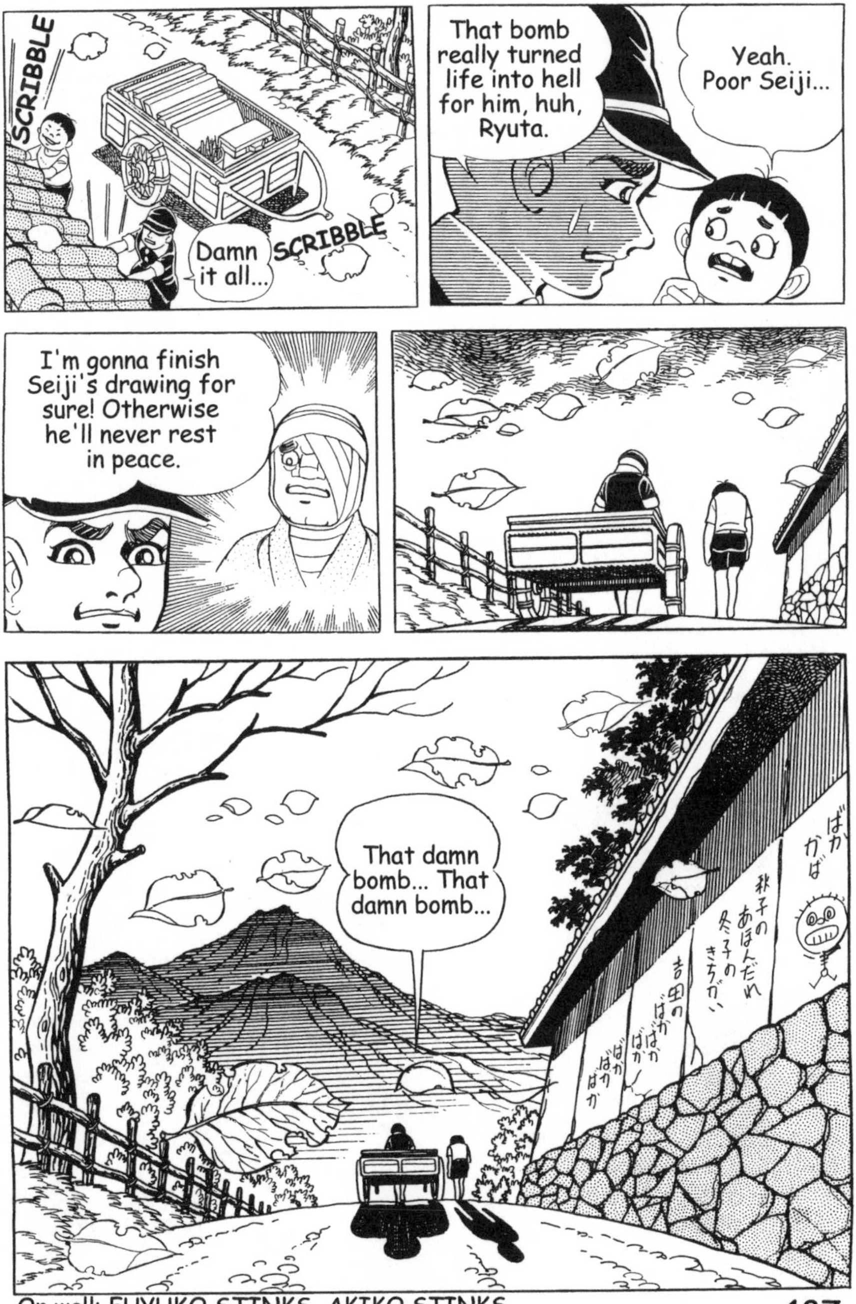
SCRIBBLE
Damn it all...
SCRIBBLE
That bomb really turned life into hell for him, huh, Ryuta.
Yeah. Poor Seiji...
I'm gonna finish Seiji's drawing for sure! Otherwise he'll never rest in peace.
That damn bomb... That damn bomb...
ばか
かば
秋子の
あほんだれ
冬子の
きちがい
吉田の
ばか ばか
ばか ばか ばか ばか

On wall: FUYUKO STINKS AKIKO STINKS
YOSHIDAS ALL STINK

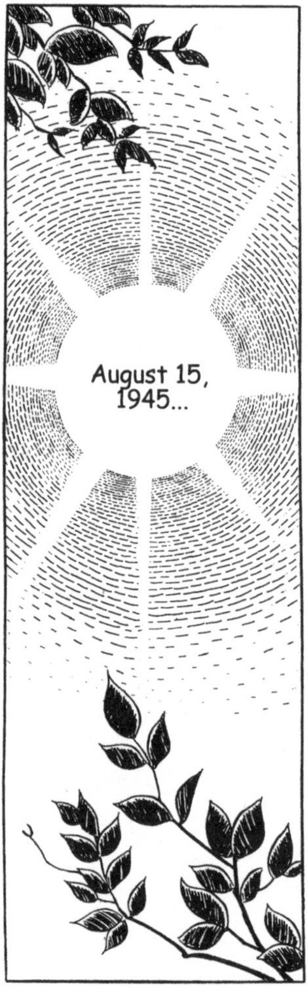
August 15, 1945...
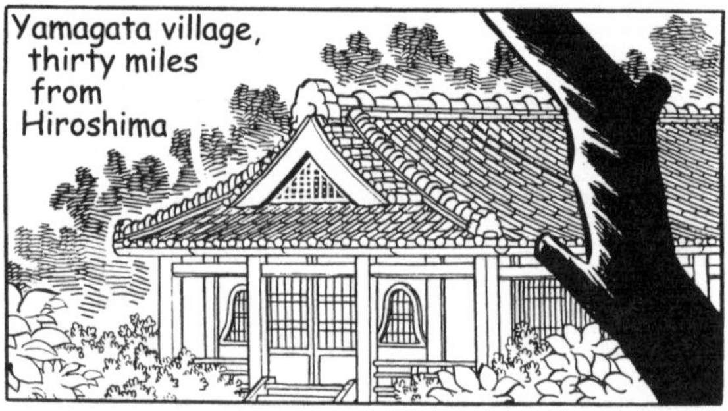
Yamagata village, thirty miles from Hiroshima
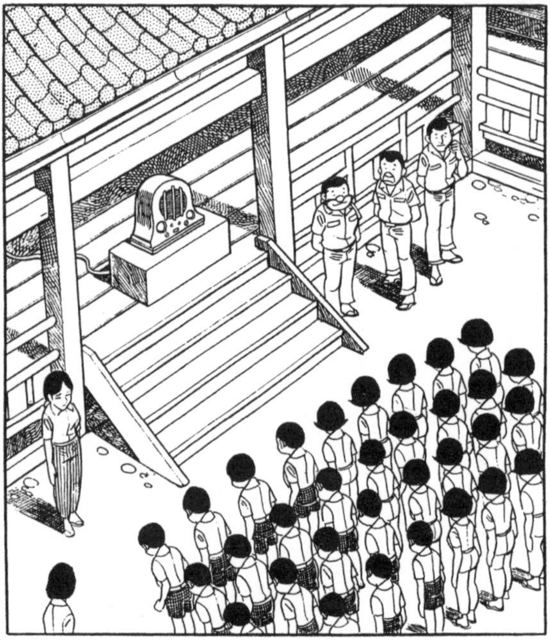
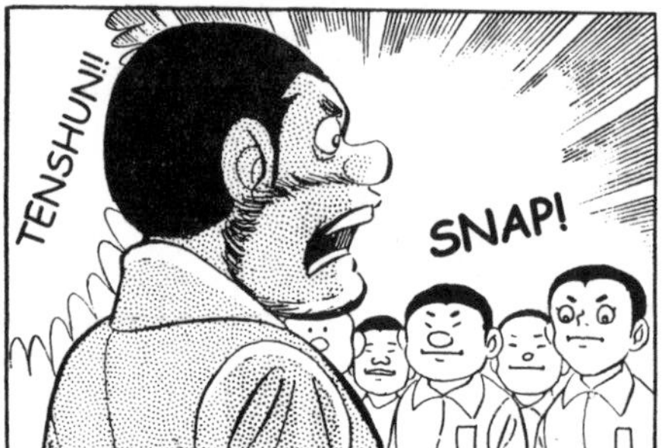
TENSHUN!!
SNAP!
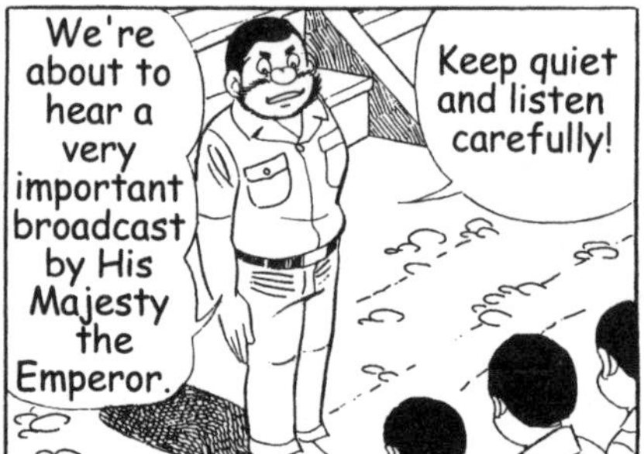
We're about to hear a very important broadcast by His Majesty the Emperor.
Keep quiet and listen carefully!

 Hey, Nakaoka, what kinda broadcast is this?

How should I know?

 I hope it's to tell us they're gonna give us lots of food!

Yeah! We never get enough to eat. My stomach feels like it's stuck to my backbone!

 Long live the Emperor, may he live a thousand, ten thousand years...

 It's starting!

 After pondering deeply the general trends of the world and the actual conditions in our empire today...

 We feel we must effect a settlement of the present situation by resorting to extraordinary measures...

 Hey, who's "We"?

That means the Emperor, dummy!

 Heh! It sounded like He was saying wee-wee!

Shut up! If the teacher hears you, he'll beat your brains out!

189

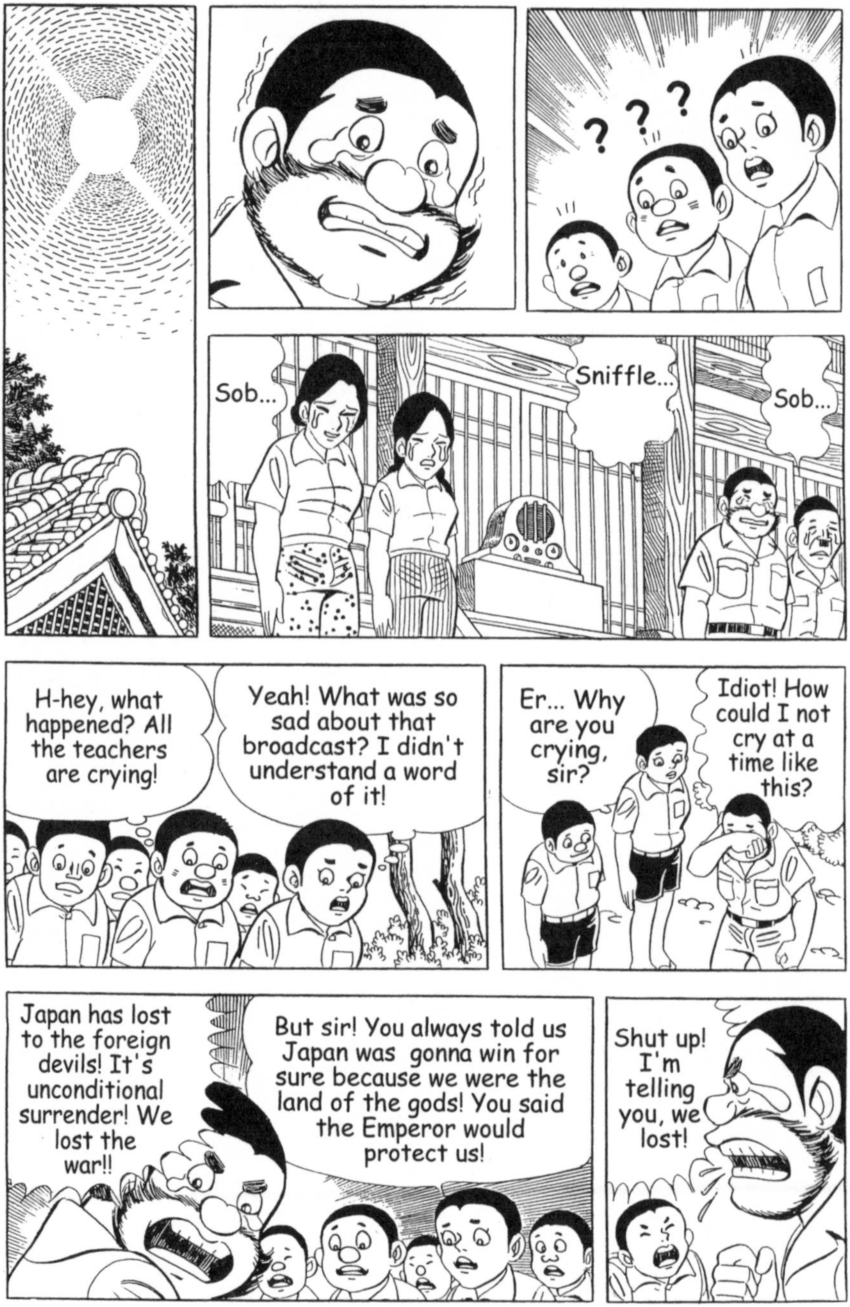
???
Sob...
Sniffle...
Sob...
H-hey, what happened? All the teachers are crying!
Yeah! What was so sad about that broadcast? I didn't understand a word of it!
Er... Why are you crying, sir?
Idiot! How could I not cry at a time like this?
Japan has lost to the foreign devils! It's unconditional surrender! We lost the war!!
But sir! You always told us Japan was gonna win for sure because we were the land of the gods! You said the Emperor would protect us!
Shut up! I'm telling you, we lost!

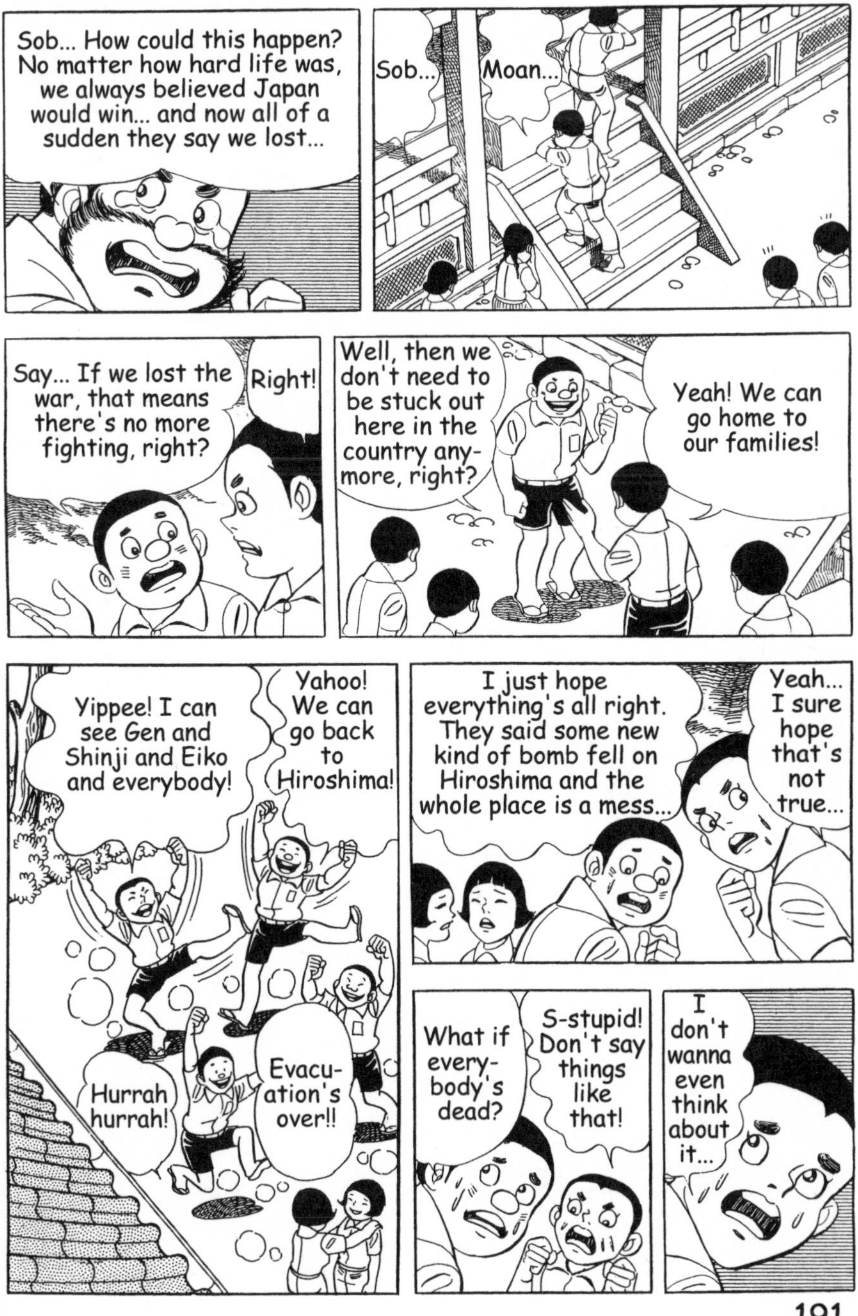

Sob... How could this happen? No matter how hard life was, we always believed Japan would win... and now all of a sudden they say we lost...
Sob...
Moan...
Say... If we lost the war, that means there's no more fighting, right?
Right!
Well, then we don't need to be stuck out here in the country any-more, right?
Yeah! We can go home to our families!
Yippee! I can see Gen and Shinji and Eiko and everybody!
Yahoo! We can go back to Hiroshima!
Hurrah hurrah!
Evacu-ation's over!!
I just hope everything's all right. They said some new kind of bomb fell on Hiroshima and the whole place is a mess...
Yeah... I sure hope that's not true...
What if every-body's dead?
S-stupid! Don't say things like that!
I don't wanna even think about it...

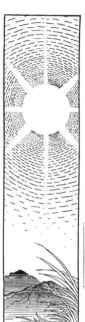

Huff
puff...

.....

Mama, they say the war's over!

Yeah, Japan lost!

I know...

They take us for complete fools! First they started the war without telling us anything... only that it was for the sake of the country and the Emperor...

And now that Japan has lost, they tell us we have to "bear the unbearable and endure the unendurable..."

Why can't they just leave us alone?!

What do we have left now? Our house is gone! Father, Eiko, and Shinji are dead!

We don't even have enough food for tomorrow. All they've left us is pain and misery...

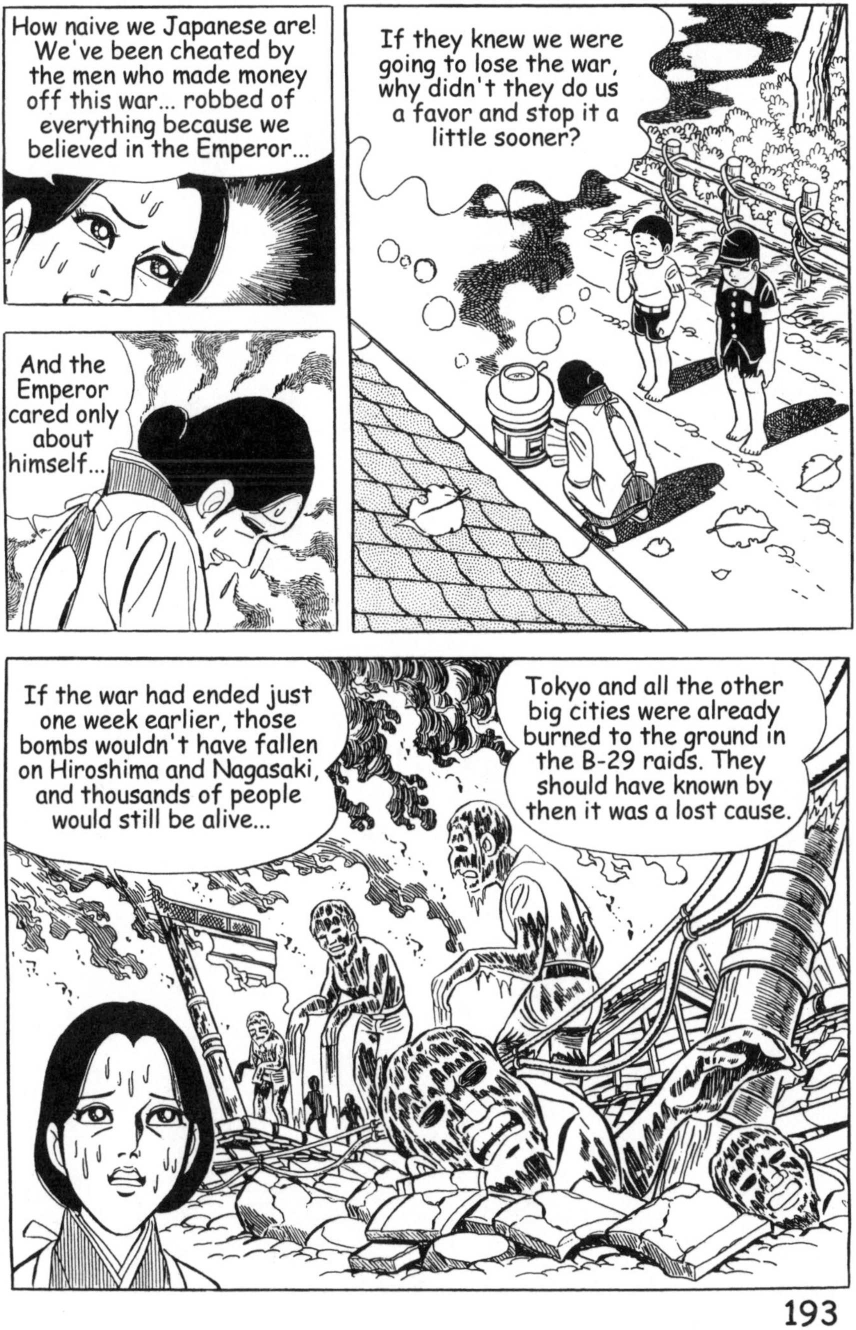
How naive we Japanese are! We've been cheated by the men who made money off this war... robbed of everything because we believed in the Emperor...
If they knew we were going to lose the war, why didn't they do us a favor and stop it a little sooner?
And the Emperor cared only about himself...
If the war had ended just one week earlier, those bombs wouldn't have fallen on Hiroshima and Nagasaki, and thousands of people would still be alive...
Tokyo and all the other big cities were already burned to the ground in the B-29 raids. They should have known by then it was a lost cause.

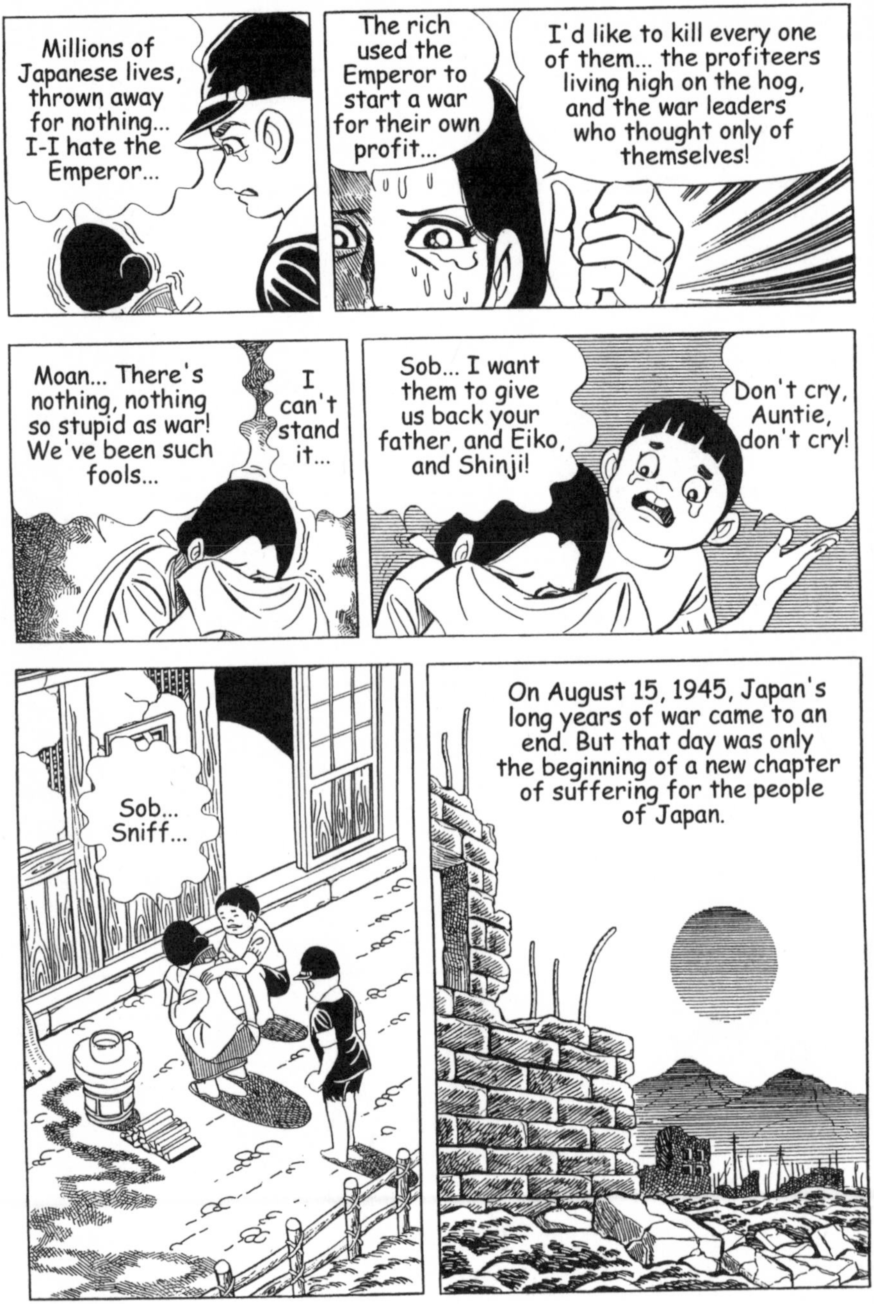
Millions of Japanese lives, thrown away for nothing... I-I hate the Emperor...
The rich used the Emperor to start a war for their own profit...
I'd like to kill every one of them... the profiteers living high on the hog, and the war leaders who thought only of themselves!
Moan... There's nothing, nothing so stupid as war! We've been such fools...
I can't stand it...
Sob... I want them to give us back your father, and Eiko, and Shinji!
Don't cry, Auntie, don't cry!
Sob... Sniff...
On August 15, 1945, Japan's long years of war came to an end. But that day was only the beginning of a new chapter of suffering for the people of Japan.

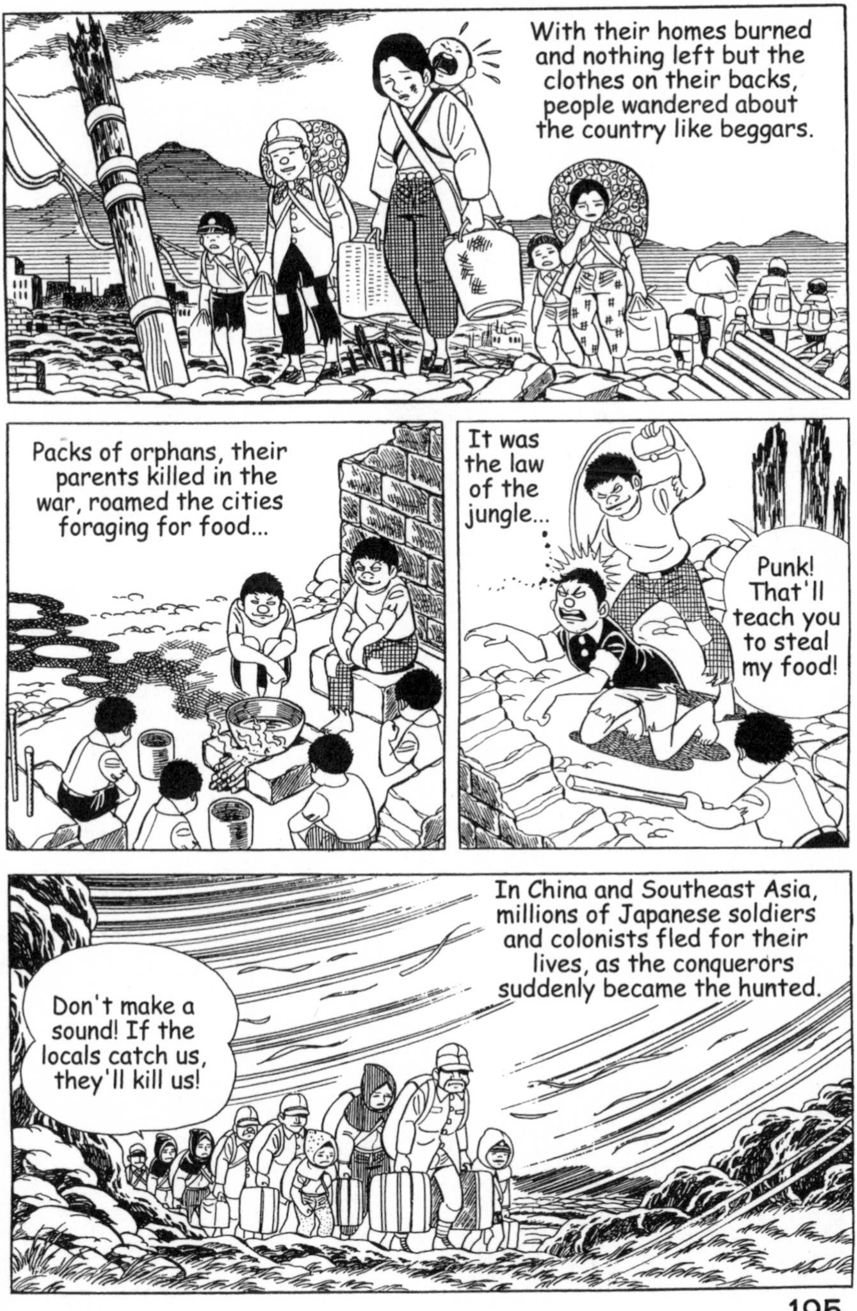
With their homes burned and nothing left but the clothes on their backs, people wandered about the country like beggars.
Packs of orphans, their parents killed in the war, roamed the cities foraging for food...
It was the law of the jungle...
Punk! That'll teach you to steal my food!
In China and Southeast Asia, millions of Japanese soldiers and colonists fled for their lives, as the conquerors suddenly became the hunted.
Don't make a sound! If the locals catch us, they'll kill us!

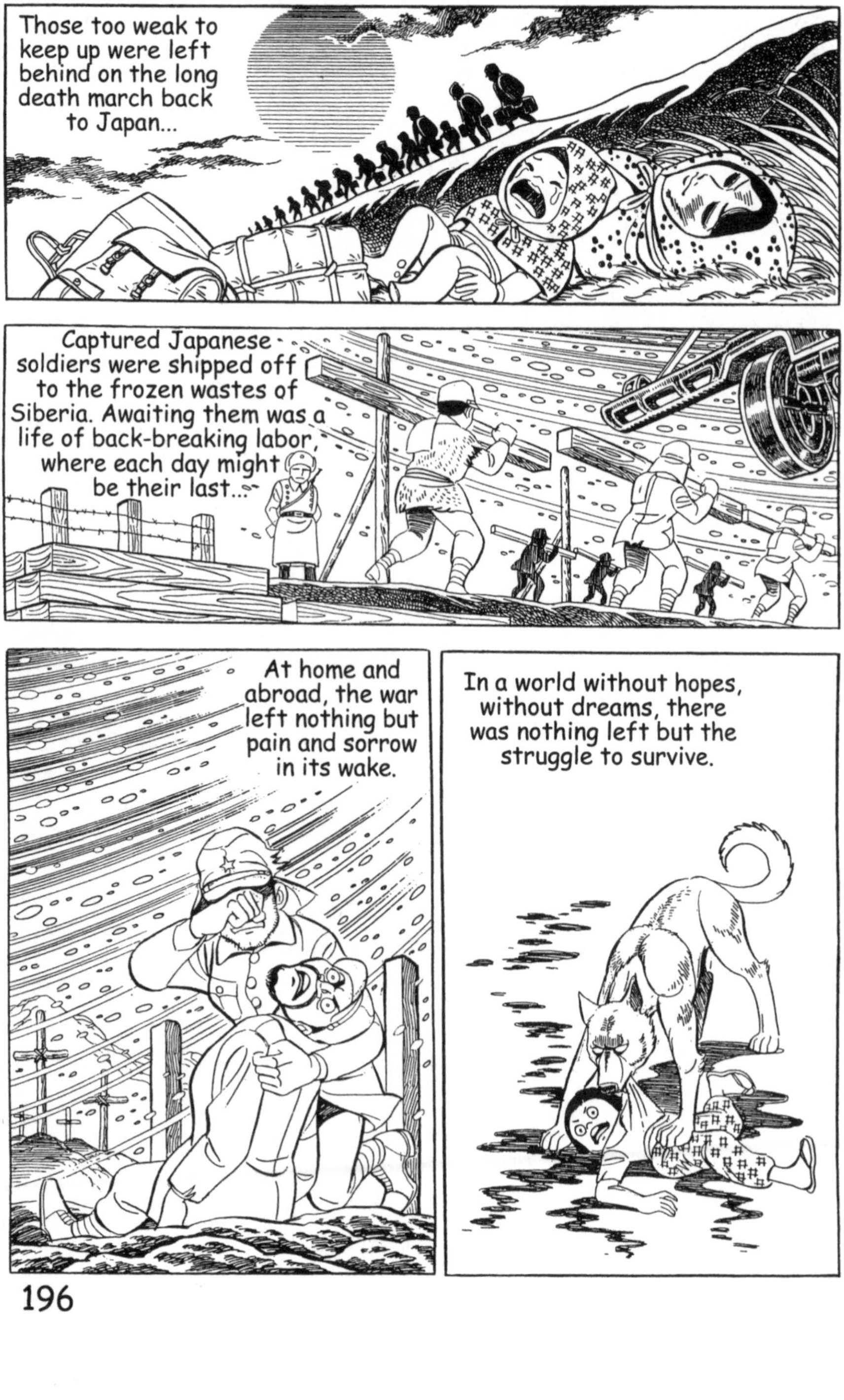
Those too weak to keep up were left behind on the long death march back to Japan...
Captured Japanese soldiers were shipped off to the frozen wastes of Siberia. Awaiting them was a life of back-breaking labor, where each day might be their last...
At home and abroad, the war left nothing but pain and sorrow in its wake.
In a world without hopes, without dreams, there was nothing left but the struggle to survive.

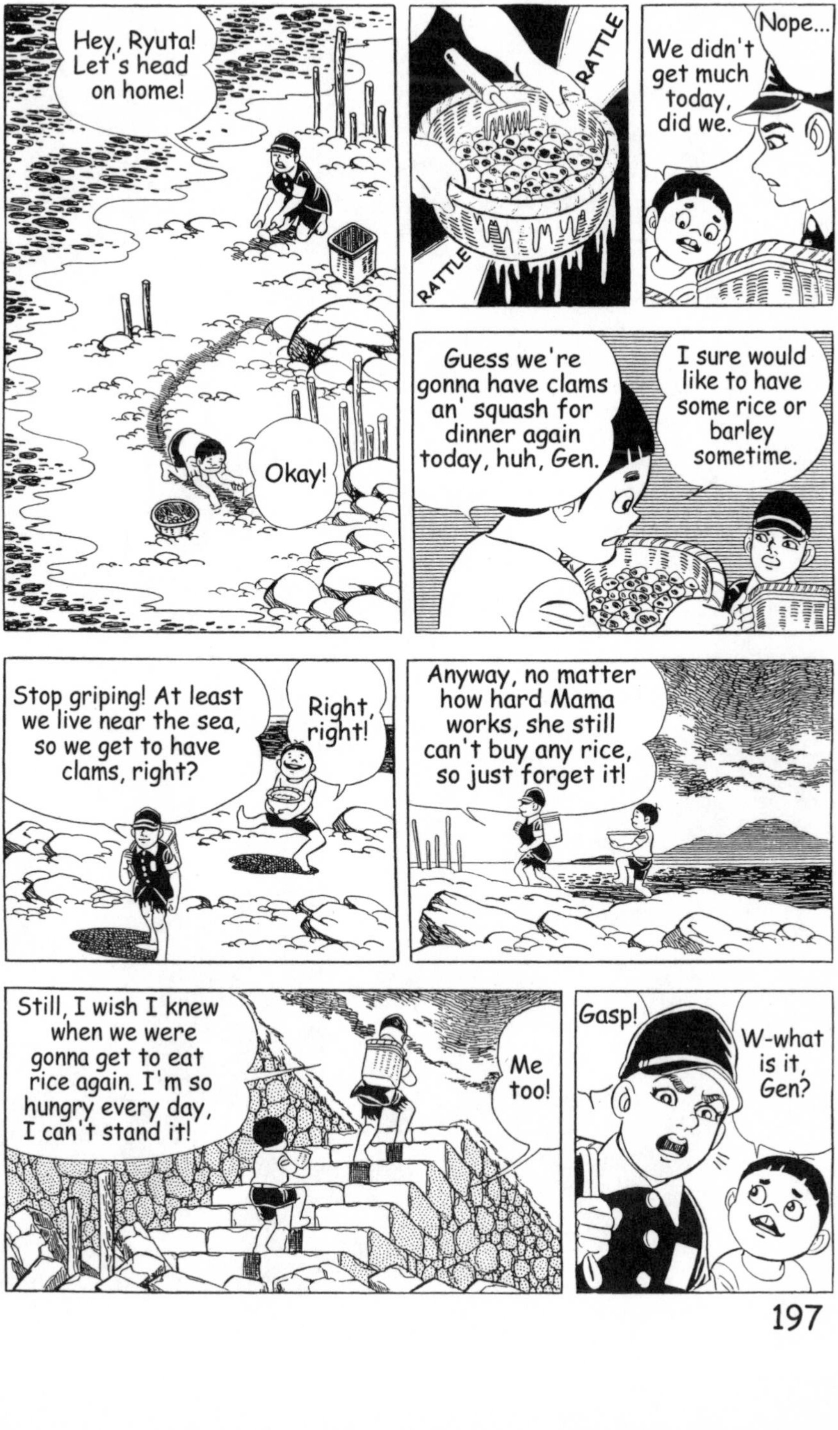
Hey, Ryuta! Let's head on home!
Okay!
RATTLE
RATTLE
Nope...
We didn't get much today, did we.
Guess we're gonna have clams an' squash for dinner again today, huh, Gen.
I sure would like to have some rice or barley sometime.
Stop griping! At least we live near the sea, so we get to have clams, right?
Right, right!
Anyway, no matter how hard Mama works, she still can't buy any rice, so just forget it!
Still, I wish I knew when we were gonna get to eat rice again. I'm so hungry every day, I can't stand it!
Me too!
Gasp!
W-what is it, Gen?

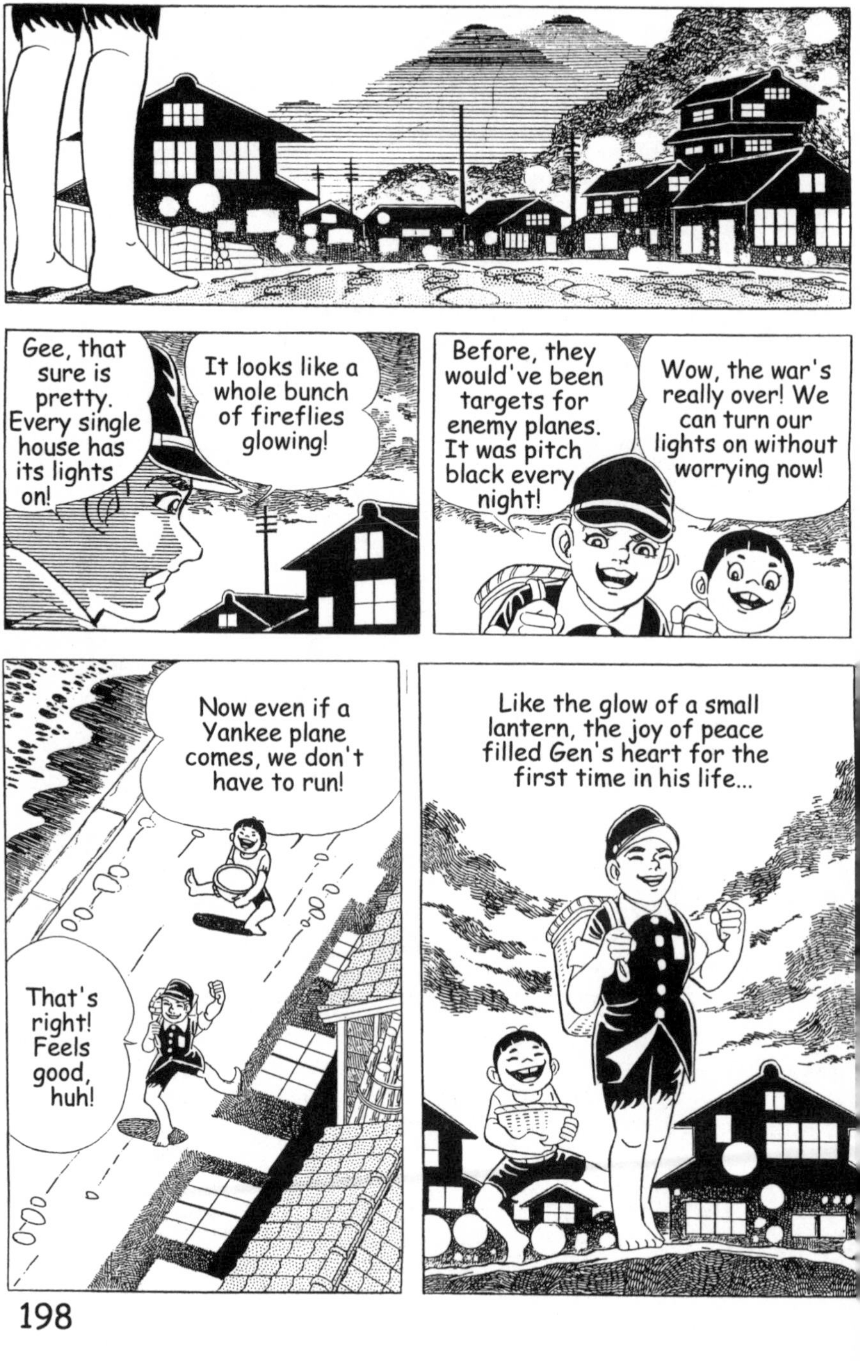
Gee, that sure is pretty. Every single house has its lights on!
It looks like a whole bunch of fireflies glowing!
Before, they would've been targets for enemy planes. It was pitch black every night!
Wow, the war's really over! We can turn our lights on without worrying now!
Now even if a Yankee plane comes, we don't have to run!
That's right! Feels good, huh!
Like the glow of a small lantern, the joy of peace filled Gen's heart for the first time in his life...

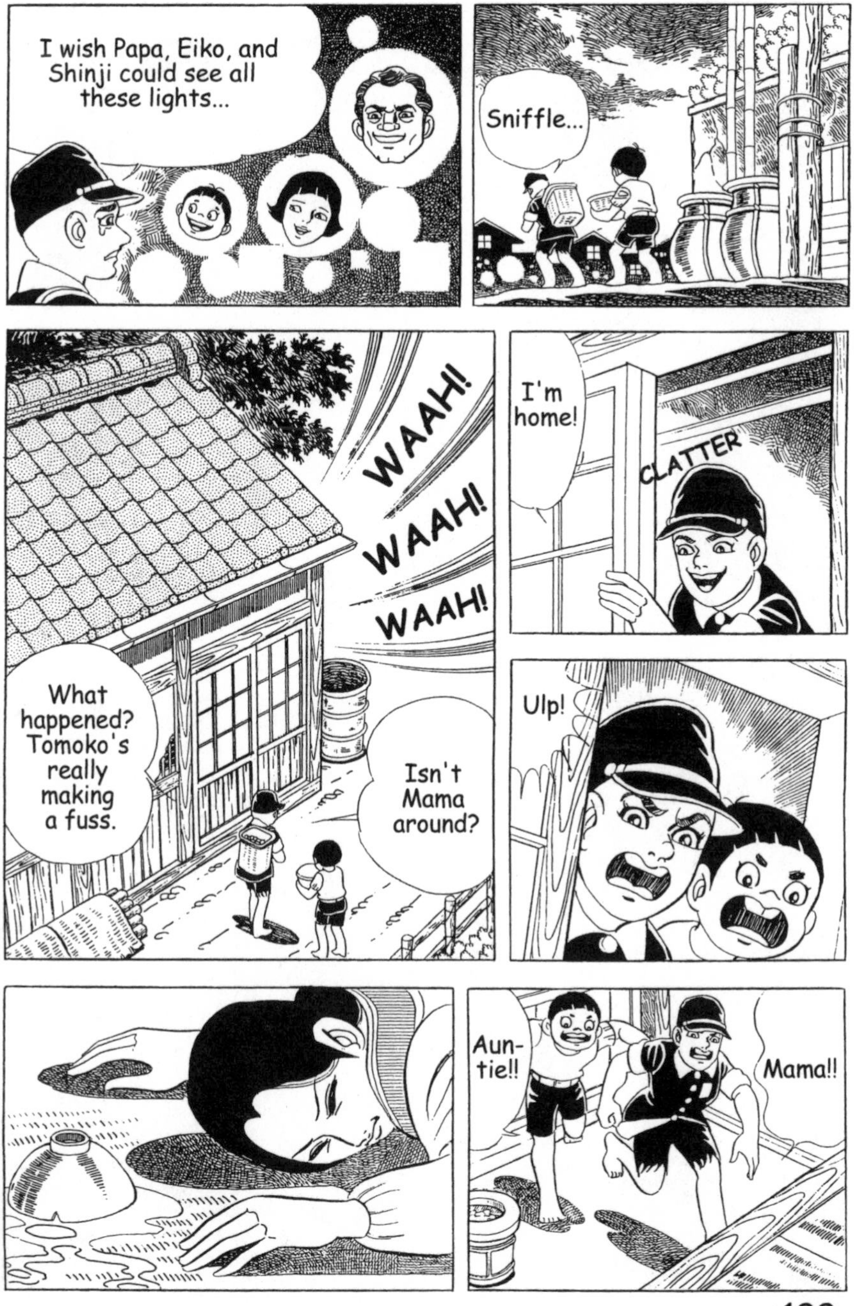
I wish Papa, Eiko, and Shinji could see all these lights...
Sniffle...
WAAH!
WAAH!
WAAH!
What happened? Tomoko's really making a fuss.
Isn't Mama around?
I'm home!
CLATTER
Ulp!
Aun-tie!!
Mama!!

WAAH! WAAH! WAAH!

Mama! What's wrong?!

Groan...

Groan... G-Gen, I'm in pain... so much pain...

Oh no! Hold on, Mama!

Look after her, Ryuta. I'll go get a doctor.

Right!

Hang on, Mama!

BAM BAM BAM

Open up, doctor! My mother's hurt! You've gotta come quick!

BAM BAM BAM

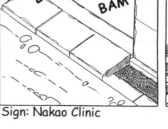

Sign: Nakao Clinic

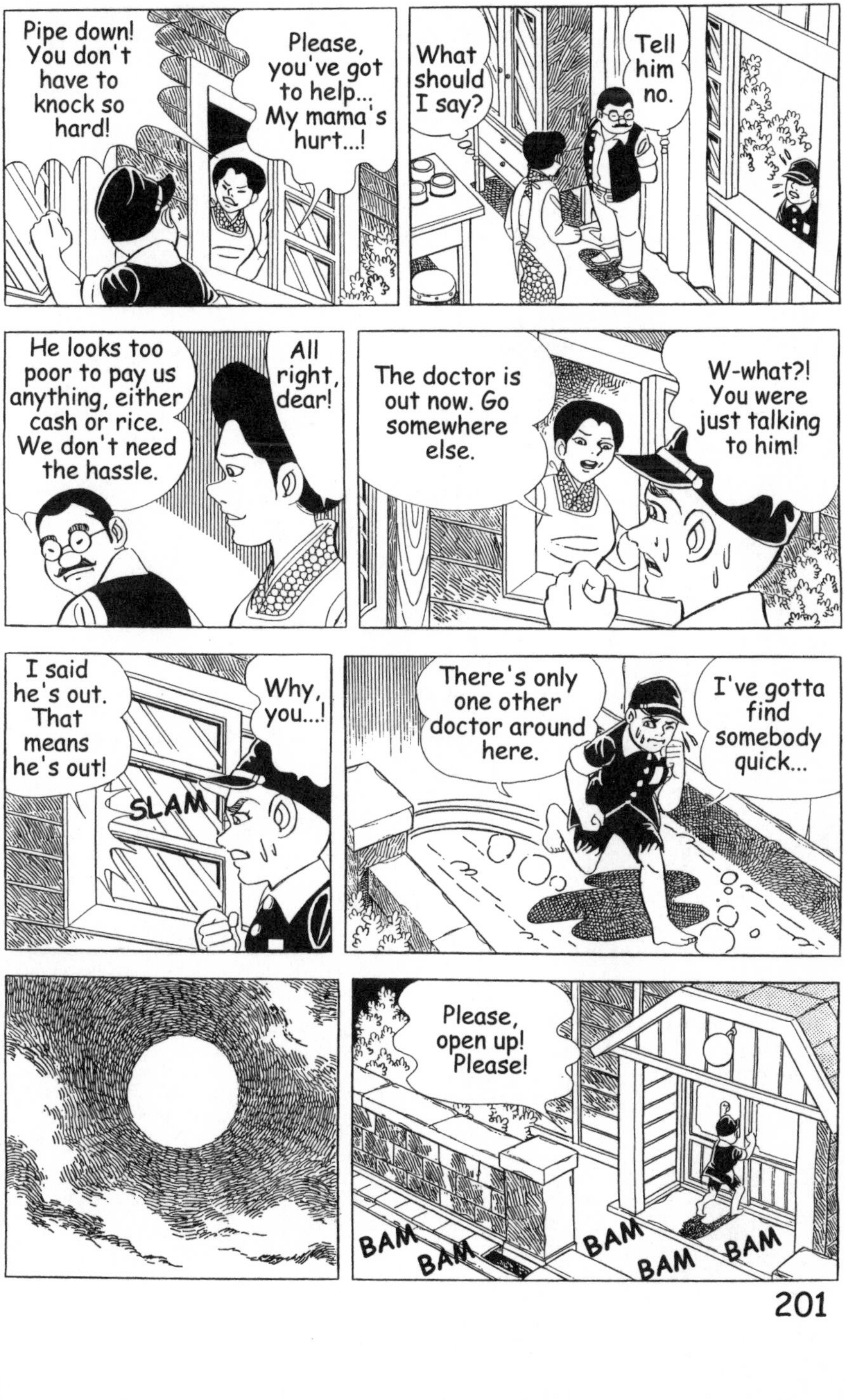
Pipe down! You don't have to knock so hard!
Please, you've got to help... My mama's hurt...!
What should I say?
Tell him no.
He looks too poor to pay us anything, either cash or rice. We don't need the hassle.
All right, dear!
The doctor is out now. Go somewhere else.
W-what?! You were just talking to him!
I said he's out. That means he's out!
Why, you...!
SLAM
There's only one other doctor around here.
I've gotta find somebody quick...
Please, open up! Please!
BAM
BAM
BAM
BAM
BAM

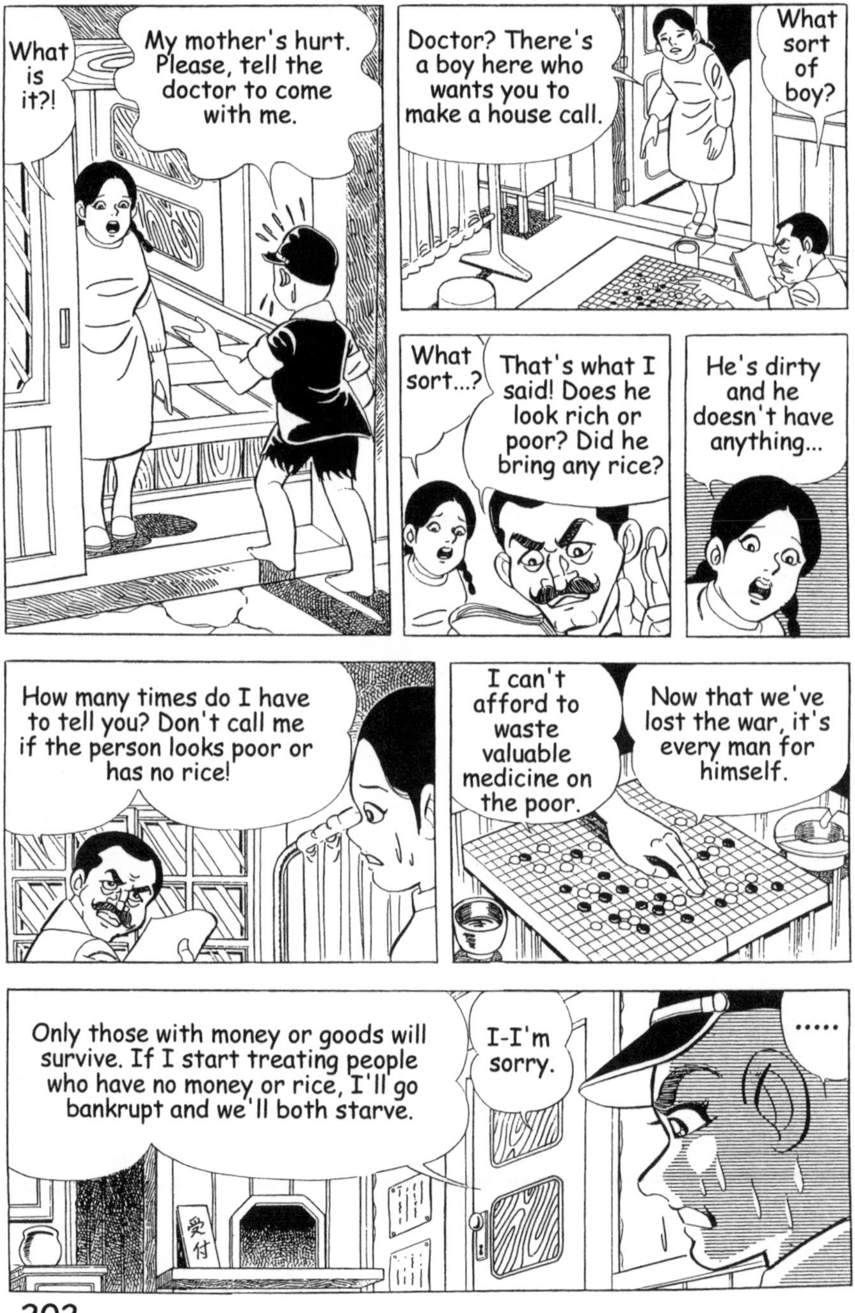
What is it?!
My mother's hurt. Please, tell the doctor to come with me.
Doctor? There's a boy here who wants you to make a house call.
What sort of boy?
What sort...?
That's what I said! Does he look rich or poor? Did he bring any rice?
He's dirty and he doesn't have anything...
How many times do I have to tell you? Don't call me if the person looks poor or has no rice!
I can't afford to waste valuable medicine on the poor.
Now that we've lost the war, it's every man for himself.
Only those with money or goods will survive. If I start treating people who have no money or rice, I'll go bankrupt and we'll both starve.
I-I'm sorry.
......
受付

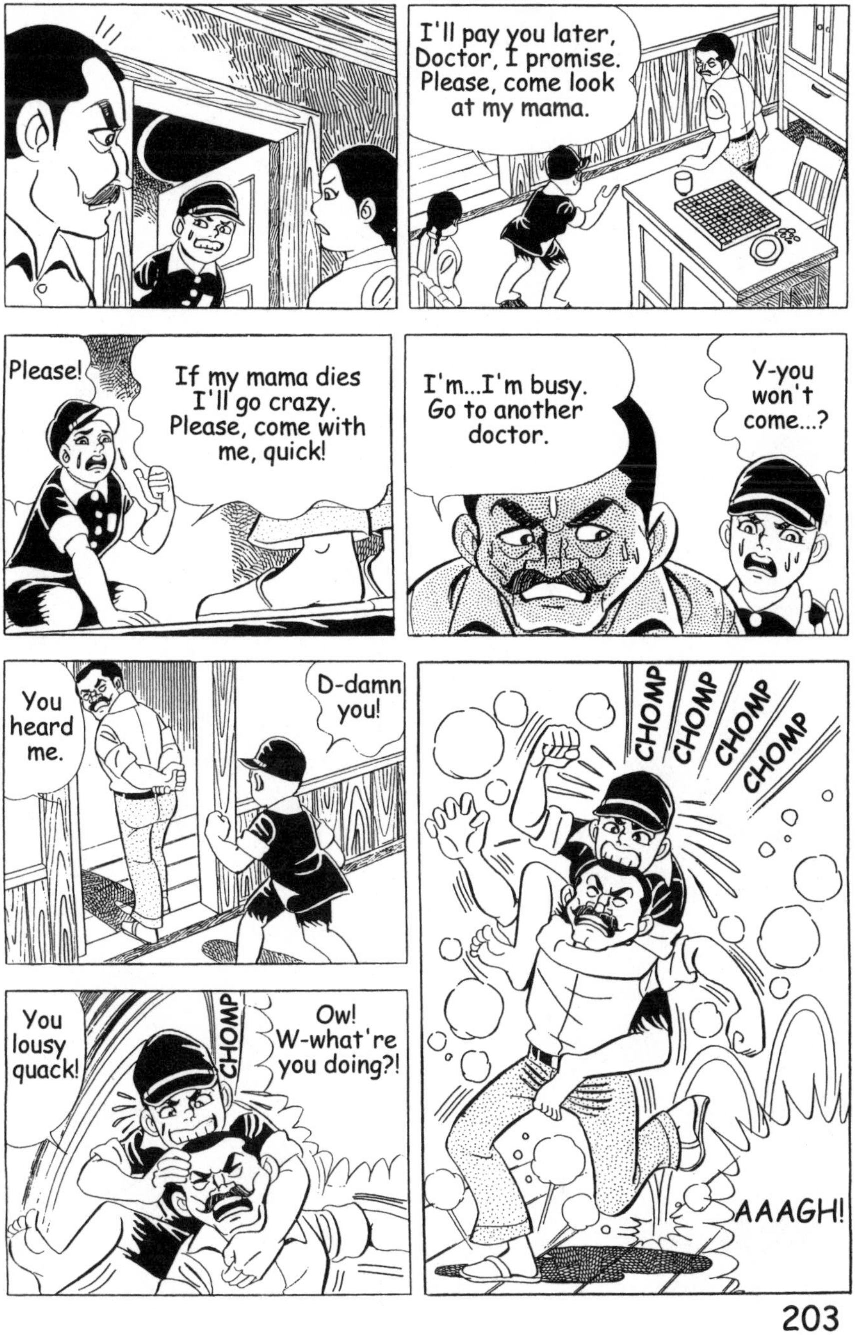
I'll pay you later, Doctor, I promise. Please, come look at my mama.
Please!
If my mama dies I'll go crazy. Please, come with me, quick!
I'm...I'm busy. Go to another doctor.
Y-you won't come...?
You heard me.
D-damn you!
CHOMP
CHOMP
CHOMP
CHOMP
AAAGH!
You lousy quack!
CHOMP
Ow! W-what're you doing?!

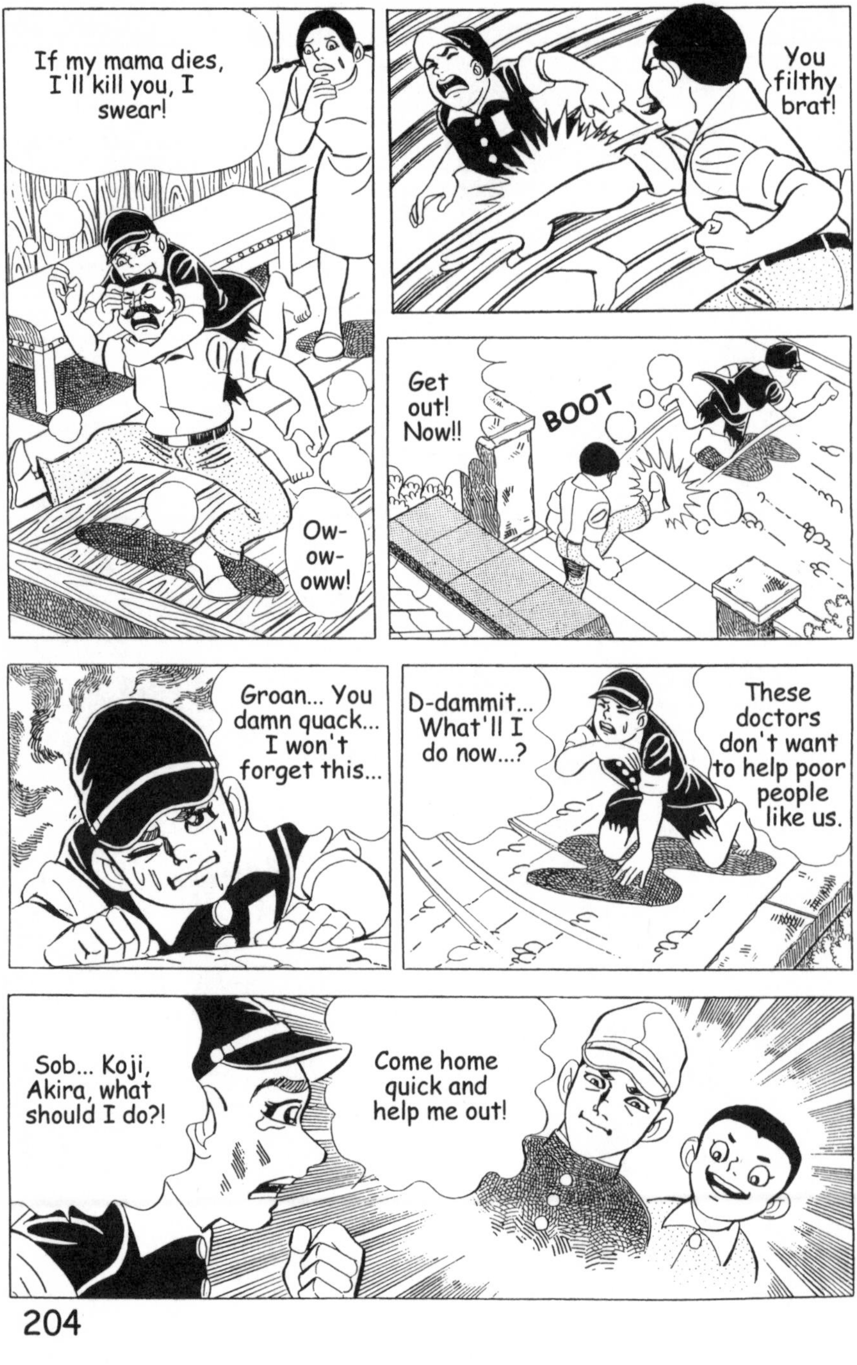
If my mama dies, I'll kill you, I swear!
Ow-oww-oww!
You filthy brat!
Get out! Now!!
BOOT
Groan... You damn quack... I won't forget this...
D-dammit... What'll I do now...?
These doctors don't want to help poor people like us.
Sob... Koji, Akira, what should I do?!
Come home quick and help me out!

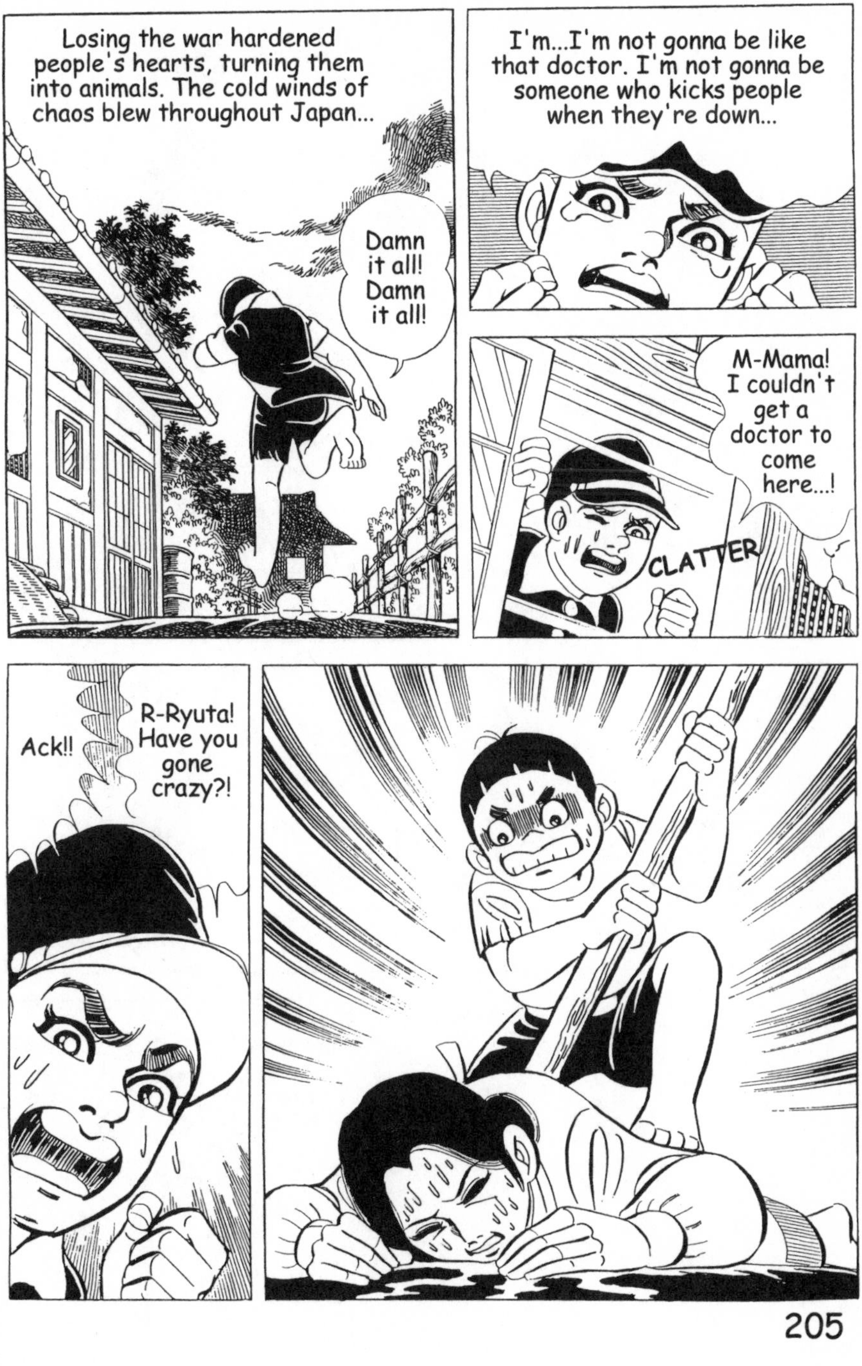
Losing the war hardened people's hearts, turning them into animals. The cold winds of chaos blew throughout Japan...
Damn it all! Damn it all!
I'm...I'm not gonna be like that doctor. I'm not gonna be someone who kicks people when they're down...
M-Mama! I couldn't get a doctor to come here...!
CLATTER
Ack!!
R-Ryuta! Have you gone crazy?!

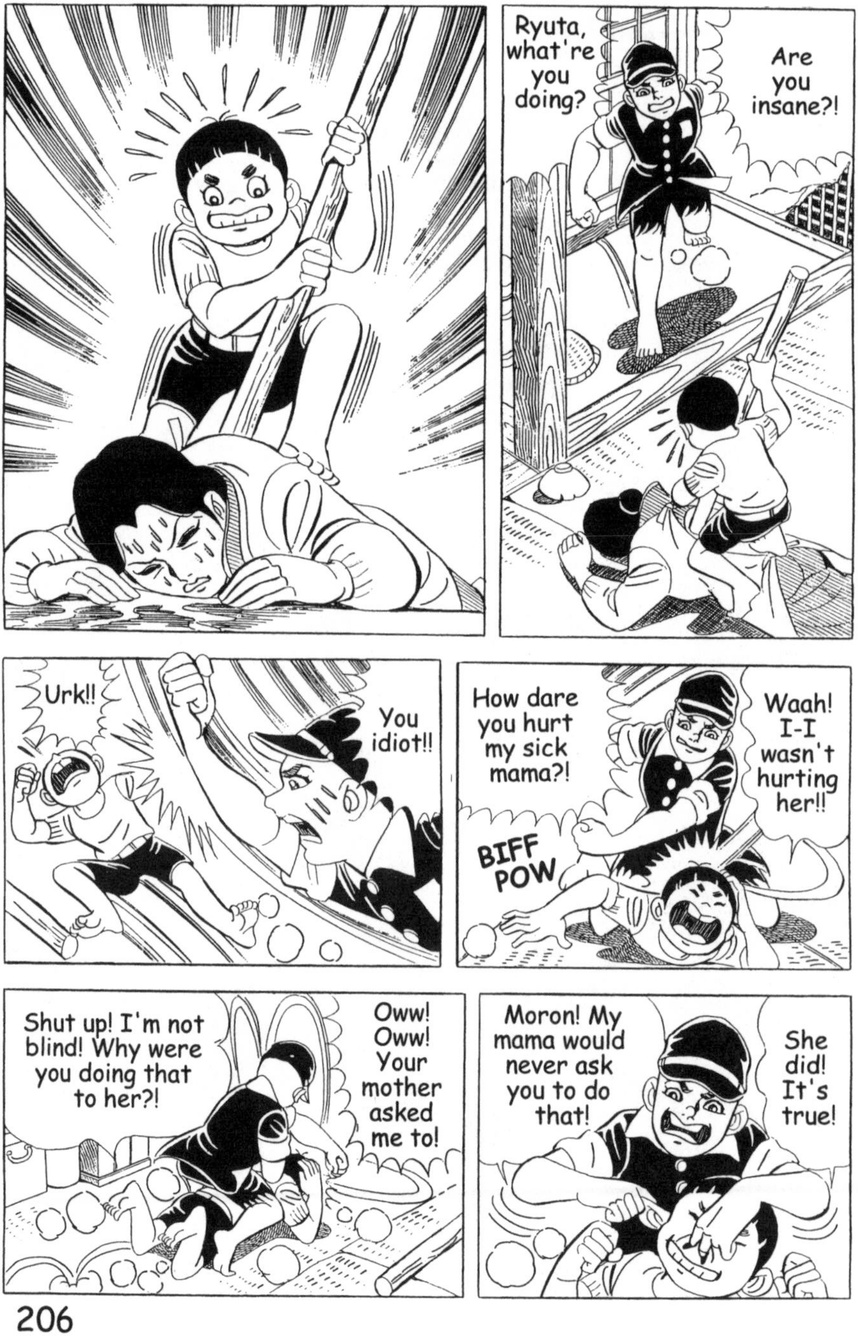
Ryuta, what're you doing?
Are you insane?!
Urk!!
You idiot!!
How dare you hurt my sick mama?!
Waah! I-I wasn't hurting her!!
BIFF
POW
Shut up! I'm not blind! Why were you doing that to her?!
Oww! Oww! Your mother asked me to!
Moron! My mama would never ask you to do that!
She did! It's true!

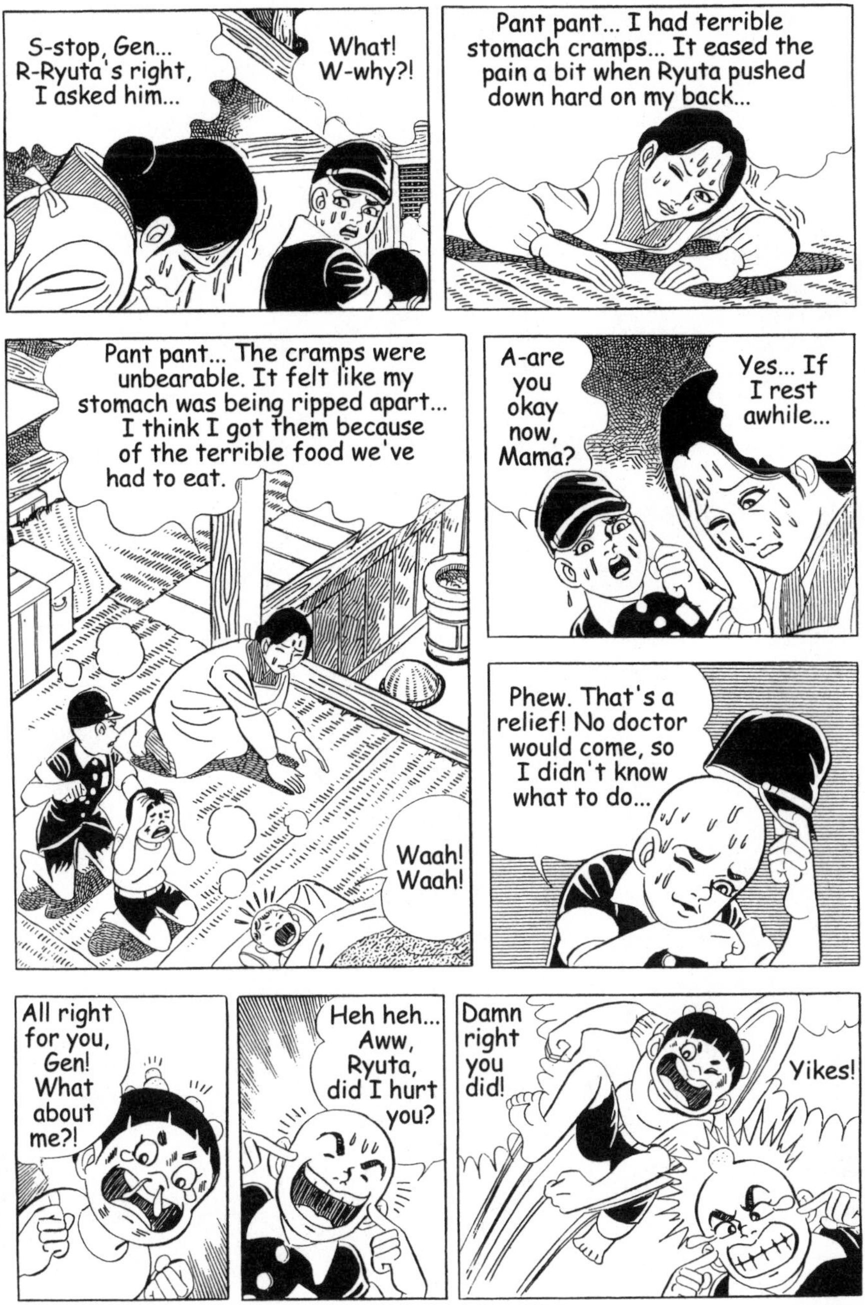
S-stop, Gen... R-Ryuta's right, I asked him...
What! W-why?!
Pant pant... I had terrible stomach cramps... It eased the pain a bit when Ryuta pushed down hard on my back...
Pant pant... The cramps were unbearable. It felt like my stomach was being ripped apart... I think I got them because of the terrible food we've had to eat.
Waah! Waah!
A-are you okay now, Mama?
Yes... If I rest awhile...
Phew. That's a relief! No doctor would come, so I didn't know what to do...
All right for you, Gen! What about me?!
Heh heh... Aww, Ryuta, did I hurt you?
Damn right you did!
Yikes!

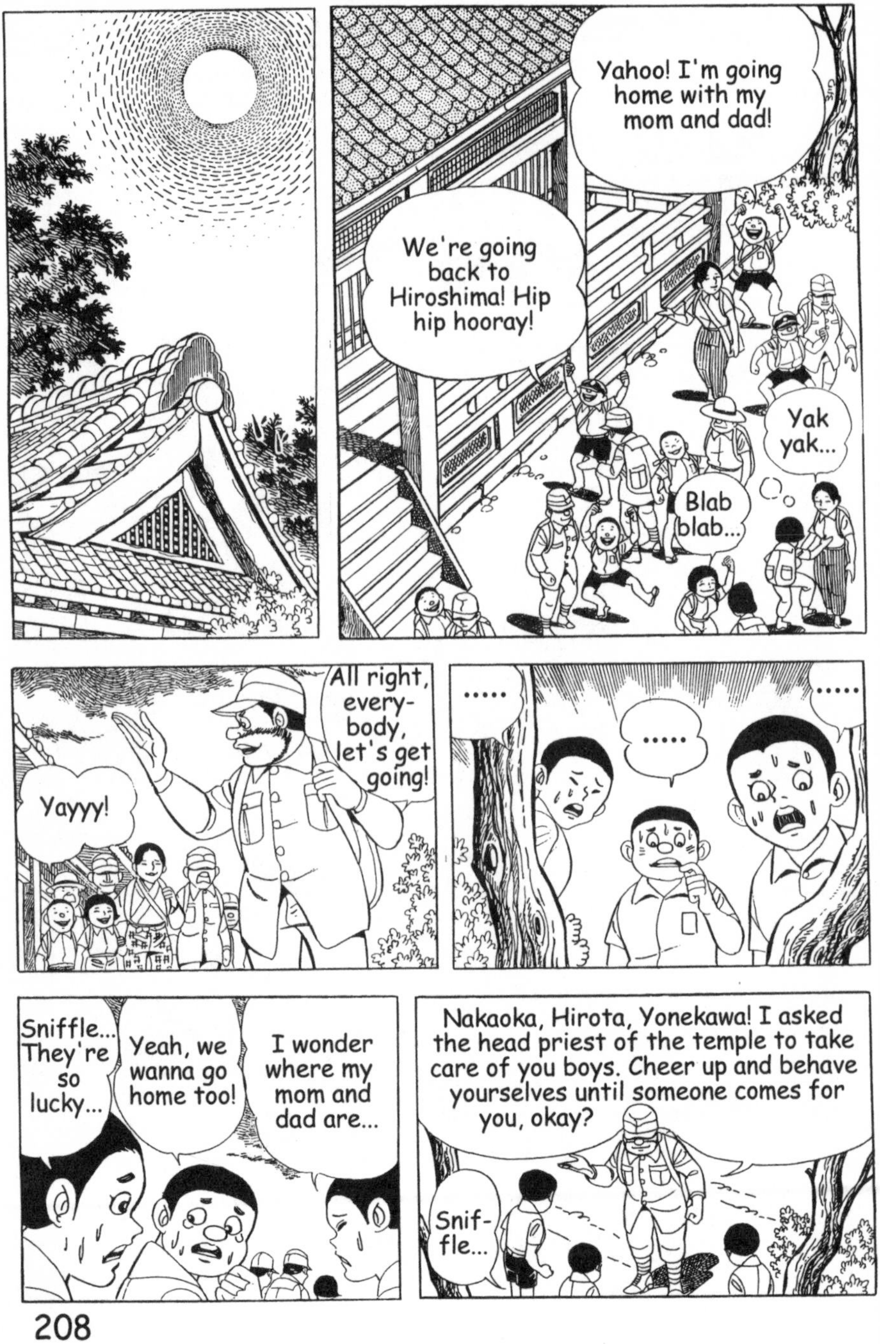
We're going back to Hiroshima! Hip hip hooray!
Yahoo! I'm going home with my mom and dad!
Yak yak...
Blab blab...
Yayyy!
All right, every-body, let's get going!
.....
.....
.....
Sniffle... They're so lucky...
Yeah, we wanna go home too!
I wonder where my mom and dad are...
Nakaoka, Hirota, Yonekawa! I asked the head priest of the temple to take care of you boys. Cheer up and behave yourselves until someone comes for you, okay?
Snif-fle...

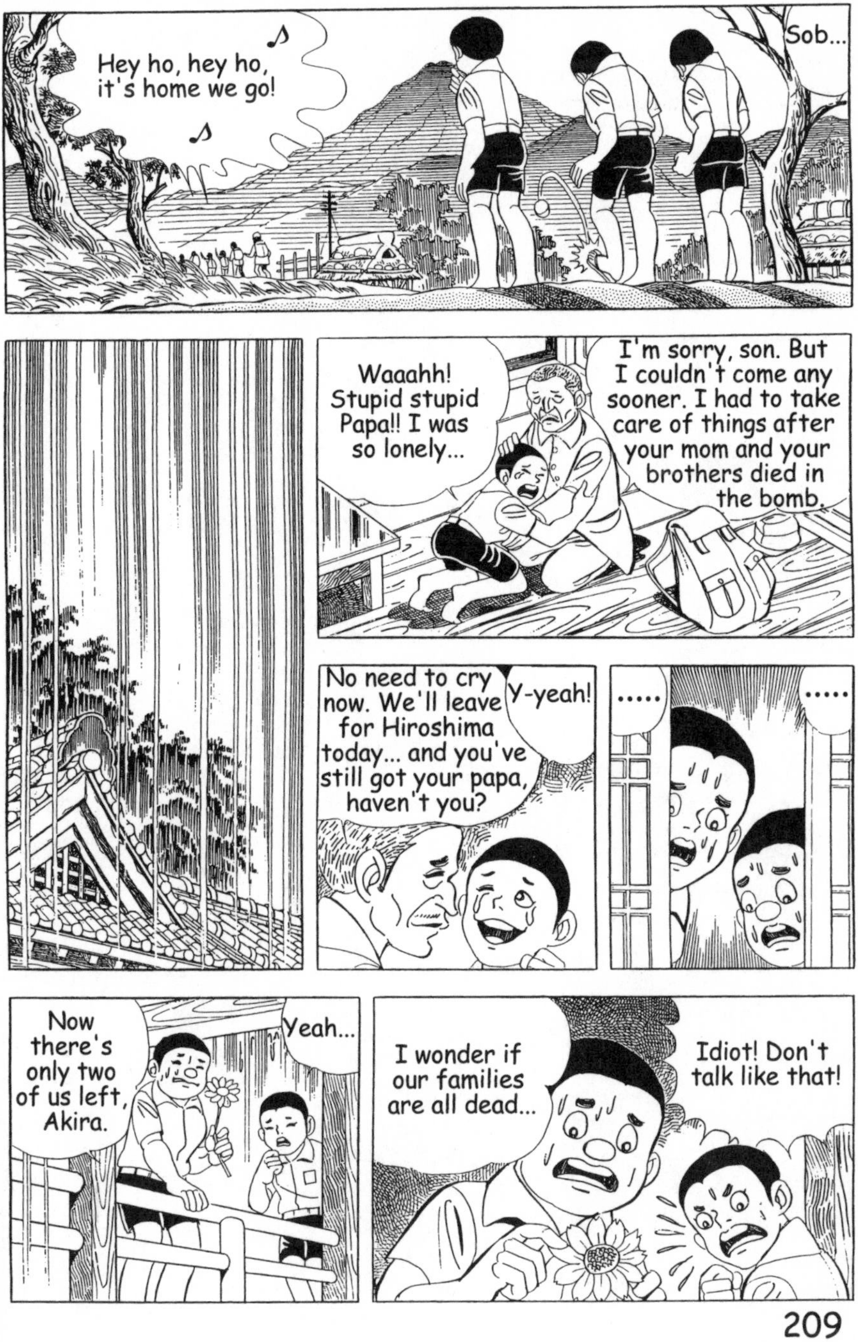
Hey ho, hey ho, it's home we go!
Sob...
Waaahh! Stupid stupid Papa!! I was so lonely...
I'm sorry, son. But I couldn't come any sooner. I had to take care of things after your mom and your brothers died in the bomb.
No need to cry now. We'll leave for Hiroshima today... and you've still got your papa, haven't you?
Y-yeah!
.....
.....
Now there's only two of us left, Akira.
Yeah...
I wonder if our families are all dead...
Idiot! Don't talk like that!

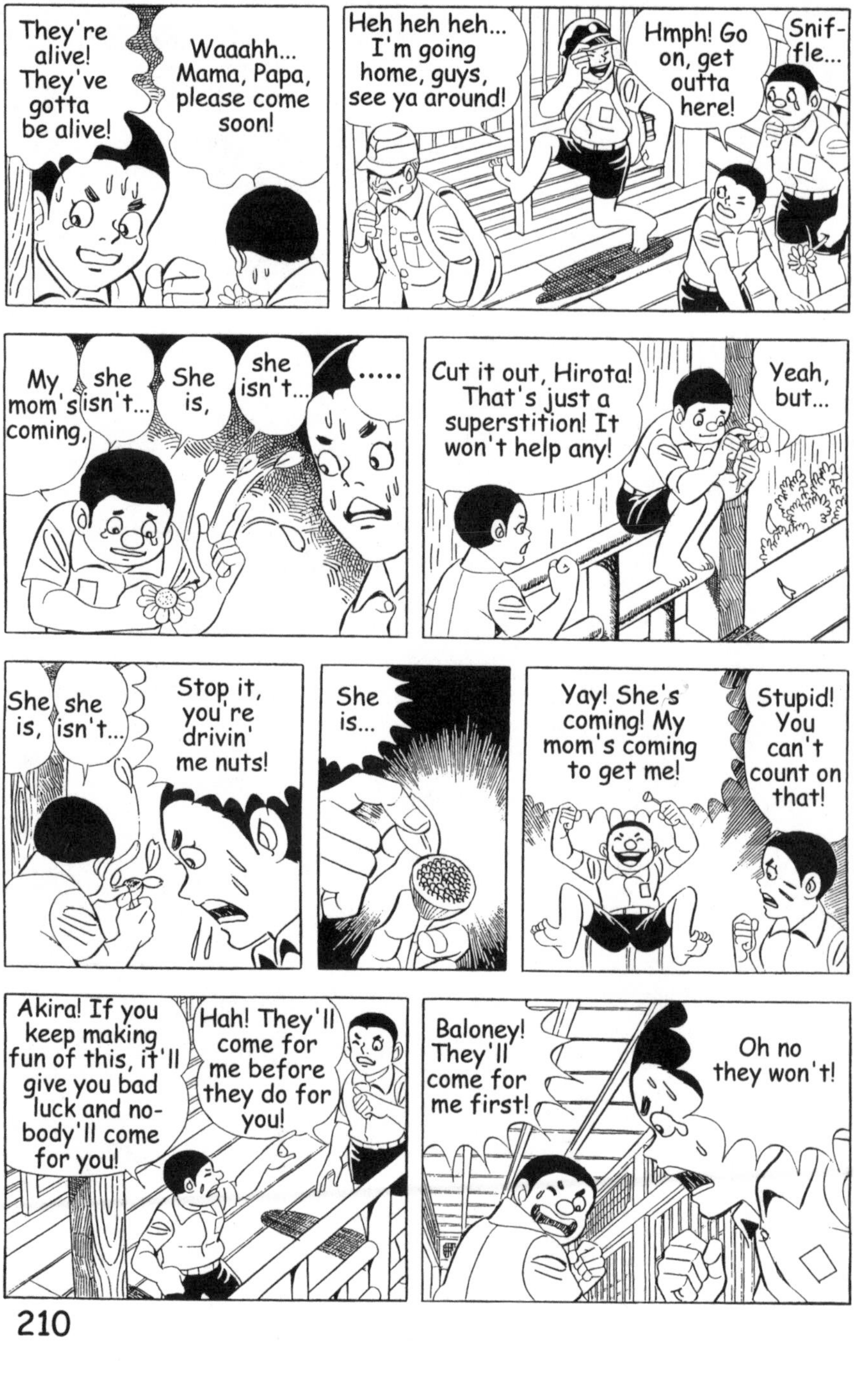

They're alive! They've gotta be alive!
Waaahh... Mama, Papa, please come soon!
Heh heh heh... I'm going home, guys, see ya around!
Hmph! Go on, get outta here!
Snif-fle...
My mom's coming,
she isn't...
She is,
she isn't...
.....
Cut it out, Hirota! That's just a superstition! It won't help any!
Yeah, but...
She is,
she isn't...
Stop it, you're drivin' me nuts!
She is...
Yay! She's coming! My mom's coming to get me!
Stupid! You can't count on that!
Akira! If you keep making fun of this, it'll give you bad luck and no-body'll come for you!
Hah! They'll come for me before they do for you!
Baloney! They'll come for me first!
Oh no they won't!

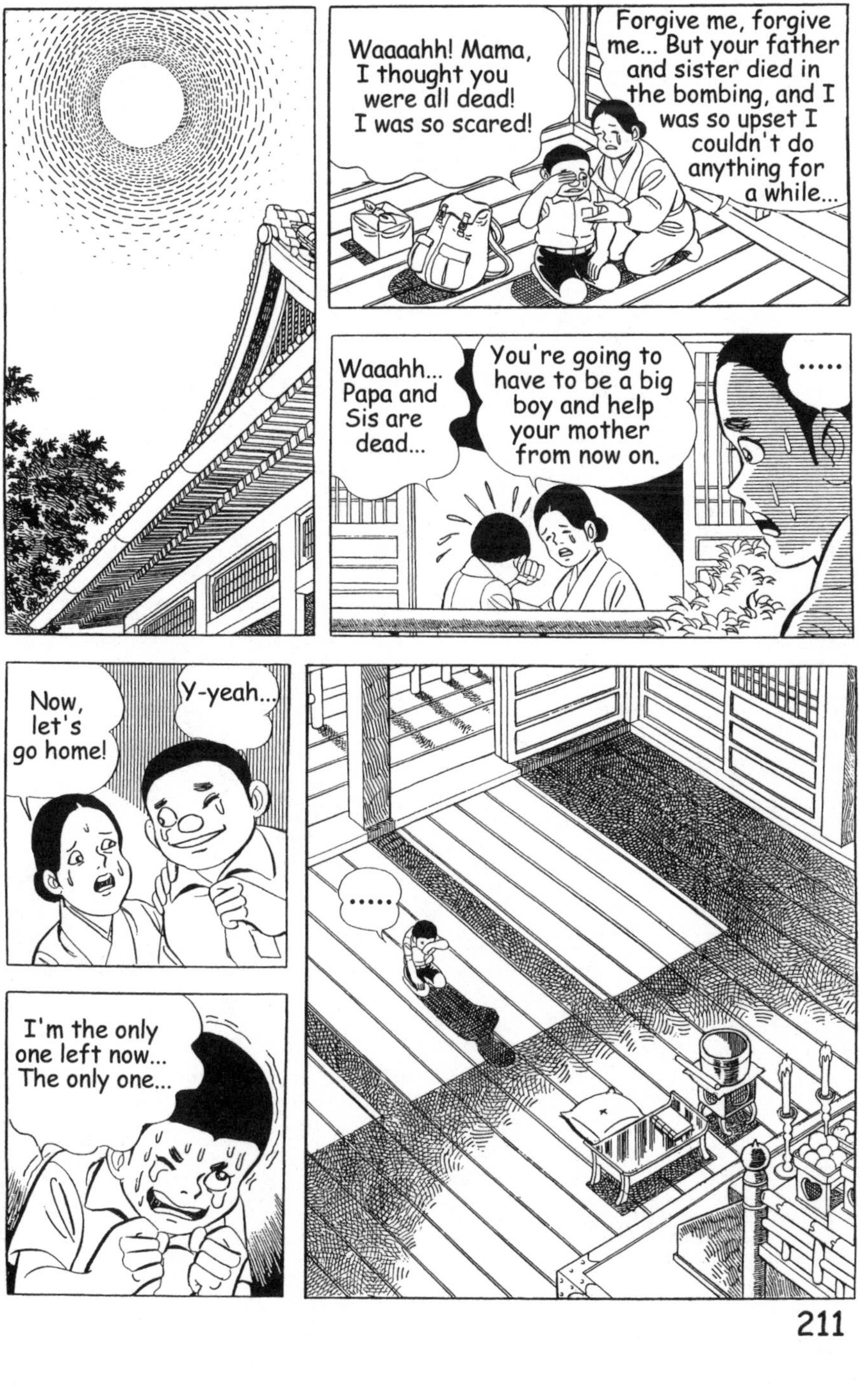
Waaaahh! Mama, I thought you were all dead! I was so scared!
Forgive me, forgive me... But your father and sister died in the bombing, and I was so upset I couldn't do anything for a while...
Waaahh... Papa and Sis are dead...
You're going to have to be a big boy and help your mother from now on.
.....
Now, let's go home!
Y-yeah...
......
I'm the only one left now... The only one...

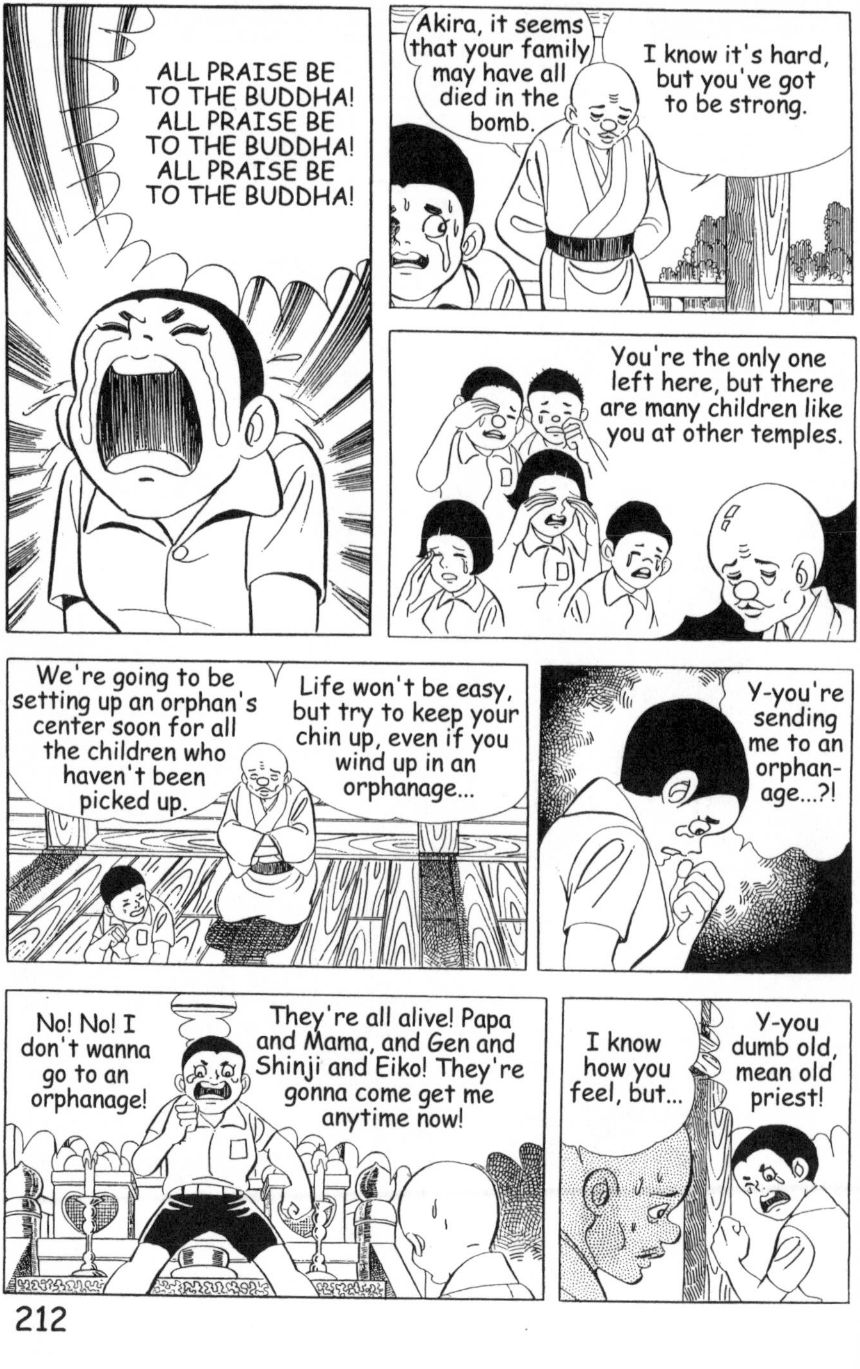
ALL PRAISE BE TO THE BUDDHA! ALL PRAISE BE TO THE BUDDHA! ALL PRAISE BE TO THE BUDDHA!
Akira, it seems that your family may have all died in the bomb.
I know it's hard, but you've got to be strong.
You're the only one left here, but there are many children like you at other temples.
We're going to be setting up an orphan's center soon for all the children who haven't been picked up.
Life won't be easy, but try to keep your chin up, even if you wind up in an orphanage...
Y-you're sending me to an orphan-age...?!
No! No! I don't wanna go to an orphanage!
They're all alive! Papa and Mama, and Gen and Shinji and Eiko! They're gonna come get me anytime now!
I know how you feel, but...
Y-you dumb old, mean old priest!

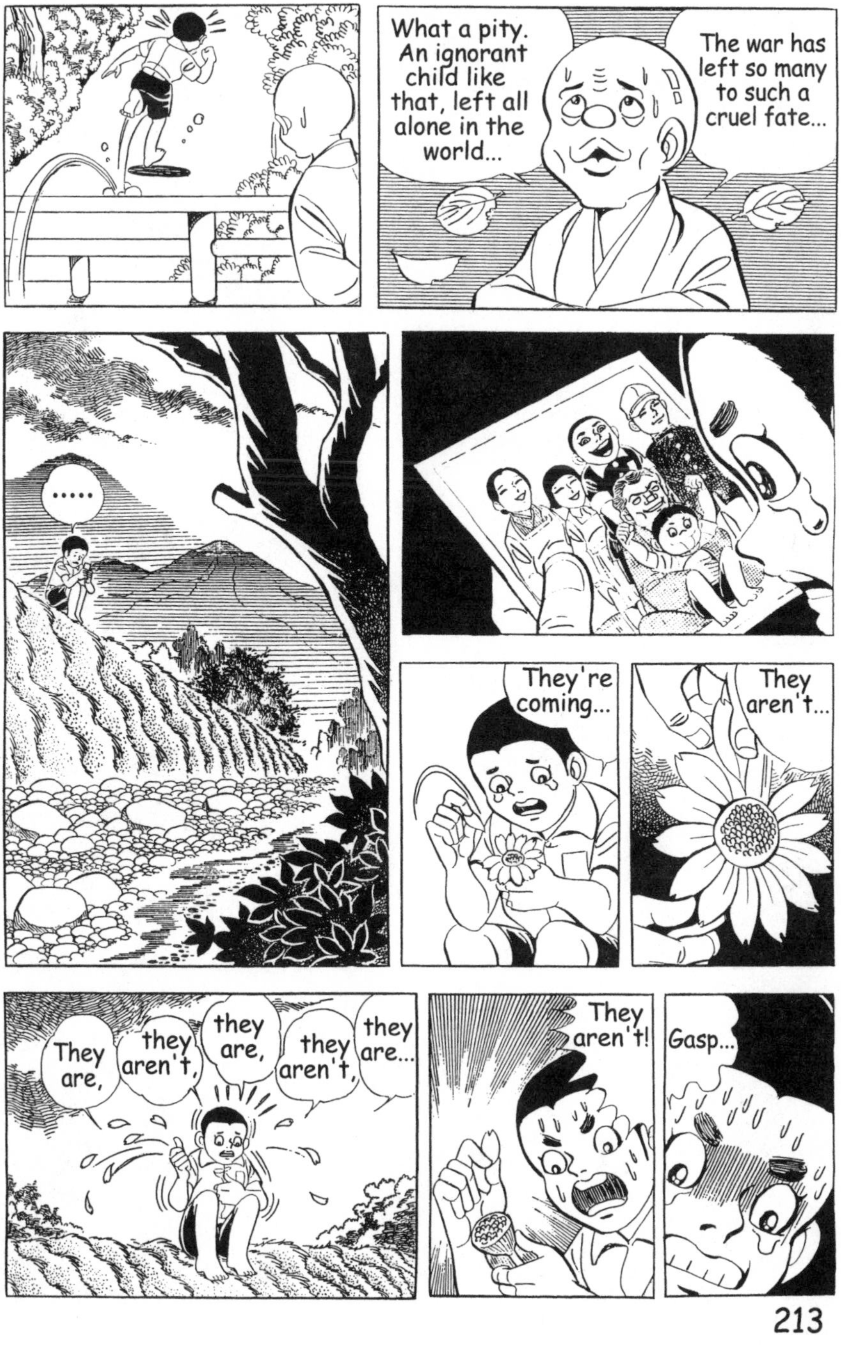
What a pity. An ignorant child like that, left all alone in the world...
The war has left so many to such a cruel fate...
......
They're coming...
They aren't...
They are,
they aren't,
they are,
they aren't,
they are...
They aren't!
Gasp...

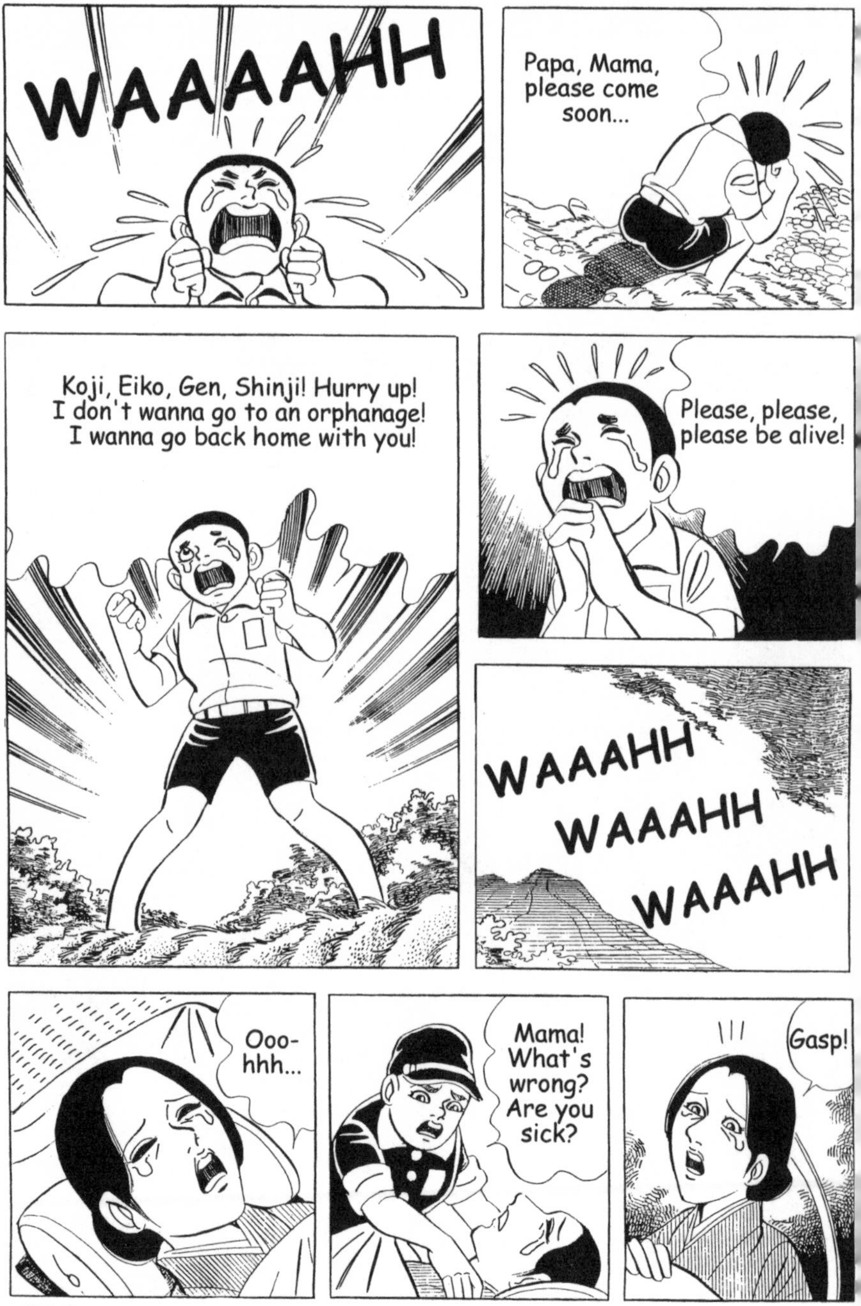
WAAAAHH
Papa, Mama, please come soon...
Koji, Eiko, Gen, Shinji! Hurry up! I don't wanna go to an orphanage! I wanna go back home with you!
Please, please, please be alive!
WAAAHH
WAAAHH
WAAAHH
Ooo-hhh...
Mama! What's wrong? Are you sick?
Gasp!

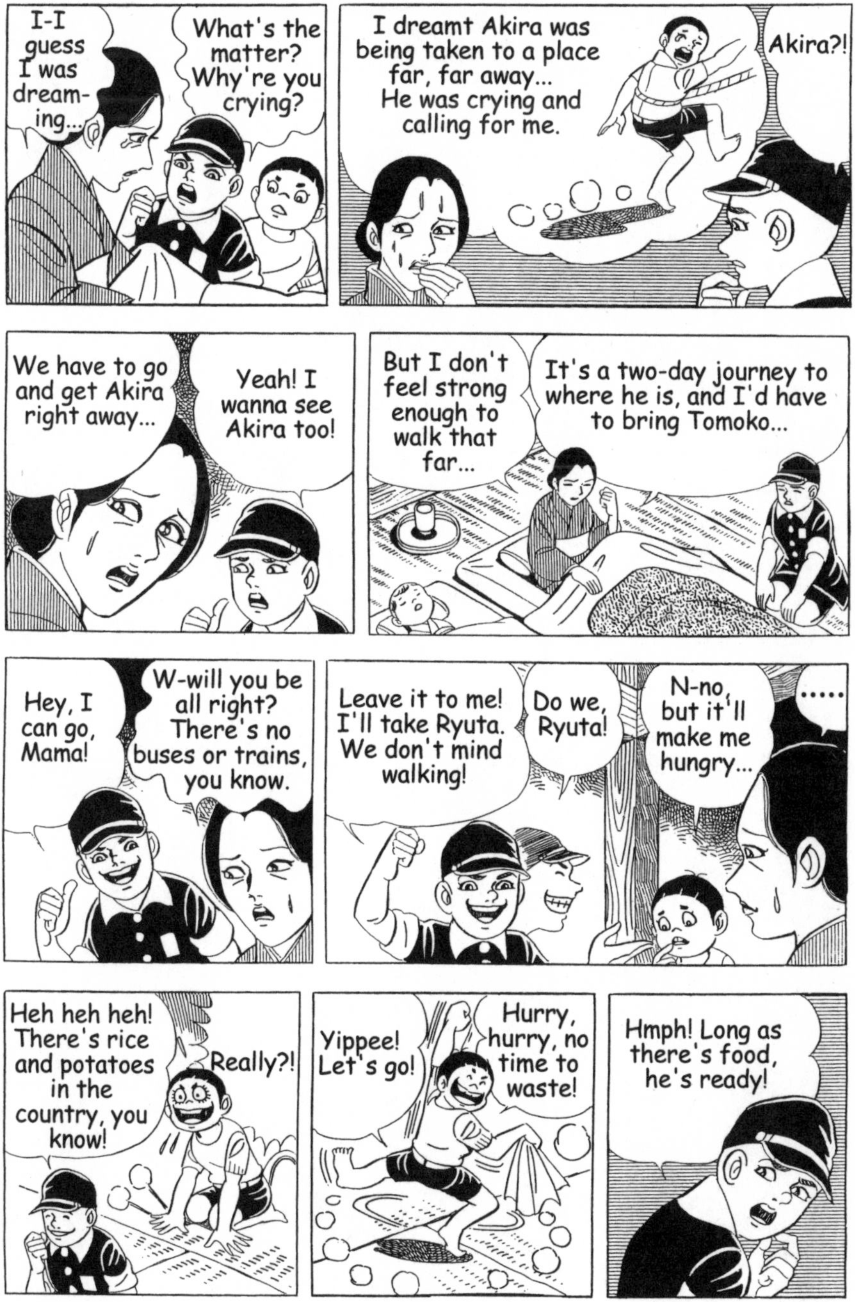
I-I guess I was dreaming...
What's the matter? Why're you crying?
I dreamt Akira was being taken to a place far, far away... He was crying and calling for me.
Akira?!
We have to go and get Akira right away...
Yeah! I wanna see Akira too!
But I don't feel strong enough to walk that far...
It's a two-day journey to where he is, and I'd have to bring Tomoko...
Hey, I can go, Mama!
W-will you be all right? There's no buses or trains, you know.
Leave it to me! I'll take Ryuta. We don't mind walking!
Do we, Ryuta!
N-no, but it'll make me hungry...
.....
Heh heh heh! There's rice and potatoes in the country, you know!
Really?!
Yippee! Let's go!
Hurry, hurry, no time to waste!
Hmph! Long as there's food, he's ready!

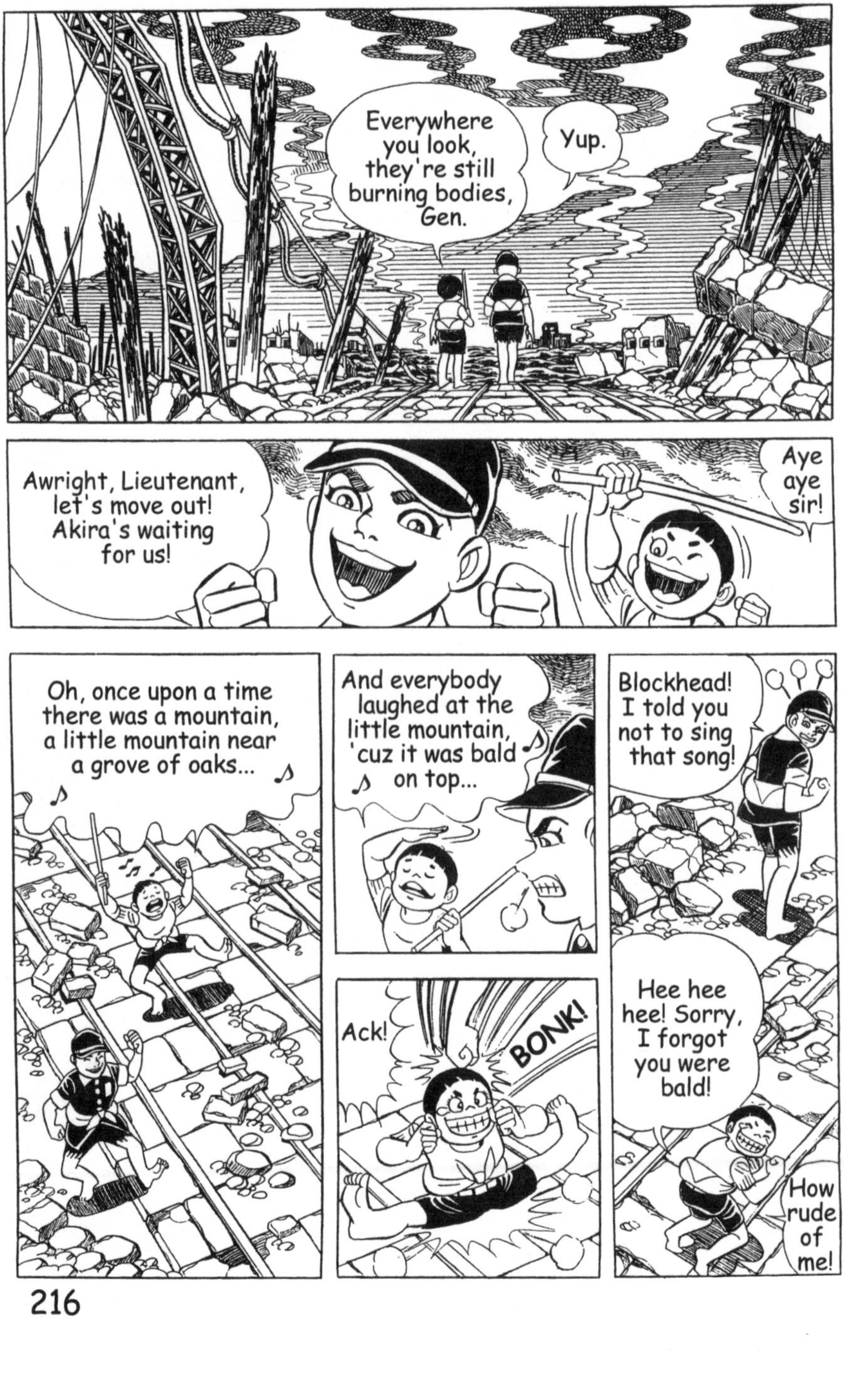
Everywhere you look, they're still burning bodies, Gen.
Yup.
Awright, Lieutenant, let's move out! Akira's waiting for us!
Aye aye sir!
Oh, once upon a time there was a mountain, a little mountain near a grove of oaks...
And everybody laughed at the little mountain, 'cuz it was bald on top...
Blockhead! I told you not to sing that song!
Ack!
BONK!
Hee hee hee! Sorry, I forgot you were bald!
How rude of me!

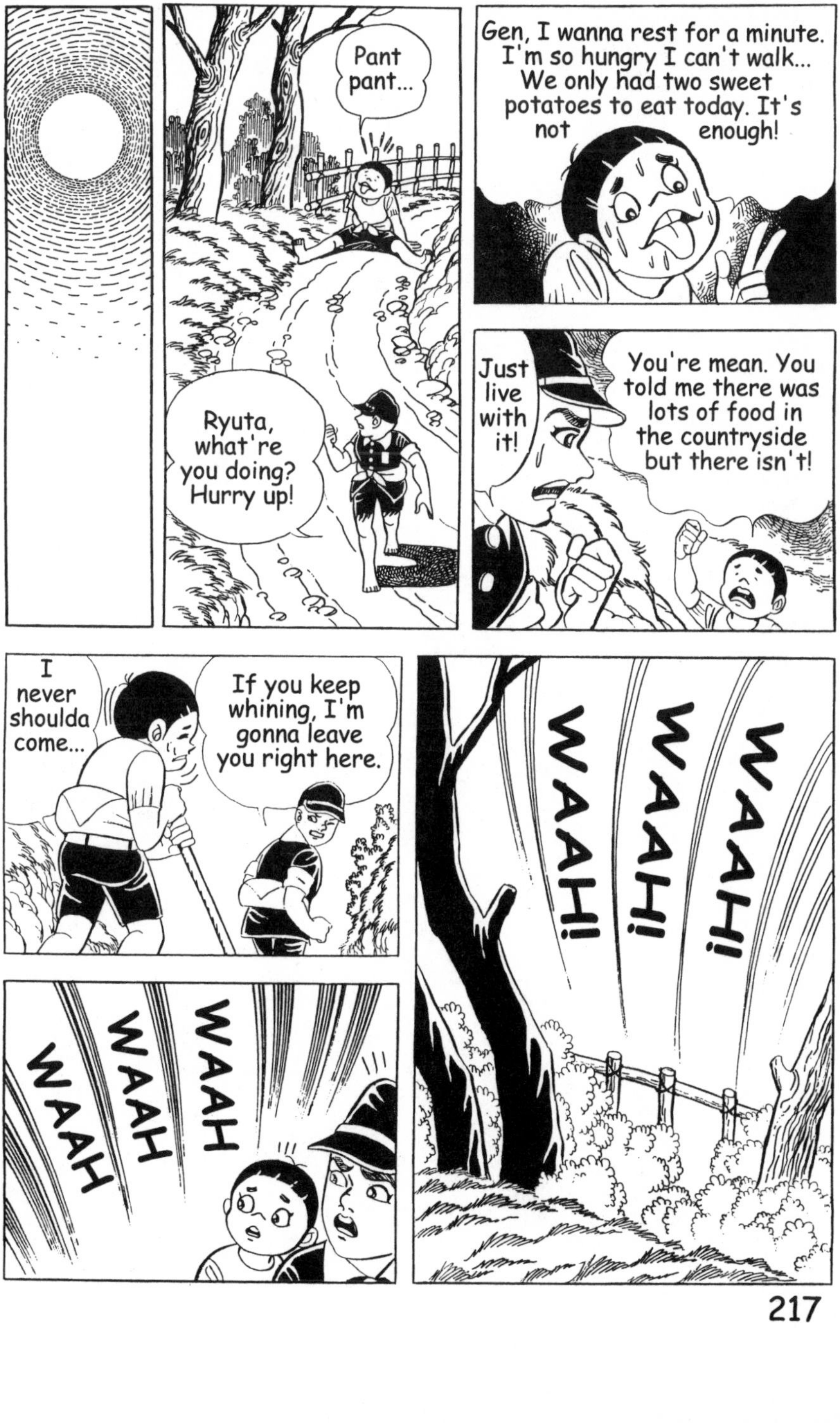
Pant pant...
Ryuta, what're you doing? Hurry up!
Gen, I wanna rest for a minute. I'm so hungry I can't walk... We only had two sweet potatoes to eat today. It's not enough!
You're mean. You told me there was lots of food in the countryside but there isn't!
Just live with it!
I never shoulda come...
If you keep whining, I'm gonna leave you right here.
WAAH
WAAH
WAAH
WAAAH!
WAAAH!
WAAAH!

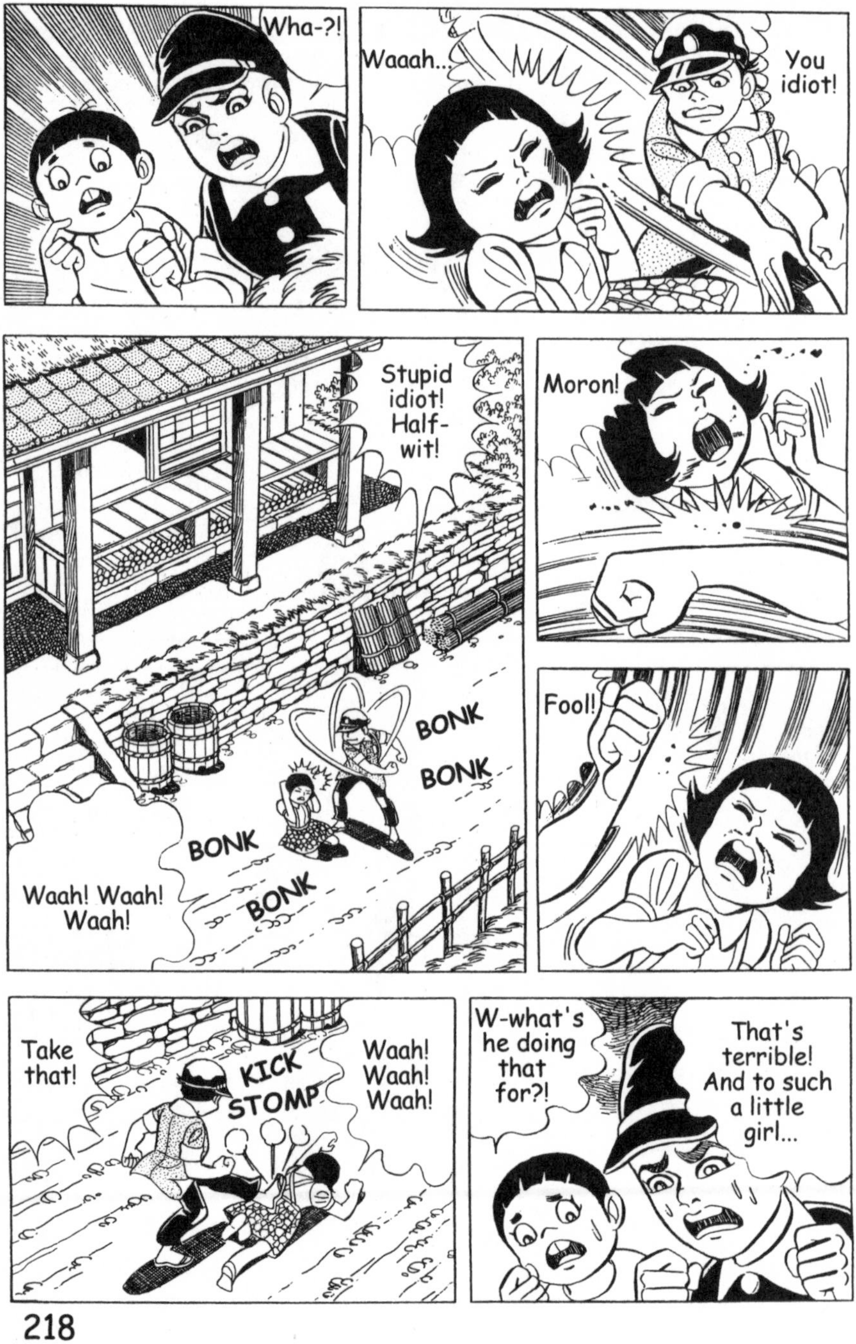
Wha-?!
Waaah...
You idiot!
Stupid idiot! Half-wit!
BONK
BONK
BONK
BONK
Waah! Waah! Waah!
Moron!
Fool!
Take that!
KICK
STOMP
Waah! Waah! Waah!
W-what's he doing that for?!
That's terrible! And to such a little girl...

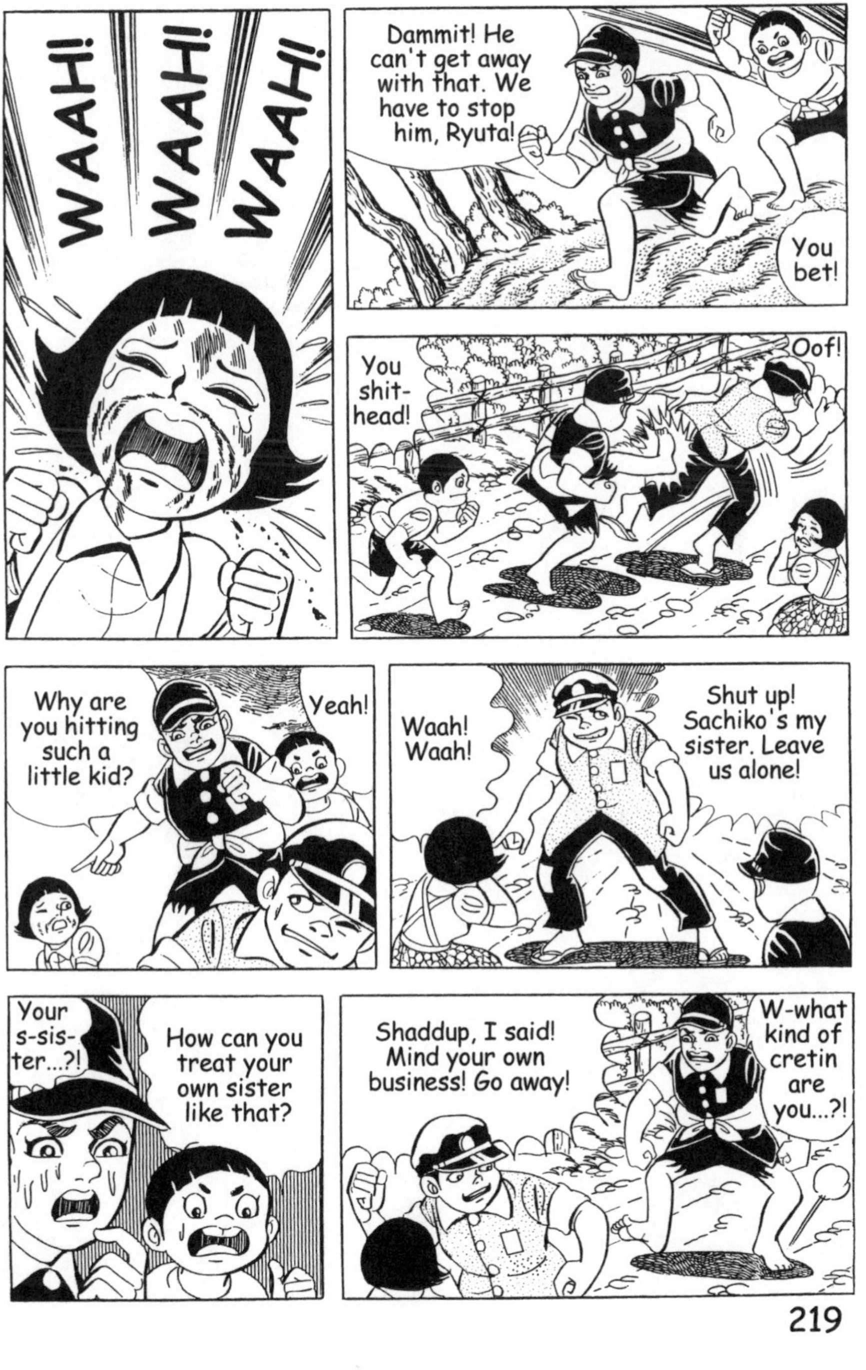
WAAAH! WAAAH! WAAAH!
Dammit! He can't get away with that. We have to stop him, Ryuta!
You bet!
You shit-head!
Oof!
Why are you hitting such a little kid?
Yeah!
Waah! Waah!
Shut up! Sachiko's my sister. Leave us alone!
Your s-sis-ter...?!
How can you treat your own sister like that?
Shaddup, I said! Mind your own business! Go away!
W-what kind of cretin are you...?!

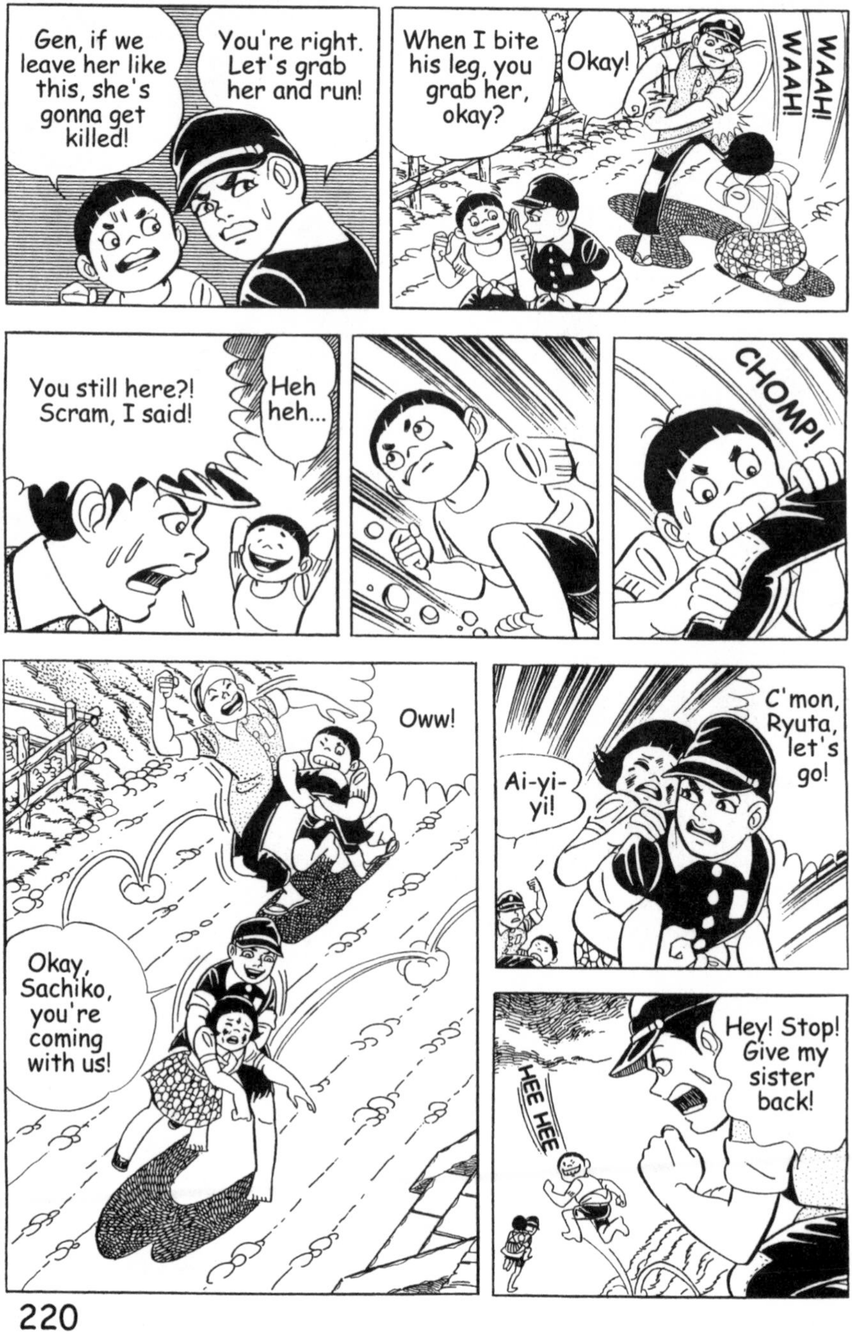
Gen, if we leave her like this, she's gonna get killed!
You're right. Let's grab her and run!
When I bite his leg, you grab her, okay?
Okay!
WAAAH!
WAAAH!
You still here?! Scram, I said!
Heh heh...
CHOMP!
Oww!
Okay, Sachiko, you're coming with us!
C'mon, Ryuta, let's go!
Ai-yi-yi!
Hey! Stop! Give my sister back!
HEE HEE

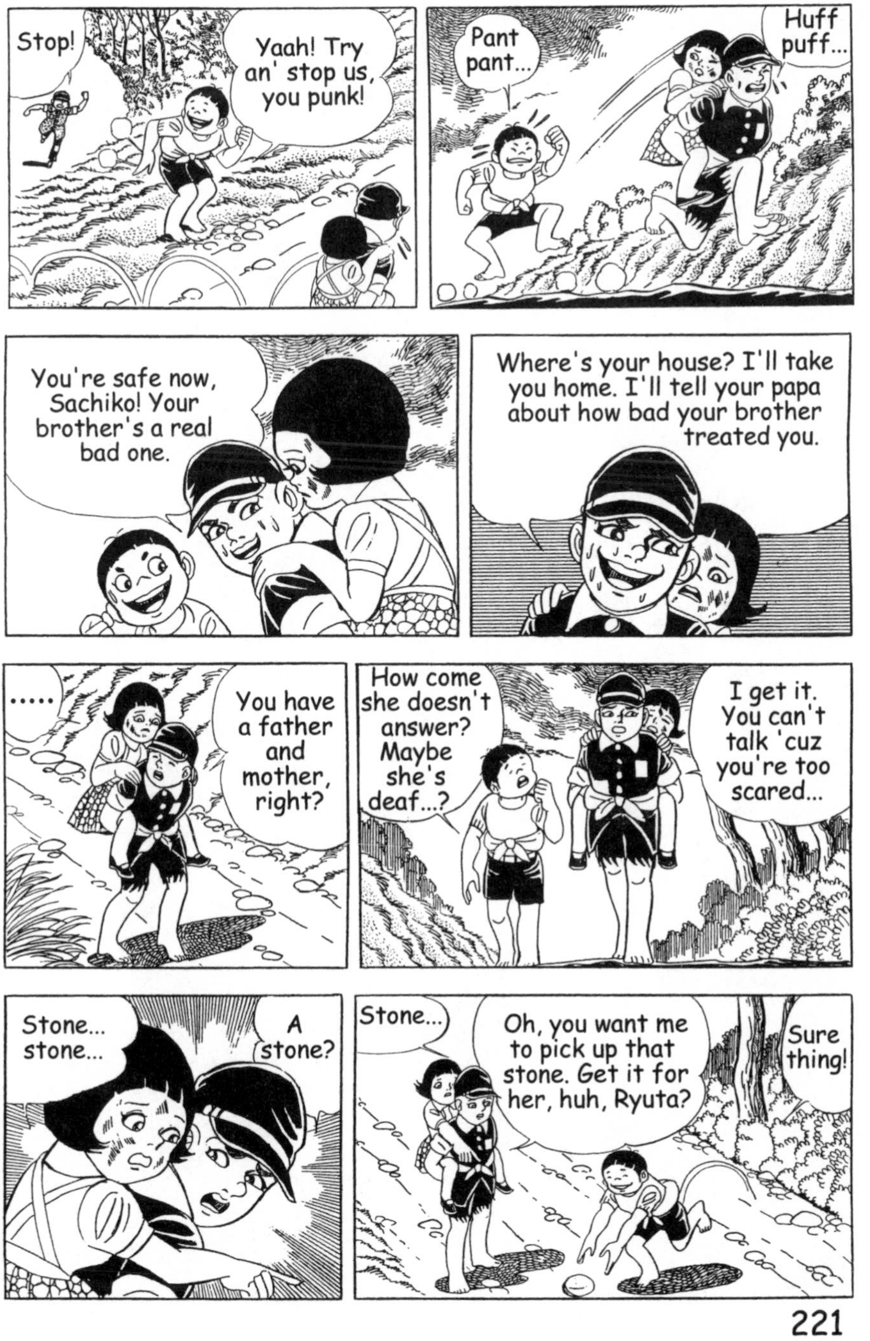

Stop!
Yaah! Try an' stop us, you punk!
Pant pant...
Huff puff...
You're safe now, Sachiko! Your brother's a real bad one.
Where's your house? I'll take you home. I'll tell your papa about how bad your brother treated you.
.....
You have a father and mother, right?
How come she doesn't answer? Maybe she's deaf...?
I get it. You can't talk 'cuz you're too scared...
Stone... stone...
A stone?
Stone...
Oh, you want me to pick up that stone. Get it for her, huh, Ryuta?
Sure thing!

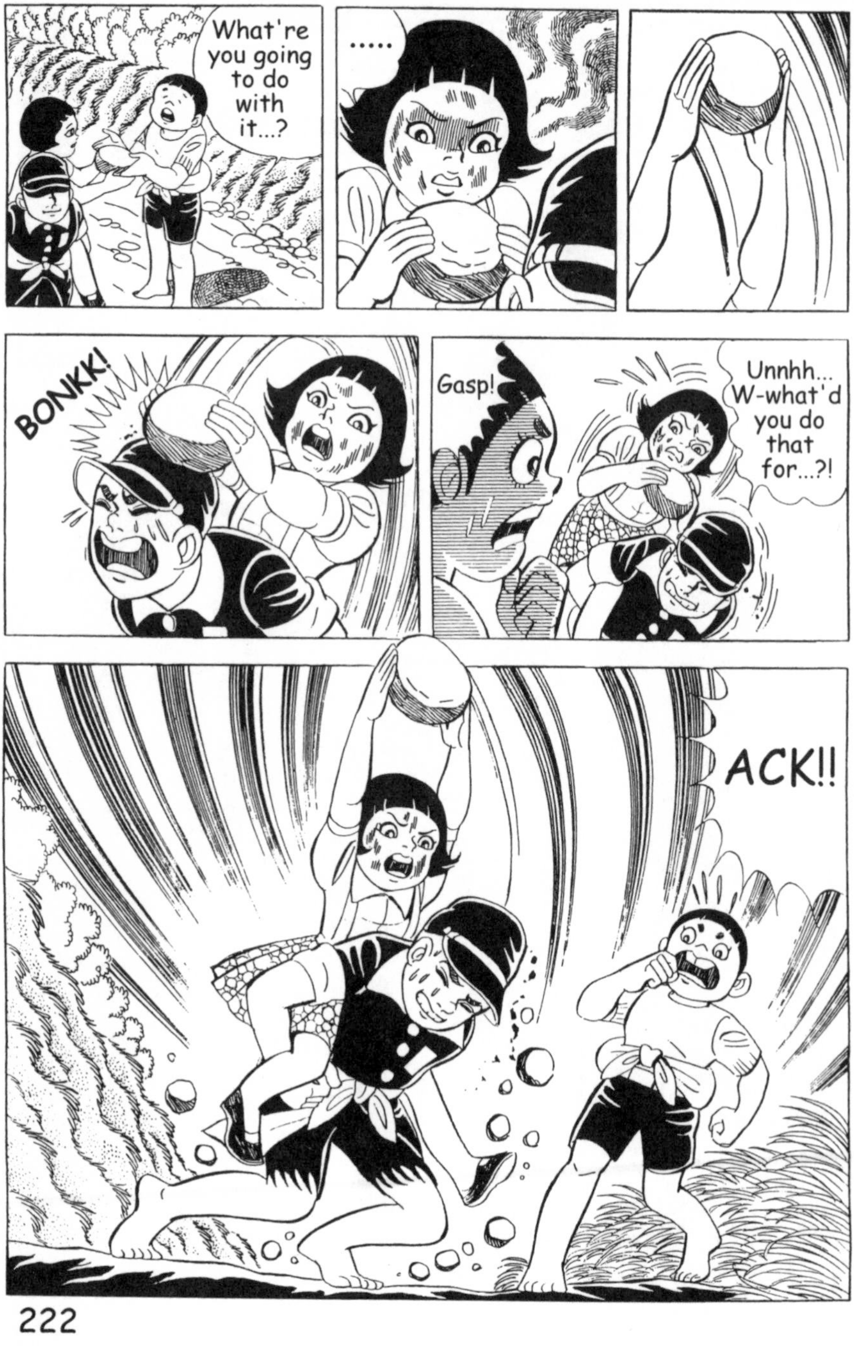
What're you going to do with it...?
.....
BONKK!
Gasp!
Unnhh... W-what'd you do that for...?!
ACK!!

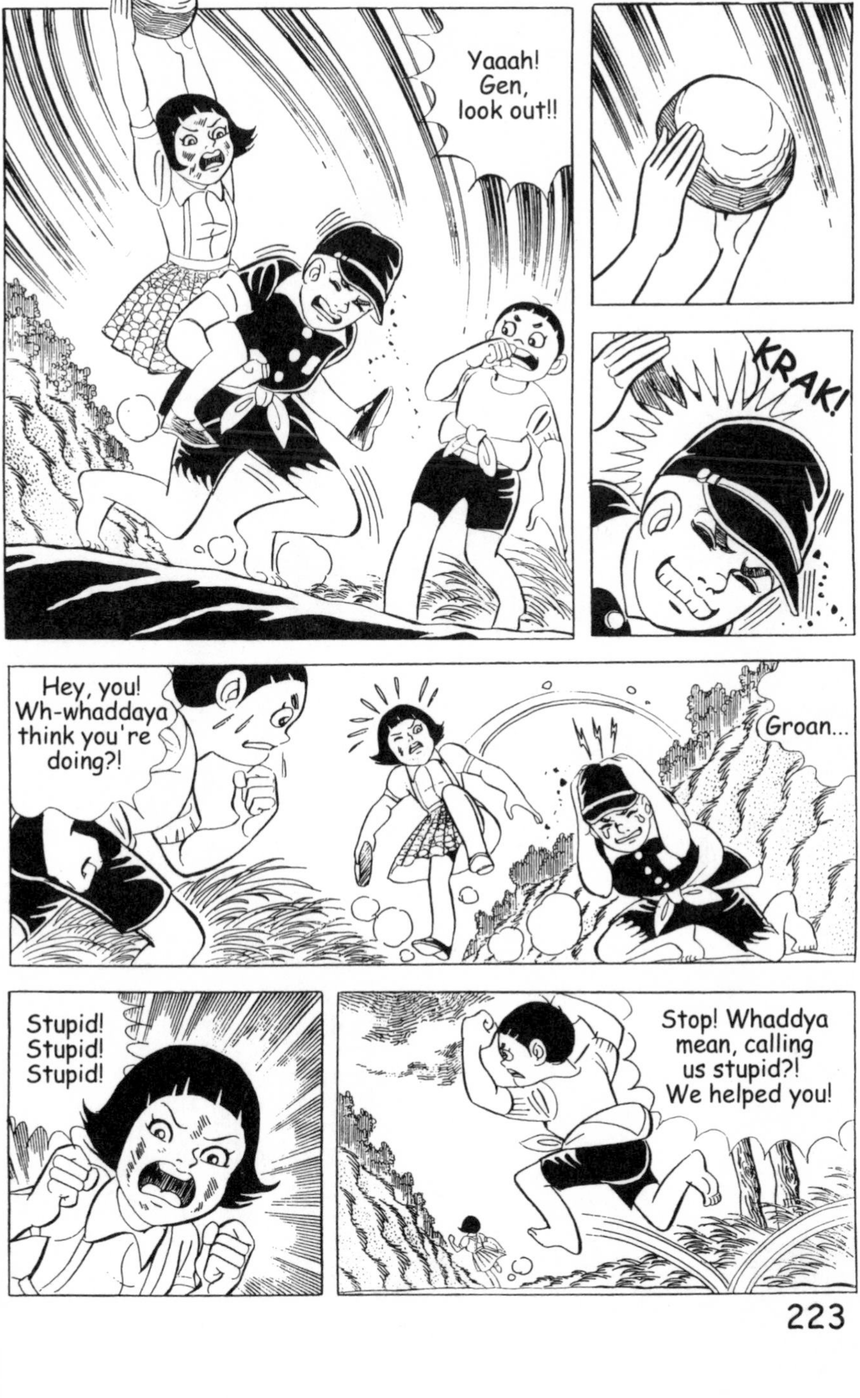
Yaaah! Gen, look out!!
KRAK!
Hey, you! Wh-whaddaya think you're doing?!
Groan...
Stupid! Stupid! Stupid!
Stop! Whaddya mean, calling us stupid?! We helped you!

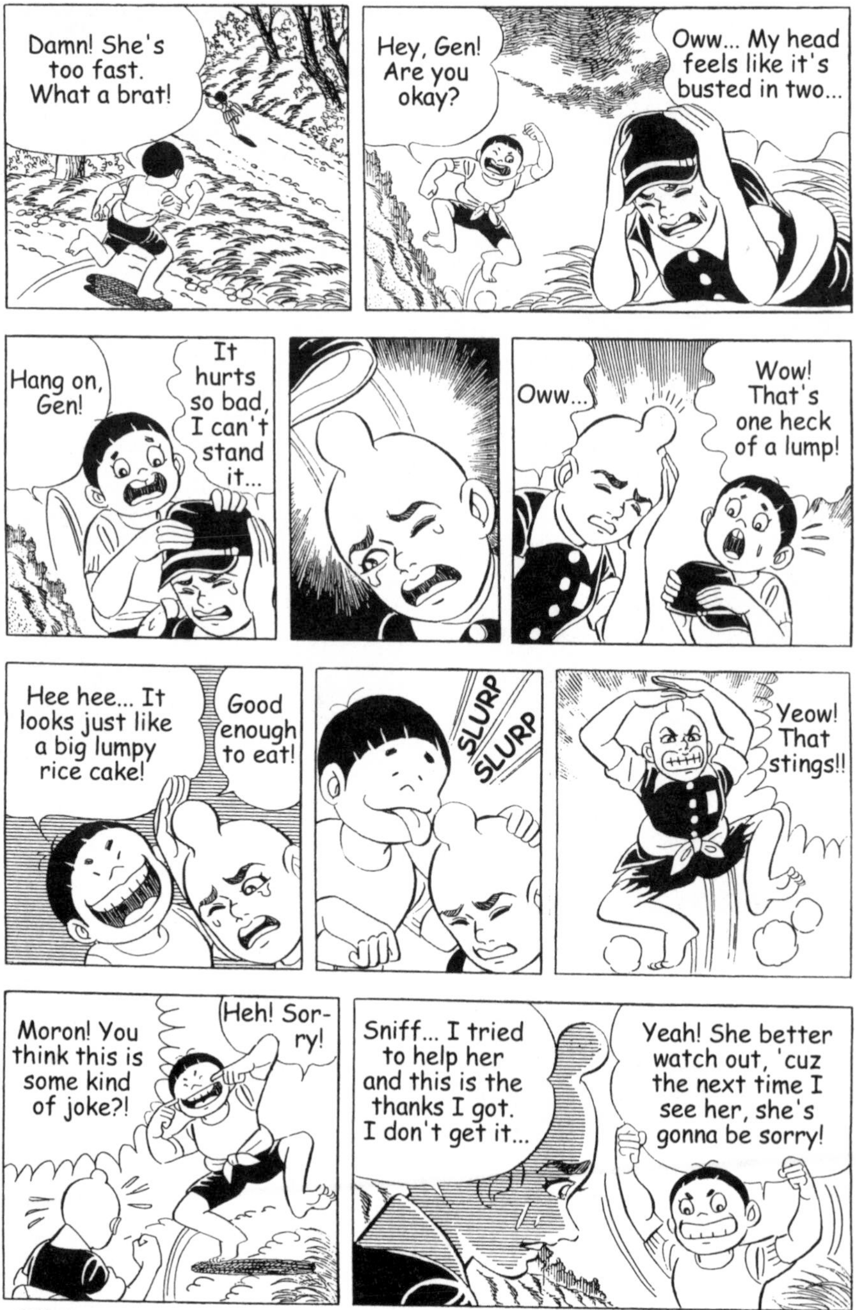
Damn! She's too fast. What a brat!
Hey, Gen! Are you okay?
Oww... My head feels like it's busted in two...
Hang on, Gen!
It hurts so bad, I can't stand it...
Oww...
Wow! That's one heck of a lump!
Hee hee... It looks just like a big lumpy rice cake!
Good enough to eat!
SLURP
SLURP
Yeow! That stings!!
Moron! You think this is some kind of joke?!
Heh! Sorry!
Sniff... I tried to help her and this is the thanks I got. I don't get it...
Yeah! She better watch out, 'cuz the next time I see her, she's gonna be sorry!

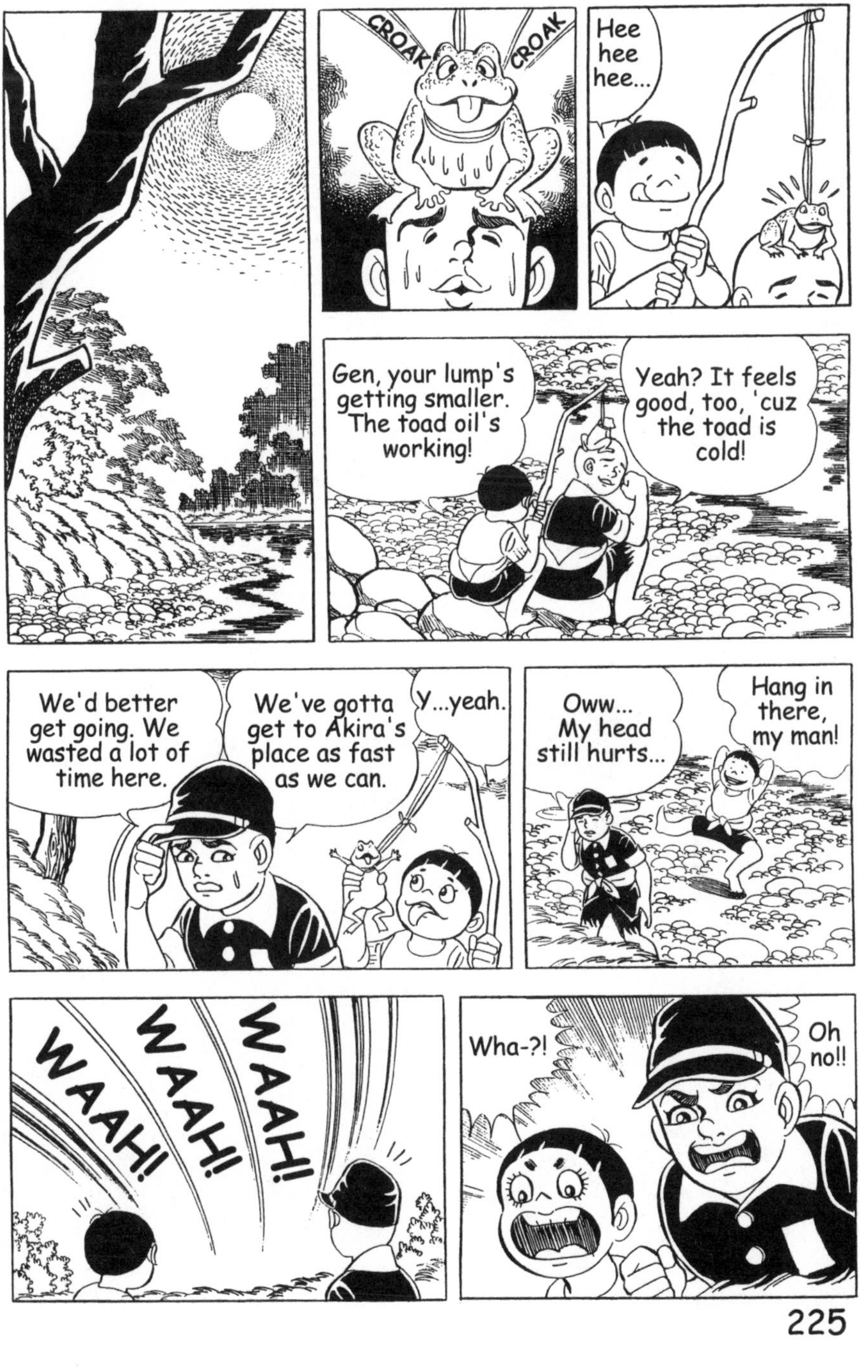
CROAK
CROAK
Hee hee hee...
Gen, your lump's getting smaller. The toad oil's working!
Yeah? It feels good, too, 'cuz the toad is cold!
We'd better get going. We wasted a lot of time here.
We've gotta get to Akira's place as fast as we can.
Y...yeah.
Oww... My head still hurts...
Hang in there, my man!
WAAAH!!
WAAAH!!
WAAAH!!
Wha-?!
Oh no!!

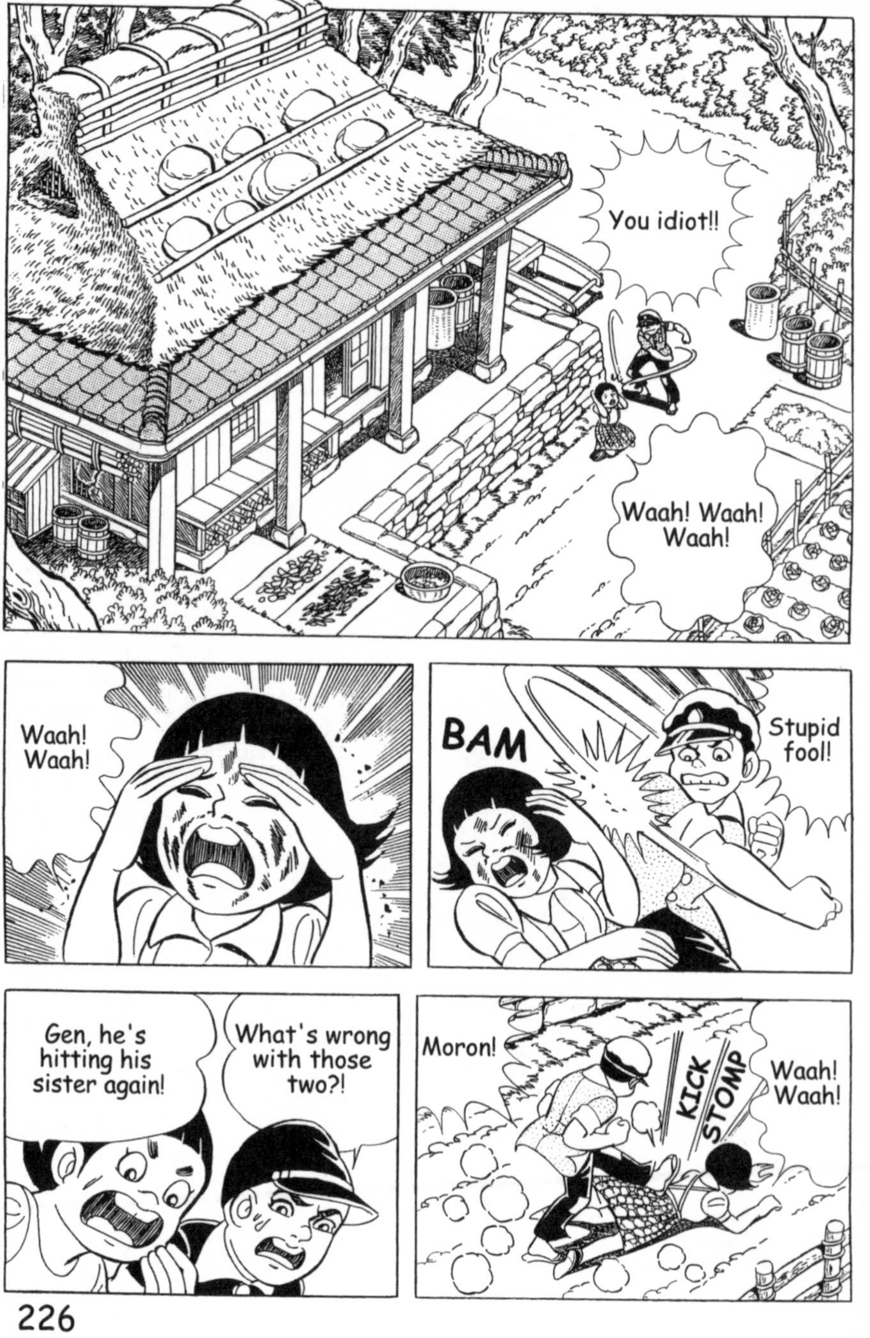
You idiot!!
Waah! Waah! Waah!
Waah! Waah!
BAM
Stupid fool!
Gen, he's hitting his sister again!
What's wrong with those two?!
Moron!
KICK
STOMP
Waah! Waah!

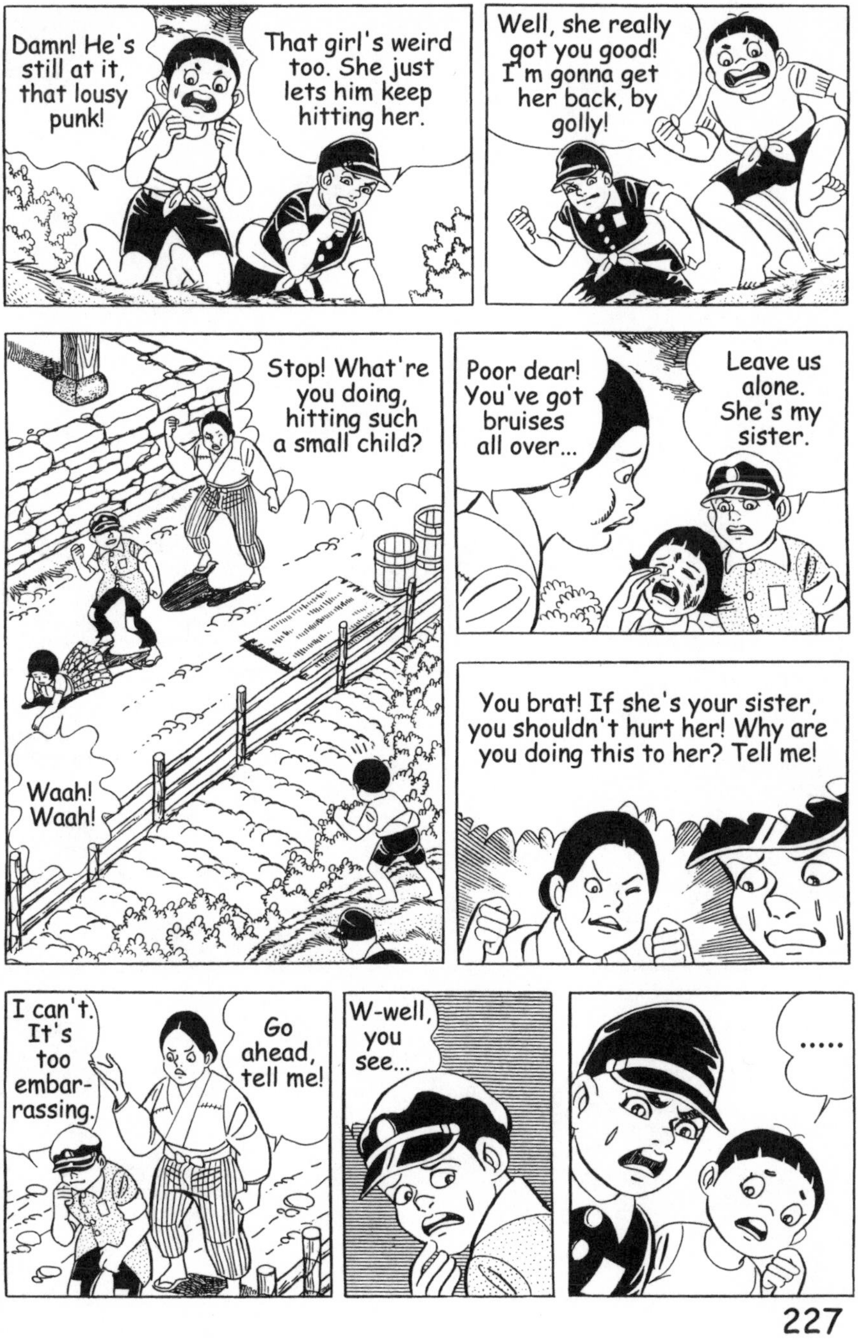
Damn! He's still at it, that lousy punk!
That girl's weird too. She just lets him keep hitting her.
Well, she really got you good! I'm gonna get her back, by golly!
Stop! What're you doing, hitting such a small child?
Waah! Waah!
Poor dear! You've got bruises all over...
Leave us alone. She's my sister.
You brat! If she's your sister, you shouldn't hurt her! Why are you doing this to her? Tell me!
I can't. It's too embar-rassing.
Go ahead, tell me!
W-well, you see...
.....

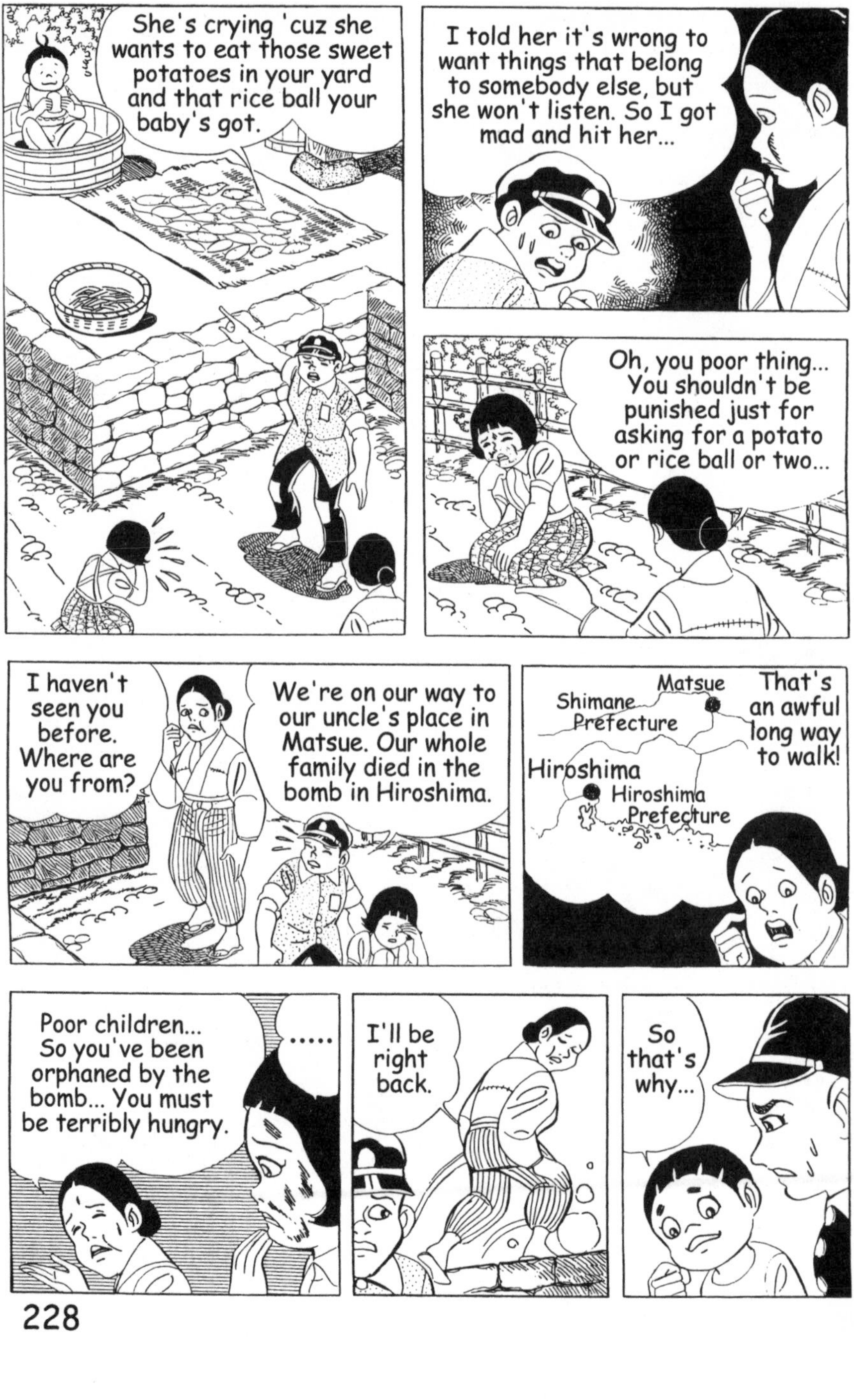
She's crying 'cuz she wants to eat those sweet potatoes in your yard and that rice ball your baby's got.
I told her it's wrong to want things that belong to somebody else, but she won't listen. So I got mad and hit her...
Oh, you poor thing... You shouldn't be punished just for asking for a potato or rice ball or two...
I haven't seen you before. Where are you from?
We're on our way to our uncle's place in Matsue. Our whole family died in the bomb in Hiroshima.
Matsue
Shimane Prefecture
Hiroshima
Hiroshima Prefecture
That's an awful long way to walk!
Poor children... So you've been orphaned by the bomb... You must be terribly hungry.
.....
I'll be right back.
So that's why...

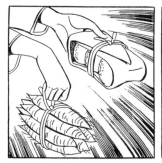

I can give you these.

Promise me you'll stop hitting your sister, okay?

T-thank you, ma'am!

Sachiko, let's go.

SNIFF

Take care, now!

Wow, Gen, those two really lucked out!

Y...yeah. But I feel sorry for them.

Whew... Gen, let's take a break.

Are you nuts? We haven't walked very far. Akira's waiting for us! We've gotta hurry!

WAAH!

WAAH!

WAAH!

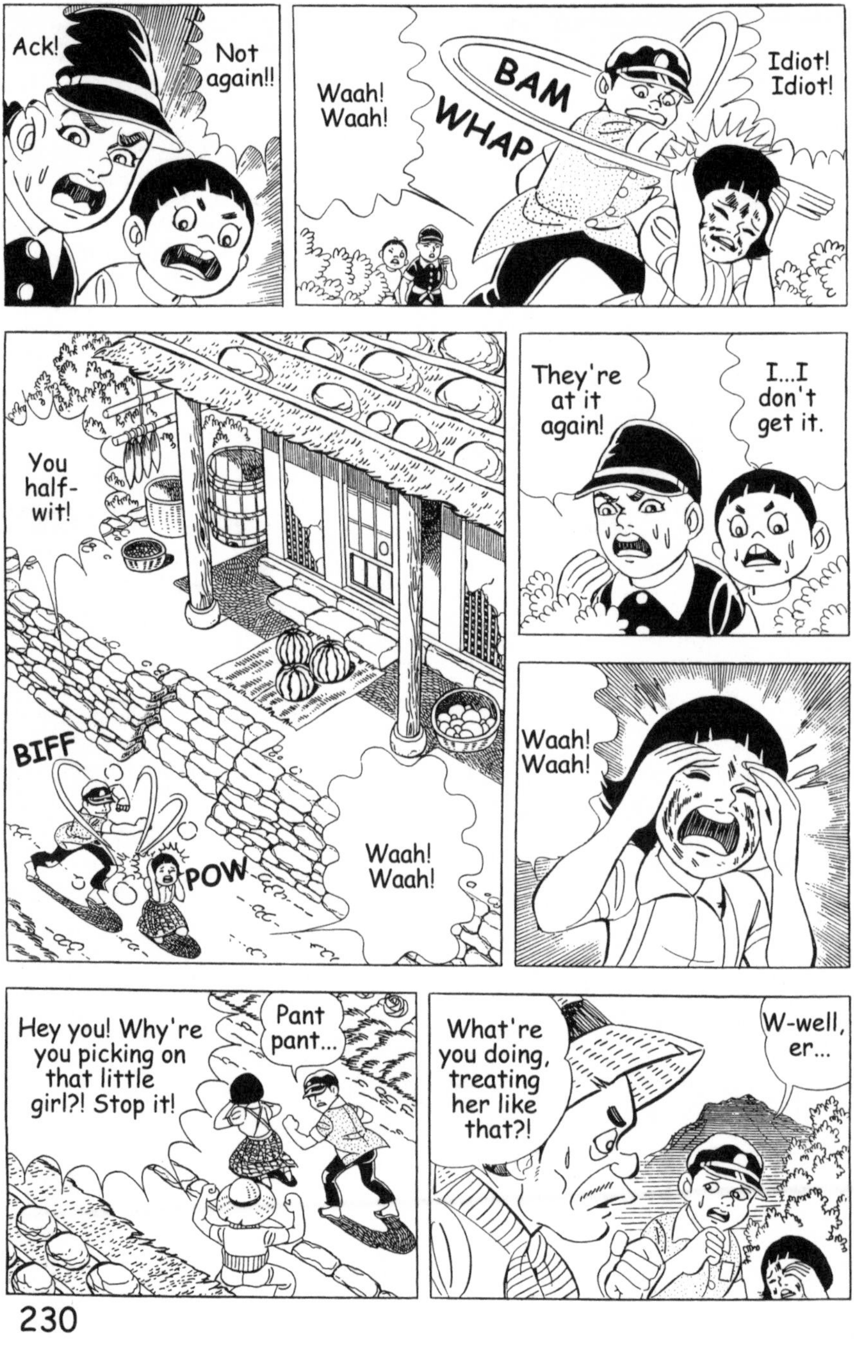
Ack!
Not again!!
Waah! Waah!
BAM
WHAP
Idiot! Idiot!
You half-wit!
BIFF
POW
Waah! Waah!
They're at it again!
I...I don't get it.
Waah! Waah!
Hey you! Why're you picking on that little girl?! Stop it!
Pant pant...
What're you doing, treating her like that?!
W-well, er...

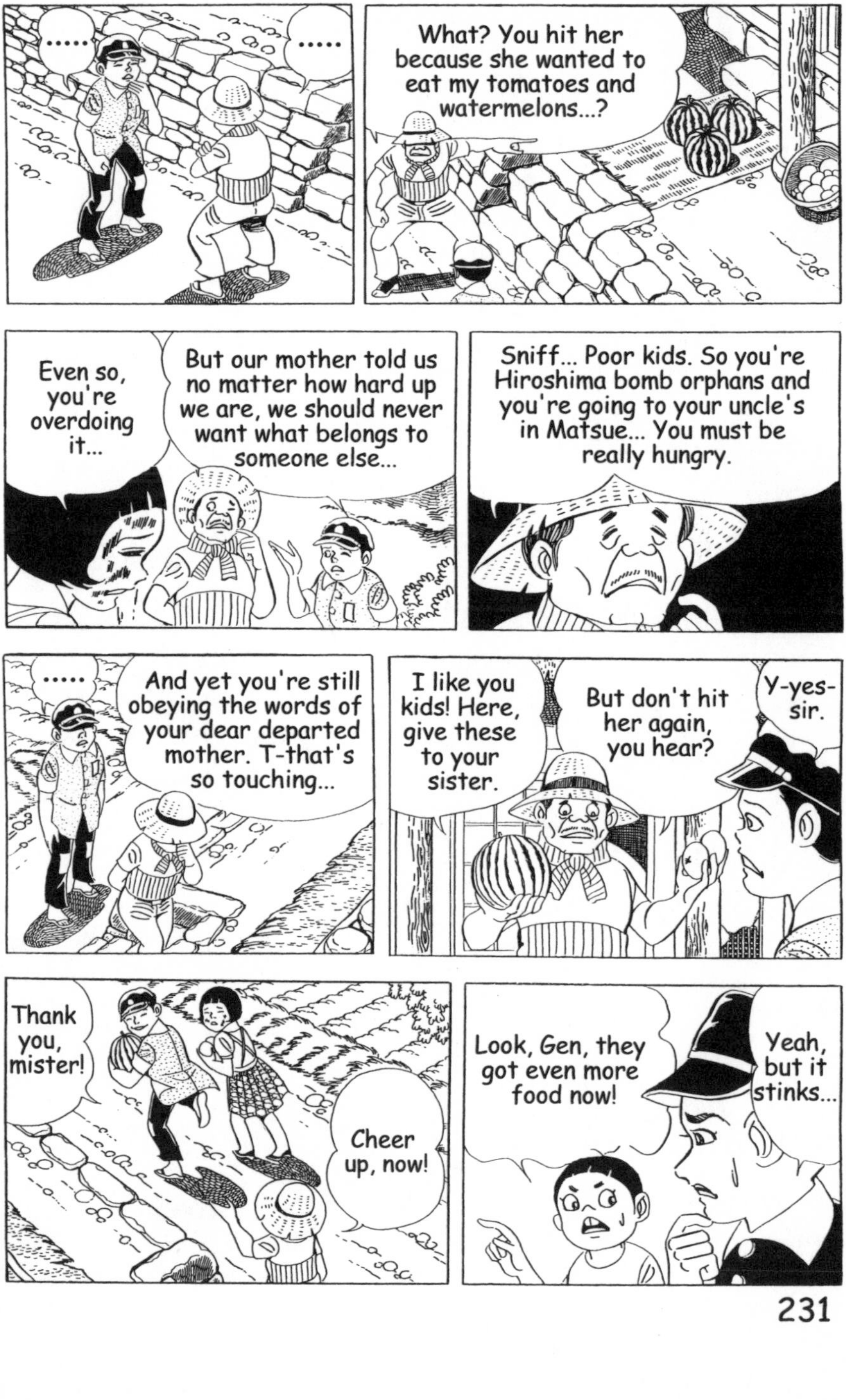
.....
.....
What? You hit her because she wanted to eat my tomatoes and watermelons...?
Even so, you're overdoing it...
But our mother told us no matter how hard up we are, we should never want what belongs to someone else...
Sniff... Poor kids. So you're Hiroshima bomb orphans and you're going to your uncle's in Matsue... You must be really hungry.
.....
And yet you're still obeying the words of your dear departed mother. T-that's so touching...
I like you kids! Here, give these to your sister.
But don't hit her again, you hear?
Y-yes-sir.
Thank you, mister!
Cheer up, now!
Look, Gen, they got even more food now!
Yeah, but it stinks...

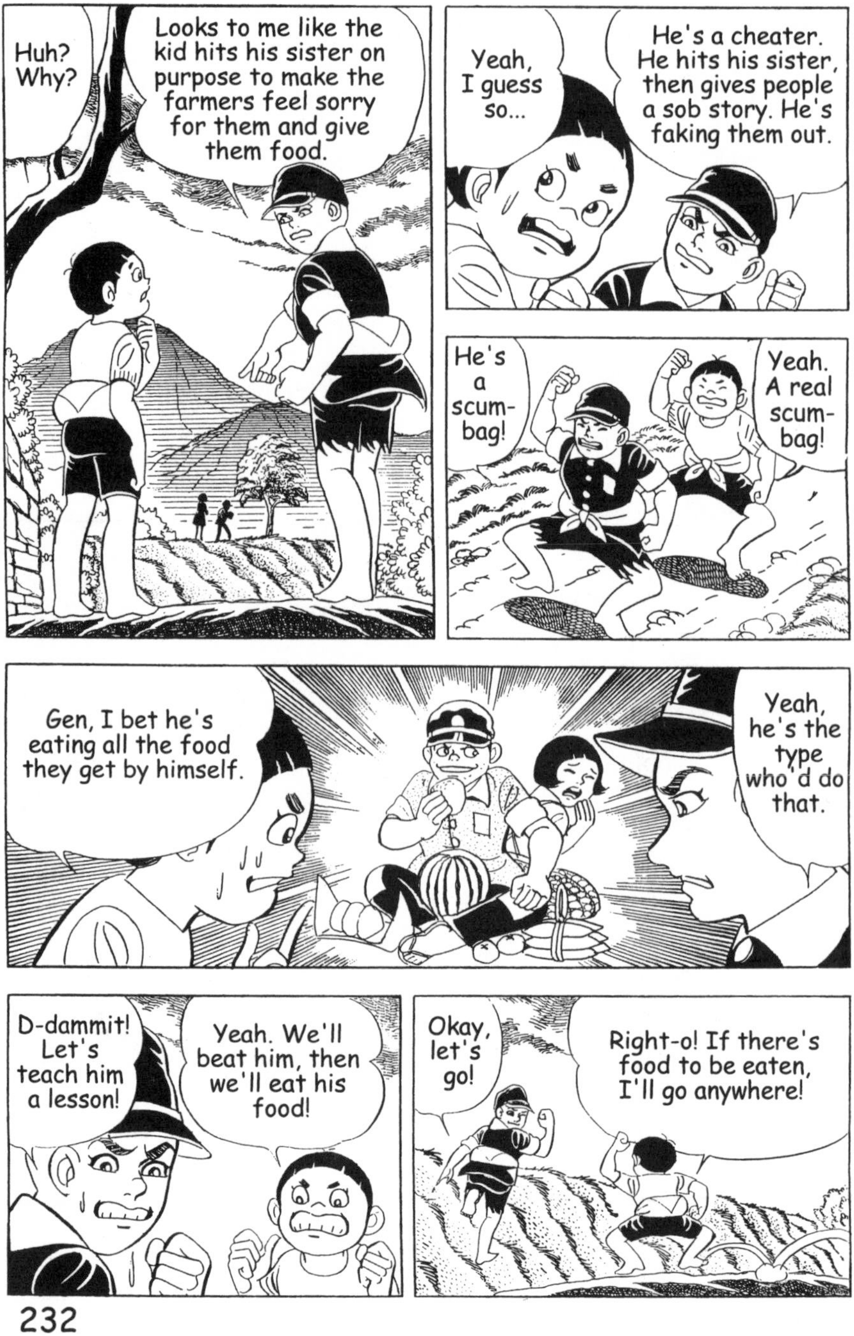
Huh? Why?
Looks to me like the kid hits his sister on purpose to make the farmers feel sorry for them and give them food.
Yeah, I guess so...
He's a cheater. He hits his sister, then gives people a sob story. He's faking them out.
He's a scum-bag!
Yeah. A real scum-bag!
Gen, I bet he's eating all the food they get by himself.
Yeah, he's the type who'd do that.
D-dammit! Let's teach him a lesson!
Yeah. We'll beat him, then we'll eat his food!
Okay, let's go!
Right-o! If there's food to be eaten, I'll go anywhere!

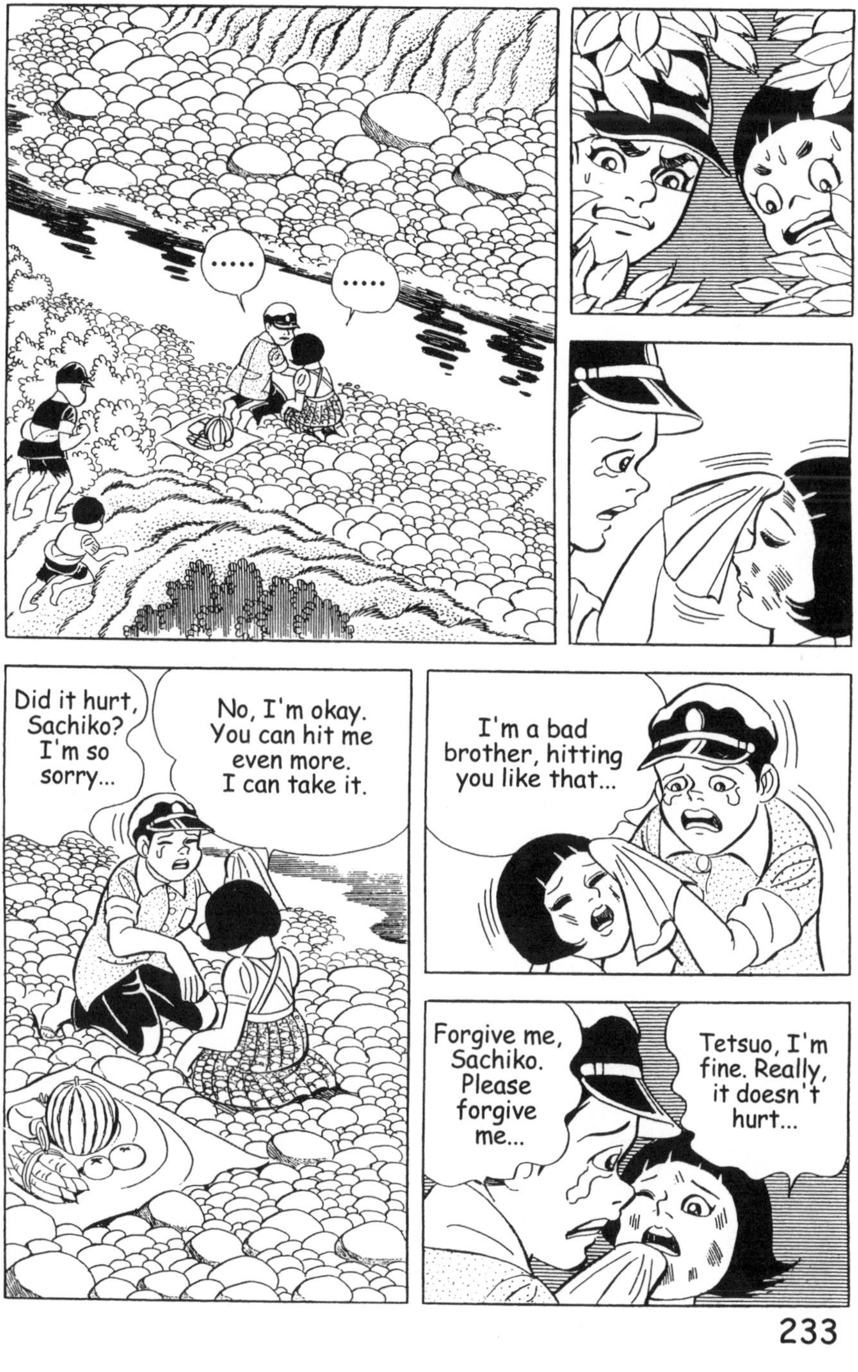
.....
.....
Did it hurt, Sachiko? I'm so sorry...
No, I'm okay. You can hit me even more. I can take it.
I'm a bad brother, hitting you like that...
Forgive me, Sachiko. Please forgive me...
Tetsuo, I'm fine. Really, it doesn't hurt...

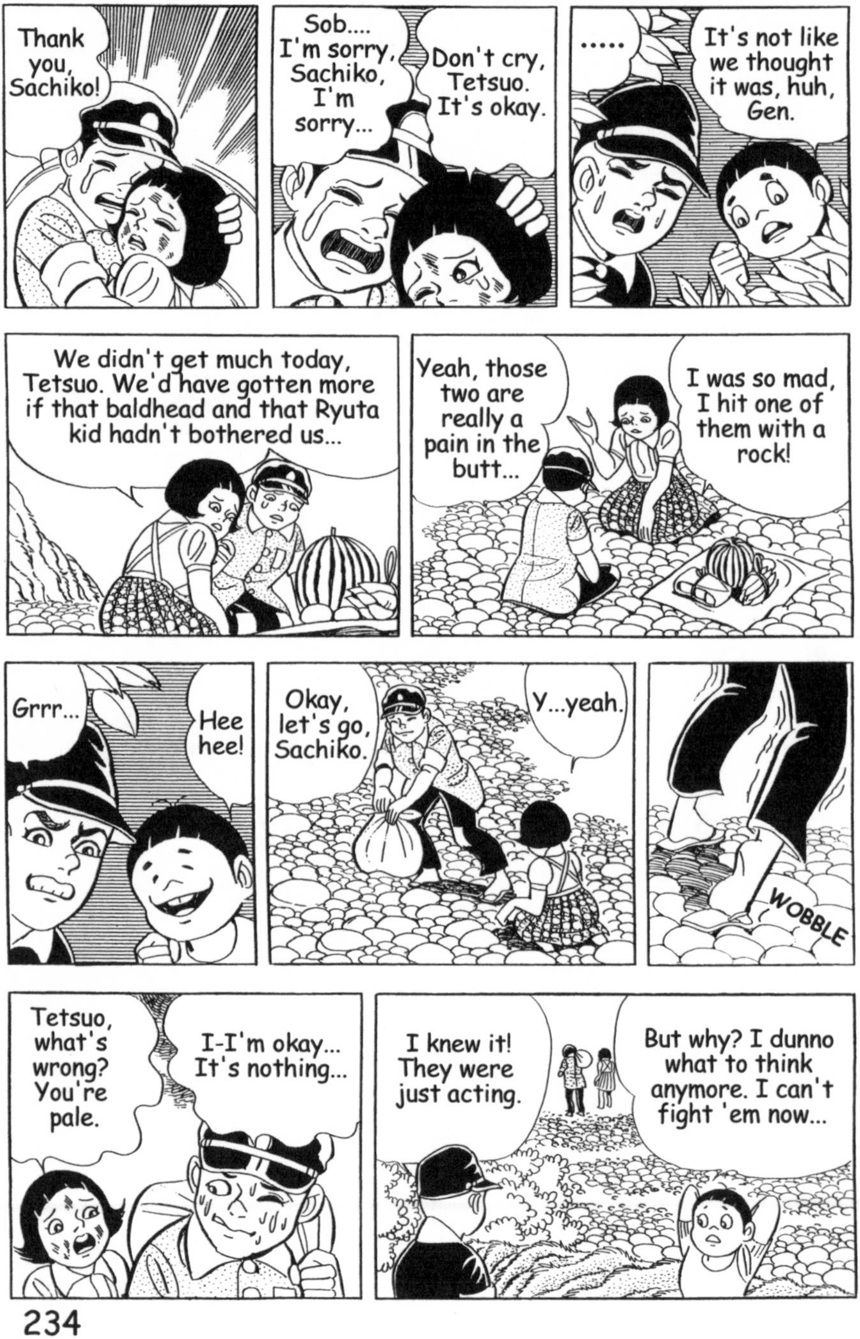

Thank you, Sachiko!
Sob.... I'm sorry, Sachiko, I'm sorry...
Don't cry, Tetsuo. It's okay.
.....
It's not like we thought it was, huh, Gen.
We didn't get much today, Tetsuo. We'd have gotten more if that baldhead and that Ryuta kid hadn't bothered us...
Yeah, those two are really a pain in the butt...
I was so mad, I hit one of them with a rock!
Grrr...
Hee hee!
Okay, let's go, Sachiko.
Y...yeah.
WOBBLE
Tetsuo, what's wrong? You're pale.
I-I'm okay... It's nothing...
I knew it! They were just acting.
But why? I dunno what to think anymore. I can't fight 'em now...

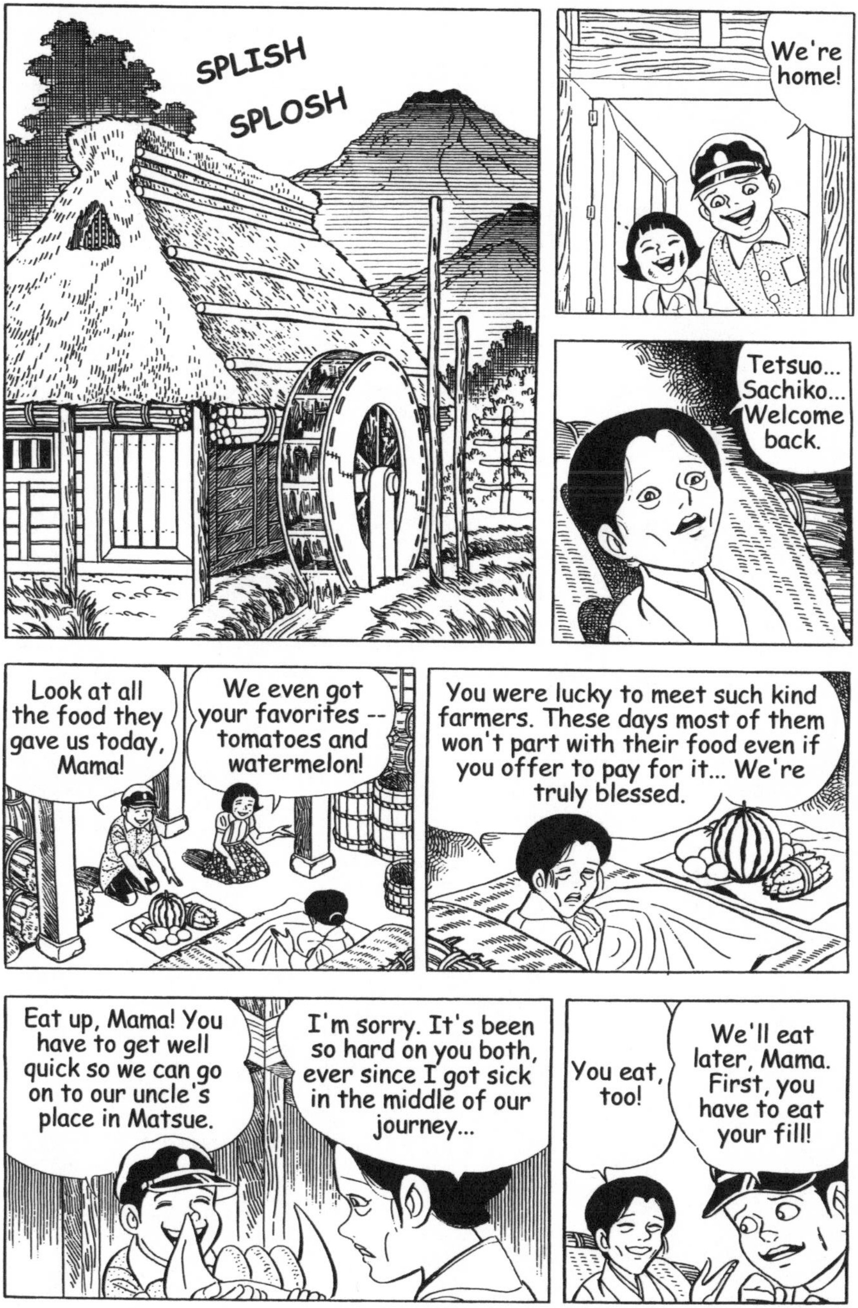
SPLISH
SPLOSH
We're home!
Tetsuo... Sachiko... Welcome back.
Look at all the food they gave us today, Mama!
We even got your favorites -- tomatoes and watermelon!
You were lucky to meet such kind farmers. These days most of them won't part with their food even if you offer to pay for it... We're truly blessed.
Eat up, Mama! You have to get well quick so we can go on to our uncle's place in Matsue.
I'm sorry. It's been so hard on you both, ever since I got sick in the middle of our journey...
You eat, too!
We'll eat later, Mama. First, you have to eat your fill!

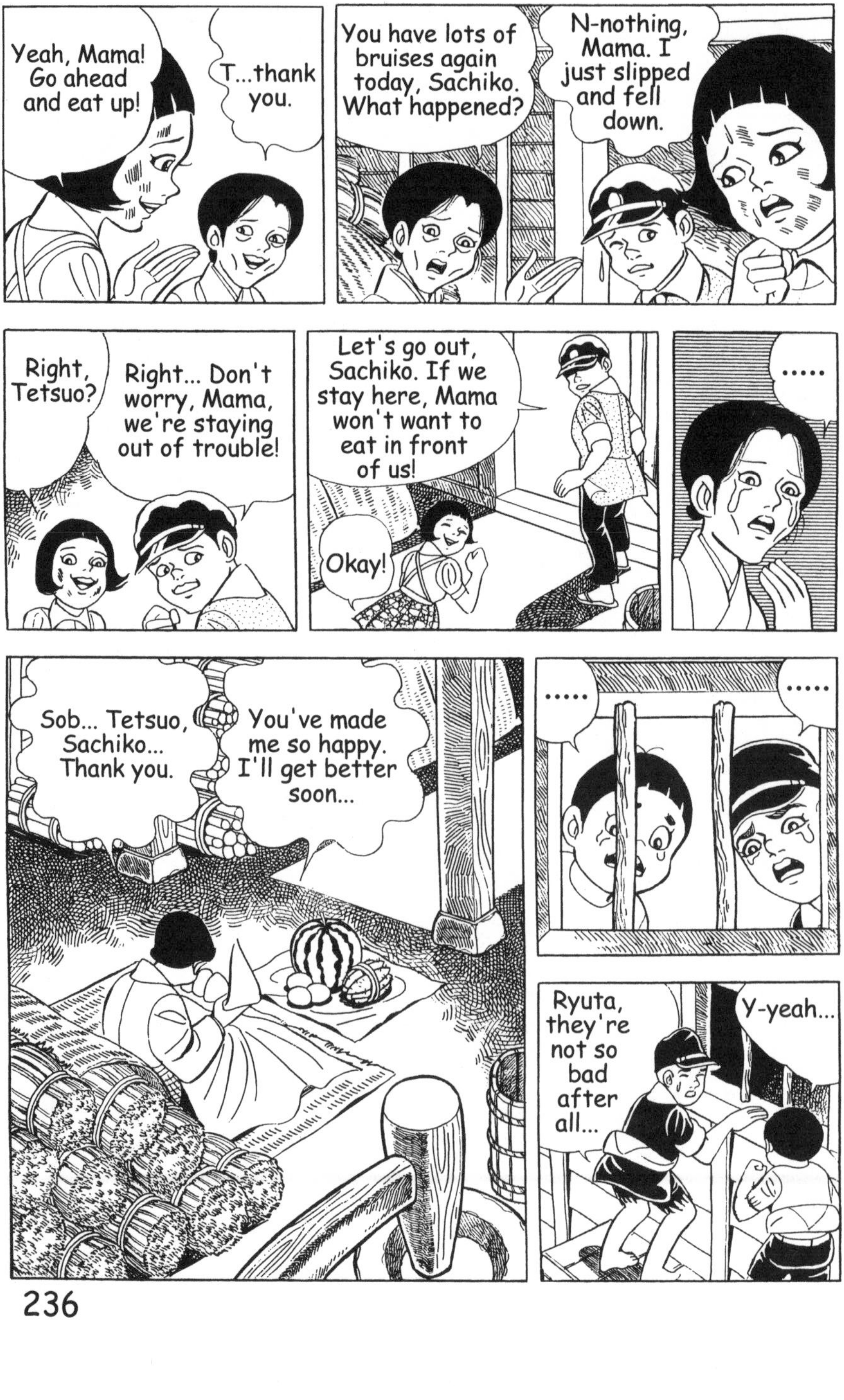
Yeah, Mama! Go ahead and eat up!
T...thank you.
You have lots of bruises again today, Sachiko. What happened?
N-nothing, Mama. I just slipped and fell down.
Right, Tetsuo?
Right... Don't worry, Mama, we're staying out of trouble!
Let's go out, Sachiko. If we stay here, Mama won't want to eat in front of us!
Okay!
.....
Sob... Tetsuo, Sachiko... Thank you.
You've made me so happy. I'll get better soon...
.....
.....
Ryuta, they're not so bad after all...
Y-yeah...

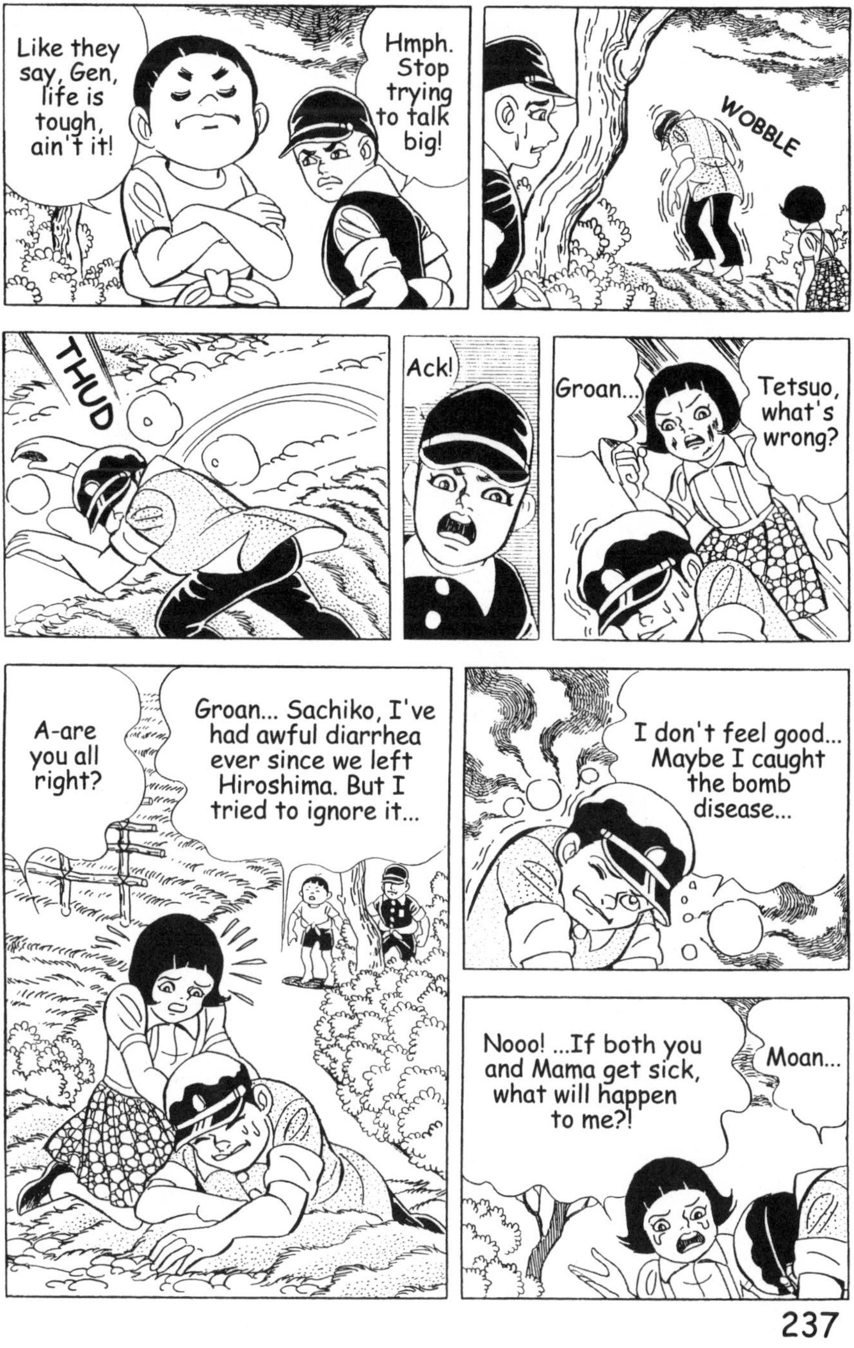
Like they say, Gen, life is tough, ain't it!
Hmph. Stop trying to talk big!
WOBBLE
THUD
Ack!
Groan...
Tetsuo, what's wrong?
A-are you all right?
Groan... Sachiko, I've had awful diarrhea ever since we left Hiroshima. But I tried to ignore it...
I don't feel good... Maybe I caught the bomb disease...
Nooo! ...If both you and Mama get sick, what will happen to me?!
Moan...

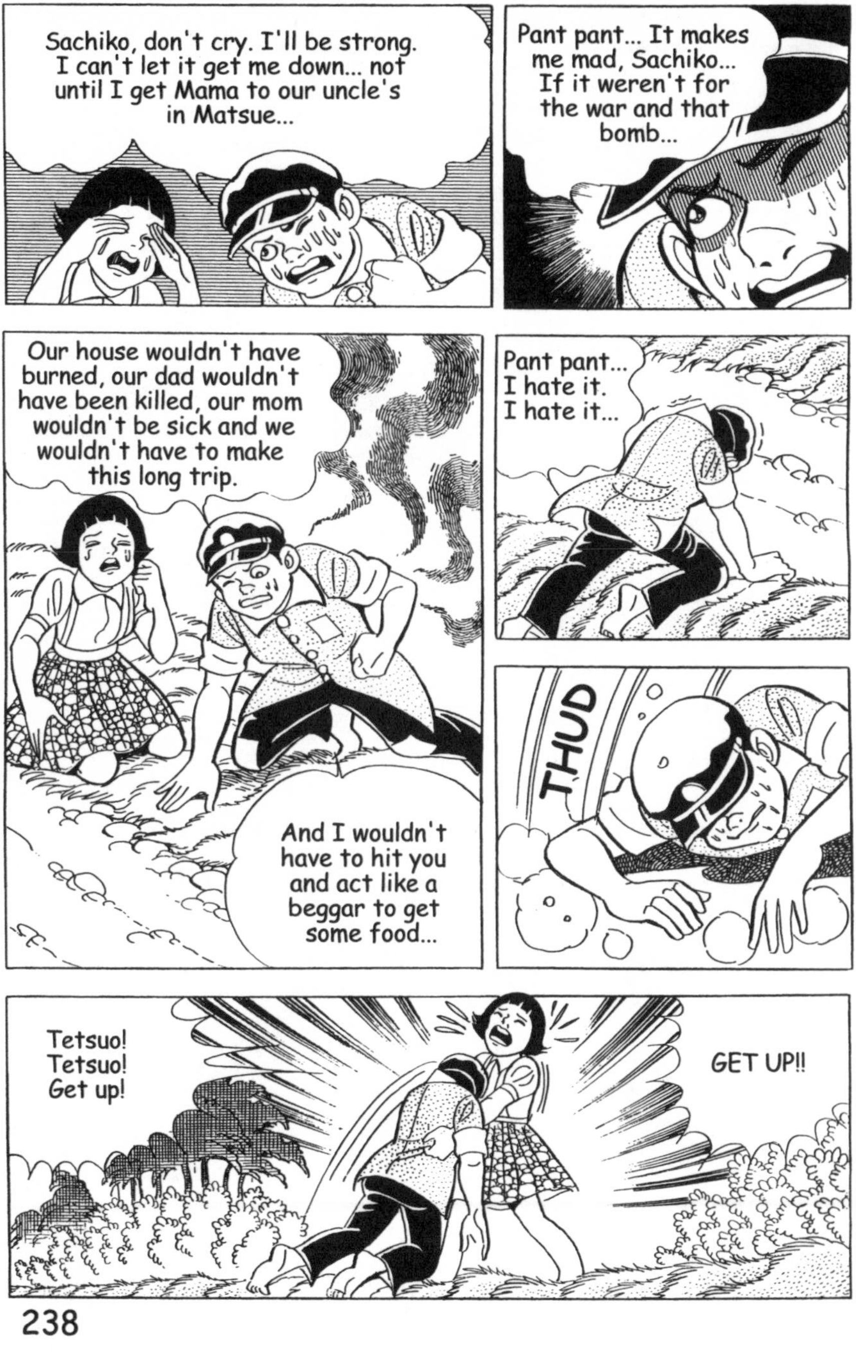
Sachiko, don't cry. I'll be strong. I can't let it get me down... not until I get Mama to our uncle's in Matsue...
Pant pant... It makes me mad, Sachiko... If it weren't for the war and that bomb...
Our house wouldn't have burned, our dad wouldn't have been killed, our mom wouldn't be sick and we wouldn't have to make this long trip.
And I wouldn't have to hit you and act like a beggar to get some food...
Pant pant... I hate it. I hate it...
THUD
Tetsuo! Tetsuo! Get up!
GET UP!!

Waah! Tetsuo! You've got to get up!

Tetsuo! If you don't hit me, we won't get any food for tomorrow and Mama will go hungry!

Waah! Tetsuo! Get up, please!

Waah! Waah!

D-damn it! Even with the war over, it just goes on...

The war and the bomb are still making life hard for people...

239

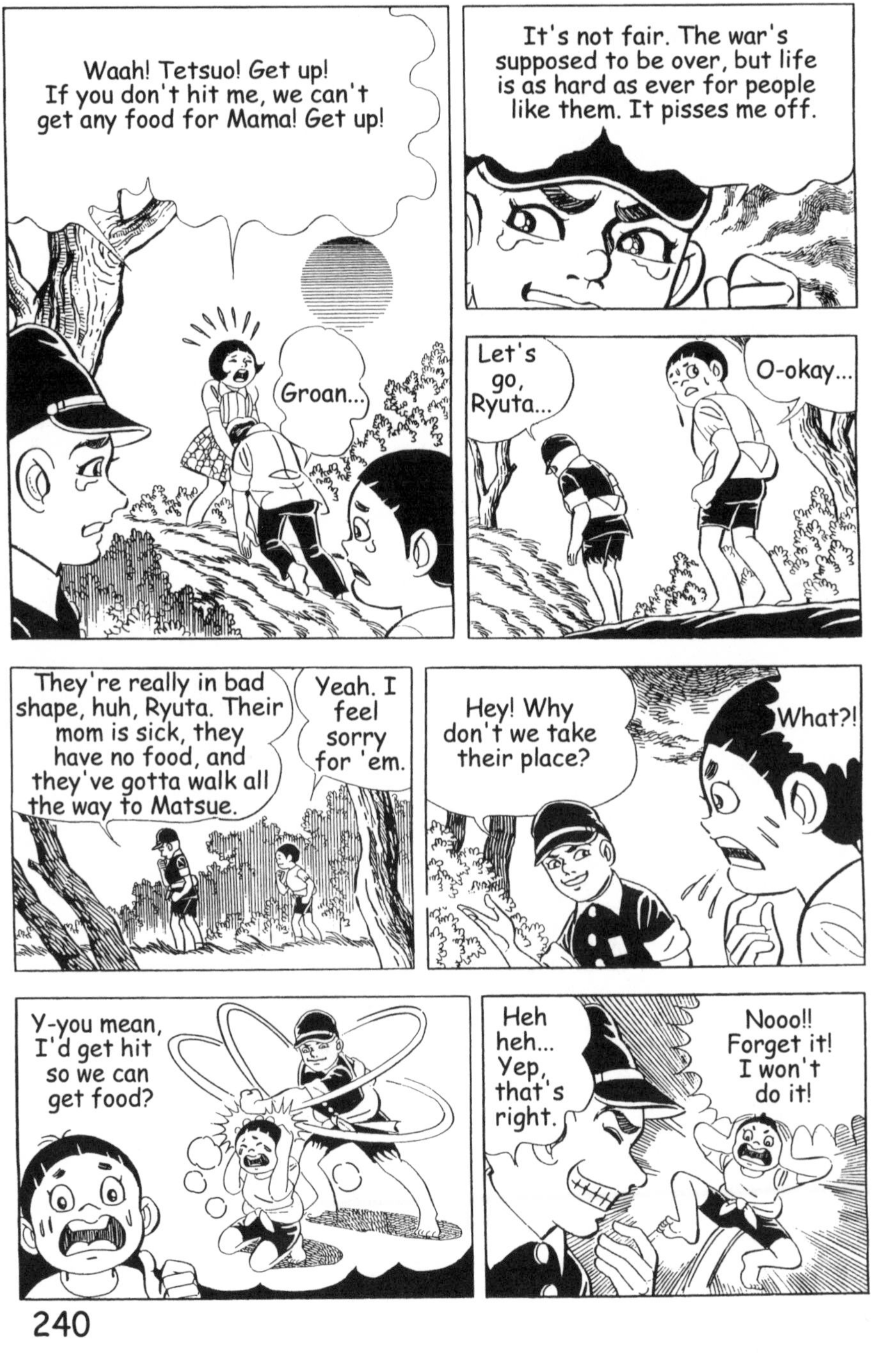
Waah! Tetsuo! Get up! If you don't hit me, we can't get any food for Mama! Get up!
Groan...
It's not fair. The war's supposed to be over, but life is as hard as ever for people like them. It pisses me off.
Let's go, Ryuta...
O-okay...
They're really in bad shape, huh, Ryuta. Their mom is sick, they have no food, and they've gotta walk all the way to Matsue.
Yeah. I feel sorry for 'em.
Hey! Why don't we take their place?
What?!
Y-you mean, I'd get hit so we can get food?
Heh heh... Yep, that's right.
Nooo!! Forget it! I won't do it!

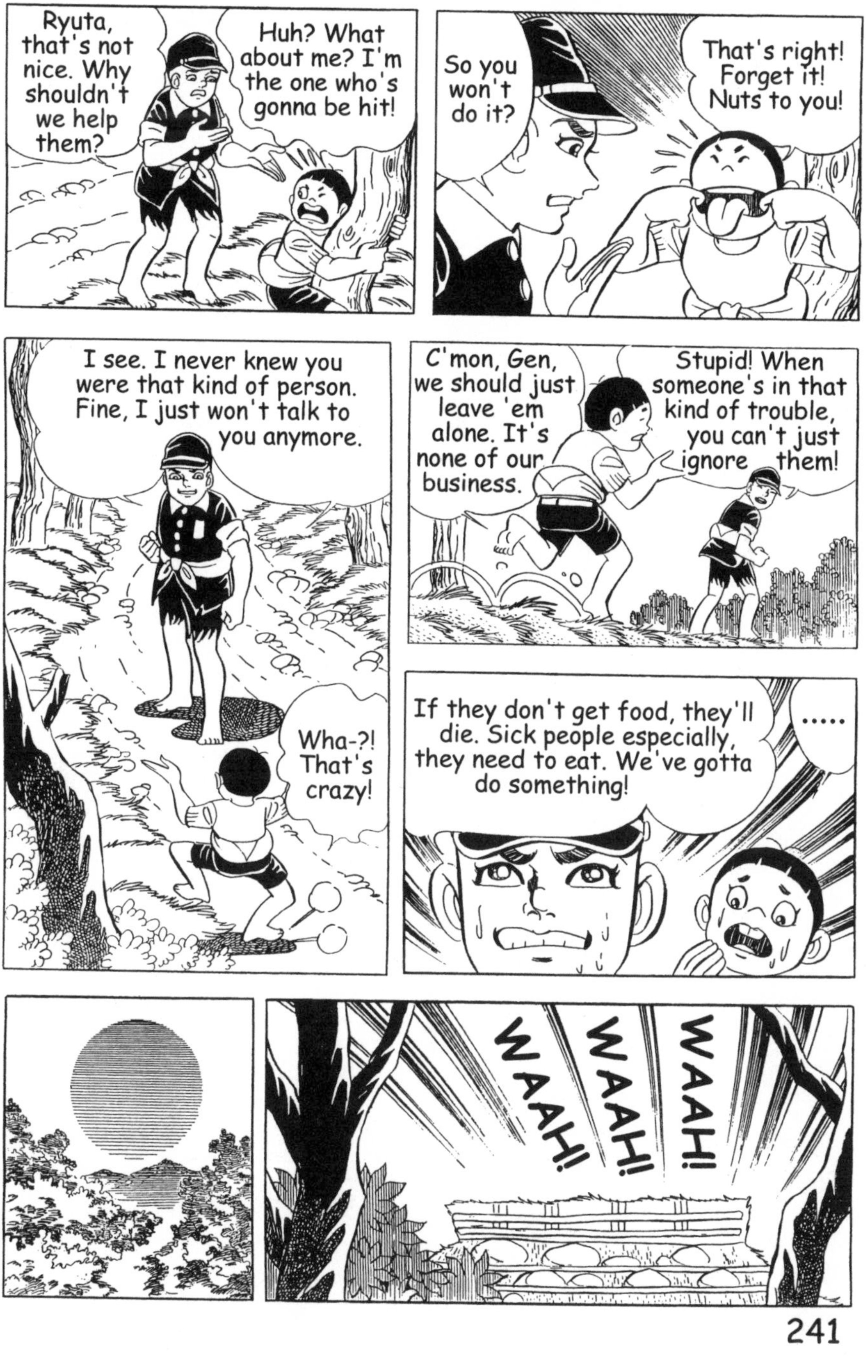

Ryuta, that's not nice. Why shouldn't we help them?
Huh? What about me? I'm the one who's gonna be hit!
So you won't do it?
That's right! Forget it! Nuts to you!
I see. I never knew you were that kind of person. Fine, I just won't talk to you anymore.
Wha-?! That's crazy!
C'mon, Gen, we should just leave 'em alone. It's none of our business.
Stupid! When someone's in that kind of trouble, you can't just ignore them!
If they don't get food, they'll die. Sick people especially, they need to eat. We've gotta do something!
.....
WAAH! WAAH! WAAH!

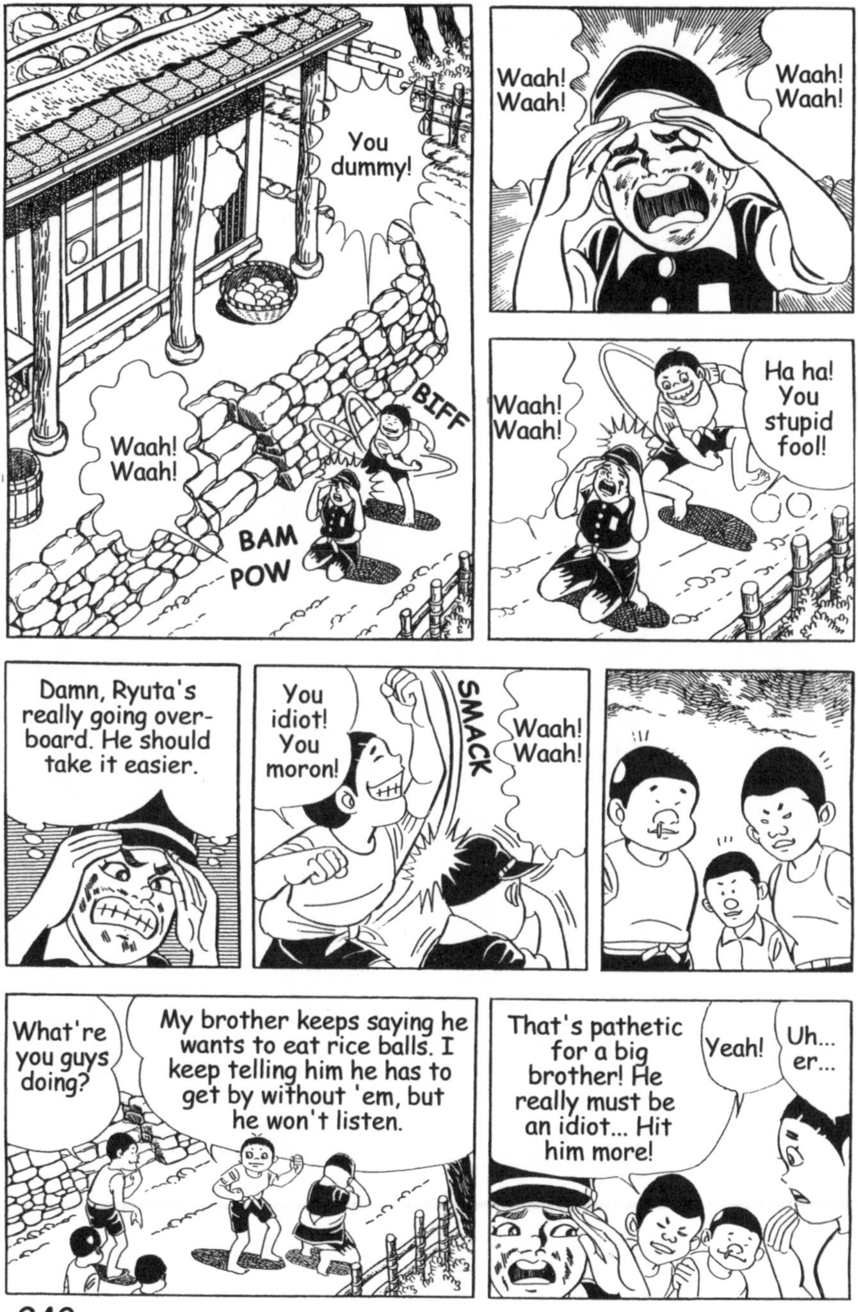
You dummy!
BIFF
Waah! Waah!
BAM
POW
Waah! Waah!
Waah! Waah!
Waah! Waah!
Ha ha! You stupid fool!
Damn, Ryuta's really going over-board. He should take it easier.
You idiot! You moron!
SMACK
Waah! Waah!
What're you guys doing?
My brother keeps saying he wants to eat rice balls. I keep telling him he has to get by without 'em, but he won't listen.
That's pathetic for a big brother! He really must be an idiot... Hit him more!
Yeah!
Uh... er...

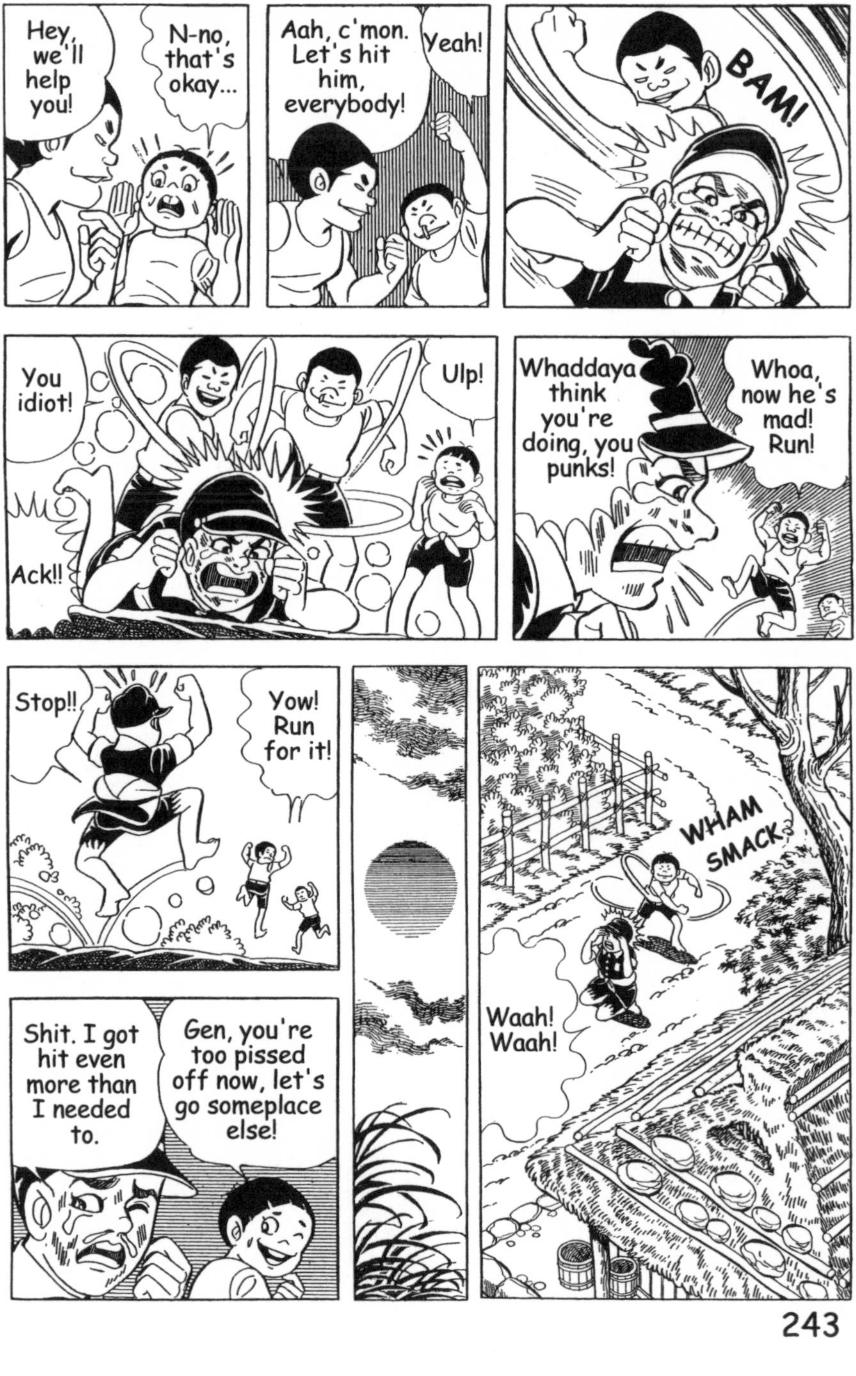
Hey, we'll help you!
N-no, that's okay...
Aah, c'mon. Let's hit him, everybody!
Yeah!
BAM!
You idiot!
Ulp!
Ack!!
Whaddaya think you're doing, you punks!
Whoa, now he's mad! Run!
Stop!!
Yow! Run for it!
Shit. I got hit even more than I needed to.
Gen, you're too pissed off now, let's go someplace else!
WHAM
SMACK
Waah! Waah!

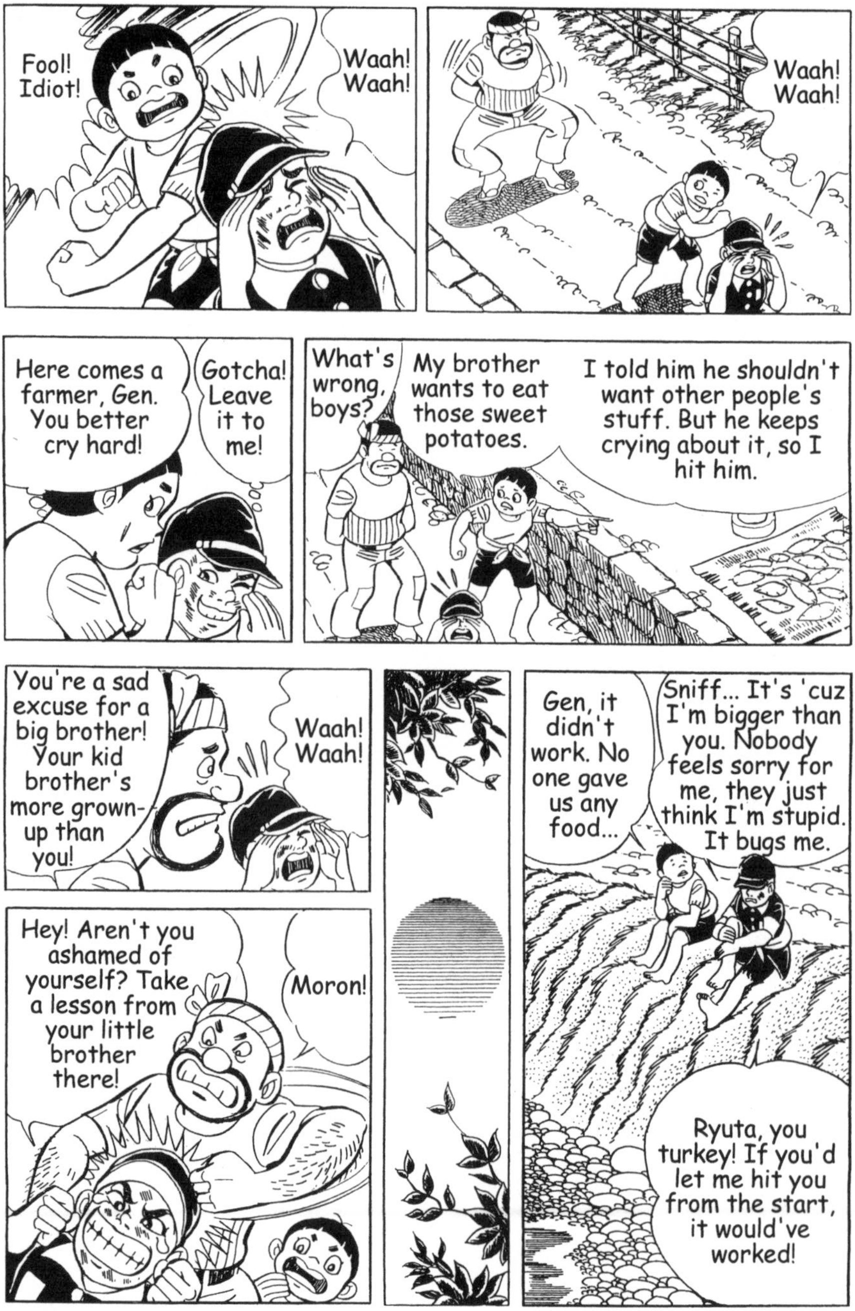
Fool! Idiot!
Waah! Waah!
Waah! Waah!
Here comes a farmer, Gen. You better cry hard!
Gotcha! Leave it to me!
What's wrong, boys?
My brother wants to eat those sweet potatoes.
I told him he shouldn't want other people's stuff. But he keeps crying about it, so I hit him.
You're a sad excuse for a big brother! Your kid brother's more grown-up than you!
Waah! Waah!
Hey! Aren't you ashamed of yourself? Take a lesson from your little brother there!
Moron!
Gen, it didn't work. No one gave us any food...
Sniff... It's 'cuz I'm bigger than you. Nobody feels sorry for me, they just think I'm stupid. It bugs me.
Ryuta, you turkey! If you'd let me hit you from the start, it would've worked!

Waah! It's not fair! Damn you, Ryuta!

Don't cry, Gen. I get it now.

Fine, okay, you can hit me.

Really, Ryuta?

But not too hard, all right?

Heh heh heh... Trust me!

Sniff... I think I'm gonna regret this...

C'mon, Ryuta, let's go!

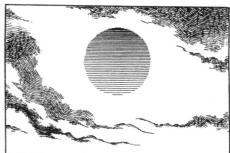

WAAH! WAAH! WAAH!

Idiot! Moron!

BONK BIFF

Waah! Waah!

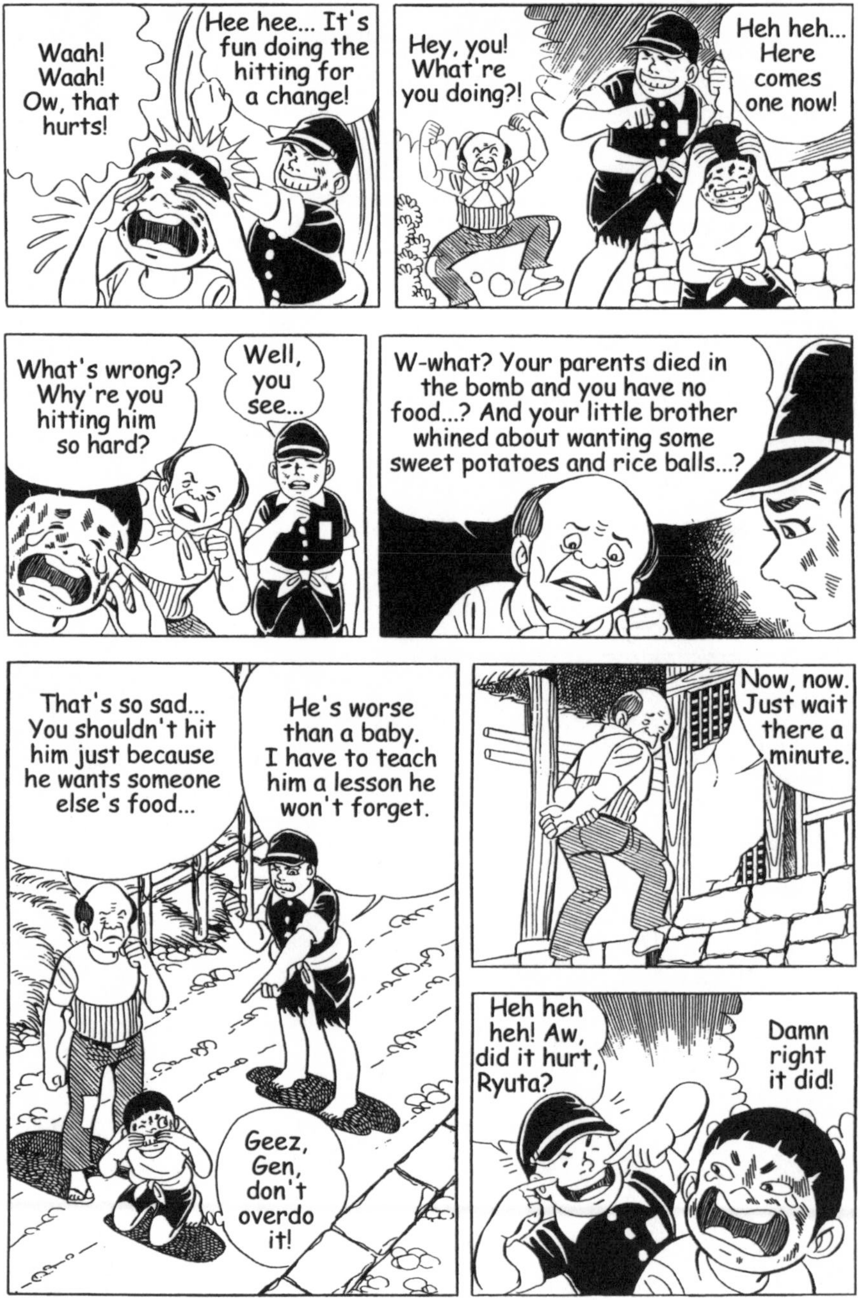
Waah! Waah! Ow, that hurts!
Hee hee... It's fun doing the hitting for a change!
Hey, you! What're you doing?!
Heh heh... Here comes one now!
What's wrong? Why're you hitting him so hard?
Well, you see...
W-what? Your parents died in the bomb and you have no food...? And your little brother whined about wanting some sweet potatoes and rice balls...?
That's so sad... You shouldn't hit him just because he wants someone else's food...
He's worse than a baby. I have to teach him a lesson he won't forget.
Geez, Gen, don't overdo it!
Now, now. Just wait there a minute.
Heh heh heh! Aw, did it hurt, Ryuta?
Damn right it did!

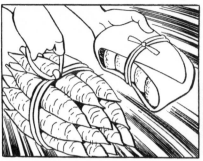

Here, give these to your little brother... and promise me you won't hit him anymore.

Wow, that much? T-thank you, mister!

Yeah, thanks, mister!

You cheer up, now!

Hee hee! See, when I hit you, it works like a charm! Isn't that great?

Not for me it isn't! Why do I have to get hit just to get food? People are crazy...

Hup hup! On to the next farmhouse!

Huh? You wanna do it again?!

You bet! The more we do it, the more food we get!

Nooo! What's my face gonna look like? I must be the unluckiest kid in Japan... Mutter... Grumble...

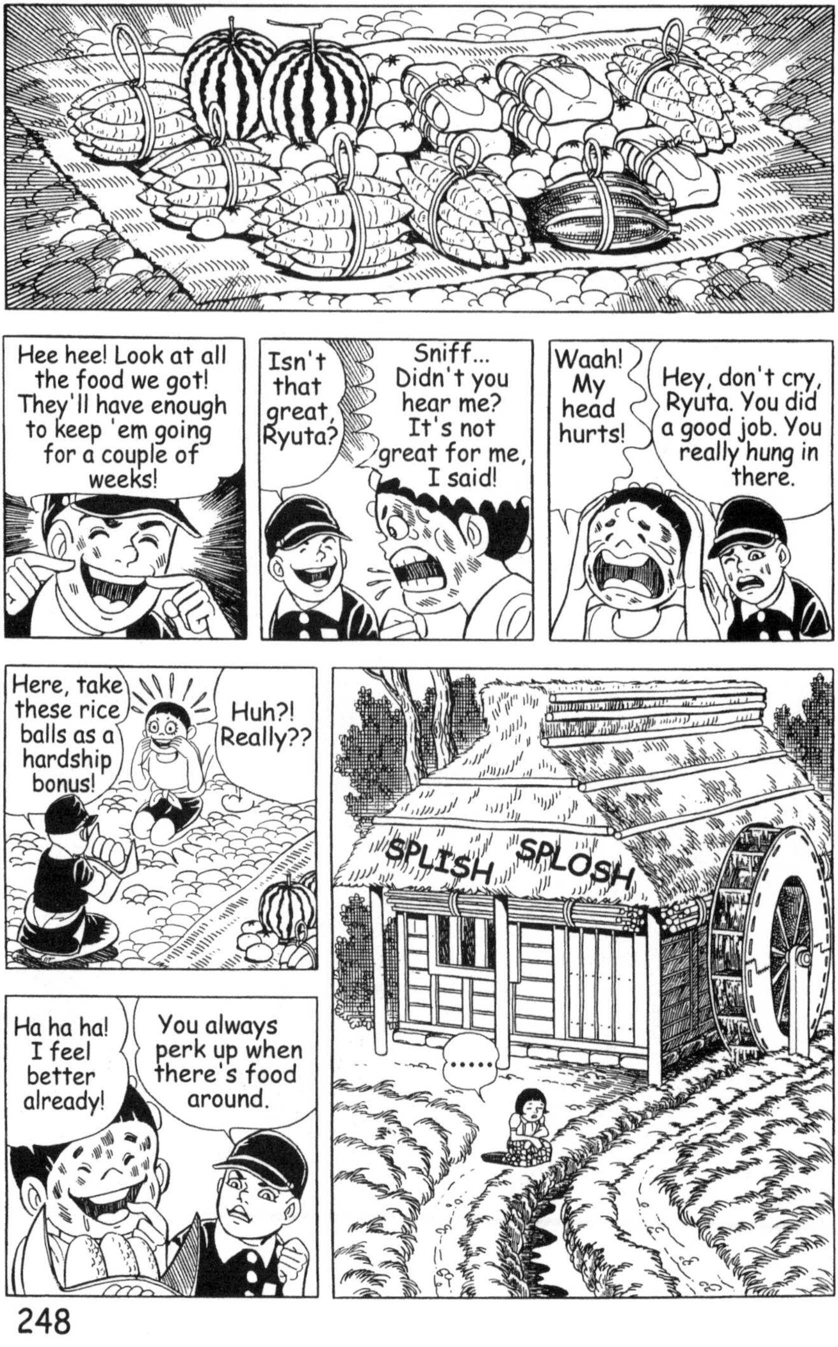
Hee hee! Look at all the food we got! They'll have enough to keep 'em going for a couple of weeks!
Isn't that great, Ryuta?
Sniff... Didn't you hear me? It's not great for me, I said!
Waah! My head hurts!
Hey, don't cry, Ryuta. You did a good job. You really hung in there.
Here, take these rice balls as a hardship bonus!
Huh?! Really??
Ha ha ha! I feel better already!
You always perk up when there's food around.
SPLISH SPLOSH
......

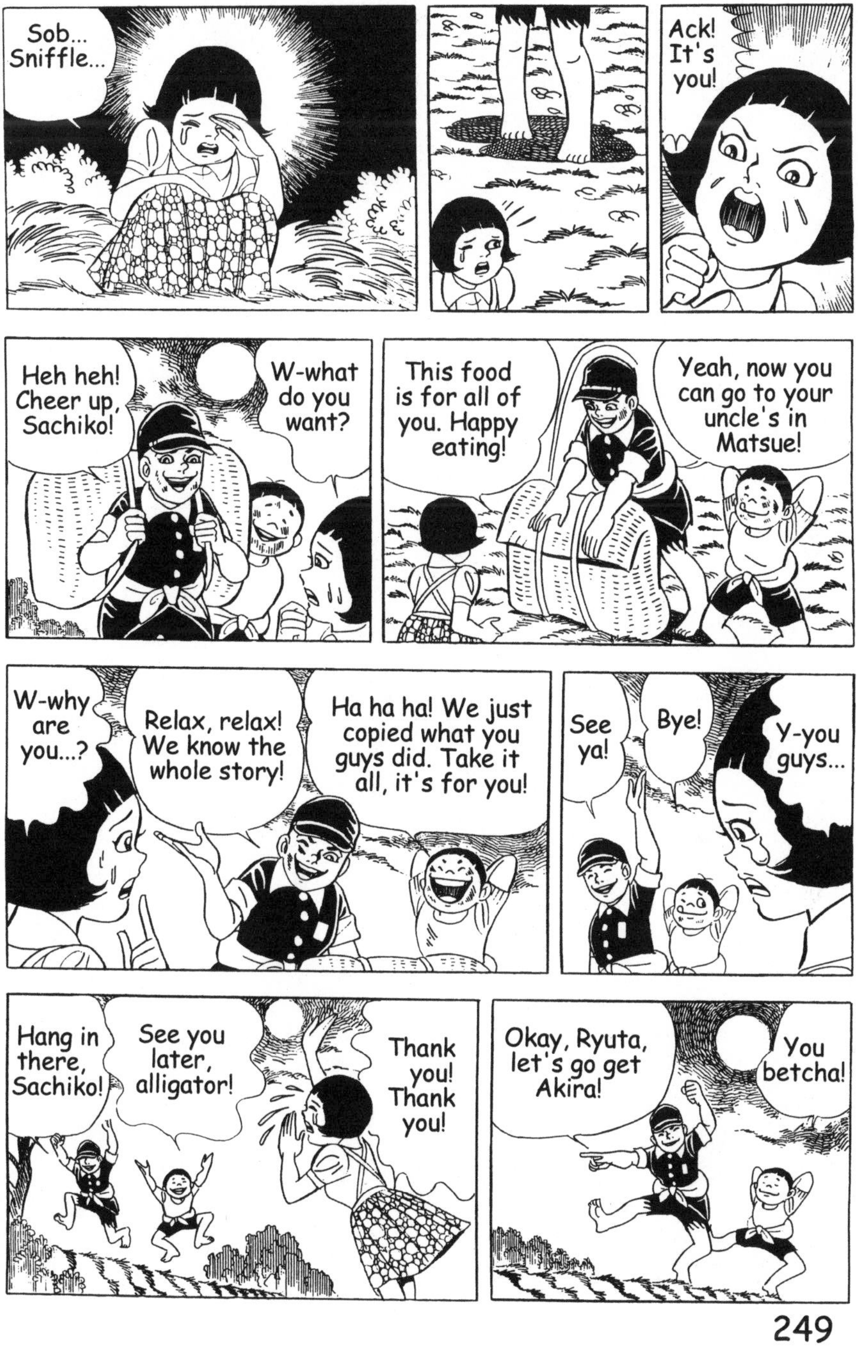
Sob... Sniffle...
Ack! It's you!
Heh heh! Cheer up, Sachiko!
W-what do you want?
This food is for all of you. Happy eating!
Yeah, now you can go to your uncle's in Matsue!
W-why are you...?
Relax, relax! We know the whole story!
Ha ha ha! We just copied what you guys did. Take it all, it's for you!
See ya!
Bye!
Y-you guys...
Hang in there, Sachiko!
See you later, alligator!
Thank you! Thank you!
Okay, Ryuta, let's go get Akira!
You betcha!

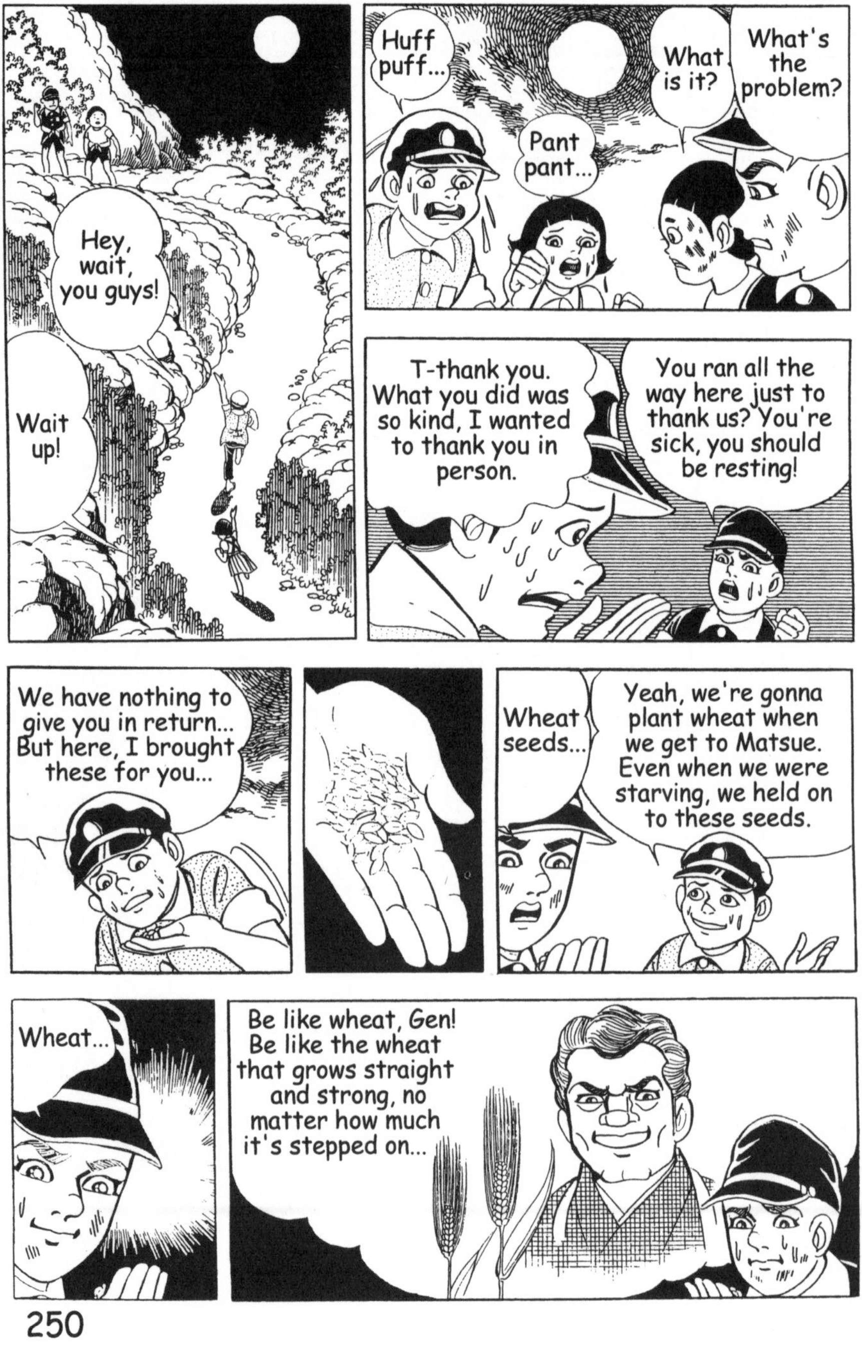
Hey, wait, you guys!
Wait up!
Huff puff...
Pant pant...
What is it?
What's the problem?
T-thank you. What you did was so kind, I wanted to thank you in person.
You ran all the way here just to thank us? You're sick, you should be resting!
We have nothing to give you in return... But here, I brought these for you...
Wheat seeds...
Yeah, we're gonna plant wheat when we get to Matsue. Even when we were starving, we held on to these seeds.
Wheat...
Be like wheat, Gen! Be like the wheat that grows straight and strong, no matter how much it's stepped on...

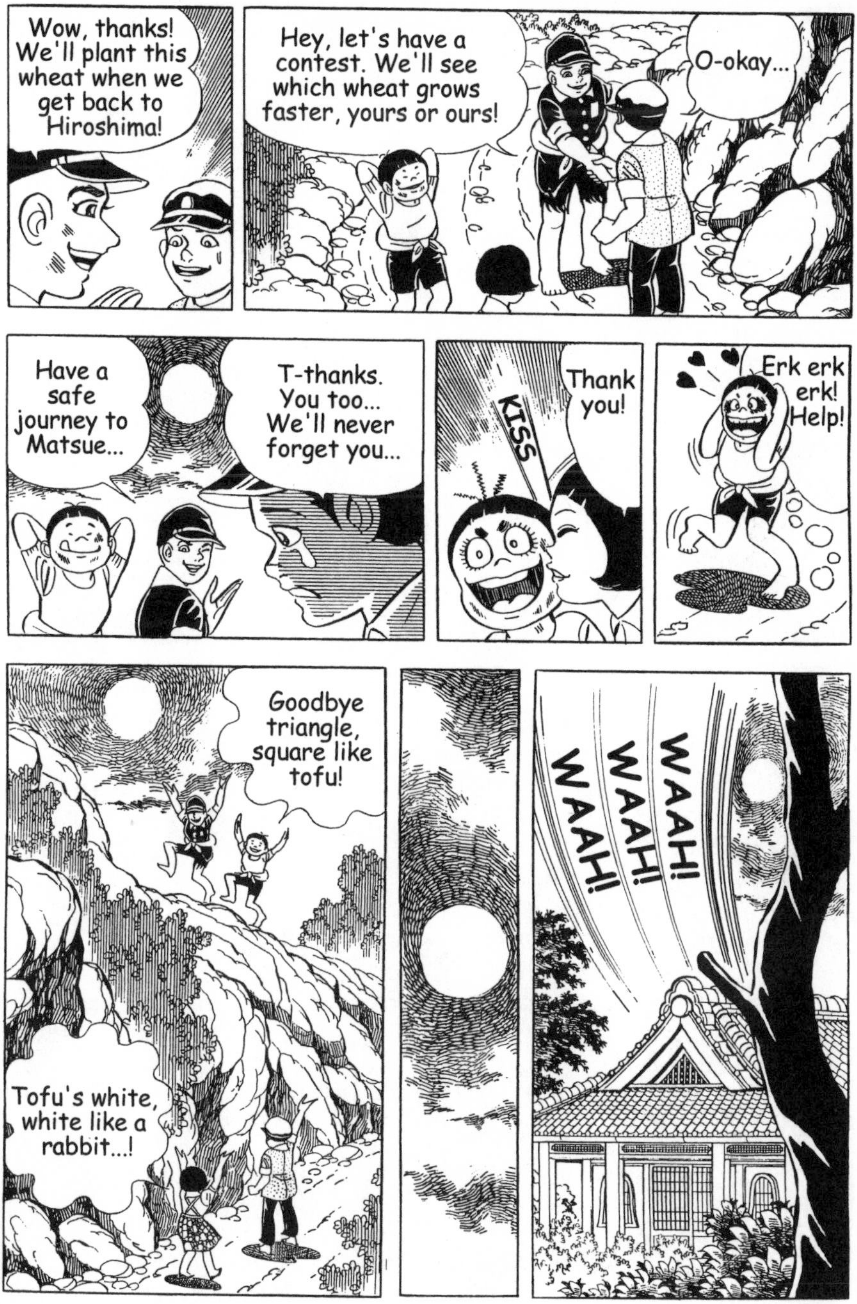
Wow, thanks! We'll plant this wheat when we get back to Hiroshima!
Hey, let's have a contest. We'll see which wheat grows faster, yours or ours!
O-okay...
Have a safe journey to Matsue...
T-thanks. You too... We'll never forget you...
KISS
Thank you!
Erk erk erk! Help!
Goodbye triangle, square like tofu!
Tofu's white, white like a rabbit...!
WAAH! WAAH! WAAH!

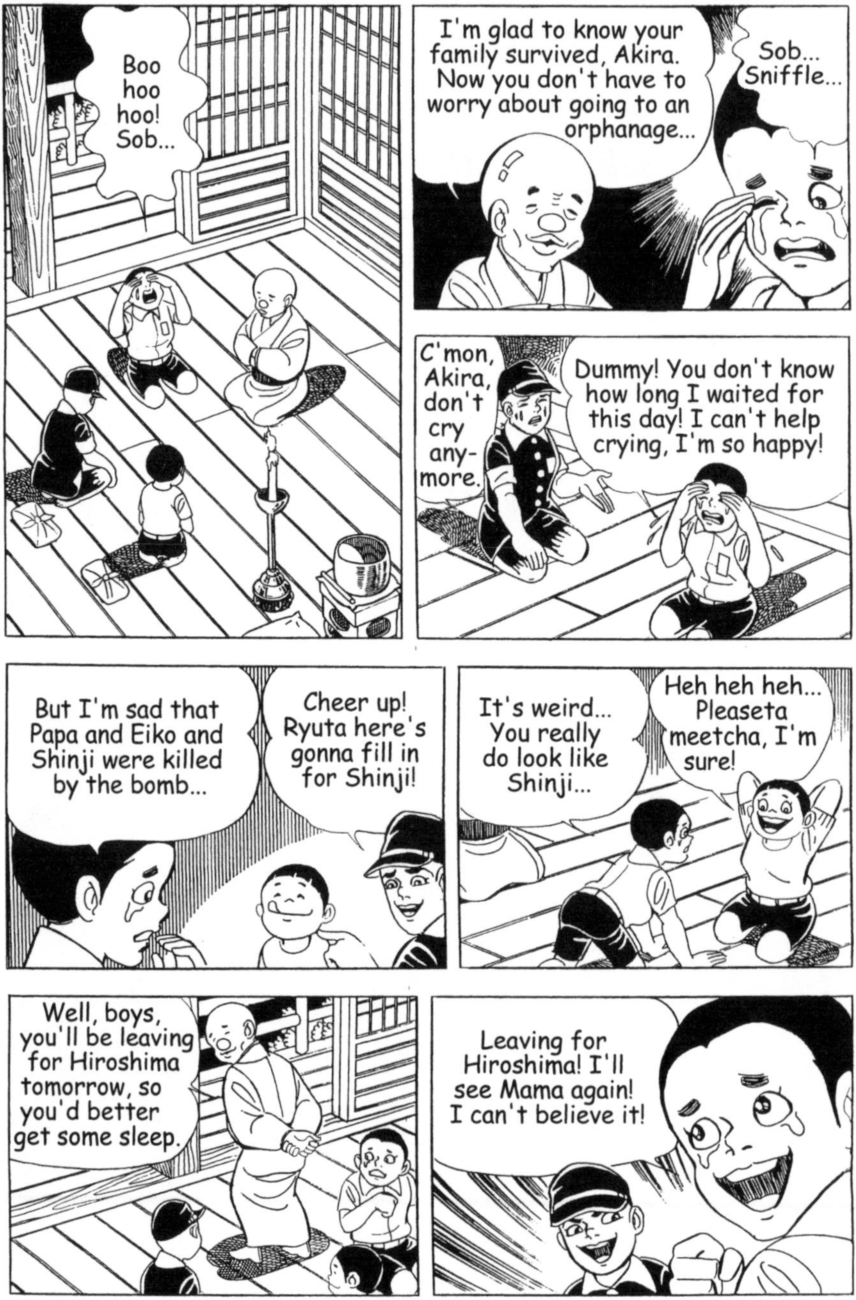
Boo hoo hoo! Sob...
I'm glad to know your family survived, Akira. Now you don't have to worry about going to an orphanage...
Sob... Sniffle...
C'mon, Akira, don't cry any-more.
Dummy! You don't know how long I waited for this day! I can't help crying, I'm so happy!
But I'm sad that Papa and Eiko and Shinji were killed by the bomb...
Cheer up! Ryuta here's gonna fill in for Shinji!
It's weird... You really do look like Shinji...
Heh heh heh... Pleaseta meetcha, I'm sure!
Well, boys, you'll be leaving for Hiroshima tomorrow, so you'd better get some sleep.
Leaving for Hiroshima! I'll see Mama again! I can't believe it!

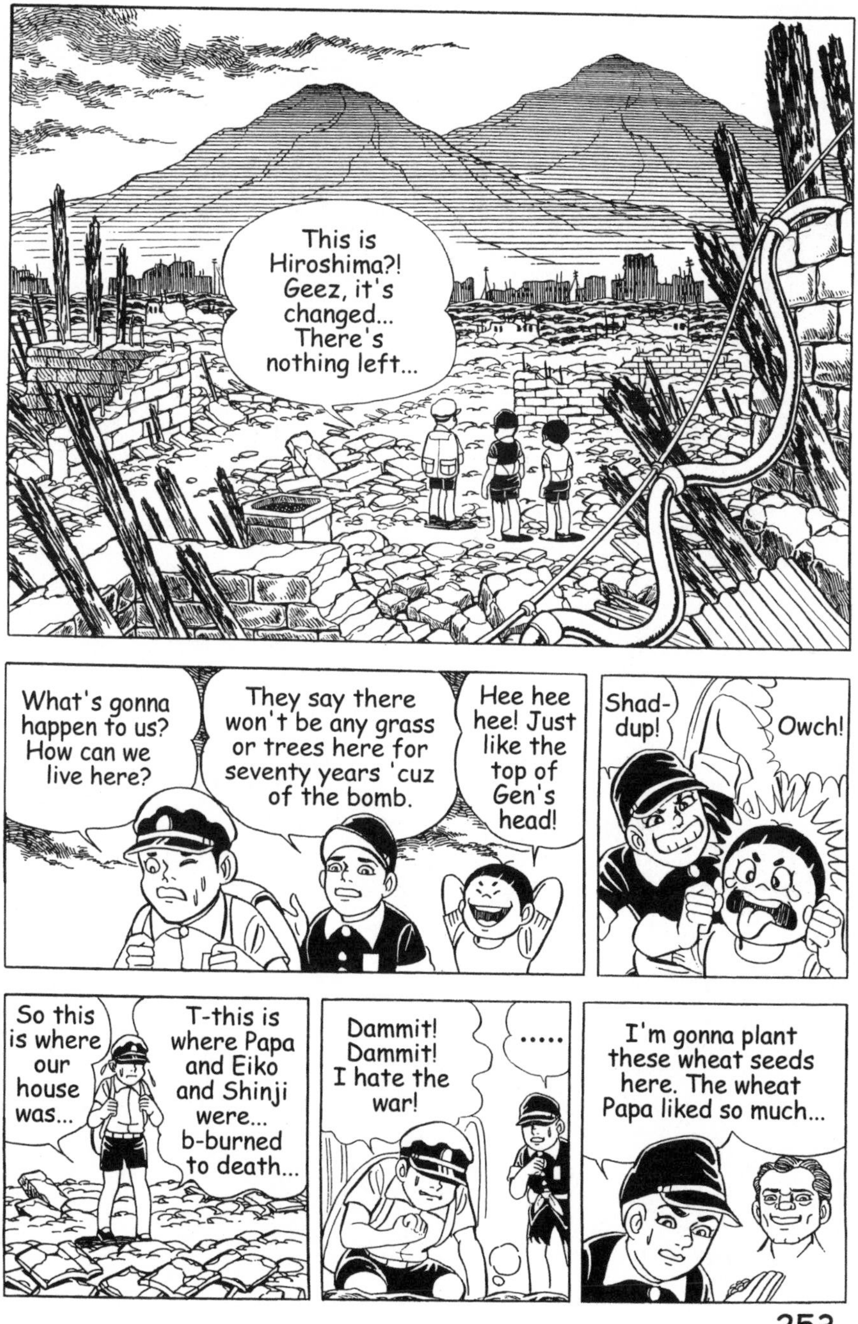
This is Hiroshima?! Geez, it's changed... There's nothing left...
What's gonna happen to us? How can we live here?
They say there won't be any grass or trees here for seventy years 'cuz of the bomb.
Hee hee hee! Just like the top of Gen's head!
Shad-dup!
Owch!
So this is where our house was...
T-this is where Papa and Eiko and Shinji were... b-burned to death...
Dammit! Dammit! I hate the war!
.....
I'm gonna plant these wheat seeds here. The wheat Papa liked so much...

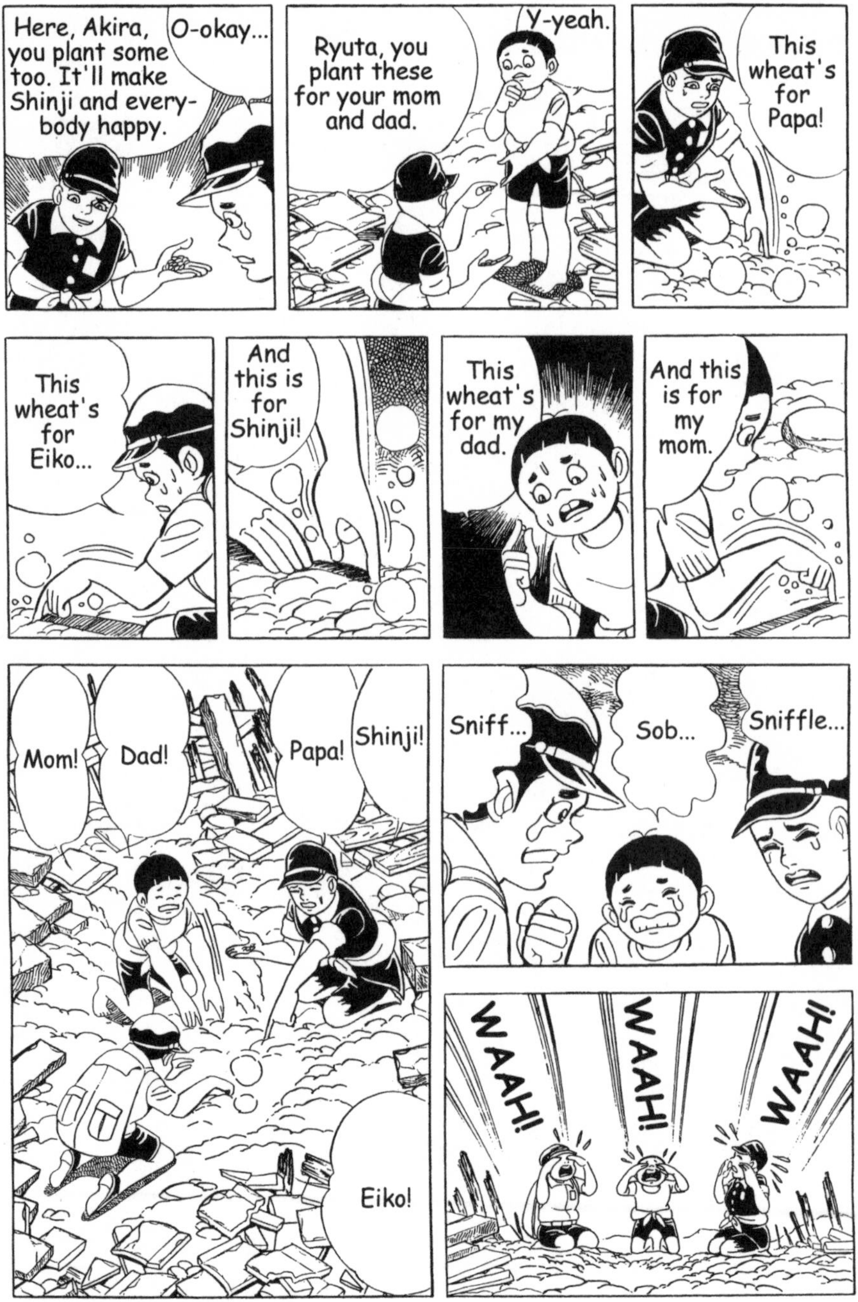
Here, Akira, you plant some too. It'll make Shinji and every-body happy.
O-okay...
Ryuta, you plant these for your mom and dad.
Y-yeah.
This wheat's for Papa!
This wheat's for Eiko...
And this is for Shinji!
This wheat's for my dad.
And this is for my mom.
Mom!
Dad!
Papa!
Shinji!
Eiko!
Sniff...
Sob...
Sniffle...
WAAH!
WAAH!
WAAH!

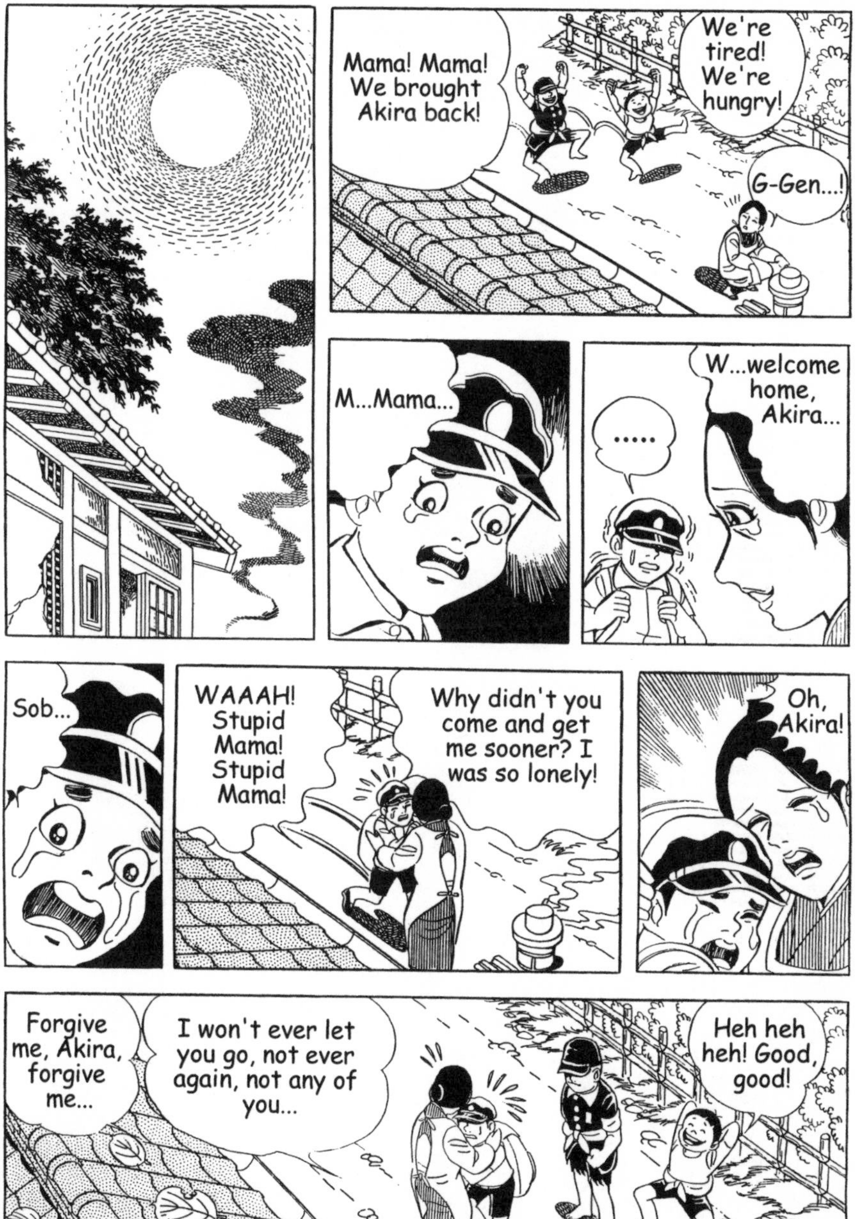
Mama! Mama! We brought Akira back!
We're tired! We're hungry!
G-Gen...!
M...Mama...
.....
W...welcome home, Akira...
Sob...
WAAAH! Stupid Mama! Stupid Mama!
Why didn't you come and get me sooner? I was so lonely!
Oh, Akira!
Forgive me, Akira, forgive me...
I won't ever let you go, not ever again, not any of you...
Heh heh heh! Good, good!

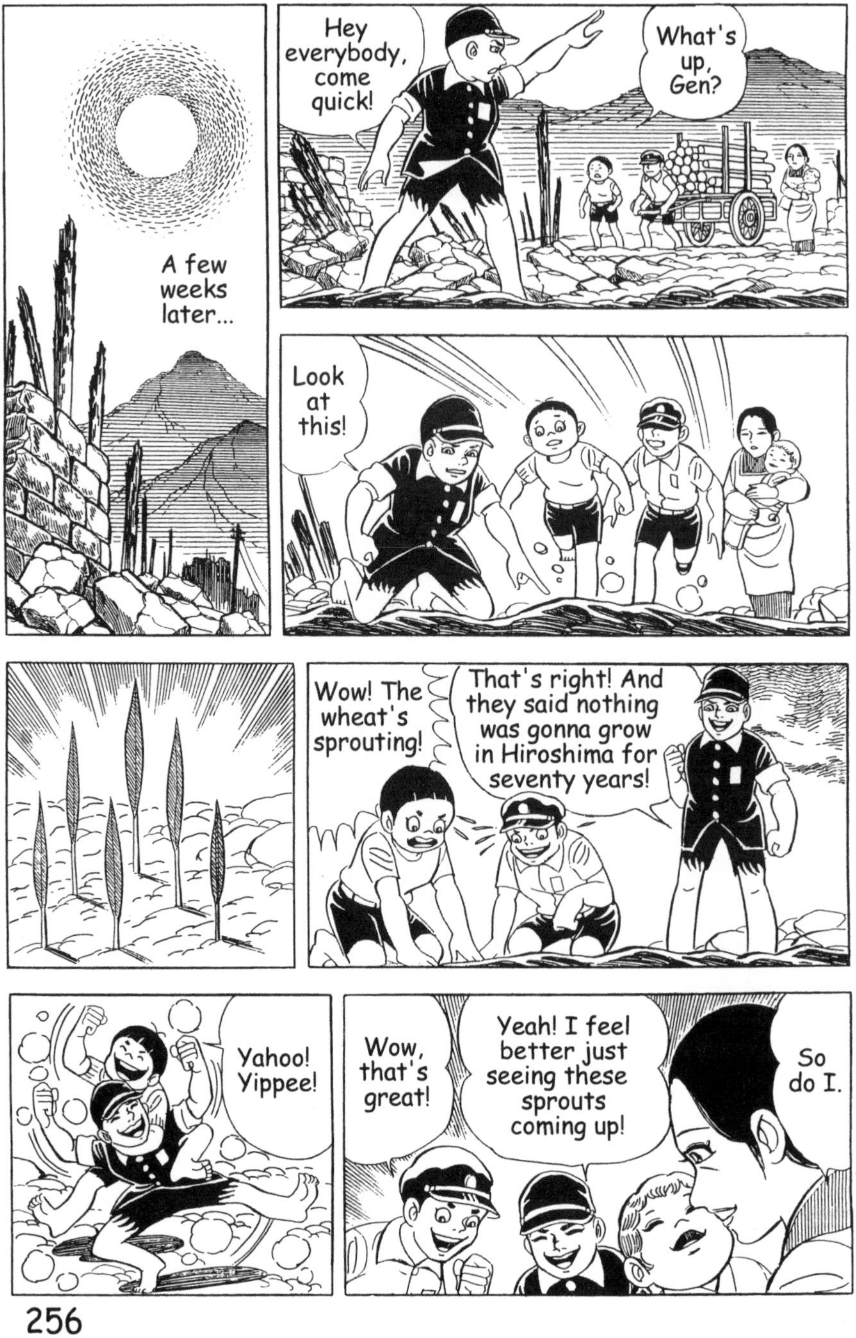
A few weeks later...
Hey everybody, come quick!
What's up, Gen?
Look at this!
Wow! The wheat's sprouting!
That's right! And they said nothing was gonna grow in Hiroshima for seventy years!
Yahoo! Yippee!
Wow, that's great!
Yeah! I feel better just seeing these sprouts coming up!
So do I.

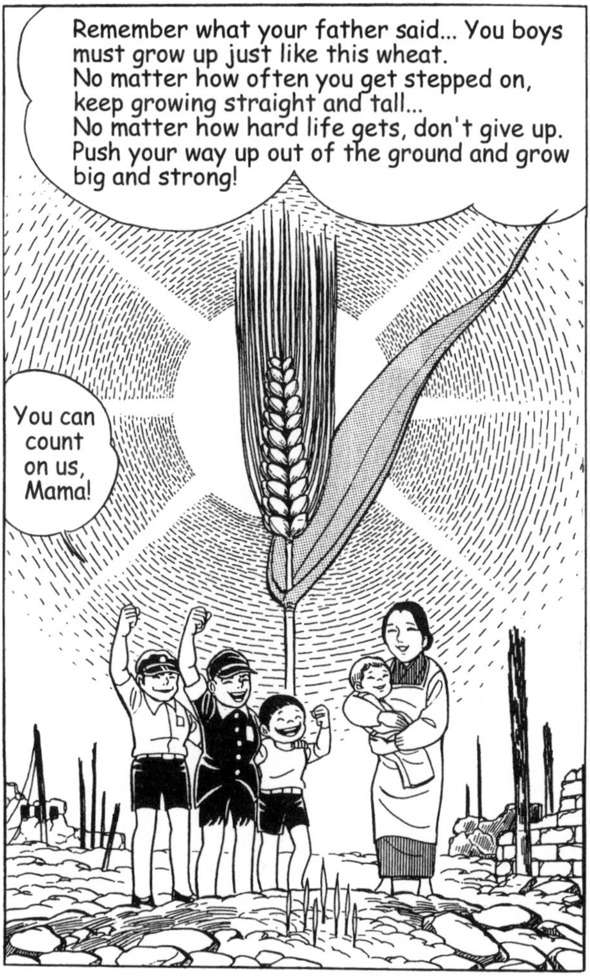
Remember what your father said... You boys must grow up just like this wheat. No matter how often you get stepped on, keep growing straight and tall... No matter how hard life gets, don't give up. Push your way up out of the ground and grow big and strong!
You can count on us, Mama!

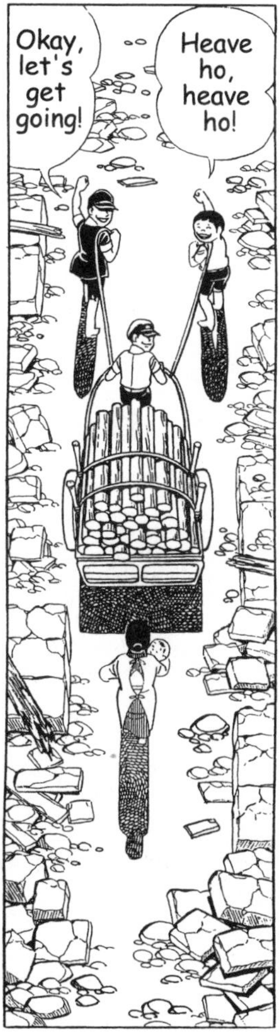
Okay, let's get going!
Heave ho, heave ho!

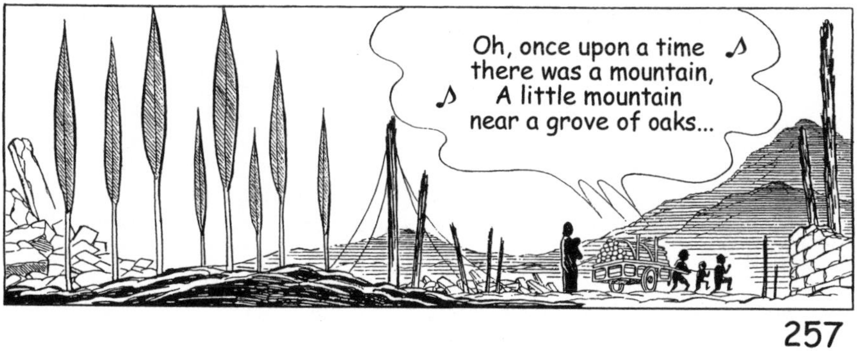
Oh, once upon a time there was a mountain, A little mountain near a grove of oaks...

About Project Gen

Namie Asazuma
Coordinator, Project Gen

In the pages of *Barefoot Gen*, Keiji Nakazawa brings to life a tragedy unlike any that had ever befallen the human race before. He does not simply depict the destructive horror of nuclear weapons, but tells of the cruel fate they visited upon victims and survivors in the years to come. Yet Gen, the young hero of this story, somehow manages to overcome one hardship after another, always with courage and humor. *Barefoot Gen's* tale of hope and human triumph in the face of nuclear holocaust has inspired volunteer translators around the world, as well as people working in a variety of other media. Over the years *Gen* has been made into a three-part live-action film, a feature-length animation film, an opera, and a musical.

The first effort to translate *Barefoot Gen* from the original Japanese into other languages began in 1976, when Japanese peace activists Masahiro Oshima and Yukio Aki walked across the United States as part of that year's Transcontinental Walk for Peace and Social Justice. Their fellow walkers frequently asked them about the atomic bombing of Hiroshima, and one of them happened to have a copy of *Hadashi no Gen* in his backpack. The Americans on the walk, astonished that an atomic bomb survivor had written about it in cartoon form, urged their Japanese friends to translate it into English. Upon returning to Japan, Oshima and Aki founded Project Gen, a non-profit, all-volunteer group of young Japanese and Americans living in Tokyo, to do just that. Project Gen went on to translate the first four volumes of *Barefoot Gen* into English. One or more of these volumes have also been published in French, German, Italian, Portuguese, Swedish, Norwegian, Indonesian, Tagalog, and Esperanto.

By the 1990s Project Gen was no longer active. In the meantime, author Keiji Nakazawa had gone on to complete ten volumes of *Gen*, and expressed his wish to see the entire story made available to non-Japanese readers. Parts of the first four volumes had also been abridged in translation. A new generation of volunteers responded by reviving Project Gen and producing a new, complete and unabridged translation of the entire Gen series.

The second incarnation of Project Gen got its start in Moscow in 1994, when a Japanese student, Minako Tanabe, launched "Project Gen in Russia" to translate *Gen* into Russian. After publishing the first three volumes in Moscow, the project relocated to Kanazawa, Japan, where volunteers Yulia Tachino and Namie Asazuma had become acquainted with *Gen* while translating a story about Hiroshima into Russian. The Kanazawa volunteers, together with Takako Kanekura in Russia, completed Russian volumes 4 through 10 between 1999 and 2001.

In the spring of 2000, the Kanazawa group formally established a new Project Gen in Japan. Nine volunteers spent the next three years translating all ten volumes of *Gen* into English. The translators are Kazuko Futakuchi, Michael Gordon, Kyoko Honda, Yukari Kimura, Nobutoshi Kohara, Kiyoko Nishita, George Stenson, Michiko Tanaka, and Kazuko Yamada.

In 2002, author Keiji Nakazawa put the Kanazawa team in contact with Alan Gleason, a member of the first Project Gen, who introduced them to Last Gasp of San Francisco, publisher of the original English translation of *Gen*. Last Gasp agreed to publish the new, unabridged translation of all ten volumes, of which this book is one.

In the hope that humanity will never repeat the terrible tragedy of the atomic bombing, the volunteers of Project Gen want children and adults all over the world to hear Gen's story. Through translations like this one, we want to help Gen speak to people in different countries in their own languages. Our prayer is that *Barefoot Gen* will contribute in some small way to the abolition of nuclear weapons before this new century is over.

Write to Project Gen c/o Asazuma, Nagasaka 3-10-20, Kanazawa 921-8112, Japan

Special Acknowledgement

The following people (as well as many who wish to remain anonymous) contributed generously to our Kickstarter campaign and made these hardcover editions of *Barefoot Gen* possible.

A. MacBride

A. T. Warren

A. Waller Hastings

Aabra Jaggard

Aaron B Reiser

Aaron Diamond

Aaron J. Schibik

Abhilash Sarhadi

Ada Palmer

Adam Christopher Bryant

Adam Doochin

Adam Meyers

Adrienne Marie Núñez

Agustin Chancusi

Akio Duffy

Alan Zabaro

Alenka Figa

Alex Fitch

Alex Ponomareff

Alex Stevenson

Alexander Hoffman

Alexis A Candelaria

Ali T. Kokmen

Alison Davila

Alok Karande

AM

Amanda Burdic

Amanda, Keagan, and Andromeda O'Mara

Amberly Maxwell

Amy Heaney

Amy Rachels

Amy Watson

Andrea Peitsch

Andrew Lohmann

Andrey Novoseltsev

Andy Holman

Angela Bacchi

Anne-Scott Whitmire

Annie Koyama

Arianne Hartsell-Gundy

Arthur Murakami

Asahiko Matsuda

Ash Brown

Ashley Hernandez

Avelino Morais

Avi Finkel

B. Wilks

Badou Jobe

Barbara Lindsey

Bears Den Mountain Lodge

Ben Laverock

Benjamin Sussman

Benjamin Woo

Bernd the Anon

Beth Campbell

Beth Lonsinger

billy pete

Blue Delliquanti

Bob Culley

bowerbird!

Brad Ander

Brent Van Keulen

Bryan Gaffin

Cabel Sasser

Caitlin Huddleston

Candise Branum

Cara Averna

Carl K.H.

Carlos Bergfeld

Cedric Tisserand

Chikada, Hibiki (fireworks.vc)

Chris Lepkowski

Chris Patti

Chris Shepard

Christian Kaw

Christopher Charles
Reed

Clay Nash

Cody Billings

Corey Proft

Cynthia Oshiro

dajomu

Dan and Ellen Wasil

Daniel Cahill

Daniel Oliveira Carn

Daniel Schneider

Daniella Orihuela-Gruber

Danielle Keenan

Dave Johnston

David & Sinda Eggerman

David Lee

David Toccafondi

Denise Larson

Dennis Smith

Derick Peterson

Deter Clawmute

Don Van Horn

Donald Scott

Donna Almendrala

Dorian Bell

Doug Redway

Doug Wilder

Douglas Candano

D-Rock

Dus T'

Dylan Cheung

Dylan Fields

Eileen Kaur Alden

Elaine Loftus Loeb

Eleanor Walker

Elisha Rush

Ellen Jane Keenan

Ellen Power

Ellen Yu

Elliott Walker

Emily Hui

Emily Lakin

Emmanuel D'Hoop

Eric Agena

Eric Kim

Eric Phipps

Erick Reilly

Erika Ray

Evan Ritchie

Eve Turner-Lee

Eyeball Kicks

Fred Burke

G.M. Harvey

Gabe Lowendick

Gabriel Bravo Gallardo

Gary D. Simmons

Gary Tanigawa

Genta Mochizawa

George Peter Dimos

Gina Curtice

Graham Kolbeins

Gregory Prout

Guy Thomas

H.Dannoue

Hans Eric Svensson

Harris Fish

Hart Larrabee

Heather Skweres

Heidi von Markham

Helen Koyama

Hikky Yoshida

Hillary Harris Moldovan

Holly Tomren

Hollyann Wood

Ian Harker

Isabel Samaras

Ismael F. Salazar Jr.

Ivory Madison &
Abraham Mertens

J. Christina Smith

J. Driscoll

J. Torres

J.R. Pas

Jackie Fox

Jackie Z.

Jacob Ryan Larson

Jake Pushinsky

James A. Hardi

James Prevott

James R. Bradshaw

James Turnbull

James Wight

Jane Mahoney

Jared Brock

Jared Konopitski

Jason beirens

Jason Tuason

Jay Perry

JB Segal

Jeff Newelt

Jeffrey Kahn

Jeffrey Meyer

Jen Crothers

Jen Propst

<3 Jeska Kittenbrink

Jill DeLong

Jim DelRosso

Jim Kosmicki

Jingran Wang

Jocelyne Allen

John "Boother" Booth

John Kyritsis

John Madigan IV

Johnny Mayall

Jon Kelly

Jon Parrish

Jonathan Shaver

José Loureiro

Joseph Kurachi Luk

Joseph P. Young

Joshua Drescher

Joshua Dunh

Julian Khaw

Julie Reiser

Julitta R. McIntire-Federico

Junko Mizuno

Justin Harman

Karin Wilson

Karl Brian Arcadio

Kat Kan

Katy Costello

Kayoko.A

Kazue Evans

Kelly Winquist

Kelsey C

Kendell Briggs

Kent K. Barnes

Kevin J. Maroney

Kevin Robinson

Kimberly A. Gordon

Kimiaki Suzuki

Kohji 'osa' Osamura

Kory Cerjak

Kristina Elyse Butke

Kristine Anstine

Kumar Sivasubramanian

Kurtis Ray Foster

Kwame N. Akosah

Leanna Lucas

Leen Isabel

legalmoon

Linda Stevens

Linda Yau

Lisa Martincik

Liz Davis

Loren Rhoads

Luan Resende

Lucas Aubrey Paynter

Luke White

Lynne Wooddell and Family

M

M. Griffiths

M.R. Innes

Maggie Young

Mahlon Landis

Maiji/Mary Huang

Marc Escanuelas

Marc Lee

Marc St-Jacques

Marcel Wienen

margaret miller

Mariell Leniuk

Marisa McFarlane

Mark Hartsuyker

Marla Greenwald and
Erin Sparling

Mary C. Carroll

Masahiro Kitagawa

Masako I.

Matt Adrian

Matt Parrillo

Matteo Gilebbi

Matthew and Crystalyn
Hodgkins

Matthew Mizenko

McCausland

Meagan Lowell Phillips

Mel Smith

Melanie Gillman

Michael Arroyo

Michael C. Stewart

Michael Czobit

Michael John
Constantine

Michael MacBride

Michael Pang

Michael Rock

Michael Tannenbaum

Michael Thaler and Inna
Guzenfeld

Michelle C.

Michelle Stoliker

Michiko Byers

Mike Borch

Mike Davis

Mike Dawson

Mission: Comics & Art

Monique G.

Naadir Jeewa

Nancy Chan

Nancy Ruan

Nathan Schreiber

Nathan Young

Nathaniel Merchant

Niall John James
MacDougall

Nicole Compliment

Nicole Fabricand-Person

Nina Matsumoto

Odette Christensen

Odyssey Publications

Olivia Eirene Luna

Olivia Rohan

Olivia Tai

Omar Pineda

Óscar Morales Vivó

OYAJIHAHA

Pascal Hamon

Patricia Wakida

Patrick King

Patrick Leahy

Patrick Montero

Pattie Piotrowski

Paul Freelend

Paul J Hodgeson

Pete Goldie

Peter Munford

Petey Rave

Phaedra Risher

Philip Kinchington

Priya Ananthasankar

Pual N

R Evans

R. Sikoryak

R. Todd Crockett

R~

Rachel "Nausicaa" Tougas

Raina Telgemeier

Rebecca Boldes

Renzo Adler

Richard J. Neil III

Richard Wesley Hooper

Rob Reger

Robert Altomare

Robert Duncan

Robert Paul Weston

Robert Rosendahl

Rochelle Claire Brown

Rodrigo Ortiz Vinholo

Ronald Stewart

Rosanne Nagy

Royce Engemann

Russell Martens

Ruth Ilano

Ryan Lynch

Ryan Sands

Sadie McFarlane

Samuel Henley

Sarah Rich

Sawa Hotta

Scott Rubin

Sean C Kershaw

Sean Kleefeld

Seiko Yoshina

Sergio Goncalves Proenca

Sergio Segovia Cervantes

Sharon Leong

Shaun Huseman

Shelby McGowan

Shervyn

Shiro H.

Siddharth Gupta

Soko Yamamoto

Sonia Harris

Sophie Muller

Stacey Ransom & Jason Mitchell

Stephen Schloss

Steve & Ana Hart

Steve Laflef

Steve Leialoha and Trina Robbins

Steven Darrall

Steven M. Jankowski

Susanna Hough

Sutter Kane Haggblom

T.M. Finney

Tabi Joy

Takahiro and Molly Kitamura

Tatsuo Senshu Ph.D

Terry W. McCammon II

Tetsuya Ishibashi

The Beguiling Books & Art

The Chou Malpicas

The Hoffman Family

The Kostelecky Family

The Land of Obscusion

theRat

Thomas Lloyd

Thomas Pand

Thorsten Gruber

Timothy Rottenberg

Tomislav Jelenkovic

Tony Bennett

Torsten Adair

TOUYAMA Jun-ichi

Treve Hodsman

Tshihide Satoh

Tsuyoshi Ogawa

Tyler Bibbey

Varun Gupta

Vivian Kokot

W.Schiller

Wesley Holtkamp

Wilma Jandoc Win

Yellow T

Zac Clarke

Zach Powers

Zach Van Stanley

Zach Von Joo

Zachary Clemente

Zack Davisson

琴線計画

近田火日輝

"I named my main character Gen in the hope that he would become a root or source of strength for a new generation of mankind—one that can tread the charred soil of Hiroshima barefoot, feel the earth beneath its feet, and have the strength to say "no" to nuclear weapons... I myself would like to live with Gen's strength—that is my ideal, and I will continue pursuing it through my work."

— Keiji Nakazawa (1939-2012)

Keiji Nakazawa retired from cartooning in 2009. He continued to lecture throughout Japan about the experience of atomic bomb victims, until his death in Hiroshima in 2012, at age 73. He is survived by his wife, daughter, and grandchildren.

Y Nak
Nakazawa, Keiji.
Barefoot Gen. 3, Life after
 the bomb